■ AURAL REHABILITATION ■

Second Edition

Edited By

■ RAYMOND H. HULL, PH.D. ■

SINGULAR PUBLISHING GROUP

SAN DIEGO, CALIFORNIA

Singular Publishing Group, Inc.
4284 41st Street
San Diego, CA 92105

First edition © 1982 by Grune & Stratton under the title *Rehabilitative Audiology*
Second edition © 1992 by Singular Publishing Group, Inc.

Library of Congress Cataloging-in-Publication Data

Aural Rehabilitation — 2nd ed. / edited by Raymond H. Hull.
    p.   cm.
  Includes bibliographical references and index.
  ISBN 1-879105-35-7
  1. Deaf — Rehabilitation.   2. Aged. Deaf — Rehabilitation.
3. Audiology.   I. Hull, Raymond H.
  [DNLM: 1. Hearing Disorders — rehabilitation.   WV 270 R345]
RF297.R43 1991
362.4'28—dc20
DNLM/DLC
for Library of Congress
          91-4884
          CIP

Printed in the United States of America

■ CONTENTS ■

PART II: AUDIOLOGIC REHABILITATION:
THE ADULT WHO IS DEAF OR HARD OF HEARING

CONSIDERATIONS FOR THE OLDER ADULT CLIENT

■ PREFACE ■

The purpose of this book is to provide comprehensive information on the management of children and adults who are hearing impaired. The book is divided into three parts, which examine the problems and procedures for intervention on behalf of three complex populations of persons who are hearing impaired. The Introduction presents information that is fundamental to the provision of services on behalf of all persons who are hearing impaired, including an introduction to the handicap of hearing impairment that differentiates between handicap and impairment, an introduction to hearing aids and their components, a psychological and economic profile of persons who are hearing impaired, and an examination of the vocational impact of hearing impairment on persons who are hearing impaired.

Part I concentrates on the child who is hearing impaired. The information centers on the importance of the family and their involvement in serving the child who is hearing impaired, considerations for amplification for children, the development of auditory skills for children who are hearing impaired, language and speech development, and their educational management.

Part II concentrates on adults who are hearing impaired. Chapters in the first section address the impact of hearing impairment on adults and procedures for counseling; hearing aid orientation; assistive listening devices for adults who are hearing impaired; the history, theory, and application of aural rehabilitation for adults; and strategies for speech conservation on behalf of adults who are hearing impaired. The second section of Part II addresses special considerations for the adult who is hearing impaired. The chapters in this section present information on the special nature of hearing loss in older adulthood, psychosocial factors of aging, the impact of hearing loss in older adulthood, counseling the older adult who is hearing impaired, considerations on hearing aid use for older adults, techniques of aural rehabilitation for older adults who are hearing impaired, and considerations for serving the older adult who has both auditory and visual impairments.

Part III presents information on the process of evaluating the communicative function of adults who are hearing impaired and the measurement of their success in aural rehabilitation treatment. Included is an extensive compilation of scales and tests of communicative function for use with adults who are hearing impaired, many of which are included in the Appendixes.

The majority of the contributors to this book are audiologists. It is important, however, that a comprehensive treatise on the management of children and adults who are hearing impaired includes professionals from other fields as well. For example, in Part I, a doctoral-level specialist in vocational rehabilitation for adults who are hearing impaired prepared the chapter on the vocational rehabilitation counseling of the adult who is hearing impaired. It is critical for students and professionals in audiology and deaf education to be aware of the role of the vocational rehabilitation counselor as a team member in the aural rehabilitation of persons who are hearing impaired. In Part II, other professionals also were involved. A well known psychologist whose specialty is the counseling of elderly persons was asked to write the chapter titled "Who Are These Aged Persons?" A psychologist/sociologist, who has tremendous expertise on the elderly who are multiply impaired, was asked to write the chapter on "Visual and Multiple Impairments in Older Adults." This is the only chapter of its kind in a book on the aural rehabilitation of adults who are hearing impaired.

The 19 authors who contributed to this comprehensive treatise on aural rehabilitation bring with them a wealth of experience and knowledge. They were asked to contribute information on concise, restricted topics so that each topic would receive equal attention. In this way, the comprehensive nature of the book could be achieved within a reasonable number of pages. The combination of the contributors' knowledge and the editor's efforts to meld the topics has, we hope, been fruitful in achieving this goal.

The topics selected were by no means arbitrary. Professionals in audiology, deaf education, and vocational rehabilitation, along with students in training and graduate students, were consulted about the topics they felt were critical in preparing to work with children and adults who are hearing impaired. Although few persons suggested the same topics, a general consensus was reached.

We have attempted to cover the topics considered the most important in preparing to serve children and adults who are hearing impaired. Therefore, a diverse range of vocabulary and sophistication is acknowledged in regard to both the content of the chapters and the book's intended readership. The book has been designed for use by a broad range of readers, primarily upper level undergraduate students and graduate students in speech-language pathology and audiology and professional speech-language pathologists, audiologists, and deaf educators. Other interested readers include physicians, nurses, gerontologists, vocational rehabilitation counselors, psychologists, and sociologists.

Preparing this book was an enjoyable and rewarding experience. Hopefully, students, professors, and professionals will find it a valuable source of information for serving children and adults who are hearing impaired.

Raymond H. Hull, Ph.D.

▪ CONTRIBUTORS ▪

Dale V. Atkins, Ph.D.
Psychologist in Private Practice
Green Farms, Connecticut

Jill L. Bader, Ph.D.
Director, "Hear At Home"
Denver, Colorado

Frederick S. Berg, Ph.D.
Professor, Department of Communicative Disorders
Utah State University
Logan, Utah

Karen L. Dilka, Ph.D.
Assistant Professor, Deaf Education
Division of Special Education
Eastern Kentucky University
Richmond, Kentucky

William R. Hodgson, Ph.D.
Professor of Audiology
Department of Speech and Hearing Sciences
University of Arizona
Tucson, Arizona

Raymond H. Hull, Ph.D.
Professor of Communication Disorders, Audiology
Department of Communication Disorders
College of Health and Human Sciences
University of Northern Colorado
Greeley, Colorado

Pamela L. Jackson, Ph.D.
Associate Professor of Audiology
Department of Communication Disorders
Northern Illinois University
DeKalb, Illinois

Harriet F. Kaplan, Ph.D.
Associate Professor
Department of Audiology and Speech-Language
  Pathology
Gallaudet University
Washington, DC

Roger N. Kasten, Ph.D.
Professor of Audiology
Department of Communicative Disorders and
  Sciences
Wichita State University
Wichita, Kansas

Jack Katz, Ph.D.
Professor
Department of Communicative Disorders and
  Sciences
State University of New York at Buffalo
Buffalo, New York

Robert K. Lightfoot, M.S.
Audiologist
Birmingham Veterans Administration Medical
  Center
Birmingham, Alabama

Daniel Ling, Ph.D.
Dean, Faculty of Applied Health Sciences
Elborn College
University of Western Ontario
London, Ontario, Canada

James F. Maurer, Ph.D.
Professor of Speech and Hearing Sciences
Portland State University
Portland, Oregon

Robert M. McLauchlin, Ph.D.
Associate Dean and Professor
School of Education, Health and Human Services
Central Michigan University
Mount Pleasant, Michigan

Maria Montserrat-Hopple, M.S.
Instructor, Rehabilitative Audiology
Speech and Hearing Sciences
Portland State University
Portland, Oregon

Jane E. Myers, Ph.D.
Professor, Counselor Education
University of Florida
Gainesville, Florida

Judah L. Ronch, Ph.D.
Psychologist in Private Practice
Poughkeepsie, New York

Lois Van Zanten, M.A.
Clinical Coordinator, Day Treatment Program
Rehabilitative Programs, Inc.
Poughkeepsie, New York

Gwenyth R. Vaughn, Ph.D.
Audiologist
Birmingham, Alabama

Thomas P. White, M.A.
Assistant Professor of Audiology
Department of Communicative Disorders and
  Sciences
State University of New York at Buffalo
Buffalo, New York

Introduction to
Rehabilitative Audiology

■ CHAPTER 1 ■

What Is Aural Rehabilitation?

■ RAYMOND H. HULL, Ph.D. ■

Deafness is worse than blindness, so they say —it is the loneliness, the sense of isolation that makes it so, and the lack of understanding in the minds of ordinary people. The problem of the child deaf from birth is quite different from that of the man or woman who has become deafened after school-age or in adult life. . . . But for all of them, the handicap is the same, the handicap of the silent world, the difficulty of communicating with the hearing and speaking world.

— Scott Stevenson[1]

The aim of aural habilitative/rehabilitative efforts for the hearing impaired is to overcome the handicap. In discovering the existence of a hearing impairment, assessing its type and degree, and referring the person who possesses it for medical treatment, the audiologist makes that referral with the possibility in mind that the physician can correct it through medical services. The referral is made on the premise that the hearing impairment, per se, may be overcome.

If the hearing impairment cannot be medically treated, the audiologist then works with the client as the expert in remediating the handicapping effects of the hearing loss and to help the child or adult overcome the communicative, social, and psychological effects. A team of professionals may become involved, including vocational rehabilitation counselors, teachers, psychologists, sociologists, and speech pathologists, with the audiologist coordinating the team. The client's family will also be involved in the aural rehabilitation treatment process. This task, in its totality, holds tremendous responsibility for all who are involved.

Why, then, is this important area in so many instances presented as a single chapter in books that deal entirely with the subject of hearing impairment? Only recently have entire books been written and published that concentrate on aural rehabilitation. Books that deal with the effects of hearing impairment on children, adults, and aging persons, including

[1] From Ballantyne, J. (1977). *Deafness* (p. 215). New York: Churchill Livingstone.

approaches to counseling, the psychosocial and vocational impact of hearing impairment, and approaches for remediation did not exist to any degree until two decades ago.

The three parts of this textbook provide theoretical and practical information on serving children, adults, and the elderly who are hearing impaired and address the issues and needs unique to each age group.

WHAT IS AURAL REHABILITATION?

What is aural rehabilitation? It has for so many years been discussed from within the framework of speechreading, lipreading, visual communication, auditory training, and other subcategories that we have occasionally strayed from the totality of the habilitative and rehabilitative process.

The first sentence of this chapter contained a statement by Ballantyne which, as paraphrased, was, "The aim of aural habilitative/rehabilitative efforts for the hearing impaired is to overcome the handicap." What is the handicap? Elements of the result of hearing impairment may have a great impact on one person, but may not be a handicap to another. One person may remain despondent over his or her partial loss of hearing, but another may rebound and work with vigor to overcome the communication difficulties caused by the hearing impairment. One person may demonstrate great social handicap as the result of a relatively mild high-frequency hearing impairment, while another person, who possesses a more severe hearing loss, may reveal only a mild occupational or social handicap. A child who possesses a mild loss of hearing that is not detected until school age may suffer as great a handicap as one who possesses a greater loss of hearing that was discovered earlier. Two children who possess equal amounts of hearing loss may experience different degrees of impairment due to the psychosocial and interactive/communicative environment in which they are raised.

If the catalyst for a psychosocial, educational, and/or occupational handicap resulting from either acquired or congenital hearing impairment could be pinpointed, it would probably revolve around the term "communication," and the interference either receptively, expressively, or both, caused by a hearing impairment. A child who possesses a severe congenital hearing loss, whether remediation is begun early or late, will possess a language deficit to some degree that will retard educational and occupational potential; and language delay is the basis for that communication deficit. An adult who acquires a hearing impairment that is of sufficient degree to interfere with the reception of the speech of others may become despondent over his or her difficulties in maintaining a current occupation or functioning socially. Again, the problem centers around interference with communication as the result of the auditory deficit.

Aural rehabilitation and the strategies utilized in the process of aural rehabilitation center around the impact of a loss on adults and elderly persons who are hearing impaired. The majority have probably possessed normal hearing at some time in their lives and will probably possess normal, or near normal, language function. In that regard, the impact of the hearing impairment on communicative function reveals itself from innumerable dimensions and avenues.

Children who are hearing impaired, in the majority of instances, have not experienced normal language, and will respond to their hearing loss, their environment, and communication in differing ways. Further, they also have parents, siblings, and relatives who respond to them and interact with them and their hearing loss in complex and differing ways.

In relation to acquired hearing loss, each adult and elderly person responds in different ways to the hearing impairment. Each has different demands, either self-imposed or externally imposed. Some will have families who are also affected by the hearing deficit, and others will not. For some individuals, their occupations may require precise and in-depth communication with other professionals or clients, while other persons' occupations require little communication. Some persons may have been greatly involved on a social basis, while others' social lives have revolved around home and family. A Harvard School of Business graduate whose spouse and parents have always had great expectations of him or her for success in the business world may feel a greater impact as the result of acquired severe hearing impairment than someone who desires to be a good rancher, but is not required to communicate as much on his or her ranch in northern Montana. Each child who is hearing impaired is born into families and environments that differ. A child who is born into a family in which deafness has not occurred before, and whose parents become impotent and noncommunicating out of self-pity and anger, will not fare as well as a child who is deaf born to parents who are deaf and who accept their child in a nurturing, communicating environment.

SERVING CHILDREN WHO ARE HEARING IMPAIRED

HISTORICAL BACKGROUND

Aural rehabilitation services on behalf of children have a much longer and more diverse history than services for adults who are hearing impaired, although much of the history centers on education of people who are deaf and the early oralism versus manualism debates. However, the history is an important one as we learn about the procedures utilized to serve children who are hearing impaired.

The recorded history of philosophical treatises on hearing impairment, children who are hearing impaired, their apparent ability to learn, and the "methods debate" on how children who are hearing impaired most efficiently learn language and speech began prior to

the development of Hebrew law, that is, prior to 500 B.C. (Bender, 1981).

One of the first recorded philosophical opinions on the potential of children who were deaf to learn and to speak was rendered by Aristotle (355 B.C.). His theories and philosophies on most topics carried so much weight in his day that others hesitated not only to question them, but even to venture into the topical areas at all. This situation was particularly disastrous for the hearing impaired, because, interpreted, Aristotle's opinion on the "deaf" was as follows:

Those who are born deaf all become senseless and incapable of reason. Men who are born deaf are in all cases dumb; that is to say, they can make vocal noises, but they cannot speak. (Giangreco, 1976, p. 72)

Unfortunately, the words *kophoi*, meaning "deaf," and *eneos*, meaning "speechless," had, at the time, taken on the additional meanings of "dumb" and "stupid" in some instances, and so a misinterpretation of Aristotle's statements could have become the interpretation that cast the mold for all children and adults who were deaf or hearing impaired for many centuries.

By the sixteenth century some prominent individuals, primarily priests and physicians, began to challenge the opinions of Aristotle. For example, Giralamo Cardano (1501–1576) of Italy braved the opinion that he could see no reason why people who were deaf could not be taught. In *De inventione dialectica*, Cardano wrote that he had observed a man who was born deaf who had learned to read and write, and in that manner could learn and could communicate with others. In that regard, he felt people who were deaf were capable of reason (Farrar, 1923).

During the seventeenth century, rapid advancements occurred in many areas, particularly in the development of educational philosophy, intellectual growth, political theory, and scientific thought. In relation to people who were deaf, such names as Lock (1632–1704),

Bacon (1561–1626), Bonet (1579–1629), Bulwer (1614–1684), and others dominated the scene. The quarrel between John Wallis (1617–1703) and William Holder (1616–1698) concerning the best method for teaching people who were deaf created the beginning of public interest in the area of deafness (Bender, 1981; Giangreco, 1976; Hodgson, 1953).

During the eighteenth century, great growth occurred in services on behalf of the individuals who were deaf. Jacob Pereira (1715–1780) was recognized as the first teacher of the deaf in France. de l'Epee (1712–1789), also of France, became the first person to make deaf education a matter of public concern. He wrote about his work and brought attention to the potential of children who are deaf to learn (Bender, 1981; Giangreco, 1976), as did Samuel Heinicke (1727–1790) of Germany, a contemporary of de l'Epee (Hodgson, 1953). Jean Itard (1774–1838) of France conducted research into the hereditary nature of deafness. He concluded that, indeed, deafness can be inherited, although it can skip generations (Bender, 1981).

In the nineteenth century, other significant strides were made in the detection and understanding of hearing loss and education of people who were deaf. Some were important to the future of services on behalf of individuals who were deaf in America. The Braidwoods and the Watsons were the operators of nearly all of the schools for the deaf in England, both adhering to an oral method of teaching, emphasizing oral speech (Bender, 1981; Deland, 1931). At this same time, deaf education in France was under the direction of Sicard who emphasized a manual approach to teaching language to children who were deaf (Bender, 1981; Deland, 1931).

In America, the first school for people who were deaf, the American Asylum, was begun by Thomas Gallaudet (1781–1851) who is considered to be the father of deaf education in America and a proponent of manualism (Bender, 1981; Giangreco, 1976), so the first school for the deaf was manual in orientation. In an effort to begin an oral school in this country on March 16, 1864, Gardiner Green Hubbard, a

concerned and influential citizen, and Samuel Howe, Superintendent of the Massachusetts School for the Blind, petitioned the Massachusetts General Court to incorporate an oral school for the deaf in that state. Governor Bullock of Massachusetts listened to Hubbard, and after receiving a letter from philanthropist John Clarke offering $50,000 to establish an oral school for the deaf, Governor Bullock persuaded the state legislature to approve the establishment of the school. It was later named Clarke School for the Deaf and was established in October, 1867 (Bender, 1981).

Alexander Graham Bell strongly influenced the future of services on behalf of children who were hearing impaired in the United States. Bell's mother was deaf due to illness, and Alexander married Mabel Hubbard who was deaf due to scarlet fever in early childhood. When he invented the telephone, Bell also saw its potential for electrically amplifying sound for the hearing impaired. Further, he was moved by the impressive way his mother and wife were able to communicate without using manual sign, and so he openly differed with Gallaudet's manual approach to teaching the deaf. With $200,000 that he received from the Volta prize for his work with electricity, Bell initiated the Volta Bureau in Washington, DC in 1867. Out of the Volta Bureau arose the Alexander Graham Bell Association for the Deaf.

The debates of Gallaudet and Bell regarding manualism and oralism remain in existence today. However, their ultimate goal was the best and most efficient method for language development and communication for children who are deaf.

CURRENT THEORY AND PRACTICE

The twentieth century has brought us more eclectic approaches for the development of language among children who are hearing impaired. The various approaches have as their goal the utilization of the most efficient sensory avenues available to children. However, although the individual philosophies are all felt to be in the best interest of children who are hearing impaired, they are structured around six general philosophies, or methodologies (Boothroyd, 1982).

1. *Emphasis on Speech.* This philosophy centers on speech as the avenue for communication that provides a person with the requisite independence that we strive for on behalf of the deaf (Bader, 1991; Calvert & Silverman, 1975; Fry, 1978; Hochberg, Levitt, & Osberger, 1983; Kretschmer & Kretschmer, 1978; Ling, 1978, 1980, 1984a, 1984b; Ling & Milne, 1980; Osberger, Johnstone, Swarts, & Levitt, 1978; Pollack, 1970; Sanders, 1982; Vorce, 1974).

2. *Emphasis on Hearing.* This primarily unisensory approach emphasizes the earliest possible identification of hearing impairment in children and the earliest uses of amplification so that the child's auditory system can play its natural role in the enhancement of auditory perceptual skills, and, thus the development of speech and language (Boothroyd, 1982). The goal is for hearing to play as great a role as possible in the development of speech and language (Bader, 1991; Boothroyd, 1982; Calvert & Silverman, 1975; Chase, 1968; Hirsh, 1966; Ling, 1980; Ling & Milne, 1980; Markides, 1983; Pollack, 1970, 1985; Simmons-Martin, 1977).

3. *Manual Supplements to Speech.* Cued speech is a manual supplement to lipreading. It is used as a manual supplement to an oral approach to the development of communicative competence (Cornett, 1967; Ling & Ling, 1978).

4. *Emphasis on Language and Communication.* This philosophy emphasizes that the mastery of language, no matter what the mode, is critical for the cognitive, emotional, and social growth of the child. It supports total communication and the simultaneous use of hearing, speech, and manual communication. It is believed that the use of manual communication will provide a base for communication, and that speech will emerge out of it since communicative competencies will have been more highly developed (Boothroyd, 1978; Fry, 1978, 1982; Groht, 1958; Harris, 1963; Kretschmer & Kretschmer, 1978, 1984; Ling, 1980; Simmons-Martin, 1972).

5. *Cognitive Emphasis.* With this philosophy, the modality for language stimulation is de-emphasized. The primary concern is placed on providing children who are hearing impaired optimal opportunities for cognitive skills development. However, proponents generally have their preference relative to the modality emphasized (e.g., manual, auditory, total) (Blank, Rose, & Berlin, 1978; Boothroyd, 1982; Grammatico & Miller, 1974; Moeller & McConkey, 1984; Stone, 1980; Taba, 1962).

6. *Emphasis on the Child and His or Her Parents.* Successful intervention on behalf of children who are hearing impaired depends, at least to more than a moderate degree, on the emotional well-being of the child, which, in turn, depends on the emotional well-being of the parents (Boothroyd, 1982). No matter how great the expertise of the clinician, parents exert the greatest impact on the social, communicative, and emotional growth of their child (Bader, 1991; Boothroyd, 1982; Lillie, 1969; Luterman, 1987; Mindel & Vernon, 1977; Moses, 1985; Phillips, 1987).

These philosophies are presented as individual approaches that are found to one degree or another throughout this century. However, it is seldom one observes a professional who works with children who are hearing impaired utilizing a single approach. It is most common to observe the wise clinician utilizing the best of several approaches to the benefit of the child and his or her family.

SERVING CHILDREN WHO ARE HEARING IMPAIRED

THE PROBLEM

In discussing aural habilitation services for children, we are in most instances referring to children who possess hearing losses that are prelingual in nature. According to Boothroyd (1982), these children generally possess a primary impairment of hearing that will, if left untreated, result in several possible impairments that are secondary to the hearing loss. For example, if a child possesses a congenital hearing loss that is severe enough to prevent him or her from hearing speech prior to being fitted with a hearing aid, the result may, according to Boothroyd (1982), include any or all of the following:

1. *A Perceptual Problem.* The child may have difficulty identifying objects and events by the sounds that they make.

2. *A Speech Problem.* The child does not learn the connection between the movements of his or her speech mechanism and the resulting sounds. Consequently, the child has difficulty acquiring control of speech.

3. *A Communication Problem.* The child may not learn his or her native language. He or she has difficulty understanding what people say, and cannot participate in conversational exchange.

4. *A Cognitive Problem.* The child has difficulty acquiring auditory/oral language. Children without language must learn about their world only from concrete aspects, not the elements that normally hearing children use, for example, the abstract elements of language.

5. *A Social Problem.* The child who is hearing impaired, as a toddler, does not hear the verbal signals that may signal the fact that he or she is about to transgress parental limits. At a later age, this child cannot have social rules explained to him or her, unless alternative avenues for communication have been established.

6. *An Emotional Problem.* If the child is unable to satisfy his or her evolving needs through spoken language, unable to make sense of the seemingly precipitous and capricious reactions of parents and peers, and constantly feeling acted upon rather than feeling in charge, the children who are hearing impaired become confused and angry and may develop a poor self-image.

7. *An Educational Problem.* The child with limited language gains minimal benefit from formal educational experiences.

8. *An Intellectual Problem.* The child will be deficient in general knowledge and language competence — both of which are included in a broad definition of intelligence.

9. *A Vocational Problem.* Lacking in verbal skills, general knowledge, academic training, and social skills, the hearing impaired child will reach adulthood with limited possibilities for gainful employment.

10. *Parental Problems.* The instinctive reaction of parents to a baby's failure to develop language is to withdraw language input and to reduce interaction. When they discover the true nature of the deficit, they may well enter into a state of denial and confusion, which reduces their general effectiveness as parents and further undermines the social and emotional development of their child.

11. *A Societal Problem.* The withdrawal of interaction by the parents will be repeated later by society.

THE PROCESS

To reduce these potential outcomes of a prelingual hearing loss to the extent possible, a comprehensive program of aural rehabilitation will need to be introduced. In fact, all children who are hearing impaired will require habilitative intervention in some form and to some extent. These steps are, in many instances, the same as those for adults. The difference lies in the time of onset of the hearing loss and the impact on language development. The components include some or all of the following:

1. *Parental Guidance.* It is critical that the child who is hearing impaired have well-adjusted parents, that is, parents who have overcome the anxiety and apprehension that they felt upon diagnosis of their child's hearing loss; who have accepted their child as a child, not as a burden; and who have accepted their role in the development of their child. This requires continuity of support from the day of diagnosis and every step along the way (Sanders, 1982).

2. *Audiologic Services.* Early audiologic management is extremely important for both the child who is hearing impaired and his or her parents. For the child, it is critical that amplification is offered as early as possible. Each day that amplification is not provided is a day lost in auditory development. A hearing aid, or hear-

ing aids, should be fit and the performance evaluated by the audiologist who will be involved in services for the child on an long-term basis. The clinician should do all that can be done to make the fitting of the hearing aid(s) a happy occasion. The joy is in observing the child respond and attend to sound, perhaps for the first time, and to celebrate this first day in the hearing life of the child. On the other hand, a solemn atmosphere surely will be reflected in both the child's and the parents' acceptance of the hearing aids.

3. *Auditory Development.* This aspect involves providing the child the opportunity to develop an awareness of sounds in his or her environment and to develop the ability to recognize things by the sounds they make; to make judgments about what is heard; to make judgments about where sounds come from; and to use hearing not only for recognizing speech, but for understanding and producing speech.

4. *Cognitive/Language Development.* Although auditory development cannot be separated from cognitive development, since much of what we are doing is involved in the cognitive/linguistic development of the child on an auditory basis, the components involved in language development must be spoken to independently. As Boothroyd (1982) observed, we are not only assisting the child to develop a "world model," or a conceptual model of his or her world — the raw materials from which to construct their internal world models — but the language required to interact with it and those within it. The child must have access to a rich linguistic environment to not only understand language, but also to express it.

5. *Speech Development.* The child must also have the opportunity for access to speech, no matter what earlier expressive mode of communication was used. Of course, if the child has no access to auditory sensitivity because of the severity of the hearing loss, we should not force the child to use a communication mode that is doomed to failure. However, if the child appears to have access to the hearing and motor skills that will permit speech development, it should be encouraged in a natural and interactive way. If it is forced and drilled, it will be-

come a dreaded and punishing experience to the child.

AURAL REHABILITATION FOR ADULTS

HISTORICAL BACKGROUND

Because the field of audiology had its origin as an aural rehabilitation service during World War II, it has been interesting to note its progress, forward and backward, in that regard. Its history is important as we study the process of aural rehabilitation on behalf of adults.

Military aural rehabilitation programs provided the birthplace for the field of audiology. The Veterans Administration expanded the role of the audiologist and the standards for professionals and equipment. The first training program for audiologists was developed at Northwestern University in the 1940s, and programs expanded rapidly through the 1950s and 1960s. As a young profession, growing pains were experienced. As instrumentation became more elaborate during the 1950s and particularly during the 1960s, and the field became more sophisticated in the area of research, a shift of emphasis toward pure and applied research and in the diagnosis of site of lesion of auditory disorders in medical environments became evident. It was apparent that the emphasis among the majority of professionals and training programs was turning toward diagnosis, instrumentation, and research and away from aural rehabilitation. Results from an automated piece of equipment or from a research project were more tangible than the emerging signs of improvement in social communication observed in an adult client who was hearing impaired.

The course of working with clients who are hearing impaired on the improvement of communication skills can be a difficult one. Interaction with adults or elderly clients who are hearing impaired, helping them to deal with the emotional impact of hearing impairment and their frustrations and fears, requires that the audiologist become involved on a close professional basis with clients and their families.

Unfortunately in the 1950s and 1960s, research and diagnostics became popular, and interest in aural habilitation/rehabilitation of the hearing impaired declined. Courses within training programs in the areas of differential diagnosis of auditory problems, speech and hearing sciences, instrumentation, and experimental audiology expanded rapidly, and new faculty were hired to teach them. Amid the array of those courses and the blinking lights of the equipment, training programs generally offered a course or two titled Aural Rehabilitation. When it came to finding a faculty member to teach the course, often the lowest ranked faculty member or a doctoral assistant would submit to the task. Students generally reflected the same negative feeling, not only in regard to the course, or courses, but also to the aural rehabilitation practicum experiences with children and adults who were hearing impaired.

However, that attitude in most instances does not prevail today. A more humanistic desire to work with people is becoming predominant among practicing professionals and professors of auditory training programs and, thus, their students. Prospective students are searching for graduate programs in audiology that permit them to concentrate on learning to provide aural (re)habilitation services. So the field of audiology appears to be achieving a healthy balance.

The Academy of Rehabilitative Audiology

Probably one of the most positive steps taken during the past two decades toward strengthening the professional stature of aural rehabilitation, the professionals who provide those services, and students in training who desire to provide them after graduation was the origin of the Academy of Rehabilitative Audiology in 1966. The academy has done much to bring about a renewed awareness of the importance of professional training in aural rehabilitation and those services on behalf of the child, adult, and elderly client who are hearing impaired.

As procedures for providing aural rehabilitative services for children, adults, and aging persons who are hearing impaired become more sophisticated, along with increased emphasis on the need for professional involvement in the fitting and dispensing of hearing aids, the professional prominence of the rehabilitative aspects of audiology continues to expand. But as a primary health care service, both the diagnostic and habilitative/rehabilitative aspects of audiology must carry an equal share of the responsibility in caring for clients who are hearing impaired. This is also true in the conduct of research to discover new and more effective ways of providing those services.

THE PROCESS OF ADULT AURAL REHABILITATION: DEFINITIONS AND CONSIDERATIONS

What is aural rehabilitation and the provision of aural rehabilitation services on behalf of adults who are hearing impaired? Aural rehabilitation is an attempt to reduce the barriers to communication that result from hearing impairment and facilitate adjustment to the possible psychosocial, educational, and occupational impact of the auditory deficit. In discussing aural rehabilitation, we are generally referring to serving those who had normal to near-normal hearing postlingually, but have sustained hearing loss that will, if left untreated, result in increasing levels of impairment. In most instances, these persons range from younger to older adulthood. If viewed from the provision of aural rehabilitation services, those services include the following facets.

Assessment

Assessment of the individual's threshold levels for hearing, per se, and determination of his or her ability to hear and understand speech, are the first important steps in the aural rehabilitation process. In the past, in all too many instances, this step was the first and last, except for possible referral for a hearing aid if one appeared warranted. Few other avenues for remediation of the auditory deficit were taken. According to Rosen (1967),

As he [the client] takes leave of the audiologist he knows that he has a hearing problem. . . . It is true that the audiologist may have mentioned lipreading, auditory training, or training in the use of a hearing aid, but probably did not offer those services himself. Furthermore, the advice was likely to be offered half-heartedly, as if the audiologist was really not aware of or convinced of its value. (p. 42)

This attitude is not as widespread as it appeared to be in the early sixties, but it does still exist to some degree. If the attitude of the audiologist who conducted the audiologic evaluation is such that he or she is not convinced of the value of aural rehabilitative services, the individual who possesses the auditory deficit either may not be referred for such services, or may become so discouraged from the audiologist's attitude that, even though a referral is made, the client may not keep the appointment. It is discouraging to find audiologists, who apparently entered the field of audiology because it is a helping profession, feel uncomfortable when they must relate with people who are hearing impaired on a face-to-face basis.

Nevertheless, the accurate assessment of the extent of the hearing deficit, per se, is the first step in the process of aural rehabilitation. With that information, the assessment of the handicapping effects of the hearing loss, the initiation of a hearing aid evaluation, if deemed necessary, and the other steps involved in the total aural rehabilitation program can begin.

Assessment of the Benefits of Amplification

If warranted, assessment of the benefits of amplification for individual clients should be the second step in the aural rehabilitation treatment program, and, if indicated, the fitting and dispensing of the instruments. Correspondingly, with the hearing aid evaluation, assessment of the handicapping effects of the hearing loss should be made. In that regard, steps one, two, and three in this sequence must go hand in hand.

In the hands of a skilled audiologist who can not only sift through audiometric data, including those of speech discrimination and the client's dynamic range, but also assess the emotional, social, and occupational consequences of each client's hearing loss and communicative needs, an accurate determination as to their candidacy for a hearing aid can be made. The hearing aid evaluation and/or evaluation for other assistive devices is only one part of the total aural rehabilitation program, but it is a critical part.

Assessment of the Impact of the Hearing Deficit

Assessment of the impact of the hearing deficit on individual clients is, again, critical for formulating a viable aural rehabilitation program based on individual client's needs. The assessment may include attempts at determining the impact of the hearing loss on the individual emotionally, socially, occupationally, and educationally. In most instances, when dealing with adults and elderly persons who are hearing impaired, the potential impact of the hearing deficit on the educational aspects of life may not be the most important. For young, school-age adults it becomes extremely important, as it does for those adults or elderly clients who desire to be involved in continuing education programs for occupational advancement or simply for the enjoyment of learning.

There are, at present, a number of scales and procedures that have been outlined for the assessment of the handicap of hearing impairment on the adult or elderly client. In light of the probability of possession of normal to near-normal communicative function prior to the onset of the hearing loss, the impact of the hearing loss on their personal lives and their occupational or educational goals is, in many ways, a personal thing. Everyone is affected differently.

The results of the audiometric evaluation provide the audiologist with information regarding expected communicative levels resulting from the hearing loss, particularly when observing the shape of the audiogram notations, the degree of hearing loss, and the client's ability to hear and understand speech. The client's response to that hearing loss must be evaluated and taken into consideration as his or her aural rehabilitation treatment program is being developed. The perceptive audiologist will be able to observe the more obvious behaviors and respond appropriately to them from the first contact with clients.

Evaluation of the impact of the hearing impairment on adult or elderly clients is an important part of the ongoing aural rehabilitation program. It is, however, a difficult task and one that is probably never finished because as clients face new situations, their responses to them may be different also. As physical, occupational, and personal environments change so do the responses of persons with hearing impairments. Evaluation, therefore, is ongoing, and clients must also be taught to evaluate themselves and their reactions to new communicative environments. Perhaps the most important component of the evaluation process prior to services, and upon the decision to terminate them, is the client's opinions of his or her ability to function communicatively in his or her communicating world. Scales and procedures for evaluating communicative functions are in the appendices of this textbook.

The Treatment Program

A formal aural rehabilitation program is, of course, not separated in any way from the procedures previously discussed, but is an extension of them. It involves extensive counseling to facilitate adjustment to the hearing loss, facilitating increased efficiency in communication, including establishment of client priorities in communication and a treatment program centering around them. The procedures used may involve efforts toward greater efficiency of the use of the client's residual hearing, greater awareness and use of visual clues in communication, manipulation of the client's communicative environments, and other specific tasks. The client's family and significant others are important elements in the total process of aural rehabilitation.

The formal treatment program is certainly not the most important aspect of the aural rehabilitation effort, but for those clients who can benefit from treatment strategies that may enhance communication in their most difficult environments, it is an important aspect of the total pro-

cess. The most successful aural rehabilitation treatment programs, however, are those in which counseling and hearing aid orientation are carried over as an integral part.

Involvement of Other Professionals

Involvement of other professionals, including the vocational rehabilitation counselor, the social worker, educational personnel, the speech/language specialist, and the psychologist is important to the ongoing aural rehabilitation program for individual clients who require their services. For elderly clients who reside in a health care facility, involvement of facility personnel is necessary. Included may be the activity director, occupational therapist, social worker, nurses, nurses' aides, and others who are necessary for a successful treatment program.

It is incumbent on the audiologist to call on other professionals to facilitate the rehabilitation process. It is also important to know when the problems an adult or elderly person is facing are beyond the scope of the audiologists' knowledge and skill, and to be aware of proper referral sources. As a team leader in the aural rehabilitation process, the audiologist can function as the catalyst in the development of a truly comprehensive rehabilitation program for clients who require additional services.

Involvement of the Family

A positive involvement of the family and/or a significant other in the client's life can be one of the most strengthening aspects of the aural rehabilitation program, both for the adult and elderly client. The words "positive involvement" are stressed because involvement by a nonunderstanding family member, or a friend who in the end decides that he or she "does not have the time" or who otherwise does not desire to become involved, can be damaging. If a spouse, another family member, or another significant other is to be a part of the client's aural rehabilitation program, it is important that he or she be involved from the initial evaluation, but particularly during the period of assessment of the handicapping effects of the hearing loss on the client. As the significant other becomes aware of the impact of the hearing deficit, that person can become an important strengthening component in facilitating adjustment and enhancing the communication abilities of the client.

SUMMARY

What is aural rehabilitation? According to Costello et al. (1974), in a paper developed by them as members of the Committee on Rehabilitative Audiology of the American Speech-Language-Hearing Association, "audiologic rehabilitation is designed to assist individuals with auditory disabilities to realize their optimal potential in communication regardless of age, or the age of the person at the onset of the disability" (p. 68). It is a complex process which has as its goal the reduction of the barriers to communication that have resulted from hearing loss. Within the process, a number of professionals may be involved, with the audiologist functioning as the coordinator, or facilitator, of the team. The client's family will be a critical element in the process. The process is as complex as the client and the handicapping effects of his or her hearing impairment, and unquestionably, it carries great responsibility. Only those audiologists who are willing to accept that responsibility should provide those services. That means, coming face-to-face with people — children, adults, elderly persons, siblings, and the family who require a close professional relationship and a service that will enhance their abilities to function communicatively in a complex and changing world.

REFERENCES

Bader, J. L. (1991). Language development in hearing impaired children. In R. H. Hull (Ed.), *Rehabilitative audiology*. San Diego, CA: Singular Publishing Group.

Ballantyne, J. (1977). *Deafness*. New York: Churchill Livingstone.

Bender, R. E. (1981). *The conquest of deafness*. Cleveland, OH: Press of Western Reserve University.

Blank, M., Rose, S., & Berlin, L. (1978). *The language of learning: The preschool years*. New York: Grune & Stratton.

Boothroyd, A. (1978). Speech perception and sensorineural hearing loss. In M. Ross & T. Giolas (Eds.), *Auditory management of hearing impaired children* (pp. 92–101). Baltimore, MD: University Park Press.

Boothroyd, A. (1982). *Hearing impairments in young children*. Englewood Cliffs, NJ: Prentice-Hall.

Calvert, D., & Silverman, S. (1975). *Speech and deafness*. Washington, DC: Alexander Graham Bell Association for the Deaf.

Chase, R. A. (1968). Motor organization of speech. In S. J. Freeman (Ed.), *The neuropsychology of spatially oriented behavior*. Homewood, IL: Dorsey Press.

Cornett, R. (1967). Cued speech. *American Annals of the Deaf, 112*, 3–13.

Costello, M. R., Freeland, E. E., Hill, M. J., Jeffers, J., Matkin, N., Stream, R. W., & Tobin, H. (1974). The audiologist: Responsibilities in the habilitation of the auditorily handicapped. *Asha, 16*, 68–70.

Deland, F. (1931). *The story of lipreading*. Washington, DC: The Volta Bureau.

Farrar, A. (1923). *Arnold on the education of the deaf*. London: Francis Carter.

Fry, D. B. (1978). Language development in the deaf child. In F. Bess (Ed.), *Childhood deafness: Causation, assessment and management*. New York: Grune & Stratton.

Giangreco, C. J. (1976). *The education of the hearing impaired*. Springfield, IL: Charles C. Thomas.

Grammatico, L., & Miller, S. (1974). Curriculum for the preschool deaf child. *Volta Review, 79*, 19–26.

Groht, M. A. (1958). *National language for deaf children*. Washington, DC: The Alexander Graham Bell Association for the Deaf.

Harris, G. (1963). *Language for the preschool deaf child*. New York: Grune & Stratton.

Hirsh, I. J. (1966). Teaching the deaf child to talk. In F. Smith & G. A. Miller (Eds.), *The genesis of language* (pp. 129–138). Cambridge, MA: MIT Press.

Hochberg, I., Levitt, H., & Osberger, M. J. (Eds.). (1983). *Speech of the hearing impaired*. Baltimore, MD: University Park Press.

Hodgson, K. (1953). *The deaf and their problems*. New York: Philosophical Library.

Kretschmer, R., & Kretschmer, L. (1978). *Language development and intervention with the hearing impaired*. Baltimore, MD: University Park Press.

Kretschmer, R., & Kretschmer, L. (1984). Habilitation of language of deaf children. In W. H. Perkins (Ed.), *Current therapy of communication disorders: Hearing disorders.* New York: Thieme-Stratton.

Lillie, S. M. (1969). *Management of deafness in infants and very young children.* Presentation before the 47th Annual International Convention, Council for Exceptional Children, Denver, CO.

Ling, D. (1978). Auditory coding and recoding: An analysis of auditory training procedures for hearing-impaired children. In M. Ross & T. Giolas (Eds.), *Auditory management of hearing-impaired children: Principles and prerequisites for intervention.* Austin, TX: Pro-Ed.

Ling, D. (1980). Early speech development. In G. T. Mencher & S. E. Gerber (Eds.), *Early management of hearing loss.* New York: Grune & Stratton.

Ling, D. (1984a). *Early intervention for hearing-impaired children: Oral options.* San Diego, CA: Singular Publishing Group.

Ling, D. (1984b). *Early intervention for hearing-impaired children: Total communication options.* San Diego, CA: College-Hill Press.

Ling, D., & Ling, A. (1978). *Aural habilitation: The foundations of verbal learning in hearing-impaired children.* Washington, DC: Alexander Graham Bell Association for the Deaf.

Ling, D., & Milne, M. M. (1980). The development of speech in hearing-impaired children. In F. Bess (Ed.), *Amplification in education.* Washington, DC: Alexander Graham Bell Association for the Deaf.

Luterman, D. (1987). *Deafness in the family.* San Diego, CA: College-Hill Press.

Markides, A. (1983). *The speech of hearing-impaired children.* Oxford, UK: Manchester University Press.

Mindel, E. D., & Vernon, M. (1987). *They grow in silence: The deaf child and his family.* Silver Spring, MD: National Association for the Deaf.

Moeller, M. P., & McConkey, A. J. (1984). Language intervention with preschool deaf children: A cognitive/linguistic approach. In W. H. Perkins (Ed.), *Current therapy of communication disorders.* New York: Thieme-Stratton.

Moses, K. L. (1985). Infant deafness and parental grief: Psychosocial early intervention. In F. Powell et al. (Eds.), *Education of the hearing-impaired child.* San Diego, CA: Singular Publishing Group.

Osberger, M. H., Johnstone, A., Swarts, E., & Levitt, H. (1978). The evaluation of a model speech training program for deaf children. *Journal of Communication Disorders, 11,* 293–313.

Phillips, A. L. (1987). Working with parents. A story of personal and professional growth. In D. Adkins (Ed.), *Families and their hearing-impaired children. Volta Review, 89*(5), 131–146.

Pollack, D. (1970). *Educational audiology for the limited hearing infant.* Springfield, IL: Charles C. Thomas.

Pollack, D. (1985). *Educational audiology for the limited hearing infant and pre-schooler.* Springfield, IL: Charles C. Thomas.

Rosen, J. (1967). *The role of the audiologist in aural rehabilitation.* Unpublished manuscript, University of Denver.

Sanders, D. A. (1982). *Aural rehabilitation* (2nd ed.). Englewood Cliffs, NJ: Prentice-Hall.

Simmons-Martin, A. (1977). Natural language and auditory input. In F. Bess (Ed.), *Childhood deafness: Causation, assessment and management.* New York: Grune & Stratton.

Stone, P. (1980). Developing thinking skills in young hearing impaired children. *Volta Review, 82*(6), 345–353.

Taba, H. (1962). *Curriculum development: Theory and practice.* New York: Harcourt, Brace and World.

Vorce, E. (1974). *Teaching speech to deaf children.* Washington, DC: Alexander Graham Bell Association for the Deaf.

CHAPTER 2

Introduction to the Handicap of Hearing Impairment:

Auditory Impairment Versus Hearing Handicap

■ JACK KATZ, Ph.D. ■
■ THOMAS P. WHITE, M.A. ■

To understand the aural rehabilitative needs of a client, a careful interview should be carried out as well as a battery of audiometric procedures. An in-depth interview or questionnaire and specialized diagnostic tests might be required to obtain the broadest possible understanding. In the end, however, there will always be an element of uncertainty. This limitation in precise prediction may be due to the client's motivation and personality factors and the severity of the hearing loss.

The audiologic assessment provides audiologists with data with which to compare a client to a control population. The person with a hearing impairment will do less well on most tests, but we are left with many questions regarding the person's rehabilitative needs. For example, audiologists do not know with whom the person communicates and whether it is within a large lecture hall, over a taxicab CB radio, or if it involves extensive psychiatric interviews. Tests do not tell clinicians if a child has a well developed vocabulary and language system or optimal classroom conditions. Unless audiologists test further, they will not know how well individuals are able to use visual information to supplement auditory information.

At this point, it is well to consider terminology. Sometimes cause and effect and measurement is confused with function.

FUNCTIONAL TERMINOLOGY

In certain conversations, people are likely to use the terms hearing loss, hearing level, hearing impairment, and hearing handicap interchangeably. This chapter will delineate them.

HEARING LEVEL VERSUS HEARING LOSS

Hearing level (HL) is a measurement made on an audiometer and reported in decibels (dB re ANSI, 1989). Hearing levels obtained in a controlled acoustical environment compare the client's performance to the responses of individuals in a standard population, that is, a population that possesses normal hearing. In essence, it is the dial reading on an audiometer at which an individual responds in a specified manner. *Hearing loss* will be used to indicate the type of problem (e.g., conductive vs. sensorineural), or that hearing ability has been lost (Davis & Silverman, 1970). A person's 40 dB threshold is labeled as a 40 dB HL (hearing level). However, if initial threshold was known to be −5 dB, then one could indicate a 45 dB hearing loss.

HEARING IMPAIRMENT VERSUS HEARING HANDICAP

Hearing impairment is closely associated with hearing level, and the terms are sometimes used interchangeably. Hearing impairment can also relate to measures that are not in dB, such as discrimination scores for speech. Hearing impairment implies that performance is poorer than normal. It is generally categorized as mild, moderate, or severe. *Hearing handicap* refers to the interference in hearing that results from the hearing loss. Thus, the influence of the hearing impairment is the hearing handicap. For example, an individual with a hearing level of 50 dB may have more difficulty in his or her communicative environment than another individual with a 30 dB HL because that person may have greater communicative demands in his or her occupational or personal life.

RELATIONSHIPS OF TERMINOLOGY

The terms just described can best be understood as they relate to individual cases. Two case presentations clarify their use.

A 42-year-old woman was seen by an audiologist following a sudden onset of tinnitus and hearing loss. The audiometric results revealed a flat sensorineural hearing loss. The pure-tone speech frequency average was 45 dB hearing level in each ear. According to a pre-employment audiogram, the patient essentially had normal hearing with an average of 8 dB HL in each ear. Thus, there was a 37 dB hearing loss associated with the incident. Her hearing impairment is classified as moderate. The actual hearing handicap is greater than this because the patient reports considerable difficulty in communicating. The problem is more acute in this case because the client works as a librarian, and people tend to speak softly in libraries.

A 5-year-old child is being mainstreamed in a regular kindergarten class. He has normal hearing until 1000 Hz in each ear, but at this point his thresholds fall off markedly. The hearing level at 2000 Hz is 35 dB poorer than his 0 dB threshold at 1000 Hz. Although there is a mild hearing impairment according to standard classifications, this child has major difficulties in distinguishing high-frequency consonants from one another and developing age-appropriate verbal concepts. This problem is increased because the child has been placed in a relatively noisy classroom with a teacher who has never had a child who is hearing impaired in her class. In addition, she does not know the special accommodations that should be made for this particular youngster. Thus, the level of difficulty is underestimated by simply looking at the hearing level.

CONGENITAL VERSUS ACQUIRED HEARING LOSS

One factor that influences the effect of a hearing loss is *when* it occurs. Severe congenital or prelingual hearing losses (losses prior to the development of oral speech and language) have a great impact on language, voice, and articulation because the individual does not develop these skills normally. The person does not have the constant language stimulation and accurate feedback of his or her own speech production. As an adult the person may continue to have limitations in language as well as in voice and articulation. Prelingual hearing disorders also have a more deleterious effect on social, educational, and vocational aspects of the person's life, than if the hearing loss occurred after oral speech and language have developed.

The same type of loss at an older age, especially a sudden catastrophic loss of hearing, will be likely to have a profound influence on the individual, but of a much different type. There will be no diminution of the person's language ability and relatively little change in his voice quality. Over a period of time, articulatory movements will tend to become less precise, typically affecting the high frequency sibilant sounds first. Because the individual is not able to monitor articulation and voice effectively, he or she may compensate for this by increasing speech volume.

The sudden catastrophic loss is usually more devastating than one of gradual onset in two ways. First, the psychological impact of isolation is much greater because of the suddenness of the onset. Second, the person who experiences a sudden onset of hearing loss will tend to have difficulty utilizing his or her residual hearing to make fine distinctions among, for example, the sounds of speech. Clients with progressive hearing loss have been able to alter their auditory perceptions in a gradual manner. The person with a sudden loss may not know how to listen for clues to distinguish, for example, the singular form of a word from the plural, whereas the person whose hearing has diminished over time may have developed strategies for doing so.

Obviously, the complex interactions of people, their needs and environments, and the various test indicators provide infinite possibilities about the person who possesses the

hearing loss. Audiometric results will give us some guidance and general knowledge about the patient, but in the end, they fail to reveal things that the patient or his family can tell the audiologist. The contribution of audiometric test results in predicting hearing handicap will be discussed in the following section.

TYPE OF HEARING LOSS

CONDUCTIVE LOSS

Knowing the type of hearing loss can aid in predicting the handicap that the client is experiencing. For example, conductive losses, particularly when the client possesses normal to near normal bone conduction, are associated with good discrimination ability for speech. Clients with a conductive hearing loss may achieve very good speech discrimination simply with increased volume. Although the communicative effects of conductive loss in the adult are not as severe as an equivalent sensorineural loss, there is growing evidence that a mild conductive loss early in life may have significant long-term effects (Dalzell & Owrid, 1976; Holm & Kunze, 1969; Secord, Ericson, & Bush, 1988). Furthermore, in some cases, ear drainage may contraindicate the use of an earmold for a hearing aid, and a conductive overlay on top of a sensorineural problem can complicate the use and types of amplification.

COCHLEAR LOSS

Most cochlear (sensory) losses reveal some diminished word discrimination ability. There is usually a direct relationship between hearing level and discrimination ability (Thompson & Hoel, 1962). The more depressed the hearing level, the poorer the discrimination score. Disorders of the cochlea produce a variety of audiometric patterns, which provide clues to their etiology. Detection of these problems can lead to preventative measures and thus minimize any further hearing loss. Most cochlear hearing losses are greater in the high frequencies than in the low frequencies. This is because presbycusis (age related) and noise induced hearing loss, the most common causes of sensorineural disorder, primarily affect the higher frequencies. Cochlear losses associated with Meniere's disease, however, are greater in the low frequencies than in the high frequencies. A flat audiometric configuration may be seen also in ototoxic-related disorders. These patterns are not mutually exclusive and thus may overlap one another.

Another characteristic of sensory losses is an intolerance for loud sounds. Consequently, this factor must be considered in the use of amplification. In cases with extremely small dynamic ranges, the use of amplification could be contraindicated. That is, some individuals with sensory losses have an intolerance for sounds only slightly above their threshold levels.

Cochlear losses may also affect the speech and voice of the individual. Because the inner ear functioning is decreased, the internal feedback loop is reduced to the extent that the clients are unable to monitor their own speech and voice patterns normally. This can lead to some articulation disorders as well as reduced vocal inflection and quality. The effect is related to the extent and duration of the hearing loss.

NEURAL LOSS

The effects of a neural hearing loss, that is caused by a decline in function of the auditory nerve (VIII cranial nerve) and beyond, are generally more a problem of clarity than of sensitivity. Consequently, audiometric findings will usually show more significantly depressed word recognition scores. This in turn may disrupt not only normal communications, but also the use of a hearing aid that is designed to alleviate the communicative breakdown. Another characteristic of neural losses is the presence of tone decay, or the inability to maintain the audibility of sounds. For example, Costello and McGee (1967) discussed clients who behaved as either deaf or aphasic individuals, although their pure-tone thresholds were quite good. These cases were found to have severe discrimination losses associated with rapid tone decay. It should be noted that many cases with brainstem dysfunction, as well as those with eighth nerve losses, display poor discrimination of speech and significant tone decay.

CENTRAL DYSFUNCTION

Peripheral hearing disorders may be due to disease at the conductive, cochlear, or eighth nerve levels of the auditory system. Dysfunction in the brain or brainstem results in a central disorder. Although it also might produce a hearing loss, central dysfunction is generally associated with more subtle changes, including figure-ground processing and localization problems. These difficulties may compound the problems associated with a coincidental hearing loss; however, central auditory dysfunction by itself can produce sufficient difficulty to cause a person to seek evaluation by an audiologist.

Stach (1989) points out that a high percentage of people who fail to benefit from hearing aids, at least among the elderly, have central processing problems. Thus, the audiologist should consider this possibility when an individual does not demonstrate the expected degree of benefit from amplification, or when the amount of auditory disability far outweighs the person's amount of hearing loss as shown on the standard audiometric tests.

UNILATERAL VERSUS BILATERAL HEARING LOSS

The problems experienced from hearing loss may be increased or minimized depending on whether the loss involves one or both ears. The difficulties associated with unilateral hearing impairments generally are not limited to the amount of loss alone. Although the thresholds in the affected ear are lowered, one would think that if either ear could hear the sound, that the individual would benefit fully by its presence. In this way, the better ear would be expected to dominate and greatly reduce the adverse influence of the poorer ear. However, the handicap resulting from a unilateral loss is due not only to the loss of sensitivity, but even more likely to the imbalance between the ears which tends to disable important central processes.

Individuals who have unilateral losses often experience some listening problems. One obvious difficulty is the lack of hearing when someone is speaking on the person's impaired side. Two other problems are not associated with the problem of hearing sensitivity. For one thing, people with unilateral losses can be expected to have trouble in localizing the source of a sound. But, perhaps the most important problem associated with this type of loss is difficulty understanding speech in a background of noise or when the acoustical conditions are poor. Similarly, a person with a bilateral loss who wears a monaural hearing aid tends to lose the benefits he or she might derive from the binaural system. Thus, that person cannot benefit fully from the central functions that enable someone, for example, to separate foreground from background and to locate sounds in space.

Unilateral losses in children, although they might not be as devastating as when lost suddenly in adulthood (Bardon, 1986), have potentially important consequences. A complete journal issue was devoted to the work of Bess and his colleagues, dealing with unilateral hearing loss in children (Bess, 1986). Their work confirms that unilateral losses are associated with poor localization of sound in space, as well as with difficulty on speech-in-noise tasks. The greater the loss in the poorer ear, the greater the difficulty.

WHAT AUDIOMETRIC DATA REVEAL

In their simplest form, hearing disorders can be viewed as changes in sensitivity, frequency range, and fidelity. Sensitivity can be likened to the decibel variations produced by an attenuator. A reduced range is similar to the effects of an acoustic filter that selectively impedes the passage of some frequencies and permits others to pass. A lack of fidelity refers to the distortion caused by the nonlinear transmission of a sound due to the breakdown of either peripheral or central structures.

The influences of sensitivity (degree of loss) and frequency range (configuration) will be described first because they represent the most reliable audiometric information. The disorders of fidelity (clarity), while vitally important, are not as quantifiable. Fidelity and other factors that are less precise reduce a clinician's ability to predict the handicap from the pure-tone information. The audiologist and the client will be best served when all of the available information is used.

DEGREE OF LOSS

One of several things that audiometric data reveal is the degree of loss. This information is important because it provides a general indicator of the handicap the individual may experience. One way of putting the obtained hearing threshold levels into perspective is to relate them to general guidelines that categorize various hearing levels along with their predicted handicaps (see Table 2–1). By doing this, the audiologist may be able to make general statements about the person's hearing function and probable needs. However, the clinician cannot state with great accuracy the specific effect of the loss. Thus, a table should be used only as a guideline, not as an absolute.

Many methods of categorization have been proposed, including those of Davis and Silverman (1970), Green (1978), and Hodgson (1978). The emphasis of each table varies according to its purpose. These purposes include medical-legal definitions, handicapping effects, rehabilitative needs, and the impact on children versus adults.

The overall influence of the degree of loss may not be as obvious as it appears. Generally,

TABLE 2–1. RELATIONSHIP OF THREE FREQUENCY SPEECH AVERAGES TO TYPICAL HEARING DIFFICULTIES AND AMPLIFICATION CONSIDERATIONS*

ANSI (1989) Levels in Decibels	Classification	Approximate Discrimination** (%)	Typical Speech Understanding (Unaided)	Typical Adult Amplification Considerations	Typical Child Amplification Considerations
0–24	Essentially normal	92	No significant limitations	Generally none but depends on configuration; high frequency loss may benefit; possible special fittings such as CROS or BICROS	Generally none but preferential seating is recommended; mild gain FM system optional on case by case basis
25–39	Mild	82	Difficulty with faint speech especially from a distance	Recommended based on reported degree of difficulty; mild gain canal and in-the-ear units are appropriate	Preferential seating required; mild gain hearing aid may be considered; in-the-ear or behind-the-ear units recommended based on degree of difficulty; FM systems to be considered
40–54	Moderate	70	Frequent difficulty with normal speech	Frequent to full-time hearing aid use; canal aids useful; in-the-ear and behind-the-ear instruments are more effective; assistive listening devices may be considered	Full-time use of amplification; in-the-ear style is possible but behind-the-ear instrument is preferred; supplemented in school with FM system
55–69	Moderately severe	60	Constant difficulty even with loud speech	Full-time hearing aid use; patient acceptance related to word discrimination ability; behind-the-ear styles most appropriate to yield best performance; direct audio input may be considered	Minimum choice is behind-the-ear units; may require special class and speech therapy; use of FM system is essential

70–89	Severe	36	Severe difficulty; loud or amplified speech might be understood	Full-time binaural hearing aid use; behind-the-ear aid is appropriate style; assistive devices considered such as closed caption TV decoder	Minimum choice is behind-the-ear instruments; may consider body hearing aid; FM system use is mandatory
90+	Profound	20	Understanding of speech severely limited even with amplification; use of amplification provides mostly environmental and speech clues	Minimum choice is power behind-the-ear instruments; may require body instrument; cochlear implant may be recommended in post-lingually deafened	Powerful behind-the-ear units may be possible; body instrument may prove better consideration; cochlear implant or vibrotactile aids may be considered; often requires special education program

* This information is based in part on that published by Goetzinger (1978). It should be pointed out that this table refers to limitations and needs related to cochlear hearing losses. Conductive, retrocochlear, and central disorders may follow a different pattern of handicap and needs. The three frequency speech average refers to the average dB value for pure tones 500 Hz, 1000 Hz, and 2000 Hz in the better ear. When appropriate, binaural amplification is preferred to monaural.

** W–22 scores at PB–Max for cochlear cases from Thompson and Hoel (1962), and Mongelli (1978).

the rule of thumb is, the greater the hearing level the greater the handicap. However the actual *handicap,* when compared to the *degree* of loss, may vary considerably. Important factors contributing to these differences include personality, intelligence, motivation, occupation, and environmental conditions. Individuals who rely heavily on communicative function for their work, such as salespersons, attorneys, and teachers who possess relatively mild hearing loss may notice significantly greater handicap than those whose jobs are not as verbally demanding (e.g., truck drivers, plant workers). Individuals who tend to socialize more (those who go to parties and plays) will notice slighter hearing losses sooner than people who tend to stay home and read, watch television, and relate only to close family members.

The influence of the degree of hearing loss is even more critical in the case of young children, especially when the problem occurs before the development of language, in the first few years of life. In cases of profound hearing loss, voice, speech, and language are likely to be substantially influenced. Abnormal breathing patterns and improper use of the vocal folds will influence intonation and stress patterns (Whitehead & Barefoot, 1983). Also, the fundamental frequency of the voice is generally higher than normal (Gilbert & Campbell, 1980). Vocal onset confusions, which result from not knowing how to produce the sounds, affect both a child's understanding of and production of voiced and voiceless consonants (Mashie, 1980). Vowels often are substituted for one another, and final consonants frequently are omitted (Levitt & Stromberg, 1983).

Less severe hearing losses have correspondingly fewer communicative consequences; however, in any given group there will be notable exceptions. Often, due to unknown reasons, an individual with relatively little hearing loss will perform especially poorly, or one with a severe problem will perform especially well. This is most obvious in classrooms for the hearing impaired in which students with the poorest hearing may perform better in dealing with verbal information than those who possess hearing losses that are less severe.

CONFIGURATION OF LOSS

The shape of the audiogram helps to determine the frequency characteristics of the auditory information the individual receives. When both the audiometric configuration of the client's hearing and the energy distribution of the incoming auditory signals are known, the audiologist can better understand the frequency information the client is receiving. An audiologist often looks at the client's binaural hearing to determine the sounds that he or she will hear best. This is done by noting the better threshold at each frequency for the two ears. Although this approach is a valid one, it is limited in a number of ways. While it does consider HL, it does not consider the locus of lesion, the unilateral/bilateral nature of the loss, and the clarity of the incoming information.

The configuration of the hearing loss will be considered as if it were produced by acoustic filters. Despite the limitations of the acoustic filter approach, the audiologist can obtain an important source of information that can be used in understanding a client's communicative abilities and deficits. Other variables that influence performance will be discussed later.

Flat Configuration

A flat configuration refers to a pure-tone audiogram in which there are relatively small differences in thresholds obtained across the frequencies on the audiogram. This does not imply the same dB hearing level throughout. In fact, slightly sloping and jagged patterns are frequently considered flat because they are not extreme enough to be classified as high- or low-frequency curves.

The audiologist can assume that a flat loss will limit the input evenly across the frequencies. The major energy component of speech is in the low frequencies (250 to 500 Hz). Despite the power of those frequencies, they contain relatively little information for identifying words. There is little speech energy in the high frequencies. In the normal listener, essentially complete and accurate intelligibility comes from the frequencies 300 to 3000 Hz. The frequencies of speech that contribute most to intelligibility are between 1000 and 3000 Hz (Hodgson, 1978). This information can help clinicians to understand hearing loss as a filter effect. For example, because speech contains little high-frequency energy, a flat loss is likely to affect the high-frequency information most severely and the low-frequency information least of all.

High-Frequency Configuration

While the flat configuration tends to impact heavily on the high-frequency portion of speech signals, a high-frequency loss has an even greater adverse effect. This type of loss is analogous to a filter with a sharply sloped rejection for the high frequencies. In other words, the low frequencies are passed on to the listener, while the high frequencies are impeded and not heard, or heard less clearly.

A person with a predominantly high-frequency hearing loss is keenly aware of speech and environmental sounds that contain a preponderance of low-frequency energy. Thus, he or she is able to hear such life saving sounds as a car horn or a verbal warning, but misses nuances, confuses words, and may not understand the punch lines of jokes. These individuals also have difficulty in locating the source of a sound, understanding speech from another room, and blocking out background sounds.

When there is a major difference between a person's hearing in the low- and middle-frequencies versus those in the upper-frequency range, this difference may create a problem for the audiologist in planning appropriate amplification. The specific frequency at which the loss drops off is most important, especially if it is within the speech frequencies.

Individuals with high-frequency losses are often accused of hearing just what they want to hear. For example, they may easily recognize their names and familiar phrases from the low-frequency components, but fail to understand when the language or concepts become complex or abstract. Furthermore, their level of understanding can be expected to fall sharply when the listening environment is noisy.

Low-Frequency Configuration

Low frequency audiometric configurations are the least common and have the fewest disadvantages. Low frequency information is the most powerful and the most expendable portion of the speech signal. Thus, from a simple filter effect, the patient retains the most important part of the frequency range and should have good discrimination for speech. The one exception to this rule is when the low-frequency loss is associated with brainstem pathology, which may result in reduced speech discrimination. Even in those instances, the client's voice is generally unaffected and articulation usually remains normal.

Saucer-Shaped Configuration

Occasionally, a saucer-shaped audiometric curve is observed. This pattern is characterized by better thresholds for the high and low frequencies than those in the mid-range. Thus, the sounds that are most important for speech recognition are diminished the most. Although this configuration of loss would appear to be extremely handicapping, we often find good speech thresholds and very good speech discrimination scores. This may be because saucer-shaped losses are frequently congenital in nature. Therefore it is likely that, over the years, the individuals refine their ability to derive phonemic cues from the higher and lower frequency information.

SPEECH RECEPTION AND DISCRIMINATION TESTS

Audiologists make use of standard speech threshold and discrimination (recognition) tests in order to understand a person's hearing ability under optimum conditions, such as those found in a sound-treated environment. Suprathreshold measures such as most comfortable loudness (MCL) and uncomfortable loudness (UCL) tests can be administered to help predict how comfortably an individual will handle amplified speech (e.g., a hearing aid).

Good speech recognition along with a moderate speech threshold and a wide dynamic range of comfortable listening encourages audiologists to think that the individual will be relatively easy to fit with a hearing aid. However, poor word discrimination with very poor pure-tone thresholds may complicate the achievement of excellent aided results. The hypersensitivity to moderate levels of speech may call for complex solutions to enable the individual to benefit fully from amplification.

Because the standard speech threshold and discrimination measures generally employ single word tasks, they are not representative of normal conversation (not to mention the lack of background noise and the benefit of a professional speaker). They do not take into account the context of conversations, inflections, and visual cues. Thus, a variety of speech measures is needed to represent accurately a person's normal listening conditions. The Central Institute for the Deaf's Everyday Speech Sentence lists (Davis & Silverman, 1970) and the Harvard Psycho-Acoustic Laboratory (PAL) question-and-answer type materials are often used for these purposes (Hudgins, Hawkins, Karlin, & Stevens, 1947).

Early tests of speech discrimination failed to address the difficulties experienced by people with losses that primarily involved the high frequencies. This problem has been resolved somewhat by the introduction of tests such as the California Consonant Test (Owens & Schubert, 1977), a multiple choice procedure that requires careful attention to the high-frequency consonant sounds.

The evaluation of young children poses additional challenges to the audiologist. Speech threshold and recognition measures generally require modification, if they can be used at all. If time tested materials such as the Haskins Phonetically Balanced Kindergarten Word Lists (PBKs) (Haskins, 1949), or the Word Intelligibility by Picture Identification test (WIPI) (Ross & Lerman, 1970) are not successful, informal procedures may be employed.

OTHER TESTS

A group of other audiometric tests, many of more recent origin, is available to the audiologist to provide a better understanding of the client. Acoustic immittance measurements are of great value in determining the need and type of rehabilitative services for an individual. Tympanometry, which measures the mobility of the tympanic membrane, permits us to determine if the status of the middle ear is normal. If so, then medical intervention to remediate otitis media and other conditions of the outer and middle ear is likely to be unnecessary. Rather, attention can be focused on other types of medical, audiological, or other forms of management. If a middle ear problem, such as otitis media, does exist, this situation might influence whether an ear mold or bone conduction vibrator should be used to conduct the auditory signal. Acoustic reflex thresholds may be used as a general guideline when selecting the maximum output level of an aid for an individual who cannot communicate his or her intolerance for loud sounds (Keith, 1979).

Another important procedure that is useful for young children and the difficult-to-test is the auditory brainstem response (ABR). Although hearing aid evaluations with those who can communicate effectively do not need such elaborate procedures to verify the benefit of a hearing aid, this might be necessary for young children and others who may not provide reliable responses to the test stimuli. ABR audiometry utilizes minute electrical potentials that can be measured on the scalp to monitor the activity of the acoustic nerve and central auditory system when auditory signals are presented to the ears. The audiologist can assess the levels at which the auditory system produces acceptable electrical responses from the eighth nerve and brainstem. This will help the audiologist to ascertain whether there is a functional auditory system, if the aid is to be of benefit, and at what level the aid should be set.

A number of behavioral tests also can be of importance when assessing a patient for rehabilitative purposes. Tests of central function may explain why a particular individual does not make good use of amplification (Stach, 1989). When central tests show that one ear is especially deficient (regardless of the peripheral test performance), then the other ear might be considered more strongly for amplification.

A number of tests that provide speech signals embedded in competing noises may be used as a more realistic measure of performance in life situations. The Synthetic Sentence Identification (SSI) (Speaks & Jerger, 1965) and the Speech Perception In Noise (SPIN) (Kalikow, Stevens, & Elliot, 1977) tests are particularly applicable for this purpose.

LIMITATIONS OF AUDIOMETRIC INFORMATION

Audiometric data can accurately describe a person's hearing status, but cannot reveal with any precision how well the individual gets along in his or her personal and professional communication environments. The specifics and complexities of real-life situations are too idiosyncratic for audiologists to make accurate predictions about how a complex and idiosyncratic individual will perform or react. Thus, audiologists can make assumptions and generalizations, but they must validate them through interviews and informal testing. Certain information may never be known. The following examples illustrate these uncertainties:

A college student inadvertently pushed a cotton swab through his tympanic membrane. He was tested audiometrically over time until his hearing levels improved to a level of about 10 dB above his normal ear. At this point, both ears were within normal audiometric limits. After five years, the client continues to feel that the hearing deviation has affected him greatly. He is annoyed because the two ears sound different and he is highly distracted by the background noise.

At the other end of the continuum is the child who is severely-to-profoundly hearing impaired who performs better than other individuals with normal hearing could be expected to perform. He excels in foreign languages, plays a musical instrument, and communicates without obvious handicap when facing the speaker at a distance of no greater than 15 feet. It the belief of this chapter's authors that this is due to early binaural amplification and a mother who was determined that her child would develop normal speech and language.

EDUCATIONAL AND VOCATIONAL CONSIDERATIONS FOR THE HEARING HANDICAP

EDUCATIONAL

The child or adult who is hearing impaired will be subject to limitations in a mainstreamed class perhaps more than any other setting. Despite the numerous potential advantages of integrating a child with a hearing impairment into a regular class, the challenge may be considerable. By definition, school is a setting in which new information and unfamiliar concepts are presented. Unlike the rest of the class, the person who is auditorily impaired must attempt to determine what was said and then deal with it at the cognitive level that the teacher intended.

In recent years, many forms of assistive listening devices have become available to help people who are limited in their auditory function to pursue their education along with normally hearing individuals. These devices and approaches will be discussed in greater length throughout this textbook.

VOCATIONAL

Like the classroom, the workplace provides many challenges to the person who is hearing impaired. People choose careers that are suited to their abilities and are least affected by their limitations. People who are hearing impaired generally avoid jobs that require intensive communication. However, in recent years we have seen a growing number of students who are handicapped enter fields that were considered out of their reach not too many years ago. For example, individuals who are partially sighted or hearing impaired, now can pursue careers as physicians and lawyers. New vocational openings make the need for efficient and innovative management strategies even greater than in earlier times when a person's options were more severely limited by his or her hearing impairment.

SUMMARY

This chapter discussed the implications of audiometric findings on the needs of individuals who are hearing-impaired. Much information can be obtained from basic audiometric procedures which shed light on the auditory status and auditory capabilities of these people. This, in turn, aids in developing a rehabilitative plan that can address their communicative needs.

Although audiometric data provide crucial information in understanding the client's problems, the audiologist must also be aware of their limitations. It is often difficult to generalize from formal tests to the person's day-to-day life. To fill in those gaps, audiologists must seek information from interviews, questionnaires, and other sources.

REFERENCES

American National Standards Institute (1989). American National Standard Specifications for Audiometers. ANSI S3.6-1989, New York.

Bardon, J. I. (1986). Unilateral sensorineural hearing loss: From the inside out, a patient's perspective. *The Hearing Journal, 39,* 13–17.

Bess, F. (Ed.). (1986). [Special Issue]. *Ear and Hearing, 7*(1), 1–54.

Costello, M. R., & McGee, T. M. (1967). Language impairment associated with bilateral abnormal auditory information. In A. B. Graham (Ed.), *Sensory processes and disorders.* Boston: Little, Brown.

Dalzell, J., & Owrid, H. L. (1976). Children with conductive deafness: A follow-up study. *British Journal of Audiology, 10,* 87–90.

Davis, H., & Silverman, S. R. (1987). *Hearing and deafness.* New York: Holt, Rinehart & Winston.

Gilbert, H. R., & Campbell, M. I. (1980). Speaking fundamental frequency in three groups of hearing-impaired individuals. *Journal of Communicative Disorders, 13,* 195–205.

Goetzinger, C. P. (1978). Word discrimination testing. In J. Katz (Ed.), *Handbook of clinical audiology* (pp. 149–158). Baltimore, MD: Williams & Wilkins.

Green, D. (1978). Pure tone testing. In J. Katz (Ed.), *Handbook of clinical audiology* (pp. 98–109). Baltimore, MD: Williams & Wilkins.

Haskins, H. (1949). *A phonetically balanced test of speech discrimination for children.* Unpublished master's thesis, Northwestern University, Evanston, IL.

Hodgson, W. R. (1978). Disorders of hearing. In P. Skinner & R. Shelton (Eds.), *Speech, language and hearing.* Reading, MA: Addison-Wesley.

Holm, V. A., & Kunze, L. H. (1969). Effects of chronic otitis media on language and development. *Pediatrics, 43,* 833–839.

Hudgins, C. V., Hawkins, J. E., Karlin, J. E., & Stevens, S. S. (1947). The development of recorded auditory tests for measuring hearing loss for speech. *Laryngoscope, 47,* 57–89.

Kalikow, D. N., Stevens, K. N., & Elliot, L. L. (1977). Development of a test of speech intelligibility in noise using sentence materials with controlled word predictability. *Journal of Acoustical Society of America, 61,* 1337–1351.

Keith, R. (1979). An acoustic reflex technique of establishing hearing aid settings. *Journal of the American Auditory Society, 5,* 71–75.

Levitt, H., & Stromberg, H. (1983). Segmental characteristics of speech of hearing-impaired children — Factors affecting intelligibility. In I. Hochberg, H. Levitt, & M. J. Osberger (Eds.), *Speech of the hearing-impaired: Research, training and personnel preparation* (pp. 32–41). Baltimore, MD: University Park Press.

Mashie, J. J. (1980). *Laryngeal behavior of hearing-impaired speakers.* Unpublished doctoral dissertation, Syracuse University, Syracuse, NY.

Mongelli, C. (1978). Central auditory involvement in two geriatric populations measured with the staggered spondaic word test. Unpublished manuscript, University of California, Santa Barbara.

Owens, E., & Shubert, E. (1977). Development of the California Consonant Test. *Journal of Speech and Hearing Research, 20,* 463–474.

Ross, M., & Lerman, J. (1970). A picture identification test for hearing impaired children. *Journal of Speech and Hearing Research, 13,* 44–53.

Secord, G. J., Erickson, M. T., & Bush, J. P. (1988). Neuropsychological sequelae of otitis media in children and adolescents with learning disabilities. *Journal of Pediatric Psychology, 13,* 531–542.

Speaks, C. & Jerger, J. (1965). Method of measurement of speech identification. *Journal of Speech and Hearing Research, 8,* 185–194.

Stach, B. (1989). Hearing aid amplification and central processing disorders. In R. E. Sandlin (Ed.), *Handbook of hearing aid amplification. Vol. II. Clinical considerations* (pp. 87–111). Boston, MA: College-Hill Press.

Thompson, G., & Hoel, R. (1962). Flat sensorineural hearing loss and PB scores. *Journal of Speech and Hearing Disorders, 27,* 284–287.

Whitehead, R. L, & Barefoot, S. (1983). *Air flow characteristics of fricative consonants produced by normally hearing and hearing-impaired speakers.* Unpublished manuscript, National Technical Institute for the Deaf, Rochester, NY.

CHAPTER 3

Introduction to Hearing Aids

■ RAYMOND H. HULL, Ph.D. ■

The fitting and dispensing of hearing aids and other amplification systems is one of the very important aspects of the process of aural habilitation/rehabilitation. When a child or adult's impaired auditory system is brought to a more efficient level of function through the appropriate fitting of a hearing aid, then the other components of the auditory habilitation or rehabilitation program will be facilitated.

This discussion of hearing aids will encompass the topics of (1) the basic components of hearing aids, (2) their electroacoustic properties, (3) types of hearing aids, and (4) ear molds and their types and properties. Considerations of hearing aid evaluation and fitting procedures, along with hearing aid orientation for children, are found in Chapter 7 of this textbook. Hearing aid orientation for adults is found in Chapter 13, and considerations regarding hearing aids for older adults are found in Chapter 21. A thorough discussion of other assistive listening devices is found in Chapter 14.

COMPONENTS OF HEARING AIDS

Even though there are many different types and models of hearing aids available for fitting,

their basic components are the same. They possess: (1) a microphone, (2) an amplifier, (3) a receiver, (4) a power source in the form of a battery. Figure 3–1 provides a diagram of the basic configuration for a hearing aid. Figure 3–2 presents an "exploded" behind-the-ear (BTE) hearing aid, revealing (a) the battery compartment, (b) the amplifier, (c) the volume control, (d) the receiver, and (e) the earhook.

THE MICROPHONE

The sound energy from a source is received by a microphone to be transduced (changed) into an electrical form of energy. Historically, the microphone portion of a hearing aid has evolved to a state of substantial sophistication.

Magnetic Microphones

In the early stages of the development of transistor hearing aids, the magnetic microphone was the standard for the industry. Figure 3–3 shows a schematic of a magnetic microphone. The magnetic microphone is made up of (1) magnetic poles designated north and south, or + and −, to which a small electrical charge is

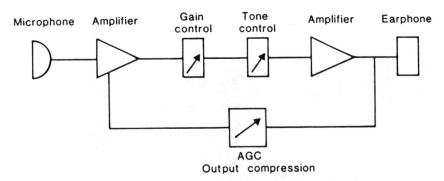

Figure 3–1. Basic diagram of a hearing aid with compression circuitry.

placed, (2) a magnetic armature that has a coil of copper wire wrapped around it, and (3) the microphone diaphragm that is attached to the armature by a small rod. As sound strikes the diaphragm, it moves in synchrony with the waveform. The rod moves with the diaphragm movements, causing the armature to move correspondingly in an alternate fashion between the magnetic poles. The signal that results contains the same waveform as the signal that originally struck the microphone diaphragm.

These magnetic microphones were a great improvement over earlier forms, but were a source of frustration for those who fit hearing aids and those who wore them due to variable distortion of the signal.

The Electret Microphone

Electret microphones are found in virtually all hearing aids today. The electret microphone (Killion & Carlson, 1974) is far superior to the earlier magnetic and crystal microphones due to its excellent response to a wide range of frequencies, even at low intensity levels; a low sensitivity to mechanical vibration; and low noise. The early crystal microphone used in the 1930s and 1940s was susceptible to damage by humidity and temperature factors; and the magnetic microphone, although well suited for use in transistor hearing aids, was incapable of maintaining as smooth and as wide a frequency response as the electret mi-

crophone. It was also more susceptible to mechanical vibration.

An electret microphone is made from fluorocarbon material that is permanently electrically charged, so an outside source for the charge is not required. A very thin diaphragm that is covered with a metallic coating is suspended just above the electret material layer. As sound strikes the diaphragm, the action causes a small symmetrical charge to be generated and then amplified by a small transistor in the microphone housing. (See Figure 3-4 for a diagram of an electret microphone from Killion & Carlson, 1974.)

THE AMPLIFIER

The purpose of the amplifier in a hearing aid, as in radios, television sets, and stereos, is to increase the magnitude of the incoming signal. In early hearing aids, the size of the amplifier greatly increased the size of the hearing aid. With the advent of the transistor, hearing aids were greatly reduced in size. With the development of the silicon chip, hearing aid size has been reduced further.

Today, hearing aid amplifiers are designed around numerous transistors, resistors, and diodes that are formed on a single silicon chip, providing the opportunity for various configurations of intensity and frequency responses, signal compression, and expansion in concert with the microphone and receiver of the hearing aid.

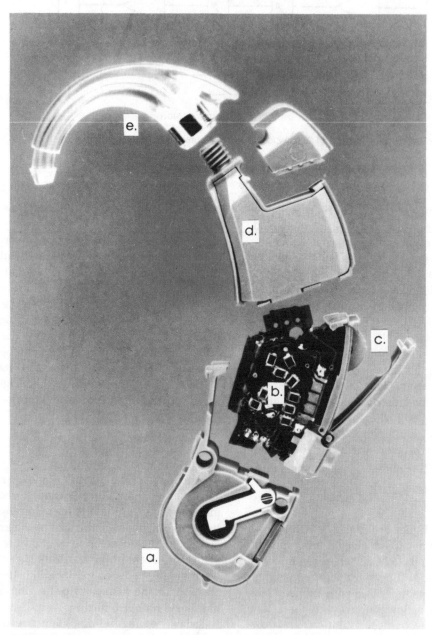

Figure 3-2. "Exploded" behind-the-ear (BTE) hearing aid. (Courtesy of Telex Communications, Inc.)

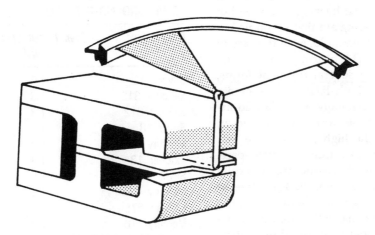

Figure 3-3. Schematic of a magnetic microphone.

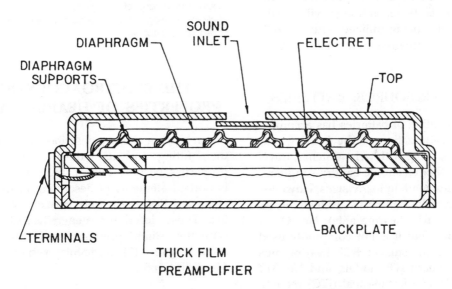

Figure 3-4. Diagram of an electret microphone. (Reprinted with permission from M. S. Killion, Etymotic Research, 61 Martin Lane, Elk Grove Village, IL 60007.)

The amplifier is responsible for the gain (amplification potential) of the hearing aid. The gain of hearing aids generally is controlled manually by the wearer. Also changes in output and frequency response generally are made manually, but those controls are less visible to the wearer, and changes in those aspects of the signal generally are made by the dispenser in accordance with the needs of the client. With the advent of digitally programma-ble hearing aids, changes in frequency response and output can be *programmed* into the amplifier to suit the needs of the wearer.

THE RECEIVER

The receiver, which converts the signal from electrical form back to its acoustic form to be received by the ear, is either found in the casing of the hearing aid that is coupled directly to the wearer's concha and ear canal, as in the case of the all-in-the-ear hearing aid, or within the casing of the hearing aid that is coupled to plastic tubing and an earmold, as in the case of a behind-the-ear (BTE) hearing aid.

Receivers come in several different forms, but those found in both BTE and in-the-ear (ITE) hearing aids generally are balanced armature magnetic type receivers (Lybarger, 1985), because of the high performance that they can achieve in an extremely small space.

Bone conduction receivers are basically magnetically driving systems that are free to vibrate within a casing that is held against the listener's head. The magnetic vibrator transduces the acoustic energy of sound into vibration that is transported to the concha by way of the temporal bone, although vibrotactile systems are also being utilized with the profoundly hearing impaired on the hands, wrists, or fingers.

THE POWER SOURCE: BATTERIES

The miniaturization of batteries has accompanied the miniaturization of the hearing aids that use them, along with wrist watches, travel alarms, and other electronic battery-run items. These batteries come in many sizes. However, for hearing aids the standard sizes include No. 675 (for larger BTE hearing aids); No. 41 for some BTE aids (but it is not commonly used today); No. 13 for smaller BTE hearing aids and many standard ITE models; and No. 312 for smaller ITE and in-the-canal (ITC) models.

Hearing aid battery types are generally those of zinc-air and mercury. With the advent of batteries with increased useful battery life, the battery has become one of the less stressful aspects of hearing aid use. And, with the advent of air-activated batteries, shelf life is also less of a concern. The actual life of a hearing aid battery, however, depends on the output level required by the hearing aid user, and the ambient noise levels in the environment in which the hearing aid is used (Lybarger, 1985). Table 3–1 presents the voltages and life of several types of hearing aid batteries (from Lybarger, 1985).

TABLE 3–1. VOLTAGES AND LIFE OF SEVERAL TYPES OF HEARING AID BATTERIES.

Battery Type	Open Circuit Voltage (volts)	Capacity mAh
Silver 312	1.5	37
Mercury 312	1.3	45
Zinc-air 312	1.3	70
Silver 13	1.5	75
Mercury 13	1.3	85
Zinc-air 13	1.3	170
Silver 76	1.5	180
Mercury 675	1.3	180–245
Zinc-air 675	1.3	400
Mercury 401	1.3	800

Source: From Lybarger, S. F. (1985). The physical and electroacoustic characteristics of hearing aids. In J. Katz (Ed.), *Handbook of clinical audiology* (p. 858). Baltimore: Williams & Wilkins. Reprinted with permission.

THE ELECTROACOUSTIC PROPERTIES OF HEARING AIDS

When hearing aids are described in relation to their fitting and use, their electroacoustic properties become critical. Indeed, the most important elements in describing hearing aid characteristics are their electroacoustic properties. Those descriptors generally include (1) saturation sound pressure level (SSPL), (2) acoustic gain, (3) frequency response, and (4) distortion.

SATURATION SOUND PRESSURE LEVEL

The saturation sound pressure level (SSPL) used to be referred to as the maximum power output (MPO) of a hearing aid. This is the greatest amount of sound pressure that a given hearing aid can produce. The SSPL is usually measured with the gain of the hearing aid at its full-on position, and the input at 90 dB SPL. The average SSPL-90 across the frequency spectrum is computed observing the average of the output at the frequencies of 1000, 1600, and 2500 Hz (ANSI S3.22–1987).

ACOUSTIC GAIN

The gain of a hearing aid is determined by measuring its output across the frequency spectrum when compared to an input intensity of a specified amount. The gain represents the amount of intensity the wearer receives at various frequencies in comparison with the intensity of those incoming signals. A person with a severe hearing loss will require a hearing aid with a higher gain than one who possesses a milder hearing loss. A person who possesses most of his or her hearing loss in the higher frequencies will be satisfied with a hearing aid that produces its greatest gain in those frequencies.

The acoustic gain of a hearing aid is the difference in decibels between the input signal *to* the hearing aid, and how much the hearing aid amplifies it. This is measured to determine how much amplification the wearer of a specific hearing aid can expect when the hearing aid volume control is set at a specific level and when the input signal is at a generally expected level, for example, for conversational speech at 50 to 60 dB SPL. The ANSI S3.22–1987 standard contains the official processes and methods by which gain and other acoustical parameters of hearing aids are to be measured.

FREQUENCY RESPONSE

In practical terms, gain and frequency response cannot be separated, since in measuring the frequencies that a given hearing aid will respond to, one must also know how much those frequencies can be amplified by that hearing aid. In this way, the dispenser will be aware of whether a given hearing aid can be expected to meet the amplification needs of specific clients.

Frequency response, according to the ANSI S3.22–1987 standards, is to be measured across a wide frequency range by way of a sweep frequency audio oscillator of a hearing aid test system, rather than at the three frequencies specified for measurement of gain. This, then, gives a picture of the frequency/gain relationship across the frequencies that each specific aid can provide at selected settings. The input signal setting is specified by the ANSI standard

Standard Frequency Response 007 HX-RPC-1

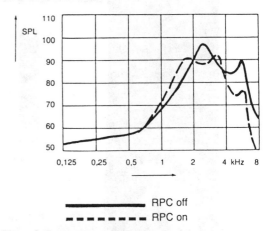

Figure 3–5. Frequency-gain characteristics of a representative ITE hearing aid. (Courtesy of Siemens Hearing Instruments)

to be 60 dB, with the gain set below maximum, that is, at 17 dB less than the high frequency average SSPL-90. The frequency/gain characteristics of an ITE hearing aid are shown in Figure 3–5.

DISTORTION

The clarity of the signal that hearing aids reproduce is critical to the success that clients who are hearing impaired will experience with their hearing aids. The ability of a hearing aid to deliver a clear signal is a product of its harmonic distortion characteristics, that is, to be as distortion free as possible. Harmonic distortion is the result of electrical and/or mechanical components of a hearing aid that are overstressed, or are not functioning as they otherwise could, resulting in nonlinearity of the signal. The result is sound produced by a hearing aid that is unclear to the listener, contributing to poorer speech discrimination than would otherwise have been noted, and a hearing aid wearer will complain of a decrease in clarity.

Harmonic distortion is routinely measured as a part of the test battery through standard hearing aid measurement systems. The amount

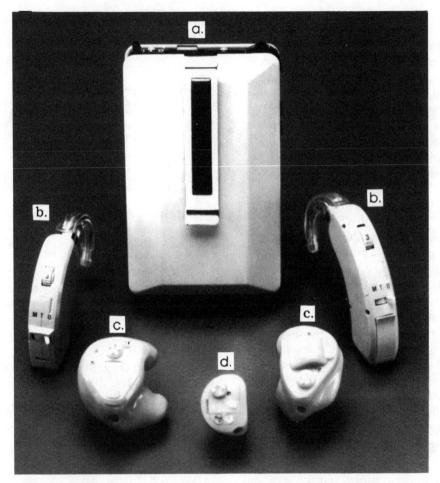

Figure 3–6. Representative hearing aids: (a) body-type; (b) behind-the-ear (BTE); (c) in-the-ear (ITE), (d) in-the-canal (ITC). (Courtesy of Telex Communications Inc.)

of total harmonic distortion (THD) is stated as a percentage across a wide frequency spectrum.

TYPES OF HEARING AIDS

With the advent of the telephone, invented by Alexander Graham Bell in 1876 and carbon transmitters by Blake and Hughes in 1878, the amplification technology for an assistive hearing device became available (Lybarger, 1988).

The first commercially available carbon hearing aid in the United States was made by Miller Reese Hutchinson in 1902 (Berger, 1984). It was made up of three parts, including

(1) a carbon microphone, (2) a magnetic receiver, and (3) a battery.

The first hearing aids were quite large, even larger than the size of current stereo systems. Even through the late 1940s, they were larger and more cumbersome than most people desired. With the advent of the vacuum tube in the early 1900s, and the transistor era which began in 1952, the size of hearing aids, and all amplification systems for that matter, were greatly reduced. By 1955, the size of hearing aids had dropped dramatically.

Today, five general models of hearing aids constitute the available market: These are (1) body-type hearing aids, (2) eyeglass hearing aids, (3) over-the-ear hearing aids, also called behind-the-ear (BTE) hearing aids, (4) in-the-ear (ITE) hearing aids, and (5) in-the-canal (ITC) hearing aids. Figure 3–6 shows four of these hearing aids. These are (a) the body-type aid, (b) the BTE aid, (c) the ITE aid, and (d) the ITC aid. The eyeglass aid is not shown in this figure.

BODY-TYPE HEARING AIDS

Body-type hearing aids (Figure 3–7) make up only approximately 2% of current hearing aid sales (Berger, 1984; Lybarger, 1988). Although this type of hearing aid is primarily designed for persons with severe-to-profound hearing losses, over the past three decades it has been used primarily to amplify the hearing of children who are hearing-impaired.

EYEGLASS HEARING AIDS

According to Berger (1984), in 1959 approximately 50% of the hearing aids worn in the United States were the eyeglass type. Cosmetically, this type of hearing aid was appealing to many adults who were hearing impaired. With the advent of smaller and more convenient hearing aids, the eyeglass type currently constitutes only about 4% of sales. Figure 3–8 depicts an eyeglass hearing aid with the microphone, amplifier, and receiver all built into the temple piece of the glasses.

A major drawback of this type of hearing aid was that the wearer was forced to wear his or her glasses when the hearing aid was to be used. Clear lenses were ground for those who did not require visual correction. To eliminate these and other drawbacks, the BTE hearing aid was developed as an outgrowth of the eyeglass model.

BEHIND-THE-EAR (BTE) HEARING AIDS

An ear-level hearing aid was desirable for many reasons. Included was the elimination of

Figure 3–7. A body-type hearing aid. (Courtesy of Telex Communications, Inc.)

clothing noises that had to be endured by wearers of body-type hearing aids, improved sound localization, particularly through binaural fittings, and the convenience of a comparatively smaller size.

Figure 3–9 presents the components of a BTE hearing aid with the microphone, amplifier, and receiver all housed within the casing of the instrument. Further, various fitting adjustments are available, including those for frequency configuration, gain, and output limitation.

IN-THE-EAR (ITE) HEARING AIDS

With the advent of ITE hearing aids, the hearing aid market quickly turned away from the comparatively larger BTE hearing aids toward the smaller, more cosmetically appealing ITE models. According to Mahon (1987), ITE and the smaller ITC hearing aids now constitute approximately 80% of hearing aid sales. The ITE hearing aid was made possible by miniature electret microphones, the miniaturization of receivers, and smaller yet longer lasting batteries.

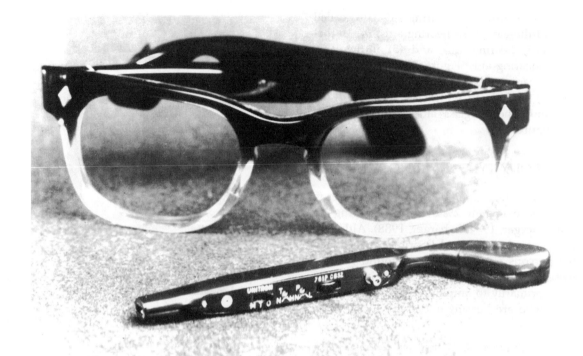

Figure 3–8. An eyeglass hearing aid. (Courtesy of Unitron Industries, Inc.)

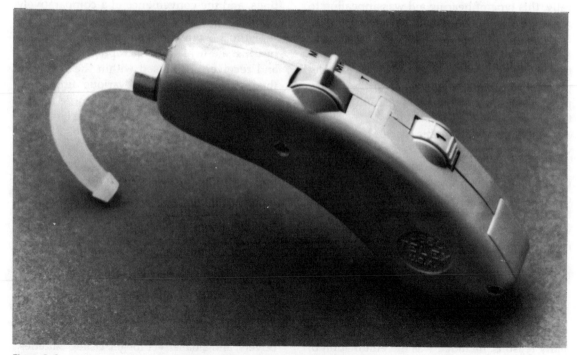

Figure 3–9. A behind-the-ear (BTE) hearing aid. (Courtesy of Telex Communications, Inc.)

Figure 3–10. An in-the-ear (ITE) hearing aid. (Courtesy of Unitron Industries, Inc.)

As can be seen in Figure 3–10, the entire hearing aid is contained within the earmold piece which is inserted into the concha and canal of the ear. Even though the typical ITE hearing aid is quite small, it is large enough to include such options as a telephone coil, frequency modification controls, and a resonance peak control which allows for slight modifications in gain/frequency response and the control of acoustic feedback. Further, hearing aids that fit all in-the-ear allow for the middle-to-high frequency resonance characteristics of the pinna to function naturally.

IN-THE-CANAL (ITC) HEARING AIDS

With further miniaturization of components and modifications in manufacturing tech-niques, hearing aids that fit in the ear canal of the wearer were made possible. Figure 3–11 showns an ITC-style hearing aid.

The ITC hearing aid quickly caught the attention of hearing aid wearers who were looking for hearing aids that were even more miniaturized and cosmetically appealing. Some hearing aid companies primarily used the cosmetic appeal to dispense these aids. However, with such miniaturization, drawbacks were quickly discovered. Some drawbacks are the restriction of gain for those who require moderate to high gain hearing aids, the reduced size of the aid which can cause some older adults and people with disabilities to experience difficulty inserting and/or removing the hearing aid from their ear, and the miniature batteries that are difficult for some people to insert correctly and that

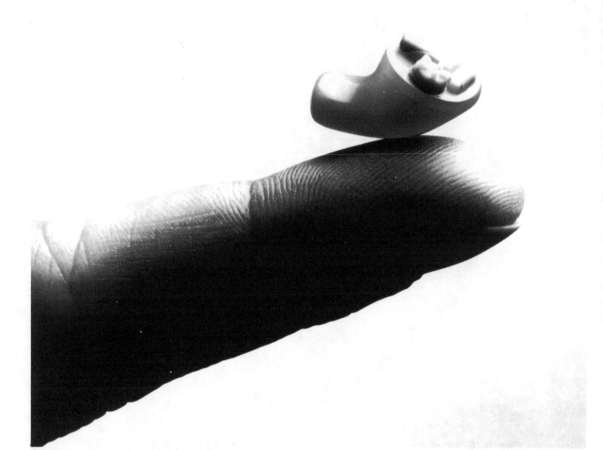

Figure 3–11. An in-the-canal hearing aid. (Courtesy of Memorex Hearing Aids)

disappear into the carpet if dropped. On the positive side, the ITC hearing aid allows for the natural benefit of the pinna/concha resonance characteristics that not only enhance certain middle and high frequencies, but also enhance sound localization.

EAR MOLDS

The ear impression taken as part of the hearing aid evaluation and selection process and the resulting ear mold are critical elements in the fitting and use of any type of hearing aid. For example, the typical hearing aid coupling system comprises a transfer from a high impe-

dance hearing aid receiver to a low impedance ear canal. With such a system, the probability of changing the output characteristics of the signal as received by the wearer's ear canal is always present; thus, the critical nature of the ear mold (Cox, 1979; Leavitt, 1986; Mueller & Grimes, 1987). Figure 3–12 depicts the frequency response curves of a single hearing aid when fitted with six different ear mold plumbing arrangements (Killion, 1980).

According to Mueller and Grimes (1987), the effects of the earmold and its plumbing (modifications and tubing) can be divided into those of (1) venting (affecting primarily the lower frequencies), (2) damping (influencing primarily the mid-frequencies), and (3) horn-

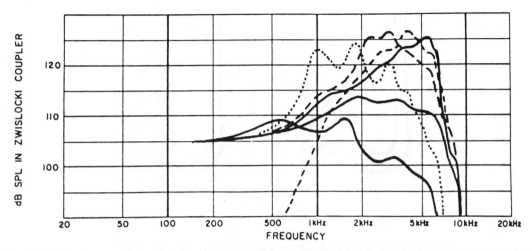

Figure 3-12. The frequency response curves of a single hearing aid when fitted with six different earmold plumbing arrangements. (From Killion, M. C. [1980]. Problems in the application of broadband hearing aid earphones. In G. Studebaker & I. Hochberg (Eds.), *Acoustical factors affecting hearing aid performance* (p. 259). Baltimore, MD: University Park Press.

ing (influencing primarily the higher frequencies). These factors along with tubing type, size (for BTE hearing aids), and other considerations are among the many that the dispenser must appraise during prehearing aid selection and the fitting process.

VENTING

Earmold venting is used for several reasons, including (1) to attenuate low frequencies, (2) to permit sound that does not require amplification to reach the ear, and (3) to reduce air pressure against the eardrum that is often experienced with closed ear molds, and to eliminate the feeling of fullness that can be experienced, along with the "echo" from the occlusion effect.

Depending on (1) the amount of hearing loss the client possesses, (2) the gain of the hearing aid, and (3) the reason for the venting, various sizes of openings will be required. The sizes of ventings are unlimited depending on the requirements, ranging from as wide as 3 mm in diameter, to a smaller "standard" vent of about 1.63 mm, to as small as .020 mm in diameter. The wider in diameter the vent, the greater will

be the enhancement of the high frequencies. For relief of pressure against the eardrum, a small vent may be all that is needed, for example, in the .065 mm diameter range, particularly when the hearing aid is a high gain aid and any larger opening may result in acoustic feedback.

Although the parallel versus the diagonal earmold vent debate continues in some circles, the parallel vent generally is found to be the most successful. Diagonal vents tend to attenuate sounds in the high frequencies, and this is not desirable for clients with high frequency hearing losses.

DAMPING

Damping is simply the inclusion of an occluding type filter (or damper) to the tubing of BTE hearing aids to smooth out the sound signal as it passes through to the person's ear. Most damping reduces the output of the signal primarily for the middle frequencies. Even though damping is used by many fitters of hearing aids, the use of mechanical dampers in hearing aid tubing or ear hooks is probably not necessary in the majority of hearing aid fittings, and

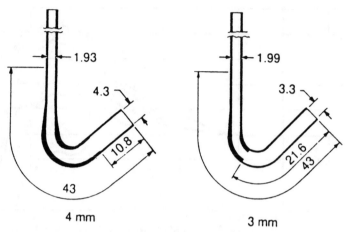

Figure 3–13. One-piece Libby horn arrangements. (From Lyberger, S. F. [1985]. Earmolds. In J. Katz, [Ed.], *Handbook of clinical audiology* (p. 898). Baltimore, MD: Williams & Wilkins. Reprinted with permission.)

can, indeed, be more of a nuisance than a benefit. The dispenser must be ready to change or replace dampers fairly frequently; they tend to attract moisture, dust, and other debris and become clogged, causing the signal of the hearing aid to become attenuated. Damping can in most instances be done through internal hearing aid adjustments, through the use of resonance peak control circuitry, through earmold modifications, or through adjusting the frequency response of the hearing aid.

HORNS

Horns are principally designed for use in BTE hearing aids. Designed by Killion (1976a, 1976b) and Libby (1981), such horns provide for an enhancement of higher frequencies as they are emitted to the ear by the hearing aid receiver. Horns, as seen in Figure 3–13, range in size from a bell of 4.3 mm in diameter, to a fitting end of 1.93 mm in diameter at the earhook of the hearing aid, usually with a total length of 43 mm. This type of one-piece horn has been found to shift the energy of sound to around 3000 Hz to enhance the frequency response for persons who possess high frequency hearing losses.

SUMMARY

The subject of hearing aids is extensive. The advances in hearing aid technology that occur even monthly are staggering as our knowledge and the development of amplification systems and devices continue to increase. However, even in light of the advances that continue to emerge, we must remember that children and adults who are hearing impaired are the reasons and the beneficiaries of our advances in knowledge and technology.

REFERENCES

American National Standards Institute. (1987). *Specifications for hearing aid characteristics, S3.22–1987.* New York: Author.

Berger, K. W. (1984). The hearing aid: Its operation and development. Livonia, MI: The National Hearing Society.

Cox, R. (1979). Acoustic aspects of hearing aid ear canal coupling systems. *Monographs on Contemporary Audiology, 1,* 1–44.

Killion, M. C. (1976a). Experimental bandwidth hearing aids. *Journal of the Acoustical Society of America, 59,* S62 (A).

Killion, M. C. (1976b). Earmold plumbing for wideband hearing aids. *Journal of the Acoustical Society of America, 59,* S62 (A).

Killion, M. C. (1980). Problems in the amplification of broadband hearing aid earphones. In G. Studebaker & I. Hochberg (Eds.), *Acoustical factors affecting hearing aid performance.* Baltimore, MD: University Park Press.

Killion, M. C., & Carlson, E. V. (1974). A subminiature electret-condenser microphone of new design. *Journal of the Auditory Engineering Society, 22,* 237–243.

Leavitt, R. (1986). Earmolds: Acoustical and structural considerations. In W. Hodgson (Ed.), *Hearing aid assessment and use in audiologic habilitation.* Baltimore, MD: Williams & Wilkins.

Libby, E. (1981). Achieving a transparent, smooth wideband hearing aid response. *Hearing Instruments, 32,* 9–12.

Lybarger, S. F. (1985). Earmolds. In J. Katz (Ed.), *Handbook of clinical audiology* (pp. 885–910). Baltimore, MD: Williams & Wilkins.

Lybarger, S. F. (1988). A historical overview. In R. E. Sandlin (Ed.), *Handbook of hearing aid amplification* (Vol. I, pp. 1–29). Boston: College-Hill Press.

Mahon, W. J. (1987). U.S. hearing aid sales summary. *The Hearing Journal, 40,* 7–13.

Mueller, G. H., & Grimes, M. A. (1987). Amplification systems for the hearing impaired. In J. G. Alpiner & P. A. McCarthy (Eds.), *Rehabilitative audiology: Children and adults* (pp. 115–160). Baltimore, MD: Williams & Wilkins.

CHAPTER 4

A Psychosocial and Economic Profile of the Hearing Impaired and Deaf

■ PAMELA L. JACKSON, PH.D. ■

Loss of hearing is the most common of all physical impairments. Yet until recently it has received little attention in terms of the psychosocial and economic handicaps that it imposes on the life of the individual. In 1974, Schein and Delk published the results of the National Census of the Deaf Population in a comprehensive book titled *The Deaf Population of the United States*. This work presents numerous data that describe the extent and the characteristics of the hearing-impaired population.

Table 4–1 summarizes prevalence and prevalence rates for hearing losses occurring at various ages. The figure 13,362,842 for the prevalence of all hearing impairments emphasizes the extent of the overall problem. The increase in incidence figures is also apparent if the data are compared to past figures. For example, since the early 1930s, the prevalence rate for

deafness has been reported as approximately 1 per 1,000. The 1971 rate, however, reported by Schein and Delk (1974) indicates a rate for prevocational (prior to 19 years of age) deafness of 2 per 1,000, or more exactly, 203 individuals who are deaf per 100,000. This doubling of the rate in 40 years is attributed to three factors: (1) possible inaccuracies in past counts; (2) differences in definitions which alter the population sampled; or (3) an actual increase in the occurrence of deafness. While all of these do play a part, it is important to add that survival rates of high-risk infants have also increased in recent years and will contribute to an overall increase in the number of adults who are deaf who in the past might not have survived beyond early childhood.

The prevalence and prevalence rates for significant bilateral hearing impairment as they

TABLE 4-1. PREVALENCE AND PREVALENCE RATES FOR HEARING IMPAIRMENTS IN THE CIVILIAN NONINSTITUTIONALIZED POPULATION BY DEGREE AND AGE OF ONSET: UNITED STATES, 1971

Degree	Age at Onset	Number	Rate per 100,000
All hearing impairments	All ages	13,362,842	6,603
Significant bilateral	All ages	6,548,842	3,236
Deafness	All ages	1,767,046	873
	Prevocational[a]	410,522	203
	Prelingual[b]	210,626	100

Source: From Schein and Delk (1974).
a. Prior to 19 years of age.
b. Prior to 3 years of age.

relate to age and sex are shown in Table 4–2. Schein and Delk define significant bilateral hearing impairment as one in which the loss is present in both ears and the better ear has some problem hearing and understanding speech. This category includes deafness which Schein and Delk define as "the inability to hear or understand speech" (p. 133).

Inspection of the data in Table 4–2 indicates the expected prevalence of hearing impairment in the 65-and-over age range. The decline in hearing sensitivity with age is well known. The rates in the 24-and-under age range are the ones that must be concentrated on, however, especially when future program needs are being considered. Vocational, social, and geriatric programs can then be made aware of their long-range responsibilities.

PSYCHOLOGICAL PROFILE

The presence of a hearing impairment affects the entire life of the individual, not just his or her ability to perceive auditory cues. The extent of this influence can be illustrated by examining Table 4–3. Even if only the most severe cases are considered, 18,500 individuals who are deaf are in need of psychological services. Compare that figure with Goulder's (1977) estimate that only 727 persons are being served by mental health programs for

the deaf, and the problem becomes evident. The psychological needs of the hearing-impaired population cannot be ignored.

Studies that have attempted to describe psychological and personality traits of persons who are deaf have been hampered by the communication problem imposed by the hearing loss. Enough information has been gathered, however, to permit several summary statements concerning the psychological profile of the adult who is more severely hearing impaired. This information compiled from Schlesinger and Meadow (1972), Levine (1976), Bolton (1976), Schein (1977), and Schein (1978) shows that:

1. They tend to be immature.
2. They tend to withdraw, especially from communication situations.
3. They tend to be less flexible than a normal hearing adult.
4. They tend to adhere rigidly to a set routine.
5. They tend to demonstrate a negative self-image; this is due in part to a general lack of information concerning the nature of hearing impairment.
6. They tend to have a narrow range of interests.
7. They tend to show a lack of social judgment.
8. They tend to exhibit a lack of regard for the feelings of others.

TABLE 4–2. PREVALENCE AND PREVALENCE RATES FOR SIGNIFICANT BILATERAL IMPAIRMENT BY AGE AND SEX: UNITED STATES, 1971

Sex/Age	Number	Rate per 100,000
Both sexes	6,549,643	3,237
Under 6	56,083	262
6–16	384,557	852
17–24	235,121	862
25–44	642,988	1,356
45–64	1,870,356	4,478
65 and over	3,360,583	17,368
Females	2,706,124	2,583
Under 6	23,661	227
6–16	155,738	701
17–24	81,923	568
25–44	243,403	990
45–64	610,741	2,783
65 and over	1,590,818	14,257
Males	3,843,519	3,938
Under 6	32,267	295
6–16	228,819	997
17–24	153,198	1,191
25–44	399,585	1,749
45–64	1,259,885	6,535
65 and over	1,769,765	21,606

Source: From Schein and Delk (1974).

9. They tend to be more naive than the hearing adult.
10. They tend to be more dependent than the hearing adult.
11. They tend to be irresponsible.
12. They tend to be impulsive.
13. They tend to be passive and overaccepting, especially if the loss occurred early.
14. They tend to be depressed, but generally in cases where the hearing impairment occurred later in life.

It must be stressed, however, that a description of the typical profile of an adult who is hearing impaired is impossible. The characteristics are offered only as possibilities, and no one will fit the mold exactly. These traits are frequently observed, but their emergence in any one case will depend on several factors, primarily age of onset and degree of hearing loss. The psychological characteristics of a hearing impaired population are as varied as they are in a normal hearing group. This point is stressed by Bolton (1976) when he concludes that the personality characteristics of a hearing-impaired population are not due to hearing loss, but rather they are due to the environment in which the loss places an individual.

SOCIAL PROFILE

The social characteristics of the hearing-impaired population can be described in part by examining geographic distribution. Table 4–4 contains a breakdown of this population by region. The highest prevalence rate for the deaf and for the prevocationally deaf groups occurs in the North Central area. The West, however, has the highest prevalence for all hearing impaired. The lowest rates occur in the Northeast for all three groups (hearing impaired, deaf, and prevocationally deaf), and these rates appear to be significantly lower than the other regions. These figures allow at least rough predictions to be made concerning the location of deaf communities that will be in need of rehabilitation services.

Social characteristics of adults who are hearing impaired have received more emphasis in recent years. According to Schein and Delk (1974) the following summary statements can be made:

The majority of deaf adults have hearing parents. The National Census of the Deaf Population figures show that 91.7% of adults who are deaf fall into this category. Schein and Delk stress the importance of this finding by emphasizing that the majority of parents of these individuals probably had little or no contact with or understanding of hearing impairment prior to its occurrence in their child. This lack of understanding of the problem can affect the social development and adjustment of the individual.

TABLE 4–3. NEED FOR MENTAL HEALTH SERVICES AMONG PEOPLE WHO ARE DEAF (THE 1%, 2%, AND 10% CLASSES REPRESENT DECREASING DEGREES OF SEVERITY OF THE PSYCHIATRIC PROBLEM.)

Degree of Hearing Loss	Total Number	Number Needing Services		
		1%	2%	10%
Hearing impaired	13,975,000	139,750	279,500	1,397,500
Significant bilateral loss	6,850,000	68,500	137,000	685,000
Deaf	1,850,000	18,500	37,000	185,000
Prevocationally deaf	430,000	4,300	8,600	43,000

Source: From Goulder (1977).

TABLE 4–4. DISTRIBUTION OF THE HEARING-IMPAIRED POPULATION BY REGIONS: UNITED STATES, 1971

United States and Regions	Hearing Impaired	Deaf	Prevocationally Deaf
United States	13,362,842	1,767,046	410,522
Northeast	2,891,380	337,022	83,909
North Central	3,683,226	541,465	135,653
South	4,280,177	562,756	123,260
West	2,508,059	325,803	67,700
Rates per 100,000 Population			
United States	6,603	873	203
Northeast	5,977	697	173
North Central	6,563	965	242
South	6,807	895	196
West	7,170	931	194

Source: From Schein and Delk (1974).

When compared to the general population, individuals who are deaf marry less often and, when they do, they tend to marry at a later age. This is especially true for men. These data are summarized in Table 4–5. It is interesting to note that the divorce rate in the two populations is very similar. Data from the census also indicated that persons who are deaf frequently marry other persons who are deaf, as opposed to hard of hearing or normal hearing individuals, 79.5% of the time.

There are fewer children born to deaf women than to normal hearing women. Also, children born into families in which at least one parent is prevocationally deaf have normal hearing 88% of the time.

Additional data on the social characteristics of people who are deaf were compiled by Emerton (1977) at the National Technical Institute for the Deaf (NTID) and were described by Johnson (1978). The information was gathered through a battery of tests that was designed to obtain a social profile of an individual who was deaf within five areas. Although it was stressed that the data were preliminary, the following statements by John-

TABLE 4–5. PERCENTAGE DISTRIBUTION OF MARITAL STATUS OF DEAF POPULATION COMPARED TO GENERAL POPULATION[a] BY AGE AND SEX: UNITED STATES, 1972

| | Marital Status | | | | | | | |
| | Single | | Married[b] | | Widowed | | Divorced | |
Respondents' Sex and Age	Deaf	General	Deaf	General	Deaf	General	Deaf	General
Total	34.1	18.5	60.0	74.3	2.1	3.5	3.8	3.6
16 to 24[c]	83.9	57.6	15.4	40.9	0.2	0.2	0.5	1.3
25 to 34	28.3	13.6	77.6	82.0	0.3	0.4	3.8	3.9
35 to 44	17.9	6.3	76.4	87.6	–	1.5	5.7	4.6
45 to 54	13.6	5.9	77.1	84.5	4.1	4.9	5.2	4.7
55 to 64	18.3	6.1	70.1	77.3	7.1	12.8	4.4	3.8
Male	40.3	21.8	55.7	74.3	1.0	1.0	3.0	2.9
16 to 24[c]	88.4	67.3	10.6	31.9	0.4	–	0.4	0.7
25 to 34	38.3	17.6	58.5	79.2	–	0.1	3.2	3.0
35 to 44	22.8	7.5	72.0	88.5	–	0.5	5.2	3.5
45 to 54	16.3	7.3	77.5	87.2	1.1	1.5	5.1	4.0
55 to 64	20.8	5.8	73.7	87.4	4.2	3.5	1.4	3.3
Females	27.5	15.4	64.5	74.3	3.3	5.9	4.7	4.3
16 to 24[c]	78.1	48.8	21.3	49.2	–	0.3	0.6	1.8
25 to 34	24.6	9.7	71.5	84.7	0.3	0.9	3.6	4.8
35 to 44	12.0	5.2	81.7	86.7	–	2.5	6.3	5.6
45 to 54	11.1	4.5	76.7	82.0	6.9	8.0	5.3	5.4
55 to 64	16.0	6.4	66.7	68.2	10.0	21.2	7.3	4.1

Source: From Schein and Delk (1974).
a. From Statistical Abstract of the United States (1972).
b. Includes persons who are separated.
c. General population rates do not include persons 16 and 17 years of age.

son were made based on profile results from 295 of the entering students at NTID.

1. In terms of social knowledge, about 13% performed at a level expected for college students, 32% performed at a high school level, and 55% performed at an unsatisfactory level for employment.
2. In terms of social decision making, 95% needed improvement, while 84% needed improvement in social reasoning.
3. In terms of various levels of interaction, interpersonal was significantly better than group interaction, but it was still relatively low.
4. In terms of social behavior, about 66% were considered to be performing at a college level, while 34% needed improvement.
5. In terms of career development, 78% were below college level. This included performance on tests that measured work-related skills and attitudes.

Again, as with psychological factors, it is important to stress that these characteristics must be considered only as general trends. Rehabilitative programs must still be tailored to individual needs and not to a stereotyped group.

ECONOMIC PROFILE

The economic problems of adults who are severely hearing impaired appear to involve both unemployment and underemployment. A large part of the problem may be attributed to the myths concerning deafness and ignorance on the part of many employers as to the capabilities of the hearing impaired. In a survey of Baltimore manufacturing firms, 32% of the employers indicated that deafness was the disability that would most likely prevent them from hiring an applicant. Total deafness ranked fourth after total blindness, mental retardation, and epilepsy (Fellendorf, Atelsek, & Mackin, 1971).

The unemployment data compiled by Schein and Delk (1974) indicated that the problem was less severe for men who were deaf than for the general population. Men who were deaf showed 2.9% unemployment compared

to 4.9% for men in general. Women who were deaf showed 10.2% unemployment compared to a general female unemployment figure of 6.6%. The greatest unemployment for people who were deaf was seen in the 16- to 24-year-old age group for both men and women.

If the principal occupations of the severely hearing-impaired population are compared to the principal occupations of the general population, part of the unemployment problem is revealed. This comparison is made in Table 4-6. The majority of workers who are deaf are in the craftsman and operatives areas and have traditionally been in positions that allow little upward mobility. Occupations requiring a great deal of communication, on the other hand, are seldom held by an individual who is deaf.

A primary indicator of the economic status of the hearing-impaired population is individual income level. Schein and Delk (1974) report a median personal income level for individuals who are deaf of $5,915, compared with a median level of $8,188 for the general population. Those in the professional and

TABLE 4-6. PERCENTAGE DISTRIBUTION OF EMPLOYED DEAF VERSUS GENERAL POPULATION, ADULTS (16 TO 64 YEARS OF AGE), BY PRINCIPAL OCCUPATION: UNITED STATES, 1972.

	Percentage of Population	
Principal Occupation	Deaf	General
All occupations	100.0	100.0
Professional and technical	8.8	14.2
Managers and administrators (nonfarm)	1.4	11.0
Sales	0.5	6.4
Clerical	15.0	16.9
Craftsman	21.3	12.7
Operatives, nontransit and transit	35.9	16.2
Laborers (nonfarm)	6.2	5.0
Farmers, farm managers, and farm laborers	1.6	4.0
Service workers	9.2	13.5
Private household workers	0.2	–

Source: From Schein (1978).

technical occupation category earn the most, as might be expected. The authors also note that yearly earnings were the least for the congenitally impaired population, while income was the highest for those whose hearing loss occurred after the age of six.

Studies cited by Meadow-Orlans (1985) involve employment and employability of workers who have been deafened in Europe, the Netherlands, and Scandinavia. Beuzart (1982) found that in one inquiry in France, 50% of those workers lost their jobs. Others remained, but earned lower salaries. A survey by Thomas and Gilhome-Herbst (1980) found 236 respondents were significantly "less happy at work" than matched hearing controls. Breed, van den Horst, and Mous (1981) found members of a Dutch hard of hearing organization were most likely to do "lonely" work.

Meadow-Orlans (1985) cites two studies in detail that elaborate on the impact of hearing loss on a person's economic future. A study by Kyle and Wood (1983) consisted of an interview with 105 persons ages 25 through 55 years with onset of hearing loss in the previous 10 years. According to Meadow-Orlans (1985), 91% of those persons could, with their hearing aid(s), "hear normal speech across a room." Despite their usable hearing, 35% "felt that promotion at work was relatively impossible." Sixty-three percent of persons who were prelingually deaf felt the same, compared with only 16% of those who possessed normal hearing. Kyle and Wood (1983) state that acquired hearing loss affects the quality of working life more than the level of earnings. In this study, it was found that when the workers discovered their hearing losses, only 39% informed their employers.

Another study described in detail by Meadow-Orlans (1985) involved adults who are hearing impaired in greater London. The study was conducted by Thomas, Lamont, and Harris (1982). All subjects were of employment age and possessed hearing loss greater than 60 dB. The study involved interviews with the workers and surveys. Representative responses by the workers as it relates to the

impact of their hearing loss on their ability to work included (1) difficulty coping with the public; (2) difficulty with the telephone; (3) difficulty *doing* their job; (4) difficulty with colleagues; (5) given less responsibility; and (6) altered job assignment.

The impact of hearing loss on vocational success and job satisfaction varies with the person involved, interacting with degree of loss. Needless to say, however, hearing loss can have a negative impact on a person's job performance and on vocational satisfaction.

SUMMARY

The information presented in this chapter offers an emerging profile of the psychosocial and economic characteristics of the adult deaf population. It must be stressed that this is also a changing profile. In light of new educational opportunities, improved training programs for professionals who deal with deafness, and the emergence of advocates for the rights of the handicapped, the profile will be altered. Hopefully, in time, the differences created by a loss of hearing will be minimized.

REFERENCES

Beuzart, J. G. (1982, November). *Deafened workers in France: Characteristics and conditions.* Presentation before the International Congress of Audiophonology, Besancon, France.

Bolton, B. (1976). Introduction and overview. In B. Bolton (Ed.), *Psychology of deafness for rehabilitation counselors* (pp. 1–18). Baltimore, MD: University Park Press.

Breed, P. C., van den Horst, A. P., & Mous, T. J. M. (1981). Psychosocial problems in suddenly deafened adolescents and adults. In H. Hartmann (Ed.), *Congress report.* Hamburg, Germany: First International Congress of the Hard of Hearing.

Emerton, R. G. (1977). *Socialization profile: Prototype 1976.* Paper presented to the National Advisory Group of the National Technical Institute for the Deaf.

Fellendorf, G., Atelsek, F., & Macklin, E. (1971). *Diversifying job opportunities for the adult deaf.*

Washington, DC: Alexander Graham Bell Association for the Deaf.

Goulder, T. J. (1977). Federal and state mental health programs for the deaf in hospitals and clinics. *Mental Health in Deafness, 1,* 13–17.

Johnson, D. D. (1978). The adult deaf client and rehabilitation. In J. G. Alpiner (Ed.), *Handbook of adult rehabilitative audiology* (pp. 172–221). Baltimore, MD: Williams & Wilkins.

Kyle, J. G., & Wood, P. L. (1983). *Social and vocational aspects of acquired hearing loss.* Final Report to the Ministry of Social Concern. Bristol, England: School of Educational Research Unit, University of Bristol.

Levine, E. S. (1976). Psycho-cultural determinants in personality development. *Volta Review, 78,* 258–267.

Meadow-Orlans, K. P. (1985). Social and psychological effects of hearing loss in adulthood: A literature review. In H. Orlans (Ed.), *Adjustment to adult hearing loss* (pp. 35–58). San Diego, CA: Singular Publishing Group.

Schein, J. D. (1977). Psychology of the hearing impaired consumer. *Audiology and Hearing Education, 3,* 12–14, 44.

Schein, J. D. (1978). The deaf community. In H. Davis & S. R. Silverman (Eds.), *Hearing and deafness* (4th ed., pp. 511–524). New York: Holt, Rinehart & Winston.

Schein, J. D., & Delk, M. T., Jr. (1974). *The deaf population of the United States.* Silver Springs, MD: National Association of the Deaf.

Schlesinger, H. S., & Meadow, K. P. (1972). *Sound and sign: Childhood deafness and mental health.* Berkeley: University of California Press.

Thomas, A., & Gilhome-Herbst, K. (1980). Social and psychological implications of acquired deafness for adults of employment age. *British Journal of Audiology, 14,* 76–85.

Thomas, A., Lamont, M., & Harris, M. (1982). Problems encountered at work by people with severe acquired hearing loss. *British Journal of Audiology, 16,* 39–43.

■ CHAPTER 5 ■

The Vocational Impact of Hearing Impairment and Vocational Rehabilitation Counseling of the Hearing Impaired

■ KAREN L. DILKA, Ph.D. ■

The purpose of rehabilitation is to provide comprehensive services to individuals with mental, physical, sensory, or emotional handicaps with the intent that they will "attain usefulness and satisfaction in life" (Wright, 1980, p. 3). This broad definition asserts that determination of a recipient's goals and objectives will vary along a continuum from those who have achieved independent living skills to those who have achieved gainful employment. The rehabilitation process encompasses a series of prioritized steps tailored to the unique needs and circumstances of the individual client. Therefore, the associated time limit for successful completion of the rehabilitation process will depend on the extent and diversity of designated services. The expectation for accomplishment of the client's initial goal(s) is correlated with his or her stamina, capabilities, motivation, and support base, which includes his or her family and significant others.

Unfortunately, the hearing-impaired population does not have equivalent sociological, educational, and linguistic advantages that are inherent in the hearing society. Undoubtedly, this is due to the fact that an auditory loss, regardless of the type of remedial treatment proposed, significantly restricts the acquisition and comprehension of information that is readily accessible to the hearing majority. Divisional gaps deepen with demographic data indicating inferior educational and socioeconomic status of persons with impaired hearing compared to their hearing counterparts (Phillipe & Auvenshine, 1985; Schein & Delk, 1974; Wootton & Mowry, 1986). To complicate the situation further, members of this minority group do not necessarily have homogenous characteristics. For example, school environments, parental acceptance and leadership, exposure to cultural experiences, onset and degree of loss, and most importantly self-esteem are all variables that affect individual growth and development. Hence, the accumulation of the above factors compounds any career dynamics associated with occupational choice, mobility, adjustment, and work-related functions.

The literature regarding technological advancements in business and industry is replete with references that detail the rapid changes and breakthroughs in industrial mechanization. The forecast of career profiles reflects this shift, with a move from manual labor toward administrative and executive positions. Concurrently, a concentrated effort must be made by all professionals serving individuals who are hearing impaired to empower and prepare them to take advantage of these trends.

THE VOCATIONAL REHABILITATION PROCESS

The structural framework of vocational rehabilitation is mandated by public law (PL 93–112, PL 93–516) and consists of specific phases. The preliminary phase combines client referral, an intake interview, and evaluations to determine the client's eligibility or potential for employment. Two critical components are *the interview* in which valuable personal, educational, vocational, and financial information is collected; and an aggregate of *evaluations* (medical, audiological, visual, vocational, and psychological) to assess the client's physical, mental, and work-related abilities and limitations. Consideration of appropriate testing instruments and administra-

tion procedures with persons who are hearing impaired inundate this phase of the rehabilitation process. A wide range of communication possibilities and cultural experiences collectively influences the sequential movement of preparation toward vocational achievement. Emphasis is placed on individual assets and liabilities. However, regardless of the client's circumstances, the following requirements must be met to receive further specialized assistance through this governmental program.

1. The individual is mentally, physically, or sensory impaired or disabled.
2. The disability creates a barrier or handicap to attainable employment.
3. The individual will obtain and sustain employment on completion of services provided by vocational rehabilitation.

The next phase entails the development of an Individualized Written Rehabilitation Plan (IWRP) to focus on pertinent occupational goals and establish a course of action. Vocational guidance, under the direction of the vocational rehabilitation (VR) counselor, is imperative at this stage to develop a realistic perspective regarding preparation, duration of the task, extent of provisions, and monetary subsidy. At this juncture, the client and counselor jointly decide on career aspirations, orientation, timeliness, and procedures. The data gathered on job placement for persons with impaired hearing consistently indicate that they tend to be underemployed rather than unemployed (Schroedel, 1987; Steffanic, 1982; Williams & Sussman, 1976). Job stereotyping and employer discrimination have contributed to this situation (Phillips, 1975). Individuals who are hearing impaired are predominantly hired in the operative and clerical areas (El-Khiami, 1986). Therefore, a severe underrepresentation of persons who are hearing impaired exists in what is considered to be high status professions (Schroedel, 1987).

Although all phases of the vocational rehabilitation program comprise essential elements, the categories of restoration and training are exclusively oriented to the needs of the client and, therefore, considered the core of the process. Auditory devices such as hearing aids, telephone accessories, and other assistive equipment/appliances for the purpose of communication or personal management are necessary. Additionally, medical, surgical, or prosthetic intervention may be necessary, as well as the correction of visual problems to enhance clients' communicative effectiveness via sign language and/or lipreading. Another option might be classes to improve these communication techniques; auditory training and speechreading, manual communication systems, and/or American Sign Language (ASL) when they will assist the client.

As the client progresses, formal training begins. Training activities will vary for the person who is hearing impaired depending on the results of previous evaluations and his or her occupational interests. Support services are interwoven throughout the rehabilitation process; however, access to information imparted during training is crucial to the application of new skills. Individuals who are hearing impaired may derive benefit from the availability of interpreters, oral or manual. Other auxiliary resources may be requested to participate fully in community or educational settings. Notetakers and tutors also facilitate instruction and learning for a person with impaired hearing.

For the client who is more severely hearing impaired or deaf, the final phase of vocational rehabilitation solidifies the original plan by the formulation of a tangible conclusion — employment or independence. Job opportunities have, at this point, been solicited and placement of the client proceeds. Continual observation provides the counselor with insight into the success or failure of the arrangement. Clients' freedom to express themselves and be understood by management contributes to their performance level. Both client and employer satisfaction determine which procedures a counselor will select for follow-up sessions. If the situation is unfavorable, then an attempt to gain employment elsewhere is

investigated. It must be noted that provisions are made in each phase to disqualify a client from services and receiving further assistance through vocational rehabilitation if extenuating circumstances arise.

The vocational rehabilitation process is designed to offer counseling and personal or career consultation at all phases. At times, the counselor's role involves intensive therapeutic interaction with the client to resolve personal issues that interfere with the ultimate goal of employment. Therefore, demonstrated proficiency in the preferred language of the individual who is hearing impaired, irrespective of the mode or method, creates an atmosphere of trust and respect vital for a positive client-counselor rapport. Rehabilitation counselors provide direction, supervision, and advocacy for the client while arranging, organizing, and monitoring the delivery of an array of services. These responsibilities cover a gamut of vocational, educational, and professional transactions (operations).

CASE STUDIES

The following vignettes are presented to illustrate the diversity of service alternatives within the realm of vocational rehabilitation and the individualization embedded in the system. The three clients described represent a spectrum of the hearing-impaired population whose needs are interwoven into the IWRP. The ability of the rehabilitation counselor to tailor the IWRP is one of the unique strengths of the rehabilitation process.

ACQUIRED HEARING LOSS (REHABILITATION)

Wendy was a skilled home economics teacher. She had enjoyed teaching high school students for 12 years. Her goal was to continue teaching for 13 more years and then retire with her husband. As Wendy was driving to work one morning she had a serious car accident and was hospitalized for several weeks. Although she recovered from her physical injuries, Wendy was left with a severe bilateral sensorineural hearing loss. This traumatic experience left Wendy angry and frustrated. Her acquired hearing loss created obstacles which she found extremely difficult to cope with both emotionally and physically. Wendy tried to return to work only to discover she no longer had control of her classes and could not communicate with her students or colleagues. Subsequently, Wendy chose to give up her teaching position.

Wendy's home life was also affected by her postlingual loss of hearing; family relationships were strained due to the lack of spontaneous communication or compensatory techniques. Misunderstandings frequently arose and she began to remove herself from social gatherings with family and friends. Feeling isolated and seeking alternatives, Wendy decided to contact a local organization for the hearing impaired. She was eventually referred to a vocational rehabilitation counselor where she gained information about her hearing loss and opportunities for revised career development.

After the initial interview and application procedure, Wendy was sent to an otologist for a thorough examination of the hearing mechanism and to her family physician for a current medical update. The next step entailed an audiological evaluation to assess the extent of the hearing loss sustained in the accident and an ophthalmological evaluation to ascertain the integrity of her visual system. With relevant information obtained from the audiologist, Wendy became aware of a wide range of assistive devices, hearing aids, and communication strategies to enhance adjustment to her hearing loss.

Wendy met all the necessary requirements for eligibility for vocational rehabilitation and proceeded to develop, in conjunction with the counselor, an individualized written rehabilitation plan (IWRP). Wendy identified an aspect of home economics she wanted to pursue (fashion editor) and the IWRP document detailed her new career direction including training, resources, essential materials, a proposed schedule of activities, and anticipated out-

comes. At this time it was recommended that Wendy return to the audiologist to purchase bilateral hearing aids. She also inquired about the purchase of a telephone device for the deaf (TDD) and a light system for her house so she would know when the doorbell or telephone rang. Vocational rehabilitation approved and paid for these items on Wendy's behalf. Concurrently, arrangements were made for Wendy to enroll in an auditory training and lipreading class sponsored by a local speech and hearing clinic. Wendy's preference was to continue to use an oral method of communication, and the aforementioned instruction was designed to maintain speech production and diminish the frustration of adjustment to auditory stimuli. Vocational rehabilitation contributed financial support to Wendy's endeavors; however, the amount was based on her income and economic status reports.

The relationship between Wendy and her counselor developed into a warm, respectful exchange of thoughts, ideas, and information. Communication became less of a challenging receptive task and more of a relaxed auditory and visual acquisition of messages. Personal and career counseling were an integral part of Wendy's IWRP. The onset of a sudden hearing loss can evoke emotional turmoil for which an individual is not psychologically prepared to manage without the expertise of a professional trained in the area of hearing loss. Gradually, Wendy began to acknowledge and ultimately accept her disability. She gained confidence in her communication abilities, focusing on the positive aspects of change. This significant progress was due, in part, to the effective guidance and monitoring techniques employed by her vocational rehabilitation counselor.

Due to the level of communication required in her previous teaching position, Wendy could not return to it. However, through specialized courses, Wendy studied interior design. She assumed responsibility for payment of all supplies and materials for the courses; however, she was reimbursed for tuition by vocational rehabilitation. Wendy finished the program within one year and later found employment at a woman's publishing company. The VR counselor proceeded to conduct an in-service for the manager of the publishing company on practical communication strategies and disseminated similar information to departmental employees. Wendy's goals were consequently achieved in a 2-year time frame, resulting in an occupational shift and successful rehabilitation closure.

CONGENITAL HEARING LOSS (HABILITATION)

Dustin was born with a profound bilateral sensorineural hearing loss. The cause of his prelingual hearing impairment was traced to maternal rubella. As a senior, Dustin attended the state school for the deaf and his preferred mode of communication was American Sign Language (ASL). Dustin's strong academic performance, talent as an artist, and interest in drafting led him to explore the field of architecture. With encouragement from the high school principal, Dustin arranged an appointment to discuss future educational/career goals with the vocational rehabilitation counselor.

Dustin applied to several universities and was accepted by two. His final decision was to attend an institute recognized for its highly acclaimed architectural school. The VR counselor explained the procedure to request a sign language interpreter for classes. The week of his arrival, Dustin contacted Disabled Student Services on campus and submitted his semester itinerary. He noticed a circular tacked on the bulletin board announcing a tutorial program on English proficiency for second language learners. English was always a laborious subject for Dustin, yet he clearly understood the importance of English competency. Therefore, with an avid endorsement from the VR counselor, Dustin applied for the private instructional sessions.

Vocational rehabilitation subsidized Dustin's educational expenses including interpreting services for extracurricular activities. Costs for interpreting and notetaking in the classroom setting were absorbed by the university.

Incidentals were furnished by Dustin's parents, and he commuted to and from school, which decreased the overall financial obligation incurred by both the agency and his family. The only stipulations for receiving aid were the maintenance of a cumulative grade point average consistent with program standards and enrollment in the minimum semester credit hours equivalent to full-time status. Dustin was responsible for contacting the counselor regarding any changes to this agreement.

During the summer months, Dustin worked for a small architectural company. Because his co-workers did not have an understanding of the cultural or linguistic aspects of sign language, the VR counselor authorized an interpreter for a period of several weeks to facilitate communication. This gave Dustin an opportunity to become familiar with his surroundings and foster an atmosphere of fluent, spontaneous interaction.

When Dustin graduated, he continued to receive vocational rehabilitation services including interpreter assistance for interviews, and tools to construct a portfolio. After Dustin secured a position with a larger architectural firm, an interpreter was requested to orient Dustin to his duties and establish a positive rapport with his fellow employees. The VR counselor conducted inservice presentations and dispensed information regarding methods of communication with adults who are hearing impaired. Dustin's work-related progress was confirmed by his supervisor, and within several months he was successfully terminated from the vocational rehabilitation process.

GENETIC CONDUCTIVE HEARING LOSS — APERT SYNDROME (INDEPENDENT LIVING)

Stanley was born with an autosomal dominant disease diagnosed as Apert syndrome. He had multiple handicapping conditions, including a moderate hearing loss (SRT of 50 dB HL), skull and facial malformations, decreased cognitive capacity, fusion of the hand and toe digits (syndactyly), and spina bifida. Stanley's extreme high forehead and syndactyly were primary indicators of the genetic syndrome upon delivery. Therefore, Stanley received early medical, otological, and audiological intervention.

Throughout the developmental years, Stanley underwent numerous surgeries to correct cranial and facial anomalies. The multidisciplinary management team also performed several operations on Stanley's hands and feet to separate the digits. However, only the thumb and smallest finger could be detached from the solid mass. This allowed Stanley to manipulate objects even though he did not have optimal functioning of his hands. Otological intervention was necessary to improve his hearing acuity for the acquisition of speech and language. The stapes footplate was removed and a prosthesis put in place; however, further reconstructive surgery to remediate his hearing loss was not possible. After treatment, Stanley had an audiological evaluation that signified an increase in his hearing ability to within the mild range on the audiogram. Simultaneously, Stanley was fitted with a bone conduction hearing aid.

Education for Stanley was difficult. His mobility was restricted because he had spina bifida and therefore he used a wheelchair. During his school years he was assigned to a self-contained classroom for the trainable mentally handicapped and later transferred to the district's vocational setting. Stanley enjoyed the hands-on work that was expected of him in this new environment. The precision with which he assembled products was recognized by his teachers. The quality of his workmanship was consistently above average. Prior to graduation, Stanley's instructor contacted the VR counselor, starting the vocational rehabilitation process. Stanley was 21 years old.

Diagnostic data were collected regarding Stanley's medical, audiological, educational, and vocational history. Fortunately, current information was available in all these specialty areas, expediting the determination of eligibility. The years of training and work experience gained at the vocational school were noted for consideration when Stanley's future placement was discussed. Together with scores from a battery of work sample evaluations to measure Stanley's occupational aptitudes and input from the immediate family, an IWRP was developed. This document focused on independent living skills and extended employment at a sheltered workshop.

It was decided that a combination of community resources would benefit Stanley in his pursuit of independence. An occupational therapist taught Stanley functional self-care tasks. This helped him attain a higher level of autonomy within the family unit. The services of a physical therapist were contracted to administer a therapeutic exercise program aimed at strengthening body parts, enhancing circulation, and reducing the possibility of muscular atrophy. Of course, it was apparent to Stanley's family that he would always need additional support since he had multiple disabilities affecting his mental, physical, and emotional health. Restorative devices rendering freedom of movement were purchased, including an automatic wheelchair and a contemporary bone conduction hearing aid. These items were deemed essential for Stanley to cope constructively with the barriers that exist in the environment. This significant expenditure of money was shared by vocational rehabilitation and Stanley's parents.

Job placement at a local sheltered workshop for rehabilitation clients complied with Stanley's IWRP objectives. He was tentatively accepted at the facility and a conference was scheduled for the VR counselor and appointed supervisor to exchange relevant competency-based information. A brief transitional period from school to work was allotted before actual training sessions were set up. Stanley's performance was assessed for several weeks. It was eventually established that he met the criteria for extended employment. The counselor remained in contact with the center until closing Stanley's file. Follow-up conferences were positive, and his supervisor reported he was an asset to the facility.

As indicated in the preceding case study examples, a distinction is evident between the terms, rehabilitation and habilitation. The first implies that an individual becomes disabled, due to a medical condition or a deliberate or accidental injury, after possessing work-related skills. In contrast, the latter term signifies that the individual has a congenital disability and must be introduced to the complexities of employment. Although these terms are used synonymously throughout the literature, the difference is considerable when selecting appropriate facilitative methodology.

Wendy, Dusty, and Stanley obviously have very different needs, idiosyncratic qualities, and lifestyles. Optimally, a VR counselor will develop a plan for the delivery of services that accentuates each recipient's aptitudes and talents, as depicted in the vignettes. Often this will require unlimited resources and a longer period of training than is usually allocated for completion of the VR process. Consequently, the enormous challenge facing both client and counselor necessitates a creative flexible program to derive maximum benefits that will lead to a profitable future.

COMBINING VOCATIONAL REHABILITATION AND AUDIOLOGY

Networking between professionals, their sponsoring agencies, and organizations affiliated with hearing loss is a powerful tool for the collection and dissemination of information. Many VR counselors recognize networking as the key to a smooth vocational transition for the client who is hearing impaired. It expands client opportunities while negating bias factors that have, in the past, prohibited the participation of those with hearing loss. Networking breaks down the barriers involved in "turf guarding" and allows for positive interaction and valuable input into the rehabilitation process (Woodrick, 1984). Without this cooperative working relationship among service providers, the client will experience delayed progress due, in part, to external

matters beyond the locus of his or her control. Additionally, the lack of communication and/or miscommunication between professionals interupts the continuity and flow of services. In return, this affects the client's personal motivation and has a profound impact on the client's perspective toward specialized personnel. Confidence in the system and associated professionals begins to deteriorate. Therefore, prompt and accurate information, exchanged in an efficient and timely manner, eliminates conflict and unnecessary obstacles. Through the avenue of networking, many of these intrusive problems can be avoided or resolved.

Given the continuum of audiological needs exhibited by persons with hearing loss, the role of the audiologist is significant in all phases of the vocational rehabilitation process. Considering the prolific rate at which new developments in technology occur, the audiologist's knowledge and expertise is vital to programming success. Contemporary hearing aids and devices are capable of refining a client's auditory skills and enabling the individual to incorporate strategies for the enhancement of overall communication. A VR counselor cannot possibly keep abreast of the latest improvements in hearing aids and devices and for this reason must regularly consult with the audiologist. This is especially true for adult clients who have recently acquired a hearing loss. Most often the VR counselor is the clients' first contact, so they have not been introduced to these sophisticated instruments. They, therefore, may required in-depth counseling by the audiologist. It becomes apparent in these particular situations that the charge for both professionals is interrelated with counseling and supervision as shared responsibilities. However, the VR counselor and audiologist's complementary roles have distinctive knowledge bases from which each can solicit useful information. The VR counselor is accountable for the client's vocational habilitation/rehabilitation, whereas the audiologist's focus is primarily on the auditory aspects of habilitation/rehabilitation.

SUMMARY

The placement and retention of individuals who are hearing impaired in quality work environments is the ultimate goal of vocational rehabilitation. Counselors are trained in the areas of hearing impairment and deafness to diligently seek out new frontiers for employment, liaison with other professionals, and provide assistance to clients in their efforts to obtain personal and occupational independence. The underlying commonality that VR counselors share is the advancement of people who are hearing impaired in the labor market.

REFERENCES

El-Khiami, A. (1986). Selected characteristics of hearing-impaired rehabilitants of general VR agencies: A socio-demographic profile. In D. Watson, G. Anderson, & M. Taff-Watson (Eds.), *Integrating human resources, technology and systems in deafness: Proceedings of the Tenth Biennial Conference of the American Deafness and Rehabilitation Association* (pp. 136–144). Silver Spring, MD: American Deafness and Rehabilitation Association.

Phillipe, T., & Auvenshine, D. (1985). Career development among deaf persons. *Journal of Rehabilitation of the Deaf, 19,* 9–17.

Phillips, G. B. (1975). Specific jobs for deaf workers. *Journal of Rehabilitation of the Deaf, 9,* 10–23.

Schein, J. D., & Delk, M. T. (1974). *The deaf population of the United States.* Silver Spring, MD: National Association of the Deaf.

Schroedel, J. G. (1987). The educational and occupational aspirations and attainments of deaf students and alumni of postsecondary programs. In G. B. Anderson & D. Watson (Eds.), *Innovations in the habilitation and rehabilitation of deaf adolescents: Selected proceedings of the Second National Conference on Habilitation and Rehabilitation of Deaf Adolescents* (pp. 117–139). Afton, OK: American Deaf Adolescent Conference.

Steffanic, D. J. (1982). *Reasonable accommodation for deaf employees in white collar jobs* (Monograph 10). Washington, DC: United States Office of Personnel Management Office of Research and Development.

Williams, W., & Sussman, A. E. (1976). Social and psychological problems of deaf people. In A. E. Sussman & L. G. Stewart (Eds.), *Counseling with deaf people* (pp. 13–29). New York: Deafness Research and Training Center.

Woodrick, W. E. (1984). Utilization of existing potential programs and facilities for serving multihandicapped deaf persons in region IV. *Journal of Rehabilitation of the Deaf, 18,* 17–20.

Wooton, S. C., & Mowry, R. L. (1986). A follow-up study of hearing impaired vocational rehabilitation clients closed successfully by a state VR agency. In D. Watson, G. Anderson, & M. Taff-Watson (Eds.), *Integrating human resources, technology and systems in deafness: Proceedings of the Tenth Biennial Conference of the American Deafness and Rehabilitation Association* (pp. 410–419). Silver Spring, MD: American Deafness and Rehabilitation Association.

Wright, G. N. (1980). *Total rehabilitation.* Boston, MA: Little Brown.

PART I

Audiologic Habilitation: The Child Who Is Hearing Impaired

■ CHAPTER 6 ■

Family Involvement and Counseling in Serving Children Who Are Hearing Impaired

■ DALE V. ATKINS, Ph.D. ■

Acknowledging that one's child is hearing-impaired is a long and difficult process which no one, aside from another parent of a child who is hearing impaired, can fully understand. It is the first and most important fact that each professional needs to accept before, during, and after provision of service to any family. This chapter presents information on the family of the child who is hearing impaired, the family's role in the support of the child, and the role of the professional in family involvement on behalf of their child who is hearing impaired.

There is much that professionals can do to help in the navigation of an unfamiliar and confusing road. Whether trained as teachers, doctors, speech and language therapists, audiologists, or counselors, professionals must always be mindful of who they are and what their role is in the process of working with parents and children. They may wish to make their clients' pain go away, they may wish to fix everything, see themselves as saviors, miracle workers, persons on whom parents rely in order to cope better with their situation. They may, intentionally or not, raise parents' expectations based on their own desire to have them feel better.

Certainly, it is well within a professional's realm to be encouraging, hopeful, and positive in spirit. *It is not within a professional's realm to promise what cannot be delivered.* Early in this author's career of working with families of children who are hearing impaired, a mother of a happy, popular, highly communicative 12-year-old girl who used total communication (i.e., a combination of sign language, voice, and audition) kept insisting that her daughter use her voice more instead of signing, when talking with me. Afterward, in my private conversation with the mother, she said she felt like a failure whenever her daughter chose not to speak. When asked why, she replied, "I'll never forget the first professional I met in the field of deafness. She was a therapist who told me that if I worked hard enough my daughter would speak as well as any normal child. You know, I devoted my entire life to trying to teach her to speak well. Since she doesn't, I feel as if I didn't do enough."

Another family has been waiting for life to return to the way it was before their son lost his hearing at age 26 months. The father, upon reflection of the doctor's words, recalled him saying, "Things will be as good as new; even better because you all have survived such a terrible trauma." Contrary to what the doctor predicted, things were far from better. The household was in chaos, the older, 6-year-old brother felt confused, abandoned, and neglected because of his parents' involvement with the younger boy. They were waiting for things to go back to "the way it was." It was already over 4 years and the family was still trying to sort out their lives. Things were hardly "as good as new!"

Professionals must be mindful that each person's experience is unique and that discovering that one's child is hearing impaired changes each person in some way. In all families, parental actions are heavily influenced by various factors, among which are the child's responses, the parents' family backgrounds and interpersonal histories, how they were raised, marital harmony or discord, finances, chronic or acute stresses and means of dealing with them, strengths and support of friendships, expectations for themselves and their children, knowledge about and attitude toward hearing impairment, maturity, and attitude toward life's challenges. Cultural differences exist with regard to how persons with disabilities and their families are perceived (Yacobacci-Tam, 1987).

How professionals see themselves and interpret their roles will greatly affect the course of treatment for the family as a whole and the child individually. Helping people to approach their lives from a perspective of strength, expediting their discovery and utilization of their own inner resources, while sorting out the maze in which they find themselves, is within the professionals' domain. The rate at which a family's progress occurs is outside the professional's domain and is determined by the persons themselves and their response and interaction with the long process of healing, coping, and living. Specialists need to be unintimidating, cooperative teammates who have chosen a field of study and have developed considerable experience and training in specific areas, but who are open to learning from the people who have come for help. They must present themselves as human beings who have selected a particular profession and as a result, have accumulated some knowledge. He or she cannot be all-knowing, superior, or condescending. Rather, professionals must embark, eager to learn, in a partnership with people whom they view positively and respectfully.

The family is a primary, powerful emotional system that shapes and influences the lives of its members. In Systems Theory, the family is conceptualized as a dynamic unit. The theory posits that family relationships are interdependent and mutually interactive; change in one part of the system stimulates compensatory change in other parts. Erikson (1964) found that the stability of the family hinges on the complicated and sensitive pattern of emotional balance and interchange. The behavior of each member affects and is affected by the behavior of other members. Families are the greatest potential resource for personal well-being, as well as for psychological distress.

Luterman (1979) states that in families with children who are disabled, the family as a whole may initially attempt to adjust to the disability without changing the existing family structure. However, members may eventually reach a point where they cannot continue to meet previous social, economic, and personal roles and expectations, and where they may become dissatisfied with their relationships with each other. A role organization crisis may occur, which is associated with elevated tension, in which delicately balanced family priorities may shift. Siblings may be expected to take over adult responsibilities; the quality and frequency of recreational activities may change; grandparents may shy away from sharing child care responsibilities or may offer help and be rejected; finances previously earmarked may need to be budgeted for the funding of hearing aids, tactile stimulators, private therapy, or attendance at conferences; longstanding friendships may be critically scrutinized; and personal time and energy all but disappear. When family disequilibrium persists and parents feel particularly stressed, there is a risk of severe personal or relational problems developing.

All too often the actual issues that are troubling the family are not addressed, and symptoms rather than causes are confronted. In a rather typical example, a father in one family became increasingly more involved in his work after the diagnosis of his son's hearing impairment. He attended evening work meetings, traveled more, and accepted business-related phone calls at home. Whenever he would attend a clinic appointment, invariably, someone from his office would call. This put a severe strain on his relationship with his wife. She felt she was alone, and they argued frequently. The symptoms appeared to indicate marital distress, but in truth, the man needed to become totally absorbed in his work to get his mind away from the pain he was experiencing over his child who was hearing impaired and to reassure himself of his importance. He needed to believe that he could still control much of his world even though he felt helpless over not being able to change the fact that his son was hearing impaired.

THE ROLE OF THE PROFESSIONAL

In the beginning of a professional association, the professional does not know these people (parents or children), and they do not know the professional. Professionals are looked at as "the experts." The danger of this for professionals is that they may maintain the parents' expectation of them and forget that they, too, are involved in a learning process. This "halo effect" is a dangerous illusion for the professional who does not understand the lengthy process in which the parents are immersed. Parents desperately need to know they are not lost, that their family, particularly their child, will be okay. They desire reassurance regarding the decisions confronting them. Parents are thrown into a new world and are required to make serious decisions for and about their child, based on recommendations of many professionals.

Even before the child's own hearing aids arrive, the parents need to select one of many early intervention programs representing different philosophies. "What should I do? What would you do if you were in my shoes?" asks the overwhelmed parent. The professional is often, at these moments, viewed as much more than human and asked to make decisions for the parents about their family's future. The professional's job is *to not make decisions* for the family, but rather to help the parents become sufficiently comfortable and informed so that they can make their own decisions. It is a difficult position to be in due to the nature of the counseling required.

Since speech and language therapists, teachers, and audiologists are not trained to be professional counselors, social workers, or psychologists, they sometimes feel inadequate to deal with the range of emotional responses they encounter, while performing the service for which they were "trained." Many of these professionals feel competent working with children, but find themselves interacting at length with the child's parents as well as siblings, grandparents, and babysitters. Frequently, an entire family (extended and nuclear) will show up for an appointment, and the professional feels unprepared to handle the different people and the various emotions expressed. It is essential they understand that their role is not to become counselors. However, in order to execute their roles more proficiently, they do need to be sensitive to and unafraid of the multifaceted nature of their work, which is simultaneously content and emotion based. Both aspects are equally important to the success of the interaction. At times, content may come more to the fore, but that does not mean that emotional underpinnings are absent.

THE PROFESSIONAL AS COUNSELOR

To enable professionals to feel prepared for these encounters, it is useful for them to learn basic counseling theories with the understanding that they will, for the most part, be dealing with a well patient model.

Unlike in psychotherapy, where the main goal is to help reorganize and reinterpret a client's intrapersonal conflicts which may be characterized by anxieties, depression, guilt, confusions, or ambivalence, counseling in this context is done with psychologically normal individuals who are presently trying to confront and cope with a major, or series of major disruptions in their lives. (Clark, 1990, p. 5)

The counseling that takes place is supportive and builds on renewed insights into the person, his or her family, goals, and specific aspects of their lives. For a more intense examination of the various models and their use with a population that is hearing impaired, the reader is referred to the works of Luterman (1979), Harvey (1989), and Rollin (1987). One can attempt to be familiar with a variety of theories, and then blend them, depending on the need of the client and the situation.

Whatever the professional's orientation, no response will compensate for the loss that the family is experiencing. The gaping hole cannot be filled by words. The hurt may be soothed, over time — usually years. Professionals must be active and involved listeners, committed to the process; active in that they encourage parents to express their emotions and the circumstances underlying those emotional states; involved in that they recognize when questions need a direct, informational response. Being straightforward yet compassionate and empathetic, confident yet neither pompous nor omniscient, respectful of the family and sensitive

to their plight and concerns, is essential so that the family will be able to perceive and accept the professional as a viable and trustworthy partner.

Trust has more chance of developing if the professional learns the parents' personal hopes and their goals for themselves and their children. These people have a lot to teach. Refraining from making assumptions is vital to the professional. The extent to which the news of a hearing impairment affects a family can only be discovered by listening to and observing *this* family. Yet the professional can view them against a backdrop of knowledge that has been garnered from other families.

EMOTIONAL RESPONSES OF FAMILIES

Among the research and observation of families of children who are hearing impaired, professionals find that, in the area of emotional response, these families experience reactions similar to those of children who have other disabilities. The response cycle is not unlike that experienced by any person involved in grieving a major loss. For years, this process was likened to that described by Elisabeth Kubler-Ross (1969) in *On Death and Dying.* Predictable stages were described as shock, recognition, denial, acknowledgment, and constructive action. Because parents lost the child they had envisioned, their task at hand is to adapt to the thought and reality of life with this different child. What was previously normal suddenly undergoes reassessment. Somehow, a new normalcy needs to be established. There is an ending to the relationship with the child who was believed to have normal hearing and a beginning of a new relationship with the child who is hearing impaired. With neither warning nor preparation, the parents are thrust into an unfamiliar world filled with information and people they would have gone a lifetime without confronting. To add to the predicament, there really is no choice. They enter this world reluctantly and apprehensively. The professional's function at this point is to serve as a supportive guide through the maze.

This process of parental grieving is different from that of losing a child completely. It is also unlike the discovery that one's child has a more visible disability that may have been obvious at birth. Deafness is referred to as "the invisible handicap" and thus, the extent of the disability is not known to most people. Additionally, since deafness is rarely discovered at birth, parents initially bond with the child whom they believe is 100% alright. They sing, talk, and in general relate to the baby as if there were normal function. When the suspicion that the child may have a hearing problem is confirmed, there is, understandably, much sadness, guilt, anger, and remorse on the part of the parents and other family members. These feelings frequently appear and reappear over the years, despite the fact that the families rebuild their lives and deal with their loss constructively. It is essential that parents go through, rather than avoid, the mourning process. "It enhances their parental capacity for satisfaction in childrearing" (Leigh, 1987).

HEARING THE NEWS

Often, on hearing the news, parents question their ability to parent the child, feel unprepared, and don't know what to do. They question everything they do know about their child and wonder if they will ever relate to this different child from whom they feel estranged and with whom they imagine they will be unable to communicate. Previously held feelings of competency regarding their own parenting skills are called into question as they begin to worry about what will happen to their children, their relationship, and their family. One mother mused: "I knew that music was my whole life and I had spent so much time thinking about how great it would be to have a child to sing with; I played soothing classical music during my pregnancy, sang all the time while he was an infant, and bought him every musical toy that I could find. I truly do not know what I'm supposed to do. I'm just so utterly sad." Upon the recent discovery of his fourth child's hearing impairment, one father lamented, "I don't think I can rely on anything I did with my other kids

to be right. I don't know how to deal with Mickey since he cannot hear me. How will I discipline him? How will I find out what he wants? I'm questioning everything I ever knew about children, because I see how much I don't know." The overwhelming sense that they will not know what to do or that there is too much to learn, and they are not equipped to handle all that will be required, can cause some parents to question everything they know about children.

To help parents realize their full potential, their initial perceptions of weakness and helplessness must be gradually and consistently replaced by confidence and competence. The clinician's role is to enable the parent to work effectively with the child while providing objective, individualized support, guidance, and critique. The professional's role changes over time. At first, their words are the only words of guidance and instruction that are available to the family. Later, they serve as a sounding board.

It is at this point that the message "child first and foremost" needs to be conveyed to parents gently and consistently. Usually, parents focus on the aspect of their child that is impaired rather than focusing on the whole child. This is a natural response. It is up to the professional to relate to the child as a child first, considering the hearing impairment second. Even though the family sees the professional for issues regarding the hearing impairment, the nature of the professional's interaction, questions, and manner should be that of a person interested in the functioning of a whole child within a whole family. A mother of a newly diagnosed 20-month-old daughter insisted, whenever her husband interacted with their daughter, that he wear the microphone for her FM unit. At times he resisted, especially when he wanted to "rough house" with his daughter. This incited tension between the couple. She felt she was the only one "working" with Angela, while he was just there for the fun. The mother felt they did not have time to "fool around." Without realizing it, the mother sent disapproving messages to her husband, so that he felt his way of relating to his daughter was not as valuable. Much of his time was not engaged in "teaching language;"

therefore, it was deemed unimportant. She felt he was not giving his daughter anything that she needed. He claimed, "I don't do as well as my wife does in the structured setting. At least I can still develop a relationship with my daughter. Isn't that worth something?" Intuitively he knew that he was right, but the pressure of needing every waking hour to be involved in a structured language experience had taken over and dictated their lives. The valuable, delicate balance had not yet been struck.

FEELINGS, DOUBTS, AND QUESTIONS

Feelings are complex and confusing. Doubts abound. Questions are asked. Some are unanswerable, thus adding to the frustration and the sense of feeling unfamiliar and incompetent. Parents of newly diagnosed children frequently report feeling numb; overwhelmed with a horrible sense of disbelief and shock; unable to process information they are given about hearing loss, audiograms, hearing aids, educational options, and state support services, while attempting to look attentive with tears welling up or running down, fighting enormous lumps in throats, resisting nausea and a generalized feeling of being in another place or time zone, with people who are unfamiliar (Buscalia, 1975; Featherstone, 1980; Moses, 1985).

Marcia Forecki (1985) recounted her experiences with her son, Charlie, who is hearing impaired, in *Speak to Me*. She recalled her initial experience this way:

Mourning manifested itself in not wanting to speak to Charlie, or anyone else. I unplugged my radio and refused to watch television. I surrounded myself with the absence of sound so as to make sound not exist. It was impossible to live with the fact that Charlie could not experience sound. (p. 29)

One father described hearing the news this way:

It was as if I was knifed in my stomach; my insides were threatening to come out and the more I tried to hold them in, the more I lost control. The audiologist just kept staring at me with a shocked expression on his face. I must have looked like something had snapped inside of me ... in fact, it did.

Delivering bad news is something most of us are not comfortable with. At various stages in the families' journey they will meet many professionals who will be in the position of delivering, if not bad, then difficult news. The first person to confirm the parents' suspicion of hearing impairment is usually a pediatrician, otologist, or audiologist. Although the news may be delivered gently and tactfully, it may not be received in that way.

Many professionals perceive their role to be one of delivering news and then asking the parents for questions. When the parents do not ask any, the professional assumes all is understood as it was presented and continues to talk. It is useless to deliver news and information if you do not validate that it is received and understood. Yet when the news is difficult, professionals often avoid the very probing that is necessary, not wanting to "upset" the parents more. The professional must make a serious and consistent effort to listen to what is and what is not being said. Whenever professionals are in the position of delivering news, they must be conscious of several factors among which are environment, participants, timing and sequencing, language or symbols, strength assessment, and resources (Kroth, 1987). Because the sorrow of having a child who is hearing impaired is often chronic, professionals need to be supportive and mindful of these factors throughout the years of their interactions with parents. One mother thought aloud,

Sometimes, today, 15 years later, I still feel like I did at that first meeting with the audiologist. When I hear important information about Jackie, my emotions get in the way of my being able to listen attentively, and I have a hard time hearing what is being said. I guess because we have been through so much, people expect me to have an unfeeling filter through which I hear all of the facts. It just isn't so.

If a professional is furnishing information, it is imperative that attempts be made to assist the parents in feeling less overwhelmed by making enough time to give information and to answer questions. Language needs to be carefully chosen, and words that may be unfamiliar should be explained. Few situations are more intimidating to parents than listening to professionals talk about their child, using words that are unfamiliar. In the area of hearing impairment, where there are many unfamiliar terms and symbols (e.g., interpreting an audiogram), handouts should be provided with terminology, phrases, and definitions; and resource sheets and pamphlets should be readily available. Parents need time to ingest what is discussed. They need to be assured that a follow-up meeting or phone call is scheduled to ensure clarification of points made.

ENHANCING COMMUNICATION BETWEEN PROFESSIONALS AND PARENTS

Because much of the information that is presented may or may not be heard or processed, it is essential to frequently review what was discussed previously. One mother tape recorded every session she had with the otologist and audiologist so that she could review the tape with her husband who was unable to attend many of the appointments with her. As her child grew up, tape recording became a useful habit. She taped teachers' meetings and Individualized Educational Plan (IEP) sessions. Some professionals she encountered were uneasy, but she countered by saying that she wanted to concentrate on what was being said, wanted to feel free to ask questions, and wanted to have time to review all of the answers when she was in the privacy of her own home. Professionals who feel comfortable with this idea can expand it by providing prerecorded tapes of the information to be covered or by taping their sessions and giving the parents the audiotape. Additionally families should be furnished with a packet of information sheets, booklets, lists of national and local organizations and resources, and books for home study and sharing with family members. The information packet should be available in as many languages as the community served. This practice is especially helpful when parents travel a great distance and the likelihood of frequent follow-up meetings or immediate contact with other parents is slim.

Realizing that only a portion of the message sent is going to be received is an important lesson for all professionals. Messages, particularly those that are not entirely welcome, are frequently distorted as they are filtered through our thoughts and feelings. Whenever professionals are in the position of giving news to parents, they must be aware that parents also need to hear what the possibilities are for their children and for their families. One father remembers, "The therapist seemed so upbeat, hopeful, and positive. It helped us because, like us, our friends and family were all so down and grief-stricken. Every conversation we had was about Joey and his hearing. Heaven knows what was happening in other aspects of our lives since it seems now that we didn't deal with anything else. We were sad, but we also wanted to do something constructive." Referring to his own participation he said, "I realized that I began to enjoy the sessions because I was learning while I was getting to know Joey in a different way. Instead of focusing on the fact that he could not hear, I began to think of ways I could broaden his ability to hear. It became exciting. That is when I began to feel hopeful."

Families seem to do better when they are confident that the professional is familiar and current with different educational programs. Visiting area schools and keeping up professional associations with those in the same and related fields is helpful for the clinician's personal and professional growth. It is invaluable when sharing knowledge with families. Professionals who attend conferences and participate in workshops designed for parents can develop a sensitivity to the situation faced by those parents. Teachers who visit local hearing aid dispensers and hearing and speech centers at local hospitals and clinics where families receive services have a better chance of connecting with families and understanding the complex network with which families interact. Too often, parents are the link in a large network of services. When they discover that professionals are unacquainted or unfamiliar with one another, their confidence in the professionals and the system can wane. If they perceive that there is a larger, interconnected structure of which they are a part, they feel less isolated.

EXCHANGING ROLES

A strategy at seminars and workshops is to encourage parents and professionals to assume the role of the other when involved in a particular problem-solving exercise or sensitivity-training experience. By reversing roles, empathy is likely to develop, and the process of working together can be accomplished more smoothly. In one such exercise, a speech-language pathologist expressed anger over a parent's tardiness at her son's sessions. She interpreted this chronic lateness as the mother's resistance to having her son in therapy. When the speech-language pathologist took the role of the mother, she discovered that the mother needed to travel two hours on public transportation to attend therapy. After discovering this, the pathologist became more alert to such aspects in her clients' lives. In this case, there was an effort to address the problem directly, enlisting a community ride service which helped to ease the transportation problem.

It is essential for professionals to possess sensitive communication skills that consider the families' needs and comfort. Professionals who work with children who are hearing impaired and their families are involved with them in searching for solutions to their problems. The overriding message the professional can convey is that the family will be able to cope, and the professionals the parents encounter will make their task easier. Parents' existing coping skills may enable them to deal with their situation better than professionals expect. Conversely, developing coping skills may be what is needed to facilitate better adjustment and, therefore, the professional's role may be enlarged to include helping parents

discover how to efficiently negotiate the maze of people, places, and things related to and about hearing impairment. Additionally, professionals can help them incorporate family and friends into their lives in ways that can be beneficial to them and their families. Finally, professionals can help provide a safe place where families can see and explore their fears and develop the courage to deal with them.

PARENT SUPPORT GROUPS

Most professionals know the value of connecting families with other families who are in similar situations. At times, there may be initial reluctance by clients to meet other parents. Perhaps talking to one professional is all a family can handle at the moment. Perhaps meeting with other parents is too threatening; too definite an acknowledgment that they have a child who is hearing impaired. But the eventual sharing that occurs among families is potentially the most therapeutic and healing remedy that any family can undertake. Bonds of friendship, understanding, empathy, and humor form among families who, under "normal" circumstances would not have met. They give one another strength as well as hope. Helen Keller (1954) said, "We bereaved are not alone. We belong to the largest company in all the world — the company of those who have known suffering. When it seems that our sorrow is too great to be borne, let us think of the great family of the heavy-hearted into which our grief has given us entrance, and, inevitably, we feel about us their arms, their sympathy, their understanding." It is the parents who grow together, leaving behind feelings of helplessness and despair, as they try to make sense out of the new world into which they reluctantly have been thrust.

Professionals must encourage attendance at parent support groups, and if none exist, commit to starting such a program with one or two interested families. These discussion groups augment parent-to-parent phone connections; membership in organizations; attendance at panel discussions featuring parents of teenagers and young adults who are hearing impaired, older children who are hearing impaired, grandparents, and siblings; and interaction with adults and professionals who are hearing impaired. All are of inestimable value in the adaptation of families with children who are hearing impaired.

It is other parents who can offer solace when a grandparent appears to favor one child over another and the parents do not know how to address this with their own parents. It is other parents who understand what it is like when a child who is hearing impaired is not asked for "playdates" by the neighborhood kids. It is other parents who can talk openly about their feelings of neglecting their other children in favor of the child who is hearing impaired because the "need" is greater. Other parents can truly understand the difficulty of not having the time or energy for their spouses or other children. They can notice other parents placing expectations on the hearing siblings in the family to behave maturely, accepting responsibilities beyond their ages.

Parents in a parent group can organize a "Sibling Day," arrange to have all of the families meet at a picnic site, emphasize the "normalcy" of their families so that the siblings can see other families with children who wear hearing aids (Atkins, 1987). These events help families, and siblings in particular, feel less isolated. It is in a parent group that parents can let their hair down and not have to be "supermom" or "superdad." It is in a parent group that parents can discuss what it is like to have one's personal and familial identity quickly transformed into the "father of" or "family with the deaf kid," recognizing that wherever they go people look at them and make assumptions, sometimes asking questions, sometimes not, sometimes offering suggestions, sometimes not. One mother received nods of recognition from group members when she said, "Running to the market used to be so easy. Now when I take Alex, everyone in the check-out line stares at his hearing aids. One woman asked if he was listening to a Walkman. I'm embarrassed to tell you that I said 'Yes!' "

Only other parents can identify with the sinking feeling when every eye in the store is on you when your child has a tantrum. Upon reflection of his daughter's tantrum in a toy store one father admitted, "It is worse when your kid is deaf because when she closes her eyes and pulls her hearing aids out of her ears there really is no way to reach her. While I am waiting for her to calm down, it seems like everyone in the store has passed me and I'm convinced they think I am the most incompetent father in the world."

It is also parents who are going through the same process who can encourage other parents to be patient while witnessing the progress of their friends' children and not seeing any discernible change in their own children. "Sometimes when we see my sister's kids, I can't help feeling envious of her. She has it all so easy! We were pregnant at the same time, planned it so that the cousins would be close and play together and now I wonder how they will ever get along. I don't want my nephew to feel that Billy is a drag to be around." Another mother commented, "Years ago when I saw other mothers playing with their children in the park I would feel intensely jealous. Now I know that many of my friends envy my relationship with my daughter because we really are close. Maybe that has to do with how hard we have worked at communicating. I needed a lot of patience."

OTHER FAMILY MEMBERS

In addition to parent support groups as a means of assisting parents to adapt to life with a child who is hearing impaired, parents also benefit from acknowledgment by professionals that there are other important influences in their lives. Attending to the needs of their child who is hearing impaired is often dominant, but it is not the only important aspect in their lives. Relationships with other children in the family, spouses or significant others, grandparents, friends, and the relationship with one's self need to be addressed.

Other children in the family fare better when their needs are recognized also, when they are included in family decisions, and when they are spoken to openly and honestly about what has transpired and what is happening in their family. Explanations take time and need to be repeated and broadened as children grow and develop. Books written for and about sibling issues are available, and most professionals welcome brothers and sisters attending an occasional session so that they can become informed, participate if they care to, and "listen" through hearing aids. Siblings can help in very specific ways, thus alleviating some of the pressure felt by the parents. It is imperative to remember at all times, however, that the responsibility for the child who is hearing impaired, whether with regard to lessons or care, does not lie with a sibling. In addition to making brothers and sisters feel welcome and important, professionals can offer correct, easy explanations, embellished by pictures, filmstrips, and the actual apparatus that is used for testing, while providing answers to questions that help siblings respond when their friends ask them questions about hearing loss.

Professionals and parents can organize "Sibling Days" too, devoted to the education and involvement of brothers and sisters. Age-appropriate information can be shared about facts and myths about hearing impairment, family adjustment issues, and coping techniques for specific situations. Children of all ages need to know that they are not responsible for their brother or sister's hearing impairment. They need to be reassured that their school performance, for example, is unrelated to their brother's or sister's. A 24-year-old teacher of children who are hearing impaired remembered her own household. "Everyone made such a fuss when Kristen did well in school. If she got a 'B' it was cause for celebration. I was happy for her too, but sometimes I would have liked some recognition for my hard work. Granted, things came easier for me because I had my hearing, but school was still hard. I had a straight 'A' report card throughout high school and it was as if it was expected. I was the model kid. I knew my folks had enough on their minds; I didn't want to add to their heartache, so I never brought them my problems."

To help siblings face their own feelings, parents need to be encouraged to provide full, age-appropriate explanations with emphasis on the feelings the family and siblings are experiencing. This is particularly beneficial when helping siblings deal with feelings that encompass sadness, guilt, disappointment, confusion, anger, jealousy, overprotection, fear, embarrassment, responsibility, pride, love, comfort, interest, concern, tolerance, patience, and sympathy. Encouraging siblings to express their feelings is difficult for some parents if they, themselves, have been avoiding their emotions. Allowing children to express their feelings is a gift.

It is also worthwhile to know the parents' perception of their normally hearing child's role in relation to the sibling who is hearing impaired. Is the parental perception communicated to the sibling? If so, by what means? If not, is this a problem for the sibling? Most children need to know that the feelings they are having are okay. Parents do not need to *do* anything except listen nonjudgmentally and lovingly.

When parents attempt to deal openly with their own feelings related to having a child with a hearing loss, they are more likely to be able to address the issue with their other children. Some are unable to do this. One mother who was deep in grief interpreted her normal hearing daughter's "needy requests at bedtime" for "another glass of water, and just one more story and please straighten out the dolls" as the daughter's willful attempt to be uncooperative and a pest. The daughter, however, realized that this was the only time during the entire day that her mother spent any time alone with her. She was determined to extend those moments as long as she could, even if her mother became impatient with her. It was better than nothing.

One father observed that his only chance to be with his children occurred when he returned from work in the evening and on weekends. He tried to divide his time so that he could have separate time with each of the children while still maintaining family time. "I try to make everyone feel important, emphasizing not only what they do for themselves, but what they do for each other. I try to have them develop pride in how they help one another. Everyone gives to everyone else in this household. Dana teaches us things and we teach her things. That's just the way it is. I expect the same behavior out of all the kids. It is just harder to get Dana to understand what I expect. What's funny is that frequently, the older kids understand Dana better than I do, and they are the ones who help me understand what she is trying to say. I have to be careful though, that they are not always used as her interpreter. I don't want her to become too dependent on them. They really do look out for her, though."

This father noticed many aspects of sibling interaction within his own family. Siblings in all families serve many roles — friends, playmates, caregivers, teachers, models, interpreters, socializers, and confidants. The challenge in families with children who are hearing impaired is to try to accentuate the positive aspects of sibling relationships, promote healthy bonding, while encouraging each child to develop his or her individuality, and to feel good about themselves as valuable, contributing members of the family. Their role in the family is as important as any other child in the family. Their needs are as significant. When parents are unable to be available totally to all of their children, they can enlist the help of friends or family members who may be eager to help, but may not know what they can do.

Grandparents are often a source of support for families of children who are hearing impaired. Sometimes the diagnosis facilitates the healing of old family wounds because of the need. Like parents, grandparents also have expectations for their grandchildren. They, too, have dreams about their relationship and how it will develop. One woman said, "When my daughter was pregnant I fantasized about how I would tell my grandchild stories about our life before we came to America. My English isn't very good, so I thought I would teach her Spanish and she would become bilingual and travel with me to Mexico and meet her relatives. Now I worry that she will not understand me. How will I talk to her?" This grandmother needed reassurance that she was not inadequate. The love and caring that she wanted to give her granddaughter could still be transmitted effec-

tively. She continued to talk to her granddaughter. Instead of withdrawing, she helped to encourage attendance at meetings of Spanish speaking grandparents. Her involvement with her granddaughter was invaluable, and a close relationship developed.

Grandparents can play a more consistent role in the lives of their grandchildren, especially in the case of single-parent households, when they live nearby. Their support of their children and their "extra pair of hands" can, in some families, enable parents to cope successfully with their situation. It behooves the professional to understand the role that grandparents have undertaken and interact with them respectfully and in accordance with their position. When a grandparent cares for the child all day while the parent is at work, it is advisable that both the parent and the grandparent be involved in lessons and any informational sessions that may be scheduled. This important relationship between parents of the child who is hearing impaired and their own parents is one that is a potential source of support or stress. Without a doubt, it comes under scrutiny when a child is diagnosed as hearing impaired.

PARENT SELF-CARE

Encouraging parents of children who are hearing impaired, particularly mothers, to take care of themselves, physically, mentally, emotionally, and spiritually, is of utmost importance. For women who work outside of their homes, the conflicts surrounding caring for their children and caring for themselves is profound. Arranging time off from work to attend professional meetings and appointments is frequently difficult and can cause distress, even with the most understanding employers and co-workers. One mother stated, "My performance on the job diminishes, and taking care of my own needs doesn't even make the list of 'things to do'." Another mother reflected, "My boss was wonderful to me when I discovered Hillary's hearing loss, but now I feel I have to make up the time. People assume that, once you get hearing aids, and your child is enrolled in a program, your involvement is virtually over, and you can return to your 9 to 5 job. I feel apologetic when I ask for time off to visit school programs, audiologists, and to attend a mothers' group. The mothers' group is really for me and me alone but I can't attend regularly because it meets in the daytime. Almost all of the things that I have to do for Jenny take place during working hours. Believe me, as much as I love my job, if I did not *have* to work I would not."

Single mothers are not the only ones who have difficulty with inflexible work schedules, which clearly add to the stress in their lives. Every parent who works outside of the home needs to take into account the time it takes to travel between appointments. Professionals need to be as flexible as possible when scheduling sessions if the goal is to have parents participate.

THE LONG PROCESS

Professionals are sometimes unaware of the time it takes for parents to see results and believe that a particular method will work for their child. Because auditory technology has come so far in the last several years, professionals in the field of hearing impairment have tremendous confidence in the value of hearing aids and auditory stimulation. This confidence is frequently conveyed to parents, but the context of an appropriate time frame is not. It is helpful to communicate a variety of examples illustrating the kinds of responses that have been observed with other children, so that the family has a framework within which to work. Many parents have no way of knowing that learning to attend auditorially is a process that takes years. Since assurances cannot be given, parents are asked to proceed on faith. Professionals implore them to be patient.

However, it is not only parents who become impatient for their children to begin showing progress. Professionals, at times, have a specific time frame in which a parent's acceptance of the hearing loss is supposed to fit. At a meeting of several professionals who had contact with

one family, one commented: "This mother has been denying her son's deafness long enough." Another added, in a particularly frustrated way, "I can't handle this father's anger any longer. He really should be moving on; he's known about his son's hearing loss for two years already!" Their frustration demonstrates that sometimes professionals have their own internal requirements for the "rate of recovery." But what about a mother who was doing fine with her daughter's deafness, in fact was the mother most often found comforting and helping other parents in a parent group? She was thrown into a tailspin when her mother died and began mourning the loss of her daughter's hearing all over again. The knowledge that she was now on her own, without her own mother to take care of her (even though the mother had lived 2,000 miles away) was enough to stimulate her bereavement again. Subsequent losses are felt more severely; previous losses may be reexperienced more intensely.

It is imperative that both professionals and parents are mindful of the emotional seesaw of frustration, fear, anger, denial, recognition, and adaptation. Families who overidentify with their children may attribute to them aspects of life that may be inappropriate. "Deaf people are so isolated, Annie will never be able to make friends." This mother's comment reflects her own pain and does not take into consideration Annie's personality, ability to socialize, communicate, or interact. Coming to terms with one's own feelings, as separate from those of the child and the child's situation, takes time and experience. Accepting one's feelings, no matter what they are, is imperative to establishing a healthy relationship with one's self and one's loved ones, especially one's children. Acceptance of one's feelings is a positive precursor to acceptance of one's situation. Adapting to life with a child who is hearing impaired means accepting change. By nature, some of us do this better than others, but all of us have the ability to learn.

There are numerous and varied aspects to the adjustment to life with a child who is hearing impaired. Parents and professionals need to work together to help families find a balance that suits them. Whole families can learn much about themselves as individuals and as a family unit. Among the many challenges they face is that of discovering and tapping their inner resources. This is a long process requiring courage, strength, and patience.

REFERENCES

Atkins, D. (1987). Siblings of the hearing-impaired: Perspectives for parents. *Volta Review, 89*(5), 32–45.

Buscaglia, L. (1975). *The disabled and their parents: A counseling challenge.* Thorofare, NJ: Charles Slack.

Clark, J. (1990, Spring/Summer). Counseling in communicative disorders: A responsibility to be met. *Hearsay* (pp. 4–7).

Erikson, E. (1964). *Childhood and society.* New York: W. W. Norton.

Featherstone, H. (1980). *A difference in the family: Life with a disabled child.* New York: Basic Books.

Forecki, M. (1985). *Speak to me.* Washington, DC: Gallaudet College Press.

Harvey, M. (1989). *Psychotherapy with deaf and hard-of-hearing persons.* Hillsdale, NJ: Lawrence Erlbaum.

Keller, H. (1954). *The story of my life.* Garden City, NY: Doubleday. [Originally published 1902].

Kroth, R. (1987). Mixed or missed messages between parents and professionals. In D. Atkins (Ed.), *Families and their hearing impaired children* (pp. 1–10). Washington, DC: Volta Bureau.

Kubler-Ross, E. (1969). *On death and dying.* New York: Macmillan.

Leigh, I. (1987). Parenting and the hearing impaired: Attachment and coping. *Volta Review, 89*(5), 11–21.

Luterman, D. (1979). *Counseling parents of hearing-impaired children.* Boston: Little Brown.

Moses, K. (1985). Infant deafness and parental grief: Psychosocial early intervention. In F. Powell, T. Finitzo-Hieber, S. Friel-Patti, & D. Henderson (Eds.), *Education of the hearing impaired child.* San Diego, CA: Singular Publishing Group.

Rollin, W. (1987). *The psychology of communication disorders in individuals and their families.* Englewood Cliffs, NJ: Prentice-Hall.

Yacobacci-Tam, P. (1987). Interacting with the culturally different child. In D. Adkins (Ed.), *Families and their hearing impaired child* (pp. 46–58). Washington, DC: Volta Bureau.

■ CHAPTER 7 ■

Considerations and Strategies for Amplification for Children Who Are Hearing Impaired

■ WILLIAM R. HODGSON, Ph.D. ■

Children who wear hearing aids are not a homogeneous group. A world of difference exists among the needs of the child with profound congenital hearing loss, the older child with acquired sensorineural loss, and the child with small, fluctuating conductive loss. The child with profound congenital loss faces the almost insurmountable obstacle of learning to use minimal residual hearing and of acquiring speech and language through the use of partial auditory clues to supplement those available through vision. The older child with sensorineural loss, although having the advantage of normal language and speech, faces social stigma associated with hearing loss and hearing aid use and the task of learning in school with an im-

paired sensory system. The child with small hearing loss, perhaps a fluctuating conductive disorder, may find the handicap unrecognized, misunderstood, or underestimated and may have difficulty developing the discipline required for effective hearing aid use when needed.

Because children with congenital losses are the most visible, and perhaps the most common, of this disparate group, the majority of this chapter is devoted to them. However, attention is also given to the very different but no less severe problems of children in the other two groups.

During the last 20 years, significant changes have occurred in the etiologies of hearing losses in children. Hearing losses from maternal rubella and problems associated with Rh incompatibility have been substantially reduced. The prevalence of hearing losses from unknown causes remains at 40% of identified cases (Upfold, 1988). The increased availability of genetic counseling may have had some impact on the prevalence of hereditary disorders. These factors have reduced the number of severe and profound hearing losses and increased, proportionately, the number of mild and moderate losses. Children with these latter losses are not being identified and aided at an early enough age (Matkin, 1984).

Significant improvements have been made in miniaturization and flexibility of hearing aids. Digital hearing aids that can differentiate speech and noise remain, tantalizingly, just out of reach. Better identification procedures for children with smaller hearing losses, better techniques for preventing hearing losses, and smarter hearing aids are goals toward which clinicians should work in the immediate future.

EARLY IDENTIFICATION AND ADEQUATE EVALUATION

Amplification is the foundation on which the structure of aural habilitation for children who are hearing impaired is built. If the structure is to be sound, the hearing loss must be detected early in life, for the child is faced with the task of learning the meaning and utility of sound, with developing language and speech, and acquiring an education, while all auditory stimuli are filtered through an impaired sensory system. Therefore, the impairment must be minimized as early as possible through amplification, stimulation, and training in the use of residual hearing.

Additionally, early identification is vital to provide time for parents to progress through a sequence of events commonly reported to occur in the parents of children who are hearing impaired: disbelief, grief, anger, and acceptance. Because of the crucial role parents must play in habilitation of the child who is hearing impaired, they must have time to acquire the knowledge that will make them an effective part of the aural habilitation team.

IMPORTANCE OF EARLY AMPLIFICATION

Children born with profound hearing losses may suffer from sensory deprivation. Children who acquire hearing loss may experience delay in language, speech, and educational development dating from the onset of the loss. The time that intervenes between onset of loss and amplification may increase resistance to acceptance of amplification. Because of these factors, fitting and use of amplification must begin as soon as possible. A prerequisite for amplification is detection and evaluation of the hearing loss.

STRATEGIES FOR IDENTIFICATION AND EVALUATION OF HEARING LOSS

Behavioral methods for the identification and evaluation of hearing loss in infants and young children include Conditioned Orientation Reflex Audiometry (Suzuki & Ogiba, 1961), Visual Reinforcement Audiometry (Liden & Kankkunen, 1969), and Conditioned Play Audiometry (Barr, 1955). These techniques have the advantages of eliciting frequency-specific information and being applicable to either unaided or aided testing. Therefore, in addition to quantification of the hearing loss, the amount of functional gain delivered by the hearing aid can be evaluated. Using behavioral assessment methods, Wilson and Thompson (1984) established that reliable estimations of threshold can be established in children under 1 year of age.

Although it is true that skilled clinicians experienced in the evaluation of young children can obtain useful estimates of hearing sensitivity, evaluation is an ongoing process involving continued refinement of original estimates. Final determination of the exact extent and fine details of the auditory impairment is usually not completed until the child is 2 or 3 years of age. This consideration calls for fitting of hearing aids that are flexible enough to be modified appropriately as more is learned about the child's hearing. Fortunately, hearing aids that can be modified substantially in gain, maximum output, and frequency response are available and should be used when fitting young children.

Physiologic measures, such as Auditory Brainstem Reponse (ABR), add materially to the quantification of hearing loss in young children (Jacobson, 1985). Immittance measures also help to identify the presence of conductive components as well as giving information about the sensorineural system (ASHA, 1989). In addition to service in the initial diagnostic process, immittance measures should always be part of ongoing audiologic monitoring to detect development of conductive disorders that may require treatment and which can render an otherwise appropriate hearing aid fitting inadequate.

When a hearing impairment is identified in a child, language development should be evaluated. This information may be useful in estimating the degree of handicap associated with the hearing loss and, in mild hearing loss, help to suggest whether or not a hearing aid is needed. Information regarding language development can be solicited from parents or teachers, and receptive language level can be assessed by a scale such as the Peabody Picture Vocabulary Test (Dunn, 1959).

The clinician should also be alert for the possibility of impairments in addition to hearing loss whose presence may complicate the aural habilitation plan. A parent questionnaire such as the Minnesota Child Development Inventory Profile (Ireton & Thwing, 1974) provides information about gross development, motor development, self-help ability, and personal-social development in addition to receptive and expressive language development. Low profiles in areas outside language development indicate the need for additional evaluation to explore for the possibility of multiple handicaps.

Children with significant hearing losses must learn to use vision for clues that the defective auditory system cannot provide. For this reason, screening of the child's visual acuity is important, and good visual health care must be maintained. This consideration is particularly important, because some causes of hearing loss are also associated with visual abnormalities.

It is important that preschoolers and children in regular classes from kindergarten onward enjoy a good hearing conservation program designed to prevent the development of hearing loss (e.g., through awareness of the hazard of noise exposure). Screening audiometry is part of a good school hearing conservation program to identify hearing losses that develop during the school years (ASHA, 1985). It is unfortunate that school hearing conservation programs are still needed for another purpose — to detect small, long-standing hearing losses that have gone undetected until the child started school.

PARENT COUNSELING AND EDUCATION

Without the understanding, acceptance, and commitment of the parents or other responsible adults, aural habilitation of the child who is hearing impaired cannot be successful. First, parents must understand the nature and implications of hearing loss. Hearing is taken for granted and the general public knows substantially nothing about the ears' functioning. To understand their child's hearing problem, parents must learn how the ear works and what can go wrong.

Early reactions of parents to the statement that their child is hearing impaired are likely to be emotionally driven and constitute rejection of the statement and, in addition, include feelings of doubt, anxiety, and guilt. A beginning place to reduce these negative emotions is explanation of auditory function along with discussion of the potential of residual hearing to be realized through successful aural habilitation. The advantages and limitations of amplification must be thoroughly discussed, for parents will know nothing more of hearing aids than they know of the basic auditory processes.

Many questions must be answered regarding groundless fears that parents may have. Parents should be assured that there is no causal relationship between deafness and intelligence. Research indicates a similar distribution in the hearing-impaired and hearing populations (Vernon, 1968). Audiologists should keep in mind, however, that hearing loss associated with some etiologies may be accompanied by brain damage or other organic disorders. For example, these problems have been substantiated in meningitis and the postmaternal rubella syndrome (Mindel & Vernon, 1987).

In addition, couples should be made aware of the genetic origin of some hearing disorders. Hopefully, those who carry these traits will learn of the probabilities of having children who are hearing impaired before any are born. In this way, they can make an informed decision.

Positive professional support and encouragement must accompany instruction as parents learn to accept the hearing problem and commit themselves to a long-term program of aural habilitation. Development of a goal-oriented program and the acquisition and successful use of hearing aids can reduce parents' anxiety, guilt, and feelings of helplessness as they learn about hearing loss and what can be done.

HEARING AID EVALUATION AND FITTING

After hearing evaluation has established hearing levels, the next step before hearing aid fitting is medical clearance. Hearing aids are currently classified as medical devices, and federal regulations require medical clearance prior to fitting hearing aids on children (Food and Drug Administration, 1977). This regulation merits conscientious adherence to facilitate the general otologic health of the child, to look for correctable disorders, and to establish that there are no medical contraindications for hear-

ing aid use. Following the initial medical examination and fitting of hearing aids, regular otologic examinations should be part of the aural habilitation plan. This practice will help to ensure good otologic health and reduce the probability that encroaching conductive disorders, for example, ear wax or middle ear problems, will cause further damage to the child's hearing or make the selected amplification units inadequate.

SELECTING ELECTROACOUSTIC CHARACTERISTICS

Today, there are several prescriptive procedures designed to specify overall gain, gain versus frequency, and maximum output of hearing aids. Most incorporate modification of the half-gain rule suggested by Lybarger (1963), who observed that most people with sensorineural loss preferred hearing aid gain that amounted to about one-half of their hearing loss. Subsequently, other individuals (Berger, Hagberg, & Rane, 1977; Byrne & Tonisson, 1976; McCandless & Lyregaard, 1983) modified the half-gain rule to reduce overamplification of low frequencies and make other adjustments to maximize audibility of speech. Others (Cox, 1985; Skinner, Pascoe, Miller, & Popelka, 1982) based their prescription on a most-comfortable-loudness (MCL) procedure. In general terms, all of the prescriptive procedures aim to make as much as possible of the aided speech spectrum comfortably audible.

Each prescriptive procedure could be adapted for use in hearing aid evaluation and selection for children, although some call for loudness judgments that very young children cannot make. The following paragraphs suggest ways in which prescriptive procedures designed for adults could be modified to be appropriate for evaluation for children.

Probe-Tube Microphone Measurements

Of particular interest in evaluating the function of hearing aids on children is the use of probe-tube microphone measurements. Once the hearing loss is established and a hearing aid is selected, the probe-tube system can be used in an objective fashion to measure quickly and definitively the real-ear performance of the hearing aid. Desired changes in response can then be made and again measured, the process continuing until the ideal response is realized. These measures are much faster than behavioral testing, during which the child may become restless and inattentive before the evaluation is completed. Hawkins, Morrison, Halligan, and Cooper (1989) have presented a plan to use probe-tube microphone measurements to evaluate hearing aids in children. They reported success in their goal of amplifying and packaging the long-term speech spectrum into the child's residual hearing.

Use of the 2 cm³ Coupler

The relationship between hearing aid electroacoustic performance as measured in the 2 cm³ coupler and the human ear is not very good when adult ears are considered, because of coupler-real ear differences. This disparity may be increased in the child's ear. Because of the smaller size of the child's ear canal relative to the adult, greater sound pressure levels (SPLs) will be generated in the child's aided canal. Jirsa and Norris (1978) reported SPLs about 5 dB greater in the canals of preschool children relative to those of adults. Although these values may be accurate on average, they cannot account for the considerable variability in the volumes of ear canals of different children. A decided advantage of probe tube measures in hearing aid evaluations is the measure of the SPLs actually generated in ear canals under aided conditions.

Sound Pressure Output Levels

There appears to be a remote possibility of further change in the hearing of children who wear hearing aids because of the exposure to high sound levels. Sporadic accounts of individual cases appear in the literature. Rintelmann and Bess (1977) surveyed the lit-erature on this topic and conducted their own investigation. They concluded that sufficient evidence existed regarding isolated instances of amplification-induced threshold shift to justify careful limitation of maximum outputs according to the degree of loss and to emphasize the importance of careful audiologic monitoring. Subsequently, a federal regulation was enacted to require a warning to accompany hearing aids whose maximum output exceeds 132 dB SPL, that the hearing aid may be hazardous to residual hearing (Food and Drug Administration, 1977).

Concerned about the possibility of damage to the child's remaining hearing through amplification-induced threshold shift, Matkin (1986) recommended the following SPL limits for maximum output of hearing aids: (1) with profound loss, 125 dB; (2) with moderate loss, 120 dB; and (3) with mild loss, 110 dB. He further recommended that 5 dB be subtracted from these values when fitting preschool children. More specifically, Skinner (1988) recommended that 6 dB be subtracted from the otherwise appropriate maximum output for infants to 2 years of age and that 3 dB be subtracted for children between 2 and 5 years old. It should be noted that Kawell, Kopun, and Stelmachowicz (1988), in a study of loudness discomfort levels (LDLs) in children, did not find systematic differences between children over 7 years old and adults and concluded that there may be no reason to reduce maximum output of the hearing aid below the levels necessary for adults.

Maximum output values are usually selected when fitting hearing aids for adults by determining loudness discomfort levels and selecting output levels below the patient's LDL. Young children cannot report LDLs reliably, and it may be necessary to select output values based on those found to be uncomfortable on subjects with loss of hearing sensitivity comparable to those of the child in question. Estimated levels may be obtained by reference to the average LDLs obtained from subjects as a function of the magnitude of sensorineural loss. LDLs from one study (Kamm, Dirks, &

TABLE 7-1. SPLS AT 25, 50, AND 75 PERCENTILES FOR LDL IN 178 SUBJECTS WITH SENSORINEURAL HEARING LOSS.

Stimulus	Hearing Threshold (in dB HL re: 1969 ANSI Norms)				
	>10 dB	11–30	31–50	51–70	>70 dB
500 Hz					
75%	115.5	113.4	117.0	>124	>124
50	106.5	109.1	106.0	120.0	>124
25	97.5	102.5	100.5	115.5	>124
2000 Hz					
75%	108.0	115.0	108.6	>124	>124
50	102.0	104.3	102.4	112.3	121.5
25	97.5	98.4	98.0	108.0	114.0

Source: Adapted from Kamm et al. (1978).

Mickey, 1978) are shown in Table 7–1. It should be remembered that these values are from adult subjects, and appropriate corrections should be made, as discussed previously. In addition, the investigators reported considerable variability in LDL for subjects in each hearing loss group, necessitating caution when using the averages to limit hearing aid output. Finally, it should be noted that appropriate procedures may permit assessment of LDL in older children. Kawell, Kopun, and Stelmachowicz (1988) reported reasonably reliable LDL measures on children as young as 7 years. They used five loudness categories from *too soft* to *hurts*. While listening to signals at various levels, children judged loudness by pointing to pictures of human faces whose expressions represented typical reactions to each of the five loudness levels.

BINAURAL AMPLIFICATION

It is generally recognized that most adults with bilateral hearing losses and aidable hearing in each ear perform better with two aids than with one. Advantages include improved localization ability, reduction of the head shadow effect obtained with one hearing aid, improved audibility of speech in noise (the squelch effect), more

natural "three dimensional" sound quality, and the ability to set the volume controls at a lower level because of binaural summation (about 5 dB, according to Byrne, 1981). However, some individuals who are hearing impaired appear to function better with one hearing aid than with two, possibly because of defects in the central auditory system that prevent the interaction of signals coming from each ear as they ascend in the central pathways. Adults may be able to judge whether they function better with two aids, but small children cannot. Skinner (1988) suggested careful observation while the child is aided with one versus two aids. She recommends that these observations involve the child's ability to localize, to respond to speech and language, and if possible the degree of speech development during trial periods with both monaural and binaural amplification.

TYPE OF HEARING AID

As is the case with adults, when fitting children decisions must be made about the type or style of hearing aids. Concern about cosmetics plays a large role in this respect when adults are fitted. The same will be true for older children and for the parents of younger children. This concern must be considered, for aids considered stigmatic may not be worn. However, every attempt should be made to reduce these concerns on the part of the child and the parents, so that appropriate amplification is the basis on which the decision of hearing aid type is made.

Today, behind-the-ear (BTE) aids are available with sufficient power and flexibility to fit most hearing losses. They offer the advantage of ear-level hearing, which may be important in binaural functions, and reduction of clothing noises and cord problems previously associated with body-type aids. However, for the very young child, it is easier for parents to see and manipulate controls of body aids. Body-type amplification is more feasible for the infant prior to the time the child sits and walks. For the child who requires extremely high gain, serious feedback problems may limit effective amplification if BTE aids are used. For example, Matkin (1984) reported that 8 of 11 preschoolers surveyed were receiving inadequate gain from ear-level aids because the volume controls were turned down to avoid feedback problems.

To receive maximum gain without feedback, ear molds must be well designed and frequently replaced. Full-shell ear molds should be used, and soft material such as polyvinylchloride, in addition to reducing the risk of injury if a child falls or is struck on the head, is thought to reduce feedback problems (Seewald & Ross, 1988). Especially with ear-level aids, frequent replacement of ear molds is necessary to maintain adequate gain without feedback. Constant monitoring of gain and earmold adequacy is necessary. Matkin (1984) suggests that children under the age of 3 years may need new ear molds at 3-month intervals to maintain an adequate seal.

As children grow older, particularly as they approach adolescence and changes in size and shape of the external ear are reduced, cosmetic concerns may lead them to ask for in-the-ear (ITE) aids. Such a change is justifiable if the hearing loss is appropriate for this type of aid, remembering that ITE aids generally do not provide as much overall gain or high-frequency amplification without feedback.

Children who are hearing impaired, especially those with more serious losses, should

not be confined to conventional wearable amplification. Systems used in the classroom, and others designed for personal use and generally classified as "assistive listening devices," are designed to improve signal-to-noise ratio and reduce effects of reverberation by moving the system's microphone closer to the person who is speaking. Examples include the FM radio transmitting-receiving unit designed for either classroom or personal use. Another common unit is the induction loop system, which sends an electromagnetic signal from the person speaking to the child's hearing aid. It is necessary that the hearing aids that are selected be compatible with whichever of these classroom or personal units are to be used. That is, if an induction loop system is to be used in the class or in the home, the child's hearing aids must have induction coils ("telephone switches"), which pick up the electromagnetic signals. These coils should be evaluated to ensure appropriate function, because hearing aids may operate quite differently with induction coil function than when the microphone is the input transducer.

The child's hearing aids should have input jacks to "hardwire" external microphones, which can be located close to the mouth of the person speaking. An example of such an aid, with direct audio input via an external microphone, is shown in Figure 7–1. The result will be vastly improved signal-to-noise ratio in situations where hard-wired arrangement is feasible. Moreover, when FM transmitting-receiving units are used, the hearing aid can be wired directly to the FM receiver output. Alternatively, a neck-worn loop can deliver the signal to the hearing aids' induction coils via electromagnetic energy, but the hard-wired arrangement is preferable, because each additional transduction of the signal increases the chances for reduced quality or increased noise.

Consistent with the child's age and auditory needs, other assistive devices, such as telephone and television aids, should be introduced. The former may consist of telephone amplifiers or visible print-outs of telephone messages (TDDs). In the latter case, various systems improve pickup of TV audio. The sig-

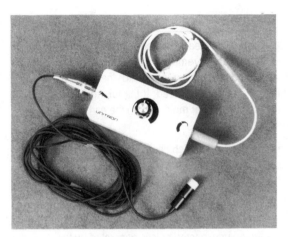

Figure 7–1. Hearing aid with "hardwired" external microphone. (Courtesy of Unitron Industries, Inc.)

nal may be sent directly to the child's amplification system via hardwire, FM, or induction loop. These arrangements avoid amplification of room noise. For children who are more severely impaired, a close-captioned decoder will reveal on the TV screen the printed subtitles, which are available on many TV programs. A complete amplification program should consider these, and the many other alerting, warning, and auditory devices that are available, as appropriate.

LEARNING EFFECTIVE HEARING AID USE

The following three principles will help to ensure effective hearing aid use on the part of the child: (1) the parents must learn how to operate and care for hearing aids; (2) the child must learn and assume responsibility for hearing aid use and care, learning as soon as possible optimum setting of controls and reporting hearing aid problems; and (3) an effective monitoring system must be in place involving the audiologist, the parents, the child, and others, such as teachers, who are a part of the aural habilitation team.

Parents, and children as they are able, must become aware of the physical components of the hearing aid and their functions. They must

learn to operate the switches, rotate the volume control dial, and replace the battery. Prior to first hearing aid use, all concerned should be warned of the toxic nature of batteries and the danger of accidental ingestion. Parents should be instructed to call their doctor if a battery is accidentally swallowed and given the national hotline number, (202) 625-3333, which they can call for help.

Parents must learn how to place the ear mold in the ear and remove it. They should be assisted in teaching the child to assume this responsibility as early as possible.

Care and maintenance of the aid and troubleshooting of simple problems must be learned by the parents and assumed by the child in a gradated fashion, beginning with the concept of responsibility for the hearing aids.

Beyond learning the physical aspects of hearing aid manipulation and care, parents and the child must learn good hearing aid use in terms of effective listening strategies. They must learn to survey the environment and assess factors that contribute to or detract from successful communication. They must learn to help the hearing aid by coming closer to desired speech signals and moving further away from interfering noises. They must learn to reduce background noise levels when possible and to adjust hearing aids' volume controls for maximum intelligibility in various noise levels. They must even learn the degree of assertiveness necessary to inform those who talk to them of the presence of the hearing loss and how to improve communication. Their strategies may include getting the attention of the child who is hearing impaired before speaking, limiting conversation to line-of-sight situations when possible, speaking more slowly, and interpreting signs that indicate whether these strategies to improve communication are successful or if additional effort is needed.

Of vital importance is the development of a program of hearing aid monitoring involving the audiologist, the parents, the child, and others who are in frequent contact with the child. With remarkable consistency, surveys taken over the years to determine how well hearing aids worn by children are functioning

TABLE 7-2. THE HEARING AID CHECK

1. *Visual inspection of aid, tubing,and ear mold.* Each should be clean and free of wax. All can be wiped clean with a dry tissue. The earmold and tubing can be removed from the earhook of the aid, washed in warm soapy water, rinsed, and dried completely. Afterward, the earhook, not the hearing aid, should be held firmly while the tubing is replaced. If the tubing is discolored, cracked,dry and brittle, or loose where it fits into the ear mold or onto the earhook, a trip to the dispenser is needed to replace the tubing.

2. *Battery check.* The battery should deliver its specified voltage, which can be learned from the dispenser, and discarded if it does not. It should be free of corrosion, as should be the battery case.

3. *Listening check on the parental ear.* Using the hearing aid stethoscope or a custom ear mold, the parent should ascertain that speech is understandable through the aid, that speech quality has not deteriorated from its usual level, that there are no unexpected noises generated by the aid, and that the expected loudness is delivered when the volume control is rotated. While turning the volume control, the parent should ascertain that there are no scratchy noises or dead spots. Speech should smoothly grow louder as the volume control is rotated. The parent should tap the case of the aid and listen for intermittency, suggesting loose battery contacts. Additionally, with body aids, the cord where it inserts into the aid and into the earphone should be twisted gently, for the same purpose. Problems in any of these areas necessitate a visit to the dispenser.

4. *Listening check on the child's ear.* Separately, each aid should be inserted and the volume control rotated to the level recommended by the audiologist. Feedback (squealing) should not occur. Parents should learn that feedback results when too much sound leaks out of the aided ear canal and re-enters the hearing aid microphone. Causes of feedback at recommended volume control setting are (1) wax in the ear canal, which reflects too much sound back to the hearing aid; (2) an incompletely inserted ear mold; (3) loose connections along the sound delivery route between hearing aid, earhook, tubing, and ear mold; (4) an ear mold that no longer fits well enough to create an adequate seal; and (5) internal causes, which occur when the acoustic isolation between the hearing aid microphone and earphone is destroyed. Additionally, feedback can occur momentarily when a hand is cupped over the hearing aid or the child stands close to a wall or other reflecting surface. The listening check on the child's ear should be completed by making sure the child can hear and understand speech in the usual fashion, consistent with the amount of hearing loss that is present.

have shown that, at any given time, about half of them are defective or set inappropriately (Blair, Wright, & Pollard, 1981; Gaeth & Lounsbury, 1966; Porter, 1973). These surveys also suggest little knowledge on the part of parents about hearing aid function. For example, in the Gaeth and Lounsbury study, when asked how long the batteries in the child's aid lasted, 9% of the parents answered longer than a year. Eleven percent were more honest and admitted that they didn't know. While it is of great importance that parents learn to monitor the hearing aids and help to keep them operating well, it is most critical that the child learn to assume this responsibility, because the wearer is the only person who can monitor the hearing aids full time.

The guide provided in Table 7-2 may be helpful to assist parents in a check of the child's hearing aids to be performed daily and, in addition, whenever problems are suspected. Initially, the audiologist should instruct parents and

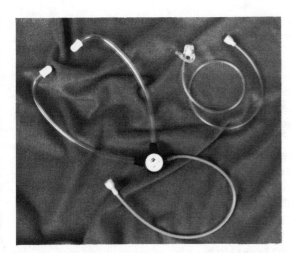

Figure 7–2. Hearing aid stethoscope and parental ear mold for hearing aid listening check. (Courtsey of Hal-Hen).

provide supervised practice in this hearing aid check, and parents should instruct the child to assume this responsibility in those areas where normal hearing is not a requisite. Some equipment is needed for this hearing aid check. For listening to the hearing aid, the parent will need a hearing aid stethoscope or a custom ear mold that fits the parental ear. The method of coupling these devices to the child's hearing aid is shown in Figure 7–2. A voltmeter for testing the battery is useful. Batteries have been improved so that they deliver almost their full voltage until near the end of their lives, and then die suddenly. For these reasons, a battery that delivers anything less than its specified voltage should be discarded, and spare batteries should always be carried in case a battery dies between hearing aid checks. Figure 7–3 illustrates an inexpensive battery tester. As shown in Figure 7–4, a small brush and a wire loop may be helpful to remove accumulated wax from the sound channel of the ear mold. Also illustrated is a hand syringe that is useful to dry out tubing after the ear mold has been removed and washed. Fluids other than water should not be used on the ear mold; and, of course, the hearing aid itself should never be exposed to fluids of any kind.

Parents must learn, and assist the child in learning, simple troubleshooting procedures

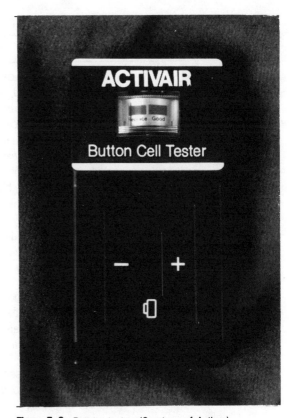

Figure 7–3. Battery tester. (Courtesy of Activar)

Figure 7–4. Brush and wire loop for removing wax from ear mold, and hand syringe for clearing water and debris from earmold tubing. (Courtesy of Starkey Electronics)

which may correct some problems and prevent a visit to the dispenser when problems arise. Some of these are presented in Table 7–3. Parents should not try to go beyond these simple

TABLE 7-3. HEARING AID TROUBLE SHOOTING

Symptom	*Possible Causes*
No sound	Off-on switch may be set to off or to the T (telephone) position. Battery may be wrong kind, dead, or inserted backwards. Corrosion on the battery contacts may be responsible and may be cleaned gently. There may be a mechanical blockage of the sound route, such as perspiration in the tubing, which may be dried with a hand syringe after the tubing is removed from the ear mold. Aids fitted with acoustic filters are particularly prone to this problem since the filter consists of a very small opening, which is easily blocked. If the problem persists, a drying kit can be purchased, into which the aid can be placed each night. The earmold sound channel may be blocked by wax, which can be removed with the wire loop described earlier. It is possible, with the aid on the ear, that a kink or twist may close the tubing and block sound, necessitating correct placement, or a new tube.
Weak sound	Weak battery, sound channel partially blocked by moisture or wax, or the tubing may be bent partially closed. These problems can usually be corrected by the parents. If these causes are not evident, there may be an internal problem that will require repair by the dispenser.
Intermittent sound	Loose battery caused by bent contacts. With body aids, broken cords or loose connections may be the problem. Solutions are best left to the dispenser.
Loudness does not change appropriately as volume control is rotated.	Volume control rotation may be accompanied by noise, no change in loudness, or a sudden loudness at a given rotation. Dirty or broken volume control, requiring repair by the dispenser.
Unnatural sound quality or noise	Remembering that all hearing aids sound different than unamplified speech and that some audible noise is present in normal function, the parent must learn to discern abnormalities that develop. Dirty controls can produce noise, and turning them back and forth may dislodge the dirt responsible for the problem. Unnatural sound quality may result from a nearly dead battery or from an inappropriately set tone control. Other noise and quality problems will require attention by the dispenser.
Feedback (squealing)	Ear mold incompletely inserted, volume control set above recommended level, loose connections between earhook, tubing, and ear mold. These problems may be solvable by the parents. Other causes of feedback, for which parents must seek help, are wax in the ear canal and poorly fitting ear molds. Internal feedback can be diagnosed by removing the earhook and holding a finger over the sound outlet while rotating the volume control on. If the feedback is internal, the squealing will continue.

TABLE 7-4. HEARING AID CARE AND MAINTENANCE

1. Do not drop the aid. Hearing aids today are more resistant to shock than earlier models, but a long fall onto a hard surface may damage the case or contents. It is a good practice to sit on the bed or other soft surface when inserting or removing the aid.

2. Moisture, heat, and dirt are damaging to hearing aids. Therefore, the aid should be removed before showers or before applying hair spray. If the child forgets and takes a dip in the pool while wearing the aid, a trip to the dispenser is necessary. As mentioned elsewhere, a kit which contains a drying agent is available from the dispenser if moisture from perspiration is a problem. Opening the battery cases after removal of the aids each evening may permit some drying out, and will ensure that the aids are turned off. Batteries should be removed if the aids are to be unused for a period of time. The aid should never be left in a really hot place, such as a window sill or the dashboard of a car.

3. Ear molds and their tubing can be removed from the earhook of the aid and washed. A hand syringe is useful to blow water out of the tubing before replacing it. Brushes and wax picks should be used to keep the earmold sound channel and vents free of wax. Small "pressure equalizing" vents are especially liable to become occluded by wax, and a broom-straw may be helpful to clean them. A wire should not be used, especially with soft ear molds, because vents are not always straight, and the material is easily damaged.

4. A safe place should be reserved to keep the aids when they are not in use. Audiologists who have been dispensing for a very long time have witnessed the problem of temporarily or permanently lost hearing aids, or aids damaged or completely ingested by the family dog. As an additional safeguard, parents may want to consider insurance for the hearing aids.

5. Parents should institute a regular schedule of visits to the audiologist where, in addition to evaluation of the child's hearing, the performance of the aids and the integrity of the ear molds can be evaluated. Retubing of the molds and minor repairs to the aids may prevent development of more serious problems.

procedures and should never attempt to open the case to repair the aid.

Finally, because hearing aids are expensive and repairs or replacements are costly, parents and the child must learn certain fundamentals of care and maintenance. Some of these fundamentals are detailed in Table 7-4.

SUMMARY

Amplification is the foundation on which aural habilitation is built. Hearing aids are the best tool to implement the habilitation process. For children born with hearing loss, early identification and amplification are crucial. Today, behavioral and electrophysiologic test batteries can reliably establish hearing loss even in infants, and provide estimates of the magnitude and configuration. After fitting with hearing aids, a period of continuing evaluation and modification of amplification characteristics will follow. For this reason, it is important to prescribe flexible hearing aids with provision for considerable modification in electroacoustic characteristics. At the same time, parents must learn about hearing and hearing loss, the advantages and limitations of amplification, and become dedicated to the long-term habilitation process.

Parents must learn efficient use of amplification, including the physical manipulation of hearing aids and environmental strategies for effective listening. They must learn about the care and maintenance of the hearing aids, how to assess functioning of the aids, and how to detect problems and correct them when possible. The child who uses the aids must assume all of these responsibilities as soon as possible. There must be an effective program for monitoring the hearing aids' function and regular audiologic and otologic attention to the aids, the child's hearing, and hearing health.

REFERENCES

American Speech-Language-Hearing Association. (1985). Guidelines for identification audiometry. *Asha, 28,* 49–52.

American Speech-Language-Hearing Association. (1989). Guidelines for screening for hearing impairment and middle ear disorders. *Asha, 31,* 71–76.

Barr, B. (1955). Pure tone audiometry for pre-school children. *Acta Oto-laryngologica* (Suppl. 121).

Berger, K., Hagberg, E., & Rane, R. (1977). *Prescription of hearing aids: Rationale, procedures, and results* (4th ed.). Kent, OH: Herald Publishing.

Blair, J., Wright, K., & Pollard, G. (1981). Parental knowledge and understanding of hearing loss and hearing aids. *Volta Review, 83,* 375–382.

Byrne, D. (1981). Clinical issues and options in binaural hearing aid fitting. *Ear and Hearing, 2,* 187–193.

Byrne, D., & Tonisson, W. (1976). Selecting the gain of hearing aids for persons with sensorineural hearing impairments. *Scandinavian Audiology, 5,* 51–59.

Cox, R. (1985). Hearing aids and aural rehabilitation: A structured approach to hearing aid selection. *Ear and Hearing, 6,* 226–239.

Dunn, L. (1959). *Peabody Picture Vocabulary Test.* Circle Pines, MN: American Guidance Service.

Food and Drug Administration. (1977). Hearing aid devices — Professional and patient labeling and conditions for sale. *Federal Register, 42,* 9286–9296.

Gaeth, J., & Lounsbury, E. (1966). Hearing aids and children in elementary schools. *Journal of Speech*

and Hearing Disorders, 32, 289–293.

Hawkins, D., Morrison, T., Halligan, P., & Cooper, W. (1989). Use of probe tube microphone measurements in hearing aid selection for children: Some initial clinical experiences. *Ear and Hearing, 10,* 281–287.

Ireton, H., & Thwing, E. (1974). *Minnesota Child Development Inventory.* Minneapolis, MN: Behavior Science Systems.

Jacobson, J. (Ed.). (1985). *The Auditory Brainstem Response.* San Diego, CA: College-Hill Press.

Jirsa, R., & Norris, T. (1978). Relationship of acoustic gain to aided threshold improvement in children. *Journal of Speech and Hearing Disorders, 43,* 348–352.

Kawell, M., Kopun, J., & Stelmachowicz, P. (1988). Loudness discomfort levels in children. *Ear and Hearing, 9,* 133–136.

Kamm, C., Dirks, D., & Mickey, R. (1978). Effect of sensorineural hearing loss on loudness discomfort level. *Journal of Speech and Hearing Research, 21,* 668–681.

Liden, G., & Kankkunen, A. (1969). Visual reinforcement audiometry in the management of young deaf children. *International Audiology, 8,* 99–106.

Lybarger, S. (1963). *Simplified system for fitting hearing aids.* Canonsberg, PA: Radioear Corporation.

Matkin, N. (1984). Wearable amplification: A litany of persisting problems. In J. Jerger (Ed.), *Pediatric audiology* (pp. 125–145). San Diego, CA: Singular Publishing Group.

Matkin, N. (1986). Hearing aids for children. In W. Hodgson (Ed.), *Hearing aid assessment and use in audiologic habilitation* (3rd ed., pp. 170–190). Baltimore, MD: Williams & Wilkins.

McCandless, G., & Lyregaard, P. (1983). Prescription of gain/output (POGO) for hearing aids. *Hearing Instruments, 34*(1), 16–17, 19–21.

Mindel, E., & Vernon, M. (1987). *They grow in silence: Understanding deaf children and adults* (2nd ed.). San Diego, CA: College-Hill Press.

Porter, T. (1973). Hearing aids in a residential school. *American Annals of the Deaf, 118,* 31–33.

Rintelmann, W., & Bess, F. (1977). High-level amplification and potential hearing loss in children. In F. Bess (Ed.), *Childhood deafness: Causation, assessment and management* (pp. 267–293). New York: Grune & Stratton.

Seewald, R., & Ross, M. (1988). Amplification for young hearing-impaired children. In M. Pollack (Ed.), *Amplification for the hearing impaired* (4th ed., pp. 213–271). New York: Grune & Stratton.

Skinner, M. (1988). *Hearing aid evaluation.* Englewood Cliffs, NJ: Prentice-Hall.

Skinner, M., Pascoe, D., Miller, J., & Popelka, G. (1982). Measurements to determine the optimal placement of speech energy within the listener's auditory area: A basis for selecting amplification characteristics. In G. Studebaker & F. Bess (Eds.), *The Vanderbilt hearing-aid report* (pp. 161–169). Upper Darby, PA: Monographs in Contemporary Audiology.

Suzuki, T., & Ogiba, Y. (1961). Conditioned reflex audiometry. *Archives of Otolaryngology, 74,* 192–198.

Wilson, W., & Thompson, G. (1984). Behavioral audiometry. In J. Jerger (Ed.), *Pediatric audiology* (pp. 1–44). San Diego, CA: Singular Publishing Group.

Upfold, L. (1988). Children with hearing aids in the 1980s: Etiologies and severity of impairment. *Ear and Hearing, 9,* 75–80.

Vernon, M. (1968). Fifty years of research on the intelligence of the deaf and hard-of-hearing. A survey of literature and discussion of the implications. *Journal of Rehabilitation of the Deaf, 1,* 1–11.

CHAPTER 8

Development of Auditory Skills in Children Who Are Hearing Impaired

■ JILL L. BADER, M.A. ■

Auditory development is the process by which children learn to recognize and understand auditory signals available to them. Aural habilitation programs for young children with limited hearing must promote the optimal use of residual hearing, by development of the auditory modality for acquisition and maintenance of spoken language. Children's optimal use of residual hearing requires (1) early identification of hearing loss, (2) consistent use of appropriate amplification, (3) parents committed to the belief that their child's auditory capacity can be developed, and (4) an educational program with skilled professionals equally committed to the same belief.

A holistic approach to children's auditory-speech-language development ensures parallel development of children's cognitive, socio-emotional, motor, and self-help abilities (Cole & Mischook, 1986). This approach enhances the integration of auditory listening skills with cognitive experiences and social interactions throughout a child's day. It is the child's use of, not the amount of, residual hearing that is valuable to functional communication (Stone, 1983). In the preschool years, it is the parent who becomes the primary habilitative agent for maintaining the child's hearing aids and structuring an auditory learning environment rich with listening experiences and expectations.

This chapter outlines the stages and levels of auditory development. Appropriate amplification is briefly discussed, while the critical role played by parents and professionals in the aural habilitative process of children under 3 years old is discussed at length.

APPROPRIATE AMPLIFICATION

The first step toward optimal auditory development is early identification of hearing loss, because a child's capacity for language learning is at its peak in the first 3 years of life. Significant difficulty in acquiring spoken communication skills can be encountered, especially by the child with a severe-to-profound hearing loss that goes undetected through the first few months of life (Cole & Mischook, 1986). Since the dramatic deprivation studies of the early 1960s, more recent evidence further suggests functional or even physiological atrophy from lack of early auditory stimulation. Although early auditory deprivation is not impossible to overcome, early identification greatly facilitates the integration of auditory information with the other sensory information a young infant receives. Early identification usually results in early amplification, but does not always ensure optimal selection of amplification or consistent use. The consistent use of functional, appropriately selected hearing aids or a cochlear implant (to be discussed later in this chapter) is the second necessary step to optimal auditory development.

HEARING AIDS

Hearing aid selection is far from an exact science and requires the collaborative expertise of audiologist, parent, and educator (Stone & Adams, 1986). The audiologist offers knowledge of a variety of hearing aids' capabilities and the skill to conduct a full audiologic assessment. The parents provide the intimate knowledge of their child's response patterns and will be responsible for the maintenance and the child's consistent use of the hearing aids. The educator ideally possesses a combined understanding of speech acoustics, child development, and family dynamics (including the diagnosis reaction discussed in Chapter 5). This professional combination of skills affords the parents the appropriate guidance and encouragement necessary to their family's health and their child's optimal development.

Once hearing aids are recommended and purchased, regular evaluation of hearing aids must be ongoing. A number of earmold modifications exist which also may assist some children who are hearing impaired in a variety of ways. As young children's auditory responses expand and become more consistent, acoustic horns and filters or different shapes and materials used in ear molds may be beneficial.

Properly fitting ear molds are of the utmost importance to ensure the maximum gain from powerful aids. A poor acoustic seal can produce feedback and lead parents to decrease the volume of the hearing aid to solve the annoying problem. This solution allows parents to avoid embarrassment in public places, but the child loses the auditory information that links the child to his or her world. A more common solution used by parents of newly diagnosed infants is to remove the hearing aids altogether. Infants and toddlers are active, wiggly little creatures who dislodge the best fitting ear molds many times a day. Parents, still adjusting to their new role as parents of a child who is hearing impaired, may be clumsy with ear mold insertion or simply glad for a temporary reprieve. In this immediate postdiagnostic state, parents and children require the encouragement of a supportive educational habilitative program.

Hearing aids should be purchased with the necessary adaptation for FM use, which can be an important contributor to promoting auditory development. FM systems allow a consistent optimal auditory input of the parent's voice free of masking by background noise. The use of FM systems over the early learning years can accelerate children's use of their residual hearing and often generates a greater recordable frequency range later in life (Ling, 1984). As children enter the toddler and preschool years, the FM system can be used for a good portion of each day. FM systems can also be adapted for use with cochlear implants.

Children who demonstrate no auditory progress after an extended period of consistent hearing aid use and appropriate aural habilitation may be candidates for a cochlear implant. These children's aided and unaided responses remain the same or nonexistent over time, but with training they will learn not only about the existence of sound, but also the differences and subtleties of sound. A lengthy discussion of cochlear implants is not possible here, but many articles describing implant devices, surgical and programming procedures, and noted auditory benefits to young children exist in current publications. A cochlear implant represents the most advanced form of otologic/audiologic technology available that allows sound reception for this small subgroup of children who are profoundly deaf (or non-auditory). Intensive aural habilitation for cochlear implant children who are congenitally deaf is even more critical due to the years of preoperative auditory deprivation.

It cannot be overemphasized that hearing aids and/or cochlear implants must be worn and in good working order for a young child to learn how to use them. However, simply providing the child with hearing aids does not ensure that he or she will learn to listen. Learning to listen requires time, attention, practice, and adults who create an environment conducive to the child's development of audition.

ELEMENTS OF AUDITORY DEVELOPMENT

Normal development of audition proceeds through the same stages for normal hearing children and children who are hearing impaired, albeit at a slower pace for the latter. The infant who is hearing impaired must wait for identification and consistent, optimal amplification of the hearing loss before he or she can embark on what Pollack (1985) describes as the first "listening year."

During the first year of life infants develop an affective bond with parents who reinforce the infants' social, motor, and vocal responses to auditory events. As parents attach communicative intent to these responses, the infant begins to associate sounds with their source and meaning. Toddlers then attempt verbal reproductions of the sounds they have heard for at least a full year. Those sounds include their own babble, which Fry (1978) described as functionally important to integrating the auditory and kinesthetic feedback functions in the brain. The development of that auditory feedback mechanism is the means by which children

learn to approximate adult forms of spoken language. Naturally, more speech dimensions are available to those children with more hearing and to those children appropriately amplified.

The key elements to auditory development include: (1) detection, (2) discrimination, (3) identification, and (4) comprehension.

DETECTION

Detection involves children becoming aware that sound exists and learning to attend to those sounds. At the detection level, the child simply responds to the presence or absence of sound. For most children who are hearing impaired, this only happens with amplification and parents who have learned to draw their child's attention to the linguistic and nonlinguistic sounds in the environment. In this way, parents represent their child's first feedback mechanism. The most important job of a parent is to assist their child who is hearing impaired to attend and respond to speech (Simmons-Martin, 1981).

DISCRIMINATION

Discrimination develops as children learn to perceive the differences in sounds. Suprasegmental discriminations of intensity, duration, pitch, and timing appear first. Children can discriminate, for example, that their parent's conversation conveys excitement before they can understand the cause or content of their parent's excitement. Children at the discrimination level also discover that different objects, people, and situations have different sounds associated with them. Discrimination allows children to tell whether two auditory patterns are the same or different. How they differ and what the sound means comes later in the developmental schema.

IDENTIFICATION

Identification is the stage at which children can repeat or point to a representation of a specific set of sounds. Identification requires memory, but not understanding of the sounds. For example, children can identify a toy cow in response to "moo-o-o" and a toy pig to "oink," simply because one is a long set of sounds and the other is short. However, with only this long versus short identification ability, a child may identify any one of many other toy animals (e.g., a sheep) which also represents a long set of sounds (i.e., "baa-a"), but which is not semantically correct to the auditory signal presented (i.e., "moo-o-o"). This occurs because the child has not yet gained comprehension of the sound's specific meaning nor identification of the specific sounds.

COMPREHENSION

Comprehension of acoustic signals sent to the child by the linguistic and nonlinguistic sounds in his or her environment is the final and most complicated stage of auditory development. At this stage, children must be able to repeat the auditory set and also demonstrate that they understand the meaning of the sounds received. Erber (1982) stated that a child's demonstrations of comprehension are "usually referenced to his or her knowledge of language." Very young children will initially use nonverbal behaviors to indicate their understanding. Specifically, when the parent hurriedly says, "Let's go bye-bye," a child may wave or get his or her coat. This child, on a detection level, is aware that sound exists. On a discrimination level, the child knows that the parent is in a hurry and the child's identification skills allow him or her to look to the parent as the source of sound, even before linguistic skills allow a verbal approximation to "bye-bye." Finally, the comprehension demonstrated by the child that he or she understands the act of leaving completes the cycle of connecting sound to meaning. The auditory stimulus (i.e., "Let's go bye-bye") has integrated with cognitive functioning (i.e., the memory of the experience of going bye-bye) and elicited an appropriate motor response (i.e., waving).

This lengthy process of auditory development begins with attention and ends in comprehension. The very best hearing aid selection will not totally compensate for the hearing loss

nor guarantee the child's acquisition of spoken communication through audition. Audition must be viewed as the desirable primary modality for (re)habilitation, but not the only modality available. Hearing aids can enhance the child's hearing, but the act of listening is a behavior that must be learned.

CREATING A LISTENING ENVIRONMENT

The world of a child in utero is far from silent. The auditory system (cochlea) becomes functional at four months prenatally (Furuhjelm, Ingelman-Sundberg, & Wirsen, 1986) and the amniotic fluid provides a better source of sound conduction than air does after birth. One might say that neonates emerge with almost a half year of listening in their experience. No research is presently available with which to draw conclusions about the impact of prenatal auditory experiences, so this discussion will, for now, be confined to the postnatal period.

THE LISTENING ENVIRONMENT

Parents, and later educators, will become primarily responsible for a listening environment that neither limits the quality nor quantity of the child's auditory experiences. Prior to receiving hearing aids, the sensorimotor child has experienced how things look, feel, taste, and smell without integrating how things and people sound, as well. After receiving hearing aids, the child must attach new auditory information to past perceptions and to future learning experiences via an imperfect input system. Vygotsky (1962) explained that parents direct their child's attention to certain aspects of experiences and thereby determine the way the child perceives and responds to his or her world.

THE NONLINGUISTIC LISTENING ENVIRONMENT

Parents of an infant who is hearing impaired must direct their child's attention to the auditory aspects of ongoing daily experiences as soon after hearing aid fitting as possible. For the young infant, attention to sound is a difficult, but necessary task. Parents can enhance their infant's ability to make auditory responses by controlling the sound distractions present in their home. For example, the running of a nearby dishwasher or television during mealtime should be delayed. The use of the radio and stereo should be confined to nonconversation periods of the day. The acoustic quality of language input, impoverished by hearing loss, is thereby increased for the infant's reception when parents provide a noise-controlled environment.

Parents' heightened awareness of sound also allows them to draw their child's attention to the numerous, common everyday environmental sounds (e.g., toaster, running water, toilet, garage door) that parents take for granted in their home. For the very young, inattentive toddler in his or her first listening year, association of sounds with their source and meaning requires focused attention and repeated exposure. Van Uden (1979), Simmons-Martin (1981), and Dunst (1981) have described an effective strategy whereby parents and teachers "stage" or "structure" situations to ensure that auditory learning events occur and reoccur daily. For example, parents may instruct frequent visitors to ring the doorbell two or three times before expecting an answer, thus allowing ample opportunity for parents to direct their child's attention to the sound until one day, the child spontaneously responds. Parents may stage bathtime so that the child's hearing aids are not removed until after the child has had a chance to listen to the language of undressing, the bath water running, and the toys splashing in the tub. Parents can learn to apply this staging strategy to virtually every moment of their child's day, given the professionally guided practice necessary to the creation of an optimal listening environment.

While attention to nonlinguistic auditory events is certainly a worthwhile component to a child's aural (re)habilitation, the primary focus must be on linguistic events since the ultimate goal for the child is spoken language competence. An optimal listening environment is linguistically rich with parents who provide a running verbal commentary on the people, objects, and activities in their child's life. These verbal descriptions are simple, meaningful, interesting, repetitive phrases and sentences. They match the child's thoughts, feelings, and interests. Such acoustic input affords children phonemes and words in a prosodic envelope steeped with the suprasegmental features available auditorally to nearly all children who are hearing impaired. These are the features that will be imitated first by young children and that will maintain the child's natural-sounding voice quality and contribute to intelligibility into adulthood.

PARENT-CHILD INTERACTION

Because early optimal auditory learning requires an exchange between a child and an adult, learning will be broadened and accelerated by a positive parent/child relationship. The young infant who is hearing impaired must be viewed as an active participant in audition, capable of increasing his or her contributions to the communicative exchanges that develop between parent and child. Many investigators cite turn-taking exchanges, wherein parents and child alternate the role of speaker and listener, as precursors to language and social development. Balanced turn taking is achieved by parents who follow their child's lead, interact on the child's level, and match their child's pace of interaction (Mahoney & Powell, 1986). The resultant reciprocity and synchronization in the parent/child dyad increases mutual enjoyment (Brazelton, 1986) and lays a solid foundation for auditory learning.

A FULL RANGE OF LISTENING EXPERIENCES

The final component to creating a listening environment for young children is to provide a full range of listening-learning experiences. This cannot be achieved in the preschool years without the help of parents. A wide variety of experiences, shared by a monitoring parent, will greatly expand a child's learning horizons (Vaughn, 1981). Fortunate is the child who is hearing impaired who has been given the opportunity to learn to listen to the sounds of the circus, the carwash, a whisper, a parade, and the singing of Christmas carols.

Since the critical period for learning is in the first three years of life, the provision of an optimal listening environment must not be left to chance. Caring, skilled professionals must help parents establish positive interaction patterns with their toddler, which promote the quality and quantity of learning situations necessary to optimal auditory development.

AURAL INFANT INTERVENTION MODEL

Auditory responses, especially from infants and toddlers unsophisticated to the world of behavioral audiometry, cannot always be obtained in the audiologist's clinical setting. Young children exhibit auditory responses first in familiar settings with familiar adults. Because infant and parent are bound in an inseparable dyad, aural habilitation is most effective when it goes through the parent to the child. Infant habilitation programs, therefore, must simulate the most conducive environment possible for both optimal parent and child responses. That first learning environment is the home.

The preferred infant intervention model is a Home Demonstration Center. This model operates aural habilitation programs in a center-based house with a modestly furnished kitchen, living room, baby's bedroom, and bathroom. The center-based advantage of professional control over the physical environment and availability of training materials is not sacrificed to provide the comfortable "home" environment advantage of home-based programs. The Home Demonstration Center offers a warm, safe, stimulating learning environment for both group parent support sessions and individual parent-child therapy.

Auditory learning is most effective during a child's ongoing daily activities (Erber, 1982; Simmons-Martin, 1981). At a Home Demonstration Center, children are immediately at ease to interact naturally with their parents while watering flowers, unloading the dishwasher, fixing lunch, getting dressed, or mopping up spills. Participation in these simulated daily household chores, under the guidance of a trained professional, allows sensorimotor children to learn by doing (Northcott, 1972; Piaget, 1952), and allows parents to modify their behaviors more effectively by being placed in a doer rather than an observer role (Brazelton, 1986). Strategies learned and practiced by parents at the Home Demonstration Center can be transferred easily into their own daily activities at home. It is in the pleasures of being dressed, fed, and played with that infants establish socially communicative skills, which assist the acquisition of language and stimulate the elements of auditory development.

Parents gain confidence in their own competence to affect their child's optimal development when they receive reinforcement for effective parenting skills from a trained professional during parent-focused habilitation. The professional's expertise in a child-centered program may benefit the child for an hour or two a week, but optimal progress occurs when children have parents who have been helped to develop their own expertise with their child all day long, everyday — not by becoming teachers, but by becoming confident, competent parents.

SUMMARY

It is critical that professionals involved in the auditory habilitation of very young children have a broad base of knowledge about child development, speech acoustics, and family dynamics into which can be meshed the specificity of strategies parents must learn to enhance a child's listening and language development. Listening is not an isolated skill, and a child's auditory development must not be approached in a segmented way.

Each child's unique family system and the dyadic interaction patterns therein must be assessed by the infant habilitator. Internal to that knowledge the professional can guide parents to establish appropriate expectations, to capitalize on auditory learning opportunities that arise naturally during a child's routines, and to stage situations that accelerate their child's progress through the levels of auditory development.

During those critical first three years, aural (re)habilitation programs must regard the family and not the child as an entity. Parents make a huge commitment of time and energy to aural habilitation that helps their child to integrate listening into daily life, as they become active members of the hearing world. Both the parents and child need support and guidance from professionals whose holistic approach balances auditory learning with the parallel development of the child's other learning domains.

REFERENCES

Brazelton, T., M.D. (1986). *Infants and mothers.* New York: Dell Publishing.

Cole, E., & Mischook, M. (1986). Auditory learning and teaching of hearing impaired infants. *Volta Review, 88,* 67–81.

Dunst, C. J. (1981). *Infant learning.* Hingham, MA: Teaching Resources.

Erber, N. P. (1982). *Auditory training.* Washington, DC: Alexander Graham Bell Association for the Deaf.

Fisher, E., & Schneider, K. (1986). Integrating auditory learning at the pre-school level. *Volta Review, 88,* 83–92.

Fry, D. B. (1978). The role and primacy of the auditory channel in speech and language development. In M. Ross & T. Giolas (Eds.), *Auditory management of hearing impaired children.* Baltimore, MD: University Park Press.

Furuhjelm, M., Ingelman-Sundberg, A., & Wirsen, C. (1986). *A child is born* (pp. 116–117). New York: Dell Publishing.

Ling, D. (1984). *Early intervention for hearing impaired children: Oral options.* San Diego, CA: Singular Publishing Group.

Mahoney, G., & Powell, A. (1986). A teacher's guide. *Transactional Intervention Program* (Monograph 1). Farmington, CT: University of Connecticut, School of Medicine.

Northcott, W. H. (1972). *Curriculum guide: Hearing-impaired children birth to three years — and their parents.* Washington, DC: Alexander Graham Bell Association for the Deaf.

Piaget, J. (1952). *The origins of intelligence in children.* New York: International University Press.

Pollack, D. (1985). *Educational audiology for the limited hearing infant and preschooler.* Springfield, IL: Charles C. Thomas.

Simmons-Martin, A. (1981). Acquisition of language by under-fives including the parental role. In A. M. Mulholland (Ed.), *Oral education today and tomorrow* (pp. 253–273). Washington, DC: Alexander Graham Bell Association for the Deaf.

Stone, P. (1983). Auditory learning in a school setting: Procedures and results. *Volta Review, 85,* 7–13.

Stone, P., & Adams, A. (1986). Is your child wearing the right hearing aid? Principles for selecting and maintaining amplification. *Volta Review, 88,* 45–55.

van Uden, A. M. J. (1979). Hometraining service for deaf children in the Netherlands. In A. Simmons-Martin & D. R. Calvert (Eds.), *Parent-infant intervention* (pp. 165–177). New York: Grune & Stratton.

Vaughan, P. (1981). (Ed.), *Learning to listen.* Ontario, Canada: General Publishing.

Vygotsky, L. (1962). *Thought and language.* Cambridge, MA: MIT Press.

CHAPTER 9

Language Development for Children Who Are Hearing Impaired

■ JILL L. BADER, M.A. ■

Language development, like auditory development discussed in Chapter 8, must be viewed within the context of a child's developmental domain, including the learning environment provided in early childhood. This decade's focus, for those of us involved in facilitating receptive and expressive language development of young children who are hearing impaired, must be directed toward a global view. This vantage point allows a treatment focus on auditory and language learning in relation to the child's other developmental areas and the family system within which the child will learn. Acquisition of language is enhanced by integration of the emerging auditory, social, motor, self-help, and cognitive functionings within the transactional/interactive/pragmatic relationship that parent and infant form.

Audition is the most efficient sense modality for initial development of functional verbal communication skills during the first three years of life (Ling & Ling, 1976; Pollack, 1985).

Children who are hearing impaired, regardless of degree of hearing loss, who can use hearing as their main avenue of learning, must be given the opportunity to do so. Children assured of the appropriate amplification and auditory learning environment described in Chapter 8 are learning to use their hearing for acquisition of spoken language. Erber (1972) states that audition has proven to be a complementary skill to lipreading (and vice versa), which is also a valuable avenue of effective communication for some children.

As the habilitative process unfolds, professionals need to be alert to the learning preferences exhibited by the child and to the "teaching" styles most comfortable to parents. Parents need a great deal of professional guidance and practice in making effective modifications in their interactional styles. The rich linguistic climate required by a preschool child who is hearing impaired can be effective only if it is developed through the child's parents.

This chapter will review the stages of language development, in a global and ecological fashion, that are related, but not restricted, to a child's auditory development. It is hoped that the reader will come to view as symbiotic the relationship of the child's learning domains, parent competence, and effective professional guidance that shape the process of language acquisition for children who are hearing impaired during their preprimary years.

DEFINITIONS AND TERMS

Communication is defined here as *the exchange of ideas, information, and feelings between two or more individuals. Spoken language* refers to *the orderly arrangement of verbal symbols to convey meaning.* Each part of the definition serves as a reference point to what decades of psycholinguistic research and habilitative discussion have established as the three basic components of language: *Meaningful symbols* refers to the **semantic content** (Bloom & Lahey, 1978) of language, *orderly arrangement* refers to the **syntactic form** of language, and *conveyance* is the **pragmatic use,** which must be functional (Simmons-Martin, 1981) with respect to the context in which it is spoken. Therefore, this chapter will refer to the three basic components of language as: (1) semantic content, (2) syntactic form, and (3) pragmatic use. Spoken language falls within either a receptive or expressive realm. Simply defined, *receptive language is the information that a person receives with comprehension. Expressive language is the information sent to a listener.*

THREE COMPONENTS OF LANGUAGE

Language is truly three-dimensional and multifaceted. For young children learning language, these components must mesh in an integrated fashion (Bloom & Lahey, 1978) to achieve conversational competency (Stone, 1988). These components of language have been separated here for brief examination, but are learned interdependently (Bruner, 1983).

SEMANTIC CONTENT

Semantic content is the element of language that concerns meaning. As cognition's linguistic component, semantics involves much more than acquisition of word meanings. It involves words related to other words in sentences that represent relationships between people, actions, and objects.

Over the first two years of a child's life, parents follow a conversational model which begins at birth with short, simple, interesting, redundant, comprehensible sentences (Snow, 1976). The semantic simplicity of parents' verbal interactions with their infants indicates clearly their intent to match the infant's ability to receive meaning. Infants must extract meaning from these verbal actions before attempts at expressive language can begin. Nonverbal counterparts (i.e., positioning, pointing, proximity, visual gaze), therefore, become the first semantic carriers and continue into adulthood to exert a communicative influence. It is from those nonverbal frames, established between parent and infant, that mastery of even the simplest form of verbal self-expression emerges (Bruner, 1975).

Riding in the rumble seat of nonverbal language behaviors are suprasegmental features that are semantically laden. These phonological aspects include intensity, pitch, timing, intonation, and duration. Suprasegmentals are understood and imitated by infants prior to demonstrated comprehension of words. With the possible exception of pitch, these suprasegmental features are available to children who are profoundly hearing impaired and carry the emotion of communication on an acoustic waveform. Simmons-Martin (1981) described intonation as "the vehicle one rides to syntax."

SYNTACTIC FORM

The form component of spoken language includes syntactic, phonologic, and morphologic features that parents choose to enhance meaning. Syntax refers to the grammatical rules one applies to alter words and arrange them into meaningful sentences in an orderly fashion (Pollack, 1985). Every language has its syntactic rules governing the order of adjectives, nouns, and verbs, but describing form requires phonologic and morphologic descriptions, too. Morphological inflections (e.g., ed, ing, ly) or single sounds (phonemes) carry their own unique set of rules and acoustic elements that vary in the combinations chosen for use. The act of choosing the form of sentences directed to a young child is dictated to some degree by the parent's perception of their child's cognitive and linguistic abilities (Bruner, 1975). This leads us to the third component of language, pragmatic use.

PRAGMATIC USE

Pragmatics, the least tangible component of language, has a socially related ingredient that involves the contextual appropriateness, functionality, and intent of language. Parents' alteration of their language away from complex words and forms for use with infants is pragmatically controlled by their perception of their young listener's level of understanding (van Uden, 1979).

Pragmatic use is also controlled by the parent's intent. For example, a speaker uses *"an authority"* when the intent is a nonspecific, one-of-many authority. If the desire is to direct one's attention to a specific authority, then he or she is *"the authority."* If a vocal stress is added to the article, *the,* a speaker believes that authority to be the best among many. Furthermore, if that someone is *the* authority him- or herself, then humor or sarcasm may be intended as well. The correct use of articles is listed among the most common errors presented in the verbalizations of children who are hearing impaired (Erber, 1982). The fact that articles gain their semantic value from their syntactic use, which is pragmatically controlled, may serve to explain this phenomenon more than the low acoustic feature aspect.

HIERARCHICAL DEVELOPMENT

Receptive language develops from an increasing awareness of and attention to the verbal signals to which a child is exposed. Those features of language to which the child attends, are imitated. Although this stage of receptive language development is not connected yet to meaning, the child is absorbing information. The comprehension stage is reached when children can demonstrate their understanding with an action. These ongoing, cyclic stages are the means by which children and adults process the components of language.

A child's expressive language passes through orderly, predictable stages of development, each of which appears for a fairly short period of time and then becomes an integral part of the next stage. Infants' vocalizations begin with reflexive crying and cooing and proceed to babbling consonant/vowel chains, then combinations, over the first year of life. This verbal exercise cultivates the ability to imitate increasingly complex prosodic patterns used by parents. When these imitative vocalizations carry meaning and intent, they begin to approximate single words. Single words lead in turn to inflected jargon, wherein children combine the babble and suprasegmental imitations into long vocalizations that, over time, are interspersed with single words. As single words increase, children combine two then three together into telegraphed phrases, which eventually become part of complete sentences.

GENESIS OF LANGUAGE

Children are introduced to language at the moment of birth, even before caregivers direct conversation to them. Neonates embark upon a quest for neurological organization that requires sensorimotor refinement before a child can process or produce spoken language.

During the first 2-year sensorimotor period, language emerges from the thoughts a child has about the objects and people in that immediate experience. The infant picks up toy keys to feel, taste, hear, and see. Through his or her senses, the child has inferred meaning related to the object. Parents accompany their child's sensory experiences with linguistic symbols. Over time and with repeated exposures, the child attaches that verbal symbol ("keys") to the object. The child's thought now has receptive language. Expressive production by the child of that linguistic symbol will follow soon.

So, young children's language stems from thought, and that thought has its roots in the child's experiences. Because the sensorimotor child's thought is extremely concrete and self-referenced, so is the first language understood and later expressed by the child (Piaget, 1952).

BIRTH TO 6 MONTHS OLD

During the first six months of life there is no symbolic representation. The infant's expressive verbal language proceeds from reflexive random vocalizations toward more purposeful sounds cooed with socioemotional intent. The child socially engages caregivers by initiating vocalizations directly at others to express displeasure. These vocalizations contain patterns other than crying and are primarily vowels, although consonant/vowel babble chains do emerge. The infant's nonverbal language is far more advanced and includes reaching, directed visual gaze, and body positioning.

6 TO 12 MONTHS OLD

Receptive language development proceeds from a reflexive point, as well. The startle responses of infants in the first month of life become quite deliberate, and are directed toward the source of sound; and by the sixth month they are followed by a social smile. The child not yet identified as having a significant hearing loss may not have heard auditory signals well enough to search for the location of the sound and, instead, may exhibit the social smile as a response only to the visual presence of an object or caregiver. Measurement tools of receptive language development evidence a prominence of social as well as auditory response behaviors. The 6 month old demonstrates a general contextual understanding (angry vs. friendly vs. danger) that is conveyed through the suprasegmental features of lan-

guage. He or she also has attached meaning to words with situational clues like "bye-bye," as evidenced by an emerging nonverbal response of a social waving behavior. The child who is hearing impaired, and fortunate enough to have full-time hearing aid use during this time, benefits from the accompanying auditory and language labels for his or her sensorimotor experiences.

12 to 18 MONTHS OLD

By the end of the first year of life, the toddler's behaviors have become coordinated, goal-directed, and imitative. A full year of object orientation and attention toward the effect of actions on the child's environment has contributed to the development of symbolic representation of objects independent of self. With the development of internal language, the toddler can carry the memory of familiar objects and people when they are not present, and demonstrate receptive comprehension of concrete verbal labels for them. The child begins to coordinate nonverbal behaviors of pointing, reaching, and looking from an object to a parent and back to the object again to communicate social intent. These nonverbal manifestations of cognitive growth and increased social awareness dictate parents' continued use of naming ("That's a bunny") and descriptive language ("It's so soft") strategies in verbal interactions with the child.

As the toddler's imitative powers mature, the verbal contributions of intonational parameters of conversations increase. Motoric imitations of the physical actions of speech gesture games (Patty cake and Peek-a-boo) soon are accompanied by the highly audible prosodic features of parents' verbal expressions. A 1-year-old child may delight his or her parents by speaking his or her first words and taking his or her first steps all at once. A motor preoccupation with newly gained walking and climbing skills can decrease the toddler's quantity of vocalizations for a few weeks. It is important that parents of children who are hearing impaired be forewarned of this natural phenomenon, lest they assume the possibility of a progressive loss of hearing or decreased efficacy of intervention.

18 TO 24 MONTHS OLD

As the sensorimotor toddler actively explores the way to 18 months of age, he or she gains a new separation of people-oriented acts and object-oriented acts. The child begins to use communicative behaviors (e.g., pointing, nodding, vocalizing, eye contact) more frequently with people and motoric behaviors (e.g., grasping, tasting, manipulating) more often with objects. As a toddler, the earlier repetition of object manipulatory acts now yields to social pleasure gained from imitation of people's acts. These imitations are often repeated to re-engage an adult in joint play. Object permanence allows the 16-month-old child to carry out verbal requests for an object that is absent from direct view.

Receptively, the 18-month-old child who is gaining on symbolic representation can match objects to pictures and identify those pictures when they are named. He or she appears to understand more words each week. By 18 months, the toddler has an expressive vocabulary of approximately 20 words and babbles intricate inflections that evidence increased consonant use. Pointing and gesturing now have a vocal counterpart. Babbling and nonverbal imitations abound, but verbal imitations are less frequent and not semantically connected. As the toddler moves into the second half of the second year of life, these parroted vocal imitations provide a household echo.

Imitations and gestural representations (e.g., hold telephone to ear, hugging baby doll, putting shoe to foot) explode in the last few months of the 2-year sensorimotor period, allowing the world of make-believe to emerge. There is an increased interest in books and pictures, which now carry meaning for the child and can be connected to objects and word labels. The prosodic rhythms of nursery rhymes and fingerplays lure the 2 year old to an accelerated level of repetition. The 1 year old's babble, which bred a handful of single words, is temporarily superceded by the 20 month old's practice of suprasegmental jargon. This jargon often accompanies a 2 year old's fantasy play. It is characterized by inflectional similarities to adult conversation, but with a noted lack of intelligible words.

At 18 months, the normal hearing toddler can imitate two-word phrases and many environmental sounds. By 22 months, four-word phrases are often imitated, but not spoken spontaneously. Nouns, verbs, and modifiers all appear in the child's expressive vocabulary, but are still used as noun labels (e.g., food may be called "banana" or "eat"). Receptively, this toddler can give appropriate responses to a series of two or three simple, but related commands. The child appears to listen to the meaning and reason of language utterances, not just to words or sounds, as his or her receptive word vocabulary grows steadily.

The semantic focus of parents' and toddlers' verbal interactions over the first two years of a child's life results in the use of spontaneous two word "telegraphs" about the objects, actions, and events with which he or she is actually involved. These concrete utterances reflect the cognitive level of concrete thought. Telegraphic utterances require verbal expansion by the parent that adds syntactic fill-ins. The use of correct word order gives form to the semantic intentions (Bloom & Lahey, 1978) that the child formerly could express only suprasegmentally through pitch, inflection, and intensity.

24 TO 36 MONTHS OLD

During the third year of life, the child embarks on development of *Wh* question forms (Brown & Bellugi, 1964). Expressive language gives clear evidence of morphological additions of pronouns, prepositions, articles, plurals, and word endings. The 2-year old's verbal use of pronouns and plurals demonstrates his or her social possessiveness. The child is no longer content with one block, but desires all the "blocks" that are "mine." Prepositions come to life as the motorically coordinated and socially independent toddler goes in, under, around, and behind things in his or her world. Phonemic features gain clarity of articulation, and most basic syntactic forms are used; however, errors are frequent, and telegraphic phrases still are present.

Receptively, the child demonstrates word associations and categories. Conceptually and linguistically, the child understands size, shape, color, and location. A preoperational child whose thinking is becoming representational demonstrates comprehension of early number concepts and is able to talk about things not physically present. Learning remains experience-based and the range of opportunities afforded the child serves as his or her learning catalyst.

4 TO 5 YEARS OLD

Over the fourth and fifth year of life, the three interwoven components of language (semantic content, form, pragmatic use) receive their expansion and refinement. This transformational period of language development coordinates with a child's increased comprehension of attribution, quantity, causality, and time concepts. The child engages his or her semantic knowledge of word meanings and calls an umbrella, an "underbrella." McNeill's (1966) Language Acquisition Device (LAD) illustrates how semantically and syntactically sensible words can work pragmatically in context, but nevertheless be incorrect.

The child has gleaned the generalities of form rules and may simply apply them universally (Ling, 1976). For example, as time concepts emerge, children learn that the morpheme "ed" is added to action words that describe events that have already happened (e.g., "I throwed it in the sink"). The well-intentioned parent who attempts to correct form errors, may say (e.g., "No, you threw it. Threw") only to have their transformational LAD simply apply the same rule again (e.g., "I threw it in the sunk"). For the

child who is hearing impaired, who may have no auditory information available from these visually and acoustically low morphological endings, the progress toward linguistic competence becomes even more challenging.

TRANSACTIONAL BREEDING GROUND

The first three years of life represent the critical period for language acquisition and for the formation of interactional patterns conducive to optimal learning. As active, information-seeking infants become neurologically organized and integrated, their learning is molded by the experiences afforded them through their senses in interactions with adults. A milieu of infant research in the 1980s confirmed these interactions between parent and infant to be transactional in nature, because both participants alternate the roles of initiator and responder.

The infant exhibits a behavior that elicits a response from the parent. The quality of that response and the speed with which it occurs, in turn, shape the infant's subsequent response over time. Conversely, parents initiate behaviors that elicit a response from the infant, which, in turn, shapes the parents' subsequent response over time.

A child with an impaired auditory sense is receiving impoverished data about his or her world through the prediagnostic period of no amplification and the postdiagnostic period of inconsistent or inappropriate amplification (Friedlander, 1979). The infant and toddler who are hearing impaired, therefore, proceed to explore the world with auditorily diminished semantic connectors to the transactional patterns and learning concepts being formed. In other words, the "whole" of learning is simply not available for this child's sensory integration or socialization.

Educational peer pressure for audiological advancement toward earlier identification and ever-improving amplification was a natural concommitant. Despite the presence of those audiologic advancements, appalling statistics exist that relate to the numbers of children still not identified in the first year of life, when some critical milestones of emotional bonding should occur.

Auditory signals (e.g., singing lullabies) contribute to the bonding of parent and child (Bowlby, 1982) much like social signals (e.g., smiling) do. Even with the benefit of appropriate amplification, auditory signals initiated by the parent out of the child's hearing range can go unnoticed by the infant and toddler who are hearing impaired. This lack of response may encourage parents to cease the use of auditory signals rather than to modify them. Undetected auditory signals of endearment will neither add to the promotion of the child's self-worth nor reap the parents' desired cuddly response from their infant. Undetected signals of danger could have even more disastrous consequences. Infant habilitation programs strive to help parents understand this transactional phenomenon and modify their behavior. Transactional intervention can prevent the erosion of mutually satisfying interactions that teach children appropriate behaviors to communicate effectively later in life.

Communicative behaviors acquired transactionally in the first few months of life are predominately nonverbal. Parents learn to match their infant's attention, imitate their behaviors, and "read" their child's thoughts. A synchrony of pace and emotion occurs as parents increasingly become tuned in to their infant. Parents soon can match their child's thoughts, actions, and perceptions with spoken language descriptors appropriate to their child's focus of attention. Nonverbal imitative games lead to verbal turn-taking games. Children's language thus emerges from warm, mutually pleasurable, social transactions with their parents.

Since language has a social interactional intent, parents are wise to acquire the firm, clear, reasoned behaviors characteristic of the authoritative guidance cited by Baumrind (1971, 1975) to promote social competence in school-age children. An authoritative parental style, rather than a permissive or authoritarian one, allows realistic parental expectations for the child of developmentally and socially appropriate toddler behaviors. Preschool children learn by doing (Northcott, 1975), and it is the parents who control whether their child will be an active participant or passive observer in learning experiences.

This transactional breeding ground for language development can be affected greatly by parents' diagnosis reaction. This reaction can result in grieving parents who unwittingly undermine their own relationship with their child and with subsequent intervention. Denying parents may delay the early consistent use of hearing aids and the beginning of active auditory-verbal stimulation. Depressed parents may seriously limit their children's exposure to those natural prosodic intonation patterns so critical to an infant's early understanding of language. Luterman's (1985) contention that "parents of hearing impaired children are the first clients" is valuable from both a linguistic and family health perspective.

Habilitative progams are best served by addressing the family's emotional agendas and the parent/child transactional pattern with the same aggressiveness audiologists employ in fitting amplification. Then, within the context of this type of habilitative intervention, the child can concentrate on the language acquisition task at hand.

SUMMARY

Professionals involved in the audiologic habilitation of young children who are hearing impaired require a broad base of knowledge about child development and family dynamics into which can be meshed the specificity of strategies to enhance a child's listening and language development. Parents are responsible for the wealth or poverty of their child's experiential base — some parents are caretakers, other are caregivers. Optimal language development in young children is accelerated by warm, nurturing transactional relationships with parents and later, by teachers who can follow a child's lead in experiential exploration of the world around him or her.

The length of auditory deprivation can be as devastating to a child's language development as the diagnosis of deafness is to the emotional health of the child's primary language input source — his or her parents. Consistent, appropriate amplification for the child, individualized grief counseling for parents, and early transactional parent-child intervention, are parallel first steps in the audiological habilitation of young children who are hearing impaired. Devoted, effective parents and professionals together help children gain the communicative competence needed for full participation in an integrated society in later years.

REFERENCES

Baumrind, D. (1971). Current parent patterns of parental authority. *Developmental Psychology Monographs, 4*, 1–2.

Baumrind, D. (1975). Child care practices anteceding three patterns of preschool behaviors. *Genetic Psychology Monographs*, 43–88.

Bloom, L., & Lahey, M. (1978). *Language development and language disorders*. New York: John Wiley.

Bowlby, J. (1982). *Attachment*. New York: Basic Books.

Brown, R., & Bellugi, U. (1964). Three processes in the child's acquisition of syntax. *Harvard Educational Review, 34*, 133–151.

Bruner, J. (1975). The ontogenesis of speech acts. *Journal of Child Language, 2*, 1–21.

Bruner, J. (1983). *Child talk: Learning to use language*. New York: W. W. Norton.

Erber, N. P. (1972). Speech envelope cues as an acoustic aid to lipreading for profoundly deaf children. *Journal of the Acoustical Society of America, 51*, 1224–1227.

Erber, N. (1982). *Auditory training*. Washington, DC: Alexander Graham Bell Association for the Deaf.

Friedlander, B. (1979). Finding facts of value and value in facts. In A. Simmons-Martin & D. Calvert (Eds.), *Parent-infant intervention: Communication disorders*. New York: Grune & Stratton.

Ling, A. H. (1976). The training of auditory memory in hearing-impaired children: Some problems of generalization. *Journal of the American Audiologic Society, 1*, 150–157.

Ling, D., & Ling A. (1976). *Speech and the hearing-impaired child: Theory and practice*. Washington, DC: Alexander Graham Bell Association for the Deaf.

Luterman, D. (1985). *Deafness in the family*. San Diego, CA: College-Hill Press.

McArthur, S. H. (1982). *Raising your hearing-impaired child: A guideline for parents*. Washington, DC: Alexander Graham Bell Association for the Deaf.

McNeill, D. (1966). Developmental psycholinguistics. In F. Smith & G. A. Miller (Eds.), *The genesis of language* (pp. 15–85). Cambridge, MA: MIT Press.

Northcott, W. (1975). *Curriculum guide: Hearing impaired children (0–3 years) and their parents*. Washington, DC: Alexander Graham Bell Association for the Deaf.

Piaget, J. (1952). *The origins of intelligence in children*. New York: International University Press.

Pollack, D. (1985). *Educational audiology for the limited-hearing infant and preschooler*. Springfield, IL: Charles C. Thomas.

Simmons-Martin, A. (1981). Acquisition of language by under-fives including the parental role. In A. M. Mulholland (Ed.), *Oral education today and tomorrow* (pp. 253–273). Washington, DC: Alexander Graham Bell Association for the Deaf.

Snow, C. (1976). Mother's speech research: From input to interaction. In C. Snow & C. Ferguson (Eds.), *Talking to children: Language input and acquisition* (pp. 132–137). New York: Cambridge University Press.

Stone, P. (1988). *Blueprint for developing conversational competence: A planning/instruction model with detailed scenarios*. Washington, DC: Alexander Graham Bell Association for the Deaf.

van Uden, A. M. J. (1979). Hometraining service for deaf children in the Netherlands. In A. Simmons-Martin & D. R. Calvert (Eds.), *Parent-infant interventions* (pp. 165–177). New York: Grune & Stratton.

CHAPTER 10

Speech Development for Children Who Are Hearing Impaired

■ DANIEL LING, Ph.D. ■

For several centuries, children with various degrees of hearing impairment, including many who were totally deaf, have been taught to communicate through the use of spoken language. Nowadays, speech development is included on the curricula of most special schools and classes for children who are hearing impaired. The extent to which such teaching succeeds depends not only on the characteristics of the children enrolled, but also on the importance assigned to speech in any given educational program and on the relative competence of the professionals undertaking the work (Markides, 1983).

Until the years immediately preceding World War II, speech development among children with hearing impairment was promoted mainly by teachers of the deaf in the course of their classroom work. Among the most famous of such teachers was Alexander Graham Bell (1916), who contributed many specific speech-teaching techniques to the field. In more recent years, speech-language pathologists and, to a lesser extent audiologists, have become increasingly involved in developing spoken language skills, often through working in clinical settings with very young children and their parents.

ADVANCES IN SPEECH PERCEPTION AND SPEECH PRODUCTION

SPEECH AS A SENSORY-MOTOR PROCESS

Speech acquisition is a perceptual as well as an oral process. Perception pervades speech communication. For people to understand the speech addressed to them, they must, through the ears, the eyes, and/or the skin, be able to detect, discriminate, and identify sufficient information in the spoken message to permit them to comprehend it. For acquiring accuracy of expression, a talker requires some form of sensory feedback involving conscious or unconscious awareness of the sensations generated in the act of talking. The sensory modalities that are most appropriate for the development of speech vary from one child to another, mainly according to the degree of hearing impairment and the type of educational or habilitation program that has been, or is being, followed (Boothroyd, 1982; Ling, 1989; Reed, 1984).

The work of "speech teachers" until about 50 years ago was based almost exclusively on speech reading, the use of tactile cues, and awareness of internal feedback cued by kinesthesia (Silverman, 1983). Now, as a result of research and the technology developed over the past few decades, much more is known about spoken language and its acquisition. Clinicians can identify hearing impairment and enhance speech communication skills through working with parents and their children who are hearing impaired during the earliest stages of infancy. Modern speech development procedures are supported by ever more sophisticated devices and strategies to measure hearing and to provide amplification. Through the use of cochlear implants, clinicians can now stimulate the neural receptors in the inner ear of children who would formerly have had to function as individuals who were totally deaf, thus permitting many of them to perceive a good deal of spoken language and other acoustic stimuli in their environments. During more recent years, it has become possible to transmit speech to the skin through wearable vibrotactile and electrotactile devices (Blamey & Clark, 1985; McGarr, 1989; Proctor, 1984). As a result, clinicians are now in a much better position than at any other time in history to promote the development of speech communication skills among children who are hearing impaired (Lauter, 1985; Ling, 1989).

THE RATIONALE FOR PROMOTING SPOKEN LANGUAGE

Speech skills are associated strongly with superior educational achievements (Jensema &

Trybus, 1978); and educational achievements, in turn, are influenced strongly by how effectively children can read and use English (Hanson, Liberman, & Schankweiler, 1984). In reviewing the evidence relating to speech and memory, Quigley and Paul (1984, p. 50) concluded that "speech recoding is important to reading development" and that "faithful representation of English structure seems to be particularly sensitive to speech recoding." At a more general level, it is clear that individuals with hearing impairment who can communicate through the use of spoken language, whether or not they also use sign language, have many advantages. They can interact more freely with other members of society, most of whom talk. They can, therefore, function more independently in most of the everyday situations that they are likely to meet in employment, leisure, and family life (Subtelny, 1980). Legislation and social awareness have improved the lot of most people who are hearing impaired in Western societies but, even so, the advantages lie with people who can talk. With spoken language, opportunities for higher education are less restricted, a more extensive range of careers is open, and there is greater security of employment. People who can talk also face fewer limitations in the personal and social aspects of their lives (Silverman, 1983). To talk badly rather than well can, however, be disadvantageous to individuals with hearing impairment relative to their employment. Doggett (1989), for example, found that there was a high correlation between employers' ratings of the comprehensibility of speech and their ratings of a person's independence, likability, and competence. Her subjects who were hearing impaired received poorer ratings than those who were native or foreign speakers, and the poorest ratings were received by the poorest speakers.

THE SPEECH ACHIEVEMENTS OF CHILDREN WITH HEARING IMPAIRMENT

The speech of children with moderate (50 to 70 dB HL) or severe (70 to 90 dB HL) hearing impairment usually reflects the quality of their auditory management. Such children, when appropriately aided and stimulated, are able to acquire much of their spoken language spontaneously through the use of their residual hearing (Ling, 1989). The speech of children who are profoundly (>90 dB HL) hearing impaired tends to reflect not only the type of information provided by the device(s) a child is using (hearing aid, cochlear implant, and/or tactile aid), but also the amount and quality of systematic teaching received. The more the child is profoundly hearing impaired, the more difficult it is to acquire speech spontaneously. In general, the more profound the degree of hearing impairment, the greater the amount of formal speech teaching a child will require in order to acquire spoken language (Markides, 1983).

Various levels of speech and spoken language achievement by children with impaired hearing have been reported in the literature. On one hand, the many advantages of early perceptual-oral treatment have led some children who are profoundly hearing impaired to acquire normal or near-normal speech (Ling & Ling, 1978; Ling & Milne, 1981). Conversely, several large-scale demographic studies have shown that, overall, scant improvement in the average standards of speech production by school children who are hearing impaired has occurred during recent years, in spite of the technical and educational advances in speech science and allied fields (Wolk & Schildroth, 1986). There is clearly a great deal of unrealized potential for better speech and language among children who are hearing impaired.

SPEECH IN THE CONTEXT OF SPOKEN LANGUAGE

The traditional method of teaching speech to children with hearing impairment has been to develop the production of sound patterns largely in isolation and then to combine them to form syllables, words, and sentences; but over the last few decades, authors such as Ewing and Ewing (1964), Vorce (1974), Calvert and Silverman (1975, 1983), among others,

have recognized that, under conditions that favor speech reception and language learning, some speech skills usually can be acquired spontaneously by many such children. Accordingly, authors such as Clark (1989), Cole (1990), and Ling (1989) have advocated a greater focus on promoting the acquisition of speech in the context of spoken language as it is used in natural communication.

Individual differences among children who are hearing impaired are often greater than those among children who hear normally, because degree and age at onset of hearing impairment are additional and important variables affecting development. Consequently, no one type of speech development program can suit the needs of all such children. Some children, with appropriate parental participation and professional support, can learn to hear (and even overhear) people talking to them and around them, and by this means acquire most of their speech and spoken language skills much as normally hearing children do. Others require highly organized training in order to develop effective speech communication (see Ling, 1976, 1989; Stone, 1988). Most children require at least some remedial help to gain mastery over the production of certain sound patterns, for abnormalities commonly develop in the speech of children whose hearing impairment is severe (about 70 to 90 dB HL) or profound (>90 dB). Remedial help usually is focused on particular speech patterns and on strategies for their carryover into everyday communication practices.

Carryover from lessons to life is least difficult to orchestrate when speech lessons and speech-language therapy closely relate to real life conditions. It is most difficult to manage effectively when lessons or therapy are organized around the use of devices and procedures that are not part and parcel of everyday communication (Ling, 1989, pp. 250–255). Generalization problems facing children who are hearing impaired can, therefore, if certain devices are used extensively and exclusively in formal teaching or therapy, become even more serious than those facing normally hearing children who have language deficits. A far-reaching analysis of issues affecting generalization from lessons to life has been undertaken by various writers in a clinical forum section of *Language, Speech and Hearing Services in Schools* (Fey, 1988).

FACTORS AFFECTING SPEECH DEVELOPMENT

Both intrinsic and extrinsic factors influence the acquisition of speech skills among children who are hearing impaired. Factors that are intrinsic to each child cannot, in general, be changed or greatly improved through direct intervention. These include unaided sensorineural hearing levels, age at onset of hearing impairment, visual acuity, integrity of or damage to the central nervous system, integrity of or damage to the peripheral speech mechanisms, and so on. Extrinsic factors may be defined as devices, procedures, people, and life experiences that, either by design or chance, serve to affect the development of children's communication skills. They include hearing aids, cochlear implants, tactile aids, glasses, socioeducational practices and experiences, environmental communication modes, parents' management skills, teacher/clinician competence, availability of support personnel, and the extent and type of children's contacts with peers (Ling, 1989). Orchestration of such extrinsic factors so that they operate most effectively to enhance the development of spoken language skills should be regarded as an extremely important part of any speech development program. *To be optimally effective, developmental and remedial speech training programs for children who are hearing impaired cannot be confined within the walls of a clinic or classroom, or by professionals' involvement within their normal working hours.*

CRUCIAL BASES FOR OPTIMAL SPEECH DEVELOPMENT

EARLY DETECTION OF HEARING IMPAIRMENT

Over the past few decades, the use of computers has become widespread in the fields of speech, language, and hearing (Curtis, 1987). They have allowed the development of various forms of electrophysiological hearing tests that are now in widespread clinical use, not only as a diagnostic tool, but also for screening the hearing of children at birth (Jerger, 1984). Further, relatively recent and highly significant contributions to tests of hearing in early infancy have been the development of the immittance battery (Popelka, 1981) and Visual Response Audiometry (Wilson & Thompson). Such tests, together with the use of probe-tube microphone systems in hearing aid selection, permit the effective use of hearing aids, or other sensory aids, with increasingly more children from a few months of age (Jerger, 1984; Stelmachovicz & Seewald, 1990).

When spoken language development is begun in the first year of life rather than later, children can be provided with more natural exposure to their mothers' spoken commentaries on objects and events that interest them, and they are enabled also to monitor and preserve the quality of much of the reflexive vocalization and repetitive babble they produce during the first year of life (Oller, Eilers, Bull, & Carney, 1985). Such auditory or alternative sensory access to their own early utterances promotes the children's production of an extended range of vocalization (Mischook & Cole, 1986). It also provides them with the essential foundations for feedback on the quality of their voices and the accuracy of the spoken language that they will acquire later (Ling & Ling, 1978). The ultimate development of children's spoken language has long been known to be most effectively triggered by appropriate stimulation during the first few years of life (Friedlander, 1970; Fry, 1966; Lenneberg, 1967; Studdert-Kennedy, 1984).

The acoustic environment of most homes approaches the ideal for speech acquisition by children under a year of age. With carpets on the floors, relatively little noise is created by movement. With drapes at the windows, and soft furnishings around the house, reflection and reverberation of sounds are at minimal levels in most rooms. Most important, however, is that mothers are usually quite close to their infants when they are talking to them. Conditions that predominate in most homes thus make for clear speech signals at babies' ears — signals that are not degraded by background noise. Speaking while the child is within earshot is clearly an essential for auditory learning (Ling, 1981).

After their first year, children's acoustic environments are less stable. As they become able to move over considerable distances without help from or contact with their mothers, they tend to have less speech addressed to them at close quarters. Nevertheless, young children are more frequently at home in good acoustic conditions than out and in noise. The emphasis in early speech habilitation over the past few decades has, therefore, shifted to the guidance of parents rather than direct intervention with infants. Descriptions of exemplary programs having such emphasis have been provided by the several contributors to a book edited by Ling (1984a). Many ways in which parents can be involved in the aural habilitative process also are discussed in this text (see Chapters 5, 6, and 7).

PROVISION OF APPROPRIATE SENSORY AIDS

Devices and Speech

The three senses through which we can gather information about speech are audition, vision, and touch. When aided hearing does not provide adequate sensory information about speech, vision and touch can be used as supplementary or alternative sensory channels. Cochlear implants and tactile aids, both of which have become available only recently, now are frequently prescribed as alternatives to hearing aids for children who have little or no residual hearing over all or part of the frequency range of speech. Either type of instrument can be of single- or multichannel design, and both vibro- and electrotactile devices are available. No currently available cochlear implant or tactile device can compensate fully for severe, profound, or total deafness so, like hearing aids, they are found to be most effective when used to supple-

ment speechreading (Carney & Beachler, 1986; DeFilippo, 1984; Pickett & McFarland, 1985).

Some children use both a hearing aid and a cochlear implant, and many children who hear nothing beyond 1000 Hz find that a multichannel tactile device will supplement aided audition in speech perception. These devices, and what they can contribute to children's speech and spoken language acquisition, have been discussed in detail in a recent book by Ling (1989), and are discussed also by Hodgson in Chapter 7 of this textbook. The selection of appropriate sensory aids (hearing aids, cochlear implants, and tactile devices) will depend on the needs of individual children. *To use any one of them to the utmost effect in developing speech skills, the teacher/clinician must be familiar with the acoustic properties of speech, know exactly what speech patterns a given sensory aid can be expected to provide for each particular child, ensure that the sensory aids for each child have been appropriately selected and adjusted, and see that the devices are consistently used under good acoustic conditions.*

Vision and Speech

Speechreading is the art of understanding the visual cues that occur as talkers move their tongues, lips, and jaws, and produce related facial expressions and body postures in the act of speaking (Ijsseldijk, 1988). Unfortunately, only comparatively degraded information on speech production is available through speechreading. This is because there are no visible correlates of some speech patterns. For example, vocalization (the use of voice), prosody, and nasality cannot be perceived through speechreading alone, because adjustments and positions of the larynx, the tongue, and the velum are partially or completely obscured by the lips and the teeth. Thus, there are severe limitations to learning speech through visual imitation. Also, several other sounds have the same visual (homophenous) patterns and on this account are frequently confused (see De Filippo & Simms, 1988; Dodd & Campbell, 1987). Although speechreading by itself provides a very impoverished signal, it is, nevertheless, a natural and often effective supplement to hearing in the development of spoken language. This is because the cues that speechreading provides, such as those relating to place of consonant production, can usefully augment a message that is heard only in part (see Erber, 1972). Many of the sensory aids such as tactile devices and cochlear implants produced in recent years serve, or have been designed, to supplement speechreading. If vision is to be used in helping children who are hearing impaired to talk, the teacher or clinician must know exactly what components, if any, of a given speech pattern can be clearly seen and how such components complement the information provided by the sensory aid or aids used by each individual.

Numerous visual aids, some involving sophisticated technology, have been produced for the purpose of enhancing children's speech production in the course of clinical training. There are at least three major problems inherent in their use. First, visual displays that represent the complete speech signal are hard to perceive, whereas simpler displays poorly represent the dynamic nature of communicative speech. Second, because they provide information that is quite unlike that required for communication in everyday life, it becomes essential for the teacher or clinician to design and supervise an extended range of generalization procedures in order to ensure that speech skills acquired through the use of such devices are carried over into the children's meaningful use of spoken language. Third, teaching through reference to a visual representation of only part of the normally complex speech signal has to be done under the close supervision of a professional if one skill is not to be learned to the detriment of another. Although one can easily show that children can learn particular skills through the use of visual speech training aids (and it is on this account that they are recommended), there have been no convincing studies demonstrating that the use of such devices leads to improved speech communication abilities in the everyday lives of the children. It is difficult to promote the carryover of speech skills into everyday life when they are learned through strategies that are not primarily based

on interpersonal communication (Perigoe & Ling, 1986).

EARLY INTERVENTION

To be optimally effective in developing perceptual-oral communication, professionals and parents must adopt developmental strategies for speech perception and speech production that differ according to each child's unique sensory capacities and needs. Special attention to such needs should, ideally, be initiated from the first few months of life. Such early intervention, in which parents become the primary agents in the process of fostering their children's development, is discussed by Atkins in Chapter 6 of this textbook.

Children can acquire optimal speech communication skills only when they use personal hearing aids and/or other selected sensory aids during all waking hours. A further requirement is that the speech addressed to children relates closely to their cognitive levels, motor development, self-help skills, and their personal and social experiences. Such experiences normally abound in the meaningful situations that pervade the activities of everyday living (Grant, 1987; Ling & Ling, 1978). Early speech development should not be based initially on the formal teaching of particular speech patterns, but on children's desire to communicate through speech and on their approximations to adult sentence patterns in the various areas of discourse — conversation, narration, questions, explanation, and description (Ling, 1989).

The first step in the process of learning speech informally usually will result in vocalizations in which desirable intonation contours, rather than consonants or vowels, are imitated. Appropriate perception and production of segmental features are likely to follow naturally under such circumstances if, according to their individual needs, children are using acoustic hearing aids, more than one sort of sensory information, or a different sort of sensory aid. Even with children who start their program somewhat later — for example, at 3 or 4 years old — developing speech through the meaningful use of spoken language in interactive situations is likely to result in later speech skills that are superior to those developed through more formal teaching (Ling, 1989).

SYSTEMATIC PROGRAMMING

Many different levels of skill have to be acquired before intelligible words can appear (Murry & Murry, 1980). In much the same way that a variety of vocalizations and canonical (repetitive) babbling patterns precede speech in normally hearing babies, so do such pre-speech patterns help to lay the foundations for the speech of children who are hearing impaired. Just as control of a wide range of vowels and diphthongs precedes mastery of most consonants and blends in the speech of normally hearing children, so do they create a similar groundwork for consonant production in people who are hearing impaired. The order of speech pattern development presented in the model described and discussed by Ling (1976, 1989) appears to be optimal for both informal and (the later) formal development and remediation of speech among children with hearing impairment. The model suggests that speech development should be promoted in seven somewhat overlapping sequential stages progressing from control of vocalization, to production of prosodic patterns, vowels and diphthongs, consonants differing in manner, consonants differing in place, consonants differing in voicing, to consonant blends (clusters). Such organization can save substantial amounts of time and increase efficiency, because systematic programming ensures that behaviors that are prerequisites for the production of any given pattern are already present, and that new skills can be developed with reference to other skills that have been acquired previously. For example, children who, because of their hearing impairment, have failed to develop a /g/ spontaneously, can, as explained by Ling (1989), more easily learn to produce it through reference to the production of /b/ and /d/ than through description, direct imitation, or any other strategy (see the following).

EVALUATION

Children's potential for learning to talk, particularly during the early stages of habilitation, should be assessed mainly through ongoing evaluation in the course of treatment in a program that features wholehearted commitment to the development of spoken language. Many factors contribute to young children's speech acquisition and, apart from a relatively few essentials such as hearing levels and basic oral-peripheral function, they cannot be assessed simply through formal clinical evaluation. For example, it is only following a period in which counseling, education, and support services are provided for parents that one can determine the extent to which they are able to help their children. Also, it is only when children have sufficient experience of speech reception through an appropriate sensory aid that their capacities for speech recognition can be assessed. In short, diagnostic training under optimal conditions is a prerequisite for a valid prognosis and the planning of therapy or teaching (Cole & Gregory, 1986).

Evaluation of both speech reception and speech production are essential aspects of any program directed toward children's speech development. Tests of either aspect can be norm-referenced (designed and standardized to permit comparisons) or criterion-referenced (designed to determine what skills a particular child has acquired). The latter tests provide the most appropriate guides for therapy or teaching.

To evaluate speech reception abilities, one must have tests that determine whether children can detect, discriminate, and identify the elements of speech (prosodic features, vowels, and consonants) as well as tests that determine how well running speech is perceived. Audiological tests of these types have been discussed by Beasley (1984) and Bess (1988). Such tests, as currently performed, however, can provide only part of the necessary information, for speech reception measures also must encompass appraisal of children's performance not only with hearing aids, but with cochlear implants, tactile aids, speechreading, or a combination of these (see Geers & Moog, 1989).

Various tests of speech production exist, and procedures that measure speech intelligibility through listener judgments and rating scales commonly are used in research studies (Subtelny, 1980; Wolk & Schildroth, 1986). For therapy and teaching purposes, however, one needs to use tests that permit the assessment of each child's ability to produce both the elements of speech (vocalization, suprasegmental features, vowels, and consonants) and to use speech meaningfully in everyday discourse. If one can identify the precise deficits that exist, one can select the most appropriate remedial measures to overcome them. The Ling (1976) Phonetic Level and Phonologic Level Evaluations are criterion-referenced tests designed to provide the necessary diagnostic information for effective speech development; the program of which they are a part is also in widespread use (Cole & Mischook, 1985).

TEACHING AND LEARNING: SOME STRATEGIES

INFORMAL AND FORMAL PROCEDURES

Informal speech development procedures may be defined as those that involve activities with children (particularly young ones) that are largely unplanned by adults, that are primarily determined by the children's interests and needs, and that lead to the spontaneous acquisition of spoken language. Informal procedures usually involve parents, caregivers, and/or peers to a greater extent than professionals. Formal procedures are those in which learning and teaching activities are planned and carried out in accordance with a predetermined program of speech development, usually by teachers or clinicians (Ling, 1989).

The basic techniques, tactics, and tools involved in the teaching and learning of speech communication by children who are hearing impaired are summarized in Table 10–1. The content of this table is illustrative rather than exhaustive. It simply lists the major elements

of effective speech development programs that are discussed in this chapter, and it illustrates the somewhat sequential nature of the techniques and strategies that can be applied. Note that the tools of greatest importance are sensory aids — primarily hearing aids, but for some children, cochlear implants or tactile devices. Table 10–1 maps the relationship between material already presented and the discussion that follows.

Whether speech acquisition programs are formal or informal in nature, perception must either precede or accompany production. Speech addressed to, used in the presence of, or produced by children with hearing impairment must be processed through devices that permit the child, as Hirsh (1940) put it, to detect, discriminate, identify, and comprehend as much as possible of the utterance. Among the most important cues for the acquisition and maintenance of speech by children who are hearing impaired are tactile and kinesthetic sensations that are produced as they themselves talk. Just as every speech pattern in the language sounds different to a normal listener, so does every such pattern feel different to a normal talker. It is the tactile and kinesthetic codes that are established in the course of speech acquisition that permit older children who lose all of their hearing to maintain most, if not all, of their speech skills. Making sure that children who are (or become) hearing impaired encode accurate tactile and kinesthetic patterns to guide their speech production must be treated as an essential part of informal or formal learning and teaching (Ling, 1976).

Informal learning takes place as children receive stimuli from their environments and try to derive meaning from them. Speech normally is addressed to (or used within earshot of) children in the context of activities that permit them to derive meaning from what has been said. The effective use of appropriate sensory aids, supplemented or not by speechreading, provides optimal opportunities for children who are hearing impaired to learn a great deal about speech reception and speech production in much the same way as their normally hear-

TABLE 10–1. TECHNIQUES, TACTICS, AND TOOLS INVOLVED IN TEACHING AND LEARNING COMMUNICATION

Techniques	Focus of Tactics	Tools
Informal learning (early infancy)	Early detection Early intervention Parental involvement Enhancement of speech reception Reinforcement of speech production Development of communication Personal social growth	Appropriate sensory aids
Informal Teaching (from early childhood onwards)	Context-based spoken language Perception of message Refinement of dialogue Perception of meaning Clarity of expression Spontaneous discourse Integration of personal-social skills	Appropriate sensory aids Everyday objects and events
Formal teaching (following optimal exposure to informal techniques)	Evaluation Systematic programming Development of specific skills Remediation of specific faults Use of anticipatory set Training to automaticity Programming generalization Promoting carryover Developing discourse Extending communicative competence	Appropriate sensory and teaching aids Tactile and visual skills
Formal learning (school-age through adult life)	Conscious and deliberate acquisition of knowledge or skills by an individual	Sensory and learning aids as required

Note: Certain techniques may be more appropriate at one stage of development than at another, but some tactics may be applicable at any stage.

ring peers (Wood, Wood, Griffiths, & Howarth, 1986).

Informal teaching is usually provided by parents in the course of everyday activities around the home, where repetitive situations, such as daily dressing, food preparation, feeding, and housework, as well as caregiving, supervision, and play activities, contribute abundant opportunities for both children and parents to initiate spoken language and for the children to acquire speech perception and speech production skills. With appropriately selected sensory aids, children who are hearing impaired can be encouraged to interact effectively and verbally with parents, caregivers, siblings, and peers. Informal teaching of children by others in the home can be enhanced through parent guidance work and, even with children whose hearing impairment is profound, at least result in approximations to adult forms of speech that provide the idea base for more formal teaching.

Informal teaching is not only a part of parent guidance programs. It can also be provided in the course of therapy or education, in which the principal purpose of the play or other activity is to promote the acquisition of spoken language through interaction and the encouragement of increasingly complex vocalizations and spontaneous approximations to mature forms of speech. Informal teaching procedures strongly feature the positive reinforcement of sound patterns that occur involuntarily, such as those in crying (boo-hoo), laughing (ha-ha), giggling (hee-hee), and babbling, with a view to enhancing awareness and feedback of such sounds through the sensory aid(s) that have been selected and through the tactile/kinesthetic patterns generated in their production. Thus, the groundwork can be provided for the voluntary production of such sound patterns and their inclusion in speech.

Formal learning usually is undertaken only by quite mature children in the presence of a peer or adult who serves to monitor production, because feedback on correctness is an important aspect of formal learning in speech acquisition. If sufficiently accurate feedback is not directly available to the child, then it must be provided through an external source. Feedback provided on the basis of analysis by a skilled listener is preferable to that derived through instrumental analysis, because whether speech patterns are perceived as acceptable or "correct" depends largely on how they interact with other sounds (i.e., coarticulation) in the context in which they are produced.

Formal teaching involves an adult's planned instruction of a child. The purpose of such instruction is to develop knowledge or skills that the child previously has not acquired. Most schoolwork and a great deal of therapy is of this type. Formal teaching of speech may be considered a remedial procedure that has two major objectives; first, helping children to produce particular sounds or sequences of sounds that, even after extensive and appropriate stimulation, have not been acquired through informal procedures, and second, the correction of errors. Formal teaching is not appropriate as the first step in promoting children's acquisition of speech skills. Further, if formal teaching of speech is begun before a child is using sentence

approximations consisting of at least two or three words to communicate, the development of natural sounding speech may be inhibited. *Every opportunity should, therefore, be afforded for children to acquire a wide range of speech patterns spontaneously, through the use of suitable sensory aids, before formal work is attempted.*

The extent to which children acquire speech skills spontaneously will depend largely on the degree to which sensory aids selected for them compensate (with or without speechreading) for their hearing impairment. It follows that when particular patterns have not emerged (or have emerged in a distorted form) following extensive informal teaching, devices and procedures other than those previously used will be required to elicit them. Because there are only three sensory modalities through which speech can be perceived — hearing, vision, and touch — and because the use of hearing and vision (and possibly tactile devices) will have been promoted already in the course of informal teaching, direct use of touch clearly will have to be the basis of much formal speech teaching. Indeed, many tactile strategies are available for guiding speech production. They include having children feel vibration of the chest when vocalizing; the movement of the larynx as intonation changes; and the duration, intensity, and temperature of the breath stream as different vowels, fricatives, and plosives are produced. A finger tap on the hand, or a finger drawn slowly or quickly along the arm can be used to signal durational cues that a given child can neither hear nor see, such as the difference between /m/ and /b/. Of course, care should be exercised to ensure that the children receive such cues without feeling that the clinician or teacher is invading their personal space.

ANTICIPATORY SET

The most natural and effective process in learning and teaching speech is to ensure that children acquire new patterns as an extension of those that are already mastered. Indeed, all children proceed from one stage of development to the next using previously established skills that, in many instances, are actually pre-requisites for new behaviors. For example, control over vocalization has to precede controlled production of prosodic patterns and vowels. In turn the production of vowels has to precede the mastery of consonants, because consonants in the dynamic stream of speech are, by and large, merely different ways of initiating, interrupting, or releasing vowels. Encouraging the development of speech through formal teaching based on the recognition of natural ordering has been advocated for some time (see McDonald, 1964).

The use of anticipatory set is a strategy based on both natural ordering and the propensity of human beings to anticipate required future responses on the basis of immediately preceding stimuli. To provide an example of such anticipation, ask literate people to produce the two letters *i* and *g* as a syllable and they will say "ig." Then ask them what they call an artificial head of hair and they will say "wig." Finally, ask them to name a large piece of wood broken from a tree and, because anticipatory set is such a compelling force, most will say "twig" even though "branch" would be more accurate.

Anticipatory set can be applied at all stages of speech development. To apply it to the development of consonants, for instance, first establish manner of consonant production with an early occurring speech sound. Then, through the use of anticipatory set, elicit the other consonants sharing that manner of production one by one. Thus, first have the child produce /b/ in repeated syllables such as /ba/, /bi/, and /bu/. This establishes an anticipatory set for manner of production. Then, by reference to /b/, establish /d/. Once this can be produced easily, sufficient anticipatory set is usually established so that when asked to make a sound like /d/ with a finger placed behind the teeth, children will produce a /g/. Similarly, for unvoiced fricatives, establish the /θ/ first, then have the children draw their tongues back slowly over either their top or bottom teeth and the likelihood is that /s/ will be produced. When the /s/ can be produced with ease, repeating the procedure but taking the tongue back even further will usually elicit the /ʃ/. Eliciting sound patterns in this way is, of course, a formal teaching procedure and one that has to be followed up by a generalization program to ensure the necessary transfer of training from lessons to life. Detailed procedures for using anticipatory set in the development of these and numerous other speech patterns are provided by Ling (1989).

One can usually capitalize on the use of residual audition in using and generalizing from early occurring speech patterns, because most children with impaired hearing have better hearing levels for the lower frequencies, those that carry the most salient cues relating to vocalization, prosodic elements, vowels and diphthongs, and manner of consonant production. In contrast, cues on place of consonant production are carried in the frequency range above 1500 Hz for which most such children have less, if any, hearing. Because many children with severe and profound hearing impairment are quite able to hear unvoiced fricatives or cues on place of production, formal teaching that employs both direct touch and the use of anticipatory set is recommended for those who have difficulty with these aspects of speech (Calvert & Silverman, 1983; Ling, 1976, 1989).

Essentially, a seven-step program is needed to ensure the effectiveness of formal teaching. These steps are specified below:

1. Ensure the presence of prerequisite behaviors;
2. Decide on the set to be used;
3. Select the child's most appropriate sense modality;
4. Choose the strategies to be used;
5. Achieve production of the targeted sound;
6. Provide reinforcement of the behavior; and
7. Generalize production to other contexts, including spoken language.

AUTOMATICITY

Ability to concentrate on what one is saying rather than on how one is saying it is an essential aspect of spoken language. Speech should therefore be developed in such a way that it can be produced automatically, that is, without conscious effort. Speech patterns are acquired by children over at least five distinct stages, with production at first being novel (and difficult), then variable (but easier), controlled, practiced, and finally habitual. Effective formal teaching ensures the development of speech skills through all five of these stages.

To ensure the automaticity of acceptable, coarticulated speech patterns in the variety of contexts in which they occur in spoken language, they must, if taught formally, be developed so that their production meets four basic criteria: *accuracy, speed, economy of effort,* and *flexibility.* Accuracy is the first requirement, for rehearsal of an inaccurate pattern can make a speech problem habitual. The rate at which a speech pattern can be repeated or alternated with others is important for a child's ability to integrate it appropriately into the stream of speech. Speech patterns produced with economy of effort do not involve extraneous musculature unduly and are not exaggerated. Thus, they provide a better base for developing further speech patterns and lead to more normal sounding speech. Flexibility in the production of speech has been acquired only when children can produce spoken language patterns appropriately in any context (see Ling, 1976).

GENERALIZATION AND CARRYOVER

When children have learned a skill in one situation and then applied it in another, they are said to have generalized that skill. Generalization and carryover are not serious problems when speech is acquired as a result of informal learning, because most such learning occurs in the context of spoken language communication in everyday situations. The less formal the intervention, the more closely lessons and real life are related. This is not the case when speech is acquired through formal teaching. Consider the production of a /g/ as described previously. When it is elicited through formal teaching in one vowel context, such as /a/, children usually will have to be helped to generalize its production to other vowel contexts, particularly those in which the /g/ has to be produced with the high-back and high-front vowels /u/ and /i/. This is because the point of contact between tongue and palate shifts according to vocal tract configuration for the vowel. To ensure that such generalization occurs, children should repeat several syllables, first with /a/, as in /gagaga/, then repeat the sound with each of the intervening vowels, one by one, moving gradually further and further away from the /a/, until /gugugu/ and /gigigi/ can be produced with ease. Production of such syllables may be a necessary speech skill, but unless it is deliberately carried over into real-life usage through integration into words, sentences, and discourse, it will remain far from an effective tool in communication (Calvert & Silverman, 1983; Fey, 1988; Perigoe & Ling, 1986).

PREVENTION AND REMEDIATION OF FAULTS

The most all-embracing statement on deviant speech due to hearing impairment must be that of Black (1971, p. 156) who wrote "The speech of deaf children differs from normal speech in all regards." The literature since that date indicates that Black's statement still holds true for the majority of children with hearing impairment, in spite of the technological advances that have been made over the past 20 years (Hochberg, Levitt, & Osberger, 1983). Nevertheless, in this writer's experience, the application of current knowledge about speech and language acquisition, present-day technology, and up-to-date educational practices would prevent many of the speech faults that are reported to be present among children who are hearing impaired (Ling, 1984a; Ling & Milne, 1981). In this section, various examples of the faults that led Black to make his statement are examined, and this writer's suggested treatments and expectations for higher level expectations are discussed.

Vocalization and Voice Patterns

One of the primary requirements for controlled vocalization is adequate breathing. Among speakers who are hearing impaired, voice production tends to be begun at — rather than sufficiently above — lung resting level (Forner & Hixon, 1977). Audition is not required for feedback on speech breathing. Sufficient tactile and kinesthetic cues are available for control of breathing patterns in the act of speech production. This fault is not, therefore, an inevitable outcome of hearing impairment. Instead, it appears to be a product of inappropriate speech development procedures. Such faults occur when a great deal of formal teaching of isolated speech patterns or single words is undertaken. They are less likely to occur when sufficient approximations to mature forms of speech based on multiword utterances have been developed through informal strategies.

Voices characterized by pharyngeal tension, abnormal pitch and prosody, and hypernasality are not uncommonly associated with hearing impairment (Hochberg, Levitt, & Osberger, 1983; Monsen, 1979). Such problems are, indeed, likely to result when there is lack of auditory perception and auditory feedback and insufficient appropriate teaching or therapy. However, because the harmonics associated with voicing and the nasal murmur are present in the low frequency range (250 Hz plus or minus a half-octave), they should be rendered audible in spite of even profound hearing impairment by the use of appropriately fitted hearing aids. These components of speech are also relatively simple to transmit through other forms of sensory aids. It follows that such abnormalities would be reduced or avoided for many children if more attention was given to the selection and application of suitable devices to improve the reception of these components. Indeed, such abnormalities are found less frequently in the voices of children who have used appropriate sensory aids in the development of spoken language from an early age (Ling, 1989).

Vowel Production

The most common faults with vowel production by children who are hearing impaired are neutralization, prolongation, diphthongization, and exaggeration (Calvert & Silverman, 1983). Residual audition that extends up to at least 2500 Hz is required for the auditory detection of the first two formants of all vowels. On the other hand, the first formants of all vowels can be detected if residual audition is present to about 1000 Hz and most identified if speechreading is used. Many fewer vowel errors are likely to occur if adequate use is made of residual hearing, multichannel cochlear implants, or multichannel tactile aids — if necessary, in conjunction with speechreading (Ling, 1989). However, an overly strong focus on speechreading can lead to these faults rather than prevent them, because they relate mainly to tongue movements, which cannot be clearly seen. Neutralization (the predominant use of a central vowel), diphthongization (moving toward a central vowel from other vowels), and prolongation can be due to either inadequate feedback, inappropriate teaching, or both. Exaggeration is almost always due to inappropriate teaching involving static rather than dynamic strategies. All four problems can be overcome by focusing remedial speech work on nonvisual feedback, increased tongue and reduced jaw movements, and the rapid alternation of different vowels, as well as syllables and words containing different vowels (Ling, 1976).

Consonant Production

In addition to normal developmental errors, the major faults in consonant production among children who are hearing impaired are reported to be omission, substitution and distortion, voiced-voiceless confusions, and implosion of stops. Such problems were reported almost half a century ago by Hudgins and Numbers (1942) and have been reported to persist, but to a much smaller extent, in the phonology of orally taught children today. In the group studied by Abrahams (1989), the best levels of correct consonant production were found among the children who had the best hearing levels at 2000 Hz. This finding is not surprising in view of the fact that place cues are available in, but not below, the octave band centered on 2000 Hz. The acquisition of acceptably produced consonants can be enhanced through the effective use of hearing aids by those who have useful residual hearing for frequencies above 1500 Hz. It can also be augmented by other sensory aids that provide relevant information, such as cochlear implants (Owens & Kessler, 1989) and tactile devices (Weisenberger, 1989). When sensory aids do not provide sufficient information for the development of certain consonants, systematic formal teaching of the type described by Ling (1976, 1989) usually can lead to their acquisition.

FUTURE TRENDS

PROSTHETIC DEVICES AND PROGRAMS

With advances in technology, new and improved sensory aids that can lead to better perception and production of speech will become available. It follows that one may expect a greater amount of research effort to be devoted to assessing the potential and the limitations of various sensory aids in the development of speech. One can, on the basis of recent advances in technology, reasonably predict a trend toward greater use of various devices in promoting the acquisition of speech among children with impaired hearing. The extent of that trend will depend not only on how well future sensory aids can be designed to transmit information, but on the number of educational programs committed to the development of spoken language. There is every reason for the variety of programming that currently exists to be preserved. Paradoxically, however, during recent years, when technology has offered greatly improved opportunities for successful acquisition of spoken language, there has been a trend toward the increased use of sign language, and this trend is likely to continue. Indeed, it has been suggested that American Sign Language programs should now begin to replace both oral and total communication programs (Johnson, Liddell, & Erting, 1989). Such a development would certainly receive widespread support from members of the deaf community (see Sacks, 1989). However, less than 3% of children who are hearing impaired are born to parents who are deaf (Jung, 1989), and the majority of parents probably will continue to press for programs that develop spoken language as the primary mode of communication, so that their children can learn to speak.

The trend toward the use of multichannel compared with single-channel sensory aids may be expected to continue because, by and large, they appear to yield superior results (Pickett & McFarland, 1985). The thrust in hearing aid design will be toward more digital processing (Levitt, 1988), and better hearing aid selection procedures involving children will continue to be made (Seewald & Ross, 1988). Accordingly, it is likely that productive strategies for the audiological management of young children will become more widespread and thus permit more children to acquire much of their speech more naturally. Because the means are now at hand, detection and diagnosis of hearing impairment can be carried out at an earlier age. More extensive application of current practices should lead to the expansion, if not proliferation, of parent-infant treatment programs in which children's speech will be developed more frequently within the first few years of life (Cole & Gregory, 1986).

PERSONNEL

In recent years, the focus on training teachers of the deaf in simultaneous communication has reduced the pool of educational personnel who are skilled in developing all aspects of spoken language (Ling, 1984b). At the same time, more audiologists and speech-language pathologists have become involved with spoken language development among children with hearing impairments, either as support personnel or as case managers. There is a definite need for more personnel who are able to provide auditory-verbal programs, and this need is more likely to be met through the recruitment of audiologists and speech-language pathologists to this area of work than through the training of more educators to work with parents and their children. Teacher training programs are more strongly geared to work with school-age children. Regardless of their children's age and the types of professionals engaged in promoting their speech communication skills, parents will continue to create the strongest demand, and to be the greatest resource, for speech development in children with impaired hearing.

ACKNOWLEDGMENTS

Thanks are due to Richard Seewald and Kevin Munhall, University of Western Ontario, who read and suggested revisions to the first draft of this chapter.

REFERENCES

Abrahams, S. (1989). Using a phonological framework to describe speech errors of orally trained, hearing-impaired school-agers. *Journal of Speech and Hearing Disorders, 54,* 600–609.

Beasley, D. S. (Ed.). (1984). *Audition in childhood.* San Diego, CA: College-Hill Press.

Bell, A. G. (1916). *The mechanism of speech.* New York: Funk and Wagnall.

Bess, F. H. (1988). *Hearing impairment in children.* Parkton, MD: York Press.

Black, J. W. (1971). Speech pathology for the deaf. In L. E. Connor (Ed.), *Speech for the deaf child: Knowledge and use* (pp. 154–169). Washington, DC: Alexander Graham Bell Association for the Deaf.

Blamey, P. J., & Clark, J. M. (1985). A wearable multiple-electrode electrotactile speech processor for the profoundly deaf. *Journal of the Acoustical Society of America, 77,* 1619–1621.

Boothroyd, A. (1982). *Hearing impairments in young children.* Englewood Cliffs, NJ: Prentice-Hall.

Calvert, D. R., & Silverman, S. R. (1975). *Speech and deafness.* Washington, DC: Alexander Graham Bell Association for the Deaf.

Calvert, D. R., & Silverman, S. R. (1983). *Speech and deafness* (2nd ed.). Washington, DC: Alexander Graham Bell Association for the Deaf.

Carney, A. E., & Beachler, C. R. (1986). Vibrotactile perception of suprasegmental features of speech: A comparison of single channel and multichannel instruments. *Journal of the Acoustical Society of America, 79,* 131–140.

Clark, M. (1989). *Language through living.* Toronto, Canada: Hodder and Stoughton.

Cole, E. B. (in press). *Listening and talking: A guide to promoting spoken language in young, hearing-impaired children.* Washington, DC: Alexander Graham Bell Association for the Deaf.

Cole, E. B., & Gregory, H. (Eds.). (1986). *Auditory learning.* Washington, DC: Alexander Graham Bell Association for the Deaf.

Cole, E. B., & Mischook, M. (1985). Survey and annotated bibliography of curricula used by oral preschool programs. *Volta Review, 87,* 139–154.

Curtis, J. F. (1987). *Microcomputers in speech, language, and hearing.* San Diego, CA: College-Hill Press.

DeFilippo, C. L. (1984). Laboratory projects in tactile aids to lipreading. *Ear and Hearing, 5,* 211–227.

De Filippo, C. L., & Sims, D. G. (Eds.). (1988). *New reflections on speechreading.* Washington, DC: Alexander Graham Bell Association for the Deaf.

Dodd, B., & Campbell, R. (Eds.). (1987). *Hearing by eye: The psychology of lipreading.* Hillsdale, NJ: Lawrence Erlbaum.

Doggett, G. (1989). Employers' attitudes toward hearing-impaired people: A comparative study. *Volta Review, 91,* 269–281.

Erber, N. P. (1972). Auditory, visual and auditory-visual recognition of consonants by children with normal and impaired hearing. *Journal of Speech and Hearing Research, 15,* 413–422.

Ewing, A. W. C., & Ewing, E. C. (1964). *Teaching deaf children to talk.* Manchester, England: Manchester University Press.

Fey, M. (1988). Generalization issues facing language interventionists: An introduction. *Language, Speech and Hearing Services in Schools, 19,* 272–281.

Forner, L. L., & Hixon, T. J. (1977). Respiratory kinematics in profoundly hearing-impaired speakers. *Journal of Speech and Hearing Reserach, 20,* 373–408.

Friedlander, B. Z. (1970). Receptive language development in infancy: Issues and problems. *Merrill-Palmer Quarterly of Behavior and Development, 16,* 109–122.

Fry, D. B. (1966). The development of the phonological system in the normal and the deaf child. In F. Smith & G. A. Miller (Eds.), *The genesis of language* (pp. 187–206). Cambridge, MD: MIT Press.

Geers, A. E., & Moog, J. S. (1989). Evaluating speech perception skills: Tools for measuring the benefits of cochlear implants, tactile aids and hearing aids. In E. Owens & D. K. Kessler (Eds.), *Cochlear implants* (pp. 227–256). Boston: College-Hill Press.

Grant, J. (1987). *The hearing-impaired: Birth to six.* San Diego, CA: College-Hill Press.

Hanson, V. L., Liberman, I. Y., & Schankweiler, D. (1984). Linguistic coding by deaf children in relation to beginning reading success. *Journal of Experimental Child Psychology, 37,* 378–393.

Hirsch, I. J. (1940). Acoustical bases of speech perception. *Journal of Sound and Vibration, 27,* 111–122.

Hochberg, I., Levitt, H., & Osberger, M. (Eds.). (1983). *Speech of the hearing-impaired: Research, training and personnel preparation.* Baltimore, MD: University Park Press.

Hudgins, C. V., & Numbers, F. C. (1942). An investigation of the intelligibility of the speech of the deaf. *Genetic Psychology Monographs, 25,* 289–392.

Isseldijk, F. J. (1988). Speechreading tests for the deaf. *Journal of the British Association of Teachers of the Deaf, 12,* 3–15.

Jensema, C. J., & Trybus, R. H. (1978). *Communication patterns and educational achievement of hearing-impaired students.* Washington, DC: Office of Demographic Studies.

Jerger, J. (Ed.). (1984). *Pediatric audiology.* San Diego, CA: College-Hill Press.

Johnson, R. E., Liddell, S. K., & Erting, C. J. (1989). Unlocking the curriculum: Principles for achieving success in deaf education. *Gallaudet Research Institute Working Paper 89–3.* Washington, DC: Gallaudet University.

Jung, J. H. (1989). *Genetic syndromes in communication disorders.* Boston: Little, Brown.

Lauter, J. L. (Ed.). (1985). Proceedings of the Conference on the Planning and Production of Speech in Normal and Hearing-Impaired Individuals: A Seminar in Honor of Richard Silverman. *ASHA Reports, 15.*

Lenneberg, E. H. (1967). *Biological foundations of language.* New York: John Wiley.

Levitt, H. (1988). Digital hearing instruments: A brief review. *Hearing Instruments, 39,* 8–12.

Ling, D. (1976). *Speech and the hearing-impaired child: Theory and practice.* Washington, DC: Alexander Graham Bell Association for the Deaf.

Ling, D. (1981). Keep your child within earshot. *Newsounds, 6,* 506.

Ling, D. (Ed.). (1984a). *Early intervention for hearing-impaired children: Oral options.* San Diego, CA: College-Hill Press.

Ling, D. (Ed.). (1984b). *Early intervention for hearing-impaired children: Total communication options.* San Diego, CA: College-Hill Press.

Ling, D. (1989). *The foundations of spoken language for hearing-impaired children.* Washington, DC: Alexander Graham Bell Association for the Deaf.

Ling, D., & Ling, A. H. (1978). *Aural habilitation: The foundations of verbal learning.* Washington, DC: Alexander Graham Bell Association for the Deaf.

Ling, D., & Milne, M. (1981). The development of speech in hearing-impaired children. In F. Bess, B. A. Freeman, & J. S. Sinclair (Eds.), *Amplification in education* (pp. 98–108). Washington, DC: Alexander Graham Bell Association for the Deaf.

McDonald, E. T. (1964). *Articulatory testing and treatment: A sensory-motor approach.* Pittsburgh, PA: Stanwix House.

McGarr, N. S. (Ed.). (1989). Research on the use of sensory aids for hearing-impaired people. *Monograph of the Volta Review, 91*(5), Washington, DC: Alexander Graham Bell Association for the Deaf.

Markides, A. (1983). *The speech of hearing-impaired children.* Manchester, England: Manchester University Press.

Mischook, M., & Cole, E. (1986). Auditory learning and teaching of hearing-impaired infants. *Volta Review, 88*(5), 67–82.

Monsen, R. B. (1979). Acoustic qualities of phonation in young hearing-impaired children. *Journal of Speech and Hearing Research, 22,* 276–288.

Murry, T., & Murry, J. (Eds.). (1980). *Infant communication.* Houston, TX: College-Hill Press.

Oller, D. K., Eilers, R. E., Bull, D. H., & Carney, A. E. (1985). Prespeech vocalizations of a deaf infant: A comparison with normal metaphonological development. *Journal of Speech and Hearing Research, 27,* 47–63.

Owens, E., & Kessler, D. K. (1988). *Cochlear implants in young deaf children.* San Diego, CA: College-Hill Press.

Perigoe, C. B., & Ling, D. (1986). Generalization of speech skills in hearing impaired children. *Volta Review, 88,* 351–366.

Pickett, J. M., & McFarland, W. (1985). Auditory implants and tactile aids for the profoundly deaf. *Journal of Speech and Hearing Research, 28,* 134–150.

Popelka, G. R. (1981). *Hearing assessment with acoustic reflex.* Orlando, FL: Grune & Stratton.

Proctor, A. (1984). Tactile aids for the deaf: A comprehensive bibliography. *American Annals of the Deaf, 129,* 409–416.

Quigley, S. P., & Paul, P. V. (1984). *Language and deafness.* San Diego, CA: Singular Publishing Group.

Reed, M. (1984). *Educating hearing-impaired children.* Milton Keynes, England: Open University Press.

Sacks, O. (1989). *Seeing voices.* Berkeley: University of California Press.

Seewald, R. C., & Ross, M. (1988). Amplification for young hearing-impaired children. In M. C. Pollack (Ed.), *Amplification for the hearing-impaired* (3rd ed., pp. 213–271). Orlando, FL: Grune & Stratton.

Silverman, S. R. (1983). Speech training then and now: A critical review. In I. Hochberg, H. Levitt, & M. J. Osberger (Eds.), *Speech of the hearing-impaired* (pp. 1–20). Baltimore, MD: University Park Press.

Stelmachovicz, P. G., & Seewald, R. C. (1991). Probe-tube microphone measures in children. *Seminars in Hearing, 12,* 62–72.

Stone, P. (1988). *Blueprint for developing conversational competence: A planning/instructional model with detailed scenarios.* Washington, DC: Alexander Graham Bell Association for the Deaf.

Studdert-Kennedy, M. (1984). Early development of phonological form. In C. von Euler, H. Forssberg, & H. Lagercrantz (Eds.), *Neurobiology of infant behavior.* New York: Stockton Press.

Subtelny, J. D. (Ed.). (1980). *Speech assessment and speech improvement for the hearing impaired.* Washington, DC: Alexander Graham Bell Association for the Deaf.

Vorce, E. (1974). *Teaching speech to deaf children.* Washington, DC: Alexander Graham Bell Association for the Deaf.

Weisenberger, J. (1989). Tactile aids for speech perception and production by hearing-impaired people. *Volta Review, 91*(5), 79–100.

Wilson, W. R., & Thompson, G. (1984). Behavioral audiometry. In J. Jerger (Ed.), *Pediatric audiometry* (pp. 1–44). San Diego, CA: College-Hill Press.

Wolk, S., & Schildroth, A. N. (1986). Deaf children and speech intelligibility. In A. N. Schildroth & M. A. Karchmer (Eds.), *Deaf children in America* (pp. 139–156). San Diego, CA: College-Hill Press.

Wood, D., Wood, H., Griffiths, A., & Howarth, I. (1986). *Teaching and talking with deaf children.* New York: John Wiley.

■ CHAPTER 11 ■

Educational Management of Children Who Are Hearing Impaired

■ FREDERICK S. BERG, Ph.D. ■

This chapter describes educational problems of children with hearing impairment in the schools. It also discusses communicative methodologies, programmatic breakthroughs, and cost-effective classroom technologies. The importance of developing and utilizing listening skills is emphasized also.

TARGET POPULATION

Hearing impairment is associated with educational handicap or risk in the schools. By the age of two, 75% of all children have had at least one episode of otitis media, which is only one of the many etiologies that can cause hearing impairment (Richardson & Donaldson, 1981). National data obtained in audiometric test booths have revealed that between kindergarten and 12th grade, perhaps one out of every five students has some degree of hearing impairment in one or both ears (J. Willeford, Janu-

ary 1971, personal communication). More recent audiometric data obtained in the Wabash and Ohio Valley Special Education District, located in southern Illinois, revealed that 32% of students in regular classrooms at the fourth-, fifth-, and sixth-grade levels had a minimal hearing loss. Seventy-five percent of these sixth grade, minimal hearing loss students had an academic deficit in one or more of the "basic" academic areas of reading, language arts, or mathematics. Twenty-five percent of all these sixth-grade students had academic deficits (Sarff, Ray, & Bagwell, 1981).

Children with hearing impairment may be divided into two audiologic groups, A and B. Group A includes more than 60,000 children who are educationally handicapped with moderate, severe, and profound bilateral hearing losses for whom Individualized Educational Programs (IEPs) are written annually (Berg, 1987; Ross, 1985). They are eligible for services for Hard of Hearing and Deaf under Public Law

94-142, the Education of the Handicapped Act,) (U.S. Department of Education, 1988). Since the passage of the All Handicapped Children's Act and onset of federal funding for early handicapped education programs, most of the children of Group A have been educated in the regular public schools, often referred to as the least restrictive environment, rather than in schools for the deaf. Most Group A children can benefit from hearing aids and personal or sound field FM amplification systems to learn in regular or special classrooms. In many states, however, neither personal FM systems or sound field FM systems typically are used to help these children. The classrooms they are educated in usually are noisy and reverberant.

Group B includes a much larger number of children with mild bilateral hearing losses or with moderate, severe, and profound unilateral hearing losses who are at risk educationally because the verbal signals they hear in the classrooms are muffled and inconsistent (Berg, 1986b; Bess, 1984; Downs, 1988; Ray, 1989). Group B includes children with fluctuating hearing loss, chronic conductive hearing loss, permanent sensorineural hearing loss, listening difficulties in noise, attentional and behavior problems, and Down syndrome. Under Chapter 1 and EHA-B, many children of Group B receive services for learning disabled, speech impaired, and mentally retarded (Ray, 1989). These children are marginal candidates for personal hearing aids and personal FM amplification equipment, but definite candidates for sound field amplification equipment. The classrooms they are educated in are typically noisy and reverberant.

EDUCATIONAL PROBLEMS

The most frequent and basic consequence of hearing loss is listening deficit. Children with hearing impairment in both regular and special classrooms are in need of classroom listening support. In the typical classroom, it is difficult for even students with normal hearing to understand all the teacher is saying. Children with hearing impairment are even more susceptible to listening breakdown than children with normal hearing under the same conditions of poor classroom acoustics (Finitzo-Hieber & Tillman, 1978). The fact that a child with a hearing impairment may be wearing hearing aids does not help much when noise and reverberation are present. The aid amplifies unwanted sounds as well as wanted sounds. Teachers often tire their voices trying to talk above the noise level (Ray, 1989).

The more than one million elementary, secondary, and special education teachers in the United States have responsibility to educate all children enrolled in their classrooms, including youngsters with hearing problems. Before appropriate education can be provided, however, there is a need to identify and seek help for pathological ear conditions, hearing loss, and resultant educational deficits among their students. In 1975, the All Handicapped Children's Education Act was passed with the mandate: "All children who are handicapped and in need of special education and related services must be identified, located, evaluated, and assured a free appropriate education in the least restrictive environment" (Amon, 1988, p. 141). This mandate includes provision that the schools provide audiology services for children with hearing handicaps. The U.S. Department of Education issued a new initiative to broaden the definition of children with hearing impairment eligible for special services (Bebout, 1985).

Children with the greatest hearing losses often are referred to as being deaf. Twenty years ago, most of these children were enrolled in special classes or schools. More recently, great emphasis has been placed on educating these children in regular classrooms. Notwithstanding the setting, children with deafness generally are not performing well academically. A fairly recent academic profile reveals that a student considered deaf at age 14 typically reads at the third-grade level and does sixth-grade mathematics (Gaullaudet Research Institute Newsletter, 1985).

Earlier, a committee chaired by Homer Babbidge, President of the University of Connecticut, made a thorough investigation of the education of the deaf in the United States under the auspices of the Secretary of Health, Education, and Welfare (Education of the Deaf, 1965). A representative sample of residential, day school, and day class programs was visited and studied. In a summary of findings, the Babbidge Committee noted that the American people had no reason to be satisfied with their limited success in educating deaf children. One finding, for example, was that the typical graduate of a residential school for the deaf had only an eighth-grade education. This typical graduate was a student who had been in a special school or in special classes for the deaf for at least 12 years and who was more than 18 years old.

Educators at that time laid the blame for educational retardation on the distressingly low language skills of children who were deaf. Furth (1966), for example, reported the mean reading grade equivalent of a sample of 1,075 deaf children ages 15½ to 16½ to be 3.5. He went on to clarify this problem.

It should be noted that a 14-year-old deaf youngster with a reading level of Grade 3 is not comparable to a hearing peer who may have difficulty reading. The hearing individual enjoys a comfortable mastery of the language even though he may be retarded in reading. For the deaf, on the other hand, the reading level is his ceiling in linguistic competence. It is inappropriate to designate this latter condition as retardation of reading. It is properly termed incompetence or deficiency in verbal language, a condition rare among the hearing but almost universal among the deaf. (p. 15)

With the release of the "Babbidge Report," a flurry of laws were passed by the federal government that have affected the education of children who are hearing impaired (Luterman, 1985). These laws are:

■ PL 89-36 (1965). Established a national technical institute for the deaf.
■ PL 89-10 (1966). Provided for the purchase of instructional media for children who are handicapped.

■ PL 89-694 (1966). Established a model secondary school for the deaf.
■ PL 91-587 (1969). Established a model elementary school for the deaf.
■ PL 90-538 (1969). Provided grants for early education of children who are handicapped.
■ PL 91-61 (1969). Facilitated the use of new technology in handicapped education.
■ PL 93-112, Section 504 (1973). Promoted equal access of the handicapped to services available to the general public.
■ PL 94-142 (1975). Required that individualized educational programs be written annually for children who are handicapped beginning at 3 years of age.
■ PL 99-457 (1986). Amended above law to mandate services beginning at birth.

COMMUNICATION METHODOLOGIES

Educational change for children with deafness has emphasized consideration of communicative methodology. Prior to the Babbidge Report, oralism was the dominant communicative methodology in special classes for the deaf, particularly in preschool and elementary school. It featured teaching children through speech and lipreading, in addition to printed forms of language. In its place, "total communication" (TC) swept the ranks of the great majority of the teachers of the hearing impaired, leaving in many localities of the country no oral options for educating children who are deaf.

Total Communication is a philosophy requiring the incorporation of appropriate aural, manual, and oral modes of communication in order to ensure effective communication with and among hearing impaired persons. ("Total Communication" Definition Committee Report, p. 3)

In practice, total communication emphasized a form of manualism in which sign language became signed English. By 1985, the pendulum had swung almost completely to TC.

Leo Connor (1985), a former administrator of one of the oral schools for the deaf, describes this shift.

The story of oral education during the past 20 years can be paraphrased in one of Dicken's phrases. "It began as the best of times and ended as the worst of times." In 1985, oralism has been replaced as the preeminent classroom methodology by total communication for almost all special classes and schools of the United States. Oralism remains as a preferred classroom method in only a handful of selective special schools, in an unknown number of preschool programs, and in an equally unknown number of mainstreamed services in local public schools. (p. 117)

With the shift to TC, most teachers of the deaf and most educational programs have deserted speech as a major goal for children with deafness. Speech is probably the most difficult and complex of the tasks facing teachers of the deaf (Connor, 1985). In spite of the fact that among children who are deaf "speech comes hard" (DiCarlo, 1964), great efforts are being made by some educators of children who are deaf to improve speech methodology (Calvert, 1985; Ling, 1976).

The phenomenal growth and acceptance of TC has been a major factor inhibiting the widespread commitment to the use of residual hearing. Ross and Calvert (1984) point out that it is unfortunate when the label "deaf" is loosely applied to children with hearing impairment, with their great diversity of hearing losses. For most of these children, there is an alternative to being deaf; it is being hard of hearing. Ross and Calvert are concerned that parents of young children with hearing impairment entering our educational system are exposed to attitudes and overt pressures to accept their child as "deaf" and to adopt a manual system, often regardless of the extent of the child's residual hearing.

Today, educators and parents are faced with the fact that the TC method, as practiced, has not fulfilled its educational promise. Generally, there has not been a substantial advance in the depressingly low educational achievement of children with deafness, as TC advocates believed there would be. At this point, the TC effect must be judged as "not proven," and a sense of weariness, almost revulsion, exists in debating or trying to prove there exists a superior communication methodology (Luterman, 1985).

This result does not come as a complete surprise. As early as 1972, Daniel Ling indicated that TC was not going to be a panacea for the educational problems of deaf children.

What about the other point — that children taught by "total communication" do not fall behind educationally and learn high-level language skills? That is garbage. And the reason it is garbage is evident from research, also. For example, a recent study by Klopping compared three groups: one who'd been taught orally, one who'd been taught manually, and one who'd been taught by "total communication." Let me tell you that one-third of the children, regardless of the methodology used, were unable to use language meaningfully. Now, surely the point here is that what we've got to face is that poor standards are not necessarily due to the communication mode at all, but to damn poor teaching .... 40% of the people who are dealing with our children in these schools today have no professional training in teaching deaf children; and that is ghastly. And, let me add that a lot of the teachers who have this training have very little experience, and some of their training isn't worth that much. (p. 554)

It would not be surprising to see a swing of the pendulum back toward oral methodology because of the new oral emphasis on auditory rather than visual input of speech. Audiometric and spectrographic data suggest that the majority of children with hearing impairment educated in schools for the deaf have sufficient residual hearing to learn to listen and speak fluently and develop spoken language skills that underpin reading, writing, and other academic skills. The oral method is now referred to as the auditory oral (AO) or oral aural methodology (Berg, 1986b).

The AO method can be particularly effective with children with severe and profound hearing loss if used beginning with infancy. Early auditory intervention is advocated for at least three reasons: (1) to prevent the possible imperfect development or deterioration of the hearing sensory mechanism due to lack of early stimulation, (2) to take advantage of a time of life in which language develops very rapidly, and (3) to avoid disturbing the synchrony of perceptual and motor development, which proceeds on schedule despite missing sensory information.

Geers, Moog, and Schick (1984) studied the acquisition of spoken and signed English by a sample of 327 children with profound hearing loss, from AO and TC programs across the country. Each child was tested on the Grammatical Analysis of Elicited Language — Simple Sentence Level (GAEL-S), which measures production of selected English language structures. Percentage correct scores for the oral productions of TC children were substantially below scores for their manual productions and below the oral scores of AO children on all grammatical categories sampled on the GAEL-S. The data indicate either that spoken English does not develop simultaneously with manually coded English, or that efforts were not made in the TC sample to ensure that signs were correlated with oral production.

It is not known to what extent auditory or auditory-visual stimulation should be used in the acquisition of language. Unisensory auditory stimulation, often called the Acoupedic Method, has been recommended to ensure that the child with hearing impairment develops a predominately auditory orientation rather than reliance on lipreading or sign communication. Bisensory stimulation is recommended because of the combined roles of audition and vision for linguistic and cognitive development (Berg, 1986b).

If a child does not have residual hearing, Cued Speech may be used to enhance the development of lipreading and speech. In contrast with TC, this communicative approach inherently requires that the hands correlate with speech. It is only when the hand cue and lip position are correlated that a speech sound is recognized. With TC, by contrast, the sign conveys meaning independent of speech that is being used. Nicholls and Ling (1982) have described Cued Speech in some detail.

In Cued Speech the consonants are cued by eight hand configurations and the vowels by four hand positions. Diphthongs are cued by gliding from the position of the initial to the final vowel nucleus. In running speech, the consonant-vowel hand cues are coarticulated, in a one-to-one relationship with the syllables of the language. A sender is able to transmit the cues in real-time synchronously with speech, thus conveying a visual analog of the syllabic-phonemic-rhythmic patterns of spoken language. (p. 262)

Kipila and Williams-Scott (1988) indicate that Cued Speech is not a language. It is just a communication system to orally convey any spoken language. Consequently, Cued Speech may be acquired faster than sign language or signed English, which has important implications for parents and teachers trying to learn to communicate with children who are deaf. The linguist Stokoe, who discovered that American Sign Language (ASL) is a true language, also discovered the difficulty of becoming fluent with sign language (Gannon, 1981).

In a study of the use of Cued Speech for the reception of spoken language, 18 children with hearing losses from 97 to 122 dB averaged 95% recognition of key words in sentences. They had been taught through the use of Cued Speech for at least 4 years. Nicholls and Ling (1982) concluded that Cued Speech: (1) is compatible with simultaneous auditory processing; and (2) merits more widespread use as an oral option for those children who are deaf, near-deaf, or who do not progress adequately in more conventional oral programs.

PROGRAMMATIC BREAKTHROUGHS IN EDUCATING CHILDREN WHO ARE HEARING IMPAIRED

Data gathered over the last 70 years, particularly during the last 20 years, indicate that the best overall educational achievement of children with hearing impairment has been in select private oral schools for the deaf and in regular educational programs (Quigley & Paul, 1985). For many years, teachers at the Central Institute for the Deaf (CID) have asked the question, "Can typically deaf children achieve well above what is generally expected, even approaching the achievement of hearing children with improved teaching?" (Geers, 1985).

An experiment was designed and implemented at CID, called Experimental Program in Instructional Concentration (EPIC), to answer this question. An experimental group of CID students received concentrated, intense instruction, with a 2.3 student-teacher ratio. The control group students received the typical instruction of private oral schools for the deaf, with a higher student-teacher ratio. Pretreatment and posttreatment tests enabled investigators to determine progress in language and vocabulary, speech, reading, and mathematics. All students were taught through an oral-aural or AO approach. The findings showed that both the experimental and control subjects progressed in all areas of tested performance, but the experimental subjects made accelerated gains approaching the performance of normal hearing children. There was no plateauing or leveling of performance as long as these children were taught systematically.

At CID the success of the EPIC project was attributed to exceptional tutorial education and not communication methodology, new technology, or educational placement.

In conclusion, it can be suggested that the amelioration of the problems of early profound hearing loss has not been found in any one method of communication (be it oral-aural, total, cued speech, acoupedic), or device (be it powerful amplification, cochlear implant, vibrotactile stimulation, and so forth), or educational setting (schools for the deaf, segregated classes, or mainstreaming). All of these methods, devices, and settings have, at one time or another been proposed as "solutions" to the educational problems presented by deafness. Such emphasis discounts the important ingredient in effective education of the deaf child — well structured educational programs that are based on the realization that most deaf children require extremely careful, intensive, individualized instruc-tion in order to realize their potential. (Geers, 1985, p. 81)

The Central Institute for the Deaf sees EPIC as a cost-effective way ($9,500 per student in 1984) to upgrade the education of all children with severe and profound hearing impairment. In 1986, CID received national recognition as one of the 60 private elementary schools in the country named as outstanding by the U.S. Department of Education's Elementary School Recognition Program.

Another cost-effective program for children with hearing impairment is to begin their education early in life. A nationally validated, early intervention program for hearing impaired children called SKI*HI (pronounced sky high) is a case in point. SKI*HI was initiated in 1972 by Tom Clark, who believes that language is learned in the home rather than taught in school. Using a systematic and comprehensive curriculum, SKI*HI parent advisors conduct weekly visits to homes to train parents to assist their children to learn to communicate. SKI*HI provides AO and TC home training, with hearing aid usage incorporated into both methodologies (Clark & Watkins, 1985).

A SKI*HI report on 545 very young children with hearing impairment showed that these youngsters averaged a 6-month language growth in 6 months time. With the advent of the early intervention programs, children with hearing impairment ordinarily are more advanced by the time they enter school. Many children who previously would have entered special schools for the deaf are enrolled directly into regular classes in home communities. Others enter special schools or classes for the deaf with greater communication skills than they would have had 20 years ago. There is concern, however, with the social adjustment of children with hearing impairment among children with normal hearing. Many deaf adults who sign indicate that mainstreaming has the potential of isolating deaf children from their peers and from the deaf community (Davis, 1985). Steps must be taken to encourage children who are hearing impaired to mingle freely with both the hearing community and the deaf or sign-language-speaking community.

AUDITORY LEARNING IN CLASSROOMS

Many often unrecognized problems exist within school classrooms that hinder listening. Steps need to be taken by teachers to make it easier for children and youths to learn auditorily in school. The development of listening skills should receive educational priority for at least two reasons. First, our ability to speak, read, write, and master complex cognitive skills is directly and indirectly based on our ability to listen (Lundstein, 1971). Second, throughout all levels of our educational development, listening is the main channel of communication and thus plays a significant role in our educational, personal, and professional lives (Peters & Austin, 1985). Listening includes hearing, attending to the speaker, and trying to understand what the speaker is saying (Wolvin & Coakley, 1988).

Children with hearing impairment need special stimulation and training in the development of listening skills. Listening, language, and speech training should begin as early as possible in life. A listening attitude needs to be trained because children who are hearing impaired naturally learn to rely on vision. Even with profound hearing loss, stress, intonation, voicing, the oral-nasal contrast, and back tongue, cues can be recognized through residual hearing. Surface cues from lips, teeth, mouth opening, and tongue tip can be identified through residual hearing or through supplemental speechreading.

Audition has another distinct advantage over vision. Hearing and vision are the lead senses of man and reach out like antennae to bring in the close and distant environment. The hearing antenna is more encompassing than the visual antenna, however, although both are indispensable for full environmental

contact. Hearing is multidirectional, like an infinitely wide-angle lens, allowing vast sound input. Because of the reflective, diffractive, and transmitting properties of sound, a child can track events from around corners and through walls. In contrast, the visual antenna is unidirectional and would require a "house of mirrors" to compensate for audition.

A hierarchy of listening and speech tasks must be learned before a child who is hearing impaired can be expected to succeed in regular school. These tasks include learning to discriminate, recognize, and comprehend speech, with the aid of amplification (Berg, 1987).

Once a child has been trained to listen in close situations, a need exists to enhance auditory learning in school classrooms. Two new technologies are especially needed to make the transition to classroom learning: (1) reduction of classroom noise and reverberation, and (2) use of sound field FM amplification.

REDUCTION OF CLASSROOM NOISE AND REVERBERATION

Reduction of classroom noise and reverberation is a direct approach at enhancing auditory learning in classrooms. School classrooms typically are noisy and reverberant. Discrepancies exist between minimally acceptable and actual signal-to-noise (S/N) ratios and reverberation times (RTs). Minimally acceptable S/N ratios and RTs are +12 dB and 0.4 seconds, respectively. Actual S/N ratios and RTs typically range from −5 to +5 dB and from 0.4 to 1.2 seconds, respectively. Open classrooms typically have noise levels of 70 to 75 dBA, which corresponds to S/N ratios of −10 to −15 dB. Many old classrooms have hard surfaces and RTs that exceed 1.2 seconds (Berg, 1987; Bess, 1984; Finitzo-Hieber, 1988; Nabelek & Nabelek, 1985).

The effects of current classroom acoustics are documented in Table 11–1, which presents speech discrimination scores of school-age children under several S/N ratios and RTs (Finitzo-Hieber & Tillman, 1978). Listening scores are compared at 0.4 and 1.2 second RTs and with S/N ratios of 0, +6, and +12 dB. The

TABLE 11-1. AVERAGE SPEECH DISCRIMINATION OF 12 NORMAL-HEARING AND 12 HARD-OF-HEARING STUDENTS UNDER RTs AND S/N RATIOS SIMULATING VARIOUS CLASSROOM CONDITIONS.

RT in Seconds	S/N Ratio in dB	Percent Words Repeated Correctly	
		Normal Hearing	Hard of Hearing
0.4	+12	83	60
	+6	71	52
	0	48	28
1.2	+12	70	41
	+6	54	27
	0	30	11

Source: Adapted from Finitzo, T. Classroom acoustics. In *Auditory disorders in school children, 2nd Edition* (p. 31). Roeser, R. J., & Downs, M. P. (Eds.), New York, 1988, Thieme Medical Publishers, Inc. Reprinted by permission.

students with normal hearing had mean speech discrimination scores of 95%, and the students with hearing loss had 83% when tested in an audiometric booth with a very low noise level and a very short RT.

The hard-of-hearing data in Table 11-1 are for students with bilateral hearing losses. It is likely that the speech discrimination scores of students with unilateral losses would fall somewhere between the scores of the normal hearing students and the students with bilateral hearing losses. Bess (1982) found that students with unilateral hearing losses experience listening difficulty in classrooms, even when given preferential seating (i.e., teacher facing normal ear of student).

Equipment for precise and automatic measurement of signal, noise, and reverberation needs to be used in the schools. Radio Shack sells a low-cost meter for measuring overall sound intensities from 50 to 126 dB. The Larson-Davis (LD) and Ivie companies produce acoustic and vibration measuring instruments with much greater measurement capabilities. The LD Model 800 system measures intensity levels from −10 to 140 dB, from 1 to 20,000 Hz. The LD Model 700 dosimeter with printer stores and graphs time-sampled measures of sound intensity. The Ivie PC-40 analyzer with RT 60 software and the IE-208 pink and white noise generator measures RT for up to 30 frequency bands simultaneously. With help from acoustical engineers, educational audiologists who work in the schools should be trained to use this new technology to identify sources of classroom noise and reverberation and set priorities for reducing them.

Classroom noise, which emanates from many sources outside and within a school building, can be reduced. The use of motorcycles, power mowers, and similar noisy equipment can be restricted during school hours. A dense wall barrier can be placed between a heavily traveled road and the school. Doors and windows to the outside can be closed. Machine noise within a school shop can be shielded near its source with foam or fiberglass absorbent materials. Pipe and duct support structures can be serviced to prevent structureborne conduction of vibration. The floor, ceiling, and walls of a classroom can be made of dense materials to keep outside noise out.

Classrooms can have solid core and noise lock doors and double-paned windows separated by a layer of air. The noise levels of heating and cooling systems, room fans, and projectors can be controlled. School personnel and children throughout the school, especially in hallways and classrooms, can be cautioned to be as quiet as possible (Berg, 1987; Finitzo-Hieber, 1988; Hirshorn, 1988; Nabelek & Nabelek, 1985).

Classroom reverberation also can be reduced by acoustical treatment of hard surfaces to prevent the speech of the teacher from smearing. Suspending acoustical tile from the ceiling and installing padded carpet will reduce the RT to a minimally acceptable level. Adding small fiberglass panels at various wall locations will reduce the RT to a highly desirable level (Berg, 1987; Finitzo-Hieber, 1988).

USING SOUND FIELD FM AMPLIFICATION

When either classroom noise or classroom reverberation cannot be reduced to minimally acceptable levels, the educational audiologist can use sound field amplification equipment. This enhances auditory learning in the classroom by alleviating the adverse effects of classroom noise and reverberation rather than reducing noise and reverberation. The teacher uses a wireless microphone and an FM radio transmitter. Sound from an audio or audiovisual device also can be entered into the system. Students listen to the teacher through loudspeakers electrically connected to an FM receiver and amplifier. The teacher can be in any location in the classroom, facing toward or away from students, and be heard better (+5 to +15 dB signal improvement) than without the system. This is perceived as "turning on the sound," which is similar to perception of turning on the light in the classroom.

The value of sound field FM equipment was originally investigated in a three-year longitudinal project called Mainstream Amplification Resource Room Study (MARRS) conducted in the Wabash and Ohio Valley schools of southern Illinois (Sarff et al., 1981). The MARRS research compared sound field FM with resource room placement in overcoming educational deficits of fourth-, fifth-, and sixth-grade students with mild hearing impairments. The findings revealed that both treatments resulted in significant improvements in academic achievement test scores. However, students who received amplification in a mainstreamed classroom achieved gains at a faster rate, to a higher level, and at one tenth the cost of students taken from regular classrooms and placed with resource room teachers. The success of sound field FM equipment in this study led to a national validation of MARRS and continuation of funding support from the U.S. Department of Education through its National Diffusion Network (Ray, 1989). The MARRS sound field FM equipment includes the Omni 2000 and 20001 systems marketed by the Audio Enhancement Company and located in at least 400 schools throughout the nation.

The value of sound field FM equipment has been investigated more recently in the Utah schools. Worner (1988) tested the effect of this type of system on signal level in classrooms of the Utah School for the Deaf. He found that the system provided signal levels in the range of 70 to 73 dBA throughout classrooms. To obtain baseline data without sound field FM amplification, Barton (1989) studied the sound levels of occupied classrooms in Utah schools. The overall mean dosimeter reading in 25 elementary school classrooms during a five-week period was 59 dBA. Jones, Berg, and Viehweg (1989) compared the effects of distance and sound field overhead speakers on the listening efficiency of kindergarten students. They concluded that sound field treatment was superior to close (4 feet) and distant (12 feet) listening treatments without equipment.

Bateman (1989) studied the effect of exposure to sound field FM amplification on teacher and student ratings of attention, understanding, ease of listening, ease of teaching, and preference for amplification in junior high classrooms as compared with no amplification. He also compared the effects to two equipment brands, Audio Enhancement and Realistic. Both teacher and students ratings revealed: (1) the equipment improved student attention and understanding and ease of listening and teaching, (2) amplfication was preferred, and (3) equipment brand was not a factor.

Blair, Myrup, and Viehweg (1989) compared sound field FM amplification with personal FM amplification and with personal hearing aids alone. The subjects were children with mild and moderate bilateral hearing losses (50 dB average). They were seated an average of 8.5 feet from the signal source in a classroom with desirable acoustics. Their speech recognition percentages under the three treatments were 82 for sound field plus hearing aid, 87 for personal FM plus hearing aid, and 70 for hearing aid alone.

The value of sound field FM should be compared with other treatments in the broad context of the commercial market and school applications. In 1989, Claudia Anderson, National Sales Manager of Audio Enhancement, stated that sound field FM is the fastest growing segment of the FM market. Karen Anderson (1989), an educational audiologist employed by the Tacoma schools, lists multiple benefits when sound field FM is utilized:

1. The system costs slightly more than a personal FM system but it can be utilized by all of the hard of hearing students, minimal hearing loss students, and other children in the classroom, including those with listening difficulties in noise, attentional problems, and behavior problems.
2. The presence of classroom amplification is beneficial to the child with the unidentified fluctuating hearing loss, the child being managed medically who has yet to return to normal hearing, and the child with a chronic conductive hearing loss. These children may not qualify for special help, but nonetheless are having educationally significant hearing problems.
3. There is a very low malfunction rate compared to other auditory equipment. Sound field amplification equipment is not subject to student sabotage and is resistant to breakage by the teacher. This results in low maintenance costs and long equipment life.
4. The presence of a sound field amplification

system in a classroom does not necessarily stigmatize the student who is hearing impaired. Stigmatization is avoided because the amplification is beneficial to all students in the classroom and all the children who use it.
5. Because the student who is hard of hearing does not wear this amplification system, it is unlikely to be rejected for cosmetic reasons, resulting in longer use and benefit. Also, if the student's personal hearing aids are malfunctioning or absent, he or she still will receive benefit until the aids can be returned or loaner aids supplied.
6. This amplification system can be used in conjunction with a personal FM set on FM + HA, enhancing the student's ability to hear his class peers as well as a radio transmitted signal from the teacher.
7. Completed surveys indicate an 85 to 90% acceptance rate by teachers. Most teachers find that the use of classroom amplification is beneficial to their students and makes the act of teaching less of a vocal and emotional strain for them. This acceptance translates into careful and consistent use of the equipment, which is sometimes a problem when personal FM systems are used.
8. The students with normal hearing also enjoy the benefits of having classroom amplification and using the transmitter for oral reports, oral reading, and when answering questions. The child with a hearing impairment is not then set apart as the only student who uses the equipment, which helps peer acceptance.

TARGET CLASSROOMS

Gilman and Danzer (1989), an educational audiologist and a speech-language pathologist who work together in the Portland, Oregon, schools, recommend sound field FM amplification for most classrooms, including those: (1) with unusual physical configurations, (2) that are large, (3) in older two-story buildings, (4) with large class sizes, (5) in school buildings near high-noise areas, (6) that are highly reverberant, (7) in school buildings with noisy heating systems, (8) in preschools or the primary grades due to high incidence of otitis media in young children, (9) taught by teachers with voice disorders, (10) with children having language/learning problems, (11) with children identified as auditorily learning disabled, and (12) with children identified as having chronic hearing loss, unusual and/or difficult-to-fit sensorineural hearing loss, or unilateral hearing loss.

This chapter's author is currently engaged in a series of studies with sound field amplification. He notes that this technology helps teachers, students with normal hearing, and students with varying degrees of hearing impairment. This help is realized in regular classrooms in which mainstreamed children are enrolled and in special classrooms for the hearing impaired alone. Sound field FM equipment does not require that a hearing aid have a telecoil or that the child use personal FM equipment.

Johnson-Lawrence (personal communication, November 2, 1989) recently reported that the Charles County School System in southern Maryland was experiencing four problems with personal FM equipment: (1) high malfunction rate from student abuse, (2) unwillingness of children to use personal FM when they reach middle school or junior high school, (3) inability of personal FM to be used by children with fluctuating hearing loss and central auditory processing problems, and (4) the high cost of trying to use personal FM with all children with mild hearing loss.

However, one should use caution in trying to use sound field FM in extremely noisy classrooms. Sarff, Ray, and Bagwell (1981) recommended keeping sound levels no higher than 75 dBA with the equipment and reducing noise and reverberation prior to equipment installation. One should also realize that sound field FM does not provide as high a S/N ratio as personal FM equipment.

SUMMARY

There are formidable educational problems faced by students with hearing impairment. Many of these problems are largely unrecognized or misunderstood. There are a great many students with hearing impairment who currently are not being served. The services provided to children with hearing impairment who are being served need to be re-evaluated in light of recent programmatic and technological breakthroughs.

REFERENCES

Amon, C. (1988). Remediation within and beyond state and federal guidelines. In R. Roeser & M. Downs (Eds.), *Auditory disorders in school children* (pp. 141–155). New York: Thieme Medical.

Anderson, K. (1989). Speech perception and the hard-of-hearing child. *Monographs of the Educational Audiology Association, 1*(1), 15–29.

Barton, L. (1989). *Sound levels in occupied elementary classrooms.* Unpublished master's thesis, Utah State University, Logan.

Bateman, R. (1989). *Listening and teaching with wireless classroom amplification in junior high school.* Unpublished educational specialist thesis, Utah State University, Logan.

Bebout, J. M. (1985). Audiology in public education. *The Hearing Journal, 38*(5), 7–12.

Berg, F. (1986a). Characteristics of the target population. In F. Berg, J. Blair, S. Viehweg, & A. Wilson-Vlotman (Eds.), *Educational audiology for the hard of hearing child* (pp. 1–24). Orlando, FL: Grune & Stratton.

Berg, F. (1986b). Listening and speech skills. In F. Berg, J. Blair, S. Viehweg, & A. Wilson-Vlotman (Eds.), *Educational audiology for the hard of hearing child* (pp. 131–156). Orlando, FL: Grune & Stratton.

Berg, F. (1987). *Facilitating classroom listening.* Boston: Little, Brown.

Bess, F. (1982). Children with unilateral hearing loss. *Journal of the Academy of Rehabilitative Audiology, 15,* 131–144.

Bess, F. (1984). *The hard of hearing child.* Logan: Institute for Management of the Communicatively Handicapped, Utah State University.

Blair, J., Myrup, C., & Viehweg, S. (1989). Comparison of listening effectiveness of hard-of-hearing children using three types of amplification. *Monograph of the Educational Audiology Association, 1*(1), 48–55.

Boney, S., & Bess, F. (1989). Noise and reverberation effects on children with minimal bilateral sensorineural hearing loss. *Educational Audiology Association Newsletter, 6*(4), 11. [Available from F. Berg, Department of Communicative Disorders, Utah State University, Logan, UT 84322-1000.]

Calvert, D. (1985). Speech in perspective. In D. Luterman (Ed.), *Deafness in perspective* (pp. 167–191). San Diego, CA: College-Hill Press.

Clark, T., & Watkins, S. (1985). *Programming for hearing impaired infants through amplification and home intervention.*Logan, UT: SKI*HI Institute.

Connor, L. (1985). Oralism in perspective. In D. Luterman (Ed.), *Deafness in perspective* (pp. 117–129). San Diego, CA: College-Hill Press.

Davis, J. (1985). Academic placement in perspective. In D. Luterman (Ed.), *Deafness in perspective* (pp. 205–224). San Diego, CA: College-Hill Press.

DiCarlo, L. (1964). *The deaf.* Englewood Cliffs, NJ: Prentice-Hall.

Downs, R. (1988). Contribution of mild hearing loss to auditory language learning problems. In R. Roeser & M. Downs (Eds.), *Auditory disorders in school children* (pp. 186–199). New York: Thieme-Stratton.

Education of the Deaf. (1965). *A report to the Secretary of Health, Education, and Welfare by his Advisory Committee on Education of the Deaf.* Washington, DC: U.S. Government Printing Office.

Finitzo-Hieber, T. (1988). Classroom acoustics. In R. Roeser & M. Downs (Eds.), *Auditory disorders in school children* (pp. 221–233). New York: Thieme-Stratton.

Finitzo-Hieber, T., & Tillman, T. (1978). Room acoustics effects on monosyllabic word recognition. *Journal of Speech and Hearing Research, 21,* 440–458.

Furth, H. (1966). A comparison of reading test norms of deaf and hearing children. *American Annals of the Deaf, 111,* 461–462.

Gallaudet Research Institute Newsletter. (1985, May). Washington, DC: Gallaudet College.

Gannon, J. (1981). *Deaf heritage: A narrative history of deaf America.* Silver Spring, MD: National Association of the Deaf.

Geers, A. (1985). Assessment of hearing impaired children: Determining typical and optimal levels of performance. In F. Powell, T. Finitzo-Hieber, S. Friel-Patti, & D. Henderson (Eds.), *Education of the hearing-impaired child* (pp. 57–82). San Diego, CA: College-Hill Press.

Geers, A., Moog, J., & Schick, B. (1984). Acquisition of spoken and signed English by profoundly deaf children. *Journal of Speech and Hearing Disorders, 4,* 378–388.

Gilman, L., & Danzer, V. (1989, November). *Use of FM sound field amplification in regular schools.* Poster session presented at the National Convention of the American Speech-Language-Hearing Association, St. Louis, MO.

Hirshorn, M. (1988). *Noise control reference handbook.* Bronx, NY: Industrial Acoustics Company.

Jones, J., Berg, F., & Viehweg, S. (1989). Close, distant, and sound field overhead listening in kindergarten classrooms. *Monograph of the Educational Audiology Association, 1*(1), 56–65.

Kipila, E., & Williams, Scott, B. (1988). Cued speech and speechreading. [Special issue on new reflections in speechreading]. *Volta Review, 90*(5), 179–189.

Ling, D. (1972). Panel presentation on audition, speech, and methodology. *Volta Review, 74*(9), 554.

Ling, D. (1976). *Speech and the hearing-impaired child: Theory and practice.* Washington, DC: Alexander Graham Bell Association for the Deaf.

Lundstein, S. (1971). *Listening: Its impact on reading and other language arts.* Urbana, IL: National Council of Teachers of English, Educational Resources Information Center.

Luterman, D. (1985). Editor's introduction. In D. Luterman (Ed.), *Deafness in perspective.* San Diego, CA: College-Hill Press.

Nabelek, A., & Nabelek, I. (1978). Principles of noise control. In D. Lipscomb (Ed.), *Noise in audiology* (pp. 59–79). Baltimore, MD: University Park Press.

Nabelek, A., & Nabelek, I. (1985). Room acoustics and speech perception. In J. Katz (Ed.), *Handbook of clinical audiology* (pp. 834–846). Baltimore, MD: Williams & Wilkins.

Nicholls, G., & Ling, D. (1982). Cued speech and the reception of spoken language. *Journal of Speech and Hearing Research, 25*(2), 262–269.

Peters, T., & Austin, N. (1985). *A passion for excellence.* New York: Warner.

Quigley, S., & Paul, P. (1985). A perspective on academic achievement. In D. Luterman (Ed.), *Deafness in perspective* (pp. 55–86). San Diego, CA: College-Hill Press.

Ray, H. (1989). (Mainstream amplification resource room study). Unpublished brochure. Wabash and Ohio Valley Special Education District, Norris City, IL.

Richardson, M., & Donaldson, J. (1981). Middle ear fluid. *American Family Physician, 23,* 159–163.

Ross, M. (1985). A perspective on amplification: Then and now. In D. Luterman (Ed.), *Deafness in perspective* (pp. 35–54). San Diego, CA: College-Hill Press.

Ross, M., & Calvert, D. (1984). Semantics of deafness revisited: Total communication and the use and misuse of residual hearing. *Audiology, 4*(9), 96–120.

Sarff, L., Ray, H., & Bagwell, C. (1981). Why not amplification in every classroom? *Hearing Aid Journal, 34*(10), 11, 44, 47–48, 50, 52.

"Total Communication" Definition Committee Report. (1976). *Proceedings of the Conference of Executives of American Schools for the Deaf.* Rochester, NY: Author.

U.S. Department of Education. (1988). *Tenth annual report to Congress on the implementation of P.L. 94-142.* Washington, DC: Author.

Worner, W. (1988). An inexpensive group FM amplification system for the classrooms. *Volta Review, 90*(1), 29–39.

Wolvin, A., & Coakley, C. (1988). *Listening.* Dubuque, IA: William C. Brown.

■ PART II ■

Audiologic Habilitation: The Adult Who Is Deaf or Hard of Hearing

The Impact of Hearing Impairment and Counseling Adults Who Are Deaf or Hard of Hearing

■ HARRIET F. KAPLAN, PH.D. ■

The sense of hearing is integrally related to communication and interaction among people; to a great extent we relate to others through verbal language. For the vast majority of people who are deaf or hard of hearing, when the sense of hearing is impaired, the ability to relate may be impaired as well. Messages may not be interpreted properly because crucial words are missed or because nuances of meaning conveyed by a rising inflection, a pause, or an emphasis in a particular part of an utterance are not caught. Faulty hearing often leads to misunderstanding and inappropriate behavior. Helping the individual deal with these problems must be considered an integral part of the total process of aural rehabilitation.

The relatively small group of individuals who consider themselves culturally deaf represent a notable exception. Adults who are culturally deaf are those individuals who have chosen to use sign language as their primary means of communication and to associate primarily with others who do likewise. They identify with and obtain most of their social experiences and cultural exchange in the deaf community. Such individuals find sign language to be a complete, unambiguous communication system and find a vast array of social and cultural support systems in the signing deaf community (Kannapell & Adams, 1984).

The type of psychological problem and the degree to which it exists varies with the individual's life style, personality, and the characteristics of the hearing loss. Although there are inevitably individual differences among persons who are hard of hearing and deaf, similar adjustment problems are frequently observed.

EMOTIONAL REACTIONS TO HEARING LOSS

DEPRESSION AND FEELINGS OF INADEQUACY

People who are nonculturally deaf and hard of hearing often feel shut off from the world, not only because of difficult communication with others, but also because some or all of the subliminal auditory clues which permit one to maintain contact with the "hearing world" are no longer available. They may react to this depression by withdrawing from social situations and from contact with other people. They may even modify vocational aspirations. An example of this type of behavior is the case of the man who, as a result of a gradually worsening hearing loss, requested a transfer to a lower status, lower income position requiring minimal communication, even though such a change was clearly not what he desired.

Depression is frequently complicated by feelings of inadequacy. The person who is deaf or hard of hearing may feel that he or she should be able to cope better with the hearing loss, and that the inability to do so indicates weakness. In addition, there may be feelings of shame because of the rationalization that hearing difficulty is associated with abnormalities such as thinking, learning, remembering, or decision-making disabilities. Such people apologize for not understanding and assume that the "fault" for communication breakdown is always theirs. This is typified by the gentleman who is hard of hearing who took a trip to an area where people spoke a dialect unfamiliar to him. He automatically assumed that his communication problems were his "fault," although he acknowledged that normal hearing people were experiencing the same differences.

Depression and feelings of inadequacy tend to be lesser problems for adults who are culturally deaf, because of the many support systems within the deaf community. Many individuals who are culturally deaf, however, desire to function within the hearing community as well. Their communication problems are related to their attempts to become bilingual, bicultural people.

DEFENSE MECHANISMS

Denial

In most cases, the threat to self-esteem is handled by one or more defense mechanisms. A common defense mechanism is denial. People with mild to moderate hearing losses may simply not acknowledge the existence of a hearing loss, because to them acceptance implies abnormality. Those same individuals would probably have no difficulty accepting the reality of a visual problem, because visual problems usually are not associated with the general adequacy of the person. Denial increases the problem because it makes it more difficult to seek help or accept the need for a hearing aid, because the visibility of the hearing aid would make the hearing impairment apparent to others. Undoubtedly, we all know people who are hard of hearing who insist that their communication problems would disappear if only people would speak plainly.

Hostility and Suspicion

Persons who are hard of hearing may blame others for their difficulties, accusing them of mumbling or of deliberately excluding them from the conversation. They may become suspicious, accusing others of saying unpleasant things or planning unpleasant situations. Laughter may be misinterpreted as ridicule. People who are culturally deaf may react in that manner to people who communicate with each other in their presence, without using sign language. Suspicion or hostility is frequently directed at those who are closest such as spouses, children, or friends, further complicating adjustment. Persons who are deaf or hard of hearing may react negatively to service providers such as the doctor, the audiologist, or the hearing aid dispenser. It is very important for the helping professional to realize the true source of this unpleasant behavior and remain objective about it. It is equally important for any professional working with individuals who are culturally deaf to use sign language for communication with those clients or in their presence.

PSYCHOLOGICAL LEVELS OF HEARING

Ramsdell (1978) has described three psychological levels of hearing for the normal hearing person and the problems that exist with loss of hearing at each level.

PRIMITIVE LEVEL

At the primitive level, sound functions as auditory coupling to the world. People react to the changing background sounds of the world around them without being aware of it. As Ramsdell states:

At this level, we react to such sounds as the tick of a clock, the distant roar of traffic, vague echoes of people moving in other rooms of the house, without being aware that we are hearing them. These incidental noises maintain our feeling of being part of a living world and contribute to our own sense of being alive. (p. 501)

When this primitive function is lost, acute depression may occur. Since the primitive level of hearing is not on a conscious level, the person who is deaf may not be aware of the cause of the depression. Frequently, the depression is attributed to inadequacy in coping with the hearing impairment.

The severity of the depression will be greatest among persons who experience a sudden hearing loss, whether it is through trauma, surgery such as acoustic tumor removal, or other causes. Fortunately, hearing loss of sudden onset most frequently affects one ear only, although bilateral losses do occur.

Depression due to the loss of the primitive level will occur in the individual with slowly deteriorating hearing as well. It is more insidious, occurring more slowly, but the resulting depression may be equally great. In some instances, the depression may be more severe because the person may not be aware that hearing is deteriorating. Informing the client of the true cause of the depression will help alleviate some of the problem, although this knowledge will not eliminate it entirely. Often, properly fitted amplification can restore the primitive level, even if speech understanding is not possible. In some cases where amplification is not possible, such as with eighth nerve destruction, a vibrotactile device may serve to couple the individual who is deaf to the world of sound.

The loss of the primitive level is a problem primarily with severe to profound adventitious losses. Most adults who are culturally deaf have never experienced the world of sound and, therefore, are not aware of the absence of subliminal auditory cues.

WARNING OR SIGNAL LEVEL OF HEARING

At the warning level, sounds convey information about objects or events. The doorbell indicates the presence of a visitor. Footsteps indicate that someone is approaching. A siren indicates the presence of an emergency vehicle. A fire alarm indicates danger. Since warning sounds frequently are intense, loss of the warning level is generally found among persons who possess severe to profound losses. Some warning sounds, however, are of low intensity, and may be missed by persons with less severe hearing losses. These are mainly distant sounds, such as the whistle of an approaching train.

Insecurity

When there is an inability to hear warning sounds such as a smoke alarm, a door knock, or a child in another room, it is understandable that feelings of insecurity exist. Such problems are found within all segments of the deaf and severely hard-of-hearing population, including people who are culturally deaf. An array of electronic visual systems has been developed to deal with warning level problems. These systems can monitor the doorbell, a person in another room, the smoke alarm, and any other important sound within the home or office. More complete discussions of alerting device systems can be found in Compton (1989); Di-Pietro, Williams, and Kaplan (1984); Kaplan (1987); and Chapter 14 of this textbook.

Annoyance

Feelings of annoyance are caused by disruption of normal patterns of life due to loss of hearing at the warning level. The person who is deaf or hard of hearing who cannot hear the alarm clock may oversleep in the morning and suffer penalties at work as a result. When the ring of the telephone can no longer be heard, social activities may be affected or business opportunities lost. Visual alerting systems can be useful in overcoming these problems.

Localization

Localization problems may be considered a special type of warning level difficulty. To predict direction of sound, individuals need approximately equal sensitivity in both ears; therefore, the inability to localize sound is a special problem for persons with unilateral losses. What clinicians do not always realize, however, is that localization problems also exist for individuals who are bilaterally hearing impaired who are aided monaurally.

In addition to alerting device technology, warning level difficulties can be dealt with by training the person who is hard of hearing or deaf to become more visually aware of the environment.

Loss of Aesthetic Experience

For some individuals, music provides aesthetic experience. For some people, the inability to

hear the sounds of nature, such as bird calls, may represent significant aesthetic loss. However, amplification cannot always restore these sounds to the extent that aesthetic experiences are restored.

SYMBOLIC LEVEL OF HEARING

At the symbolic level we are dealing with sound as language and a major channel of communication. Nearly all people who are deaf or hard of hearing have difficulty at this level to one degree or another. Many children and adults who incur deafness early in childhood experience delayed language development, which later affects reading and other academic skills. Although adults who are culturally deaf tend to communicate comfortably in sign language and consider English a second language, they may have difficulties with the vocabulary and structure of English. Language deficits create a variety of communication problems for anyone who needs to function in the mainstream community.

Although adults who are hard of hearing or deafened generally do not suffer delayed language development, they do face the problem of communicating under conditions of reduced verbal redundancy imposed by impaired auditory reception. Depending on degree, type, and configuration of loss, such individuals lose linguistic cues inherent in the sentence, prosodic cues such as stress and inflection, and phonemic information. The fewer auditory cues that are available, the more likely the person is to misinterpret what is heard, with consequent embarrassment, frustration, and social penalty. This situation is worsened if the communication environment contains background noise, competing speech, or other auditory or visual distractions.

At Home

The home can be a source of tension because of communication difficulties for a number of reasons. First, there is more opportunity for interpersonal communication and consequently more opportunity for communication breakdowns. Second, the person who is hard of hearing or deaf expects the family to be more understanding of the special problems imposed by hearing loss than nonrelatives, and he or she experiences disappointment if that is not the case. Third, households tend to be noisy places. The noise level in a typical kitchen was measured at 100 dB SPL with water running at moderate speed, the refrigerator on, and the radio turned to a comfortable listening level.

Typical is the problem of a client who complained that he could use his hearing aid comfortably everywhere but at home, because his family showed no consideration for his needs. His children slammed doors when entering the house and played rock music at high intensity levels. At the dinner table everyone talked at once, making it impossible for him to sort out one conversation from another. Worst of all, his wife insisted on talking to him from another room, raising the level of her voice when asked to repeat, but not coming into his line of sight. His solution to these problems was, first, to not use his hearing aid at home, and second, to minimize communication with his family. Several conferences with the entire family, which included discussions of the limitations imposed by hearing loss, improved the situation for the client. Unfortunately, not all families are equally adaptable. When conflicts already exist in a family, the presence of a hearing loss can accentuate them. The hearing impairment can be used as a weapon by either the person who is hard of hearing or other family members. A supportive family is important to an individual who is deaf or hard of hearing; at the same time, the person with the hearing loss must be willing to assume part of the responsibility for successful communication.

An individual who is culturally deaf will not have communication difficulties with the family if the family is willing to use sign language as the primary mode of communication. However, many adults who are culturally deaf have grown up in hearing families. Unless the person who is deaf can communicate orally with the family or the family can sign to the person who is deaf, limited communication occurs in the home, and the stresses are great.

At Work

Work-related problems are common. The extent and nature of the difficulty depends on the nature of the hearing loss itself and the type of job the person holds. The greater the amount of oral communication required and the greater the need for precision of understanding, the more difficulty the client is likely to experience. The receptionist who has difficulty understanding speech on the telephone may be in danger of losing the job. The physician who finds it difficult to monitor a patient's heartbeat may find it increasingly difficult to function professionally. Large or small group meetings pose special problems because of the need to follow rapidly changing conversation, often against background noise or reverberation. If not dealt with, anxiety and frustration created by these demands complicate communication problems caused by the hearing loss itself. The vast majority of individuals who are culturally deaf work in environments where the communication system is spoken English. To function successfully, they must develop strategies to communicate comfortably with hearing people or constantly use an interpreter. If communication is limited, the person who is deaf may experience loneliness at work and may face limited opportunities for advancement. The vocational impact of hearing impairment and the role of the vocational counselor is discussed in depth in Chapter 4 of this textbook.

The Telephone

A special problem at the symbolic level is inability to use the telephone. The telephone message has become an integral part of our lives, affecting communication at home, work, school, and in social environments. The person who cannot understand speech transmitted by telephone, or who cannot hear the telephone ring, is affected in every aspect of life. Social contacts are reduced because friends and family cannot be easily contacted. Vocational opportunities are limited to the minority of jobs not requiring telephone use. The inability to use the telephone to summon help is threatening, particularly for the individual who lives alone.

Many people who are deaf or hard of hearing can learn to use the telephone more effectively by developing appropriate telephone strategies. Telecommunication devices for the deaf (TDDs) are viable options for those who cannot use the voice telephone; proper use of TDDs, however, requires telephone strategies and ability to write understandable messages. Telephone training is discussed in depth by Castle (1980) and Erber (1985). Fax machines are also viable options for telephone communication for the hearing impaired, if the recipient of the message also has access to a machine. They provide a convenient means for communication at a reasonable cost.

At School

The adult or adolescent in school often has special problems. Classrooms are rarely quiet places. Ross (1982) reported that the average noise level in 45 classrooms was 60 dBA; an optimal level for students who are hard of hearing is 35 dBA. At noise levels of 60 dBA or greater, it is often difficult for a normal hearing individual to correctly understand a teacher; the task is immeasurably more difficult for a student who is hearing impaired who must function with an auditory system that distorts the incoming speech signal, even under favorable conditions.

Not only are many classrooms noisy, but they tend to be reverberant as well because of large areas of rigid, smooth surface and few absorbent materials, such as drapes or carpets. Such room conditions further distort speech and add to the burden of the student who is hard of hearing who is trying to function with amplification. These conditions interfere with the efficient use of a hearing aid which amplifies noise, speech, and distortion caused by reverberation with equal effectiveness.

Teachers are not always aware of the special needs of the student who is deaf or hard of hearing, and they do not always project their voices adequately. Occasionally, teachers will speak with their backs to the class while writing at the blackboard, thus distorting and reducing the intensity of their voices. Speechreading becomes impossible. A barrier to both speechreading and sign language reception in class is the need to take notes; one cannot concentrate on interpreting visual information and write at the same time. All of these problems tend to limit educational opportunities for adults who are hard of hearing or deaf, with consequent vocational limitations. Assistive listening systems to minimize effects of noise and reverberation, notetakers, interpreters, and greater awareness by teachers of the needs of students who are deaf or hard of hearing are needed.

At Social Activities

For many adults, sudden or increasing hearing loss results in a restriction of social activities. The difficulty in understanding speech exposes individuals who are deaf or hard of hearing to the danger and embarrassment of misinterpreting what is said. As a result, they may react inappropriately and be exposed to ridicule. It is a rare person who possesses enough ego strength to continually explain the presence of a hearing loss and continually ask people to repeat what has been said. Even well-meaning friends do not always succeed in making the person who is deaf or hard of hearing feel comfortable. Normal hearing people feel uncomfortable themselves when they know a listener is not understanding what is being said. Often they are at a loss to know how to help the listener understand better, particularly when the person who is deaf or hard of hearing attempts to "bluff" and does it badly. Both partners in the conversation may attempt to deny the existence of the hearing loss, but communication is disrupted, and speaker and listener are embarrassed.

When the hearing loss is severe or has been present for a long time, speech may deteriorate. In that case the person who is deaf or hard of hearing may not be understood clearly, adding to the possible social penalties imposed by the hearing impairment.

Conversational difficulties increase exponentially in difficult listening situations. Following a conversation alternating between members of a group can be a very difficult experience, particularly when background noise is present. A dinner party can be extremely anxiety-provoking and a cocktail party impossible.

Social activities are further limited when a person who is deaf or hard of hearing can no longer enjoy the theater or lectures. Just as in face-to-face conversation, the person must cope with speakers or actors who may not project adequately, speech that shifts rapidly from one person to another, poor room acoustics, as well as the loss of sensitivity and distortion imposed by the hearing loss.

More and more, as social activities become restricted, the person who is hearing impaired experiences isolation and loneliness. Ultimately, this condition may be accepted with resignation, or it may be met with aggression. The individual may deny the reality of the problem and attribute a shrinking social life to the malice of others. Regardless of whether the problem is met with resignation or aggression, the person who is deaf or hard of hearing suffers deterioration in the quality of his or her life style.

Individuals who are culturally deaf do not suffer social penalties because of hearing loss so long as their social contacts remain within the deaf community. For many, that is a satisfying and healthy choice. However, people who wish to socialize outside of the deaf culture encounter the same barriers as individuals who are hard of hearing or nonculturally deaf. Generally, successful crosscultural friendships occur when the hearing person can sign comfortably, and both parties are good communicators.

Other Problems at the Symbolic Level

Every person who is deaf or hard of hearing has, at one time or another, experienced difficulties in obtaining services. This may involve mailing a package at the post office, purchasing an airline ticket, placing an order at a restaurant, or communicating effectively with a physician. Persons who are deaf or hard of hearing are at a definite disadvantage when dealing with the law. In recognition of this fact, a legal center for the deaf has been established at Gallaudet University. Most hospitals do not make special provisions for communicating with patients who are deaf or hard of hearing, nor are personnel aware of their communication problems. Often, hearing aids are removed for safekeeping, effectively destroying any possible communication.

Another problem at the symbolic level involves the ability to hear and understand television. Many persons who are hard of hearing increase the volume beyond the tolerance level of hearing family members and neighbors, thereby creating a great deal of tension. Many people who are deaf cannot understand the TV signal, regardless of its intensity. The inability to enjoy television is not only a social loss, but eliminates an important source of information. Assistive device technology can make television accessible to everyone at reasonable intensity levels. In addition, many persons who are deaf and hard of hearing find the use of a closed caption decoder very useful.

FACILITATING ADJUSTMENT

The professional faces a twofold task in helping the person who is deaf or hard of hearing adjust to the problems imposed by hearing impairment. First, through educational and personal adjustment counseling (Sanders, 1988), clients must be helped to accept themselves as people who are deaf or hard of hearing and understand the limitations imposed by the hearing problem. Once this is achieved, clients can be helped to manipulate the environment in such a way that penalties are minimized. Environmental manipulation may involve use of listening aids, modification of communication situations, and education of family, friends, and associates.

DEFINITION OF THE PROBLEM

To provide meaningful assistance to the client who is hard of hearing or deaf, it is necessary to obtain information on the specific communicative difficulties encountered in daily activities. Not only is it important to identify specific difficult listening situations, but also to assess coping strategies and attitudes of the client toward communication and toward him- or herself as a person who is deaf or hard of hearing.

COUNSELING

After the specific communicative and attitudinal problems of the client have been defined, a specific aural rehabilitation program needs to be developed to meet their needs. In addition to speechreading, auditory training, and other skill development activities, personal adjustment and informational counseling must be included in the program, as needed.

PERSONAL ADJUSTMENT COUNSELING

Although personal adjustment and informational counseling are artificially separated here for purposes of discussion, they are intertwined in the actual rehabilitative program. The personal adjustment counselor functions as a facilitator to help clients modify maladaptive attitudes about themselves as persons who are deaf or hard of hearing. Kodman (1967) discusses three facilitative conditions that must be present if the therapist is to be successful.

The first condition is referred to as **accurate empathy.** This refers to the understanding by the therapist of the true feelings that underlie statements the client might make. The therapist then responds in such a way that the client's feelings are reflected back, so that his or her difficulties can be viewed objectively. For example, a client might say, "Most people don't speak plainly these days. I'd rather read a book than talk to people." The empathetic clinician might reply, "it must be terribly frustrating not to understand people. Let's talk about some of your experiences." As the client begins to relate his or her difficult listening experiences, the therapist can continue reflecting back the

client's feelings and perhaps, in the process, lead the client to suggest ways of coping with these situations. This is a nondirective approach. The client makes decisions based on increased perception of the situation; decisions are not imposed on the client. The condition of accurate empathy is as important in a group situation as in an individual session. In the group situation, the therapist must reflect the feelings of each member as they are expressed. After a group becomes a cohesive unit, the members may begin to practice accurate empathy toward each other, providing strong reinforcement for attitudinal change.

The second condition is referred to as **unconditional positive regard.** This involves acceptance of clients as they are, regardless of any hostility, belligerance, or apparent lack of cooperation. It is sometimes difficult for the novice clinician to accept expressions of negativism from a client and not to consider this behavior a personal attack. However, it is important to realize that unpleasant actions or expressions are simply manifestations of the client's problems. Typical of this type of behavior is the woman who joined an aural rehabilitation program with the stipulation that under no conditions would she allow herself to receive a hearing test. Her terms were accepted, despite the fact that hearing testing was an integral part of the program. After a semester of group therapy, she apologized for her attitudes, explaining that she had been convinced that the hearing test was part of an attempt to sell hearing aids. She became one of the most hardworking and motivated members of the group, despite other expressions of hostility every now and then.

A third facilitative condition is **genuineness.** This condition implies a relaxed, friendly attitude toward the client, respect for the client's suggestions, ability to accept criticism, and communication with the client in a manner he or she can understand easily. A genuine clinician does not retreat into professional jargon or assume a pose of superiority because of professional stature. An example of a low level of genuineness is the following:

Client: I don't think this hearing aid will do me a bit of good.

Clinician: You're not correct. The tests show a definite improvement with the hearing aid.

A more genuine type of response might be: "Maybe you're right. Why don't you try the aid at home for a few weeks and if it doesn't help, you can return it and get your money back. Let's talk again in a week."

These facilitative conditions are especially important when working with clients who are culturally deaf. Their language and culture must be understood and respected. American Sign Language (ASL) is not English; idioms and other figurative language are different. ASL tends to be a more direct language with different pragmatic conventions and far fewer euphemisms than English; expression of ideas tends to be more direct. What may appear to be rudeness may simply reflect differences in the languages. To work effectively with a person who is culturally deaf, it is important for the clinician to have a working knowledge of the client's language and be willing to use it. Even if the clinician is not fluent in ASL, he or she should make every effort to maximize communication with the client. Most people who are culturally deaf will meet hearing clinicians halfway communicatively, if convinced of the genuineness of the relationship.

Clients who are culturally deaf sometimes make decisions from a different cultural base than clients who are nonculturally deaf or hard of hearing. Some have no desire to mainstream into majority culture; these people come to therapy with a desire to develop greater communicative independence in those situations where it is advantageous to communicate using English speech or writing. The aural rehabilitation specialist must respect such decisions and work with clients on their own terms.

The qualities of accurate empathy, unconditional positive regard, and genuineness can be developed or enhanced through experience. Taping sessions — with the permission of the client — and reviewing the client-clinician interchange later is an excellent way for the novice clinician to improve skills.

One of the most important goals of personal adjustment counseling is to help the client accept the reality of the hearing loss and the need for help. One must not assume that because the client has come to the clinic for evaluation, acceptance of amplification or therapy is a given. The client may simply be appeasing family or friends, or perhaps be taking the first tenuous steps toward seeking help while remaining very ambivalent about self-acceptance as a person who is hard of hearing. If a hearing aid is warranted, it should be recommended. If the client is not ready to accept it, however, the issue should not be forced. It is far better to persuade the individual to enroll in an aural rehabilitation program that includes discussion-counseling to help with acceptance of the reality of the hearing problem. If necessary, the group discussions can be supplemented with individual counseling. It must be made clear that participation in aural rehabilitation is not contingent on hearing aid use. It must be emphasized that the audiologist is ready to assist with selection of a hearing aid, if and when the client becomes ready.

EDUCATIONAL OR INFORMATIONAL COUNSELING

An extremely important part of informational counseling is identification of difficult communication situations and development of coping strategies that work. The group format is especially effective for identification of and practice with communication strategies, but such training can be incorporated into individual sessions, if necessary.

Assertiveness training can be incorporated easily into aural rehabilitation sessions. It is important for clients who are deaf or hard of hearing to understand that they have a right to understand, that it is acceptable to ask for help in a polite and courteous fashion, and that it is the responsibility of the person who is hearing impaired to instruct the communication partner in ways of helping. Clients need to learn to distinguish between the following kinds of behavior: *aggressive*, which involves violation of other people's rights; *passive*, which involves allowing others to violate their rights; and *assertive*, in which clients protect their rights without violating those of other people.

The aural rehabilitation specialist might pose the following problem: "Suppose you meet two friends on a noisy street who are having a conversation. They greet you and try to include you in their conversation, but you are unable to follow what they are saying. What might you do?" The therapist would then try to elicit some of the following examples of assertive behavior.

1. Ask the people to move away from the source of the noise so that you can understand better.
2. Ask one of the two people to summarize briefly what has been said before you entered the conversation.
3. Admit that you do not understand and ask for repetition or rephrasing of the idea.
4. Ask the people to speak louder.

The clients would then be asked to give examples of aggressive behavior, such as verbal or physical abuse of the speakers, and of passive behavior, such as saying nothing about the lack of understanding.

Role playing can be incorporated into assertiveness training sessions to help clients define appropriate behaviors. Homework assignments involving the use of these behaviors in actual life situations can follow the role playing and be followed up by discussions during subsequent classes.

Once clients are able to function in an assertive fashion, they are ready to learn the many behaviors that facilitate communication. There are two broad categories of communication strategies:

1. *Anticipatory Strategies.* Anticipatory strategies involve thinking about a communication situation in advance and figuring out ways to minimize difficulties. They include such things as educating speakers to keep their faces visible; coming early to a meeting to get a seat close to the speaker; identifying tables in res-

taurants that provide optimal lighting, minimal noise, and making advance reservations to secure those tables; arranging for notetakers or interpreters in classes or meetings; and obtaining assistive devices. An excellent anticipatory strategy involves predicting vocabulary or dialogue that is likely to occur in a particular situation and practicing such language in advance. Appendices A and B of this chapter contain lists of anticipatory strategies.

2. *Repair Strategies.* Repair strategies are behaviors that are used to facilitate communication when it breaks down, either because the person who is deaf or hard of hearing did not understand a speaker, or produced speech that was not understood. Included are repetition, partial repetition in which only what was not understood is repeated, rephrasing, request for key words such as the topic of conversation, request for spelling of important words such as names or numbers, repeating numbers as single digits (e.g., 1–7–2 instead of 172), or asking a general or specific question, as appropriate, to clarify misunderstanding. An example of asking a specific question in response to a lack of understanding is "What is that person's name?" All people who are deaf or hard of hearing should be taught to use the confirmation or summarizing strategy frequently. The individual states what he or she thought was said to make sure the information is correct. An example of confirmation might be "I think you said we're meeting at your house tonight at 9 P.M. Right?" The communication partner then confirms the accuracy of the statement, or corrects inaccurate information. Clients need to learn how to use these strategies and when they are appropriate. Detailed discussion of communication strategies and exercises for practice can be found in Kaplan, Bally, and Garretson (1988).

It is important to realize that it is difficult for many people who are deaf or hard of hearing to be assertive, particularly since they are rebuffed too often. Coping with difficult listening situations in the manner suggested requires practice and development of a "thick skin." Clinicians should be sure to make their clients understand that they are aware of the difficulties involved in implementing these suggestions.

AN EXAMPLE OF PATIENT MANAGEMENT

Mrs. K. is a 53-year-old woman who had had a mild bilateral hearing loss since age 30. She is bilingual, with Spanish as her native language. She had adjusted well to amplification and was able to function as an English teacher in a local high school until two years ago, when her hearing sensitivity dropped dramatically, bilaterally. The drop in hearing was accompanied by dizziness and persisted after the dizziness had subsided. Over a period of one month, hearing sensitivity improved to the level of moderate impairment, but dropped again as a result of exposure to a fire siren. Antihistamines and vasodilators were administered by her physician in an attempt to improve the hearing, but were unsuccessful.

Audiological evaluation revealed a severe bilateral sensorineural hearing loss with poor word recognition and a severe tolerance problem. The site of lesion was cochlear. Although binaural hearing aids were fitted, sufficient gain for her degree of hearing loss could not be used for fear of triggering another episode. Therefore, the hearing aids were not completely satisfactory in transmitting intelligible speech. Since her speech understanding was no longer sufficient to allow her to continue teaching, and since she could no longer tolerate the normal noise levels of a school, she was forced to retire from her teaching position.

Mrs. K.'s first visit occurred after the second sudden drop in auditory sensitivity. She was undergoing otoneurological tests to try to determine the source of the problem and had been referred for an audiological evaluation as part of the diagnostic workup. She appeared depressed and anxious, but hopeful that some medical remedy for her problem would be found. The case history interview and results of the Hearing Performance Inventory (Lamb, Owens, & Schubert, 1983) revealed:

1. Communication difficulties in almost all situations.
2. A feeling of worthlessness because she could no longer work.
3. Extreme sensitivity to what she perceived as callousness by anyone with whom she could not communicate.
4. Resentment toward her husband, because she felt he was unsympathetic toward her problems.
5. Fear that another attack of dizziness and further deterioration of hearing could occur at any time. She was eager to try any type of amplification that might improve her communication.

At the conclusion of the audiological evaluation her hearing loss was explained briefly. Detail was avoided because it was the judgment of the audiologist that she could not absorb a lengthy explanation of her hearing status at that time. It was agreed that she would experiment with different types of amplification and start a speechreading-counseling program concurrent with the otolaryngologist's attempts to treat the situation medically. Since she was not receptive to enrollment in a group, individual therapy was arranged on a twice-weekly schedule. It was suggested that she ask her husband to attend sessions with her, but she felt that would not be appropriate.

Each therapy session consisted of speechreading training, educational counseling, and discussion of her problems. Specific problem situations were defined to find strategies that might facilitate communication. Various modifications in her binaural hearing aids were tried during these sessions to find an optimal arrangement for her. A variety of assistive listening devices were also tried. Some time was spent during each therapy session in hearing aid orientation activities. Goals of therapy were:

1. To improve communication by improving speechreading skills.
2. To teach ways of better handling difficult listening situations.
3. To help her view her communication part-

ners, particularly her husband, in a more realistic and less threatening manner.

4. To help her identify warning signs of an impending attack of dizziness so that she could either leave the situation or take one of the pills her doctor had given her for control (her doctors had been able to find a medication that would prevent or minimize attacks).

5. To find one or more amplification systems that would provide maximal speech intelligibility.

6. To help her seek another source of employment or volunteer work that would restore a sense of self-worth.

During the first semester of therapy, her speechreading skills improved rapidly. That, in combination with the strategies designed to help with difficult listening situations, improved her handling of communication sufficiently to allow some increased self-confidence.

At the end of the first semester she felt she was ready to enter group therapy. At first she was fearful she would not be accepted by the group, because her hearing would be far worse than anyone else's. However, it quickly became apparent that others in the group suffered equally great or more severe hearing losses and were managing to cope with them. She found the group a source of support in her attempts to adjust to her own problems and also found that she in turn could be of help to other group members. Her ability to assist others served to enhance her feelings of worth. Initially she did not ask her husband to participate in the group, but after seeing that other spouses were present she agreed to invite him. The information that he received from the classes has brought them closer together and has eased tensions at home.

She is still a member of the group. Her speechreading skills are still improving, as is her ability to handle difficult communication situations. These skills partially compensate for the less than optimal speech understanding provided by her hearing aids. She has purchased a telephone amplifier, a closed cap-

tioned decoder for her television, and an infrared receiver for theater. She has joined a local self-help group whose purpose is to improve services for people who are hard of hearing, and she is well on her way to becoming an activist.

ACKNOWLEDGMENTS

The author would like to thank the following colleagues for their helpful input and suggestions: Scott Bally, Robin Goffen, Susanne Scott, and Mary Pat Wilson from the Department of Audiology and Speech Language Pathology at Gallaudet University, and Mary Hilley, a former member of the department. Special acknowledgments are extended to Mary Ann Kinsella-Meier of the Department of Communication, Northwest Campus, Gallaudet University.

REFERENCES

Castle, D. L. (1980). *Telephone training for the deaf.* Rochester, NY: National Technical Institute for the Deaf.

Compton, C. L. (1989). Assistive devices. *Seminars in Hearing, 10*(1), 66–77.

DiPietro, L., Williams, P., & Kaplan, H. (1984). *Alerting and communication devices for hearing impaired people: What's available now.* Washington, DC: National Information Center on Deafness, Gallaudet University.

Erber, N. P. (1985). *Telephone communication and hearing impairment.* San Diego, CA: College-Hill Press.

Kannapell, B., & Adams, P. (1984). *An orientation to deafness: A handbook and resource guide.* Washington, DC: Gallaudet University Press.

Kaplan, H. (1987). Assistive devices. In H. G. Mueller & V. C. Geoffrey (Eds.), *Communication disorders in aging* (pp. 464–493). Washington, DC: Gallaudet University Press.

Kaplan, H., Bally, S. J., & Garretson, C. (1988). *Speechreading, a way to improve understanding.* Washington, DC: Gallaudet University Press.

Kodman, F. (1967). Techniques for counseling the hearing aid client. *Maico Audiological Library Series* (Vol. 8, Reports 23–25). Minneapolis, MN: Maico Hearing Instruments.

Lamb, S. H., Owens, E., & Schubert, E. D. (1983). The

revised form of the Hearing Performance Inventory. *Ear and Hearing, 4,* 152–159.

Ramsdell, D. A. (1978). The psychology of the hard-of-hearing and deafened adult. In H. Davis & S. R. Silverman (Eds.), *Hearing and deafness.* New York: Holt, Rinehart & Winston.

Ross, M. (1982). *Hard of hearing children in regular schools.* Englewood Cliffs, NJ: Prentice-Hall.

Sanders, D. A. (1988). Hearing aid orientation and counseling. In M. C. Pollack (Ed.), *Amplification for the hearing impaired* (pp. 343–389). New York: Grune & Stratton.

APPENDIX A

HOW TO COPE WITH DIFFICULT LISTENING SITUATIONS

- Ask the speaker to speak in a good light while facing the listener so that speechreading skills can be used.

- Ask the speaker to speak clearly and naturally, but not to shout or exaggerate articulatory movements.

- If you do not understand what a speaker is saying, ask the speaker to repeat or rephrase the statement.

- If entering a group in the middle of a conversation, ask one person to summarize the conversation.

- If someone is speaking at a distance, ask that person to stand closer.

- If the speaker turns his or her head away, ask him or her to face you to permit optimal speechreading and listening.

- If you are attempting to understand speech in the presence of noise, try to move yourself and the speaker away from the source of the noise.

- When in a communication situation requiring exact information, such as asking directions or obtaining schedules for a trip, request that the speaker write the crucial information.

- If the speaker is talking while eating, smoking, or chewing, request that he or she not do so because of the difficulty of speechreading.

- A person who has a unilateral loss should be sure to keep the good ear facing the speaker at all times.

- If possible, avoid rooms with poor acoustics. If meetings are held in such rooms, request that they be transferred to rooms with less reverberation.

- If a speaker at a meeting cannot be heard, request that he or she use a microphone.

- Arrive early at meetings so that you can sit close to the speaker. Avoid taking a seat near a wall to minimize the possibility of reverberation. This is particularly important for people who use hearing aids.

- If you are going to a movie or to the theater, read the reviews in advance to familiarize yourself with the plot.

- In an extremely noisy situation, limit conversation to before the noise has started or after the noise has subsided. Normal hearing people do this all the time. For example, if a plane goes by and a conversation is going on, most people will halt their conversations and wait until the plane has gone by.

APPENDIX B

HELPING THE STUDENT WHO IS DEAF OR HARD OF HEARING

1. Preferential seating is important to anyone with a hearing problem. The adult who is deaf or hard of hearing will usually know what position in a classroom is best. However, since the focus of attention may change during a lecture, the student should be assured that any change of seat will not be considered disruptive.

2. The teacher should be careful to speak only when the student who is deaf or hard of hearing can see his or her lips. The following situations should be avoided if possible:
   - Talking with one's back to the class, as when writing on the blackboard.
   - Standing in front of a window or a bright light. The light should be shining on the speaker's face, not in the student's eyes.
   - Teaching from the back of the room where the student cannot see.
   - Walking around the classroom while talking.

3 The teacher should:
   - Speak in a careful yet natural manner. Avoid exaggerated lip movements.
   - Restate or rephrase statements when the student fails to understand.
   - Not cover his or her face with a hand or a book while reading.
   - Not stand too close to any student who must lipread. He or she might have to tilt the head back to see the speaker's face, causing unnecessary strain and fatigue.

4. Students who are deaf or hard of hearing rely heavily on written material to obtain information. It is helpful to inform them in advance what material will be covered on a particular day so that pertinent material can be read in advance.

5. It is not possible for the student who is deaf or hard of hearing to use visual cues in class and take notes simultaneously. The teacher either can prepare special lecture notes or request that a fellow student share notes with the student who is deaf or hard of hearing.

6. The teacher should use the blackboard or the overhead projector as much as possible. If the written material must be copied by the student, lecturing should not occur at the same time.

7. Oral tests should never be given to a student who is deaf or hard of hearing.

8. The teacher should be available for extra tutoring. The student who is deaf or hard of hearing should be encouraged to meet with the teacher after class for an explanation of material not understood.

CHAPTER 13

Hearing Aid Orientation for Adult Clients

■ ROBERT M. McLAUCHLIN, Ph.D. ■

Audiologists frequently express the need for hearing aid orientation (HAO) services for the persons they serve, and many say they are offering these orientation services. Problems, however, have occurred with hearing aid users availing themselves of these services, or with specialists providing services in an effective and efficient manner. ASHA (1974) "Guidelines on the Responsibilities of Audiologists in the Rehabilitation of the Auditorily Handicapped" emphasized that hearing aid users and their families should be provided information about the use of amplification. These guidelines also mentioned the need for periodic reassessment of the amplification device and the person's adjustment to it.

In addition, ASHA's (1984a) "Guidelines for Graduate Training in Amplification" specified that audiologists need to demonstrate knowledge of "the hearing aid orientation process" (p. 43) as a rehabilitative procedure. The ASHA (1984b) "Position Statement on Definition of and Competencies for Aural Rehabilitation" listed "plan and implement a program of orientation to hearing aid use as a means of

improving communicative function" (p. 38) as one of the minimal competencies for provision of aural rehabilitation. ASHA's (1989) "Standards for the Certificates of Clinical Competence" require audiology students to obtain at least 40 clock hours of supervised practicum in the selection and use of amplification and assistive devices for adults. Finally, ASHA (1990) "Position Statement on Scope of Practice for Speech-Language Pathology and Audiology" stated the practice of audiology includes "selecting, fitting and dispensing of amplification, assistive listening and alerting devices and other systems (e.g., implantable devices) and providing training in their use" (p. 2).

As early as 1972, Burney found that about 87% of 214 programs responding to a survey reported offering HAOs. More recently, Eggen (1988) found 89% of a sample of 41 Michigan audiologists assumed responsibility for HAO. According to C. M. Shewan (personal communication, February 27, 1990), 59% of responding ASHA certified audiologists (3,610 of 6,070) indicated in a 1988 Membership Update that they were dispensing hearing aids. As more audiologists engage in dispensing hearing aids, their involvement in HAO should increase correspondingly.

Many hearing aid users are in need of HAO, or at least more comprehensive and realistic orientation services. In a review of 377 Army clients, Scherr, Schwartz, and Montgomery (1983) found 32.6% of them required some follow-up orientation. These clients were experiencing minor problems, such as feedback and earmold discomfort.

According to Eggen (1988), the major complaints of hearing aid users reported by 60 Michigan audiologists and hearing aid dealers were:

■ background noise;
■ sound quality of client's voice;
■ insertion of the hearing aid;
■ feeling of fullness in the ear;
■ sounds are too loud;
■ adjusting the volume control; and
■ comfort of the hearing aid.

Maddell, Pfeffer, Ross, and Chellappa (1991) surveyed 92 clients who had returned dispensed hearing aids at the New York League for the Hard of Hearing during 1988. The most frequent reasons for returning hearing aids were: (1) less benefit than expected; (2) discomfort, and (3) problems hearing in noise. Thus, the audiology profession and clinical surveys substantiate the essential need for HAO services.

INDIVIDUALIZED PLANNING

As is the case with all rehabilitative procedures, HAO cannot be packaged for uniform use with all persons who are hearing handicapped. As early as 1967, Panel IV participants in an ASHA Conference on Hearing Aid Evaluation Procedures (Castle, 1967) recognized that a single HAO program is not adaptable for all persons. The range and extent of HAO services should vary depending on individual factors, including:

■ age of onset and progression of hearing impairment;
■ severity of impairment;
■ present age;
■ previous experience with and understanding of hearing aids;
■ attitude of hearing aid wearer about the use of amplification;
■ attitudes of family members and associates concerning the hearing aid wearer and hearing aid use;
■ personal interests;
■ intelligence and language abilities;
■ complexity of the hearing aid system being used;
■ intended use of the hearing aid;
■ the amount and success of previously received rehabilitation; and
■ the presence of any concomitant impairments such as blindness, mental retardation, psychiatric disorders, or arthritis in the hands.

An excellent model of individualized planning for persons who are handicapped is found in a federal regulation to educate all handicapped children (U.S. Office of Education, 1977). Even though the model is entitled "Individualized Education Program (IEP)" and is intended specifically for children, the major aspects of this model are applicable for planning HAO and other rehabilitative services for adults, according to individual needs. There is a written statement indicating what services are needed and appropriate: (1) present levels of performance; (2) long-range goals and short-term objectives; (3) projected dates for initiation and duration of services; (4) services to be provided; (5) appropriate objective criteria and assessment procedures; and (6) timelines for determining whether short-term objectives are being achieved.

Individualized planning is not a new concept for professionals in communication sciences and disorders. In fact, what is required in an individualized rehabilitation program is no more extensive than what has long been considered professionally appropriate practice in audiology and speech-language pathology.

INVOLVEMENT OF FAMILY AND FRIENDS

Why is it important to involve family members and friends of hearing aid users in HAO programs? There are several reasons, but perhaps the most pervasive is because communication is social interaction between persons who interchangeably speak and listen. As the sophistication of persons who interact with the hearing aid user increases relative to hearing impairment and amplification, substantial improvements in communication can be anticipated.

For example, a wife may require orientation because she habitually has raised the level of her voice for five years when speaking to her husband to accommodate his unaided moderate bilateral hearing loss. Without some advice and possibly direct orientation, the wife may continue to speak to her husband in her habitual loud voice and will be perceived by him as speaking too loudly when wearing his hearing aid. This situation could contribute to a deterioration in social interaction and satisfactory hearing aid use. An inappropriate solution is for the husband to turn the gain of the hearing aid down when listening to his wife. Resolving the situation in this way might lead to frequent adjustments of the gain control between conversing with his wife and others. It also could perpetuate any irritation the family members and friends might have been experiencing in listening to the wife's loud voice. Therefore, both the husband and wife must be advised, and preferably shown during orientation sessions, how to share in the responsibility of helping each other adjust to hearing aid use and achieve improved social interaction.

As another example, satisfactory adjustment to hearing aid use can be jeopardized by family members and friends who have unrealistic expectations about wearable amplification. This problem can happen even when the hearing aid user clearly understands the limitations of amplification for his or her type of hearing impairment and attempts to explain those limitations to family members and friends. These limitations often have to be explained and demonstrated to family members and friends before understanding occurs. More importantly, people who communicate frequently with the hearing aid user should understand how they can help to compensate for residual communicative problems, which exist even with the use of amplification by the person who is hearing impaired.

Family members need to understand the dynamics for improving or hindering the perception of a spoken message by a hearing aid user. For purposes of illustration, assume that a wife has a moderate bilateral loss in hearing sensitivity and a moderate and severe impairment in speech discrimination ability for the left and right ears, respectively, and is wearing an aid on the left ear. The husband can improve appreciably his social interaction with her by knowing that he should (1) initially gain her visual as well as auditory attention; (2) move closer to her; (3) speak to her on her left side; (4) initially identify the topic of conversation; (5) reduce the background noise or improve the speech-to-noise ratio; (6) increase the environmental light or move away from the window with the sun at his back; and (7) remove the pipe from his mouth, before she will perceive a spoken message correctly.

There are other reasons for participation of family members and close associates in HAO programs. Less confusion will occur about information provided in HAO sessions because of the presence of additional listeners who have normal hearing, and thus have less chance of perceiving spoken information incorrectly. Moreover, participation in planning and understanding orientation activities to be performed outside of a clinical setting will help in accomplishing these activities successfully.

The ultimate HAO occurs in the daily communication activities of the hearing aid user. Therefore, a successful rehabilitation program involves orientation directly or indirectly for all significant participants in the user's communication activities. Eggen (1988) found 94% of a sample of 60 Michigan audiologists and hearing aid dealers routinely include family members and significant others. Hopefully, this sample is reflective of all specialists providing HAOs.

USER EVALUATION SCALES AND SINGLE SUBJECT TRACKING

Routine employment of user evaluation scales and tracking procedures is strongly recommended in assessing HAO success. If designed appropriately, a rating scale may serve as a daily or weekly schedule for the hearing aid user to complete during the first few weeks or months of hearing aid use. For example, the user can be asked to take 5 minutes during each day to check the appropriate responses to several questions and record any comments or questions. Such a scale is useful in determining the appropriateness of the hearing aid selection and success of HAO. Moreover, the scaled data and comments provide information that is helpful in modifying future HAO programs and hearing aid selection procedures to better serve adults who are hearing impaired.

Rating scales developed for assessing communication handicap (Alpiner, 1987; Demorest & Erdman, 1987; Harless & McConnell, 1982; Lamb, Owens, & Schubert, 1983; Sanders, 1988) are useful in determining difficult listening situations from prospective or current hearing aid users and determining users' and their associates' attitudes toward their hearing impairments. Gauger (1978) developed a series of rating scales and other materials for orienting college students who are deaf to hearing aid use. The Gauger materials can be adapted easily for use with other adult hearing aid users. Walden, Demorest, and Hepler (1984) also developed a hearing aid performance inventory — making it more directly applicable to HAO. Smaldino and Smaldino (1988) combined the use of a hearing handicap scale and a cognitive learning style instrument to investigate the effects of HAO and cognitive style on the perception of hearing handicap by first-time hearing aid users. Newman, Jacobson, Hug, Weinstein, and Malinoff (1991) found the short form of the Hearing Handicapped Inventory for the

Elderly to be an expedient tool for quantifying hearing aid benefit. According to Hawkins (1985), it will be difficult to validate hearing aid selection and assessment procedures without employing user evaluation scales. Unfortunately, only 12% of a sample of 465 responding audiologists use a hearing handicap measure (Martin & Morris, 1989).

Single-subject research designs can be adapted easily for use in tracking treatment effects (McReynolds & Thompson, 1986) and specifically for use with adults who are hearing impaired (Lesner, Lynn, & Brainard, 1988). Many of the attitudes, experiences, knowledge, and performances associated with hearing aids described in subsequent sections of this chapter could be evaluated more objectively with user evaluation scales and single-subject designs.

HEARING AID ORIENTATION IN RETROSPECT

Hearing aid orientation was an extensive and integral part of aural rehabilitation programs, even at the inception of the audiology profession. Carhart (1946) described the hearing aid selection procedures used with military personnel during World War II, which included activities designed to familiarize adults with hearing aid use. These activities were all carried out prior to the final selection of an individual's hearing aid. The major emphasis on HAO in this hearing aid selection program is apparent when reviewing their three goals to (1) obtain a hearing aid having optimal efficiency in everyday situations for each client; (2) provide the client with an understanding of hearing aids, establish habits of efficient use, and initiate auricular training; and (3) help the person foster a full psychological acceptance of hearing aids.

Preliminary to the Carhart hearing aid selection, orientation activities included an explanation about the person's hearing impairment and handicapping conditions, what to expect and what not to expect from wearing a hearing aid, any special problems that might occur, and group instructions about the hearing aid selection procedures to follow.

In an effort to select a manageable number of hearing aids from the total stock of about 200 instruments for further assessment with each individual, the hearing aid selection began with an informal trial of instruments during an interview. Audiometric and case history information also were used in narrowing the selection to 7 to 10 hearing aids. Certainly, this trial also served as an orientation to hearing aids.

The second stage involved a 24-hour trial of each preselected aid with a listening hour following every trial. Frequently, 25 to 30 persons participated in a single listening hour. Individuals rated 13 different kinds of controlled sounds on a 5-point rating scale for each of the preselected hearing aids. The sounds included 6 musical, 3 speech, and 5 environmental selections. A similar rating was done for each person's ability to localize sound, listen over the telephone, and experience a 24-hour trial. Finally, a sound discrimination test was administered. Prospective hearing aid users were allowed to adjust their aids for comfort during all of these listening experiences. These ratings, with a weighted score for the discrimination test, were combined and used in eliminating all but three aids for potential selection. The final selection was made from the three remaining hearing aids based on controlled comparisons of these instruments for speech reception threshold, speech discrimination, tolerance, comfort level, and signal-to-noise ratio tests.

Granted, comprehensive HAO activities were possible with these prospective hearing aid users, because they were a captive audience for an extended period during which their full-time assignment was to be rehabilitated for return to civilian life or active duty. Moreover, the cost of such a program in its entirety for full-time employed civilians might be prohibitive. Despite these limitations for the general adult population, many aspects of this early HAO program are being adapted for use today in familiarizing prospective adult hearing aid users to wearable amplification (Hardick, 1977; Hawkins, 1985).

This lengthy review of the early Carhart hearing aid selection procedures is a tribute to the founder of the audiology profession. From the inception of this profession, HAO was an integral part of audiological services, and these early orientation procedures were comprehensive and novel.

SEVEN ESSENTIAL HEARING AID ORIENTATION SERVICES

Some services are essential to all HAOs. The user should receive the following seven key services:

1. an understanding of the function of the compoent parts and adjustments of hearing aids;
2. practice in fitting, adjusting, and maintaining amplification;
3. an understanding of the limitations of amplification;
4. knowledge of why the particular aid was selected;
5. how to begin using a newly selected hearing aid;
6. how to trouble-shoot hearing aid problems; and
7. how to exercise a hearing aid user's legal rights.

HAO need not be restricted to a limited time frame following the selection and fitting of hearing aids. Orientation may continue for several weeks or many months until persons achieve their fullest understanding of hearing aid use and maximum potential performance in operating and communicating with particular amplifying devices. Certain aspects of HAO, such as explaining the component parts and adjustments of hearing aids and the anticipated limitations and benefits to be derived from amplification, sometimes might be presented prior to performing a hearing aid selection. Miller and Schein (1987) subscribe to providing HAO before fitting hearing aids. Thus, this chapter's author suggests that HAO not be limited to any specific rehabilitative services or time frame. Moreover, some aspects of HAO can be presented efficiently in a group, and the sharing of common experiences will result in valuable rehabilitation.

UNDERSTANDING THE COMPONENT PARTS AND CONTROLS OF HEARING AIDS

It is disheartening to evaluate an intelligent adult who purchased a hearing aid a year earlier, but is unable to tell the audiologist the location of the hearing aid microphone or the purpose of this component. Adult hearing aid users should be able to name, locate, and describe the functions of the major hearing aid components, including the microphone, amplifier, battery, receiver, tubing (if it is a behind-the-ear [BTE] or eyeglass hearing aid), hook (if it is a BTE hearing aid), and ear mold (if it is not an in-the-canal [ITC] hearing aid). Similarly, hearing aid users should be able to locate and explain the function of the controls on their hearing aids, such as the gain control and on-off, tone, and telephone switches.

An effective HAO must go beyond providing information. It must determine if objectives are accomplished by assessing user understanding and performance. This author suggests employing a user performance checklist or rating scale to record whether users satisfactorily can name, locate, and describe the functions of the component parts and controls on their hearing aids.

Objectives, as always, will have to be tailored to individual needs and capabilities. For example, this author has explained the ANSI standards for evaluating the electroacoustic characteristics of hearing aids in substantial detail to an engineer for whom a hearing aid was selected.

Videotapes can be prepared by service facilities or purchased commercially (Orton, 1989) to illustrate the component parts of hearing aids and how to fit, adjust, and maintain different models of hearing aids. These tapes can be shown to individuals or used in a more effi-cient manner with groups of individuals who are hearing impaired, family members, and friends. They also can be shown in a room for family members and friends while the client is being seen for services. Only 5% of a sample of 60 Michigan audiologists and hearing aid dealers were using videotapes for HAO (Eggen, 1988). With current technology, a computerized interactive video program could be developed to assess knowledge and performance related to hearing aids.

Given the current hearing aid sales statistics (Mahon, 1989b), most of these video programs need to emphasize in-the-ear (ITE) and BTE hearing aids. During 1989, 79.2% of sales were ITE hearing aids and 20% were BTE hearing aids for a total of 99.2%.

PRACTICE IN FITTING, ADJUSTING, AND MAINTAINING AMPLIFICATION

A hearing aid user, particularly a new user, needs more than a description and demonstration of how to fit, operate, and maintain a newly selected hearing aid. To determine if orientation has been successful, an assessment of the user's ability to perform these tasks is essential. Preferably, this assessment should be done at the time the aid is fitted and again at some follow-up appointment within a month. A simple user-performance checklist or rating scale can be used to record the user's ability to perform the many fitting, adjustment, and maintenance functions associated with the user's hearing aid. For example, audiologists should rate a hearing aid user's ability to connect and disconnect tubing and ear molds to a BTE hearing aid, insert and remove the ear mold or ITE hearing aid from the ear, operate the hearing aid controls, and change a battery. Some clients will eventually need to learn how to program their digital hearing aids. This performance-based assessment should be used for all hearing aid users. Do not assume a person is oriented adequately to hearing aid use just because he or she has previously worn a hearing aid.

The hearing aid user should be given a list of maintenance suggestions can be provided an opportunity to demonstrate basic maintenance skills. The following suggestions are only examples of what might be included on a maintenance list.

- Protect hearing aids against exposure to excessive heat from sources like hair dryers, radiators, heaters, and closed cars on a hot sunny day.
- Avoid exposing hearing aids to excessive humidity which occurs in rain, saunas, steam baths, or when aids have been placed in a pocket of pants and sent to the laundry.
- Place hearing aids in a container with silica gel at night to remove the moisture, particularly for persons who perspire heavily.
- Prevent hair sprays, insecticides, and other sprays from being directed at the aids.
- Clean ear molds and tubing periodically with mild soap and water or commercially available cleaning solution. Pipe cleaners work well for clearing foreign debris and water from the tubing and earmold channel.
- Keep hearing aids away from dogs and small children when not wearing them.
- Remove hearing aids from the ear and handle them over a soft surface so, if dropped, the possibility of damage is reduced.

LIMITATIONS OF AMPLIFICATION

Prospective hearing aid users, as well as their family members and friends, frequently have unrealistic perceptions about the benefits to be derived from wearable amplification. These perceptions range from total lack of benefit to the expectation of "normal" hearing. These perceptions must be explored if audiologists hope to achieve success in acquainting hearing aid users, and the persons with whom they communicate, with amplification. A very positive, though realistic, approach may be required with the person or family member who is extremely skeptical about the benefits of amplification. Conversely, a guarded and realistic

approach may be needed for an individual who expects a hearing aid to resolve all hearing problems, especially if speech discrimination ability is significantly reduced. Two other limitations include restricted dynamic range and tolerance problems.

WHY WAS A PARTICULAR HEARING AID SELECTED?

Hearing aid users, if capable of understanding, should be told:

- why a particular type of hearing aid, such as an in-the-ear instrument was selected;
- why the aid was a particular make;
- why a monaural aid for the right or left ear or a binaural instrument was chosen;
- why the particular external controls were chosen and where they should be set;
- why the type of ear mold was selected; and
- why any special features were selected.

The inability of a new hearing aid user to tell a close friend why she or he is using the hearing aid in the right ear can result in feelings of insecurity and inadequacy. Conversely, telling the friend why he or she has insufficient hearing, or why the clarity of speech is too poor in the left ear to warrant amplification, may impart the user's understanding of the impairment and a feeling of adequacy. Moreover, if the hearing aid user then enlists the friend's help by asking him or her to walk or sit on the user's right side, this demonstrates the user's willingness to discuss and cope with the handicapping condition with friends. A thorough knowledge about one's impairment and hearing aid, combined with an open approach to using the hearing aid, can contribute appreciably to successful hearing aid use.

USING A NEWLY SELECTED HEARING AID

The length of time necessary for satisfactory adjustment to a newly selected hearing aid will vary substantially from person to person, depending on the amount and type of impairment; whether amplification has been used previously; the presence and extent of concomitant handicapping conditions such as mental impairment, spasticity, or visual impairment; the age of onset and progression of hearing impairment; and the person's daily activities. An intelligent, long-time, successful hearing aid user who has just procured a new replacement instrument might immediately begin wearing the new hearing aid during all of his or her waking hours without needing any formalized HAO beyond an explanation of any new or different hearing aid controls. Conversely, an adult who is developmentally disabled who has a long-standing hearing impairment and has never tried amplification may require many months of HAO. Typically, a satisfactory HAO can be completed for most adults who are hearing impaired within 2 to 6 weeks and include all essential services for successful hearing aid use.

New hearing aid users generally are encouraged to begin employing their hearing aids in easy listening situations and progress to more difficult listening experiences. An easy listening situation would involve listening:

- to a single, known speaker;
- in a quiet environment;
- to a familiar and easy topic;
- while watching the speaker;
- with good lighting on the speaker's face; and
- with minimal visual or auditory distractions.

After new users adjust to easy listening situations, the preceding six conditions and others may be varied to increase the difficulty of listening situations. HAO is not complete until clients have adjusted to using their new hearing aids in a variety of daily listening activities, particularly in those situations where they want and need to communicate for social, vocational, or educational purposes.

HOW TO TROUBLE-SHOOT HEARING AID PROBLEMS

If hearing aid users sufficiently understand the functions of the component parts and controls of hearing aids, they intuitively may be able to solve many of their own hearing aid problems. However, trouble-shooting ability should not be left to chance. Quite the contrary, hearing aid users should be told about possible problems that can occur, how to locate the problems, and how to seek a resolution to the problems. A set of used hearing aids exhibiting a variety of problems is very helpful in demonstrating trouble-shooting techniques. Moreover, a chart listing problems, possible causes, and remedies should be provided to hearing aid users. The clinician can ask users to study their charts and be prepared to answer questions about malfunctioning hearing aids. Clients should demonstrate their understanding of the material by locating problems and remedying them with a stock of used hearing aids when they return for another appointment. Hearing aid users should be encouraged to keep this chart with important papers for immediate reference if hearing aid problems arise. The chart might contain the following problems:

- squealing (whistling);
- no amplification;
- reduced amplification;
- intermittent amplification or scratchy, frying, crashing sound;
- sharp sound (as though through a barrel);
- "tinny" or "thin" sound;
- sound too noisy;
- reduced clarity of speech;
- ear canal hurts; or
- problem not describable, but change noticed.

Additionally, the chart should list possible causes, how to locate the problems, and the remedies. It would be helpful for clients to know that common problems with BTE hearing aids involve receivers, microphones, and wires; whereas with ITE and canal-type instruments, breakdowns involve wax-clogged receivers and volume controls (Mahon, 1989a). The chart should indicate clearly which causes can be remedied by the user and which ones should be remedied by an audiologist or hearing aid dispenser. The hearing aid user should be encouraged to call the specialist who selected the hearing instrument if problems arise that the user is unable to resolve. The specialist's address and phone number should be placed prominently on the chart where it can be seen easily.

These charts are available commercially through a variety of sources. Hearing aid manufacturers frequently include these charts in the "User Instructional Brochure" that is required by the U.S. Food and Drug Administration (FDA) (1977). Other HAO booklets and pamphlets are available from a variety of sources (Armbruster & Miller, 1986; Gauger, 1978; Gendel, 1984; Krames Communications, 1987; Madell, 1986; Self Help for Hard of Hearing People, 1986, 1987; Williams & Jacobs-Condit, 1985).

CONSUMER RIGHTS OF HEARING AID USERS

Individuals should be informed of their legal rights and options as owners or users of wearable amplification. The cost of hearing aids and most expenses associated with hearing impairment, for example, are allowed as medical expenses in computing federal income tax. Many prospective purchasers of hearing aids may qualify for public or private funds to cover the cost, such as funds available through Medicaid, Rehabilitation Services Administration, Veterans Administration, or employee health benefits. They should also be informed of their legal rights and restrictions under the Labeling and Conditions for Sale Regulation promulgated by the FDA. Certain information must be provided to prospective hearing aid users in the form of a User Instructional Brochure, as mandated by the FDA. Although many hearing aid manufacturers provided brochures with their instruments prior to this regulation, the extent and uniformity of information varied substantially. This was particularly true concerning electroacoustic characteristics of hearing aids.

As of August 15, 1977, the effective date of the FDA regulation, all hearing aids are to be accompanied by a User Instructional Brochure containing the following categories of information:

■ illustration of the hearing aid showing controls, adjustments, and battery compartment;

■ printed material on the operation of all controls designed for user adjustment;

■ description of possible accompanying accessories;

■ instructions on how to use, maintain, and care for as well as replace or recharge batteries;

■ how to and where to procure repair service;

■ conditions to be avoided in preventing damage to hearing aids, such as dropping or exposing to excessive heat or humidity;

■ warning to seek medical advice when encountering any side effects such as skin irritation or increased accumulation of cerumen;

■ statement that a hearing aid will not restore normal hearing or prevent or improve a hearing impairment caused by organic conditions;

■ statement that with most persons, infrequent use of wearable amplification will not allow them to attain full benefit from hearing aid use;

■ statement that hearing aid use is only one aspect of hearing rehabilitation and may need to be augmented by auditory training and lipreading instruction;

■ warning statement to hearing aid dispensers to advise prospective hearing aid users to see a licensed physician before dispensing hearing aids if any of eight medical conditions exist (see any User Instructional Brochure for these conditions);

■ notice to prospective hearing aid users indicating, among other things, that hearing aids cannot be sold to individuals until they have obtained a medical evaluation from a licensed physician (preferably one who specializes in diseases of the ear); a fully informed adult may waive the medical evaluation, though such action is strongly discouraged by the FDA;

■ electroacoustical data in accordance with the Acoustical Society of America's (1987) *Standard for Specification of Hearing Aid Characteristics* (this information may be included on separate labeling that accompanies the hearing aid).

Other information may be included in the User Instructional Brochure if it is not false, misleading, or prohibited by this regulation or by FTC regulations. Audiologists, hearing aid sales personnel, and physicians specializing in diseases of the ear should have a reference copy of this important FDA regulation.

In addition to the seven services disussed in this chapter, an individualized rehabilitation plan for a client might require counseling, auditory training, situational training, speechreading, motivational training, and speech production training. Although some or all of these additional five rehabilitative services might be required, they are not essential for all clients. Moreover, these latter services are discussed in more detail in other chapters of this textbook.

SUMMARY

Because of the limited survey and research data on adult HAO services, this author challenges all specialists working with the hearing impaired to make significant clinical and research contributions to improving HAOs. The prospects for improvement are great given the current rate of change in knowledge and technology. Only a commitment and expenditure of effort is needed to fulfill this challenge.

REFERENCES

Acoustical Society of America. (1987). *Standard for specification of hearing aid characteristics.* ANSI 3.22. New York: Author.

Alpiner, J. (1987). Evaluation of adult communication function. In J. Alpiner & P. McCarthy (Eds.), *Rehabilitative audiology: Children and adults* (pp. 44–114). Baltimore, MD: Williams & Wilkins.

American Speech and Hearing Association. (1974). The audiologist: Responsibilities in the habilitation of the auditorily handicapped. *Journal of the American Speech and Hearing Association, 16,* 68–70.

American Speech-Language-Hearing Association. (1984a). Guidelines for graduate training in amplification. *Asha, 26*(5), 43.

American Speech-Language-Hearing Association. (1984b). Position statement: Definition of competencies for aural rehabilitation. *Asha, 26*(5), 37–41.

American Speech-Language-Hearing Association (1989). Standards for the certificates of clinical competence. *Asha, 31*(3), 70–71.

American Speech-Language-Hearing Association. (1990). Scope of practice, speech-language pathology and audiology. *Asha, 32* (Suppl. 2), 1–2.

Armbruster, J., & Miller, M. (1986). *How to get the most out of your hearing aid.* Washington, DC: Alexander Graham Bell Association for the Deaf.

Burney, P. (1972). A survey of hearing aid evaluation procedures. *Journal of the American Speech and Hearing Association, 14,* 439–444.

Carhart, R. (1946). Selection of hearing aids. *Archives of Otolaryngology, 44,* 1–18.

Castle, W. E. (Ed.). (1967). A conference on hearing aid evaluation procedures. *ASHA Reports, 2.*

Demorest, M., & Erdman, S. (1987). Development of the Communication Profile for the Hearing Impaired. *Journal of Speech and Hearing Disorders, 52,* 129–143.

Eggen, R. E. (1988). *A survey of hearing aid orientation process in the state of Michigan.* Unpublished master's independent study, Central Michigan University, Mt. Pleasant.

Gauger, J. S. (1978). *Orientation to hearing aids.* Rochester, NY: National Technical Institute for the Deaf.

Gendel, J. (1984). *Questions most often asked about earmolds.* New York: New York League for the Hard of Hearing.

Hardick, E. J. (1977). Aural rehabilitation programs for the aged can be successful. *Journal of the Academy of Rehabilitative Audiology, 10,* 51–67.

Harless, E. L., & McConnell, F. (1982). Effects of hearing aid use on self concept in older persons. *Journal of Speech and Hearing Disorders, 47,* 305–309.

Hawkins, D. B. (1985). Reflections on amplification: Validation of performance. *Journal of the Academy of Rehabilitative Audiology, 18,* 42–54.

Krames Communications. (1987). *Hearing aids: A guide to their wear and care.* Daly City, CA: Author.

Lamb, S., Owens, E., & Schubert, E. (1983). The revised form of the Hearing Performance Inventory. *Ear and Hearing, 4*(3), 152–157.

Lesner, S. A., Lynn, J. M., & Brainard, J. (1988). Feasibility of using a single-subject design for continuous discourse tracking measurement. *Journal of the Academy of Rehabilitative Audiology, 21,* 83–89.

Madell, J. (1986). *You and your hearing aid.* New York: New York League for the Hard of Hearing.

Madel, J., Pfeffer, E., Ross, M., & Chellappa, M. (1991). Hearing aid returns at a community hearing and speech agency. *The Hearing Journal, 44*(4), 18–23.

Mahon, W. J. (1989a). A close look at hearing aid repair. *The Hearing Journal, 42*(2), 9–12.

Mahon, W. J. (1989b). 1989 U.S. hearing aid sales summary. *The Hearing Aid Journal, 42*(12), 9–14.

Martin, F. N., & Morris, L. J. (1989). Current audiologic practices in the United States. *The Hearing Journal, 42*(4), 25–44.

McReynolds, L. V., & Thompson, C. K. (1986). Flexibility of single-subject experimental designs. Part I: Review of the basics of single-subject designs. *Journal of Speech and Hearing Disorders, 51*, 194–203.

Miller, M. H., & Schein, J. D. (1987). Improving consumer acceptance of hearing aids. *The Hearing Journal, 40*(10), 25–30.

Newman, C. W., Jacobson, G. P., Hug, G. A., Weinstein, B. E., & Malinoff, R. L. (1991). Practical method for quantifying hearing aid benefit in older adults. *Journal of the American Academy of Audiology, 2*(2), 70–75.

Orton, C. (1989). *Help with your hearing aids.* [Videotape]. Stinson Beach, CA: Orton-Palmer & Associates.

Sanders, D. A. (1988). Profile questionnaire for rating communicative performance in a home environment, occupational environment, social environment. In M. Pollack (Ed.), *Amplification for the hearing impaired* (pp. 385–395). Orlando, FL: Grune & Stratton.

Scherr, C. K., Schwartz, D. M., & Montgomery, A. A. (1983). Follow-up survey of new hearing aid users. *Journal of the Academy of Rehabilitative Audiology, 1,* 202–209.

Self Help for Hard of Hearing People. (1986). *I think I have a problem. What do I do?* Bethesda, MD: Author.

Self Help for Hard of Hearing People. (1987). *ABCs of hearing aids.* Bethesda, MD: Author.

Smaldino, S. E., & Smaldino, J. J. (1988). The influence of aural rehabilitation and cognitive style disclosure on the perception of hearing handicap. *Journal of the Academy of Rehabilitative Audiology, 21,* 57–64.

U.S. Food and Drug Administration. (1977). Hearing aid devices, professional and patient labeling and conditions for sale. *Federal Register, 42,* 9286–9296.

U.S. Office of Education, Bureau of Education for Handicapped Children. (1977). Implementation of Part B of the Education of the Handicapped Act. *Federal Register, 42,* 42474–42518.

Walden, B., Demorest, M., & Hepler, E. (1984). Hearing Aid Performance Inventory (HAPI). *Journal of Speech and Hearing Research, 27,* 49–56.

Williams, P., & Jacobs-Condit, L. (1985). *Hearing aids, what are they?* Washington, DC: National Information Center on Deafness, Gallaudet University.

CHAPTER 14

Assistive Listening Devices and Systems for Adults with Hearing Impairment

■ GWENYTH R. VAUGHN, Ph.D. ■
■ ROBERT K. LIGHTFOOT, M.S. ■

Historically, society has concentrated on the education of children who are deaf or profoundly hard of hearing. Only recently have efforts been made to address the problems of adults who are mildly and severely hard of hearing. Hearing impairment seriously hampers educational achievement for younger adults and can interfere with vocational performance in older adults. Optimal health care and rewarding family and social relationships can become affected seriously for most persons who are hearing impaired. These areas of communication are of special concern to older adults.

To address multiple listening and talking problems associated with hearing loss, a comprehensive aural rehabilitation program should consider assistive listening devices and systems (ALDS) as alternative and companion devices for use with the traditional types of personal hearing aids. ALDS can bring listeners and talkers improved personal, social, educational, vocational, cultural, and recreational relationships.

LISTENER AND TALKER RIGHTS

Both listeners and talkers have the right, as well as the need, to participate in interpersonal communication. Most modern environments are so pervaded by noise and reverberation that aural and oral communication is often highly unsatisfactory. Table 14–1 sets forth a "Bill of Rights for Listeners and Talkers" (Vaughn, 1986).

TABLE 14–1. BILL OF RIGHTS FOR LISTENERS AND TALKERS

Personal Rights	Communication Rights
Entitlement to quality care	in receiving areas, hospitals, nursing homes, outpatient waiting rooms, reception areas, physicians' offices, and rehabilitative settings.
Opportunity for equal employment	during job interviews, telephone usage, and employment in professions, offices, industries, and fine arts.
Protection of legal rights	through availability of ALDS in police stations, courtrooms, and jails.
Admittance to legislative and diplomatic action	town meetings, state legislatures, Congress, and international organizations.
Participation in business activities	in negotiations, conferences, meetings, and contacts with bank tellers, telephone operators, receptionists, and managers.
Access to protection	by fire departments, emergency services, and police.
Assurance of safety	in industry, home, public and private buildings, hotels, airports, and places for public assembly.
Recognition of dignity as listener and talker	in interpersonal communication with family and friends in restaurants, social gatherings, automobiles, and over the telephone.
Freedom of religion	in worship services, counseling sessions, and confessionals.
Opportunity to travel	through accessibility to translation services, lectures by guides, recorded information at historical sites, and verbal exchange with group members.
Understanding of information	through graphic displays of ALDS in conjunction with public address systems, public telephones, radio, and television.
Obtaining of basic and continuing education	through amplification systems during tutoring, teleconferencing, and video and audio recordings.
Appreciation of entertainment	in concert halls, theaters, and movies.
Participation in recreational activities	indoor and outdoor games, active and spectator sports, and table and group games.

Source: From Vaughn, G. R. (1986). Bill of rights for listeners and talkers. *Hearing Instruments, 37,* 7. Reprinted with permission.

SPEECH SIGNAL DELIVERY

Although great improvements have been made in hearing aids, few hearing aid users find speech easily understandable when it is masked by noise, distance, and reverberation. The background noise of cocktail parties, restaurants, and other group gatherings is likely to cause problems for most persons who are hear-ing impaired. Difficulties for listeners are increased whenever poor lighting and distance interfere with speechreading.

In order to overcome the problems described in Table 14–1, assistive listening devices and systems are designed to deliver a sound from its source directly to the ears of the listener. The "lips-to-ears" speech delivery of ALDS is shown in Figure 14–1.

Figure 14–1. Delivery of speech sounds from the lips of the talker to the ears of the listener (Courtesy of Sennheiser)

SELECTION OF ASSISTIVE LISTENING DEVICES AND SYSTEMS

Selection Consider.

The successful selection of ALDS for a person who is hearing impaired usually depends on four considerations:

1. the cost of the ALDS,
2. the degree of the client's hearing loss,
3. the acceptance of the ALDS by the client and significant others, and
4. the client's life style.

When selecting a personal hearing aid for a client, audiologists must take into consideration the client's degree of loss and his or her acceptance of amplification. When dispensing ALDS, audiologists must follow the same selection protocol. In addition, however, they need to make a careful analysis of the client's life style. The successful selection of an ALDS depends not only on the satisfaction of the listener, but also that of the talkers who wish to communicate with him or her. Figure 14–2 shows a flow chart that can be useful during the selection of an ALDS (Lightfoot & Vaughn, 1988).

ALDs should be... Assistive listening devices should be portable, affordable, commercially available, and not require any architectural modification. Table 14–2 presents an ALDS checklist for listening and talking problems (Vaughn & Lightfoot, 1983). The answers to this checklist can serve as the basis for the recommendation of one or more ALDS (Vaughn & Lightfoot, 1983).

ALDS ADAPTIVE PROCEDURES

Self-wiring. There are special adaptive procedures that can be used with ALDS. These self-contained procedures permit the users of Hardwire and Frequency Modulation (FM) ALDS to place all of the components of the ALDS on their own bodies. The amplifier of the Hardwire ALDS can be put in the listener's pocket for easy access to the volume control; the microphone can be clipped to the listener's lapel; and the earphones can be placed on the listener's ears. The transmitter and receiver of an FM ALDS can be placed in the listener's pockets, or pocketbook, allowing the listeners to "wire themselves."

Self-wiring permits the person to carry his own listening/talking environment with him. Depending on the background noise levels and the loudness of the talker's voice, self-wiring can provide an easy and satisfactory solution.

Windscreen. For talking in restaurants, around conference tables, in small groups at home or in social gatherings, the ALDS microphone can be placed in a windscreen. The windscreen can then be located in the center of the table, or can be suspended above the group. The wind-

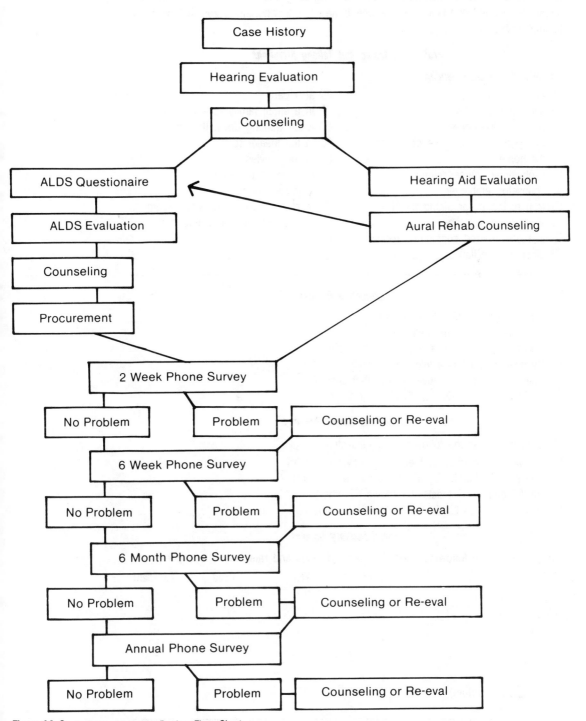

Figure 14–2. Assistive Listening Device Flow Chart.

TABLE 14–2. ALDS CHECKLIST FOR LISTENING AND TALKING PROBLEMS

Some of the information that would help in making suggestions concerning assistive listening devices is listed below. Please check the items that pertain to your listening and talking problems.

Problem Listening and Talking Situations

I have difficulty understanding:

☐ in an automobile
☐ television or radio
☐ over the telephone
☐ one person at mealtime or around the home
☐ a physician, nurse, religious counselor, employer
☐ in a restaurant or dining room
☐ at a conference table
☐ in medium-sized conference rooms
☐ other (please list) _____

☐ at a party
☐ in a small family group
☐ when walking down the street
☐ in the theater (play)
☐ in the movies
☐ in a house of worship
☐ in a classroom
☐ in a dayroom or recreation room
☐ in a conference or lecture hall
☐ on the job

Amplification Devices

☐ I do not have a new hearing aid.
☐ I am pleased with my hearing aid.
☐ I do not wish to use a regular hearing aid.
☐ My hearing aid has a telephone switch.
☐ I can afford an alternative system that costs:
    ☐ $100; ☐ $300; ☐ $500; ☐ $700

Large Area Sound Systems

My community has the following sound systems:

☐ Hardwire (☐ church ☐ theater ☐ movie ☐ other)
☐ Infrared (☐ church ☐ theater ☐ movie ☐ other)
☐ FM (☐ church ☐ theater ☐ movie ☐ other)
☐ Loop (☐ church ☐ theater ☐ movie ☐ other)

Special Sensory Devices

I use some of the following special sensory devices and rate their effectiveness as:

Device	Poor	Fair	Good	Excellent
Telecaptioning	☐	☐	☐	☐
Teletypewriter	☐	☐	☐	☐
Gongs, bells	☐	☐	☐	☐
Lights	☐	☐	☐	☐
Vibrators	☐	☐	☐	☐
Hearing dog	☐	☐	☐	☐
_____ (other)	☐	☐	☐	☐
None ☐				

Source: Adapted from Lightfoot, R. K., & Vaughn, G. R. (1989). Resource materials. In R. L. Schow & M. A. Nerbonne (Eds.), *Introduction to aural rehabilitation* (2nd ed., pp. 586–605). Austin, TX: Pro-Ed.

screen consists of a foam cover that protects the microphone from wind noise and vibrations.

CATEGORIES OF ALDS

Assistive listening devices are generally categorized in the following manner:

1. Hardwire,
2. Infrared,
3. Frequency modulation (FM),
4. Audio induction loop,
5. Sensory and alerting devices,
6. Telephone aids, and
7. Television aids.

ALD categories

The following sections include the descriptions and applications of ALDS in each of the categories.

HARDWIRE DEVICES

Hardwire devices are extremely popular because of their easy procurement, quality of sound, simple technology, and, most of all, their low cost. The basic components of a Hardwire ALDS are the following: (a) an amplifier, (b) a microphone, and (c) an earphone. Additional components may be purchased to accommodate special needs such as television or telephone listening. The name "Hardwire" is used because the listener and the sound source are physically connected by the wire. The listener usually puts the Hardwire amplifier in a pocket so that the volume control and on/off switch are accessible. He puts the earphones on his ears and places the microphone near the sound source.

Early Hardwire ALDS

Earlier generations of Hardwire systems were used in houses of worship and other public meeting places. These systems were permanently installed in designated pews or seats, usually at the front of the seating area. The earphone jacks were connected to the public address system. Users who were hearing impaired had to plug in their own earphones, or they had to use those that were installed already. As a result, listeners who were hearing impaired were unable to sit with their family members or friends.

Present Hardwire ALDS

Hardwire devices are marketed by several distributors. As prepackaged devices, they can be procured from several manufacturers. A Hardwire ALDS package usually includes the following items: (a) an amplifier, (b) a microphone, (c) a battery, (d) the instructions for using an ALDS, and (f) a carrying case. An extension cord may also be required by the listener. The length of the extension cord depends on the distance between the listener and the sound source. Other accessories may include (a) a neckloop that transmits to a telecoil in the listener's personal hearing aid, and (b) a battery charger for use with rechargeable batteries.

For the innovative consumer, the individual components for a Hardwire ALDS may be obtained from radio and television repair and parts stores. Care must be taken when personally assembling a Hardwire ALDS that the output does not exceed safe listening levels, and that the impedance between components is not mismatched.

HARDWIRE DEVICES AND SPECIAL NEEDS

Hardwire ALDS are also useful for people who only need a bit of "hearing help" in certain situations. For example, listeners who have difficulties in noisy public offices, at teller windows, in automobiles, in restaurants, when using public telephones, or when they and others are viewing television or listening to the radio, often find ALDS are excellent problem solvers.

Hardwire ALDS and Health Care

Hardwire devices are becoming a necessary piece of equipment for all types of health clinics, hospitals, nursing homes, and emergency rooms. Hardwire ALDS should be available to

Figure 14–3. A Hardwire ALDS enhances communication between a patient and a member of the health care team. (Courtesy of Williams Sound)

receptionists, bank tellers, and others who greet the public. Audiologists, speech pathologists, physicians, nurses, social workers, dentists, pharmacists, chaplains, counselors, and other members of the health care field should keep Hardwire ALDS, or other amplification devices, available for assisting persons who are hearing impaired.

One of the commercially available Hardwire ALDS is the Pocketalker. Figure 14–3 demonstrates how a Hardwire ALDS can enhance communication between a patient who is hard of hearing and a member of the health care system.

Automobile

To overcome the excessive ambient noise level in an automobile, a person who is hearing impaired can wear the earpiece of an ALDS and place the microphone in one of the following positions: (a) on the talker's lapel, or (b) on the *back* of the front seat (if he or she is in the front), thus, giving him or her access to the talkers in back. The listener may wish to pass the micro-

phone from talker to talker, if the above suggestions do not provide a satisfactory signal-to-noise ratio. Figure 14–4 illustrates the use of a Hardwire ALDS in an automobile.

Restaurant

Restaurant noise causes problems for most hearing impaired listeners. One way to carry on a satisfactory conversation with one companion at the table is to pass the ALDS microphone under the table and clip it to the lapel of the talker. The microphone may also be placed in the center of the table or suspended above the table. This placement improves effective communication for the listener who is hearing impaired when one or more talkers are present. Figure 15–4 demonstrates the use of a Hardwire ALDS in a restaurant.

Parties

The Hardwire microphone can be passed from talker to talker if the noise level is too high for

Figure 14–4. A Hardwire ALDS can provide good, amplified communication in a noisy automobile. (Courtesy of Williams Sound).

Figure 14–5. When a Hardwire ALDS microphone is placed on the table, it can provide good communication to a person who is hearing impaired in a noisy restaurant. (Courtesy of Birmingham VA Medical Center)

self-wiring. Otherwise, the listener can self-wire him- or herself and stand in an advantageous position within the small group.

Television and Radio

When one member of a family is hard of hearing, television and radio listening levels can become a source of concern. The family members complain that the person who is hearing impaired turns the volume up so high that it is uncomfortable for them, the normally hearing listeners. As a result, the normally hearing listeners often move to a separate room, leaving the person who is hearing impaired to listen alone.

There are several ways to address the problem of the volume control for the television and radio. One simple way is to clip or tape the microphone to the grille of the television or radio. If an extension cord is used, care must be taken that the cords do not pose a mobility hazard. This permits the person who is hearing impaired to independently adjust the loudness to meet his or her own needs. At the same time, normally hearing listeners are able to adjust the loudness of the television set by using the volume control on the set. Thus, both normally hearing listeners and listeners who are hearing impaired can enjoy listening in the same room to the same television or radio program.

Direct Wiring

Hardwire devices do not necessarily have to include a separate microphone and amplifier. An inexpensive approach to television and radio listening is direct wiring. This is achieved by using a direct wire between the television or radio and the earplug or earphones. In order to achieve this direct wiring, the television or radio must have a listening jack. Some televisions have two external jacks, one of which is used only for private listening. When the private listening jack is used, the internal speaker of the set is disconnected, and private listening becomes available to the person wearing the earphones. If the other jack is used, both the internal speaker and the private listening jack are operational. The volume for both jacks is adjusted by the volume control of the television set.

At times, listeners who are hearing impaired find it necessary to increase the distance between themselves and the television or radio. This distancing can be achieved by adding an extension cord with the appropriate connectors between the set and the earphones.

Telephone Amplification

The telephone can present a great problem for listeners who are hearing impaired. Hardwire devices often can alleviate this problem by replacing the microphone of the ALDS with a magnetic telephone pick-up. This pick-up is attached to the listening end of the telephone handset. Some manufacturers produce modular couplers that allow the telephone to be connected to a free standing amplifier, or to an ALDS.

Dexterity Problems

Hardwire devices also have proved to be convenient for persons who are hearing impaired who are unable to adjust traditional hearing aids because of their small controls. The volume controls of Hardwire ALDS usually are large enough for persons with dexterity problems caused by arthritis or other conditions to make the necessary adjustments. The under-the-chin stenographer type of earphone also has been very useful for persons with decreased dexterity. For those persons who do not have any difficulty in adjusting or positioning an ALDS, the more up-to-date "earbuds" usually are preferred because they are less conspicuous and are lightweight. Persons who are visually impaired also find that the manipulation of Hardwire devices is simple.

Cost

Hardwire ALDS usually cost between fifty and one hundred dollars. The price makes them accessible and more attractive to people on fixed incomes.

INFRARED DEVICES

Infrared light technology has made remarkable contributions to the field of electronics. Televisions, stereos, and VCRs employ the use of infrared light for their remote control options. Infrared light beams are now used to carry audio signals from the special light emitting diodes (LED) of the transmitters to the infrared receivers worn by normally hearing listeners and listeners who are hearing impaired. Although varying amounts of infrared light are present in *all* sources of light, technology has reduced the problems of infrared interference from incandescent and fluorescent lighting. The natural infrared light from the sun is so great that the use of infrared systems is not possible when the eye of the receiver is in direct sunlight. As a result, an infrared system is usually confined to indoor use.

The infrared receiver must be in line-of-sight with the transmitter. It is also possible for the receiver to respond to a signal that has "bounced off" a surface such as a smooth ceiling, tile floor, glossy painted wall, or other reflective surface. When considering the placement of transmitters in a facility, care must be taken that the signal is not obstructed by supporting structures or by the heads of the persons who are seated or standing between the listeners and the transmitter.

One great advantage of infrared light transmission is that it does not pass through walls or curtains, thus Infrared ALDS provide transmission privacy. Some of the locations in which this privacy is desirable include courtrooms, boardrooms, or theaters. Infrared prevents the illegal recording of a performance outside places such as those listed above or the "listening in" to proceedings in a courtroom. A second advantage of an Infrared ALDS is that it is not affected by FM or AM transmissions or by electromagnetic interference.

Infrared listening systems have been installed in many theaters and churches for pa-

trons who are hearing impaired as well as for normally hearing persons who enjoy the quality of infrared reception.

Large Area Listening

Infrared listening systems are appropriate for all situations in which the listener is in a fixed position. These situations include the large area infrared transmitter systems for houses of worship, theaters, and concert halls. The large area transmitter usually employs 119 LED. The entire listening area must be "bathed" with infrared light; the possibility of head shadows must be eliminated. Figure 14–16 shows an infrared transmitter that can cover a large area.

For small area usage, such as home television viewing or small group meetings, a 6 LED array transmitter is usually adequate. This small transmitter makes infrared listening relatively inexpensive. Figure 14–7 illustrates the use of a small infrared that is placed on the top of the television set.

Reception of any infrared signal can be accomplished by several means. The most common is by the use of an "under-the-chin" receiver that receives the infrared signal, converts it to acoustic energy, and delivers it to the ear of the listener. Figure 14–8 shows an infrared receiver. Note the volume control pictured on the left and the "eye" shown on the right. A second type of receiver is a body receiver that is worn with a cord that delivers the signal elec-

Figure 14–6. An infrared transmitter provides quality ALDS listening in a large area. (Courtesy of Siemens)

Figure 14–7. An infrared transmitter placed on top of the television provides good listening. (Courtesy of Siemens)

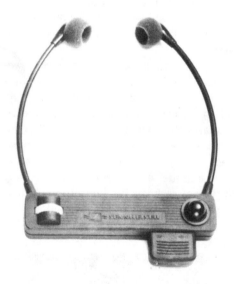

Figure 14–8. An infrared receiver can be used with large and small infrared transmitters. (Courtesy of Siemens)

tronically to (a) an earplug or earphone, (b) a magnetic induction silhouette worn behind the ear or against the T-coil of a hearing aid, (c) a magnetic neck loop, or (d) a personal hearing aid with direct audio input.

The listener who is interested in using an Infrared ALDS should experiment with the various receivers, since all of the previously mentioned modes of infrared reception are excellent.

FREQUENCY MODULATION DEVICES

Frequency modulation (FM) systems utilize radio waves to transmit the signal from the talker or sound source to the listeners. The FM transmitter may be thought of as a miniature radio station that transmits to FM receivers, similar in concept to the radios used by the general public. The FM transmitter and FM receiver must be "tuned" to each other, that is, transmission and reception must be on the same wave band.

FM systems have been used for many years in classrooms for children who are hearing impaired. These systems commonly are known as auditory trainers. The choice of FM receivers is based on the auditory need of each student. The teacher speaks into the microphone of an FM transmitter. Using this system, regular classroom activities as well as special language, speechreading, and articulation classes can be conducted through this wireless system. In the past, the receivers were collected from the students before they left the classroom. The transmitters and receivers were placed on charge, ensuring that the battery would be ready for use the next day. As a result, the students were unable to avail themselves of the extensive language exposure on the playground, in the cafeteria, and at home with normally hearing siblings and parents.

In many situations, the students did not function well with their traditional hearing aids. This was especially true in large areas such as houses of worship, theaters, auditoriums, or other settings in which distance, noise, and reverberation interfered with important auditory signals. In spite of these difficulties, FM systems were restricted to educational settings.

In 1982, the Federal Communications Commission (FCC) was finally convinced that the special needs of persons who are hearing impaired justified the approval of FM systems in settings other than educational. The new rules allowed the use of 72 to 76 MHz wave bands for general use. At present, 32 narrowband and 8 wideband channels are available for personal, social, vocational, recreational, and religious activities. During educational activities, narrowband channels are predominately used in classrooms. The simultaneous broadcast of FM signals in adjacent classrooms requires that different frequencies be used.

FM receivers interface with a variety of monaural and binaural modes to deliver the signal at ear level. Probably the most common is the "walkman" type of earphones or earplugs. Other modes include the following: (a) a snap-in earmold and transducer, (b) direct audio input to an ear level or body hearing aid, (c) an induction neck loop or silhouette used with the telecoil (T-coil) of a personal hearing aid, or (d) a bone conduction vibrator. Tape recorders also can be paired with FM receivers for simultaneous recording and listening in classroom situations.

Large Area FM Transmission

Wideband channels primarily are used in large areas, since the signal-to-noise ratio is greater than that of narrowband channels. Another advantage of wideband channels is that they provide a more natural range for speech and music. Presently, the use of only one open transmitter per channel is possible. Any number of receivers on the same channel can be used in the listening area. When using narrow- or wideband channels, the frequencies of all FM channels used in a certain listening area must be specified before additional FM systems are introduced.

FM transmission range is usually 300 to 500 feet from the transmitter, thus making the system ideal for use in large areas and outdoor recreational activities. FM ALDS provide listener freedom in seat selection. Since the FM signal will travel through walls, floors, and other barriers, FM is not the system of choice when privacy is required. The FM signal has been known to carry for miles if the FM transmission signal and the FM receivers are in line-of-sight.

FM ALDS AND SPECIAL NEEDS

FM for Interviewing

FM systems are excellent for virtually all problem listening environments. In one-to-one communication, the microphone and transmitter can be hand-held by the talker, or they can be permanently positioned on the corner of a desk or table for interviewing and counseling situations. Figure 14–9 demonstrates the FM transmitter (white) that is sending the signal of the physician's voice to an FM receiver worn by the patient. Since the patient is wearing a personal hearing aid and an FM receiver, a neck-loop is plugged into the receiver. This, in turn, provides an electromagnetic field from which the T-coil of the patient's hearing aid picks up the signal. The latter is then converted into acoustic signals by the personal hearing aid.

FM for Automobiles

For use in automobiles, or other transportation modes, the microphone of the FM transmitter can be clipped to the front or back of the car seat to be as close to as many talkers as possible.

FM for Restaurants

Restaurant noise can be overcome by placing the FM microphone as close to the sound source as possible by: (a) clipping it to the talker's lapel, (b) placing it in the center of the table, or (c) hanging it from the ceiling or light fixture above the table. Figure 14–10 shows an FM ALDS placed in the center of the table. These applications can be made for table games and boardroom tables.

FM for Groups

Comtek has developed a "sound collector" for FM transmission that is called the Conference Mate. The Conference Mate houses the FM

Figure 14–9. The FM transmitter (white) sends the physician's voice to an FM receiver worn by the patient. (Courtesy of Comtek)

Figure 14–10. An FM transmitter with microphone in a windscreen is placed in the center of a restaurant table. The gentleman is wearing an FM receiver in his pocket and an earbud in his ear. (Courtesy of Birmingham VA Medical Center)

Figure 14–11. The FM receiver "collects the sounds" from the talkers around the table and transmits them to the members of the group who are hearing impaired. (Courtesy of Comtek)

Figure 14–12. For quality listening, an FM transmitter is placed on top of the television set with the microphone located in front of the internal speaker. The gentleman is holding an FM receiver. (Courtesy of Birmingham VA Medical Center)

transmitter that broadcasts the talker's message to the FM receivers of the listeners who are hearing impaired. Figure 14–11 shows the Conference Mate positioned on a table during a group session.

FM and Television

Television and radio reception can be improved by positioning the microphone in front of the internal speaker of the television or radio. The volume level on the set should be adjusted so that it is at a listening level that is comfortable for the normally hearing listeners in the area. Figure 14–12 displays an FM transmitter on top of a television set. The microphone is shown clipped to the grille of the internal speaker of the set. The listener who is hearing impaired holds the receiver and adjusts the volume to a comfortable level.

Figure 14–13. Glass barriers can be overcome by the placement of an FM microphone held close to the opening in the glass panel. The listener wears the receiver and earpiece. (Courtesy of Birmingham VA Medical Center)

FM and Glass Barriers

One of the most difficult situations for persons who are hearing impaired is caused by the glass barriers used at teller windows and reception areas. Figure 14–13 demonstrates the use of an FM ALDS system by a person who is self-wired. He is wearing both the FM transmitter and FM receiver.

Large Area FM Applications

The problems encountered in large area listening can be overcome by giving the microphone to the talker, or by placing it at the sound source. FM transmission is highly satisfactory for activities such as religious gatherings, lectures, group meetings, classrooms, or even movie theaters. As a courtesy, permission should be given by the talker or the management of a facility prior to the placement of the transmitter. This will avoid any misunderstand-ing related to the legality of the recording. Figure 14–14 shows a minister using an FM transmitter to deliver his sermon. In the audience, there are several persons who are hearing impaired who are using FM receivers.

FM and Outdoor Activities

Outdoor instructional activities such as horseback riding, bicycling, snow skiing, and golfing can be enhanced by FM technology.

FM and Mobility Training

Blind rehabilitation specialists have included FM devices as an important tool for mobility training and other activities in which the blind person is at a distance from the instructor.

FM Advantages

Advantages of the FM ALDS include the following: (a) portability, (b) ease of use, (c) wire-

Figure 14–14. An FM transmitter with microphone sends the signal from the minister to members of the congregation who have FM receivers and earplugs. (Courtesy of Birmingham VA Medical Center)

less distance between transmitter and receiver, (d) low maintenance, and (3) lack of interference from electrical and magnetic sources.

Cost

The initial cost for the FM is one of the major disadvantages of the system for potential users of ALDS.

AUDIO INDUCTION LOOP DEVICES

The audio induction loop system is one of the oldest assistive listening devices. In Europe, loops have been used widely in conjunction with personal hearing aids. They are found in most public buildings. In several countries, the law requires the installation of this technology in churches and other public areas. The popularity of this system in Europe resulted from the widespread use of hearing aid T-coils. The use of loops spread to the United States in the 1950s. The basic components of an audio loop system include the following: (a) a micro-

phone, (b) an amplifier, and (c) a coil of wire that is looped around a room or a personal listening area. The wire generates an electromagnetic field in and around the loop of wire. This electromagnetic field is received by the telephone pick-up coil in a personal hearing aid.

Although the size of the loop can vary, it is best suited for medium and small listening areas. The loop has a number of applications: (a) it can be placed around a group of chairs in an auditorium, (b) it can encircle a single chair in a living room for television viewing, (c) it can be worn around the neck, or (d) it can take the form of a small silhouette induction loop that can be placed next to the ear level or body hearing aid with a T-coil. Figure 14–15 demonstrates the use of a loop ALDS and the television.

The major disadvantages of loop technology include interference from electric wiring, fluorescent lights, and transformers. Distance from the loop and improper head positioning can cause a reduction in the signal. Consumers report the greatest advantage to loop technology is that no special receiver is required for users who

Figure 14–15. A Loop ALDS encircles a chair for enhanced television listening. The listener wears his hearing aid with a T-coil. (Courtesy of Oticon)

have personal hearing aids with working T-coils. Loop system ALDS are easy to install, and the technology is simple and easily understood.

In the late 1970s and early 1980s, a major movement by consumer groups and health care professionals interested in the improvement of T-coil technology for personal hearing aids resulted in more efficient and sensitive T-coils in hearing aids. As a result, there has been an expanded application of Loop ALDS in the United States.

SENSORY AND ALERTING DEVICES

Persons who are profoundly hard of hearing or deaf have used alerting and signaling devices for many years. These devices also are useful for persons who are hearing impaired with high frequency losses. Sensory and alerting devices use visual, auditory, and tactile avenues. Some of these devices are discussed in the following paragraphs.

Auditory and Visual Signals

Telephones can be purchased with bell ringers that greatly increase the volume of the sound.

Horns, sirens, and warehouse bells can also be added. Signals from telephones and doorbells can be increased by attaching magnetic pick-up suction cups that are connected to loudspeakers. The same stimuli work with door knocks, doorbells, doormats, voices, crying babies, barking dogs, smoke detectors, and burglar alarms. Flashing lights in various forms are available. Remote lamps also can be installed to alert the person to a telephone that is ringing in another location. Other visual devices that can assist persons who are hearing impaired include the use of convex mirrors and peepholes. Sounds with special patterns, such as the ringing of the telephone, are easily identified through visual and auditory signals. Security alarms for driveways and gateways can alert persons who are hearing impaired of intruders. Telephone dialing for emergency and special police numbers can be activated by some of the alerting systems.

Microphones can be installed near the source of the sound. The arrangement works as an alerting system for the various needs just listed. The sensitivity of the microphone must be adjusted to pick up the immediate signal in order to cut back on unwanted responses to sounds in the area.

Assistive Listening Devices and Systems (ALDS)
Decision Circles

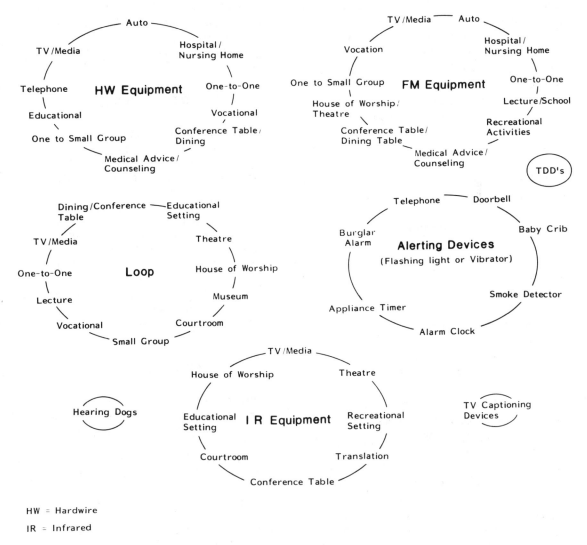

HW = Hardwire

IR = Infrared

Figure 14–16. Assistive Listening Devices and Systems (ALDS) Decision Circles suggest applications for users of ALDS. (From Vaughn, G. R., Lightfoot, R. K., & Teter, D. L. [1988]. Assistive listening devices and systems [ALDS] enhance the lifestyles of hearing-impaired persons. *The American Journal of Otology*, *9*(Suppl.), 101–106. Reprinted with permission.)

The master control unit acts as the central receiver for remote sensors such as: smoke detectors, doorbells, telephones, baby cries, and security systems. The master unit usually is connected to some form of flashing light or vi-brator. A remote lamp also can be made to act as an alerting system.

These systems also are useful for monitoring clothes dryers, washing machines, ovens, and night sounds around the house. They also serve as warning systems to indicate equipment maintenance problems.

Tactile Devices

Alarm clocks can use vibration as an alerting signal. Beds can be made to vibrate as can portable timers and wrist watches. One of the most recent tactile devices includes a wrist-worn receiver and many sensor-transmitters. The sensor-transmitter identifies a specific sound and sends a coded radio signal to a wrist-worn receiver. The wearer is alerted by the vibration of the wrist-worn receiver. The sound source is identified by a coded light on the receiver. The range of transmission is approximately 100 feet. Fans can also serve as alerting systems when attached to timers.

Hearing Dogs

Hearing dogs offer one of the most rewarding services in the area of assistance to persons who are hearing impaired. A hearing dog provides both companionship and a communication link with the normally hearing world.

SUMMARY

If quality care involving ALDS is to be made available, audiologists, hearing aid dispensers, speech-language pathologists, and other members of the hearing health care team need to be familiar with ALDS options and applications. They should also be familiar with the philosophy and practical considerations involved in the selection and utilization of these devices. Figure 14–16 shows the Decision Circles that were designed by Vaughn and Lightfoot (1988). These circles present the ALDS options that are appropriate for different listening and talking situations.

Professionals, persons who are hearing impaired, and significant others can refer to the Assistive Listening Devices and Systems (ALDS) Decision Circles (Lightfoot and Vaughn, 1988) for examples of how the various ALDS can be used. The examples are not all-inclusive, but they provide a sampling of the most popular applications. When clients are counseled concerning their special needs for hearing help, the professionals can use the Decision Circles to narrow the selection. Sometimes a single piece of equipment is sufficient; but sometimes the life styles demand a "Hearing Help Plan" that involves the future procurement of ALDS.

REFERENCES

Vaughn, G. R. (1986). Bill of rights for listeners and talkers. *Hearing Instruments, 37,* 8.

Vaughn, G. R., & Lightfoot, R. K. (1983). Lifestyles and assistive listening devices and systems. *Hearing Instruments, 3,* 128–134.

Vaughn, G. R., & Lightfoot, R. K. (1989). Resource materials. In R. L. Schow & M. A. Nerbonne (Eds.), *Introduction to aural rehabilitation* (2nd ed., pp. 586–605). Austin, TX: Pro-Ed.

Vaugh, G. R., Lightfoot, R. K., & Teter, D. L. (1988). Assistive listening devices and systems (ALDS) enhance the lifestyles of hearing-impaired persons. *American Journal of Otology, 9*(Suppl.), 101–106.

SUGGESTED READINGS

Castle, D. L. (1978). Telephone communication for the hearing impaired: Methods and equipment. *Journal of the Academy of Rehabilitative Audiology, 1,* 95.

Castle, D. L. (1983). *What you should know about TDDs.* Rochester, NY: National Technical Institute for the Deaf.

Gilmore, R., & Lederman, N. (1988, July/August). The missing link. *The Voice, 15,* 14–18.

Stoker, R. G. (1981). Telephone use by the hearing impaired: A 5-minute slide-show presentation. St. Louis, MO: Central Institute for the Deaf.

Stoker, R. G., French-St. George, M., & Lyons, J. M. (1985). Inductive coupling of hearing aids and telephones. *Journal of Rehabilitative Research, 22,* 71–78.

Stone, H. E. (1981). A report on the mini-conference: Elderly hearing impaired people. *SHHH* (pp. 1–2). Washington, DC: Self Help for Hard of Hearing People, Inc.

■ CHAPTER 15 ■

Improving Communication Through Aural Rehabilitation Treatment: History, Theory, and Application

■ RAYMOND H. HULL, Ph.D. ■

One of the basic premises in serving adults who are hearing impaired is that some form of rehabilitative activity should accompany the discovery of a hearing loss. An examination of the traditional literature dealing with aural rehabilitation procedures, however, leaves one less than satisfied in this regard. Most research in the various areas of aural rehabilitation appears marginally applicable to the process of therapy. Attempting to use these data in the determination of a treatment focus for particular clients becomes difficult. Further, in spite of subjective evaluation that certain strategies of aural rehabilitation are more effective than others, definitive validation of treatment techniques is still missing. The complexities of auditory impairment in its varying degrees of severity, along with the variability of persons affected, result in challenges that are both fascinating and frustrating.

The most successful approaches would appear to be those that address and incorporate procedures that specifically address the short-term and long-term communicative needs of individual clients. This philosophy will be stressed throughout this chapter.

Even though this chapter will address numerous avenues and approaches to aural rehabilitation, it must be remembered that the complexities observed within the population of adults who are hearing impaired require a client-oriented approach to aural rehabilitation. Using a "method" without considering the specific needs of individual clients may result in inadequate treatment.

TECHNIQUES FOR IMPROVING COMMUNICATION AMONG ADULTS WHO ARE HEARING IMPAIRED: PAST AND PRESENT

Before addressing current philosophies involved in the process of aural rehabilitation for adults, a review of issues and early approaches is important.

LIPREADING

The phonemes of speech have not been found to be visible enough for total reliance in communication for most persons. It has been difficult, however, to extinguish the term "lipreading" from its connotations of a vision-alone mode of communication.

Early definitions of lipreading, such as that by Bruhn (1949), stressed the eye as literally taking the place of the ear. Bruhn felt that the eye could be trained to distinguish the visible characteristics of the movements of the speech mechanism. Such descriptions of lipreading have been passed on through the years, and the term still tends to denote a strict concentration on the visualization of speech.

Other early methods of lipreading that stressed the primary use of vision were those of the Kinzies (1931), Bunger (1961), and Nitchie (1950). In the early to middle part of this century, however, undoubtedly it was necessary to emphasize the visual mode in communication when providing therapy for adults who were hearing impaired. As stated by McCarthy and Alpiner (1978), the visual-only methods stressed in early attempts at aural rehabilitation were necessary due to lack of efficient amplification systems.

A review of those early methods is appropriate, because it is from these methods that more current procedures have evolved or deviated.

The Mueller-Walle Method

In 1902, Martha Bruhn introduced the Mueller-Walle method (Bruhn, 1949). This method was strictly analytic in its approach. In other words, it stressed the development of lipreading skills through kinesthetic awareness of the movements in speech production. It involved rapid, rhythmic syllable drills because it was felt that the syllable is the basic unit of words, that in turn comprise sentences, and it should be subconsciously recognized. Bruhn viewed lipreading as training the eye as well as the mind, and felt that it involved visual, auditory, and motor memory. Her plans for lipreading lessons were divided into four parts:

1. Definition of the movement(s) of the new sound to be studied, contrasting the movements of the new sound with the ones studied previously;
2. Written work;
3. A story or talk that incorporated the new sound; and
4. Group practice, or a period of questions.

Jena Method

Anna Bunger and Bessie Whitaker introduced the Jena method of lipreading, which was developed by Karl Brauckman of Germany. Bunger (1944, 1961) outlined Brauckman's method, which emphasized the audible, visible, movement, mimetic, and gesture forms of communication, including syllable and rhythm. The movement form was thought of as being complete for all persons no matter what their level of hearing, because not all movements of the muscular system for speech are completely visible. The mimetic form (mimicking the lip movements of the speaker) was viewed as incomplete, but an important component of communication. Brauckman also believed that the gesture form (head, arm, hand, and body gestures) was not complete, but that it complemented all of the other forms.

Bunger (1961) stated that the first aim of persons who desire to learn lipreading is to develop awareness of the movements of speech and to learn how they feel. This was called kinesthetic awareness, and it was to become a substitute for audition.

The method included an explanation of the formation and composition of syllables. The consonants were presented and classified under the categories of production, including lips, tongue, and tongue-soft palate. The consonants were combined with words for practice. The consonants were said aloud by the clinician, and then the client said them. Clients were asked to concentrate on the manner of articulation for their production, and to categorize them in accordance with the three areas: movement, mimetic, and gesture.

The rhythmic component of this method included a basic rhythmic pattern that was established to accompany the syllable drills such as hand clapping, tapping, or ball bouncing. The aim of this aspect was to alert the client to the feeling of speech movements as he or she talked and to imitate visible speech movements as another person is speaking. The materials used included the syllable exercises, grammatical forms, stories, and conversations.

The Nitchie Approach

In 1903, Edward Nitchie introduced an approach that was intended to break away from the more analytic methods. His strategy advocated a "whole thought" approach to lipreading by emphasizing a working relationship between mind and eye. This mode of thinking paved the way toward a more psychological-synthetic basis for lipreading. Stress was placed on grasping the whole of the message, when not all auditory information was available. This was in contrast to the philosophies of Bruhn and Bunger, which stressed working with the analytic components of speech. Elizabeth Nitchie (1950), Edward's wife, later revised his materials and added additional ones. The integ-

rity of Edward's holistic approach was retained. Ordman and Ralli (1957) utilized Nitchie's approach and, with the aid of Elizabeth, developed lifelike materials for use in lipreading lessons.

The Kinzie Approach

The Kinzie sisters, Cora and Rose (1931), designed a lipreading approach and materials that evolved from a philosophy that incorporated portions of those by Mueller-Walle and Nitchie. It is considered a synthetic approach, that is, it is more eclectic in nature, involving more than lipreading. Their method involved a graded sequence of lipreading lessons based on varying levels of lipreading ability for both children and adults. The grading of the lessons was included so that individuals could progress from one level of skill to the next at their own rate.

In the developement of their materials, the Kinzie sisters established several rules. They were:

1. Sentences that were definite should be used.
2. Sentences should be natural in their structure.
3. Word selection also should be natural.
4. Sentences should be interesting, pleasing, and rhythmic.
5. All sentences must be dignified.

Within their story sections, they chose those that were short and humorous. They felt that these held the greatest value for beginners and intermediates. They also chose stories about famous people for these two levels. They felt that higher level literary selections were most appropriate for advanced clients.

In their lessons, explanations of articulatory movements for sound production were made, including sample words that contained those sounds, along with contrasting words. Vocabulary lists preceded sentence work. More advanced lessons included stories and accompanying questions. Mirror work in relation to sound production was advocated during lipreading practice. They also stressed the use of voice during lessons to aid clients in the use of their residual hearing. Their materials for adults included 36 lessons on movements of sounds, 36 lessons on stories, and 18 lessons using homophonous words.

Discussion of Early Approaches

The methods just reviewed generally were administered to clients in strict, unalterable ways. When clients had progressed through the lessons to the point of completing them, or had advanced in their lipreading skills to their apparent maximum, they were dismissed. The actual success rate is still unknown, although many clients apparently felt that they had benefitted. Some probably did. In one way or another, perhaps they were better able to understand the speech of others, in spite of the fact that they did not have the advantage of amplification devices.

According to Hull (1988a, 1988b), however, strict methods of lipreading, which were presented as a structured sequence of lessons, now are felt to be unsatisfactory for two basic reasons.

1. After the sequence has been completed, clients generally emerge unchanged in their ability to communicate with others. Even though individual clients may thank the audiologist who provided the lipreading sessions by saying, "I surely learned a lot," or "Thank you, your lessons were *very* interesting," they may have concluded that they did not improve.

2. Those approaches do not lend themselves to a basic need in the process of aural rehabilitation; that is, addressing specific communicative difficulties that clients face on a daily basis, and aiding them to function more efficiently in spite of their auditory deficit.

These strict approaches, and others like them, are based on the assumption that if the lessons are adhered to and learned, they will aid people who are hearing impaired to identify the visual clues of speech. In that regard, then, it was felt that they should likewise be able to communicate better in their everyday worlds. Although the assumption appeared rational to those who advocated the use of those strict and relatively unalterable approaches, it generally is not a valid one.

THE EFFICIENCY OF VISION IN COMMUNICATION

A number of investigators have studied the efficiency of vision in speech reception. The purpose of the majority of those investigations was to study the reciprocal benefits of vision and audition. However, studies by Heider and Heider (1940); Utley (1946); DiCarlo and Kataja (1951); O'Neill (1954); Hutton (1959); Woodward and Barber (1960); Brannon (1961); Binnie and Barrager (1969); Erber (1969); Berger (1972); Franks (1976); Franks and Kimble (1972); Hull and Alpiner (1976b); Binnie, Montgomery, and Jackson (1976); and Erber (1979) have concluded that vision alone contributes approximately 50% to speech intelligibility when no auditory information is available. Erber (1979), for example, confirmed that for essentially inaudible speech, intelligibility scores in vision-alone conditions remain at about 50% for words and sentences. Hull and Alpiner (1976b) reported that among young adults who possessed normal language function, approximately 50% of linguistically and phonemically balanced words within sentences could be identified in conditions of vision alone. They also found that about only 30% of sentences could be identified relative to their content when subjects were forced to depend on vision as the only sensory modality.

Whether adults who are hearing impaired can, through training, improve their ability to recognize the phonemes of speech and then transfer that ability to improved understanding of conversational speech continues to be a matter of debate (Walden, Erdman, Montgomery, Schwartz, & Prosek, 1977). However, the effect of training on the visual recognition of vowels and consonants (Armstrong, 1974; Black, 1957; Black, O'Reilly, & Peck, 1963; Franks, 1976;

Hutton, 1959; Walden, Prosek, Montgomery, Scherr, & Jones, 1977) generally has revealed anywhere from subtle to dramatic improvements in phoneme and word recognition. Again, whether this carries over to improved understanding of speech in everyday listening situations varies greatly from person to person and is a matter of debate. A lengthy discussion of early research on the complement vision for the hearing impaired is found in O'Neill and Oyer (1981).

THE COMPLEMENT OF AUDITION TO VISION

Erber (1979), as discussed earlier, demonstrated that vision alone under optimal conditions permits only about 50% intelligibility. For children who possessed a severe sensorineural hearing loss, vision alone attributed approximately 35 to 41% intelligibility. However, this study, like others, demonstrated the considerable complement of vision to audition and audition to vision. For example, in utilizing a systematic mechanism for manipulating the amount of visual clarity available to subjects (plexiglas placed at various distances to simulate visual acuity from 20/20 [normal] to 20/400 [severe] visual deficit), Erber (1979) found a 44% advantage when clear visual clues were available and combined with audition at a comfortable level. This advantage was maintained in spite of a simulated severe high-frequency hearing loss (450 Hz low-pass filter with a 35 dB rolloff per octave). Even with the existence of the simulated high-frequency hearing loss, scores increased from 54% intelligibility for single words in the vision-alone mode at 20/20 vision to 98% when a distorted auditory mode also was introduced, demonstrating the complement of vision to low frequency hearing when there is a simulated high-frequency hearing loss.

Erber (1979) also utilized the same procedure for the visual mode with children who were severely hearing impaired. The results relative to the identification of content words within sentences indicated that the benefit of the subjects' dominant sensory modality (vi-

sion) is great under optimal conditions (20/20 vision), but still allows only for approximately 33% intelligibility. When the subjects' amplified residual hearing was combined with clear vision, their intelligibility scores increased to 68%. For children who were profoundly hearing impaired, the contribution of the auditory modality was found to be only 6%. However, the combined auditory and visual score was 47%. When vision was reduced to replicate a severe loss of vision, scores dropped to 4%. Again, the complement of audition to vision is evident, but proportionate to the degree of auditory impairment. In working with adults who are adventitiously hearing impaired, however, the majority are found within the mild to moderate categories, where the complement of audition to vision and vice versa is very evident.

According to Hull (1988a), the reasons for the lack of definition in the visual-only reception of speech are probably that some phonemes look alike (are homophonous); some phonemes are difficult to identify because they are not visible by observing the lips (only about one third of the phonemes of American English are readily recognizable by observing the face of the speaker); and there is a general lack of redundancy of the visemes (visible phonemes and the visibility of phonemes) of speech relative to the comprehension of verbal messages. Audition, even at minimal levels, adds greatly to the synthesis and closure required to comprehend speech.

Other studies that confirm that the complement of audition to vision include those by O'Neill (1954); Sumby and Pollack (1954); Miller and Nicely (1955); Prall (1957); Hutton, Curry, and Armstrong (1969); Van Uden (1960); Erber (1971); Binnie, Montgomery, and Jackson (1976); Hull and Alpiner (1976b); Walden, Prosek, Montgomery, Scherr, and Jones (1977); Walden, Erdman, Montgomery, Schwartz, and Prosek (1981); Montgomery, Walden, Schwartz, and Prosek (1984); among others.

DISCUSSING THIS INFORMATION WITH YOUR CLIENT

Although it is important for clients to recognize the benefits of vision in communication, particularly in adverse listening environments, the efficient use of their residual hearing should be brought to a high level of awareness during aural rehabilitation. They should be made aware not only of the limitations imposed by their impaired hearing, but also of the amount of residual hearing available for use. Both should also be discussed in light of the efficient and complementary uses of audition and vision in communication.

IMPROVING COMMUNICATION SKILLS THROUGH AURAL REHABILITATION

So far, the discussions in this chapter have centered on early traditional methods used in attempts at improving the ability of persons who are hearing impaired to communicate in their worlds, and the benefits and limitations of the sensory modalities used in verbal communication and in most forms of aural rehabilitation.

As noted earlier, the approaches to aural rehabilitation for adults that appear to be most effective are those that are holistic in philosophy; that is, they address the specific communicative problems and needs of individual clients rather than a specific philosophy. There is more to resolving the communication deficit resulting from an adventitious hearing loss than learning to use residual hearing and complementary visual clues. That is not to say, however, that these aspects are not important in the process of aural rehabilitation.

The most critical element in the process of aural rehabilitation is the client. This aspect is where some of the earlier approaches may have lost their validity. Philosophies that stress holistic approaches to aural rehabilitation services for the adult include those by Fleming, Birkle, Kolman, Miltenberger, and Israel (1973); Binnie (1976); Colton (1977); Tannahill and Smoski (1978); Alpiner (1978); Hull (1982). Alpiner (1987) states that the goal of therapy for adults is to provide support, and to help clients recognize where their communication problems exist.

Hull (1982) stresses the importance of addressing the client's specific needs.

Although the majority of the problems hearing impaired adults encounter revolve around a decreased ability to communicate with others especially in adverse listening environments, each client faces uniquely individual problems as a result of his or her auditory deficit. In order for aural rehabilitation treatment to be appropriate and meaningful for clients, the approach must relate to their specific problems and communicative needs. (p. 5)

In other words, it appears that audiologists currently are adhering to philosophies that address aural rehabilitation as a multifaceted process that goes beyond speechreading and auditory training. However learning to use residual hearing with the greatest efficiency, along with supplemental visual cues, can be an important part of the process.

APPROACHES TO AURAL REHABILITATION TREATMENT

Approaches that are still traditional, but contemporary in spirit, include those of O'Neill and Oyer (1981). In their discussion of visual training, they refer to a number of avenues to train the individual who is hearing impaired to use vision more fully as a means of communication (Table 15–1).

O'Neill and Oyer suggest that the visual form of training accomplishes two purposes for the lipreading client. Those are, first, the development of visual concentration and, second, the development of synthetic ability.

O'Neill and Oyer also present a suggested approach to training clients in the combined use of visual and auditory clues. They state:

The initial stages of aural rehabilitation involve training without voice so that the hard of hearing person can focus his attention upon the visual aspects of speech. If such an approach is not employed from the beginning, the auditory channel will be used exclusively and the subject will not try to make use of the visual cues. Only because of this initial "sensory" isolation will the individual be alerted to the use of lipreading alone. (pp. 74–75)

TABLE 15–1. TRAINING EXERCISES FOR THE USE OF VISION IN COMMUNICATION

Visual perception
    Perceptual field
    Peripheral field
    Synthetic ability
    Figure ground recognition
Attention span
    Tachistoscopic training (speed of reception)
    Visual closure (training in the ability to exclude the irrelevant and to organize materials on the basis of similarities)
Predictabilities
    Sentence completion practice
    Word guessing

Source: From O'Neill, J. J., & Oyer, H. J. (1981). *Visual communication for the hard of hearing.* Englewood Cliffs, NJ: Prentice-Hall. Reprinted with permission.

Even though this rationale for the visual-only training has merit in some instances for some clients, many audiologists today are avoiding unisensory approaches, particularly with adult clients. The reasons, as discussed earlier in this chapter, include (1) the fact that clients generally emerge from therapy unchanged in their ability to communicate even though they may be more visually alert, and (2) those approaches do not address a basic need in the process of aural rehabilitation; that is, addressing the specific communicative difficulties that clients face in their daily lives.

The O'Neill and Oyer (1981) approach to the combined use of vision and audition includes beginning with combined practice in environmental noise conditions — in other words, not in an ideal communication environment. They recommend beginning at a 0 dB signal-to-noise ratio. Their approach continues as follows:

1. Progress from words utilizing lip sounds to words with open articulation (vowel) sounds;
2. Auditory discrimination of isolated sounds;
3. Amplified sound, introduced first at threshold, and then gradually increased to make a smooth transfer from vision to combined vision with audition;
4. Association of gestures and facial expression with quality and rate of speech;
5. Use of phrases, sentences, and stories;
6. Story retention (thought level rather than words or sentences), assessed by multiple-choice tests.

A summary of the first four weeks of lessons, as described by O'Neill and Oyer, follows:

■ *First day.* Explanation of purpose of program. Discussion of the value of combined practice. Demonstration of contributions of vision alone, audition alone, and vision and audition together.
■ *Second day.* Fifteen minutes of practice on "speech without auditory cues," followed by 15 minutes of practice on "speech without visual cues."
■ *Third day.* Initial listening in noise practice.
■ *Fourth and fifth days.* Thirty minutes of practice understanding individual words against interfering noises. Individual monosyllabic words in contrasting pairs are used in the practice.
■ *Sixth and seventh days.* Practice in listening without auditory cues. Paired words differing only in vowel composition. Fifteen minutes of practice with vowel discrimination against a noise background (recordings of various environmental noises).
■ *Eighth and ninth days.* Review of practice with selected consonants and vowels as incorporated in monosyllabic words.
■ *Tenth day.* Discussion of hearing aids and how they assist in lipreading. Discussion of benefits of hearing aids and effects of auditory "sets," and discussion of critical listening and viewing.
■ *Eleventh day.* Practice in speech discrimination. Sentences and phrases. Vision alone, auditory alone, and combined. Listening against noise backgrounds using phrases.
■ *Twelfth and thirteenth days.* Intelligibility practice with sentences, without voice, with voice, in noise, and in quiet.

■ *Fourteenth and fifteenth days.* Practice in rapid response to sentences.

■ *Sixteenth day.* Demonstration of "whole" approach with magazine covers. Stressed recall of thoughts. Presented description of pictures with no voice, low voice, and conversational voice.

■ *Seventeenth day.* Work on developing tolerance for noise. Discuss fact that noise has semantic as well as acoustic aspects.

■ *Eighteenth day.* Practice on colloquial forms using following subject areas: newspapers, automobiles, magazines, and cigarettes. Use of intermittent noise backgrounds with combined approach.

■ *Nineteenth day.* Situation practice. Discussion of people and objects in the clinic. Go over daily newspaper items, short stories from *Reader's Digest* and *Saturday Evening Post.* Use of white noise as background.

■ *Twentieth day.* Start incorporating tachistoscopic practice with five- and six-digit numbers presented at 1/50th of a second.

Another current, but traditional approach is presented by Sanders (1982). He believes that what should constitute a tailored management program for an adult who is hearing impaired can be facilitated by viewing the task according to a problem-solving model. His model involves the following stages:

1. Defining the problems or problems faced by the client;
2. Assessing the client's needs that are specific to those problems;
3. Establishing goals that relate to the auditory and/or visual needs of the client;
4. Determining methods for achievement of those goals; and
5. Evaluating effectiveness of those intervention strategies.

Sanders (1982) states that even though formal approaches to lipreading can be utilized for both adults and children, they "should not detract the teacher from grasping every opportunity to meet the (special) needs . . . both of

individual students and of the group" (p. 402). He stresses the importance of viewing aural rehabilitative management from the standpoint of the effects of the disability or handicap that the client is experiencing, as a result of the hearing loss. He emphasizes that a person's need for aural rehabilitation services becomes evident when: (1) communication abilities are no longer adequate to permit the client to meet the demands of his or her daily life; (2) the psychological cost of meeting daily demands is judged to be too high; (3) the present level of communicative abilities, though adequate for current demands, limits the adult in pursuit of advancement.

Sanders (1982) advocates the use of a profile questionnaire approach to probe the difficulties that the client is experiencing, and then to attempt to resolve them to the degree possible. The areas probed include the client's (1) home environment, (2) work environment, and (3) social environments, recognizing that the relative importance of these areas will differ from client to client.

The Committee of Aural Rehabilitation of ASHA (Costello et al., 1974) also presents an approach that involves more than a formal approach to the use of visual and auditory clues in communication. Even though it is over 16 years old, it emphasizes current methodologies in aural rehabilitation, and involves the following components:

1. Evaluation of peripheral and central auditory disorders;
2. Development or remediation of communication skills through specific training methods;
3. Use of electronic devices to increase sensory input (auditory, vibratory, and others);
4. Counseling regarding the auditory deficit;
5. Periodic reevaluation of auditory function;
6. Assessment of the effectiveness of the procedures used in habilitation.

McCarthy and Alpiner (1978) suggest a "progressive approach" to aural rehabilitation treatment that is based on modifying either the client's behavior and attitudes, the client's environment, or a combination of both. In modifying the client's behavior and attitudes, the emphasis is on developing the willingness to:

1. Admit the existence of the hearing loss and its handicapping effects;
2. Admit the hearing loss to others;
3. Take positive action to minimize communication difficulties by asking others to repeat and speak more clearly, and asking for selective seating.

According to McCarthy and Alpiner (1978), the sequence of their approach is as follows:

1. Audiologic and hearing aid evaluation;
2. Assessment of communication function;
3. Identification of problem areas due to hearing loss;
4. Verbal discussion with the group regarding problems;
5. Admission of hearing loss to themselves and others;
6. Modification of behavior, attitudes, and environment;
7. Willingness to utilize amplification in non-threatening therapy sessions;
8. Reduction of stress in communication situations;
9. Willingness to utilize amplification outside of therapy sessions;
10. More effective communication with normal hearing persons;
11. Termination of therapy. (p. 100)

This approach concentrates on the psychological impact of hearing impairment, and the client's response to the deficits experienced in his or her environment. The philosophy seems appropriate for portions of an aural rehabilitation treatment program and addresses important areas to be covered. It is to be stressed here, however, that not all audiologists are trained as counselors, and those audiologists should not venture into areas where problems (emotional or otherwise) require counseling by professionals trained to do so.

Hull (1982) presents a holistic approach to aural rehabilitation treatment that is presented

in its entirety in that text. It involves (1) counseling, (2) hearing aid orientation, (3) designing a program for increased communicative efficiency that is based on individual client's prioritized needs, (4) specific treatment procedures, and (5) evaluation of successes (or lack of them).

This approach lends itself to both younger and older adult clients. Its premises are: *first,* each client has special priority needs that revolve around his or her frequented communicative environments; *second,* most clients can benefit from specific treatment techniques that are based on language factors, particularly the redundancies of language, that if brought to a greater level of awareness, aid in communication; and *third,* the majority of adults who are hearing impaired complain of difficulty communicating in noisy or otherwise distracting environments. Practice in learning to cope in those environments can be of common benefit to most clients.

McCarthy and Culpepper (1987) stress that aural rehabilitation is a comprehensive process that is comprised of interacting components. They state that the purpose of an aural rehabilitation program is to focus on assisting persons who are hearing impaired in realizing their optimal potential. The important components of an aural rehabilitation program for adults who are hearing impaired, according to McCarthy and Culpepper (1987), include:

1. Visual training, including speechreading, interpretation of nonspeech stimuli such as gestures, and environmental cues;
2. Auditory training, which involves listening training, or developing attending behaviors;
3. Speech conservation; and
4. Counseling.

AURAL REHABILITATION: ITS APPLICATION FOR ADULTS

In the end, specific approaches, alone or in combination, rarely fit the needs of all clients who are hearing impaired. It is best, then, for audiologists to develop a philosophy regarding aural rehabilitation and then, taking that philosophy, extract, remold, and design programs that fit individual client's specific communicative needs.

What, then, is aural rehabilitation for adults? A holistic philosophy that would serve audiologists well was written by Braceland (1963). He states that rehabilitation, in its broadest sense, encompasses a philosophy that a person who is handicapped has the right to be helped to become a complete person, and not only to be restored as much as possible to usefulness and dignity, but also to be aided in reaching his or her own highest potential. This is a far reaching philosophy that should guide all persons who work in helping professions. In aural rehabilitation, however, such a philosophy should guide the audiologist to serve the needs of individual clients. Thus, not every adult who is hearing impaired should be placed in long-term aural rehabilitation treatment groups, nor do all require extensive hearing aid orientation or special amplification devices.

Such a philosophy suggests that, for some, the process of aural rehabilitation may involve:

1. A session or two to discuss difficult listening situations that they experience in their daily lives, and develop strategies for dealing successfully with them;
2. A few sessions of hearing aid orientation to adjust satisfactorily to their hearing aid, those with whom they communicate, and the places where they communicate;
3. A full program of auditory rehabilitation either in a group or as individual sessions. This author prefers that new clients be involved in individual work at least for several weeks to discuss and resolve communicative problems that are specific to the individual client, to discuss process and objectives, and other such matters before being introduced into a group setting.
4. Developing strategies for telephone communication, listening in church, listening in family gatherings, and environmental design to enhance communication in their home,

meeting room, or church sanctuary that may involve no more than several sessions.

APPLICATION

In any event, there are guidelines that will aid in the planning and execution of efficient aural rehabilitation programs for adult clients. The following are some principles that are important both in regard to rehabilitative procedures and to individual rehabilitation programs. They are not intended to supplant the good judgment of an individual audiologist. In the absence of an extensive body of knowledge surrounding these topics, however, the following are offered as considerations that have guided this author, and which practicing clinicians have reported or demonstrated, including those of Bode, Tweedie, and Hull (1988).

1. *Aural rehabilitation treatment should center on the specific needs of the client.* If a client is having difficulty communicating in a specific environment, then the audiologist must work with him or her to develop strategies to overcome those difficulties to the degree possible.

2. *The clinician should serve as a model of a person who functions as an effective communicator.* Clear, articulate speech without unnatural overarticulation should be the norm. Appropriate intensity levels of speech for maximum intelligibility in varying listening situations should be sought. Unintentional masking of visible speech by hand or head movements should be noted and avoided. By being an example of a good communicator, the audiologist is modeling what clients who are hearing impaired can expect among those with whom they can communicate best, or at least most efficiently.

3. *Clients should be informed of the clinician's general and specific objectives, and should also formulate their own goals, some of which should be comanaged with the clinician's objectives while the remainder are the client's responsibility.* Since auditory rehabilitation is a learning process, the client must be made aware of his or her part and responsibility in it, because in a learning, or a relearning process, the therapist is only part of the process. The client's degree of active involvement is of paramount importance. Carry-

over to real life situations cannot and will not be accomplished fully unless the client is totally aware of personal responsibility.

4. *Both individual and group therapy programs should be available to clients. Communication is a dynamic process that must be developed with varying speakers and in varying situations.* The client-therapist model is only one approach and should not be the only one considered. The group situation permits the client to discuss with peers the communication problems that may be common to each member. Each client must be evaluated carefully as to his or her potential for successful entry into the group environment. Many clients should begin treatment on an individual basis before joining group sessions, either because the difficulties they are experiencing in communication contraindicate successful group interaction, or the specific communicative difficulties that they are experiencing are not conducive to group discussion. On the other hand, group therapy can be a very powerful source for the development of an awareness of similar difficulties that others are experiencing. Group "problem solving" sessions are extremely beneficial.

5. *Counseling activity should be considered essential to the effectiveness of other components of the therapy relationship.* Audiologists are becoming more aware of this, and more training institutions are including formal courses and practicums in counseling as part of the curriculum. Counseling is one of the most important activities involved in auditory rehabilitation. In this regard, major attention and effort will need to be directed toward developing counseling skills in graduate students and in practicing audiologists.

6. *Development of assertive influence on the communication environment by the client should be an essential component of therapy.* Assertiveness, without aggression, can be an important therapy objective. The client can learn to stage-manage situations and communication events to maximize the probability of successful communication. Reducing background noise levels, decreasing the distance from a talker, optimizing lighting for speechreading cues, requesting that the talker use clearer speech and appropri-

ate gestures, and manipulating the design of the environment to one's communicative advantage are examples of areas where the client can become assertive and active in improving the communicative circumstances.

7. *Clients should be encouraged to establish and maintain a balance between assertiveness and submissiveness during communication.* The client may need counseling directed at emphasizing and demonstrating the give and take of many communication situations. Again, a balance between dominating and withdrawing behaviors might be explored during therapy. Acceptance of realistic expectations also should be addressed. Few of us can claim successful communication with even the majority of persons with whom we come in contact. In short, the client may be assuming too much personal responsibility for communication events.

8. *Clients should be instructed regarding alternative response criteria appropriate for specific communication events.* Many clients seem to adopt avoidance and/or withdrawal behaviors during situations requiring their participation in the communication act. Therapy planning might include activities that directly involve principles of effective interpersonal communication.

9. *Since successful communication is exciting and satisfying, therapy activities also should contain sufficient opportunities for similar positive interactions and experiences.* Interesting but still challenging training activities can be planned. Establishing a relaxed and satisfying communication relationship with clients is an ingredient of successful interaction. Developing and maintaining motivation are important potential effects of a relationship wherein humor, active involvement, and dynamic interaction are part of the therapy program, and not the exception.

10. *Developing technology should be incorporated into therapy activity on an experimental basis, and resulting judgments of specific equipment for specific purposes should be shared with other practitioners.* Technological aids, in addition to hearing aids, should be utilized through the aural rehabilitation program. These include, as examples, telephone amplifiers, new available assistive listening devices, prerecorded prac-

tice materials for home use, videocassette auditory-visual training systems, and radio transmission devices for specific social or vocational situations. Such existing technology can be used to enhance communication for clients with special needs.

11. *Innovative avenues for enhancing the peripheral and central auditory and visual systems of the clients should be utilized.* These include enhancement of the speed and efficiency with which clients utilize the auditory and visual information derived from communication. Time compressed speech and interactive laser-video technology is available and useful in this regard. Enhancing central auditory function in older adult clients appears to be an efficient avenue through which speech comprehension can be enhanced. Reactivating that system to regain speed and accuracy of central auditory function is not only beneficial to clients, but an exciting and challenging process as well. Activities emphasizing speed and accuracy of auditory closure, accuracy of very short-term auditory memory, and speed and accuracy of auditory/visual decision making all have proved beneficial to this author's clients.

12. *Clients should be instructed regarding alternative listening strategies appropriate for specific communication situations.* The clinician should explain to the client why certain situations are more difficult than others in which to communicate. Here the client should be informed, for example, that difficulty is to be expected in certain noise situations, and that an alternative listening approach may be to turn down the hearing aid and rely more on speechreading. Other difficult situations should be discussed to develop alternative strategies. These will add to the client's confidence in knowing that there are many ways to overcome difficult communication environments.

13. *Clinicians should establish an explicit catalog of possible methodologies to achieve specific objectives, and then review this information during planning of individual therapy.* Varying approaches to therapy should be gleaned from the literature. Novel approaches developed by colleagues or individual clinics should be evaluated for future use.

14. *Improving the speech habits of the client's family, friends, and others should be included as an important part of aural rehabilitation treatment.* Too often, it seems, clinicians concentrate exclusively on the client, with little or no attention given to significant others who are important to the client. General improvement in the communication expressiveness and effectiveness of these individuals could reduce the client's difficulties as much as, if not more than, therapy activities directed only to the client. This can be a powerful part of therapy on behalf of the client. However, diplomacy is a critical factor here. Efforts should concentrate on clarity of speech and what constitutes clear speech, including manner of articulation, intensity, and rate. Discussions of environmental design for the home, church, and meeting rooms are also important, along with the proximity of listener and speaker.

CONCLUSION

In this chapter, varying philosophies and approaches to aural rehabilitative treatment were presented. It behooves the reader to extract those portions that will be of direct benefit to his or her clients. We must continually remain vigilant to the special needs of individual clients. Some may require specific strategies that address particular problems in communication that are peculiar to them. Others may benefit from speechreading/lipreading instruction to complement their residual hearing. Whatever the assessed needs of clients, the audiologist must be flexible and knowledgeable in offering those services.

REFERENCES

Alpiner, J. G. (1978). *Handbook of adult rehabilitative audiology.* Baltimore, MD: Williams & Wilkins.

Alpiner, J. G. (1987). Rehabilitative audiology: An overview. In J. G. Alpiner & P. McCarthy (Eds.), *Rehabilitative audiology: Children and adults* (pp. 3–17). Baltimore, MD: Williams & Wilkins.

Alpiner, J., & McCarthy, P. (Eds.). (1987). *Rehabilitative audiology: Children and adults.* Baltimore, MD: Williams & Wilkins.

Armstrong, M. B. S. (1974). *Visual training in aural rehabilitation.* Unpublished doctoral dissertation, University of Illinois, Champaign-Urbana.

Berger, K. (1972). Visemes and homophenous words. *Teacher of the Deaf, 70,* 396–399.

Binnie, C. A. (1976). Relevant aural rehabilitation. In J. L. Northern (Ed.), *Hearing disorders* (pp. 213–227). Boston: Little, Brown.

Binnie, C. A., & Barrager, D. C. (1969, November). *Bi-sensory established articulation functions for normal hearing and sensorineural hearing loss patients.* Paper presented at the Annual Convention of the American Speech and Hearing Association, Chicago, IL.

Binnie, C. A., Montgomery, A. A., & Jackson, P. (1976). Auditory and visual contributions to the perception of selected English consonants. *Journal of Speech and Hearing Disorders, 17,* 619–630.

Black, J. W. (1957). Multiple choice intelligibility tests. *Journal of Speech and Hearing Disorders, 22,* 213–235.

Black, J. W., O'Reilly, P. P., & Peck, L. (1963). Self-administered training in lipreading. *Journal of Speech and Hearing Disorders, 28,* 183–186.

Bode, D., Tweedie, D., & Hull, R. H. (1982). Improving communication through aural rehabilitation. In R. H. Hull (Ed.), *Rehabilitative audiology* (pp. 101–115). New York: Grune & Stratton.

Braceland, F. J. (1963, October). *The restoration of man.* Donald Dabelstein Memorial Lecture presented at the Annual Conference of the National Rehabilitation Association, Chicago, IL.

Brannon, C. (1961). Speechreading of various materials. *Journal of Speech and Hearing Disorders, 26,* 348–354.

Bruhn, M. D. (1949). *The Mueller-Walle method of lipreading.* Washington, DC: Volta Bureau.

Bunger, A. M. (1944). *Speech reading — Jena method.* Danville, IL: The Interstate Press.

Bunger, A. M. (1961). *Speech reading — Jena method.* Danville, IL: The Interstate Printers and Publishers.

Colton, J. (1977). Student participation in aural rehabilitation programs. *Journal of the Academy of Rehabilitative Audiology, 10,* 31–35.

Costello, M. R., Freeland, E. E., Hill, M. J., Jeffers, J., Matkin, N. D., Stream, R. W., & Tobin, H. (1974). The audiologist: Responsibilities in the habilitation of the auditorily handicapped. *Journal of the American Speech and Hearing Association, 16,* 68–70.

DiCarlo, L. M., & Kataja, R. (1951). An analysis of the Utley lipreading test. *Journal of Speech and Hearing Disorders, 16,* 226–240.

Erber, N. P. (1969). Interaction of audition and vision in the recognition of oral speech stimuli. *Journal of Speech and Hearing Research, 12,* 423–425.

Erber, N. P. (1971). Auditory and audiovisual reception of words in low frequency noise by children with normal hearing and by children with impaired hearing. *Journal of Speech and Hearing Research, 14,* 496–512.

Erber, N. P. (1979). Auditory-visual perception of speech with reduced optical clarity. *Journal of Speech and Hearing Research, 22,* 212–223.

Fleming, M., Birkle, L., Kolman, I., Miltenberger, G., & Israel, R. (1973). Development of workable aural rehabilitation programs. *Journal of the Academy of Rehabilitative Audiology, 6,* 35–36.

Franks, J. R. (1976). The relationship of non-linguistic visual perception to lipreading skill. *Journal of the Academy of Rehabilitative Audiology, 9,* 31–37.

Franks, J. R., & Kimble, J. (1972). The confusion of English consonant clusters in lipreading. *Journal of Speech and Hearing Research, 15,* 474–482.

Heider, F. K., & Heider, G. M. (1940). A comparison of sentence structure of deaf and hard of hearing children. *Psychological Monographs, 52,* 42–103.

Hull, R. H. (1982). *Rehabilitative audiology.* New York: Grune & Stratton.

Hull, R. H. (1988a). Aural rehabilitation in adults. In N. J. Lass, L. V. McReynolds, J. L. Northern, & D. E. Yoder (Eds.), *Speech, hearing and language* (pp. 1278–1292). Philadelphia: W. B. Saunders.

Hull, R. H. (1988b, December). Hearing in aging. Presentation before the *National Invitational Conference on Geriatric Rehabilitation.* Washington, DC: U.S. Department of Health and Human Services, Public Health Service.

Hull, R. H., & Alpiner, J. G. (1976a). A linguistic approach to the teaching of speechreading: Theoretical and practical concepts. *Journal of the Academy of Rehabilitative Audiology, 9,* 4–19.

Hull, R. H., & Alpiner, J. G. (1976b). The effect of syntactic word variations on the predictability of sentence content in speechreading. *Journal of the Academy of Rehabilitative Audiology, 9,* 42–56.

Hutton, C. (1959). Combining auditory and visual stimuli in aural rehabilitation. *Volta Review, 61,* 316–319.

Hutton, C., Curry, E. T., & Armstrong, M. B. (1969). Semi-diagnostic test materials for aural rehabilitation. *Journal of Speech and Hearing Disorders, 24,* 318–329.

Kinzie, C. E., & Kinzie, R. (1931). *Lipreading for the deafened adult.* Philadelphia: John C. Winston.

McCarthy, P. A., & Alpiner, J. G. (1978). The remediation process. In J. G. Alpiner (Ed.), *Handbook of* adult rehabilitative audiology (pp. 88–111). Baltimore, MD: Williams & Wilkins.

McCarthy, J. P., & Culpepper, B. (1987). The adult remediation process. In J. Alpiner & J. P. McCarthy (Eds.), Rehabilitative audiology: Children and adults (pp. 305–342). Baltimore, MD: Williams & Wilkins.

Miller, G. A., & Nicely, P. E. (1955). An analysis of perceptual confusions among some English consonants. Journal of the Acoustical Society of America, 27, 338–352.

Montgomery, A., Walden, B., Schwartz, D., & Prosek, R. (1984). Training auditory-visual speech recognition in adults with moderate sensorineural hearing loss. Ear and Hearing, 5, 30–36.

Nitchie, E. H. (1950). New lessons in lipreading. Philadelphia: J. B. Lippincott.

O'Neill, J. J. (1954). Contributions of the visual components of oral symbols to speech comprehension. Journal of Speech and Hearing Disorders, 19, 429–439.

O'Neill, J. J., & Oyer, H. J. (1981). Visual communication for the hard of hearing. Englewood Cliffs, NJ: Prentice-Hall.

Ordman, K. A., & Ralli, M. P. (1957). What people say. Washington, DC: The Volta Bureau.

Prall, J. (1957). Lipreading and hearing aids combine for better comprehension. Volta Bureau, 59, 64–65.

Sanders, D. A. (1974). Aural rehabilitation. Englewood Cliffs, NJ: Prentice-Hall.

Sanders, D. A. (1982). Aural rehabilitation (2nd ed.). Englewood Cliffs, NJ: Prentice-Hall.

Sumby, W. H., & Pollack, I. (1954). Visual contributions to speech intelligibility in noise. Journal of the Acoustical Society of America, 26, 212–215.

Tannahill, J. C., & Smoski, W. J. (1978). Introduction to aural rehabilitation. In J. Katz (Ed.), Handbook of clinical audiology (pp. 442–446). Baltimore, MD: Williams & Wilkins.

Utley, J. (1946). Factors involved in the teaching and testing of lipreading through the use of motion pictures. Volta Review, 38, 657–659.

Van Uden, A. (1960). A sound-perceptive method. In A. W. G. Ewing (Ed.), The modern educational treatment of deafness (pp. 3–19). Washington, DC: The Volta Bureau.

Walden, B., Erdman, S., Montgomery, A., Schwartz, D., & Prosek, R. (1981). Some effects of training on speech perception by hearing-impaired adults. Journal of Speech and Hearing Research, 24, 207–216.

Walden, B., Prosek, R., Montgomery, A., Scherr, C., & Jones, C. (1977). Effects of training on the visual recognition of consonants. Journal of Speech and Hearing Research, 20, 130–145.

Woodward, M. F., & Barber, C. G. (1960). Phoneme perception in lipreading. Journal of Speech and Hearing Research, 3, 212–222.

■ CHAPTER 16 ■

Speech Conservation
for Adult Clients

■ PAMELA L. JACKSON, Ph.D. ■

Speech characteristics and therapy techniques for clients who are prelinguistically hearing impaired are well documented in the literature. The degree of auditory impairment and the extent of the resulting handicap for this population have drawn the attention of researchers and clinicians alike. Their efforts have resulted in a documented body of literature, which is the basis for communication training programs throughout the United States.

There is, however, another subgroup of the hearing-impaired population that is often overlooked in these descriptions of speech behaviors. That group is the *adventitiously* hearing impaired who have losses that occurred after speech and language skills had developed normally. With the onset of the hearing loss, speech monitoring ability may diminish, and in time, changes in speech production may occur. The task facing clinicians who deal with this clientele is one of conservation of already existing skills rather than the development of new ones. Maintenance of intelligibility is the goal.

FACTORS INFLUENCING
SPEECH DETERIORATION

A description of the typical characteristics of this population is nearly impossible because there is no typical case. Many factors and their interaction are responsible for the amount of deterioration that occurs after the hearing impairment develops. These factors are discussed in the following paragraphs.

DEGREE OF
HEARING LOSS

If the hearing loss is of such a degree as to allow at least partial monitoring of speech, the problem will be less severe than if no speech monitoring is possible. In the majority of cases of adventitious hearing loss, the onset is gradual, and the degree is mild enough that no change in speech production is noticed.

CONFIGURATION OF THE HEARING LOSS

Configuration and degree of hearing loss interact to impose a certain amount of distortion on the incoming auditory signal. For example, a precipitous high-frequency hearing loss will either nullify or distort sibilant or high-frequency voiceless consonants. The configuration will be a prime determiner of speech monitoring activity.

AGE OF ONSET

In general, the more years of normal hearing a client has, the better will be his or her oral speech skills. Even though this statement has been found to be true, the relationship between age of onset and speech intelligibility is still a complex one. Binnie, Daniloff, and Buckingham (1982) reported on the case of a child who incurred a profound bilateral hearing loss as a result of spinal meningitis when he was 5 years old. Prior to his hospitalization, he reportedly showed no indications of speech or language problems. Approximately 6 weeks after his illness began, the child was seen for auditory management, which included periodic tape recording, of his spontaneous speech as well as his responses to the screening portion of the Templin-Darley Tests of Articulation (1969). Testing was conducted at 2-week intervals for a period of 9 months. Phonetic, spectrographic, and perceptual analyses of the tapes were conducted and revealed increases in word duration, increases in duration variability, a rise in fundamental frequency (F_o), less variation in pitch inflection, the syllabification of final consonants, and significantly depressed speech intelligibility scores. Within a 9-month period, the speech of this 5 year old had changed markedly.

The age factor must be considered a critical determiner of speech deterioration when other, older cases are compared to this 5 year old. For example, consider the case of a client who incurred a sudden, profound hearing loss at age 21 due to antibiotic treatment for a kidney infection. Several years following the onset, speech intelligibility remained intact, with only minor sibilant distortion being noted. Prosodic factors remained unaffected. Other cases of similar etiology have been reported, however, in which speech deterioration was much more extensive and intelligibility was affected noticeably.

The influence of age of onset of hearing loss on speech intelligibility has never been explored systematically. The need for such an investigation is supported by the concluding statements made by Kent (1976) following his survey of acoustic studies of speech development. He concluded that the variability of speech motor control progressively diminishes, beginning by 3 years of age and continuing until the child is 8 to 12 years of age. At that point adult stability is achieved. This development of precise motor control occurs, therefore, after the majority of speech sounds have reached the point where they are acceptable phonetically. This statement implies that 8 to 12 years of age may be a critical dividing line for predicting speech deterioration following the onset of a hearing loss.

HEARING AID HISTORY

Ideally, amplification will be employed shortly after the hearing loss is discovered, so that speech monitoring ability is maintained. The time amplification is first initiated and the success that is achieved in restoring discrimination ability will influence how severe speech deterioration will be.

ACCOMPANYING PROBLEMS

The presence of mental retardation, learning disabilities, neuromuscular problems, and other similar disorders possibly will affect speech skills in the adventitiously hearing-impaired population just as in the congenitally hearing-impaired population.

NEED TO USE SPEECH

As with the congenitally hearing impaired, speech skills are dependent largely on the need for continued oral communication. This continued use may need to be accompanied by reinforcement and monitoring to insure that skills are maintained.

SPEECH CHARACTERISTICS OF THE ADULT HEARING-IMPAIRED POPULATION

The type of speech problem that occurs with acquired hearing loss will vary widely, and as a result, each case must be evaluated for individual patterns. The error patterns that occur may involve a combination of three different components, including articulation, voice and resonance, and rhythm and timing.

ARTICULATION

The phoneme production errors involved in the speech of the deaf have been described thoroughly in the classic study by Hudgins and Numbers (1942) and are summarized in Table 16–1.

Which of these errors appear in the speech of the adventitiously hearing impaired depends on the factors mentioned earlier. Based on a knowledge of speech acoustics, certain predictions can be made as to which speech sounds may deteriorate in the presence of a particular hearing loss. Based on that information, and according to Calvert and Silverman (1975), common errors include omissions and distortions of the sibilants, especially /s/, that are described below. These errors can be ex-

TABLE 16–1. PHONEME PRODUCTION ERRORS

Consonant Errors

Failure to distinguish between voiced and voiceless consonants

Consonant substitutions

Excessive nasality

Misarticulation of consonant clusters
Two types of errors may occur: (1) one of the sounds may be dropped from the cluster, or (2) the sounds may be produced so slowly that additional syllables are added when /ə/ is inserted between the cluster elements.

Misarticulation of abutting consonants in different syllables with /ə/ being inserted between the final consonant of one syllable and the initial consonant of the next.

Omission of initial consonants

Omission of final consonants

Vowel Errors

Vowel substitution

Misarticulation of diphthongs
Two types of errors may occur: (1) the diphthong may be produced as two separate vowels, or (2) one component of the diphthong, usually the second, may be omitted.

Diphthongization of simple vowels

Neutralization of vowels so that the production approaches /ə/

Nasalization of vowels

plained, in part, by comparing them with the acoustic characteristics of the speech signal. In general, speech sounds that are more difficult to hear are more often in error. Each sound contains energy at several frequencies, which means that a given audiometric configuration may remove only part of the identifying information and result in a distortion. The sound may be detected based on lower frequency cues but may no longer be understood, thus resulting in faulty auditory monitoring and possible distorted output.

VOICE AND RESONANCE

The disorders of voice and resonance that can occur in a hearing impaired population have been listed by Magner (1971) and can be seen in Table 16–2.

The specific characteristics of voice and resonance that occur in an individual also will vary greatly. It has been shown, however, that subtle quality and resonance differences occur early in the speech deterioration process of adults who are adventitiously hearing impaired. These changes may be due, at least in part, to the speaker's attempts to replace the decrease in auditory monitoring ability with an increase in tactile-kinesthetic feedback.

RHYTHM AND TIMING

Hudgins and Numbers (1942) reported three types of rhythm patterns that occur in the speech of the deaf: correct rhythm, abnormal rhythm, and nonrhythm. They also empha-

sized the importance of speech rhythm on overall intelligibility by indicating that its contribution was equal to that of consonant articulation.

The relationship between rhythm and intelligibility also was supported by Hood and Dixon (1969) in their study of the physical characteristics of speech rhythm of speakers who were deaf. For the purpose of their investigation, they defined speech rhythm as being composed of intonation changes, loudness changes, and two temporal factors — relative syllable duration in a sentence and rate of utterance in a sentence. They concluded that deaf speakers showed less fundamental frequency and intensity variation and greater duration of both syllables and total utterances than did normal hearing speakers. They also found that ratings of rhythm proficiency were highly correlated with the two duration measures and slightly related to intensity variation. No relationship existed between rhythm proficiency ratings and fundamental frequency variation.

A great deal of research concerning the timing and rhythm patterns of deaf speech was reviewed by Nickerson (1975). He offered the following conclusions.

1. Speakers who are deaf use a slower speaking rate than normal speakers.
2. Speakers who are deaf do not make a large enough duration difference between stressed and unstressed syllables.
3. Pauses of speakers who are deaf are more numerous, longer, and/or inserted in inappropriate places.
4. Speakers who are deaf use inappropriate rhythm or syllable grouping.

TABLE 16–2. VOICE AND RESONANCE DISORDERS IN THE HEARING IMPAIRED

Strength	Resonance	Placement	Inflection
Lacking voice	Hypernasality	High pitch	Lacking variation
Lacking control of volume	Hyponasality	Low pitch	Erratic variation
Weakness		Gutteral voice	
Harshness		Erratic changes	
Breathiness			

5. Speakers who are deaf demonstrate some timing problems related to speech sound production.

As with articulation and voice/resonance problems, the rhythm characteristics of a person who is adventitiously hearing impaired will vary considerably depending on the factors summarized earlier. It appears, however, that once speech rhythm patterns are well established, they are maintained more accurately than articulation or voice or resonance patterns. In view of their importance in speech intelligibility, however, rhythm and timing must not be overlooked.

DIAGNOSTICS FOR SPEECH CONVERSATION

RECEPTIVE SKILLS

To obtain a complete evaluation of the communication problems created by the hearing loss, both receptive and expressive skills must be explored. The initial receptive evaluation would include the items listed in Table 16–3. These data should give the audiologist information to help in medical diagnosis, to serve as a guide for aural rehabilitation recommendations, and to predict communication difficulties.

Based on the results of the initial testing, aural rehabilitation may be recommended. The receptive portion of the diagnostic evaluation would continue with a hearing aid evaluation and additional communication evaluation to assess skills with the recommended hearing aids. Additional tests or areas of exploration may include:

1. Speech recognition threshold (SRT)/speech detection threshold (SDT).
2. Discrimination in quiet and in noise using materials with different levels of redundancy. Examples of materials are word tests, such as the Central Institute for the Deaf (CID) Auditory Test W-22, the Word Intelligibility by Picture Identification (WIPI) test,

TABLE 16–3. THE INITIAL RECEPTIVE COMMUNICATION EVALUATION

Pure tone air and bone conduction testing

Speech audiometry
   A sensitivity measure such as a speech recognition threshold (SRT) or a speech detection threshold (SDT)
   A discrimination measure such as the CID W-22 word lists

Immittance testing

Site of lesion testing

and the Monosyllabic-Trochee-Spondee (MTS) test; phoneme tests (i.e., consonant and/or vowel confusion tests); and sentence tests such as the CID Everday Speech Sentences.
3. Prosodic feature tests, such as measures of stress pattern recognition in words and/or sentences.

The key point that must be remembered in performing an evaluation of receptive skills is that the examiner is looking for the starting point for auditory training, as well as attempting to obtain a measure of communication difficulty in normal listening situations. These goals may be met, at least in part, through discrimination testing using the standard W-22 word lists in quiet, but in many cases this procedure may be inappropriate. In some instances, the use of the W-22 word lists may result in scores near 100%, and yet the client reports communication difficulty. The listening task must be made more difficult in some way to find the dividing line between success and failure. This may mean increasing the difficulty of the listening task by increasing the complexity of the material (i.e., a sentence test such as the CID Everyday Speech Sentences), by reducing the redundancy of the materials (i.e., a phoneme recognition task), or by increasing the level of background noise.

In other cases, the W-22 word lists are too difficult, and the errors are so numerous and random that no patterns emerge that can be incorporated systematically into auditory training. In these instances, the task must be made easier, and this usually means selecting a closed-response set of materials. In many cases, a test such as the WIPI (Ross & Lerman, 1971) is appropriate even though the standardized norms do not apply, since the task can also be performed by adults with more severe losses. Written multiple-choice response forms can be created to eliminate a picture-pointing response for adults. The point is that in the evaluation of receptive skills for communication purposes, the audiologist must look for a level of task difficulty where some success is achieved and yet systematic errors are made. This will be the starting level for auditory training.

The final area of auditory diagnostics involves an assessment of prosodic feature perception. The importance of this area should be fairly obvious in light of the documented importance of prosodic features in the intelligibility of speech of the deaf (Hudgins & Numbers, 1942). At present, few tests exist that probe this area of prosodic feature perception in the hearing impaired. One of these is the CID-CAT or MTS test (Erber & Alencewicz, 1976) or the expanded version of the same concept, the CID-MONSTR. The MTS consists of 4 words in each of three different stress pattern categories (monosyllable, trochee, and spondee), while the MONSTR consists of 10 words in each of the three categories. In either case, the concept is the same. The test is scored two ways: *first* by percentage of words recognized correctly and *second* by percentage of stress pattern recognition. In other words, if a monosyllable is presented and a monosyllable is the response, it is counted as correct in the prosodic feature scoring even if the exact word is incorrect. In many cases of severe to profound hearing loss, the client is unable to receive enough phonetic information through the auditory channel only to recognize the words, and yet he or she can perform the stress recognition task because he or she can at least feel the patterns. Auditory training may need to start at a prosodic feature level to prevent speech deterioration in the stress and rhythm areas.

A second test that is available to probe prosodic feature perception is the Stress Pattern Recognition in Sentence Test (SPRIS) (Jackson & Kelly-Ballweber, 1979). This 48-sentence test consists of four repetitions of each of 12 simple sentences. Each sentence consists of four monosyllabic words. For each repetition of a sentence, a different word is stressed, thus giving a slightly different connotative meaning to the utterance. The subject's responses are scored in the same way the MTS is scored, first by percentage of correct sentence identification and second by percentage of correct sentence stress pattern identification. This test also has been shown to be appropriate with an adult hearing impaired population.

When the receptive diagnostic information is pulled together, the aural rehabilitationist has an indication of how much distortion the hearing loss is imposing on the incoming speech signal. This indication is derived from the audiogram, which is a frequency-by-intensity plot of sensitivity across the frequency range. The speech results are an indication of how well the client is using his or her residual hearing. Those areas of auditory perception that now are more difficult for the adventitiously hearing impaired become the core of auditory training to maintain the client's speech monitoring ability. It is this speech monitoring ability that is the key to speech conservation.

EXPRESSIVE SKILLS

Articulation

Evaluation of the expressive speech skills of the adventitiously hearing impaired population follows the same basic principles as any speech evaluation. The client's articulation characteristics are evaluated with various types of materials under various conditions. The clinician is interested in obtaining information concerning usual speech sound production, error contexts and consistency, and stimulability of error sounds.

EVALUATION OF SPEECH SOUND PRODUCTION: WORD LEVEL. Several tests are commercially available to probe phoneme production at the word level, but the general thrust of the materials is toward consonant production in a younger population with pictures being used to elicit responses. Any of these materials would serve the purpose with an adult population, if written word lists rather than pictures were used as the stimulus items.

While vowel articulation may not be of primary importance in the typical normally hearing client, it is of major concern in the speech productions of the hearing-impaired population. Errors in vowel production are common in the client who is congenitally hearing impaired, and as mentioned earlier, vowel errors in the form of resonance changes may be among the first to appear in the speech of the adventitiously hearing impaired. For this reason, it is critical that a test of articulation ability be selected that will probe vowel as well as consonant productions.

For the evaluation of the speech skills in a hearing-impaired population, Berg (1976) rec-

ommends the Templin-Darley Tests of Articulation (Templin & Darley, 1969) or his own shortened version of this test. The Templin-Darley Tests of Articulation were designed as a basic tool of the speech pathologist to assess speech production skills at the word level of children age 3 to 8 years. The stimulus materials consist of 57 cards with two to four pictures per card that are used to elicit responses. There are also printed lists of words and sentences for use with older clients for whom pictures may be inappropriate. This results in 141 items which comprise the Templin-Darley Revised Diagnostic Test. In order to increase the versatility of the test, the items are combined into two specific tests and also into several groupings of sounds to meet specific purposes in testing articulation. Various units in the test are presented in Table 16–4.

Berg's shortened version of the Templin-Darley test consists of 67 items from the 141 original words chosen to sample all vowels and diphthongs; all single consonants in the prevo-

TABLE 16–4. VARIOUS UNITS IN THE TEMPLIN-DARLEY TESTS OF ARTICULATION

The 50-item Screening Test

A 42-item Grouping of Consonant Singles, composed of 22 initial and 20 final consonants, which probes the client's mastery of consonant production.

The 43-item Iowa Pressure Articulation Test, which explores the adequacy of velopharyngeal closure by assessing the adequacy of oral pressure for speech sound production (Morris, Spriestersbach, & Darley, 1961).

Groupings of Consonant Clusters intended to determine the consistency of the speech sound production in various phonetic contexts.

A 31-item /r/ and /ɜ/ Cluster Grouping made up of two- and three-phoneme clusters

An 18-item /l/ and /l̩/ Cluster Grouping made up of two- and three-phoneme clusters

A 17-item /s/ Cluster Grouping made up of two- and three-phoneme clusters

A 9-item Miscellaneous Consonant Cluster Grouping

Groupings of Vowels and Diphthongs

An 11-item Vowel Grouping

A 6-item Diphthong Grouping made up of five diphthongs and one consonant-vowel combination.

calic position of words; the voiced stops /b/, /d/, and /g/; the sibilants /s/, /z/, /ʃ/, /ʒ/, /tʃ/, and /dʒ/, and the glides /r/ and /l/ in the postvocalic position; and several blends involving /s/, /r/, and /l/ with other phonemes. His suggested recording form and list of stimulus words are found in Table 16–5.

Each item in this table contains the phoneme to be tested and the stimulus word that is to be used in eliciting the production. Berg also presents pictures that can be used with children to elicit a verbal response. In the case of the young adult who is hearing impaired, a word list to be read by the client may be substituted. The position of the phoneme within the word is specified by the *i* (initial or prevocalic), *m* (medial or intervocalic), or *f* (final or postvocalic) beside the word.

The recording form provides a blank for scoring the acceptability of the production. Any scoring code can be used, but a suggested system would be to mark an omission with "om," a substitution with the phonetic symbol of the error sound, and an addition with the phonetic symbols. If the clinician's ear is trained to pick up fine production differences, a scaling system may be used to differentiate various levels of distortion. An example of one such system might be:

1 = *Correct production.* The sound is produced correctly with no distortion.
2 = *Mild distortion.* The distortion would be noticeable only to the trained listener.
3 = *Distortion.* The distortion would be noticeable to the layman but would not be annoying.
4 = *Marked distortion.* The distortion would distract the average listener from the speech content.
5 = *Severe distortion.* The distortion is so severe that the sound is not recognizable.

The importance of such a system must be stressed. A distortion of an articulation may occur in varying degrees, and the severity of the problem may be determined by the severity of the distortions in addition to the number of phonemes involved. The clinician must be careful to judge an articulation as a distortion even if it only mildly deviates from accepted standards. The productions of the hearing impaired must be judged relative to normal hearing articulation and not judged as acceptable as long as it is intelligible. Intelligible speech very well may be distorted speech.

Additional commercially available tests to probe articulation skills at the word level include the Fisher-Logemann Test of Articulation Competence (1971) and the Goldman-Fristoe Test of Articulation (1969). The Fisher-Logemann Test of Articulation Competence consists of 109 picture stimuli on 35 bound cards intended for use with adults as well as children. Eleven of the cards may be used as a screening test. The text explores the production of all English phonemes, both vowels and consonants, and provides for errors to be analyzed in terms of distinctive features.

The Goldman-Fristoe Test of Articulation was developed for the main purpose of assessing consonant articulation ability. The test materials consist of 35 pictures of objects or activities. The client names the pictures or answers questions to provide a total of 44 responses. Even though vowels are not specifically probed, the Sounds-in-Words Subtest contains all of the vowels and diphthongs except /ʊ/, /ɑ/, and /ɔɪ/ and, therefore, could be used for that purpose.

EVALUATION OF SPEECH SOUND PRODUCTION: SENTENCE LEVEL. When attention is focused on a particular phoneme in a word articulation test, it may be possible for the client to produce it correctly. Yet when the same sound occurs in conversation, it is omitted, distorted, or erroneously produced in some way. For this reason, it is important to explore the ability of the adventitiously hearing impaired to produce speech sounds in sentences or in conversation as well as in isolated words.

Several tests also are available to probe articulation ability at the sentence level. One is the Templin-Darley Tests of Articulation mentioned earlier. The sentence portion of this test

TABLE 16-5. RECORDING FORM FOR BERG'S SHORTENED VERSION OF THE TEMPLIN-DARLEY TEST OF ARTICULATION.

1. p (i)	pipe	_____	35. sm–	smoke	_____
2. t (i)	two	_____	36. skr–	scratch	_____
3. k (i)	cat	_____	37. –ks	socks	_____
4. b (i)	bicycle	_____	38. z (m)	scissors	_____
5. d (i)	door	_____	39. z (i)	zipper	_____
6. g (i)	girl	_____	40. z (f)	ties	_____
7. m (i)	mittens	_____	41. –lz	nails	_____
8. n (i)	nose	_____	42. ʃ (i)	shoe	_____
9. ŋ (f)	ring	_____	43. ʃ (m)	dishes	_____
10.. f (i)	fence	_____	44. ʃ (f)	fish	_____
11. θ (i)	thumb	_____	45. ʃr–	shred	_____
12. v (i)	valentine	_____	46. ʒ (i)	Zhivago	_____
13. ð (i)	there	_____	47. ʒ (m)	television	_____
14. w (i)	window	_____	48. ʒ (f)	mirage	_____
15. tw–	twins	_____	49. tʃ (i)	chair	_____
16. b (f)	tub	_____	50. tʃ (m)	matches	_____
17. d (f)	slide	_____	51. tʃ (f)	watch	_____
18. g (f)	dog	_____	52. dʒ (i)	jump	_____
19. i (m)	feet	_____	53. dʒ (m)	engine	_____
20. ɪ (m)	pin	_____	54. dʒ (f)	cage	_____
21. ɛ (m)	bed	_____	55. ə dʒ	large	_____
22. æ(m)	bat	_____	56. ɝ	bird	_____
23. ʌ (m)	gun	_____	57. r (i)	red	_____
24. ɝ	car	_____	58. r (m)	arrow	_____
25. a (m)	clock	_____	59. pr–	presents	_____
26. ʊ (m)	book	_____	60. dr–	drum	_____
27. u (f)	blue	_____	61. str–	string	_____
28. o (m)	cone	_____	62. mə	hammer	_____
29. aʊ (m)	house	_____	63. l (i)	leaf	_____
30. e (m)	cake	_____	64. l (f)	bell	_____
31. aɪ (f)	pie	_____	65. gl–	glasses	_____
32. ɔɪ (f)	boy	_____	66. –tl	bottle	_____
33. s (i)	sun	_____	67. –lt	belt	_____
34. s (f)	mouse	_____			

Source: From Berg, F. S. (1976). *Educational audiology: Hearing and speech management*, p. 168. New York: Grune & Stratton. Reprinted with permission.

consists of 141 items constructed and organized to evaluate the same speech sounds as the word portion. A second test is the sentence form of the Fisher-Logemann Test of Articulation Competence. It consists of 15 sentences printed on a single card and designed to test all English speech sounds. The sounds within the sentences are arranged so that each voiced-voiceless cognate pair of consonants is tested in the same sentence. Consonants having no cognate are grouped into sentences according to manner of production. The last four sentences probe vowel productons with the sounds being arranged in terms of place of articulation. A third test for sentence articulation is the Sounds-in-Sentences Subtest of the Goldman-Fristoe Test of Articulation. This subtest was developed to assess systematically speech sound production in a context similar to conversational speech. The material consists of two stories that are read by the examiner while the client watches sets of four or five pictures. The subject then repeats the story in his or her own words, using the pictures to guide the narrative and thus the words in the speech sample. The result is content-controlled speech that approximates conversational speech.

EVALUATION OF ERROR CONTEXTS AND CONSISTENCY. It is possible that the misarticulations that occur in a specific phonetic context do not occur in others. This inconsistency of production creates a need to examine speech sound articulation in more than one context. This type of evaluation is possible with the Templin-Darley Tests of Articulation since certain consonants occur in a number of different clusters. The results may reveal one or more contexts in which the speech sound is correctly produced. This information, in turn, will serve as an aid in the remediation process.

Berg (1976) recommends the Deep Test of Articulation by McDonald (1964) to explore error contexts in the speech of children who are hearing impaired. This test also would be appropriate for use with an adventitiously hearing-impaired adult population. The materials consist of both a picture and a sentence version with the items being designed to test the articulation of the following 13 speech sounds in several phonemic contexts: /s/, /z/, /r/, /l/, /ʃ/, /tʃ/, /dʒ/, /θ/, /ð/, /k/, /g/, /f/, and /v/.

The information obtained from such a probe may reveal one or more contexts in which the speech is produced correctly. This in turn allows selection of appropriate materials for training when kinesthetic and visual feedback mechanisms are being used to lead to correct production in all contexts.

EVALUATION OF STIMULABILITY OF ERROR SOUNDS. In planning a speech conservation program, it

is helpful if information is available concerning the susceptibility of a particular sound to remediation. Although Snow and Milisen (1954) indicate that prognostic information can be obtained by comparing productions obtained from pictorial and oral articulation tests, it is not known whether this information would apply to an adventitiously hearing-impaired population in which articulation skills are deteriorating rather than developing. It is known, however, that those sounds that are most susceptible to correction are the easiest to incorporate into a kinesthetic feedback program, since the target is already closely approximated.

The suggested procedure for stimulability testing (Milisen, 1954) involves having the client watch and listen carefully while the examiner produces the sound two or three times. Then the client is to imitate the production. This procedure is to be carried out using all sounds that were misarticulated on the previous test and should place the sounds in speech of varying complexity (i.e., in isolation, in nonsense syllables, and in words). The task is repeated twice, and the best response is recorded.

Specific materials for probing error stimulability include some of the tests already discussed. The Templin-Darley Tests of Articulation include directions for determining how well the client can produce error sounds when furnished with optimal auditory-visual stimulation. The directions indicate that each sound is to be presented in isolation, in a syllable, and in a word as well as in a consonant cluster within a word. The Goldman-Fristoe Test of Articulation also includes a Stimulability Subtest where the simplest level of production is the syllable followed by words and simple sentences.

Two tests have been designed specifically to probe stimulability of error sounds. The first is the Carter-Buck Prognostic Articulation Test (1958), which consists of a spontaneous word portion and an imitated nonsense syllable portion. The second is the Van Riper-Erickson Predictive Screening Test of Articulation (1968), which consists of nine imitation tasks, placing sounds in isolation, syllables, words, and sentences. Because both of these instruments were developed to predict which children will master their articulation errors without therapy, it is uncertain whether these materials could be applied to an adventitiously hearing-impaired population. However, even though the normative scores will not apply, the concept may still be applicable.

VOICE AND RESONANCE

Evaluation of the voice and resonance characteristics of the client who is hearing impaired could be conducted on several levels. One might be by direct observation of the laryngeal and velar mechanisms to investigate any physical change in structure. This should always be done in cases of vocal deviation to rule out any underlying pathological cause.

A second level for voice and resonance evaluation is at the listening level, where the clinician's ear is used to make a value judgment concerning the acceptability of production. Because intelligibility is seldom affected by voice or resonance changes only, the clinician must decide whether a deviant production is inappropriate based on age, sex, regional, and physical considerations.

The third level of evaluation is the acoustic level. This involves direct measurement of the various parameters of the voice or resonance, such as fundamental frequency, fundamental frequency variation, intensity, periodicity, or degree of nasal resonance. Several instruments are available for such measurement as well as for feedback in therapy and are reviewed in the appendix.

The typical voice and resonance evaluation involves systematically obtaining a representative sample of the client's communication skills. Ideally, this sample is tape-recorded for future reference. The verbal behavior should include a sample of conversational speech, impromptu speech such as telling a story, oral reading or singing, and automatic speech such as counting or naming the days of the week. The sample should be listened to carefully for deviations in laryngeal function (tension, breathiness, harshness), pitch level and variability, intensity, and resonance, with acoustic measures being made

whenever possible. This information will describe the client's typical vocal behavior.

A second part of the voice/resonance evaluation involves additional probes aimed at further assessing capabilities. Procedures designed to evaluate laryngeal function include the following:

■ Ask the client to produce an /ɑ/ with a gradual soft onset (i.e., /hɑ/). Listen for an abrupt onset of voicing at both loud and soft intensities.
■ Listen specifically for how voice is initiated in the various speech samples. That is, listen to whether it occurs with a hard or soft glottal attack.
■ Time three sustained productions of /ɑ/ using normal air intake. Listen for efficient use of air. A client with normal breath support should be able to produce the sustained vowel for 12 to 13 seconds.
■ Observe what happens to vocal quality with changes in intensity.
■ Stand behind the client and place your finger on the thyroid cartilage. Feel for the presence of laryngeal tension during phonation.
■ Have the client clear his or her throat and listen for a potential change in clarity.

Procedures aimed at evaluating pitch level and variability include:

■ Ask the client to produce a clear /ɑ/ at the lowest pitch level possible and then to slide through the scale to the highest level he or she can reach without going into falsetto phonation. This will give an indication of the client's pitch range.
■ Ask the client to produce a vocalized sigh. This should occur near his or her habitual pitch level.
■ Compare the client's pitch level during oral reading with that of a sustained vowel.
■ Compare the client's pitch level at various intensities. Look for the direction, frequency, and extent of pitch breaks.

Procedures for the evaluation of intensity include the following:

- Observe what changes occur in intensity level with changes in pitch.
- Have the client vary his or her pitch at a given intensity and observe the control that can be achieved.
- Observe the client's intensity at various rates.
- Note whether the client is using clavicular or diaphragmatic breathing during phonation.

Finally, procedures for the evaluation of resonance include:

1. Observe velopharyngeal mobility on vocalization.
2. Listen for variation of nasality with different vowels.
3. Listen for changes in nasality with increased loudness.

Because of the difficulty involved in making subjective judgments of nasality, acoustical measures of this parameter may assist the clinician in making difficult clinical decisions. The degree of nasal resonance in an individual's speech can be quantified using the Kay Elemetrics Model 6200 Nasometer. With this device, oral and nasal components of a subject's speech are sensed by microphones on either side of a sound separator that rests on the subject's upper lip. The signal from each microphone is filtered and digitized by custom electronic modules. The data then are processed by a computer and accompanying software. The resultant signal is a ratio of nasal to nasal-plus-oral acoustic energy. This ratio is multiplied by 100 and expressed as a "nasalance" score. Therefore, the Nasometer provides a numeric output indicating the relative amount of nasal acoustic energy in an individual's speech. This nasalance value has been shown to provide useful information about the speech of normal speakers (Seaver, Dalston, Leeper, & Adams, in press), patients with velopharyngeal impairments (Dalston, Warren, & Dalston, 1991), and patients with severe to profound hearing impairments (Cain, Seaver, Jackson, & Sandridge, 1989). In addition, data have been presented concerning the use of nasometry in monitoring changes in acoustic energy associated with

changes in velopharyngeal activity among normal speakers (Dalston, 1989; Dalston & Seaver, 1990; Seaver & Dalston, 1990).

Following the overall voice and resonance evaluation, specific problems in laryngeal function, pitch, intensity, and resonance will be identified in various contexts. As in articulation testing, the next step is to evaluate the stimulability of the various errors. Again, this information will influence decisions for therapy and will be beneficial when tactual-kinesthetic feedback is being stressed for the individual who is hearing impaired.

RHYTHM AND TIMING

The diagnostic evaluation of the rhythm and timing characteristics of the speech of the adventitiously hearing impaired involves analysis of the same type of speech sample that was collected for the evaluation of voice and resonance. In this case, the clinician judges the utterances for the following rhythm characteristics: overall rate (i.e., too fast, too slow, monotonous), uncontrolled variability, patterned rate, phrasing, variation in syllable duration, and variation in pause duration. Physical measurements are made again to support listener judgments.

TECHNIQUES FOR SPEECH CONSERVATION

In the 1974 report from the ASHA Committee on Rehabilitative Audiology, Costello and her associates stated that the single most important component of the aural rehabilitation program was the selection and fitting of the hearing aid. The earlier the use of amplification is initiated and the more success that is obtained in restoring usable hearing, the less chance there is that ability to monitor speech will deteriorate. However, in cases where auditory self-monitoring is lacking, auditory training and speechreading will be integral parts of the speech conservation program. If the auditory skills that are achieved with amplification are insufficient to allow auditory monitoring, kinesthetic monitoring must be substituted and may be reinforced with visual and/or vibrotactile training aids.

Speech conservation training may include several areas of emphasis depending on which expressive skills are being affected by the hearing loss. These areas include articulation, voice and resonance, and rhythm training.

GENERAL THERAPY PROCEDURES AND PRINCIPLES

The comprehensive speech perception and production diagnostic evaluation will uncover specific problems that potentially may develop or that have already started to develop with the decrease in auditory feedback. The goals in the speech conservation program, therefore, are, first, to maintain existing production skills that are in danger of deteriorating, and second, to correct any errors that have already developed as a result of the adventitious hearing loss.

Several methodologies are available for speech production training, and each varies somewhat in principle and procedures. In general, however, the majority of techniques involve presentation of a *model production* by the clinician followed by an imitated response from the client. The role of the clinician in this paradigm is one of orienting the client to the task, stimulating the production, listening carefully to the response and judging its acceptability, offering immediate feedback and reinforcement, and providing continuous evaluation of progress. The procedures are designed to shape the articulation, voice, or rhythm error into a correct production. Changes in behavior across time can be charted using procedures such as precision therapy described by Waters, Bill, and Lowell (1977).

Van Riper (1972) has outlined the stages of articulation therapy in a comprehensive way that includes numerous suggestions for training. While ear training techniques receive a major emphasis in his program, he stresses that the clinician is free to choose other techniques to stimulate correct production. This production is considered at four specific operational levels and progression from one to the next is

suggested but not required. Therapy can be initiated at whatever level seems appropriate. These four successive levels are

1. The isolated sound level
2. The syllable level
3. The word level
4. The sentence level.

From this last step, carryover into controlled conversation and finally into everyday speech is initiated.

Within this framework, Van Riper outlines four steps to be used in training the error sounds at each of the four levels. These steps can be described as follows.

1. *Have the client identify the error and the standard of production for the specific sound.* This stage normally involves ear training aimed at drawing attention to the specific characteristics of the sound in question so that the client will begin to discriminate it from incorrect productions. Obviously, this task may be difficult for the client who is adventitiously hearing impaired, so some modification is needed.

With a hearing-impaired population, this stage can be considered the one in which the client learns the characteristics of the sounds that may potentially or that have already started to deteriorate. This involves auditory training and speechreading training, which will be integral components of the speech conservation program. It also includes vocabulary building of terms such as those listed by Fisher (1975), which will be used in the correction process. This might include terms such as *harsh, hoarse, glottal attack, denasal, voiced,* and others. It must be remembered that this stage involves no production on the part of the client. It involves only structured input and comparison.

2. *Have the client scan and compare his or her own utterance with the standard.* This step also involves ear training, but now it is intended that the client carefully listen to his or her own productions rather than to the speech of others. It is assumed at this stage that the client clearly understands the characteristics of the target to which comparisons are made with his or her own approximations.

Again, at this stage, modification is needed for a hearing-impaired population. What really is involved at this level is self-monitoring through whatever perceptual channel is needed. Hopefully, residual hearing will play a major role, especially with amplification. Visual, tactual, and kinesthetic feedback information is used to supplement the auditory channel.

Van Riper stresses that this monitoring ability will occur at various times relative to each production as therapy progresses. Initially, the error will be recognized after it occurs, next while it is happening, and finally, it can be identified and hopefully corrected before the production.

3. *Have the client vary his or her production until the correct sound is achieved.* At this stage, the new sound is being taught to the client. Van Riper explains that this must occur at all levels mentioned earlier (isolation, syllable, word, sentence, and conversation) through a process in which the client is taught to vary his or her utterance. Five methods are outlined for approaching this task: progressive approximation, auditory stimulation, phonetic placement, modifications of sounds that are produced correctly, and key words.

The first method, *progressive approximation,* is Van Riper's method of choice. It involves shaping the response and rewarding productions that are progressively approaching the target.

The second method, *auditory stimulation,* involves ear training followed by imitation of the correct production. With the client who is hearing impaired, the approach should be termed auditory-visual stimulation, stressing the inclusion of speechreading cues which must be emphasized. The success of this method will vary depending on the amount of residual hearing and the success of amplification.

The third method, *phonetic placement,* involves the clinician instructing the client in the specific placement and movement of the articulators for the production of each sound. The position is analyzed, and changes in positioning are suggested. Application of this approach involves the use of a mirror, diagrams, models to guide placement, and visual speech aids for additional feedback.

The fourth method, *modification of correct sounds,* involves having the client produce a sound which he or she can do correctly and then gradually vary the production to approximate the target for the error sound. For example, the client may be instructed to slide the tongue forward from an /ʃ/ production to approximate the /s/ which normally is in error.

The fifth method, *key words,* requires utilization of words in which the defective sound can be produced correctly and thereby makes use of information obtained from the evaluation of error contexts described earlier. Emphasis is placed on the sound within the contexts where success is achieved, and the production then is introduced in isolation and in other words. Kinesthetic and auditory monitoring from one area to the next is stressed.

Another method for obtaining correct sound production is the *Motokinesthetic Method* described by Young and Stinchfield-Hawk (1955). This method has application with a hearing-impaired population since auditory stimulation is supplemented by tactile stimulation. This method is based on the assumption that by manipulation of the client's articulators, the clinician can establish tactile and kinesthetic feedback patterns. The client, therefore, passively produces the sound as the clinician manipulates the articulators until the movement pattern is established.

4. *Have the client stabilize the correct sound production so that it becomes automatic.* This stage involves activities at each level of complexity designed to strengthen the new sound production so that it occurs automatically without any conscious effort. To achieve this goal, Van Riper suggests activities such as simultaneous writing and talking, babbling, unison speech, and negative practice. It is important that this stage not be overlooked until the production has stabilized in all contexts and has become a natural part of the client's speech repertoire.

Within the framework just outlined, the clinician is free to deal with the speech production errors that have been identified. Specific techniques within the areas of articulation, voice and resonance, and rhythm are needed to accomplish various remediation goals. Several sources are now available commercially that delineate remediation techniques for individual speech sounds and various voice, resonance, and rhythm disorders. The reader is urged to refer to these sources for specifics. They include texts by Calvert and Silverman (1975), Fisher (1975), Haycock (1941), Ling (1976), Magner (1971), and Vorce (1974).

ARTICULATION TRAINING

In articulation training, the ability to imitate a correct sound depends to a large degree on the ability to perceive the model. In cases of adventitious hearing loss, this means using visual and tactile stimulation in addition to auditory stimulation. Several of the references, therefore, stress the need for the use of a mirror and somewhat slower speech to emphasize the positioning of the articulator.

Tactile cues also are outlined and described by the various authors to be used to improve feedback during stimulation. As an example, production features can be cued in the following ways:

1. Voicing (vowels and /b, d, g, v, ð, z, ʒ, dʒ, m, n, ŋ, l, r, w, j/) can be cued by feeling the vibration at the side of the throat and then contrasting it with voiceless productions.
2. Nasality (/m, n, ŋ, /) can be cued by feeling the vibration at the side of the nose.
3. Plosives (/p, t, k, b, d, g/) can be cued by the pulse of air that can be demonstrated by holding a strip of paper or the back of a hand in front of the mouth.
4. Fricatives (f, θ, s, ʃ, tʃ, v, ð, z, ʒ, dʒ/) can be cued by the flow of air that can be demonstrated by holding a strip of paper or the back of a hand in front of the mouth.

These tactile cues can be used in the initial shaping of the sound, but should soon be faded as more emphasis is placed on kinesthetic feedback. They are appropriate in isolation, syllables, or words but may not prove successful at the sentence level.

VOICE AND RESONANCE TRAINING

Remedial treatment of voice and resonance disorders involves establishing new habits or preventing bad habits from forming. The same basic therapy outline is used. First the problem must be identified and then analyzed in terms of its specific defect. Next, the voice or resonance pattern must be varied in some way, and eventually the new voice or resonance level must be located through successive approximation. Stabilization of the new pattern in communication is then stressed.

The texts mentioned earlier also offer suggestions for the remediation of voice and resonance disorders. A few examples are summarized in Table 16–6.

RHYTHM AND TIMING TRAINING

With an adventitiously hearing-impaired population, errors in rhythm and timing can be prevented or corrected (for the most part) by reviewing the importance of stress and rhythm and by reviewing some already established rules. This may be accompanied by employing some form of prosodic notation in the therapy session to stress phrasing, stress, and inflection rules.

Several such notation systems are available, but one that appears fairly straightforward is presented by Calvert and Silverman (1975). They suggest a system that indicates pitch changes with a curving line, loudness by the height of a horizontal line above a syllable, and duration by the length of the line. Slash marks are used to indicate phrasing. They then present the following illustration:

"Yesterday was a beautiful day/but

today//it's terrible."

These markings then can be incorporated into activities that draw attention to the importance of stress, rhythm, and timing in speech perception and production.

TABLE 16–6. SUGGESTIONS FOR THE REMEDIATION OF VOICE DISORDERS

To correct excessive harshness:

    Conduct exercises to reduce laryngeal tension such as head rotation and alternate tension and relaxation

    Improve speech breathing

    Emphasize easy vocalization through the use of aspirated voice onset

To correct excessive breathiness:

    Improve speech breathing

    Have the client count and increase the number he or she reaches on one inhalation

    Increase the loudness somewhat

    Have the client grip his or her chair or hold a book at shoulder height and count while the increased laryngeal tension is felt

To correct pitch problems:

    Work on sustaining vowels at an even, optimum pitch level

    Write *high* at the top and *low* at the bottom of a blackboard to give visual feedback as pitch is lowered and raised

    Use a resonating object such as a balloon, a cardboard tube, or metal, and have the client feel the high and low vibrations

To correct intensity problems:

    Improve speech breathing

    Again, use a resonating object to demonstrate intensity changes

To correct resonance disorders:

    Lower vocal pitch or increase vocal intensity slightly to reduce general nasality

    Alternate productions of /ŋ/ and /ɑ/, first slowly and then more rapidly stressing kinesthetic awareness

    Combine alternate /m/ and /n/ productions, again emphasizing the feeling of the nasal resonance

CONCLUSIONS

Even though specific programs of receptive training and speech conservation are being conducted, the client who is adventitiously hearing impaired is still faced with the problem of maintaining a healthy attitude toward communication. It is all too easy to withdraw socially and admit defeat in difficult listening or speaking situations. If this happens, a vicious circle is formed, for it is only through continuous practice that speech skills can be maintained if the hearing loss is severe. Because of this, the need often arises for assertiveness training and counseling to change attitudes toward the hearing impairment. This assertiveness training can be an integral part of the aural rehabilitation program along with hearing aid orientation, speechreading, auditory training, and speech conservation.

Communication assertiveness involves, first of all, motivation. This motivation is obvious for the client, but it should also involve family members. Their role in the maintenance of speech skills is critical, so it is important that they also understand the consequences of auditory impairment. Next, specific problem communication areas must be identified, and the client must be desensitized so that he or she no longer avoids difficult situations. At this point, the client becomes involved in receptive training and speech conservation work, so that the client learns to vary his or her behavior in positive ways and gradually to approximate more correct productions or improved speech monitoring skills. These newly learned skills then are stabilized in general communication situations.

Speech conservation, therefore, involves not only training in specific monitoring and production skills, but also support for communication in general. The clinician must be aware that a hearing loss will affect many phases of the client's life, and all need to be considered in an aural rehabilitation program.

REFERENCES

Berg, F. S. (1976). *Educational audiology: Hearing and speech management.* New York: Grune & Stratton.

Binnie, C. A., Daniloff, R. G., & Buckingham, H. W., Jr. (1982). Phonetic disintegration in a five-year-old following sudden hearing loss. *Journal of Speech and Hearing Disorders, 47,* 181–189.

Cain, M. E., Seaver, E. J., Jackson, P. L., & Sandridge, S. A. (1989, November). *Aerodynamic and nasometric assessment of velopharyngeal functioning in hearing-impaired speakers.* Paper presented at the meeting of the American Speech-Language-Hearing Association, St. Louis, MO.

Calvert, D. R., & Silverman, S. R. (1975). *Speech and deafness.* Washington, DC: Alexander Graham Bell Association for the Deaf.

Carter, E. T., & Buck, Mc K. (1958). Prognostic testing for functional articulation disorders among children in the first grade. *Journal of Speech and Hearing Disorders, 23,* 124–133.

Costello, M., N., Freeland, E. E., Hill, M. J., Jeffers, J., Matkin, N. D., Stream, R. W., & Tobin, H. (1974). The audiologist: Responsibilities in the habilitation of the auditorily handicapped. Report of the Committee on Rehabilitative Audiology. *Asha, 16,* 68–70.

Dalston, R. M. (1989). Using simultaneous photo-detection and nasometry to monitor velopharyngeal behavior during speech. *Journal of Speech and Hearing Research, 32,* 195–202.

Dalston, R. M., & Seaver, E. J. (1990). Nasometric and phototransductive measurements of reaction times among normal adult speakers. *Cleft Palate Journal, 27,* 61–67.

Dalston, R. M., Warren, D., & Dalston, E. (1991). Use of nasometry as a diagnostic tool for identifying patients with velopharyngeal impairment. *Cleft Palate Journal, 28,* 184–188.

Erber, N. P., & Alencewicz, C. M. (1976). Audiologic evaluation of deaf children. *Journal of Speech and Hearing Disorders, 41,* 257–267.

Fisher, H. B. (1975). *Improving voice and articulation* (2nd ed.). Boston: Houghton Mifflin.

Fisher, H. B., & Logemann, J. A. (1971). *The Fisher-Logemann Test of Articulation Competence.* Boston: Houghton Mifflin.

Goldman, R., & Fristoe, M. (1969). *Goldman-Fristoe Test of Articulation.* Circle Pines, MN: American Guidance Service.

Haycock, G. S. (1941). *The teaching of speech.* Washington, DC: Alexander Graham Bell Association for the Deaf.

Hood, R. B., & Dixon, R. F. (1969). Physical characteristics of speech rhythm of deaf and normal-hearing speakers. *Journal of Communication Disorders, 2,* 20–28.

Hudgins, C. V., & Numbers, F. C. (1942). An investigation of the intelligibility of the speech of the deaf. *Genetic Psychology Monographs, 25,* 289–392.

Jackson, P. L., & Kelly-Ballweber, D. (1979, November). *Auditory stress pattern recognition in sentences.* Paper presented at the meeting of the American Speech-Language-Hearing Association, Atlanta, GA.

Kent, R. D. (1976). Anatomical and neuromuscular maturation of the speech mechanism: Evidence from acoustic studies. *Journal of Speech and Hearing Research, 19,* 421–447.

Ling, D. (1976). *Speech and the hearing-impaired child: Theory and practice.* Washington, DC: Alexander Graham Bell Association for the Deaf.

Magner, M. (1971). *Speech development.* Northampton, MA: Clarke School for the Deaf.

McDonald, E. T. (1964). *A Deep Test of Articulation.* Pittsburgh, PA: Stanwix House.

Milisen, R. (1954). A rationale for articulation disorders. The disorder of articulation: A systematic clinical and experimental approach. [Monograph]. *Journal of Speech and Hearing Disorders,* (Suppl. 4), 5–17.

Morris, H. L., Spriesterbach, D. C., & Darley, F. L. (1961). An articulation test for assessing competency of velopharyngeal closure. *Journal of Speech and Hearing Research, 4*, 48–55.

Nickerson, R. S. (1975). Characteristics of the speech of deaf persons. *Volta Review, 77*, 342–362.

Ross, M., & Lerman, J. (1971). *Word Intelligibility by Picture Identification.* Pittsburgh, PA: Stanwix House.

Seaver, E. J., & Dalston, R. M. (1990). Using simultaneous nasometry and standard audio recordings to detect acoustic onsets and offsets of speech. *Journal of Speech and Hearing Research, 33*, 358–362.

Seaver, E. J., Dalston, R. M., Leeper, H. A., & Adams, L. E. (in press). A study of nasometry values for normal nasal resonance. *Journal of Speech and Hearing Research.*

Snow, K., & Milisen, R. (1954). Spontaneous improvement in articulation as related to differential responses to oral and picture articulation tests. The disorder of articulation: A systematic clinical and experimental approach. [Monograph]. *Journal of Speech and Hearing Disorders,* (Suppl. 4), 45–49.

Templin, M. C., & Darley, F. L. (1969). *The Templin-Darley Tests of Articulation* (2nd ed.). Iowa City: University of Iowa.

Van Riper, C. (1972). *Speech correction: Principles and methods* (5th ed.). Englewood Cliffs, NJ: Prentice-Hall.

Van Riper, C., & Erickson, R. L. (1968). *Predictive Screening Test of Articulation.* Kalamazoo: Western Michigan University.

Vorce, E. (1974). *Teaching speech to deaf children.* Washington, DC: Alexander Graham Bell Association for the Deaf.

Waters, B. J., Bill, M. D., & Lowell, E. L. (1977). Precision therapy — An interpretation. *Language, Speech and Hearing Services in Schools, 8*, 234–244.

Young, E. H., Stinchfield-Hawk, S. (1955). *Motokinesthetic speech training.* Palo Alto, CA: Stanford University Press.

APPENDIX: VISUAL AND VIBROTACTILE SPEECH TRAINING AIDS

One of the central concepts in speech conservation with the adventitiously hearing impaired is the effective use of amplification and auditory training to make maximum use of residual hearing. There are several cases, however, where additional sensory cues are needed to providing monitoring in speech conservation programs. Several devices are available commerically that were designed to provide visual and/or vibrotactile information. A few of these are described below in terms of their general purpose, the type of information they provide, and where additional information can be obtained.

KAY SONAGRAPH

This instrument provides visual cues for consonant and vowel articulation, duration, voice, pitch, and nasality. The cues are in the form of a sonagram, which is a time-by-frequency-by-intensity representation of the acoustic parameters of speech. A printout of this sonagram is available to become a permanent record.

Contact:
Kay Elemetrics
12 Maple Avenue
Pine Brook, NJ 07058-9798

SERIES 700 SOUND SPECTROGRAPH

This instrument provides visual cues for consonant and vowel articulation, duration, voice, and pitch. The cues are in the form of a printed spectrogram, which becomes a permanent record.

Contact:
Voice Identification Incorporated
P.O. Box 714
Somerville, NJ 08876

LUCIA SPECTRUM INDICATOR

This instrument provides visual cues designed to give feedback in vowel and voiced-voiceless fricative training. The instrument displays frequency by intensity spectral information in light displays. Intensity is represented in ten levels of 3.5 dB each, and frequency information covers a range of 180 to 6800 Hz. There is also a mirror attached to the front of the unit for speechreading cues.

Contact:
SI America
1900 Rittenhouse Square
Philadelphia, PA 19103

VISIBLE SPEECH APPARATUS

This instrument provides visual cues for the training of fricative and plosive consonants, vowels, and pitch. The display is a light indication system, which provides spectra of speech sounds. Frequency is displayed with 16 bandpass filters and covers a range of 90 to 8000 Hz. The intensity of each column is in 10 dB steps. Color coding on the display indicates fundamental frequency and first and second formants.

Contact:
Precision Acoustics Corporation
510 5th Avenue, Room 704
New York, NY 10017

VISIPITCH

This device displays fundamental frequency and amplitude information from the speech signal in real time on the screen for biofeedback information. On-screen cursors allow precise measurements of the speech sample to be made and stored for later use. A hardcopy printout is also available.

Contact:
Kay Elemetrics Corporation
12 Maple Avenue
Pine Brook, NY 07058-9798

PM SERIES OF PITCH INSTRUMENTS

This system consists of a microphone, a 12-inch video monitor, and the electronics module with keyboard which houses up to four separate programs. The available programs include (1) PM100 — split screen — speech "modeling"; (2) PM201 — split screen — pitch on the upper half, loudness on the lower half; (3) PM 300 long duration (up to 23 minutes) pitch analysis; (4) PM301 — long duration analysis of pitch, loudness, and pause time; and (5) PM302 — perturbation ("jitter") analysis. A hardcopy printout is available.

Contact:
Voice Identification, Inc.
P.O. Box 714
Somerville, NJ 08876

VOCAL-2

This instrument provides visual cues for word stress patterns, fundamental frequency, and /s/ phoneme production. The visual display is on a split screen with an example placed on the top and client trials on the bottom. It displays intensity by time patterns, frequency by time patterns, or /s/ information.

Contact:
Madsen Electronics
908 Niagara Falls Boulevard
North Tonawanda, NY 14120-2060

S-INDICATOR

This instrument provides visual and tactile information to train /s/ as well as other voiceless fricatives. The visual cues are from a display panel with a meter and a light to indicate the quality of the /s/ production. There is an optional vibrator, which also signals a correct /s/.

Contact:
SI America
1900 Rittenhouse Square
Philadelphia, PA 19103

F_o-INDICATOR

This instrument provides visual cues to train pitch level, intonation, phonation, voiced versus voiceless articulation, and breath control. The visual cues are from a meter and from red and green lights that monitor the limits of the frequency range. A contact microphone is held against the throat, and the rate of vocal fold vibration is measured within a range of 50 to 550 Hz.

Contact:
SI America
1900 Rittenhouse Square
Philadelphia, PA 19103

NASOMETER

This device is a microcomputer-based instrument designed for use in both the assessment and treatment of nasality problems. It measures the rate of acoustic energy from the nasal and oral cavities in real time and displays the resulting nasalance value on the screen of the computer monitor. This allows the device to be used as a biofeedback tool in attempts to modify abnormal nasal resonance.

Contact:
Kay Elemetrics Corporation
12 Maple Avenue
Pine Brook, NY 07058-9798

TACTAID II AND TACTAID 7

The Tactaid II is a wearable two-channel vibrotactile aid that makes use of two vibrators. It is worn in its own pouch or on a belt, and has an input jack for direct hookup to FM systems along with a built-in T-coil for telephone and audio system use. The Tactaid 7 uses seven channels and seven vibrators to produce a unique tactile pattern for every phoneme.

Contact:
Audiological Engineering Corporation
35 Medford Street
Somerville, MA 02143

VOICE LITE

This instrument provides visual and tactile cues for use in training phonation, loudness, duration, stress and rhythm, voiced versus voiceless articulation, nasality, and breath control. The visual cues are provided by a translucent dome with a light that reacts to sound. Brightness of the light is intensity related. The unit has an optional microphone that indicates nasality, and it also has an optional tactile stimulator.

Contact:
Behavioral Controls, Incorporated
3818 West Mitchell
Milwaukee, WI 53215

MONO-FONATOR, POLY-FONATOR, AND MINI-FONATOR

The mono-fonator is designed for individual use, while the poly-fonator is designed for use by one to four clients. This instrument provides tactile information for use in training stress, duration, phonation, and some phonetic features. The clinician or client speaks into the microphone, and the vibrational cues are produced by a vibrator placed on the hand. Earphones are included for auditory information. The mini-fonator is a single channel, wearable version of the device, which makes use of a wrist-worn vibrator. It is possible to use signal input from FM auditory trainers.

Contact:
Siemens Hearing Intruments
10 Constitution Avenue, P.O. Box 1397
Piscataway, NJ 08855-1397

N-INDICATOR

This instrument provides visual cues for training nasalization, denasalization, and phonation. A contact microphone is held against the nose, and the intensity of nasal vibration is shown on a meter. The panel has a green and a red light to signal when the production is blow or above a 50% deflection point.

Contact:
SI America
1900 Rittenhouse Square
Philadelphia, PA 19103

■ PART III ■

Considerations for the Older Adult Client

CHAPTER 17

Hearing Loss in Older Adulthood

■ RAYMOND H. HULL, Ph.D. ■

It is an accepted fact that many older persons have difficulty understanding speech due to declining auditory function. If we are to provide meaningful diagnostic and aural rehabilitative services on behalf of older adults, it is important that we understand the nature of the auditory problem.

INCIDENCE OF HEARING LOSS IN OLDER ADULTHOOD

There are almost as many estimates of the incidence of hearing loss in older adulthood as there are professionals assessing or treating those who possess it. Because of the complexity of the disorder involved in presbycusis, incidence studies such as the U.S. Public Health Service National Health Surveys over the past four decades have resulted in the collection of generally unreliable data. Much of this appears to be a result of a lack of reliable criteria for describing hearing impairment in older age.

It would appear that the greatest cause for the apparent inability to arrive at a consistent set of criteria are the definitions used to describe "hearing impairment" by those establishing failure criteria. We do know that elderly people are more likely to have a hearing impairment than younger people. Almost 8% of people under age 17 years have some degree of hearing impairment. Between ages 45 and 64 years, it has been estimated that the incidence rises to 12%; between ages 65 to 74 years, to 24%; and over 75 years, to 39% (National Center for Health Statistics, U.S. Department of Health and Human Services 1981 Health Interview Survey). Schow and Nerbonne (1980) found the incidence of hearing loss among nursing home patients to be over 80%, and an earlier study (Chafee, 1967) found the incidence to be nearly 90%. Even though some survey figures regarding presbycusis appear to be rather realistic, estimates reported by practicing audiologists would indicate that the incidence of hearing impairment that can interfere with communication by persons age 65 years and beyond may be greater than anticipated — as high as 60% (Hull, 1988c).

The complexities involved in the communicative deficits common to presbycusis make this disorder a difficult one to diagnose accurately. Numbers of elderly individuals who possess significant difficulties in understanding speech (a common symptom of presbycusis) also may be found to possess auditory acuity that would not be indicative of such severe impairment. These conflicting audiometric data may have contributed to the inconsistent incidence figures.

WHAT IS PRESBYCUSIS?

Of all the handicaps that affect the aged, the inability to communicate with others due to hearing impairment can be one of the most frustrating, and it can result in many other sociopsychological problems. The loss of auditory sensitivity that is the result of aging is referred to as *presbycusis.* This term has, for many years, "been used to describe the defective hearing of old people" (Schaie, Warner, & Strother, 1964).

More than three decades ago that term was accurately used to describe a multidimensional disorder that includes the pathology associated with aging, impaired auditory sensitivity, temporal discrimination, auditory judgment, and associated social and psychological difficulties (Hinchcliffe, 1959). Hinchcliffe (1962) in his early studies defined the pathology of presbycusis as (1) impairment of auditory-threshold sensitivity, frequency discrimination, temporal discrimination, sound discrimination, auditory judgment, and speech discrimination; (2) a lowering of the high frequency limit; and (3) decreases in the intelligibility of distorted speech and in the ability to recall long sentences.

While there are many physical reasons why a person's hearing may deteriorate, it is important to consider that the impairment of auditory acuity per se is not the only component of presbycusis. It also appears to involve the central auditory system, which allows for interpretation of what a person hears. The difficulties in understanding what is being said that are experienced uniquely by elderly persons with presbycusis are oftentimes disproportionately greater than one would expect in light of their measured level of auditory acuity. This discrepancy was noted nearly five decades ago by Gaeth (1948) in his doctoral research, and was coined "phonemic regression."

The literature reveals that a decline in the function of the central auditory system, including the brain stem and auditory cortex, is involved in the disproportionate decline in speech understanding that is observed among many elderly adults. According to Welsh, Welsh, and Healy (1985), for example, the resulting auditory impairment is that of a mixed type of receptive and perceptual impairment, involving both the peripheral and central auditory systems. Kasten (1980) and McCroskey and Kasten (1981) have described the auditory behaviors of the older adult with central auditory decline as similar to the perceptual and comprehension difficulties observed among learning disabled children, particularly in auditory or visually distracting communicative environments.

PAST AND PRESENT RESEARCH ON PRESBYCUSIS

According to Shaie, Warner, and Strother (1964), scientific research into changes in threshold for hearing began as early as 1894 with studies by Bezold (1894) and Zwaardemaker (1891, 1894). Most early studies consisted of observations relating to changes of hearing level in accordance with increasing age. With advances in electron microscopic technology, more detailed histopathological studies of the deterioration of function associated with aging have been made possible. The areas of interest have been the cochlea, the spiral ganglion, the brain stem auditory pathways, and the auditory cortex, although the primary area of concentration through the years has involved research on the aging cochlea.

The Cochlea

There are approximately thirty-five thousand nerve fibers in each cochlea that, when stimulated, send coded electrochemical impulses to the auditory portion of the brain by way of the auditory pathways of the eighth nerve and brain stem. If nerve fibers within the cochlea, spiral ganglion, or eighth nerve are destroyed, regeneration of function does not occur. Jorgensen (1961), while conducting post-mortem studies of the effect of aging on the ear, found a loss of ganglion cells in the basal portion of the cochlea along with thickenings of the capillary walls in the stria vascularis. This pathology was believed to be the result of arteriosclerosis. It was believed that the thickenings could affect not only the oxygen level in the cochlear duct, but also the electrical potentials in the same area.

Kirikae, Sato, and Shitara (1964) also attempted to discover the primary site of lesion of presbycusis. They feel that the cause of presbycusis principally involves lesions of the inner ear, particularly within the organ of Corti of the cochlea and the spiral ganglion cells. They describe two specific types of changes: (1) atrophy of the spiral ganglion and (2) angiosclerotic degeneration of the inner ear. In an investigation that involved 20 subjects (10 subjects from 50 to 70 years of age and 10 control subjects from 20 to 30 years of age, all with normal hearing within the speech range), it was found that auditory discrimination for distorted speech was poorer in the older subjects, even though pure-tone thresholds were equal in both groups.

The authors felt that poor auditory discrimination scores among the older subjects were due to senile changes of the auditory nervous system. It was also surmised that the elevation of pure-tone thresholds, especially at the higher frequencies, the lowered auditory discrimination thresholds, and the diminished sense of binaural hearing discovered in this study were also due to senile changes of the auditory system. Those changes also included reduction and atrophy of ganglion cells from the level of the spiral ganglion to the auditory cortex. Proctor (1961) felt that the predisposing factors for presbycusis may include arteriosclerosis and high blood cholesterol. He postulated that the progressive hearing impairment seen in aging may be due to atrophy of the eighth nerve, but that the causative mechanism in presbycusis is atrophy at the basal end of the cochlea.

Johnsson and Hawkins (1972) state that it is difficult to differentiate between the effects of ototoxic drugs, noise exposure, and the actual effects of aging when attempting to determine the effects of aging on hearing. In post-mortem studies they discovered cochlear hair-cell degeneration in newborns only a few hours old. They also found definite nerve degeneration secondary to hair-cell damage in teenagers within the extreme basal turn of the cochlea. They believe that the degeneration progresses steadily as aging occurs. Hawkins (1973), in comparing the effects of those factors on the aging cochlea, has stated:

The processes involved in ototoxic injury by aminoglycosides (ototoxic substances) and in the degenerative changes leading to presbycusis are so similar that one may serve as a model for the other. The ototoxic process resembles nothing so much as an accelerated aging of the inner ear, a sort of "galloping presbycusis." (p. 139)

Unlike Dr. Oliver Wendell Holmes' New England Deacon who built the wonderful one-horse shay, the architect of the cochlea did not design it to give perfect service for "a hundred years to a day," or even for the traditional three-score-and-ten. Its condition in old age, however, seldom represents the effects of aging alone, but rather the cumulative, combined assaults of noise and drugs, as well as time (Hawkins, 1973).

We must also consider the compounding effects of noise and drugs on the aging ear, which probably begin at birth. Schuknecht (1974) supports the concept of additive factors involved in the structural pathology of presbycusis that occur throughout life, stating, "This is deafness of aging, not of the aged."

Schuknecht (1964) described four distinct types of presbycusis that he had identified.

1. *Sensory presbycusis.* This type is caused by atrophy of the organ of Corti and degeneration of hair cells, beginning at the basal end of the cochlea and moving toward the apex. It usually affects 8000 Hz and above in the average adult, with an abrupt high-frequency hearing loss in audiometric testing.

2. *Neural presbycusis.* This type results from the loss of neurons in the auditory pathways and cochlea. It usually becomes noticeable when 30 to 40% of the neurons are lost or dam-

aged. There is a relatively more severe speech discrimination problem than with the first type. Although 90% of the cochlear nerves can be destroyed without affecting pure-tone thresholds, speech discrimination is affected much more quickly. Amplification frequently does not benefit these persons.

3. *Stria vascularis atrophy, or metabolic presbycusis.* This type is often seen where there is a family history of hearing loss and an insidious onset in the third or fourth decade of life. Degeneration takes place in the apical area of the cochlea and causes a flat pure-tone hearing loss to about 50 dB, at which point speech discrimination is affected. Schuknecht feels this is probably a genetically determined condition. Amplification often is found to benefit these persons.

4. *Inner ear conductive-type presbycusis* (somewhat theoretical). Although there are no evident histological changes, Schuknecht feels that an increase in the stiffness in the supporting structures of the cochlear duct may cause a mechanical-type of loss.

According to the Working Group on Speech Understanding and Aging of CHABA (Tobias, 1988), the four types of presbycusis described by Schuknecht (1964) have not been substantiated with any degree of certainty, except for the sensory category. The metabolic type, according to the Working Group, appears to be highly genetically determined, pure neural types are infrequently observed, while the mechanical form is still highly speculative, or at least hypothetical.

There has been some speculation over the years about a direct relationship between presbycusis and arteriosclerosis. Since the cochlea and the central auditory system are extremely sensitive to oxygen/metabolic changes, such a theoretical relationship is a natural one. Fisch, Dobozi, and Greig (1972) studied degenerative factors of the internal auditory artery. Makishima (1978) positively correlated the extent of the narrowing of the internal auditory artery with atrophy of the spiral ganglion and degree of hearing loss. Johnsson and Hawkins (1972) also found a positive relationship between stria vascularis atrophy and degenerative changes along the basilar membrane of the cochlea.

Presbycusis, as we currently understand it, then, involves: (1) the structural pathology of the aging ear, including one or several causes ranging from previous noise exposure, biochemical factors, heredity, metabolic changes, and others; (2) the auditory processing/comprehension problems seen among aging persons; and (3) the myriad of social/psychological problems facing the elderly individual with presbycusis. Schuknecht (1974) has stated that aging apparently is caused by a complex integration of inherited defects, injuries, environmental exposure, and accumulation of DNA errors, which results in a reduction of the body's capability of mitosis for repair, the person's genetic makeup, accumulation of pigment, and chemical changes in individual body cells. Schuknecht further believes that presbycusis is precipitated by an accumulation of degenerative changes within the auditory mechanism, but is "depending upon heredity, diet, environment, and use." He feels that it is difficult to differentiate between the effects of heredity and true presbycusis caused by other factors.

The Brain Stem and Auditory Cortex

It appears reasonable that a discussion of the site of lesion of presbycusis should not be restricted to the cochlea. Since presbycusis presents itself as a disproportionate inability to understand what others are saying compared to the individual's level of auditory acuity, one cannot exclude the possibility of pathology beyond the cochlea and eighth nerve, that is, along the brain stem and within the auditory cortex. A common audiologic picture includes obvious cochlear pathology, as represented by a mildly-to-moderately sloping sensorineural hearing loss with corresponding mild to moderate impairment in speech reception, as measured using spondaic word lists.

As the audiologist views these two aspects of the audiological evaluation, it generally appears that the individual should be able to function adequately. When speech discrimination abilities are assessed (the ability to understand the speech of others), a different picture becomes apparent. A greater than expected inability to understand speech is observed. The common complaint of the aging person with presbycusis is that he or she can hear people talk, but cannot understand what they are saying. The older person complains that speech sounds "jumbled," or that people seem to "mumble." The greatest difficulty is experienced in auditorily distracting environments. The problem appears to be in the sorting and synthesis of auditory-phonemic elements and difficulties in cognitive skills, not so much in auditory acuity. This significant characteristic of presbycusis is termed "phonemic regression" (Gaeth, 1948). It represents speech discrimination scores that are much lower than might be expected from the individual's threshold for pure tones and speech. According to Gaeth, this is due to a "generalized deterioration of centers within the CNS concerned with sound transmission and reception." This deterioration can exist with a relatively intact cochlea.

Hinchcliffe (1962) describes the auditory features of presbycusis and discusses the possible histological changes that cause them. He concludes that "although a number of degenerative changes throughout the auditory mechanism must contribute to the development of presbycusis, it seems more likely that changes in the brain are primarily responsible for the overall audiologic picture of presbycusis." Pestalozza and Shore (1955) included in their findings lesions located in the organ of Corti as well as in nerve fibers, spiral ganglion cells, and central pathways.

Kirikae, Sato, and Shitara (1964) report neuron loss in the cochlear nuclei and the medial geniculate bodies. They discuss the possibilities of a relationship between lowered speech discrimination and senile changes of the central auditory system, including reduction and atrophy of nerve cells and their attachments from the eighth nerve, through the brain stem, and including the auditory cortex.

Hansen and Reske-Nielsen (1965) describe neuron loss in the cochlear nucleii, the inferior colliculus, and the Heschel's gyrus. On the other hand, Konigsmark and Murphy (1972) made cell counts on the central cochlear nucleus, and concluded that there was no cell loss as related to aging. In 1982, Casey and Feldman reported their studies on rat brain stem auditory nuclei. Their findings reported no cell loss in the medial nucleus of the trapezoid body.

Ferraro and Minckler (1977) reported cell counts, and studies of glial density and cellular configuration on human brain stems, specifically the lateral lemniscus from birth to age 90 years. Hull (1977) studied the same brain stems, but included only the inferior colliculi. The conclusions were that there is a general decrease in cell size and dendritic number, but across nine decades there is little nuclei loss.

From the reports to date, there is no conclusive evidence that there are marked changes in cell density and configuration in the central auditory system. This does not, however, deny the behavioral changes that are noted among many persons in advanced age as it relates to speech understanding, including a decline in auditory processing, auditory synthesis, and cognitive/linguistic processing that interferes with one's daily communicative function. It is probable that if a basis for those changes in auditory processing is discovered, it will be found as a reduction in neurochemical/neurotransmitter processing through the auditory system, primarily in the central auditory mechanism (brain stem, auditory cortex, and the association areas of the brain).

THE EFFECTS OF PRESBYCUSIS ON HEARING

HEARING FOR PURE TONES

Bekesy (1957) stated:

In childhood some of us can hear well at frequencies as high as 40,000 cycles per second. But with age our acuteness of hearing in the high-frequency range steadily falls. Normally, the drop is almost as regular as clockwork; testing several persons in their 40s with tones at a fixed level of intensity, we find that over a period of five years, their upper limit dropped about 80 cycles per second every six months. (p. 55)

Two major manifestations of presbycusis generally are seen by the audiologist. First, a progressive bilateral reduction in sensitivity for pure tones is observed, particularly in the high frequencies. Second, decreased auditory discrimination is noted when speech is presented loudly enough for the person to hear, even though pure-tone hearing loss may be minimal. This observation is further substantiated by Jerger (1973), who states: "The aging process produces systematic changes in each of the two critical dimensions of hearing impairment — loss in threshold sensitivity and loss in the ability to understand suprathreshold speech" (p. 123). The aging person's threshold for hearing, then, reveals a typical loss of acuity for the higher frequencies, generally first seen at around 4000 Hz, and then gradually involving the lower frequencies. The most observable and debilitating aspect of presbycusis, however, is the difficulty in understanding what others are saying.

The hearing loss for pure tones seen in presbycusis generally reveals a gradually sloping pattern, with the greatest loss centering in the high frequencies around 4000 Hz. Glorig, Wheeler, Quiggle, Grings, and Summerfield (1957) surveyed the hearing of large numbers of people, ranging in age from 10 to 79 years of age. As can be seen in Figure 17–1, the greatest degree of impairment in auditory acuity for pure tones is seen in the higher frequencies for all subjects of all ages, even beginning to some degree in subjects from 10 to 19 years of age. In the age range from 50 to 79 years, some loss of acuity can be seen even in the lower frequencies.

The loss of hearing acuity in the higher frequencies in aging has been documented by numerous researchers, including Hinchcliffe (1962); Schuknecht and Woellner (1955); Schuknecht (1964); Bekesy (1957); Rosen, Bergman, Plester, El-Mofty, & Satti (1962); Rosenwasser (1964); Miller and Ort (1965); Jerger (1973); Traynor and Hull (1974). The phenomenon was reported earlier by Bunch and Railford (1931) and Beasley (1938), and much earlier by Galton (1884).

A study of Traynor and Hull (1974) established mean auditory thresholds for 120 elderly individuals who ranged in age from 65 to 90

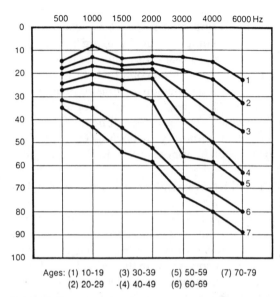

Figure 17–1. Median pure-tone thresholds for males from ages 10 to 79. Data are converted to ANSI-1969 reference. (Adapted from Glorig et al. [1957].)

years of age and who were confined to health-care facilities. These means then were compared with the results of a similar investigation by Miller and Ort (1965). The results of the two studies are presented in Figure 17–2. As can be seen, the results are quite similar. The general pure-tone audiometric configuration is revealed as relatively flat sensorineural hearing impairment, sloping gently into the higher frequencies. Speech-reception thresholds are generally equal to, and reflected by, a best two- or three-frequency pure-tone average.

Glorig and Nixon (1960) attempted to control for such contaminating factors as disease and noise (environmental exposure) by selecting 328 men out of 2,000 who had not been unduly exposed to noise or other elements that may result in a hearing loss. This was done in an attempt to obtain as reliable a picture as possible of "true" presbycusic changes in hearing. These 328 men had no presence or history of otological disease and no history of having been exposed to gunfire or noise levels high enough to make conversation difficult. Figure 17–3 shows the effect of age on hearing levels

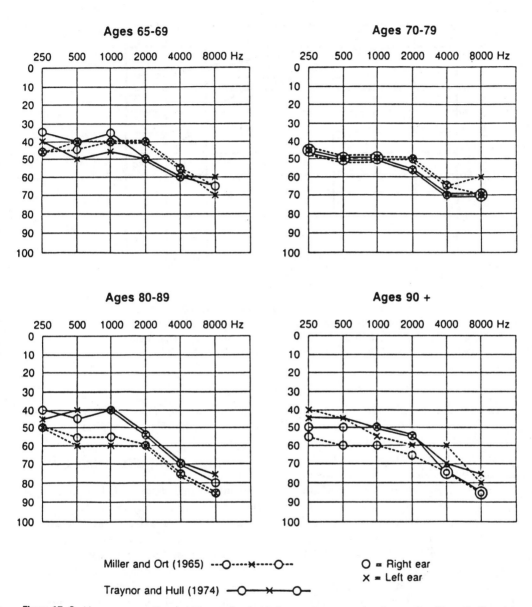

Figure 17-2. Mean pure-tone threshold for confined elderly persons, comparing the results of investigations by Traynor and Hull (1974) and Miller and Ort (1965). (All threshold levels have been converted where necessary to ANSI-1969 reference.)

for several different frequencies in that study. The aging process reveals itself by changes in auditory sensitivity at 1000 Hz beginning at age 30. On the basis of these data, the rate of decrease in auditory sensitivity for 1000 Hz is about 3 dB for every 10 years of age through 70 years. For 6000 Hz, the decrease is approximately 10 dB for every 10 years through 70 years.

Much of the research on the effects of aging on hearing has been motivated by a need for identifying the presbycusic component in noise-induced hearing loss (Corso, 1976). In an

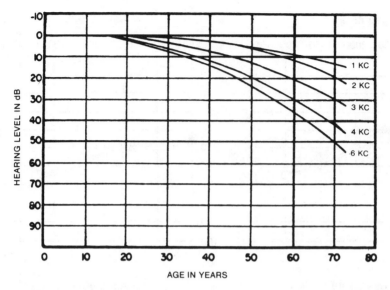

Figure 17–3. Average hearing levels as a function of age of 328 males who reported negative otologic history and no exposure to high-level noise. (Reproduced with permission from Glorig, A., & Nixon, J. [1969]. Distribution of hearing loss in various populations. *Annals of Otology, Rhinology, and Laryngology, 69,* 502.)

effort to describe the presbycusic effect on auditory sensitivity for pure tones, Spoor (1967) analyzed the results of eight studies on pure-tone thresholds as a function of age, including those by Beasley (1938); Johansen (1943); the Z24-X-2 Report of the American Standards Association (1954); Glorig et al. (1957) report of the 1954 Wisconsin State Fair; Hinchcliffe (1959); Jatho and Heck (1959); Glorig and Nixon (1960); and Corso (1976). Because these studies reported hearing levels based on reference threshold levels (SPL) in effect prior to ANSI 1969 (American National Standards Institute, 1970), Lebo and Reddell (1972) applied corrections to Spoor's 1967 data in order to show presbycusic curves relative to the ANSI 1969 standards. These curves are shown in Figure 17–4 for men and Figure 17–5 for women. These curves show that reduction of auditory sensitivity as a function of age is frequency dependent. For example, pure-tone sensitivity for 250, 500, and 1000 Hz is approximately equivalent for men and women across decade-age groups, but men experience a more

rapid decline in sensitivity than women for frequencies of 2000 Hz and higher.

SPEECH DISCRIMINATION

It becomes quite disturbing to aging persons when they feel that they can hear people talk, but have difficulty making sense of it. That is, in essence, the disorder in speech discrimination seen so commonly in presbycusis. An auditory symptom of this phenomenon, then, is revealed as a frequent inability of the elderly person to understand what others are saying when auditory acuity appears adequate for purposes of communication. A typical statement made by the elderly person is, "I can hear you, but I cannot understand what you are saying." When this statement is made, it generally can be assumed that the elderly person is describing the problem accurately. It should be noted that the loss of hearing sensitivity in the higher frequencies itself generally results in some difficulties in understanding the speech of others, especially in auditorily distracting environ-

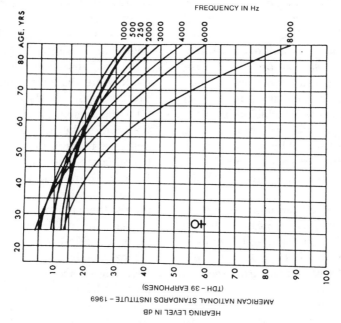

Figure 17–5. Spoor's composite female presbycusic curves modified to conform to the ANSI 1969 standard. (Reproduced with permission from Lebo, C. P., & Reddell, R. C. [1972]. The presbycusis component in occupational hearing loss. *Laryngoscope, 82,* 1402.)

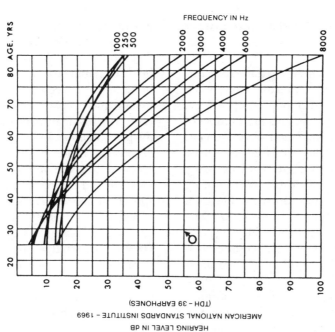

Figure 17–4. Spoor's composite male presbycusic curves modified to conform to the ANSI 1969 standard. (Reproduced with permission from Lebo, C. P., & Reddell, R. C. [1972]. The presbycusis component in occupational hearing loss. *Laryngoscope, 82,* 1402.)

ments. However, this is variable and depends on the extent of the hearing loss for those and other frequencies, and the ability of the individual to compensate for the loss of acuity for certain phonemes of speech. The cause of the more severe disability relative to auditory discrimination and comprehension among the elderly, however, cannot be restricted simply to a hearing loss for the high frequencies. The disorder exemplified in presbycusis, which appears to involve difficulties in auditory comprehension, cognition, and the sorting of both the phoneme and linguistic features of speech, must occur at some level beyond the cochlea and the eighth nerve.

To the lay person, the auditory confusion seen in aging persons may appear to take on the characteristics of confusion and "senility." It should be understood, however, that the aging person, faced with the embarrassment of these confusions, may also have considered this frightening possibility. Since the elderly person is embarrassed by his confusing of auditory verbal messages, withdrawal and a self-imposed isolation from other possible communication situations may occur. Though the older person may be alert and intelligent, he or she is faced with a devastating auditory discrimination problem.

Jerger (1973), in an investigation cited earlier, systematically studied changes in speech understanding observed among aging persons. He subjected 18 elderly persons to a number of tests for speech discrimination. Five younger people who were hearing impaired were used as controls, along with a group of normally hearing people. All individuals with hearing loss demonstrated equal sensorineural hearing loss with similar pure-tone configuration. The tests for speech discrimination included: (1) PB maximum; (2) PB scores at 5 dB sensation level; (3) sentences in competition; and (4) time-compressed speech, utilizing the Synthetic Sentence Index (SSI) in all test conditions. Mean scores are presented in Figure 17–6. Jerger found that the sensorineural hearing impairment resulted in reduced auditory discrimination scores and is not strictly related to

the age of the person. Elderly individuals did, however, demonstrate slightly depressed scores compared to the younger persons.

Jerger (1973) concluded that for the relatively easy task of repeating PB words at a level well above threshold (PB max), there is little difference among groups. When the task was made somewhat more difficult, for example by presenting the words at a very faint level (5 dB S.L.), the presbycusic group had more difficulty than either the normal or the control group. Sentence identification in the presence of ipsilateral competing message (SSI-ICM) showed an even more pronounced effect. Younger hearing-impaired subjects performed more poorly than normal controls, but older individuals showed an even greater loss for sentence identification.

Finally, subjecting the SSI sentences to time compression accentuated the effect even more. Both the hearing-impaired control and presbycusic groups showed a severe breakdown in comparison with the normal group. The presbycusic group showed a slightly greater effect than the younger hearing-impaired group.

There is, indeed, in the elderly, a disproportionate loss in speech understanding, over and above what can be accounted for by the loss in threshold sensitivity. When a hearing loss is held constant across age, the progressive effect of aging on speech intelligibility loss is easily documented. Available evidence supports a central rather than peripheral interpretation of the phenomenon. Jerger (1973) stated that if the cochlear disorders make up the majority of sensorineural loss in young adults, then we must look beyond the cochlea to explain the loss of speech understanding unique to the elderly.

Bergman, Blumenfeld, Cascardo, Dash, Levitt, and Margulies (1976) and Bergman (1980) conducted a 10-year investigation that permitted a thorough description of the disorder of auditory discrimination found among elderly persons. Two hundred and eighty-two adults, ranging in age from 20 to 80 years, were assessed, utilizing a variety of suprathreshold tasks requiring the perception of speech. Follow-up studies on the same subjects were

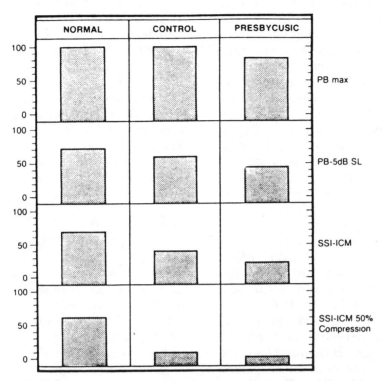

Figure 17–6. Average scores for four auditory discrimination tasks for three subject groups. (Reprinted with permission from Jerger, J. [1973]. Audiological findings in aging. *Advances in Oto-Rhino Laryngology, 20,* 115–124.

conducted at 3 years and 7 years later. The tests of degraded speech were as follows:

1. Control test of 10 CID Everyday Sentences that were undistorted.
2. Similar sentence lists interrupted electronically eight times per second.
3. Other sentences spoken at a rate 2½ times faster than the normal rate of 120 words per minute.
4. Other sentences filtered so that one ear heard them through a low pass filter extending from 500 to 800 Hz, while the other ear heard them simultaneously through a frequency band from 1800 to 2400 Hz.
5. Two-part words (spondaic words) such as *upstairs* and *downtown* presented to each ear so that the second syllable of one word overlapped the first syllable of the second word, and thereby competed for the listener's attention (dichotic listening task).
6. A test requiring the listener to attend to a message and understand it through competing speakers' voices (selective listening).
7. Simulated listening in a "lecture" hall with unfavorable (reverberant) acoustics.

The results revealed interesting findings relative to presbycusis. For example, of the original subjects, those ranging in age from 20 to 29 demonstrated definite decreases in speech understanding between the initial testing and the follow-up test 7 years later. The greatest differences were found under the conditions utilizing reverberated speech, speeded speech, selective listening task, and interrupted speech.

All subjects in age groups from 20 to 29 and ages 60 to 69 demonstrated the poorest scores for the electronically interrupted speech. There appeared to be a linear relationship between the age of subjects and the scores on all listening tasks. All subjects performed best on the control test of 10 undistorted sentences presented at a comfortable listening level. The poorest scores on all listening tasks were found among the age group of 60 to 69 years. The second poorest scores were those in the group ranging in age from 50 to 59 years, although their scores generally were significantly better than scores among the 60- to 69-year group.

According to Bergman (1980), this study indicates, "that the perception of everyday speech declines significantly with aging for conditions other than those which are optimal . . . This change is noted as early as the fifth decade, with a sharp acceleration occurring in the seventh decade of life" (p. 105).

In an earlier study by Gaeth (1948), the same phenomenon was described. Gaeth called it "phonemic regression." He founded his observation on the premise that "certain patients show much greater difficulty in discriminating the phonemic elements of speech than would be expected on the basis of their pure-tone scores" (Willeford, 1971, p. 216). Willeford (1971) presents the characteristics involved in the phenomenon as described by Gaeth (1948) as follows:

1. Otological and audiological findings indicate a hearing loss of the sensorineural type, which is either mild or moderate in severity.
2. The threshold shift in hearing for connected speech agrees with the shift for pure tones.
3. There is a greater difficulty in understanding speech as revealed by appropriate discrimination tests than the type and severity of loss would lead one to suspect.
4. The patient does not appear to evidence a general decay in mental capabilities paralleling his deterioration in phonemic perception.
5. The patient lacks insight into the quality of his discrimination problem, but tends to blame all these troubles on his deficiency in auditory acuity.

6. These symptoms appear more frequently in adults over 50 years of age than in those younger, but a substantial number of the older individuals with hearing losses do not display the difficulty. Therefore, age alone must be ruled out as the causative factor.

The studies by Jerger (1973), Bergman et al. (1976, 1980), and others generally have not supported the final statement by Gaeth (1948). They have continued to specify a relationship between the lack of ability to understand the speech of others and the age of the client.

CENTRAL AUDITORY FUNCTION AND AGING

Jerger (1985), through comparative investigations, has exhaustively studied the possibility of central involvement in presbycusis. The results of his research indicate differences between young and elderly subjects with equal auditory thresholds significant enough for him to conclude that, "We must look beyond the cochlea to explain the loss in speech discrimination unique to the elderly."

According to Hull (1988b), the premise is that (1) complementary intrinsic redundancies inherent in the central auditory system tend to decline as a function of aging; and (2) as the once natural filtering and tuning (coding) of the peripheral auditory system also declines with increased age, the disproportionate degree of impairment in auditory/communicative function experienced by older adults who are hearing impaired who also are forced to listen in a world of people and environments that degrade the extrinsic redundancies that otherwise may have facilitated auditory function, places the older adult who is hearing impaired in double jeopardy.

OBSERVATIONS OF LISTENER BEHAVIORS

This author has surveyed older listeners who are hearing impaired for the past 20 years as it relates to their descriptions of the difficulties that they experience in speech understanding, including experiences in both nondistracting and auditorily distracting environments, and how they cope in them. Generally, their descriptions, and their comparisons of their "recalled" listening skills of earlier years, center on changes that reflect an apparent decline in central auditory function within specific areas. First, they do not describe difficulty determining the existence of speech versus nonspeech in distracting environments. They describe difficulties in attending, sometimes referred to by this author as auditory vigilance, or alerting behaviors that are important in achieving an auditory "set" or readiness by the auditory system, or the person, to attend to the auditory/linguistic message. This occurs at either a cognitive level or at a reflexive level.

Older persons who are hearing impaired describe difficulties in memory, particularly as it relates to short-term storage of linguistic information, from the beginning of a message (or story) to the end. In other words, they retain the last part of the multiple word message but, under stress to remember, lose the first part in the transition. Hull (1988b) refers to this short-term storage phenomenon as "transitional storage," or "short-term storage-for-analysis and synthesis," as perhaps a more descriptive term than that of short-term, or working memory.

Another area of difficulty described by older adults is, for lack of a better descriptor, related to preanalysis, or early refinement of auditory/linguistic information after it is received. The difficulty may be related to the speed at which speech arrives at the auditory system. For example, if the peripheral and central auditory system are not provided the time necessary for preanalysis and presynthesis of the acoustic/linguistic information, then the coding of the signal both in terms of its electrical acoustical properties and the synthesis of linguistic/semantic content for translation may become lost in the process.

For the sake of brevity, the factors described by older listeners who are hearing impaired, as just presented, can, at least tentatively, be categorized as those of:

1. Sorting behaviors.
2. Attending behaviors — auditory vigilance
3. Transitional (working) memory — short-term storage-for-analysis and synthesis
4. Alerting, preanalysis and refinement of the acoustic/linguistic/semantic message content
5. Phase locking — searching — "locking on" the common acoustical characteristics of the signal for analysis
6. Speed and accuracy of processing auditory/linguistic information

These are all critical elements in the integrity of central auditory function, and all perform at the brain stem and cortical levels.

RESEARCH ON SPEECH UNDERSTANDING IN OLDER AGE

Research that involves the study of central auditory decline in older age generally centers on the use of various forms of degraded speech, or manipulating nonspeech acoustic signals or the listening environment. Most research involves reducing the redundancy of the auditory stimulus by manipulation of the physical and/or linguistic characteristics of the speech signal to make the listening task more difficult. Also, most studies involve comparisons of performance on the listening tasks between younger and older listeners.

The results of various studies involving older subjects have revealed similar findings. Those are that older subjects generally have greater difficulty on degraded speech tasks than do younger subjects, even when auditory acuity is essentially normal. For example, Bergman (1980) concludes by stating that, "... the understanding of speech in daily life undergoes gradual change with increasing age because of a combination of peripheral and central alterations, even in the absence of a significant hearing loss, and such alterations significantly affect the understanding of speech that is heard under less-than-optimal conditions" (p. 105). He continues his conclusion by stating that part of this phenomenon is a gradual delay in the ability to process rapid speech, and, thus, to understand it.

According to Welsh, Welsh, and Healy (1985), the increased difficulty in handling complex auditory tasks that is experienced by older adults is, in all probability, the result of a decline in the function of the central auditory system, including factors of:

1. Central competence;
2. Bilateral simultaneous hearing; in other words, a delay in simultaneous binaural routing of signals at the brain stem;
3. Auditory memory;
4. Failure of central fusion when there is incomplete auditory information;
5. Degeneration of neural association (e.g., between hemispheres);
6. Degeneration of neural processing at the brain stem and auditory cortex;
7. Decline in speed of processing; and
8. Neural distortion within the central nervous system (CNS).

In describing the general auditory behaviors of older listeners, Bergman (1980) states that given brief exposure to a speech signal, middle-age and older listeners will perceive only a fraction as much as the younger listener. Speeding the message either by talking faster or by electronically compressing it penalizes the older listener. In relation to filtering the higher frequencies of speech, greater reliance by older listeners than by younger listeners was found for information embedded in the frequencies above 2000 Hz.

Bergman (1980) continues by stating that selective listening declines in older age, manifesting itself in problems in hearing speech in the presence of competing auditory signals. In regard to reverberation characteristics of rooms, what is only mildly unfavorable reverberation time for young adults results in progressively greater breakdown in speech understanding for older adults. In the Bergman (1980) studies, differences in talker characteristics also impeded speech understanding among older listeners to a significantly greater degree than among younger listeners. This is particularly relevant due to the variety of people's voices that one must attend to daily and the effects of

the various forms of amplification on the acoustic characteristics of speech.

Studies by authors such as Bilger, Steigel, and Stenson (1976); Bergman (1980); Jokinen (1973); Smith and Prather (1971), Townsend and Bess (1980); Welsh, Welsh, and Healy (1985); and others have found that, in general, older subjects fare less favorably in signal-to-noise ratios that degrade the speech signal, or in situations where there are competing messages.

Studies in which speech stimuli are distorted through filtering also reveal a general decline in performance with increasing age. Studies by authors such as Bergman (1980); Bergman et al. (1976); Harbert, Young, and Menduke (1966); Palva and Jokinen (1970), however, do not confirm a significant decline that could not be explained, at least in part, by the peripheral impairment. The study by Welsh, Welsh, and Healy (1985) revealed a general decline in speech understanding with increased age through low pass filtered speech, even among those with essentially normal hearing.

Studies on the effects of time compression on speech understanding as a factor of age have generally confirmed a decline in tolerance for compression with increased age. These include studies by Konkle, Beasley, and Bess (1977); Schmitt and McCroskey (1981); Hull (1983); and others. Schmitt and McCroskey (1981) found fairly great tolerance among older subjects for up to 60% compression. On the other hand, Hull (1982) found a significant decline in speech understanding above 40% compression. In further studies, Hull (1988b) discovered that older hearing-impaired subjects could increase speech understanding scores after concentrated practice with time compression, gradually increasing their tolerance to time-compressed speech toward the 50% level. This finding has prompted this author to investigate the use of time compression as a therapy tool with older adults who are hearing impaired in an attempt to increase the efficiency of the older listener's central auditory system in making auditory/linguistic closure.

Studies in the literature consistently point to a gradual age-related decline in the auditory system's ability to utilize a speech signal when it is altered either through its temporal (McCroskey & Kasten, 1981; Kasten, 1981) or acoustical characteristics. The primary locus for the decline appears to be the central auditory system, including both the brain stem and auditory cortex. The difficulty experienced by the listener is compounded when there is an accompanying peripheral impairment of a high frequency nature.

COGNITIVE FACTORS

Changes in cognition with advancing age must certainly affect the perception of speech in oral/aural communication, and probably to a great degree account for factors that reveal themselves in the disproportionate degree of auditory difficulty observed in auditory/communicative function among many older persons. There is, however, a void of research in the literature that directly focuses on the relationship of age, cognition, and speech understanding, as concluded by the Working Group on Speech Understanding and Aging (Tobias, 1988). But, there is a growing constituency of professionals who feel that when clinicians gain greater knowledge about that relationship, they will have at their disposal an armamentarium of information that will permit the development of strategies that can be used to assist older adults in compensating for the decline in cognitive function and its impact on auditory communication.

Memory

The cognitive factor related to aging that is observed most frequently in the literature is that of memory at its various levels.

According to Poon (1985), the early stage of information flow involves sensory memory, in which new information is initially registered. This brief storage of peripheral information is referred to as iconic memory for the visual system, and as echoic memory for the auditory system. There is, however, little information available in the literature regarding echoic memory. Crowder (1980) has provided information on directions for research on sensory memory in aging. In relation to iconic (visual)

memory, for example, there appears to be only a minimal loss of sensory store for visual information, and it is postulated that echoic (auditory) memory also only declines modestly as a result of aging (Crowder, 1980). However, the types of decisions required in speech understanding appear to be beyond what is required through that peripheral form. According to Poon (1985), any decline in sensory storage as a factor of age also may be complicated by other cognitive processes referred to earlier, including those of selective attention, sorting behaviors, pattern recognition, and component integration.

Primary memory is described as the "holding," rather than storing, of information as it is being used. As stated earlier, this author has referred to this type of memory as "transitional storage," or short-term storage-for-analysis and synthesis. According to Craik (1977), this level of memory plays an important part in the control and assimilation of information, and it is an important process in the study of cognition and aging (and it is particularly important to the study of speech understanding and aging). This form of memory is, for example, an important part of the holding of preliminary information as an individual is listening to a sequence of auditory/linguistic information. The first portion is held in "storage" until the remainder is received. Hypotheses or assumptions are made about the totality of the information received and a central auditory decision is made as to the meaning or intent of the message. Manifestations of a decline in this form of memory become evident when, for example, subjects are tested for digit span memory.

Even though studies by authors such as Bromley (1958), Craik (1968), Drachman and Leavitt (1972), and others have found little difference between younger and older subjects in relation to digit span, this author notes a consistent difficulty in primary memory for digits, word lists, and item lists among his elderly clients who are hearing impaired. In fact, those clients are sufficiently concerned about those aspects of aural rehabilitation therapy that they have been found to change seating arrangements so that they will not be in a position to be first in those tasks, or will avoid that portion of therapy, even though the sessions are purposely held in a relaxed and supportive manner and environment. However, with time and practice, sensory memory for digits, words, and item lists are found to increase among the majority of elderly clients, for example, from five items to seven or eight items over a period of a few weeks.

According to Waugh, Thomas, and Fozard (1978), a principal area of decline in primary memory among elderly listeners appears to be in relation to the *speed* of performance of primary memory tasks. When one considers the speed at which speech is generally presented during conversations, lectures, stage presentations, and other situations, speed is, indeed, an important consideration. Primary memory is an important component of accuracy in listening comprehension, where holding and processing of linguistic information must be completed with efficiency *and* speed.

Significant differences between younger and older persons are found for tasks involving *secondary memory*. According to authors such as Thomas and Rubin (1973); Poon, Walsh-Sweeney, and Fozard (1980); Bowles and Poon (1981); and others, secondary memory refers to the storage of information, the use and organization of that information, and the general knowledge and vocabulary that has been stored over time. Vocabulary, the rules of language, concepts, and stored information about that person's world model are held there for retrieval and use. A decline in secondary memory, for example, may result in difficulty in the organization and free recall of recently learned information (Thomas & Ruben, 1973; Poon et al., 1980), but less difficulty when cues are provided. Again, when tasks involving secondary memory are required, elderly subjects do better when more time is provided, or when they are allowed to practice, or when the stimulus material is familiar (Canestrari, 1963). This is, again, of importance when we consider the mental gymnastics and speed required in many listening situations.

The issue of *speed* is one that appears to cross all boundaries of cognitive function as it relates to older age. The Working Group on Speech Understanding and Aging (Tobias, 1988) refers to researchers such as Birren (1974), Salthouse (1982), Salthouse and Kail (1983), and Waugh and Barr (1982) who are convinced that mental slowing is responsible for "most, if not all of the changes in cognition that occur with increased age" (p. 870).

Semantic Activation

Another aspect of memory, semantic memory activation, is described by Madden (1985) as relating to the processing of linguistic information over time, and the time required for priming to occur for vision or audition. According to Howard, Shaw, and Heisley (1986) and Madden (1985), a generalized age-related slowing in the speed of information processing could account for age differences in the retrieval of identifying information from long-term memory. This could affect all types of stimulus materials and all processing stages. The slowing should increase as processing complexity increases (Cerella, Poon, & Fozard, 1980). Although slowing of semantic activation probably will not explain all of the speech understanding difficulties of older adults, it appears to be a major contributor to age differences in cognition and communication.

Auditory/Linguistic Continuity

The continuity effect is a psychoacoustic phenomenon by which our central nervous system will "fill in the gaps" between what was heard and not heard. Early studies by Miller and Licklider (1950) and Dirks and Bower (1970) revealed that when noise was used to fill in the gaps of interrupted speech, the noise led to an improvement of intelligibility. The central auditory system does not have to contend with gaps in the acoustic wave form, and thus accepts the speech signal as more nearly whole. This phenomenon is not dependent entirely on the auditory system, however, but also depends on our knowledge of language, and our ability to make linguistic closure as a result of the predictability of our language. The Gestalt psychologists call this process *closure*. If a decline in this process occurs with advancing age, then it would affect one's ability to comprehend speech in frequently observed situations. For example, most speakers do not utter every sound in every word. Most persons both omit and combine phonemes of speech during conversational speech. They assume knowledge or meaning in some instances, when nothing is uttered, or purposely omit portions of the utterance. If there is a decline in the central auditory system's ability to make closure when auditory/linguistic information is omitted, then speech understanding would likewise be affected. This also includes the many noisy or otherwise distracting environments in which the auditory signal is interrupted frequently.

Categorical Perception

When listening to speech, in order to comprehend (understand) the message, people generally do not listen in discrete phonemic categories, but rather from one perceptual category to another (Liberman, Cooper, Shankweiler, & Studdert-Kennedy, 1967). To accomplish such a task, primary and secondary memory must be intact, along with all other cognitive functions, with the speed necessary for encoding and re-encoding to occur. Probably at the brain stem level, the system is triggered by the presence of a signal that has acoustic properties appropriate to those of speech (Stevens & House, 1972). The CNS is alerted to the speech-like signal, it identifies the signal as speech, and proceeds to categorize, compare with multiple sets of previously stored categories, and analyze the signal in terms of appropriate categories representing content and meaning.

Regarding the aging central auditory system, any slowing of the alerting, triggering, and/or processing of the speech signal would impede this complex process, disturbing and/or delaying interpretation of the message by the listener. It is proposed that this area, at both the peripheral and central levels, is one of importance for study in relation to speech understanding and aging.

SUMMARY

When one sifts through the many consistencies and inconsistencies in the results of studies regarding the relationship between the auditory/functional characteristics of presbycusis and the site(s) of lesion of this disorder, there appears to be some commonality of information. First of all, we seem to be dealing with a compounded disorder that involves the effects of (1) a sensorineural hearing loss that gradually slopes into the higher frequencies, which most certainly would disturb the ability to receive all essential phonemes of oral speech; and (2) a disorder of the higher auditory system (brain stem and auditory cortex), where the sorting and processing of auditory information takes place. A decrease in the speed of processing auditory symbols into sets of meaningful linguistic sequences would seem to represent at least a portion of the compounding difficulties seen in presbycusis. When a younger person with an equal sensorineural impairment is found to be only minimally disabled, but the aged person is disabled to the point of embarrassment and withdrawal, the principal amount of pathology involved in presbycusis most certainly cannot be restricted to the cochlea and eighth nerve. The central pathways and association areas of the brain must be involved.

REFERENCES

American National Standards Institute. (1970). *American National Standard specifications for audiometers, ANSI 3.6-1969.* New York: Author.

American Standards Association. (1951). *American standard specification for audiometers for general diagnostic purposes, Z24.5-1951.* New York: Author.

American Standards Association. (1954). *Exploratory subcommittee Z24-X-2; The relations of hearing loss to noise exposure.* New York: Author.

Bayles, K. A. (1987). *Communication and cognition in normal aging and dementia.* San Diego, CA: College-Hill Press.

Beasley, W. C. (1938). *Hearing study series* (Bulletin No. 7, National Health Survey). Washington, DC: National Institute of Health, U.S. Public Health Service.

Bekesy, G. V. (1957). The ear. *Scientific American, 44,* 1–12.

Bergman, M. (1980). *Aging and the perception of speech.* Baltimore, MD: University Park Press.

Bergman, M., Blumenfeld, V., Cascardo, D., Dash, B., Levitt, H., & Margulies, M. (1976). Age-related decrement in hearing for speech. *Journal of Gerontology, 31,* 533–538.

Bezold, F. (1984). Investigations concerning the average hearing power of the aged. *Archives of Otology, 23,* 214–227.

Bilger, R. C., Steigel, M. S., & Stenson, N. (1976). Effects of sensorineural loss on hearing speech in noise. *Transactions of the American Academy of Ophthalmology and Otolaryngology, 82,* 363–365.

Birren, J. (1974). Translations in gerontology — from Lab to life: Psychophysiology and speed of response. *American Psychologist, 29,* 808–815.

Bowles, N., & Poon, L. (1981). The effect of age on speed of lexical access. *Experiments in Aging Research, 7,* 417–425.

Bromley, D. (1958). Some effects of age on short-term learning and remembering. *Journal of Gerontology, 13,* 398–406.

Bunch, C. C., & Railford, T. S. (1931). Race and sex variations in auditory acuity. *Archives of Otolaryngology, 13,* 423–434.

Canestrari, R., Jr. (1963). Paced and self-paced learning in young and elderly adults. *Journal of Gerontology, 18,* 165–168.

Casey, M. A., & Feldman, M. L. (1982). Aging in the rat medial nucleus of the trapezoid body: I. Light microscopy. *Neurobiology of Aging, 3,* 187–195.

Cerella, J., Poon, L., & Fozard, J. (1981). Mental rotation and age reconsidered. *Journal of Gerontology, 36,* 620–624.

Chafee, C. (1967). Rehabilitation needs of nursing home patients: A report of a survey. *Rehabilitation Literature, 18,* 377–389.

Corso, J. F. (1976). Prebycusis as a complicating factor in evaluating noise-induced hearing loss. In D. Henderson, R. P. Hamernik, D. S. Dasanjh, & J. H. Mills (Eds.), *Effects of noise on hearing* (pp. 497–524). New York: Raven Press.

Craik, F. I. M. (1968). Two components of free recall. *Journal of Verbal Learning and Verbal Behavior, 7,* 996–1004.

Craik, F. I. M. (1977). Age differences in human memory. In J. Birren & K. Schaie (Eds.), *Handbook of the psychology of aging.* New York: Van Nostrand Reinhold.

Crowder, R. (1980). Echoic memory and the study of aging memory systems. In L. Poon, L. Fozard, D.

Cermak, D. Arenberg, & L. Thompson (Eds.), *New directions in memory and aging* (pp. 506–524). Hillsdale, NJ: Lawrence Erlbaum.

Dirks, D., & Bower, D. (1970). Effects of backward masking on speech intelligibility. *Journal of the Acoustical Society of America, 47,* 1003–1008.

Drachman, D., & Leavitt, J. (1972). Memory impairment in the aged: Storage versus retrieval deficit. *Journal of Experimental Psychology, 93,* 302–308.

Ferraro, J. A., & Minckler, J. (1977). The human lateral lemniscus and its nuclei. *Brain and Language, 4,* 277–294.

Fisch, U., Dobozi, M., & Greig, D. (1972). Degenerative changes of the arterial vessels of the internal auditory meatus during the process of aging. *Acta Oto-Laryngologica, 73,* 259–266.

Gaeth, J. (1948). *A study of phonemic regression associated with hearing loss.* Doctoral dissertation, Northwestern University, Chicago, IL. [Cited in Willeford (1971).]

Galton, F. (1884). [Data collected at the international health exhibition, London, England. Cited in Birren & Clayton (1975).] *History of gerontology.* New York: D. Van Nostrand.

Glorig, A., & Nixon, J. (1960). Distributions of hearing loss in various populations. *Annals of Otology, Rhinology and Laryngology, 69,* 497–516.

Glorig, A., Wheeler, D., Quiggle, R., Grings, W., & Summerfield, A. (1957). Wisconsin state fair hearing survey, 1954. [Special monograph]. *American Academy of Opthalmology and Otolaryngology.*

Hansen, C. C., & Reske-Nielsen, E. (1965). Pathological studies in presbycusis. *Archives of Otolaryngology, 82,* 115–132.

Harbert, F., Young, I., & Menduke, H. (1966). Audiological findings in presbycusis. *Journal of Auditory Research, 6,* 297–312.

Hawkins, J. (1973). Comparative otopathology: Aging, noise, and ototoxic drugs. *Advances in Oto-Rhino-Laryngology, 20,* 125–141.

Hinchcliffe, R. (1959). The threshold of hearing as a function of age. *Acoustics, 9,* 303–308.

Hinchcliffe, R. (1962). The anatomical locus of presbycusis. *Journal of Speech and Hearing Disorders, 27,* 301–310.

Howard, D. V., Shaw, R., & Heisey, J. (1986). Aging and the time course of semantic activation. *Journal of Gerontology, 41,* 195–203.

Hull, R. H. (1977). *Serial study of the inferior colliculus in humans.* Unpublished doctoral study, University of Denver, Denver, CO.

Hull, R. H. (1982). Techniques of aural rehabilitation

treatment. In R. Hull (Ed.), *Rehabilitative audiology*. Philadelphia: Grune & Stratton.

Hull, R. H. (1983). Central auditory manifestations in presbycusis. *Journal Internationale D'Audiophonologie, 15*, 61–71.

Hull, R. H. (1988a, July). *Taking charge: Research on a procedure in geriatric aural rehabilitation*. Presentation before the International Congress of the Hard of Hearing, Montreux, Switzerland.

Hull, R. H. (1988b, December). *Central auditory processing and aging*. Scientific paper presented before the Research Symposium on Communication Sciences and Disorders and Aging, American Speech-Language-Hearing Association, Washington, DC.

Hull, R. H. (1988c, February). *Hearing in aging*. Presentation before the National Invitational Conference on Geriatric Rehabilitation sponsored by the Department of Health and Human Services, U.S. Public Health Service, Washington, DC.

Jatho, K., & Heck, K. H. (1959). Schwellen audiometrische Untersuchungen über die Progredienz und Charakteristik der Alterschwerhörigkeit in den verschiedenen Lebensabschnitten. *Zeitschrift für Laryngologie, Rhinologie, Otologie, und Ihre Grenzgebiete, 38*, 72. [Cited in Spoor, A. (1967). Presbycusis values in relation to noise induced hearing loss. *International Audiology, 6*, 48–56.]

Jerger, J. (1973). Audiological findings in aging. *Advances in Oto-Rhino-Laryngology, 20*, 115–124.

Jerger, J. (1979). *Studies in central auditory processing and aging*. Presentation before the Working Group on Hearing Loss in Aging, National Institutes of Health, U.S. Public Health Service, Bethesda, MD.

Jerger, J. (1985). *The locus of presbycusis*. Presentation before the Working Group on Hearing Loss in Aging, National Institutes of Health, U.S. Public Health Service, Bethesda, MD.

Johansen, H. (1943). Den Aldersbetingede Tunghorhed, Munksgaard, Kobenhavn. [Cited in Spoor, A. [1967]. Presbycusis values in relation to noise-induced hearing loss. *International Audiology, 6*, 48–57.]

Johnsson, L., & Hawkins, J. (1972). Sensory and neural degeneration with aging as seen in microdissections of the human inner ear. *Annals of Otology, 81*, 179–193.

Jokinen, K. (1973). Presbyacusis VI: Masking of speech. *Acta Otolaryngologica, 76*, 426–430.

Jorgensen, M. (1961). Changes of aging in the inner ear. *Archives of Otolaryngology, 74*, 161–170.

Kasten, R. (1980, July). *Speed of processing as a factor in aging*. Paper presented before the Aspen Symposium on Aging, Aspen, CO.

Kasten, R. N. (1981). The impact of aging on auditory perception. In R. H. Hull (Ed.), *The communicatively disordered elderly*. New York: Thieme Stratton.

Kirikae, I., Sato, T., & Shitara, T. (1964). Study of hearing in advanced age. *Laryngoscope, 74*, 205–221.

Konigsmark, B. W., & Murphy, E. A. (1972). Volume of the ventral cochlear nucleus in man: Its relationship to neural population and age. *Journal of Neuropathology and Experimental Neurology, 31*, 304–316.

Konkle, D., Beasley, D., & Bess, F. (1977). Intelligibility of time altered speech in relation to chronological aging. *Journal of Speech and Hearing Research, 20*, 108–115.

Lebo, C. P., & Reddell, R. C. (1972). The presbycusis component in occupational hearing loss. *Laryngoscope, 82*, 1399–1409.

Liberman, A., Cooper, E., Shankweiler, D., & Studdert-Kennedy, M. (1967). Perception of the speech code. *Psychology Review, 74*, 431–461.

Madden, D. (1985). Age-related slowing in the retrieval of information from long-term memory. *Journal of Gerontology, 40*, 208–210.

Makishima, K. (1978). Anterior sclerosis as a cause of presbycusis. *Archives of Otolaryngology, 86*, 322–326.

McCroskey, R. L., & Kasten, R. N. (1981). Assessment of central auditory processing. In R. R. Rupp & K. Stockdell (Eds.), *Speech audiometry*. (pp. 126–142). New York: Grune & Stratton.

Miller, G. A., & Licklider, J. C. R. (1950). The intelligibility of interrupted speech. *Journal of the Acoustical Society of America, 22*, 167–173.

Miller, M., & Ort, R. (1965). Hearing problems in a home for the aged. *Acta Oto-Laryngologica, 59*, 33–44.

National Center for Health Statistics. (1981). *Prevalence of selected impairments* (DHHS Publication No. [PHS] 82-1562). Washington, DC: Author.

Palva, A., & Jokinen, K. (1970). Presbycusis v. filtered speech test. *Acta Otolaryngologica, 70*, 232–241.

Pestalozza, G., & Shore, I. (1955). Clinical evaluation of presbycusis on the basis of different tests of auditory function. *Laryngoscope, 65*, 136–163.

Poon, L. (1985). Differences in human memory with aging: Nature, causes, and clinical implications. In J. Birren & K. Schaie (Eds.), *Handbook of the psychology of aging* (pp. 427–462). New York: Van Nostrand Reinhold.

Poon, L., Walsh-Sweeney, L., & Fozard, J. (1980).

Memory skill training for the elderly: Salient issues on the use of memory mnemonics. In Poon et al. (Eds.), *Proceedings of the George A. Talland Memorial Conference.* Hillsdale, NJ: Lawrence Erlbaum.

Proctor, B. (1961). Chronic progressive deafness. *Archives of Otolaryngology, 73,* 444–499, 565–615.

Rosen, S., Bergman, M., Plester, D., El-Mofty, A., & Satti, M. (1962). Presbycusis study of a relatively noise-free population in the Sudan. *Annals of Otology, Rhinology and Laryngology, 79,* 18–32.

Rossenwasser, H. (1964). Otitic problems in the aged. *Geriatrics, 19,* 11–17.

Salthouse, T. (1982). *Adult cognition.* New York: Springer.

Salthouse, T., & Kail, R. (1983). Memory development throughout the life span: The role of processing rate. In P. Bates & O. Brim (Eds.), *Life span development and behavior* (pp. 256–272). New York: Academic Press.

Schaie, K., Warner, P., & Strother, C. (1964). A study of auditory sensitivity in advanced age. *Journal of Gerontology, 19,* 453–457.

Schmitt, J., & McCroskey, R. (1981). Sentence comprehension in elderly listeners: The factor of rate. *Journal of Gerontology, 36,* 441–445.

Schow, R. L., & Nerbonne, M. A. (1980). Hearing levels among elderly nursing home residents. *Journal of Speech and Hearing Disorders, 45,* 124–132.

Schuknecht, H. (1964). Further observations on the pathology of presbycusis. *Archives of Otolaryngology, 80,* 369–382.

Schuknecht, H. (1974, September). *The pathology of presbycusis.* Paper presented at a Workshop on Geriatric Aural Rehabilitation, Denver, CO.

Schuknecht, H., & Woellner, R. (1955). An experimental and clinical study of deafness from lesions of the cochlear nerve. *Journal of Laryngology and Otology, 69,* 75–97.

Smith, R. A., & Prather, W. F. (1971). Phoneme discrimination in older persons under varying signal-to-noise conditions. *Journal of Speech and Hearing Research, 14,* 630–638.

Spoor, A. (1967). Prebycusis values in relation to noise induced hearing loss. *International Audiology, 6,* 48–57.

Stevens, K., & House, A. (1972). Speech perception. In J. Tobias (Ed.), *Foundations of modern auditory theory* (p. 26). New York: Academic Press.

Thomas, J., & Ruben, J. (1973). *Age and mnemonic techniques in paired associate learning.* Paper presented before the Gerontology Society, Miami, FL.

Tobias, J. V. (1988). Working group on speech understanding and aging. *Journal of the Acoustical Society of America, 83,* 859–895.

Townsend, T. J., & Bess, F. H. (1980). Effects of age and sensorineural hearing loss on word recognition. *Scandinavian Audiology, 9,* 245–248.

Traynor, R., & Hull, R. (1974). Pure-tone thresholds among a confined elderly population. Unpublished research, University of Northern Colorado, Greeley.

Welsh, J., Welsh, L., & Healy, M. (1985). Central presbycusis. *Laryngoscope, 95,* 128–136.

Waugh, N., & Barr, R. (1982). Encoding deficits in aging. In F. Craid & S. Trehub (Eds.), *Aging and cognitive processes.* New York: Plenum.

Waugh, N., Thomas, J., Fozard, J. (1978). Retrieval time from different memory stores. *Journal of Gerontology, 33,* 718–724.

Willeford, J. (1971). The geriatric patient. In D. Rose (Ed.), *Audiological assessment.* Englewood Cliffs, NJ: Prentice-Hall.

Zwaardemaker, H. (1981). Der Verlust an hohen Tonen mit zunehmendem Alter. Ein neues Gesetz. *Archives für Ohrenheilkunde, 32,* 53–56.

Zwaardemaker, H. (1894). The presbycusic law. *Archives of Otology, 23,* 228–234.

CHAPTER 18

Who Are These Aging Persons?

■ JUDAH L. RONCH, Ph.D. ■
■ LOIS VAN ZANTEN, M.A. ■

When we work with speech, language, and hearing problems, older persons inevitably constitute a significant portion of the clients we see. Since ours is a youth-oriented society in which myths, stereotypes, and half truths about aging abound, practitioners must confront and overcome any biases about aging that they might have. Not to do so dilutes the strength of the therapeutic endeavor and disempowers older clients.

This chapter is presented so that service providers might begin to appreciate the realities of aging — both positive and negative, and to thereby better understand and serve older persons with the problems discussed elsewhere in this book.

Answers to the question, Who are these aging persons? often are based on idealizations, personal experiences, or ignorance of the realities of aging in the United States. Attitudes toward the aged can be discerned from the words people use to designate this segment of society, and by the psychological devices younger persons use to differentiate and distance themselves from "them." For many years the old have occupied a position of respect, and throughout history society's vocabulary has reflected this attitude. Terms such as senator, alderman, guru, presbyter, and veteran all have their roots in the words of various languages for "old," and denote the position of honor and privilege enjoyed by the aged. The colloquial vocabulary of aging includes expressions such as "golden age" and "senior citizen," but the aged more often are referred to by words denoting negative attitudes about being old and fears about aging. Older people are often seen as — and easily can feel — obsolete in a rapidly changing technological society. Butler (1975) termed aging people "the neglected stepchildren in the human life-cycle."

Currently, the aged constitute 12.3% of the U.S. population, about one in every eight Americans. The percentage of people 65 and older has tripled since 1900, with the largest gains being made in people over the age of 85.

In 1987 there were 29.8 million Americans over the age of 65, and the census projects that in the year 2000 there will be 34.9 million. Further, in the year 2030, when the baby boom population reaches age 65, there will be about 66 million older persons in the United States, and if birth rates and immigration rates remain stable, this will be the only group to experience significant growth.

To answer the question posed by this chapter's title, emphasis will be placed on integrating data about aging with examples of the diverse people who make up the aged group. The authors hope that those who work with the aged may begin to develop a realistic understanding of the aging process in general, as well as appreciate the diversity of aged persons as individuals. As the coming "Age Wave" (Dychtwald, 1989) brings about greater numbers and heterogeneity of older persons, service providers will have to keep finding new, more accurate answers to the question: Who are these aging persons?

DIMENSIONS OF AGING: IS THERE A TYPICAL AGED PERSON?

There are as many kinds of aging as there are aged persons. However, some characteristics of the aging population may merit attention so that the overall circumstances of the aged may be understood better.

Gerontologists have found it useful to divide the aged into the "young-old" (ages 45–64), the "old" (ages 65–74), and the "old-old" (people over 75 years of age) (Shanas & Maddox, 1976). There are significant differences in the life tasks, abilities, resources, health, and other factors between 50- or 55-year-olds and people age 75, and a greater likelihood of similarities among 65-year-olds. Still, all persons of the same age do not experience aging in the same way, and physiological, psychological, and social changes are not waiting to unfold in a fashion solely determined by chronological age.

Biological aging refers to the length of life in years, psychological aging to the adaptation capacity of the organism, and social aging to the performance of the person relative to his or her culture and social group (Birren & Renner, 1977). Rather than look solely at a person's chronological age, greater insight can be derived by looking at the multiple spheres in which a person grows, develops, and gains experience and satisfaction. People of the same biological age are quite diverse in respect to their adaptational capacity and social accomplishments. It is, therefore, important to realize that each aged person must be appreciated both in terms of his or her similarity to other elders, and the lifelong patterns of individuality brought into this stage of life.

THE INTERDISCIPLINARY PERSPECTIVE

Because the elderly person is really a complex organism attempting to interact with an equally complicated environment in a dynamic, mutually demanding way, it is necessary to understand the many factors that make up the world of the older adult. It has been said that no single discipline, whether it be psychiatry, sociology, biology, or economics, can claim to offer comprehensive explanation of how aged people act, think, and feel, or what the multiple determinants of their behavior are (Busse & Pfeiffer, 1977). The authors of this current text agree, and believe that to obtain maximal understanding of the whys and hows of behavior in the aged, knowledge must be gathered and integrated into an interdisciplinary outlook, so as to develop the most accurately parsimonious and powerful explanation available. In this light, it becomes apparent why psychologists must know that depression in an old woman who barely survives on a monthly social security check cannot be alleviated by psychotherapy alone, but that treatment of social and economic realities takes primacy over delving into her childhood experiences; and that the psychotic behavior in an old man can appropriately be alleviated by having a physician adjust his insulin dose and not give him an antipsychotic drug, or write him off as "senile." Similarly, professionals who are trained along the traditional lines of disciplinary focus must be willing and able to understand the need to know as much as possible about all of the factors that must be in harmony if the aged person is to function well and enjoy life.

QUALITY-OF-LIFE ISSUES: STRESS AND ITS SOURCES

Older age is a stage of life wherein multiple stresses are experienced, with a dwindling number of internal and external resources available to reduce stress and promote comfort. Eisendorfer and Wilkie (1977) define a stressful stimulus as one that is "perceived in some way as potentially harmful, threatening, damaging, unpleasant, or overwhelming to the organism's adaptive capacity" (p. 252). Different events will be variably stressful depending on the time of life they are experienced (Neugarten, 1973), and the prior experience of the person with such stimuli. Many sources of stress can be perceived as consequences of the objective reality of the aging process, and the biological, psychological, and social changes that may occur (Lawton, 1977). These changes induce further stress depending on the individual's personality and characteristic response to change and resultant helplessness or loss of control. The period of life beginning in the fifth decade and continuing for the rest of one's life is a time during which many aspects of a person's world undergo change. Typically, there are significant, stressful changes in the following areas (among others):

- The family of origin: parents, brothers, and sisters become ill or die, children relocate or die.
- Marital relationship: death or illness of spouse, estrangement due to empty-nest syndrome, pressures due to retirement.

- Peer group: friends die or become separated by geographical relocation for health, family, or retirement reasons.
- Occupation: retirement and loss of work-role identity.
- Recreation: opportunities may become scarce due to physical limitations or unavailability due to historical lack of interest, lack of opportunity, or few resources.
- Economic: income reduced by retirement; limited income tapped by inflation or medical costs not covered by insurance.
- Physical condition: loss of youth with concomitant biological aspects of body function causing greater risk of poor health and its emotional consequences.
- Emotional/sexual life: loss of significant others through death, separation, and reduction in sexual activity due to societal expectations, personal preference, or death of partner.

DEGREE OF STRESS

Old age is a difficult and stressful time because two things occur in a complementary and simultaneous manner. The various domains of life, as suggested previously, are prone to stresses in greater numbers. At the same time, each domain is the source of a greater degree of stress than in the past. When experienced in combination with the all-too-often limited biological, psychological, and societal resources available to alleviate stress quickly and efficiently, the organism's ability to adapt is compromised. In other words, older persons may experience more stress in so many more domains of life (with fewer internal and societal supports available to them to promote a comfortable readaptation) that they have a greater likelihood of becoming disorganized and feeling incapable of coping. It then becomes imperative that stress be reduced as much as possible if the older person is to successfully negotiate the potentially treacherous period of old age and still derive pleasure from living.

If treatment is to be appropriate, effective, and dignified, it must be borne in mind that rarely can a person of any age, and surely not an aging person, benefit from a helping relationship that does not recognize the total life situation of the client. It is only when the *total person* is addressed and understood that discrete problems may be most beneficially remediated and stress effectively reduced.

THE PSYCHOLOGICAL EXPERIENCE OF AGING

Aging is a biopsychosocial experience and, as such, requires that we understand what occurs as a series of mutually interactive processes rather than as discrete events (Cohen, 1988). The changes of physical aging, for example, produce both a discrete decrement in organ efficiency (e.g., heart output, visual ability, hearing acuity, gastrointestinal motility) and a subjective emotional reaction to the functional disability that results. Thus, it is not how much physical, psychological, or social loss a person experiences, but what that particular loss means to that individual that is the key to understanding the personal, subjective impact of the loss. An avid reader whose vision is failing due to macular degeneration, a social gadabout who cannot hear well, and a housekeeper who can no longer dust when she gets anxious because she fractured a hip and cannot walk are three of the many possible individual examples of persons at risk for strong emotional reactions including anxiety and depressions.

The many physical changes that accompany aging have a psychosocial impact not only on the person's subjective sense of well-being and self-esteem (i.e., they must potentially confront the experience of their "agedness") but on service providers as well. The service providers' usual techniques, communication habits, style of helping, and ability to provide services in their usual settings may have to be modified to assist some older persons. This may prompt providers to think about (consciously or unconsciously) their feelings about aging and youth, control and power, emotions about aging persons they care about, and other psychosocial issues relevant to the caregiver.

PSYCHOLOGICAL CHANGES: MYTH AND REALITIES

The myth that cognitive and emotional regression are inevitable with advancing years still persists with surprising tenacity, in spite of a growing body of evidence to the contrary. Sadly, many health care professionals and the lay public adamantly hold on to the old stereotypes about "normal senility" and a "second childhood" phase of selfishness, childlike dependency and stubbornness, or passivity in the older person. These nihilistic notions not only lower the self-esteem of older persons who believe these to be the cause — rather than the result — of psychosocial and/or physical problems, but often contribute to the exclusion of older persons from sources of potential help for their difficulties.

Cognitive Abilities

Normal aging does not bring with it an inevitable, clearly demonstrable decline in cognitive abilities. Measures of cognitive performance used to investigate age differences in phenomena such as memory, learning, and intelligence are complicated by the intervening effects of sociocultural factors, for example, educational experience, ethnicity, test motivation, and overall physical health of individuals used in these studies. Changes in learning capacity, intelligence (as reflected on a standardized test performance), or memory ability that are purely a function of chronological aging have been difficult to demonstrate. It is even less clear how any changes found by those investigations reflect actual changes in everyday functional abilities of older persons in the general population.

Anyone working with the older person would probably find it beneficial to ascertain each older client's ability to attend to, remember, and integrate new information in an appropriate and consistent way as they work together. The client's sensory difficulties, comfort in a helping relationship, fear of failure, embarrassment at receiving assistance or having a problem, or personality variables (see the following paragraphs) will frequently have a more significant effect on his or her ability to change behavioral patterns than will any change in cognitive ability. A factor such as cognitive style (how one attempts to understand, analyze, and solve problems) is usually an important dimension that has more relevance to how older persons adapt to new demands than do intelligence, memory capacity, or learning ability in the cognitively intact older person.

Emotions and Aging

The emotional life of older persons is the product of how lifelong personality traits and tendencies are affected by the experiences one has while aging. Longitudinal stability of personality, interests, sources of emotional gratification, comfort with emotional expression, and characteristic defenses used against anxiety appears to be a consistent research finding (see Britton & Britton, 1977; Neugarten, 1973; Butler & Lewis, 1982). Thus, the myth that older people develop rigid, cantankerous, infantile, or controlling personalities *because they have grown old* is not substantiated, and it may reflect observations of older people who are unhappy, powerless, ill, debilitated, or responding emotionally to their life circumstances. Rather than being a personality change, these are more likely either an exacerbation of lifelong personality traits, or a response to stress and helplessness not exclusive to later life in any particular older person or the aging population as a whole. (How many times do younger persons react similarly when angry, depressed, helpless, or sick?) People at any age will react to unpleasant or upsetting circumstances in their own characteristic fashion, and it is stereotyping the aged to conclude that because a particular response is seen in an older person that it is a universal, age-related reaction.

Oberleder (1966) observed many years ago that emotional characteristics of older persons

seem to fall into four basic kinds. They are:

1. The psychological characteristics that result from societal expectations about old age, to which the aged adhere to expedite conformity and acceptance (social aging).
2. The psychological reactions to the losses and deficits incurred as a result of the aging process.
3. Those characteristics that are independent of age and arise from poor health.
4. The psychological characteristics that are basic to the elderly person, and have been so throughout the life span.

Later life is like other phases of the life span in that the person has much developmental work to do if a sense of well-being is to be attained. Some developmental tasks of later life include (Butler & Lewis, 1982):

1. The desire to leave a legacy and develop a feeling of continuity (through money, land, ideas, children, or students).
2. The need to serve an "elder" function, and to share their knowledge and experience (a task made difficult by the information explosion and rapid obsolesence of old knowledge by new technology).
3. An attachment to familiar objects (as in the case of Mr. W., who wanted to leave his awful rooming house but feared losing his books, clothes, and other treasured possessions if he couldn't find a new room of adequate size).
4. A change in the sense of time, resulting in a sense of immediacy with emphasis on the "here and now."
5. A sense of the finite life cycle, and a need for completion resulting in a renewed emphasis on religion and culture. (In Japan, old men frequently begin to write poetry as a way of expressing their relationship to life.)
6. A sense of consummation and fulfillment, described by Erikson (1959) as the drive toward ego-integrity. Some authors (Butler & Lewis, 1982; Lieberman & Tobin, 1983) have observed that it is not uncommon for

the elderly to seek to escape their identities through the continuous process by which people "create the self" (Scheibe, 1989), using distortion and other devices that help a person look better in his own eyes.

The continuity of emotional development in later life has been described as occurring along multiple lines of development rather than as a unitary dimension (Colarusso & Nemiroff, 1981). This provides a more accurate notion of the complexity of emotional issues faced by aging persons and allows clinicians to help clients focus on specific issues that, either alone or interactively, are producing emotional distress. Domains such as: (1) intimacy, love, and sex; (2) the body; (3) time and death; (4) relationship to children; (5) relationship to parents; (6) work; (7) finances; and (8) play are dimensions that are operative throughout the adult years, and which require a person's ongoing psychological work to continue, if he or she is to attain mastery and well-being. An individual's ability to meet the many, often taxing demands made by the realities of aging are central in determining an older person's emotional satisfaction and personal development.

Affectional and Sexual Needs

It is widely believed that sexuality in the aged is (or ought to be) nonexistent, and that if it does exist it is surely a sign of aberrant, senile, "second childhood" regression. This belief is based on many subjective feelings, such as that old people are physically unattractive, or that any sexuality in older persons is wrong and shameful (a notion probably rooted in the anxieties young people have about the sexual activity of their parents).

Actually, sex is a matter of great concern in later life, and is the source of many satisfactions as well as emotional problems. Masters and Johnson (1966) found that sexual response in old age diminished in speed and activity, but not in the capacity to achieve orgasm. They also found that like most aspects of the behavior of older persons, levels of sexual activity tended

to be stable over a person's lifetime. Consistent with the cultural values of this cohort, older men may be more active sexually than are women. However, the preponderance of women and the lack of sexual partners among the older population, as well as older people's belief in their asexuality, are strong influences working against sexual satisfaction in the aged.

PSYCHOLOGICAL DYSFUNCTION IN LATER LIFE

It is noteworthy that while our generalizations about aging are becoming more accurate as a result of recent methodologically sophisticated research, there is no universal aging experience. While psychological problems are not inevitable or universal in older persons, there are certain realities that predispose older persons to being particularly vulnerable to mental dysfunction. Notable among these is the likelihood that physical problems will have an impact on mental functioning, and vice versa, in a dynamic fashion. Cohen (1988) illustrates four paradigms of effect.

1. Severe psychological stress leads to compromised physical health. For example, depression leads to dehydration, which can cause electrolyte imbalance and a resulting dementia that looks like Alzheimer's disease.
2. Physical disorder leads to psychiatric disturbance. For example, hearing loss leads to delusions (and possibly late-life paraphrenia).
3. Coexisting mental and physical disorders develop a mutual, dynamic influence on the clinical course of each. For example, congestive heart failure leads to depression with indirect suicidal behavior, specifically, failure to take medication properly. Further deterioration of cardiac status may result in deepened depression.
4. Psychosocial factors affect the course of physical health problems. For example, elderly persons with diabetes living in isolation are at risk for complications as a result of inadequate monitoring of diet and medi-

cation. Physical sequelae (e.g., infection of an extremity) may result, exposing the patient to the risk of amputation.

Thus, it becomes prudent to consider a "multifactorial basis" for emotional and physical disorders in the elderly (Cohen, 1988), and to engage in interdisciplinary treatment modalities and procedures in a coordinated approach when emotional difficulties occur. Older persons faced with psychosocial, physical, economic, existential, and other stressors are at risk of developing anxiety disorders, depression, and other serious but treatable psychological disturbances.

Drugs and Older Persons

Since more medications are used by the elderly than by any other age group (Lamy, 1980), it is likely that service providers who treat the older person will frequently encounter potential or actual side effects of the many drugs older people take. Medication for cardiovascular problems and psychotropic prescriptions are the most frequently prescribed and have a high potential for side effects in older persons (Salzman, 1984). This latter group includes antidepressants, antianxiety drugs, antipsychotics (neuroleptics), sleeping medications, and lithium (for bipolar disorder).

The dynamics of drug action in the older person's body changes in such a way that psychotropic drugs are particularly likely to take longer to work, stay in the body for a longer period of time, and are more potent than they would be in a younger person's body (Cohen, 1988). Older persons also are at risk for drug-drug and drug-food interactions. With the great numbers and variety of drugs used by older persons, it is not rare that an older person experiences confusion, depression, and other changes in psychological functioning due to the mind-altering effects of psychotropic and nonpsychotropic medications. This picture is further compounded when older persons use drugs differently than how they are prescribed. Sensory problems (a person is unable to read the small print on the bottle), difficult-to-open

containers, "informal" prescriptions given out by neighbors, self-medication (if the doctor says one pill works, two will work more quickly), and other factors underlie medication usage errors that have been found to be rather significant in older persons (Vestal, 1985).

Too frequently, drugs are used to achieve the impossible in the lives of older persons, and the risk-to-benefit ratio of using each drug must be considered. Drugs will not erase the effects of aging. They will not make a person suddenly pleasant or amiable, or get them to change their lifelong personality traits.

SOCIAL PATHOLOGIES: ISOLATION, POVERTY, HOMELESSNESS

Social isolation may be the most significant cause of mental illness in the aged. It can occur as a result of losses and from the lack of opportunity to form new relationships. This problem is especially severe for women over the age of 65, nearly half of whom are widows, and who, by the age of 75, outnumber men nearly two to one. Both men and women frequently experience the loss of their role in society, their sense of being needed, and a concomitant loss of self-esteem. The aged usually are not abandoned by family and friends. In 1987, according to the U.S. Bureau of the Census, 67% of older non-institutionalized elders lived in a family setting. These living arrangements, however, may be undesirable, and family conflicts may arise under the pressure of new stresses. As the number of frail elderly increases, so does the strain on family relationships, health, and resources.

Economic conditions under which the majority of aged must survive further compound the stresses of old age. The major source of income for older families continues to be Social Security, which does not compensate for present increases in the cost of living. According to the U.S. Bureau of the Census, in 1987 the median income for men over the age of 65 was $11,854 and $6,734 for women. About 3.5 million elderly persons were below the poverty level. Poverty brings with it an increased risk of chronic disease, dental problems, poor vision, and hearing impairments, along with poorer medical care.

Thus, isolation, poverty, and other social pathologies may contribute to psychological dysfunction in later life. For half of the older persons, poverty does not become reality until after they reach age 65. While each cohort of aged persons is coming to later life with more financial resources, better education, increased longevity, and better prospects for a longer and healthier retirement, many older persons find that retirement and the accompanying loss of income (about 50%) exposes them to poverty or near-poverty conditions.

RETIREMENT

The primary factor in producing a drastic change in economic status for the aged is retirement. While this is an event that is sometimes eagerly sought, it is regarded as an achievement in principle, but dreaded as a crisis when it actually occurs. There are many reasons for this, particularly in our work-oriented society. One is that retirement is actually a two-pronged process, wherein a person "retires" both economically and socially and loses a work role, a source of identification, and frequently the social contacts and relationships the work situation provided (Back, 1977). In addition, retirement in a society like that in the United States involves withdrawal from productive activities and the transfer of control over resources to others. With the latter, power is yielded to the next generation, and the formerly powerful must cope with a new degree of powerlessness.

The newer, more youthful cohorts of older persons increasingly have discovered that one must retire *to* something, be it leisure or a second career (often lasting 20 years). Not all people feel that unstructured leisure time is satisfying. With increased longevity, growth in numbers, and rising pension incomes, more middle- and working-class elders are finding

that they retain a greater proportion of their power than did the generations before them. Thus, older persons are increasingly better prepared for an active retirement phase of life by virtue of improved economic, political, and educational opportunities.

ETHNICITY AND AGING

To be old and poor is bad enough. To be old, poor, and a member of a racial or ethnic minority (particularly if one is a woman), places the aged person in "multiple jeopardy" (Butler, 1975). Blacks, Hispanics, Native Americans, Asians, and other minority groups are overrepresented among the old poor and underrepresented among the nation's elderly. Blacks, for example, comprise 10% of the population but only 8% of the elderly population, and they are disproportionately represented among the poor aged, especially if they are women.

The situation is worse for elderly Hispanics who comprise only 4% of this population. There are about 11.2 million Hispanic elderly in the continental United States, including persons of Cuban, Mexican, Puerto Rican, and South American origin, and this number does not include the almost 8 million illegal aliens of Latin origin. Wherever they live, their life expectancy is significantly lower than their Caucasian counterparts. In Colorado, for example, the average white resident lives to be about 67.5 years old, while an Hispanic lives an average of only about 56.7 years (Butler & Lewis, 1982).

Native Americans get to be old much less frequently than any other group. In 1970, there were estimated to be almost 800,000 Native American elderly, nearly half of whom lived in the western United States, although there are no reliable estimates of the number of elderly among the group. One is shocked to discover that their average life expectancy is only 47 years. Those few Native Americans who do grow old are left impoverished and cut off from traditional family supports (Butler & Lewis, 1982).

Ethnicity

Blacks, Asians, Hispanics, Native Americans, and other minorities continue to be outnumbered by white elderly, but this minority population has been growing, and by the year 2025 it will comprise 15% of the elderly population. Assistance with health care costs is of special concern to these minority elderly because of social discrimination which has resulted in poverty, malnutrition, and resulting health problems. Cultural and language differences often keep the minority elderly from using available public programs. Quality of life for these elderly is, therefore, bleak due to lack of educational opportunities, low level employment with few benefits and small pensions, and poor health care. These circumstances are not likely to improve in the near future.

Many minority elderly speak English as their second language. As they age, they find it difficult to adjust to the differences in language and culture between themselves and the rest of society. For many, English gradually loses its effectiveness as they begin to experience difficulty in the way that their central nervous system processes their second language. This can be compounded in persons with hearing loss and/or dementia whose anxiety approaches panic and terror as they are less and less able to understand what they hear, and they increasingly revert to their native language in an attempt to make order out of linguistic-cognitive chaos.

THE AGED AND THE FAMILY

The family life of older persons does not escape change as people age, and as in other aspects of life, there is a high likelihood of loss. Stresses take their toll on marital relationships, for example, when one spouse becomes ill and thereby creates a "disequilibrium" in the marriage and old role relationships. Whether it be a physical or emotional illness that is the problem, the "patient" can come to be resented for all of the demands for care (realistic or exaggerated) he or she makes on the healthier spouse. The latter, in turn, may become depressed and angry and also develop physical and/or psychiatric symptoms. Typically, the woman becomes the one "in charge" and is confronted with her own feelings about being a caregiver and decision maker. In some relationships, however, men play this role, or two friends of the same sex who share a household may assign roles based on the realities of need and not gender.

When a spouse is not available or capable of providing needed supports, the next most sought resource is a child. Four fifths of older persons have living children (Butler & Lewis, 1982), and about 83% of these aged live less than an hour's distance away from one child (Sussman, 1976). Almost 30% of the elderly reside with their children, a phenomenon reported to be on the increase in rural areas (Sussman, 1976). Usually it is a daughter to whom older persons turn in times of crisis (Brody, 1981), a choice based on long-standing family dynamics. The one chosen may be the one who lives closest, is the wealthiest, was the most- or least-favored as a child, wishes to increase his or her favor with the parents, or who historically could be prevailed on by the siblings to do almost anything.

Many older persons are now developing alternative living arrangements, which involve cohabitation of unmarried men and women (because either their children or social security regulations discourage marriage), moving in with a friend of the same sex to allow for companionship and reduced expenses, or entering communal residences where tasks are shared by all residents.

Relationships between aged parents and their children (who are usually in "middle age," that is, caught in the middle of their parents and their children) do not necessarily deteriorate, nor do all marriages. While some families are able to be involved positively and happily with each other no matter what stresses arise, others are fraught with tension, guilt, anxiety, and multigenerational unhappiness. In most cases, the outcome is influenced significantly by the nature of the family relationship as it had been for years, and not a result of the aging process of some of its members.

FEELINGS OF CAREGIVERS ABOUT AGING PERSONS

Butler (1975) has coined the term "ageism" to denote the "systematic stereotyping of and discrimination against people because they are old, just as racism and sexism accomplish this with skin color and gender" (p. 12). Much of this bigotry functions to distance younger generations from their own eventual aging, though long-lived ageists stand to become objects of their own prejudice (Butler & Lewis, 1982). Comfort (1977) points out that "even Archie Bunker confines his bigotry to groups he will never join." People with negative attitudes about the aged also tend to have more negative attitudes toward people who are physically or mentally disabled and ethnic minorities, especially blacks (Kogan, 1961). The vulnerability for elderly persons with such "multiple jeopardies" is significant. Professionals in many fields have definite prejudices against treating elderly patients (Butler & Lewis, 1982). Some of the reasons for this may be that the aged stimulate the anxiety and conflicts professionals have about their own aging and aging relatives, the belief that old people cannot be helped so professional expertise and time is wasted on "senile" or soon-to-be-dead patients, that it is a waste of their good training, or that they are uncomfortable "giving" to an emotionally demanding older person in what is unconsciously perceived as an incongruous role reversal (Group for the Advancement of Psychiatry, 1971).

On a realistic level, many professionals find it difficult to give as much of themselves as the aged client or patient demands of their nurturing or social interaction. An older person often will want to talk about his or her children, tell old stories, or do anything to hold the attention of the often overworked professional. When one does not have an audience or a responsive and regular conversation partner, the "ticket of admission" often can be a physical complaint. Usually seen as hypochondriasis, a depressive equivalent, the complaint of physical illness or other symptom really can be understood as a safe way of saying "I want to be taken care of" (Pfeiffer, 1973). These complaints usually are about a physical problem, as psychological or emotional problems are too stigmatic or too threatening to talk about.

Just as all older persons are not sick or needy, it is equally unrealistic to perceive aged persons as all being "lovely," "wonderful," and otherwise without human faults. Such stereotyping usually hides fears about one's own aging and an inability to see older persons as people first. The tendency to idealize and romanticize aging and aged persons projects a wish for one's own future and projections about how lovely it would be to be treated as faultless and ideal. It is essentially demeaning and infantilizing — hence dehumanizing.

CONCLUSION

The aged person, though undergoing changes in almost every aspect of life, is no less like him- or herself than in the past. In this period of life, as in every other which precedes it, individual differences are maintained with no reduction in the dimensions or magnitude of difference. Despite myths, stereotypes, and prejudicial distortions to the contrary, people retain their essential personalities and continue to manifest most of their essential abilities to adapt and change as they become old. Major sources of interference to coping or adequate adaptation come mainly from the severe stresses and limited resources that the elderly experience in a variety of ways depending on genetics, life experiences, past and present environment, and traditional ways of dealing with life.

Knowing older persons as people who possess characteristic individuality and a lifetime of experience permits the most productive possible relationship with them. In addition, it aids in establishing fertile ground for the development of their trust and thus encourages the older person to assume an optimistic, progress-oriented approach toward treatment as well as toward life. Nothing is worse than for older persons to perceive the negative, impatient attitude of those who purport to help them, but who have, in fact, given up hope of providing appropriate aid simply because the person in need is old. In many cases, calming reassurance and objective listening do wonders in promoting reduced anxiety and encouraging older persons to mobilize their own resources to help produce improved functioning.

Who, then, are these aging persons? The question might be rephrased to ask not only who, but what are they like, and why are they so. The answers are crucial not only to the achievement of a full understanding of the aged, but on a most personal level, to ourselves, for we are all aging persons.

REFERENCES

Back, K. W. (1977). The ambiguity of retirement. In E. W. Busse & E. Pfeiffer (Eds.), *Behavior and adaptation in late life* (pp. 78–98). Boston: Little, Brown.

Birren, J. E., & Renner, V. (1977). Research on the psychology of aging. In J. E. Birren & K. W. Schaie (Eds.), *Handbook of the psychology of aging* (p. 4). New York: Van Nostrand Reinhold.

Britten, J. H., & Britten, J. O. (1972). *Personality changes in aging.* New York: Springer.

Brody, E. (1981). "Women in the middle" and family help to older people. *The Gerontologist, 21,* 471–480.

Busse, E. W., & Pfeiffer, E. (1977). Functional psychiatric disorders in old age. In E. W. Busse & E. Pfeiffer (Eds.), *Behavior and adaptation in later life* (pp. 158–211). Washington, DC: American Psychiatric Association.

Butler, R. W. (1975). *Why survive? Being old in America.* New York: Harper & Row.

Butler, R. N., & Lewis, M. (1982). *Aging and mental health* (3rd ed.). St. Louis, MO: C. V. Mosby.

Cohen, G. (1988). *The brain and human aging.* New York: Springer.

Colarusso, C., & Nemifoff, R. (1981). *Adult development.* New York: Plenum.

Comfort, A. (1977, April 17). [Review of *Growing old in America* by D. H. Fischer.] *New York Times Book Review.*

Dychtwald, K. (1989). *Age wave.* Los Angeles, Jeremy P. Tarcher.

Eisdorfer, C., & Wilkie, F. (1977). Stress, disease, aging and behavior. In J. E. Birren & K. W. Schaie (Eds.), *Handbook of the psychology of aging* (pp. 251–275). New York: Van Nostrand Reinhold.

Erikson, E. (1959). The problem of age identity, in Identity and the life cycle. *Psychological Issues, 1,* 101–164.

Group for the Advancement of Psychiatry. (1971). *Aging and mental health: A guide to program development* (Vol. 8). New York: Author.

Kogan, N. (1961). Attitudes toward old people: The development of a scale and an examination of correlates. *Journal of Abnormal Psychology, 62,* 616–626.

Lamy, P. (1980). *Prescribing for the elderly.* Littleton, MA: PSG Medical Books.

Lawton, M. P. (1977). Impact of the environment on aging and behavior. In J. E. Birren & K. W. Schaie (Eds.), *Handbook of the psychology of aging* (pp. 276–301). New York: Van Nostrand Reinhold.

Lieberman, M., & Tobin, S. (1983). *The experience of old age.* New York: Basic Books.

Masters, W. H., & Johnson, W. E. (1966). *Human sexual response.* Boston: Little, Brown.

Neugarten, B. L. (1973). Personality changes in late life: A developmental perspective. In C. Eisdorfer & M. P. Lawton (Eds.), *The psychology of adult development and aging* (pp. 311–335). Washington, DC: American Psychological Association.

Oberleder, M. (1966, November). *Psychological characteristics of old age.* Paper presented at the U.S. Department of Public Health Geriatric Training Conference, Philadelphia, PA.

Pfeiffer, E. (1973). Interacting with older patients. In E. W. Busse & E. Pfeiffer (Eds.), *Mental illness in later life* (pp. 5–18). Boston: Little, Brown.

Salzman, C. (1984). *Clinical geriatric psychopharmacology.* New York: McGraw-Hill.

Scheibe, K. (1989). Memory: Identity, history and the understanding of dementia. In L. E. Thomas (Ed.), *Research on adulthood and aging: The human science approach.* Albany, NY: SUNY Press.

Shanas, E., & Maddox, G. L. (1976). Aging, health and the organization of health resources. In R. H. Binstock & E. Shanas (Eds.), *Handbook of aging and the social sciences* (pp. 592–618). New York: Van Nostrand Rienhold.

Sussman, M. B. (1976). The family life of old people. In R. H. Binstock & E. Shanas (Eds.), *Handbook of aging and the social sciences* (pp. 218–243). New York: Van Nostrand Reinhold.

U.S. Bureau of the Census. (1988. [Data published in *A profile of older Americans.*] Long Beach, CA: American Association of Retired Persons.

Vestal, R. (1985). Clinical pharmacology. In R. Andres, E. Bierman, & W. R. Hazzard (Eds.), *Principles of geriatric medicine.* New York: McGraw-Hill.

CHAPTER 19

The Impact of Hearing Loss on Older Persons: A Dialogue

■ RAYMOND H. HULL, Ph.D. ■

From the information presented in Chapter 18 regarding the process of aging and its effect on the aging person, we become aware that we are dealing with special people. The effects of aging on individuals are as unique as their responses to the process. When the effects of aging begin to impact negatively on the sensory processes that have in the past permitted efficient personal and social functioning, then older age may become even more difficult to cope with.

THE IMPACT

Whatever the cause of the disorder called presbycusis, the effects on the some 17 million persons who possess it are in many respects the same. The difficulties that they experienced in attempting to understand what their children and grandchildren were saying at the last family reunion were frustrating, to say the least. It becomes easier to withdraw from situations where communication with others may take place, rather than face embarrassment from frequent misunderstandings of statements and inappropriate responses. To respond to the question, "How did you sleep last night?" with "At home of course!" is embarrassing, particularly when other misinterpretations have occurred in the same conversation and are occurring with increasing regularity. The older person, who may be an otherwise alert, intelligent adult, is also understandably concerned over those misunderstandings of conversations. Many elderly adults who experience such difficulties feel that perhaps they are losing their "senses," particularly when they may not know the cause for the speech understanding problems that they are experiencing. Perhaps their greatest concern is that their family may feel they are losing the ability to function independently, and that those personal aspects of life for which they are still responsible will be taken away.

Communication is such an integral part of financial dealings, for example, that elderly persons also may question their own ability to maintain a responsible position in the family, although in the end they may not wish to withdraw from those responsibilities. The self-questioning that may occur can be further aggravated by well-meaning but demeaning comments by others. A comment by a concerned son or daughter as, "Dad, why don't you think about selling the house and moving into a small apartment? You know this house is too much for you to care for," can be defeating. Even though an elderly family member may be adequately caring for the house, cooking nutritious meals, and looking forward to each spring so that he or she can work in the garden, a seed of doubt has been planted regarding his or her ability to maintain the house and other life requirements because of age. A statement by his or her physician such as, "Of course you are having aches and pains, you're not a spring chicken any more," can bring about doubts of survival. Such doubts are the beginning of defeat among many elderly, unless they are uniquely resilient.

Compounding these self-doubts may be a growing inability to understand what others are saying as a result of presbycusis and the embarrassment that results. It becomes easier, for lack of other alternatives, to withdraw from those situations where embarrassment or fear of embarrassment may occur than to enter them. If forced into such a situation, the easiest avenue is to become noncommunicative rather than to attempt responses to questions and fail, thus instilling further doubts in younger family members' minds regarding their elder's ability to maintain independent living. If forced to respond to a question that is not understood fully, because an important word is not heard or processed correctly, frustration on both the part of the elderly person and the family can ensue. Anger and embarrassment on both sides is usually the result.

HOW DO ELDERLY PERSONS REACT TO THEIR HEARING IMPAIRMENT?

Feelings of embarrassment, frustration, anger, defeat, and ultimate withdrawal from situations that require communication are very real among older persons who are hearing impaired and people who interact with them. When so much else is taken away from many older adults, including leadership in a family, a steady income, a spouse or friend who may have passed away recently, convenient transportation, and a regular social life, a gradual decrease in the ability to hear and understand what others are saying can be debilitating. As one elderly person said, "I would like to participate socially, but I feel so isolated when I cannot hear." Many feel so agonized by their inability to understand what the minister is saying at church, what their friends are saying at the senior center, or what the speaker at a meeting they were looking forward to attending is saying, that they do withdraw and become shells of what they used to be. They are described by their family or others with whom they associate as "confused," "disoriented," noncommunicating, uncooperative, and "angry, old _____," withdrawn, and most unfair of all, "senile." In some instances, a hearing aid does not provide the help that was expected for the person who possesses presbycusis, because of the complex nature of that auditory disorder. The inability to use amplification may result further in a resolution that perhaps the disorder is mental rather than simply auditory.

It has been observed by this writer that, in many instances, a portion of the depression experienced by the elderly who are hearing impaired is brought about by that person's feelings that the breakdowns in communication that are being experienced, "are all my fault because I possess the hearing impairment." It does not occur to them that the disor-

THE IMPACT OF HEARING LOSS ON OLDER PERSONS ■ 249

der of hearing may be magnified by family members who do not speak plainly, or by being placed in communicative environments that are so noisy and otherwise distracting that only a person with normal auditory function would be able to hear and understand what was being said. Those environments, for example, may include attempting to listen to a speaker in an auditorium that possesses poor acoustics and the only seat left is toward the rear of the room, or attempting to understand what his or her shy 3-year-old granddaughter is saying.

Some older persons who are hearing impaired become so defeated in their attempts at communication that it does not dawn on them that they might be able to understand what others are saying if those with whom they communicate would improve their manner of speaking or improve on the communicative environment. However, many elderly persons have resigned themselves to "not be a bother," rather than asserting themselves by criticizing their family's manner of speaking or the environments in which they are asked to communicate. Instead, older adults may simply visit their families less frequently, even though they desire to talk to a daughter, son, or grandchildren. In the end, however, they may withdraw into isolation at home rather than attempt to maintain social or family contacts where they have felt frustrated and embarrassed.

HOW DO OTHER PEOPLE REACT TO THE ELDERLY WHO HAVE PRESBYCUSIS?

One elderly person who is hearing impaired has eloquently stated, "For every poor ear, there is at least one poor speaker." In regard to the reactions of others to the elderly person who is hearing impaired, he may be quite accurate.

As stated earlier, many elderly persons have placed themselves in a position of "not being a bother," perhaps not realizing that a portion of their difficulties in communication with others may be the result of talking to persons who do not speak clearly, or being asked to communicate in environments that may cause even a

person with normal hearing to have difficulty. Even though, for example, an elderly person's adult son may not possess good speech skills, the blame for miscommunication or misunderstanding by the elderly parent is placed on the parent and his or her hearing deficit and not on the speaker, without attempting to *analyze* the problems of communication per se.

Generally, the initial visible frustration at the elderly person's inability to understand what is being said is observed in the listener. Any lesser reaction may have resulted in a simple request for repetition or rephrasing of the statement for clarification. When the elderly listener who is hearing impaired fails to understand a statement after several repetitions of a difficult word, it is usually he or she, rather than the speaker, who first notices the apparent frustration. Increased self-imposed pressure to succeed in understanding the problem word in the speaker's sentence tends to increase anxiety and heighten the probability of failure to ultimately understand the word. One of two reactions generally follows. The most frequent reaction on the part of the elderly listener is to become equally frustrated, apologize, and withdraw from the situation. The second probable response is a feeling of anger coupled with frustration and embarrassment, and either an inner or overt expression of, "Why don't you speak more plainly!"

Who initiated this difficult situation? In all probability it was the speaker rather than the elderly listener. The speaker's initial unspoken display of frustration at the elderly listener's inability to understand the statement or question caused heightened anxiety on the elderly person's part. Anxiety, in that situation, breeds failure, failure breeds frustration, frustration breeds further failure, and so on, until some resolution to cease the conversation, leave the situation, or continue to display anger and frustration is reached.

Did the initial attempt at conversation prompt this less-than-tolerable situation? Probably not. The elderly person who has experienced frustrating attempts at conversation on prior occasions usually develops an immediate awareness of signs of anxiety, frustration, or concern that are reflected in the speaker when a misunderstood word or phrase causes a delay in the conversation. After failure in various communicative environments has occurred on other occasions, and perhaps is now occurring with greater regularity, the elderly person begins to anticipate the speaker's response, perhaps in some instances prematurely, in anticipation of a *possible* negative response. In any event, a speaker at some time has planted the seed of suspicion that he or she was frustrated, concerned, and perhaps even angry at the elderly person's failure to understand or interpret what he or she was saying.

The second person's negative response to the older person's difficulty in understanding what he or she is saying may be the result of either an unanticipated interruption in the flow of the conversation, a lack of tolerance for a disorder that is not readily visible and therefore disconcerting to the nonimpaired person, or a lack of knowledge regarding ways in which the situation could be more comfortable for both the listener who is impaired and the speaker.

A nonimpaired person typically will react to assist a person who is physically handicapped across a busy street, or guide a person who is visually handicapped through a maze of chairs. In those situations, however, the impairment and the manner in which assistance can be offered are obvious to a person who may, in fact, know little about the handicapping effects of those disabilities. But verbal communication, which is generally experienced as an ongoing set of events, when interrupted by a nonvisible disorder such as hearing impairment, is usually disconcerting to the nonimpaired person. This situation is particularly true when a hearing aid is not worn or otherwise displayed, and it generally occurs when the speaker suddenly realizes that his or her verbal message was misunderstood. Communication for that brief instant no longer exists. At that point, the hearing person is suddenly perplexed about what to do. The misunderstood word or phrase is repeated, but perhaps to no avail. The person who is hearing impaired still misinterprets the verbal

message. A natural response is to repeat the word or phrase once again in a louder voice, perhaps with emphasis and facial expression that reveal at least some frustration, since the speaker may not have determined why the listener is having such difficulty. The evident frustration may, in turn, concern the listener who is hearing impaired, and communication is at a stalemate.

If the impaired auditory system of the listener was as noticeable as the impaired limbs of the paraplegic or the eyes of the blind person, perhaps the perplexing frustrations that occur could have been softened. Presbycusis is so complex, however, that simply raising the intensity of one's voice may do little to ease the difficulty. In fact, in some instances, the misinterpretations actually increase, either by further distorting an already distorting auditory system, or as the result of recruitment. In other words, the frustrations experienced by persons who communicate with *any* person who is hearing impaired do exist, and, thus, also exist among the persons themselves who are hearing impaired.

ELDERLY PERSONS WHO ARE HEARING IMPAIRED VERSUS OTHERS WHO ARE HEARING IMPAIRED

Why do family members, friends, or spouses of elderly persons who have presbycusis appear to experience greater frustrations than those persons who, for example, must communicate with children who are hearing impaired? Adults and children, perhaps, tend to be more compassionate toward children and young adults who have difficulty communicating as the result of hearing impairment. That is not to say that there are not instances where communicating with a child who is hearing impaired ends in frustration for both the child and the speaker. Accommodations by nonimpaired children and adults, however, appear to be made willingly in most instances, because they know that the child is likely to have difficulty understanding their verbal message, either because of the hearing impairment per se or as the result of language delay. On the other hand, the nonimpaired person who is frustrated at attempts to communicate with an elderly person who is hearing impaired may rationalize the reason as being because the person is simply "old."

Are the frustrations and resulting tension expressed because the listener is simply an older person? Perhaps in a few instances this may be true, but probably not as a general rule. The frustration experienced by those persons who may have known the elderly person for some time prior to the onset of the auditory difficulties may arise from the fact that this person "was always quite alert." For reasons unknown to them, however, frustrating and failed attempts at "communicating with Dad" are causing friction in their family. "Dad's mind seems to be failing. I told him yesterday to get the safety inspection sticker for his car renewed, and he replied, 'Who was safe?' Maybe we should get him a hearing aid, or take his car away from him." When a hearing aid is purchased for him by a well-meaning son or daughter, and he refuses to wear it because, as he says, "it doesn't help," then he may be described by his family as stubborn. Or they may feel that "he refuses to do anything to improve himself," when in reality the hearing aid did not provide significant improvement. So how do others who associate with the elderly person who has presbycusis react to him or her? As one family member said to this writer:

We are concerned about Dad. We used to have a good time talking about "the good old days," and about what he wanted to do after he retired. Now that he cannot seem to hear us or understand what we say, we all get angry. He cannot understand what we are saying no matter how loud we talk, and all he does is get mad because no matter how many times we repeat what we say, he still cannot get it. We tried a hearing aid, but he will not wear it. He says it does not help. For $700, it *should* do something for him, but we all feel that he just cannot get used to something new. Besides, he is just stubborn, we think. Our whole lives have changed since this hearing problem has gotten worse. We do not communicate anymore. We do not even like to have him over anymore, and no one goes to visit him. He just sits. We are embarrassed to take him out to restaurants be-

cause he cannot understand the waiters and then he becomes angry when we try to interpret what they are saying. So we just let him sit at his house. We told him to sell the house and move into an apartment complex where older persons live. He says that if we try to sell his house he will lock the doors and windows and never come out until the hearse takes him away. His hearing problem has changed all of our lives for the worse. We really are at our wits' end.

Statements such as these are made many times by concerned and frustrated children, friends, and spouses of elderly persons who are hearing impaired. But many of these persons can be helped if those who serve them take the time to listen to their responses to the auditory disorder and their state in life, and to carefully evaluate their hearing disorders. From this information, viable service programs can be developed, not only for the older person who is hearing impaired, but also for those who most closely associate with them.

REACTIONS OF OLDER PERSONS TO THEIR HEARING IMPAIRMENT: A DIALOGUE

How do older adults who possess hearing impairment react to the disorder and the difficulties they experience while attempting to communicate with others? The following statements from clients reflect their feelings about their hearing loss. They are taken from initial pretreatment interviews with eight older clients who are hearing impaired, and were recorded on videotape by this author. This type of personalized information provides important insights into the feelings and desires of elderly clients that are not only important in the counseling process, but also in developing treatment programs on their behalf.

THE INTERVIEWEES

All but one of the persons presented in this section are from northern Colorado; one client is from Albuquerque, New Mexico. All are from an average socioeconomic level, and all are articulate older adults.

Occupational History

Two women were teachers, one at the elementary school level and one at the high school level. One man managed a grain elevator in a small town. He acquired no education past the sixth grade. One man is a retired agricultural agent for Weld County, Colorado. One man was a farmer, with no education past third grade. Two women still consider themselves to be housewives — one retired and one not retired. One man is a retired missionary. Three of these clients presently reside in a health care facility, and the other five are living in the community in their own homes.

State of Health and Mobility

The five clients interviewed who reside in the community all describe themselves as being well. They feel they are mobile, although only one of the women drives a car. Each of the men who reside in the community drives his own car. The woman who does not drive, said that transportation was occasionally a problem, but that city bus service generally was adequate. All clients interviewed, except one man who was troubled with the gout, stated that they sometimes walked where they needed to go, mostly for the exercise.

The clients interviewed who resided in health care facilities do not drive cars. Transportation was stated as being adequate generally through local bus service or by the health care facility's "ambulobus" service. The clients who reside in health care facilities generally described the reason for placement there as health, except for one who felt that she simply was deposited there. Physical problems among those confined persons include heart problems, kidney dysfunction, Parkinson's disease, cataracts, and hearing loss. Walking was described by all as difficult. One client was confined to a wheelchair due to Parkinson's disease.

Age

Ages of the clients ranged from 66 to 95 years. The mean age was 76 years.

Reason for Referral

All persons interviewed for this discussion had been referred for aural rehabilitation services, or had sought out the service. All had consented to participate in aural rehabilitation treatment on an individual or group basis after an initial hearing evaluation and counseling.

THE DIALOGUE

The following are the persons' descriptions of themselves and the impact of their hearing impairment on them. The dialogue is taken from videotaped responses by each client to the question, "How do you feel about yourself at this time and your ability to communicate with others?" Such videotaped interviews are held with each client seen by this author prior to aural rehabilitation services and again at their conclusion. The purpose for all pre- and postservice videotaped interviews is to allow clients to confront themselves and their feelings about their ability to cope in their communicating world. Changes in their opinions of themselves and their ability to function auditorily are thus more easily mapped. Clients are allowed the opportunity to note changes in themselves and their opinions of their ability to communicate with others by watching and listening to their own statements. The following are brief but descriptive excerpts of statements by these clients.

Case 1

Age. 70 years
Sex: Female
Residence: Community (in own house)
Marital Status: Never married
Prior Occupation: Elementary school educator
Health: Good
Mobility: Good. Drives own car.
Dialogue:

I try to say, "What did you say?" but sometimes they begin to appear angry. I become frustrated — so, so frustrated that I then become angry at myself because I have become angry at those with whom I am talking. Do other people have problems where they cannot understand what people are saying? Am I the only one?

I didn't know why I had begun to dislike going to meetings until I realized that I was not understanding what people were saying. I had been blaming my friends, and they had been secretly blaming me. I hope I can retain their friendship after I explain to them that the problems were not all their fault.

This woman's comments indicate concern over the difficulties she is experiencing in her attempts at interacting with others. She is, however, not resigned to the fact that she will continue to fail. She is still striving to retain friendships with others. Further, she is still enrolled in aural rehabilitation treatment and making satisfactory progress in learning to make positive change in her communication environments.

Case 2

Age: 76 years
Sex: Male
Residence: Community (in own house)
Marital Status: Widower
Prior Occupation: Grain elevator manager
Health: Generally good. Has known cardiovascular problems. Some dizziness noted on occasion.
Mobility: Good. Drives own car and is physically mobile. He is mentally alert and always seems to have a joke for the occasion. But, in most respects, he is a man of few words.
Dialogue:

It is embarrassing. When people find out that you have trouble, they do not seem to want to talk to you anymore. If you ask them to speak up sometimes they look angry.

I feel that time is lost when I go to a meeting I have looked forward to going to, and I cannot understand a word they are saying. Most people do not seem to have good speech habits. On the other hand, my poor hearing does not help a bit either.

My main goal in coming here is to learn to hear a woman's voice better — maybe a woman's compan-

ionship will not be so hard to come by . . . . As they say, a woman's voice may not be as pretty as the song of a bird, but it is awful darn close.

This man possesses a significant speech discrimination deficit, and strongly desires that aural rehabilitative services be of help to him. He feels he has much to live for and is willing to work to improve his auditory problems. Assertiveness training and manipulation of his communicative environments has supported those efforts.

Case 3

Age: 95 years
Sex: Female
Residence: Health care facility
Marital status: Widow
Prior Occupation: Housewife (retired)
Health: Parkinson's disease
Mobility: Severely limited. Is confined to a wheelchair. Effects of Parkinson's disease are progressing rapidly.
Dialogue:

I would like to be free, to drive, to go visit children and friends. I would like to get away from confinement. I would like to be able to hear again, to be able to be a part of the conversations that take place in this home. It would be pleasant to hear the minister again, or to talk to my children. They live far away, though, and cannot come often.

My main concern is death right now. I know that the infirmity I have will end in death. I don't know if I am ready. If I could hear the minister, maybe I would know.

These comments are typical of many elderly persons who are confined to the health care facility. They feel so many needs but few can be fulfilled. This woman is alert, however, and can respond to aural rehabilitation treatment. If, for example, accommodations can be made in the chapel so that she can participate in those services, then one of her desires would be fulfilled. Further, if learning to manipulate her more difficult communicative environments can be achieved so that she can function better in the confines of the health care facility, then she would feel less isolated.

Case 4

Age: 72 years
Sex: Male
Residence: Health care facility (post-hospitalization)
Marital Status: Married
Prior Occupation: County extension agent
Health: Intestinal blockage. Arthritis. Otherwise in generally good health.
Mobility: Generally good. Drives own car on occasion. Walks to many places.
Dialogue:

I feel lost sometimes. If I look people straight in the eye, then sometimes I get what they say. I get angry sometimes, but I have finally figured out that for every poor ear, there is a poor speaker!

It is rough to have poor ears. I have trouble hearing women's voices. I wish I could hear them since I'm around women more now than ever before. Maybe it's me; maybe I don't have good attention.

I wish I could hear my preacher. I go to church every Sunday, but I do not get much out of it. I wish I could understand what people are saying in a crowd, like when our children and our grandchildren come back home. If I'm talking to only one person, sometimes I do okay.

This man expresses a great many "wishes," but so far has not extended himself a great deal in aural rehabilitation treatment. In other words, he desires to improve, but seems to feel that either he does not possess the capability to regain greater communication function, or simply does not want to put forth the effort. He appears to have great communicative needs, but does not yet seem to be convinced of their importance.

Case 5

Age: 71
Sex: Male
Residence: Community (in own house)

Marital Status: Widower
Prior Occupation: Farmer
Health: Excellent, except for gout, which restricts his mobility.
Mobility: Not as mobile as desired due to gout. Drives own car. Is an avid fisherman.
Dialogue:

In a crowd, I have my worst trouble. Riding in a car drives me crazy!

People do not talk with their mouth open. My ears "hum," and that hurts too, in terms of my ability to understand what people are saying. Some people talk with their hands in front of their mouths; that is very disturbing. I do not think my children understand that my problem is my hearing — not my mind.

It just seems like the voice does not come through. I went to the doctor and he says my hearing is ruined. My hearing is my only handicap. My minister has an English brogue and I cannot understand a word of what he is saying. Groups sound kind of like a bee hive. I feel embarrassed. Someone speaks to you and you give them the wrong answer. I like to go to social gatherings, but I still get embarrassed. I certainly am not going to give up.

This man represents almost the ideal older client for aural rehabilitation services. He is alert and active, and desires to maintain himself as an active social person. He has also found a female companion who is also an avid fisherman. What an ideal motivational factor for aural rehabilitation!

Case 6

Age: 81 years
Sex: Male
Residence: Community (in own house with his spouse)
Marital Status: Married
Prior Occupation: Missionary. Still functions as part-time minister for local church. He receives many requests to serve on community and church committees.
Health: Excellent
Mobility: Excellent. Walks a great deal and drives own car.

Dialogue:

My greatest concern is my inability to participate in council meetings at church. In some cases, I am in charge of the meeting, but if I cannot understand what the members are saying, then my participation is made almost impossible. It distresses me tremendously that in some instances I cannot perform my duties. Maybe it's me? Maybe my concentration wanders. Maybe my mind is not working as well now — although I feel that it is. I have 20 to 30 members in the Sunday School class that I teach. I find that I have terrible problems determining what their questions are. If I do not know what their questions are, how can I respond to their needs?

These statements are made by an obviously frustrated man. "How can I respond to their needs?" This man has a great deal to offer his community and church, but is beginning to feel defeat. The audiologist must consider this type of older client as a high priority and intervene as a strategist to aid the person to function more efficiently in those prioritized communicative environments.

Case 7

Age: 66 years
Sex: Female
Residence: Community (in own house)
Marital Status: Single
Prior Occupation: High school educator
Health: Excellent
Mobility: Excellent
Dialogue:

I was feeling concern inasmuch as when people would ask me a question. I would know they were speaking, but I couldn't make sense out of it. I was afraid that my mind was going. I felt closed in, not comfortable; like I would hear, but little of it made sense; like I was losing my mind. I think sometimes that people want me to go away.

When I found out that my problem was with my hearing and not my mind, the relief was wonderful. Now I feel that I have something I can try to handle, where before I did not think I had a chance again. If people will bear with me, I will be able to talk with

them. I am going to stay in there just as long as I can.

This woman benefitted greatly from an initial counseling session regarding her auditory problem and some reasons for the difficulties she was encountering. After she found that the communicative problems she was experiencing were not so much the result of her mind, but rather her hearing, she was a ready candidate for a formal auditory rehabilitation treatment program.

Case 8

Age: 79 years
Sex: Female
Residence: Health care facility. Stated that she thought her daughter was looking for an apartment for her, but found herself there.
Marital Status: Widow
Prior Occupation: Housewife (nonretired)
Health: Generally excellent except for broken hip two years ago.
Mobility: Somewhat restricted due to fear of falling. Otherwise excellent. She takes the bus to those places she desires to go.
Dialogue:

I used to blame others for my inability to hear, but someone the other day told me it was my fault —me and my inability to hear. A speaker at a concert meeting the other evening spoke for 45 minutes and I did not understand what she was saying. The disturbing thing was that she refused to use the microphone!

I was in a car with two friends the other day. I rode in the back seat. They were talking in the front seat. They were talking about a person I had not seen for quite a while. I heard them say something about a ball game, something about Omaha, and something about someone becoming very ill. I finally felt that I had to say something, so I asked, "She is well, isn't she?" Well, what they had said was that my friend had died! She became very ill during a ball game in Omaha and died while being taken by ambulance to the hospital. It was terribly embarrassing, but they did not become angry with me. It is so frustrating to try to do well, but continually fail. I try not to be irritable. I think I can overcome it.

This is an example of an alert older woman who, because of factors beyond her control, fell and found herself unable to provide for her physical needs. She was placed in a health care facility — hopefully for a relatively short period of time. She has accepted such placement because of the evident short stay. She is responding well to aural rehabilitation treatment services, particularly in regard to learning to cope within her most difficult environments. She has analyzed the reasons for her communicative difficulties well, and is aware of her limitations.

SUMMARY

Auditory deficits as the result of presbycusis are as real as the people who possess the disorder. The disorder, however, affects each person in unique ways. One common denominator is evident, however, and that is the resulting communication problems can be terribly frustrating, and in many instances debilitating. The most common strain among the confessions of these elderly persons, however, is the pain caused by the isolation and loneliness they experience as the result of their inability to communicate with other people.

CHAPTER 20

Counseling the Older Adult Who Is Hearing Impaired

■ James F. Maurer, PH.D. ■
■ Maria Monserrat-Hopple, M.S. ■

A hearing impairment experienced during the later years of life represents more than an imposition on the ability of the individual to communicate receptively. For many, it represents the superimposition of degraded auditory reception on a small galaxy of concomitant problems, ranging from other sensory deficits to necessary changes in lifestyle. Presbycusis compounds the consequences of coexisting physical and social limitations. Psychiatrist Robert Butler (Butler & Lewis, 1973) describes it as "potentially the most problematic of the perceptual impairments, (because) it can reduce reality testing and lead to marked suspiciousness, even paranoia" (p. 73).

Stress factors which interface with this handicap may be reduced to three categories: (1) coexisting health problems and impairments, (2) environmental stimulation, and (3) financial status and mobility. Specific psychosocial problems arising from presbycusis cumulatively suggest that these categories are, more often than not, interrelated.

One of the many outcomes of becoming older is a frequently observed difficulty in understanding speech. The loss of brain cells, as seen in persons with atherosclerosis and forms of dementia, demonstrates this difficulty (Kelly, 1985). In studying the effects of aging on comprehension, Davis and Ball (1989) demonstrated that the ability to correctly understand spoken messages was reduced in the older age group. A breakdown in syntactic ability is evident during tasks involving comprehension of implausible events, such as "The hostage *that handcuffed the policeman* untied the kidnapper." However, no significant effect was noted on the comprehension of semantic components. This has implications on the demands central aging produces on short-term memory span.

COUNSELING THE OLDER ADULT WHO IS HEARING IMPAIRED

THE IMPACT OF ENVIRONMENT

No communication environment is a conducive one for persons with hearing impairments. Some are simply better than others. The institutionalized aged, which constitutes about 5% of the population, would seem to be residing in environments that generally are most disturbing for human communication. However, many senior adult centers also fall into this category. Moriarity (1974) surveyed 25 group living environments for the elderly, including nursing homes, high-rise apartments, extended-care facilities, and senior adult centers, concluding:

1. Most were located in high traffic areas, where average outside noise levels exceeded that of normal conversational speech.
2. Most were poorly insulated against the intrusion of outside noise.
3. Only 4 of the 25 facilities were adequately equipped with acoustic tile, drapes, and carpeting to dampen inside noise.
4. Nearly half of the buildings contained noise-producing sources, such as vibrating fans and kitchen and laundry appliances, which were in close proximity to both recreation and meeting areas.

Too few places of worship have been architecturally designed to accommodate individuals with hearing difficulties. Older persons generally are faced with vaulted ceilings, hard, flat resonating walls, and an unfavorable distance from the speaker to the listener. Sanctuaries that provide wall-mounted speakers and a pulpit microphone may offer some assistance, provided that listeners who are hearing impaired are situated in close proximity to the speakers. Assistive listening devices, including FM and infrared systems which transmit directly to pew monitors, such as earphones and hearing aids, generally offer greater noise-free intelligibility of the messages. However, "fortunately for most elderly worshippers, the familiarity of the message content may be the greatest blessing" (Maurer, 1976, p. 12).

Private residences of low-income, aging persons are often located in heavily populated urban areas where intrusion from outside noise sources is common. A sample of 100 such residents who moved from private dwellings to quality high-rise apartments were questioned about changes in the extent of unwanted sound. Fifty-one percent reported quieter sound levels in their new apartments, and nearly all indicated increased life satisfaction (Cain, Fine, & Maurer, 1974).

The nucleus of individuals associated with the older person who is handicapped in the living environment is a key ingredient in psychosocial adjustment. What Comfort (1978) described as "childrenization" of the elderly all too frequently occurs within family constellations in private residences and among staff members in collective environments. That is, there is a tendency to regard the older person from the standpoint of being elderly, rather than attending to his or her needs. This attitude, when associated with ignorance about the problems of hearing impairment, may lead to dangerous misconceptions about the individual and his or her social communicative potential. As Hull (1973) has observed:

Hearing impairment as seen by the "lay person" is often mislabeled as senility because the elderly person will often times respond to questions or statements with wrong or inappropriate answers. Senility is without question seen among the geriatric patients, but non-senile hearing impaired patients often seem to demonstrate similar symptoms with inappropriate responses to questions, depression, anxiety, suspiciousness and withdrawal. (p. 298)

In some environments there is virtually a collusion of anonymity operating against the person who is handicapped. Although collectively sharing in his general welfare, no member of the nursing staff or family personally accepts responsibility for the older individual's auditory difficulties.

Such a milieu has a powerfully decremental effect on an individual's frequency of social interaction. People communicate less because the older person does not understand them. The older person communicates less often to them, because of their lessening interest. They reciprocate by ignoring the older person's social presence. The older adult adjusts to this deprivation of interaction by interacting inwardly through thoughts and imageries that are intrinsically more reinforcing than the extrinsic social environment. Although the person is not regarded by family as "deaf," he or she often appears "preoccupied, unsociable, absent-minded, or paranoid" (Joensen & Saunders, 1984). In the presence of other functional limitations, the person who is hearing impaired may suffer from depression, often closely followed by self-isolation (LaFerle & LaFerle, 1988). Observers may remark how he or she has changed and how "he or she lives in a world of his or her own."

The Use of Validation Therapy in Serving These Clients

In validation therapy, which has evolved since its inception in 1967 (Fiel, 1967), the goal is to understand what time-locked factors may be underlying the disorientation, rather than focusing on awareness of reality, since the older person may be restoring the past in order to resolve it (Dietch, Hewett, & Jones, 1989; Fiel, 1967).

Incorporation of this form of therapy in aural rehabilitation of persons with severe dementias may be a fruitful area for future research. In particular, validation therapy would seem to be a useful strategy for reaching and gaining acceptance of persons whose mental disorientation would otherwise reject the reality orientation of hearing aid fitting.

THE INFLUENCE OF FINANCES AND MOBILITY

The financial profile of older Americans was discussed in detail in Chapter 17. Aging persons who are more self-sufficient financially, albeit equal in other respects, seem to be better

adjusted to their hearing handicaps than those who have fewer means (Maurer, 1974). More alternatives for psychosocial adjustment are available to people who are more affluent. The cost of clinical and medical services, hearing aid purchases, and special monitoring equipment, such as telephone amplifiers, are within their financial means. While the auditory impairment may dampen their enthusiasm for some activities, a sound economy creates more options for compensating for the hearing loss. The case is reversed among low-income persons, who have fewer alternatives available to them. In a comparative study made between the hearing levels of low- versus higher-income elderly seeking intervention for hearing deficits, aging persons with low incomes demonstrated poorer hearing sensitivity by the time they obtained hearing aids (Project ARM, 1983).

Persons from both minority and low-income groups fare even worse. Data reflecting a hearing survey in low-income neighborhoods, Table 20–1, reveal that among those with communicatively significant hearing impairments, more blacks failed to seek professional intervention than Caucasians. Blacks with low incomes also more frequently reported stress associated with hearing loss than did Caucasians with low incomes.

TABLE 20–1. REACTIONS TO HEARING IMPAIRMENT: A COMPARISON BETWEEN BLACK AND CAUCASIAN ELDERLY, 60–65 YEARS

	Black	Caucasian
Failed to seek professional help	61%	18%
Hearing problem produced stress	70%	53%
Average hearing loss of group (PTA)	36 dB	32 dB
of those seeking professional help	42 dB	34 dB

Source: Project ARM. Data from Multi-Service Center, Action Center, Albina, Dahlke, Campbell Hotel, Portland, OR: Portland State University.
Note: N = 262 low-income persons, 81 black, 181 Caucasian.

Aging individuals who are economically more sufficient also tend to be more mobile. They can travel to community clinics for weekly aural rehabilitation sessions. They can seek more immediate adjustments for a hearing aid in need of repair. They can avail themselves of others, friends and family members in distant places, who can provide therapeutic understanding of their problem.

Financial restrictions and lack of mobility create a cul-de-sac around the hearing impairment. Compensatory behaviors engaged in to avoid the stress of faulty communication become increasingly entrenched. As Miller (1967) has observed, when given an opportunity to extricate themselves from this situation, "some older persons would rather not 're-enter the world of sound' because, apart from their hearing problem, they feel rejected by their environment" (p. 20).

ATTITUDES AND FEELINGS

Unlike blindness, deafness fails to make a visible appeal to human compassion. In fact, responses of family and friends to the hearing loss may be antagonistic. The communication breakdowns associated with the difficulty frequently become frustrating for the family as well, often accounting for the impetus for seeking intervention.

Admission of the Hearing Loss

Admission of hearing problems is also difficult because the present generation of elderly is not far removed from the stigmatic association of deafness and dumbness that prevailed only a century ago. They are in an age bracket in which a number of friends and relatives have tried hearing prostheses, often with reported marginal success. Even when educational information pertaining to hearing loss is provided prior to rehabilitation, it does not guarantee commitment to hearing aid wear (Warren & Daily, 1984). It seems that the desire to pass in social groups as "normal" or younger than one's years negates acceptance of hearing

aid devices, which in turn diminishes public awareness of the disability. Many hearing aid manufacturers continue to emphasize the concealability of the devices, a strategy that both pays homage to and abets potential negative self-concepts among wearers.

Some older persons, on the other hand, appear to be more accepting of the problem and less resistant toward intervention. One reason for this is that therapeutic gains are significantly greater for biologically younger individuals than for very old persons. Another reason is that amplification is gaining in popular acceptance, and younger old persons are more likely to move with the tide of public sentiment than individuals who are psychosocially older.

Nonetheless, stress factors do operate to a greater or lesser extent among all persons with hearing handicaps, whether they realize the source of their difficulty or not. Even a mild loss of hearing sensitivity or a mild degeneration in central processing would manifest itself in situations where the normal hearing mechanism would respond with greater accuracy. The gradational nature of most presbycusic losses is the very antithesis of their detection. It is not surprising, therefore, that some older persons might not report hearing difficulties. Powers and Powers (1978) examined a sample of 172 aging individuals whose self-reported absence of hearing difficulties did not change substantially over a 10-year period. Although hearing threshold levels were not given, the losses were presumably mild enough to go unnoticed by the respondents. However, unnoticed losses are not necessarily unheeded problems.

One must question why, for example, a most common method of adjustment to stresses associated with presbycusis seems to be projection (Maurer & Rupp, 1979). Older persons commonly attribute their own problems with faulty registration to the failure of others to speak clearly. This seems to be particularly true for mild hearing loss cases, where hearing sensitivity is most depressed in the high frequencies. Thus, perhaps it is the low frequency information that sustains the individual in his or her belief that their hearing per se is normal, and that the distortion belongs to someone else.

Stress associated with hearing impairment does reveal itself clinically through intensive counseling of older adults. It surfaces in the adjustive techniques employed to relieve anxiety and is, therefore, of more than passing interest to the audiologist who is interested in patient management. Methods of adjustment are acquired early in life as mechanisms for defending against or escaping from stressful situations (Cameron, 1947). Since they are employed to relieve tension, the audiologist rightfully may question what factors or events in the geriatric environment are discriminative for their appearance.

PSYCHOSOCIAL RESPONSES TO HEARING LOSS IN OLDER AGE: TYPES AND CASE STUDIES

DEFENDING AGAINST THE HEARING IMPAIRMENT

Case Study. Mr. J. arrived at the clinic dressed for a dinner party and accompanied by his wife. The audiologist was prompted by his appearance to compliment him on his attire. Mr. J. beamed, exhibiting some au courant head and torso movements while proclaiming, "Well, this should go smoothly. What do you want me to do?"

Mrs. J. stared at her husband in disbelief. Later, she acknowledged, "I don't know what got into him this morning. He hasn't worn that suit since we took an ocean voyage four years ago."

Comment. Since Mr. J.'s impeccable dress and youthful behaviors were inconsistent with his usual attire and demeanor, one might justifiably raise the question whether these efforts were designed to reduce stress by drawing attention away from the real problem. Later, when the test results became known, Mr. J. appeared deflated, and the youthful mannerisms were no longer in evidence.

Case Study. Mrs. R. listened patiently while the audiologist gave instructions regarding pure tone testing. Then she announced, "I didn't sleep well last night, so I doubt if you would get very good results on me today." After the examination, she reflected, "I'm not sure I pushed the button every time I heard the sound. Those earphones pressing on my head really bothered me."

Comment. Mrs. R. presented very good reasons for not performing well in the test suite. However, the validity of her excuses is highly questionable. The real message of her rationalizing might be summed up as "My hearing is quite normal. I'm just having a bad day."

Attention-getting and *rationalization* are defense techniques that avoid the stress or anxiety of a perceived problem. In these two cases, they represented mechanisms for drawing attention away from or denying the possible existence of a hearing impairment. They are avoidance behaviors in the sense that they are aimed at preventing the occurrence of a potentially aversive consequence. Other defense techniques that act in similar ways are identification, compensation, and projection.

Identification relieves stress in the individual who temporarily assumes other roles or attributes. As examples, a 74-year-old woman, about to undergo a hearing test, announced that she had "the ears of a cat." A 61-year-old man, about to start a hearing evaluation, irrelevantly indicated that he had just completed a thorough physical examination, and the diagnostician had told him he "had the arteries of a 40 year old."

Compensation avoids stressful encounters by substituting less aversive activities in their place. A 74-year-old retiree rejected the need for amplification because, "I don't go out much anymore. I mostly just watch television."

Projection defends the individual against the problem by referring it to others. Clinically, it seems almost commonplace to hear variations on the statement, "I can hear others fine, but my wife doesn't speak clearly."

ESCAPING FROM THE IMPAIRMENT

Case Study. Mrs. O. was asked, during the counseling session which followed the hearing test,

"What changes in your life have been necessary because of your reduced hearing?"

"Quite honestly," she began, "the only change I deeply regret is church attendance. Our pastor has a soft voice and the services always contain a lot of music. And there's something about that building — that sanctuary — that makes it difficult to hear. I reached the point where I would spend most of my time sitting there, thinking about other things." She shook her head. "Finally, I just gave up on it."

Comment Mrs. O. seems to recognize that in this situation she has insulated herself from her problem by avoiding certain stimuli that produce it. *Insulation* represents a retreat from situations that interact negatively with the impairment. A very positive aspect of her conversation is that she has not insulated herself from her clinician. She is willing to discuss her actions. Moreover her possessive description of "our pastor," and her use of present tense verbs suggest that she really hasn't "given up on it."

Another example of insulation was observed in the behavior of a woman who was hearing impaired when she was seated at a group dining table in a nursing home. In the midst of conversations around her, she maintained a stereotyped expression on her face, avoiding any eye contact with others at the table. Her expression seemed to convey the message, "I am thinking about something terribly important and do not wish to be disturbed."

Negativism, on the other hand, reduces stress by opposition. Older persons may argue that they "can't learn to lipread," or they "can't stand any object" in their ears.

Some potentially stressful situations or events are simply eliminated from the elderly person's repertoire. At least momentarily, *repression* reduces anxiety by excluding the problem. The individual may selectively forget to wear the hearing aid, although the eyeglasses are never forgotten. In addition, auditory experiences that have not been perceived for a number of years may be inhibited. One older man was asked, "How long has it been since you heard a whisper?" The question provoked a smile, and then shaking his head incredulously, he replied, "A whisper! I've never even thought of it until you mentioned it. Why, it's been years!"

Regression is a mechanism which permits the client to retreat from a problem by assuming a dependent role, one that contraindicates participation in the conflict.

As another method of adjustment to stress, *fantasy* is often equated with daydreaming. Although this behavior reportedly is not more frequent in the aging population than in younger age groups, its frequency has not been studied among the elderly who are hearing impaired (Giambra, personal communication, 1989). Clinically, fantasy is manifested in the older person who, frustrated by not being able to keep up with or comprehend a group conversation, simply tunes it out and permits thought to wander to other topics; in brief, the "geriapathy syndrome":

The individual feels disengaged from group interaction and apathy ensues, the product of the fatigue which sets in from the relentless effort of straining to hear. Frustration, kindled by begging too many pardons, gives way to subterfuges that disguise misunderstandings. The head nods in agreement with conversation only vaguely interpreted. The voice registers approval of words often void of meaning. The ear strives for some redundancy that will make the message clearer. Finally, acquiescing to fatigue and frustration, thoughts may stray from the conversation to mental imageries that are unburdened by the defective hearing mechanism. (Maurer, 1976, p. 60)

The changes that occur during senescence with accompanying hearing impairment may range from subtle to profound. Similarly, the adjustive behaviors expressed may vary from minor irritation to self-imposed isolation. If there is one thread of professional continuity between such extremes, it must be the discipline of audiology.

It was in this spirit that the following "Open letter to the older person who has hearing difficulties" was written.

"You don't listen to me"
An Open Letter to the Older Person
Who Has Hearing Difficulties

Dear Grandperson:

Your problems are very real. They are witnessed a thousand times in countless places where people are talking to you. Their mouths move, and sounds reach your ears, but somehow they don't say what they are talking about. Or their message arrives on a slow train, and you respond too late to avoid the flashing signals of concern. Sometimes they frown, their voices kindling a spark of exasperation that illuminates everyone's attention on your dilemma. Too often they take the path of lesser effort, and oblivious to the strain of your forward head movements and raised eyebrows, they continue to mouth their sounds to others. The space you occupy is disregarded.

Is it any wonder that you sneak an occasional rendezvous with yourself? At least your inner thoughts are not burdened by speakers that mumble and patchwork conversations that have no meaning.

Your complaints are altogether familiar. The television newscaster seems bent on cramming as many words into a minute as is humanly possible. The musical background gets in the way of the actor's voice. Everyone talks at once on that show. Who decided that woman should appear on national TV? And when did they take the tick out of watches?

Places are annoying, too. The city transit service is a foreign country, where people seem to speak in tongues against the drones and hisses of spasmodic motion. Restaurants — couldn't we find a quiet place where the dishes don't clatter, the music doesn't swell, and the waitress was once a state elocution champion? Churches — the architect who designed them must have borrowed the plans from the Tower of Babel. The open banking system — whatever happened to the dignity of discussing one's fixed income in the quiet confines of a private office?

People — those teenage children who converse in short, accelerated bursts of unintelligible enthusiasm. Conversation stoppers, such as "Don't you remember?" Heart stoppers, such as the voice that appears suddenly at your elbow or the bicycle that materializes on soundless tires. Whisperers — their secrets are well guarded, since you don't have the remotest idea what they are talking about.

Your complaints are very reasonable, and the communication problems that you are experiencing extend well beyond your diminishing hearing ability. They are your listeners' responsibility as well.

But how do you tell them to speak slowly and clearly without shouting, to call your name before addressing you so that your attention can surface, to turn the noise down so you can understand? How do you tell them without exposing the "old person" in you? How do you project your difficulties on a society that is one or two generations away from sharing your experiences? If only for a moment they could listen to the future through your ears!

Unfortunately, they cannot. However, there are a number of things they can do. They can learn to speak to you more slowly and clearly. They can select quiet places to communicate with you. They can turn off distracting noises before addressing you. They can touch you to gain your attention and look at you when they talk. And they can pause in their conversation long enough for your train of thought to catch up with their meaning. These things they can do for you if you will muster the courage to step outside of your older person and assert yourself. Your problem must be shared with your listener.

You must not give up. You must not relinquish one listening experience that contains a shred of satisfaction. You must not withdraw from one conversation that invites your participation. Communication must be regarded as your personal invitation to learning, your private insulation against mental aging.

Finally, you will need to adopt the attitude that the emotional cost of trying to hear again is miniscule compared to the depersonalizing experience of disengagement. Once you have resolutely determined to master your handicap, you will find that you are no longer a helpless spectator in the traffic of language, but a willing participant in the wonderful word transaction that is human communication.

And the next time someone says, "You don't listen to me," try responding with a smile and the gentle reminder, "Perhaps you were not talking to me."

REFERENCES

Butler, R., & Lewis, M. I. (1973). *Aging and mental health.* St. Louis, MO: C. V. Mosby.

Cain, L. D., Fine, M. A., & Maurer, J. F. (1974, November). *Responses of elderly to socialization demands in the move to public highrise housing.* Paper presented at the 27th annual scientific meeting of the Gerontology Society, Portland, OR.

Cameron, N. (1947). Basic adjustive techniques. In N. Cameron (Ed.), *The psychology of behavior disorders* (pp. 141–186). Boston: Houghton-Mifflin.

Comfort, A. (1978, April). Keynote address. Presented at the 24th annual meeting of the Gerontology Society, Tucson, AZ.

Davis, G. A., & Ball, H. E. (1989). Effects of age on comprehension of complex sentences in adulthood. *Journal of Speech and Hearing Research, 32,* 143–150.

Dietch, J. T., Hewitt, L. J., & Jones, S. (1989). Adverse effects of reality orientation. *Journal of the American Geriatrics Society, 37,* 974–976.

Fiel, N. W. (1967). Group therapy in a home for the aged. *The Gerontologist, 7,* 192–195.

Hull, R. E. (1973). Preface to the workshops on geriatric rehabilitation. Hearing aids and the older American. *Hearings before the Subcommittee on Aging, United States Senate* (pp. 298). Washington, DC: U.S. Government Printing Office.

Joensen, J., Jerger, S., Oliver, T., & Pirozzolo, F. (1989). Speech understanding in the elderly. *The Hearing Journal, 37*(3), 39–41.

Joensen, J. P., & Saunders, D. J. (1984). Psychological correlates of geriatric hearing loss. *The Hearing Journal, 38*(5), 24–27.

Kelly, L. S. (1985). Hearing loss in the older person. *The Hearing Journal, 38*(5), 24–27.

LaFerle, K. R., & LaFerle, K. (1988). Senility and its impact on the hearing instrument delivery. *Hearing Instruments, 39*(2), 32–35.

Maurer, J. F. (1974). [Report to the Oregon Program on Aging.] Unpublished report.

Maurer, J. F. (1976). Auditory impairment and aging. In B. Jacobs (Ed.), *Working with the impaired elderly* (pp. 59–84). Washington, DC: The National Council on Aging.

Maurer, J. F., & Rupp, R. R. (1979). *Hearing and aging: A guide to rehabilitation.* San Francisco, CA: Grune & Stratton.

Miller, M. H. (1967). Audiological rehabilitation of the geriatric patient. *Maico Audiological Library Series* (Vol. 2, p. 3).

Moriarity, M. (1974). *A survey of noise levels in senior adult environments.* Unpublished paper, Portland State University, Speech and Hearing Sciences Program, Portland, OR.

Powers, J. K., & Powers, E. A. (1978). Hearing problems of elderly persons: Social consequences and prevalence. *Asha, 20,* 79–83.

Project ARM. (1983). [Reaction to hearing impairment: A comparison between black and Caucasian elderly]. Unpublished raw data.

Warren, V. G., & Daily, L. B. (1984). Efficacy of aural rehabilitation with geriatric hearing impaired. *The Hearing Journal, 37*(3), 15–19.

CHAPTER 21

Considerations for the Use and Orientation to Hearing Aids for Older Adults

■ ROGER N. KASTEN, Ph.D. ■

When hearing loss is coupled with the other maladies associated with advancing age, individuals realize that this might be an ideal time of life, but it certainly may not be a perfect time. If for no reason other than financial considerations, older individuals must be cautious about their advancing age and their opportunity to enjoy this period of life. Hearing loss is simply one of many possible physical problems that may affect these persons, and frequently it is downgraded because it has been judged as having little importance on the extension of life. While this statement may be true, for many older individuals hearing loss can have a major impact on the extension of a truly enjoyable and meaningful life. Also, for many older individuals, a properly fitted and properly used hearing aid will allow a closer touch with the environment and an ability to

interact more freely and more enjoyably in their social and personal world.

FACTORS AFFECTING SUCCESSFUL HEARING AID USE AMONG THE ELDERLY

MOTIVATION

Rupp, Higgins, and Maurer (1977) consider motivation as the most important factor in their feasibility scale for predicting hearing aid use. They point out that if individuals develop their own high level of desire for obtaining help in the use of amplification, those who show less personal motivation and depend more on the urging of others have a corresponding reduction in the likelihood of successful use of amplification. Likewise, the individual who has a great desire to continue to lead a mentally, physically, and emotionally active life and to participate in society is likely to be one who is a successful hearing aid user. On the other hand, those who have lost interest in their surroundings and are willing to withdraw from society have little motivation or desire to be successful in the use of amplification. Thus, the probability of these persons being successfully rehabilitated becomes correspondingly less.

ADAPTABILITY

One of the more important factors concerning use of amplification is the expectation of the individual. Until the person becomes hearing impaired and finds that he or she may need some type of amplification, or until he or she deals with a spouse or friend who is hearing impaired, it is unlikely that the person will have a clear-cut idea about what to expect from using a hearing aid. Average potential new hearing aid users are sometimes quite surprised when they realize what it is like to hear with amplification. It is likely that some people expect a hearing aid to restore their hearing to the efficiency it had previously, while others probably expect it to be nothing but a nuisance and of little value. Neither of these levels of expectation is realistic or correct. If an individual expects complete correction of the hearing deficiency, he or she almost certainly will be disappointed. Conversely, if the individual has little optimism and thinks the hearing aid will be of no help, then he or she is likely to be unwilling to make the effort to adjust to, and consequently wear, the instrument. In other words, he or she may simply be unwilling to give it a chance. If a person is unwilling to try something that is new or unusual, then major changes in attitude are necessary before successful use will be noted.

PERSONAL APPRAISAL

The individual's personal assessment and emotional feelings about his or her communication problems are important factors with respect to degree of success in the use of amplification. Rupp et al. (1977) approached this matter with the attitude that audiological assessment data are correct in determining the true degree of communication handicap, but it is their feeling that self-assessment is also important and should be carried out by one of the available self-assessment scales. Among the scales to be considered are those by High, Fairbanks, and Glorig (1964); Nobel and Atherly (1970); Berkowitz and Hochberg (1971); Hull (1982); Demorest and Erdman (1987); or Ventry and Weinstein (1983). Another possibility would be to use one of the abbreviated scales designed by Shotola and Maurer (1974) or Allen and Rupp (1975).

It is the opinion of Rupp et al. (1977) that older adults who are hearing impaired are likely to minimize the handicapping effect of their hearing loss and, therefore, may be unwilling to do anything to alleviate the condition. On the other hand, the problems of pseudohypoacusis or emotional hearing loss, where the individual views his or her communication difficulties as being more severe than can be justified on the basis of audiometric data, are well known. However, many cases exist where there is agreement between the degree of handicap, as determined by audiological data, and by a self-inventory using one of the self-assessment scales. It is the conviction of Rupp et al. that successful use of amplification is most likely when there is agreement between the two sets of information, that is, audiometric data and client self-assessment. It seems reasonable that those authors are correct in that assumption. It also seems evident that one who is able to appraise his or her personal handicap objectively and with accuracy is in a position to understand the resulting problems in communication and comprehend a realistic approach to the possibilities, as well as to the specific procedures needed in rehabilitation.

MONEY

The financial status of a person certainly can have a profound effect on his or her interest in a hearing aid. For many older people the words "hearing aid" have the same connotation as the words "Rolls Royce" have for most of us. For the majority of potential users, however, the purchase of a hearing aid probably is not nearly as impossible as this example would indicate. On the other hand, the hearing aid still may be in the category of a luxury or near luxury and probably would be purchased only if the person who is hearing impaired were convinced that it would meet his or her needs. Many people are aware that their friends, and perhaps they themselves, have spent thousands of dollars for one or more hearing aids that proved to be unsatisfactory and were relegated to a dresser drawer or closet shelf. Thus, many people are unwilling to spend the money necessary to obtain a hearing aid. When an individual is living on a fixed income that is only meeting living expenses, then a hearing aid purchase can become overwhelming. It is true that those who are eligible for Medicaid assistance sometimes can obtain help from that source in buying a hearing aid (if their state Medicaid laws provide for hearing aids), or there may be other possibilities for financial assistance by civic organizations. However, these sources also sometimes have restrictions that present problems in making the purchase.

SOCIAL AWARENESS

The elderly client who is hearing impaired, as with any hearing person, may fit anywhere along a continuum from one who is socially active to one who is extremely withdrawn. Those who are active in various aspects of social life are the ones who are likely to maintain contact with other people and may be able to communicate actively. Those who are withdrawn, on the other hand, may have lost interest in such contact. It seems reasonable to assume that those who are sociable would be the people most likely to succeed in rehabilitation utilizing hearing aids. At least they would be motivated for this type of achievement. Conversely, those who are withdrawn or who lack social awareness would be the ones least likely

to succeed in such rehabilitation. The large remaining group are people who are neither active socially nor completely withdrawn. They are, in fact, the ones who are losing interest in social contact, because too great an effort is needed to maintain communication with their friends. Although their lagging interest in social affairs would make them less than ideal candidates for the use of amplification, it is also highly possible that satisfactory selection of amplification and use of all rehabilitation procedures would improve their opportunity to socialize, if they so desire.

MILIEU

The attitudes, interests, and activities of the friends of the elderly client who is hearing impaired certainly can have a great deal of influence on the attitudes and desires of that person. If the person is still employed or active in volunteer or avocational activities that involve him or her with communications, and if the people who are associated with the person who is hearing impaired are sympathetic, understanding, and also stimulating in their conversations, then it will encourage the elderly person to fully utilize amplification. Conversely, if the older person's life lacks stimulating friends and situations, then the individual who is hearing impaired is likely to have little reason to obtain or adjust to the use of amplification.

MOBILITY

The ability of the person who is hearing impaired to move about and be involved in daily activities has a great effect on the elderly client who might desire a hearing aid. For example, if the individual is able to go to various functions, then he or she is likely to be a good candidate for the use of amplification. On the other hand, those who are limited in mobility and who rarely leave their residences for social or business contacts, have less desire or apparent need for communication and, therefore, less obvious need for amplification. There are those who essentially live alone and seem to have little desire for communication with others. They may feel a great deal of loneliness, and yet they are unable or unwilling to make the effort to maintain contact with other human beings.

These people have a need for the help and communication that might be available through amplification, yet they often are physically and emotionally limited in their ability and/or desire to become involved in social activities. They might be victims of arthritis, a cardiac condition, or some other debilitating problem in addition to hearing impairment, yet they *could* participate in social activities if properly motivated. However, the hearing problem presents an additional barrier, and the combination results in greater physical isolation, which means that they are less likely than others to be successful in using amplification.

VANITY

Vanity is an aspect of human nature that can greatly affect a person's interest in trying to adjust to a hearing aid. The use of eyeglasses can illustrate how a prosthetic appliance can be accepted or rejected by various individuals. Most people would prefer not to wear eyeglasses, but a large portion of society needs to wear glasses. In fact, most people accept corrective lenses quite readily, at some time in their lives. Once an individual has accepted eyeglasses, he or she may go to the extreme of purchasing large or gaudy eyewear that calls attention to the wearer. On the other hand, they may try to use contact lenses to conceal the problem. A similar situation occurs in the use of hearing aids, but with one exception. It is most unlikely that anyone would buy an overly large or conspicuous hearing aid to call attention to this item in the same way that some people buy large eyeglasses.

In general, people are interested in getting hearing aids that are inconspicuous. This seems to be true for all people, regardless of their age or life style. Even a behind-the-ear instrument is oftentimes rejected in favor of an all-in-the-ear model, simply because the person feels this would be less conspicuous. Some older per-

sons state strongly that they might accept an ear-level instrument, but they would not even consider a body-type hearing aid, even though it might provide better hearing. Problems with the presence of a cord undoubtedly contribute to the dissatisfaction, but general appearance is undoubtedly the major factor why people dislike or reject the body-type hearing aid. Regardless of whether a person might use a body-type, an ear-level, or an all-in-the-ear model, many are unwilling to wear an instrument of any kind, because they do not want to advertise their hearing problem. They would prefer to try to "get by" and conceal their problem. An attitude of this type certainly presents a large barrier in acceptance of amplification.

DEXTERITY

Beginning with the first instruments that were built, hearing aids and their controls have become smaller. This reduction in size has made hearing aids more acceptable to a larger number of people than ever before. For the majority of our population, this reduction in size has presented no great problem, since most people are able to make proper placement of the instrument and set the controls with little difficulty. However, with advancing age, the smaller dimensions of the instruments and the resulting decrease in the size of the controls frequently present a serious problem.

With age, people lose their acuity of touch, and they find it difficult to know whether they are or are not getting the hearing aid in the proper location and the ear mold seated correctly into the concha. Many an elderly person can be seen with a hearing aid hanging precariously from his or her ear, or with an ear mold that is far from being seated properly. In most cases, the individual is completely unaware that this situation exists, even though he or she has just put on the hearing aid. Likewise, the older person may have such a poor sense of touch that he or she is unable to find the gain control or the on-off switch with his or her finger. When an effort is made to move one of them to a desired location, the elderly person is not certain whether or not he or she actually has been able to make such a change. In addition, it frequently is the case that these people have reduced mobility of their fingers because of poor muscle control or arthritis. They find it very difficult to manipulate the controls even if their sense of touch is such that they can be made aware of what they need to do. Thus, good manual dexterity and a good sense of touch can help in the successful use of amplification, but reduced dexterity and sense of touch can be a strong deterrent to success and almost certainly requires the help of some relative or other assistant to overcome this difficulty. A mandatory portion of every hearing aid fitting with an older individual should include a dexterity check to determine whether the person can use the controls, affix the hearing aid to the ear, and actually handle and change the batteries.

ASSESSING THE POTENTIAL SUCCESS OF HEARING AID USE

As mentioned previously, in 1977, Rupp and colleagues proposed "A Feasibility Scale for Predicting Hearing Aid Use with Older Individuals." Their scale incorporated eleven prognostic areas or factors that should be taken into consideration when dealing with aged persons. The scoring sheet used with this feasibility scale is shown in Figure 21–1, and a guide for using the scoring scale is presented in Figure 21–2. One should note that their prognostic areas are not only listed and explained, but they are also weighted according to their relative importance as determined by Rupp and colleagues. One should note similarities between the prognostic areas associated with the feasibility scale and the factors listed earlier in this chapter. The important consideration for all individuals who deal with hearing aid fittings with older persons is the realization that complex and interactive issues must be dealt with to ensure successful, or partially successful, hearing aid use.

To a large extent, clinicians who work with the older potential hearing aid user must be able to examine his or her probable success within the various factors or prognostic areas. Clinicians also must learn to accept certain guideline factors as they relate to successful hearing aid use. Many older individuals view themselves as being in a position where they have completed the most active phases of their lives and they are now living out the remainder according to their own prescribed rules. Many view themselves as having made it through the rigors and difficulties of adult life, and they, therefore, feel that they have an insight into life that is more complete and comprehensive than their younger counterparts. They have established their own game plan for the coming years, and they feel strongly that the game plan should not or must not be modified. They look back on their previous years as authority figures, either in occupations or in families, and realize that oftentimes their existing authority is only an honorary award. More specifically, they acknowledge that many of their aged counterparts exhibit difficulties with hearing, and this particular deficit is one that simply should be accepted and tolerated. Most importantly, however, they frequently know or have heard of any number of individuals who have invested sizable amounts of money from their generally limited resources in the unsuccessful search for improved hearing through amplification.

It is relatively easy to visualize the effects these circumstances can have on the older individual's outlook toward the successful use of amplification. Further, they frequently hesitate to believe that a prosthetic device can allow them to change their life style and social awareness, and they are not fully certain that a change really will be beneficial to them. They not uncommonly feel that a device that small can only be of limited benefit to them, but at the same time appear firmly convinced that this small device will call undue attention to the fact that yet another physical affliction has taken its toll. In short, the aged person often has a sizable number of apparently logical arguments against the use of amplification, and these arguments must be successfully countered before they totally negate any potential for successful hearing aid use.

PROGNOSTIC FACTORS/DESCRIPTIONS (continuum, high to low)	ASSESSMENT 5-High: 0-Low	WEIGHT	WEIGHTED SCORE (Possible) Actual	
1. Motivation and referral (self . . . family)	5 4 3 2 1 0	×4	(20)_____	1.
2. Self-assessment of listening difficulties (realistic . . . denial)	5 4 3 2 1 0	×2	(10)_____	2.
3. Verbalization as to "fault" of communication difficulties (self caused . . . projection)	5 4 3 2 1 0	×1	(5)_____	3.
4. Magnitude of loss: amplification results				4.
A. Shift in spondaic threshold: _____	5 4 3 2 1 0	×1	(5)_____	
B. Discrimination in quiet: _____at _____BB HTL	5 4 3 2 1 0	×1	(5)_____	
C. Discrimination in noise: _____at _____dB HTL	5 4 3 2 1 0	×1	(5)_____	
5. Informal verbalizations during Hearing Aid Evaluation Re: quality of sound, mold, size (acceptable . . . awful)	5 4 3 2 1 0	×1	(5)_____	5.
6. Flexibility and adaptability versus senility (relates outwardly . . . self)	5 4 3 2 1 0	×2	(10)_____	6.
7. Age: 95 90 85 80 75 70 65 < (0 0 1 2 3 4 5)	5 4 3 2 1 0	×1.5	(7.5)_____	7.
8. Manual hand, finger dexterity, and general mobility (good . . . limited)	5 4 3 2 1 0	×1.5	(7.5)_____	8.
9. Visual ability (adequate with glasses . . . limited)	5 4 3 2 1 0	×1	(5)_____	9.
10. Financial resources (adequate . . . very limited)	5 4 3 2 1 0	×1.5	(7.5)_____	10.
11. Significant other person to assist individual (available . . . none)	5 4 3 2 1 0	×1.5	(7.5)_____	11.
12. Other factors, please cite				12.

Client _____ FSPHAU:

Very limited	0 to 40%
Limited	41 to 60%
Equivocal	61 to 75%
Positive	76 to 100%

Age_____

Date_____

Audiologist_____

_____ %
Total Score

Figure 21–1. A feasibility scale for predicting hearing aid use: An analytic approach to predicting the probable success of a provisional hearing aid wearer. (Reprinted with permission from Rupp, R. R., Higgins, J., & Maurer, J. F. [1977]. A feasibility scale for predicting hearing aid use [FSPHAU] with older individuals. *Journal of the Academy of Rehabilitative Audiology, 10,* 95.)

1. Motivation/Referral	5.	Completely on own behalf	
	4.	Mostly on own behalf	
	3.	Generally on own behalf	
	2.	Half self; half others	
	1.	Little self; mostly others	
	0.	Totally at urging of others	
2. Self Assessment	5.	Complete agreement	
	4.	Strong agreement	
	3.	General agreement	
	2.	Some agreement	
	1.	Little agreement	
	0.	No agreement	
3. Verbalization as to "fault" of communicative difficulties	5.	Clearly created by hearing loss	
	4.	Usually by loss	
	3.	Loss and others	
	2.	Environments and others	
	1.	Mostly of others	
	0.	Others totally at fault	

4. Magnitude of loss; and results of amplification*		ST shift	in quiet at —dB HTL	in noise at —dB HTL
	5.	30 + dB	90%	70%
	4.	25	80–88	60–68
	3.	20	70–78	50–58
	2.	15	60–68	40–48
	1.	10	50–58	30–38
	0.	5	48	28

5. Informal verbalizations during hearing aid evaluation re: quality of sound, mold, size, weight, look	5.	Completely positive
	4.	Generally positive
	3.	Somewhat positive
	2.	Guarded
	1.	Generally negative
	0.	Completely negative
6. Flexibility and Adaptability A. Questionnaire and observation B. Raven's Progressive Matrices C. Face/Hand Sensory Test	5.	90th percentile
	4.	70
	3.	50
	2.	25
	1.	10
	0.	5
7. Age	5.	65 years
	4.	70
	3.	75
	2.	80
	1.	85
	0.	90 +

continued

Figure 21–2. Scoring the FSPHAU factors. (Reprinted with permission from Rupp, R. R., Higgins, J., & Maurer, J. H. [1977]. A feasibility scale for predicting hearing aid use [FSPHAU] with older individuals. *Journal of the Academy of Rehabilitative Audiology, 10, 97.*)

8.	Manual/Hand Dexterity via Purdue Peg Board and Symbol Digit Modalities Test	5.	Superior
		4.	Adequate
		3.	Slow but steady
		2.	Slow and shaky
		1.	Slow and awkward
		0.	"Arthritic"
9.	Visual Ability (with glasses)	5.	Very good—no problems
		4.	Corrected, adequate
		3.	Adequate but safeguarded
		2.	Limited visibility
		1.	Very limited
		0.	Blind
10.	Financial Resources	5.	Unlimited resources
		4.	Generally unrestricted
		3.	Adequate
		2.	Adequate but close
		1.	Dipping into savings
		0.	Poverty level, on assistance
11.	Significant other person	5.	Always available
		4.	Often
		3.	Sometimes
		2.	Occasionally
		1.	Seldom
		0.	Never

*Alternate scoring scheme for factor 4 in cases where the ST shift was minimal due to loss in high frequencies only.

(Average threshold shift at 2000 and 3000 Hz)	5.	25 + dB
	4.	21–25 dB
	3.	16–20 dB
	2.	11–15 dB
	1.	6–10 dB
	0.	0–5 dB

Figure 21–2. (continued)

MODIFICATIONS OF HEARING AID EVALUATION AND FITTING PROCEDURES FOR ELDERLY CLIENTS

Since the development of the wearable hearing aid, efforts have been made and procedures have been developed for the purpose of comparing the performance of different hearing instruments (Alpiner, 1975; Carhart, 1946, 1950; Hayes & Jerger, 1978; Jeffers, 1960; McConnell, Silber, & McDonald, 1960; Reddell & Calvert, 1966; Ross, 1972). This has been done to provide as much assurance as possible that the potential wearer would obtain a hearing aid that would be of substantial benefit to him or her. In some cases, it is not possible to state unequivocally that every recommended instrument was the ultimate of perfection for each individual, but procedures have been developed that take into account many different factors in an effort to approach that goal as nearly as possible. The degree of success in obtaining this goal undoubtedly varies, but it is sincerely believed that these procedures avoid selection of an instrument that would be unsuitable for the individual concerned.

It has been pointed out in this book that aging individuals have hearing impairments that present unique problems as a result of their age. These problems are particularly evident when one considers procedures to be used in the selection of hearing aids. There is no question that the same purposes and philosophies apply to the selection of hearing aids for this group as for any other group. But their unique needs, abilities, and limitations demand that the selection and fitting procedures be modified. The selection procedures used in choosing amplification for older clients must take those special characteristics of aging persons into account. With the aging population, clinicians find themselves in a position of more frequently having to mold the evaluation to fit the individual.

Clinicians cannot talk about a single evaluation procedure, nor can they talk about a single population of aging individuals. In short, it is necessary for the evaluator and fitter of hearing aids, when working with an aging population, to utilize a variety of evaluation procedures, and tailor those procedures to the specific requirements of each potential hearing aid user.

Great care must be taken to see that all clients are able to handle and adjust their own instruments. They must be given opportunities during the evaluation procedure to work with a specific hearing aid model and to demonstrate their ability to both use it and adjust it. If they are unable to accomplish these tasks on their own, they must understand that successful hearing aid use will require either a larger instrument or the continual assistance of significant other persons. These facts must be emphasized to prevent the individual from later rejecting the instrument as an unsuitable device. Some other individuals will be perfectly willing to rely on a significant other person, and in this case clinicians can do their best to satisfy clients' desires. Those who are strongly independent in terms of their personal care, however, must be made aware that the hearing aid should be of a size and construction that will allow them to make all necessary manipulations.

It is important to convince the potential hearing aid user that he or she is not being pushed into purchasing an instrument that is not desired or will not be personally satisfactory. Be-cause the elderly client has a lifetime of knowledge and experience behind him or her, it is important for the person to have the opportunity to experience aided listening and to make a decision without undue pressure from the evaluator or dispenser.

During the trial period, it is imperative that the potential hearing aid purchaser receive counseling to ensure that everyone concerned with the aged person who is hearing impaired really knows how to help him or her get the most from the hearing aid. This period also provides the opportunity for the clinician to make any necessary adjustments of the instrument and for the client to adjust his or her attitude to become a truly successful hearing aid user.

MODIFICATIONS ACCORDING TO DIFFERENCES AMONG POPULATIONS

There are several populations included among the older adult population (e.g., independent, semi-independent, dependent, extremely dependent), and the differences among these populations influence the potential use of hearing aids. Likewise, the differences among these populations influence the procedures that can be used for selecting a suitable hearing aid.

Independent Older Adult Population

Older individuals in the independent-living group frequently are the easiest to work with and the most successful in terms of hearing aid use. They are still in control of their life styles, and they enter the process of hearing aid use with their eyes wide open, albeit sometimes reluctantly. It is with this particular group that a high score on the feasibility scale of Rupp, Higgins, and Maurer (1977) is most encouraging. For the factors or prognostic areas that predict hearing aid use, individuals in this population are most frequently amenable to change. These individuals still see many varied opportunities available to themselves and frequently are willing to exert themselves to modify behavior and attitude for their own betterment and for the benefit of spouses or friends.

With this independent-living population, *motivation* is the critical factor. If motivation exists, even to a limited degree, appropriate counseling and sufficient success experiences can serve to bring about change relating to other factors. Sympathetic involvement on the part of a spouse or friend can help to enhance the degree of communicative success that can be achieved. Also, sympathetic involvement can soften the impact of knowing that certain desirable conditions may remain unattainable, due to their inherent difficulty.

To a large degree, potential success with a hearing aid will be tied directly to the extent that the potential hearing aid user can see and experience success in significant and meaningful situations. Success in communication can cause a heightened social awareness and can lead to a genuine desire to expand social horizons and to modify the individual milieu.

Semi-Independent Older Adult Population

When clinicians deal with the semi-independent population, they are faced with a different set of circumstances. These individuals frequently have large portions of their life styles dictated by those who control the environment in which they live. Very often, this direction is provided by well-meaning but communicatively naive sons or daughters in whose homes the older people may find themselves. All too often, this group of elderly individuals find themselves existing in a relatively comfortable, albeit controlled, environment, and they recognize completely that their only other option is a nursing home or care-home placement. As a result, their psychological set and their attitude toward the factors relating to successful hearing aid use are subconsciously dictated to them by the individual or individuals governing their living accommodations.

With this population, it is frequently necessary to spend more time with the persons who control the living environment than with the older individuals themselves. If the well-meaning son or daughter is not sold on the value of a hearing aid, odds are better than

even that the older individual will not be able to be sold. If the son or daughter feels that a hearing aid is too expensive to warrant purchase, the likelihood is quite high that the older individual will find no way to afford that purchase. If the son or daughter strongly states that the older person does not seem to have enough problems to warrant hearing aid use, then chances are that the older person will at least verbalize this same statement. If the son or daughter feels that the older person does not have a wide enough range of activities or experiences to benefit from a hearing aid, then the likelihood is quite high that the older person will reflect the same belief and, even worse, may demonstrate it. In spite of the apparent needs of the older individual, decisions regarding amplification and attitudes toward amplification may be shaped or totally formed by others who are not directly experiencing the problem.

This particular situation creates an awkward position for the older individual who is hearing impaired. He or she may readily recognize the need for the kind of assistance that can be obtained from amplification, but genuinely fear the consequences of a decision that goes contrary to the power structure in his or her environment. Although often not intentional, the older individual in the semi-independent population may become the *recipient* of attitudes and decisions rather than the *originator* of the attitudes and decisions.

Dependent Older Adult Population

The dependent living population frequently requires a totally different approach and demands serious moral judgments on the part of the audiologist or the hearing aid dispenser. Individuals in this population are oftentimes totally controlled and cared for as the result of their physical, emotional, mental, or financial condition. If this population is viewed objectively in terms of hearing aid use, clinicians are faced with the brutal facts that these people frequently have poor motivation, markedly little adaptability, limited insight in terms of personal appraisement, little available money, poor social awareness, and restricted milieu as well as limited mobility and finger dexterity.

In addition to these factors, clinicians must realize that these people oftentimes are cared for by well-meaning and hard-working staff members who know almost nothing about hearing aid use and who are concerned primarily with physical factors relating to the extension of life. Taken as a group, the prospects for successful hearing aid use are limited. This fact has been substantiated in the reports of Grossman (1955), Alpiner (1963), and Gaitz and Warshaw (1964). In particular, Alpiner (1963) discusses three general attitudes that appear among dependent older individuals who chose not to become involved in hearing aid use. These individuals presented a definite denial that a problem was present, displayed a general attitude of hopelessness, and expressed a recognition of the hearing loss, but indicated no desire for any type of rehabilitation. It should be emphasized again that this situation is confounded further by the fact that many of the individuals who deal with the dependent older individual know little or nothing about hearing aid use and oftentimes are occupied fully in providing the necessities for meaningful life support.

SUCCESSFUL HEARING AID USE

For this group, the key to any successful hearing aid use will be the staff members who care for the individual or the volunteers who are present for daily activities. These people must be trained in proper hearing aid use and maintenance and must be made aware of the importance of communication experiences. A statement this author always makes when dealing with the staff of care homes is, "A person reacts to people who react." By explaining in detail the methods and procedures they can use to convey information to the older individual who is hearing impaired, this author and colleagues provide them with extensive knowledge regarding hearing aid care and use. They are encouraged to work with hearing aid users in an attempt to elicit the maximum response from this group of people.

Clinicians must realize, however, that generally there is a relatively high turnover of staff in many health care facilities. As a rule, the work is hard, the hours are long, and the pay is often not commensurate with the work involved. As a result, many individuals stay with a particular job only until they are able to find something else that will provide them with more satisfaction or more money. With this in mind, clinicians must realize that inservice training that deals with hearing aid use and care must be performed on a recurring basis and must include a great deal of demonstration and some systematic follow-up in response to questions.

With the dependent group, clinicians must continually remember that a well-fitted hearing aid is not an end unto itself. Successful hearing aid use will result only if there is a need for communication, a desire for personal interaction, and support that includes family and staff encouragement and understanding. Successful hearing aid use will result only when the older individuals can demonstrate to themselves a real benefit from the process.

Extremely Dependent Older Adult Population

These are individuals who are truly physically, mentally, or emotionally dependent. In many cases, they will have very limited ability to communicate, but it may be possible to make their care easier and provide them with some additional contact with the outside world. With individuals of this group, formal testing procedures are often impossible, and decisions concerning the value of amplification may be made purely by observation. Before actually attempting the use of a hearing aid, it is necessary to make some type of estimate concerning the degree of hearing impairment. It may be necessary for this test to be conducted with the presentation of various sounds combined with subjective observation of any type of response the individual produces. Predictive acoustic reflex testing should also be accomplished, when possible. Although this may provide only an approximation of the hearing capability, it will give the audiologist some indication as to whether amplification is indicated. Obviously, any type of information concerning the degree of hearing impairment would be most helpful.

As soon as the degree of hearing impairment has been determined, it would be appropriate to evaluate performance with a series of listening devices, while the audiologist carefully observes responses to sound. One might notice whether the individual responds to voice or environmental sounds, or whether the use of both visual and auditory means are used in making contact with those around him or her. The observer should also watch for any behavioral changes, tolerance reactions, vestibular effects, or aggression toward amplification. Real-ear analysis can provide an objective analysis of hearing aid performance without requiring responses from the client.

Except for the real-ear analysis, the procedures discussed may appear to lack the true objectivity audiologists generally strive for in evaluating a hearing aid. But, if one can observe and document behavioral changes that result from amplification, there would appear to be reason to recommend use of an instrument based on these results. However, if one can observe no changes between the unaided and aided behavior, one can state that there is no evidence of any improvement and recommendation of a hearing aid could not be justified, even though evidence of hearing loss suggests that the amplification is needed.

A FINAL CONSIDERATION FOR THE EXTREMELY DEPENDENT POPULATION. One final factor is absolutely essential to consider when dealing with the extremely dependent aged population. By definition, individuals in this group are incapable of caring for themselves and require the constant ministrations of others. For the hearing aid user in this group, this means that the significant other person must be somewhat knowledgeable and proficient in terms of hearing aid use. He or she must be able to ensure that the hearing aid is working properly, and the aid is set as it should be for the individual. While these do not seem to be overwhelming

tasks, they can be major hurdles for a health care facility staff member who has no experience with hearing aid use.

Because there is a relatively high turnover in nursing home staff, this means that an ongoing program of hearing aid familiarization will be necessary to ensure proper hearing aid use for both dependent and extremely dependent individuals. It will accomplish little if clinicians provide only a one-time orientation for staff members at the same time that the hearing aids are actually evaluated and fitted on elderly individuals. While these staff members may be able to provide adequate care for individuals who are hearing impaired, this care will cease if the staff members move on to other occupational settings. The audiologist will need to maintain close contact with the care facility administrators so that they can be available immediately when staff turnover requires a new staff training program, so that continuous care can be provided for the hearing aid users.

SUMMARY

The geriatric individual who is hearing impaired may belong to one of several different populations having any of a wide range of skills and abilities. Because skills and abilities vary so much, frequently it is necessary to modify the procedure for selecting and fitting hearing aids to meet amplification needs successfully. However, even while modifying the test procedures to fit individual needs and capabilities, it is possible to carry out relatively objective test procedures that can aid greatly in the selection of a particular hearing aid for an individual.

It matters little which dependency category an aged person may fit into. The individual presents a unique set of abilities and capabilities, and the audiologist must be fully aware of the major characteristics of the elderly population to deal effectively with individuals within the population. Aged individuals have experienced long and meaningful lives in which they frequently have functioned in an independent manner. As such, they have formed opinions of their own, and these opinions must be respected. When aged clients reject amplification and the evaluation of amplification because of their own individual biases, these biases cannot be dismissed casually with the thought of a rapid evaluation procedure. The elderly individual (and in some cases the significant other person) must be dealt with as mature and knowledgeable individuals who possess unique capabilities and frequently present distinct disabilities. Hearing impairment may be only one of many problems that face the older individual, and clinicians must approach the remediation of the hearing impairment with this fact firmly in mind.

Clinicians frequently must modify the length of the hearing aid evaluation, rate of presentation, and type of presentation so that the procedure itself becomes meaningful. In addition, they must take into account the tendency on the part of some elderly individuals toward conservatism and rigidity. The procedures utilized in an evaluation of amplification systems must be conducted in a manner that will instill confidence and a willingness toward adaptation.

The large population of aged individuals poses a unique challenge to all persons involved in the hearing health team. The audiologist must be particularly aware that he or she is not dealing with one large group of homogeneous individuals, but rather with several subgroups that have advanced age as a common factor.

REFERENCES

Alpiner, J. G. (1963). Audiologic problems of the aged. *Geriatrics, 18,* 19–26.

Alpiner, J. G. (1975). Hearing aid selection for adults. In M. Pollack (Ed.), *Amplification for the hearing impaired.* New York: Grune & Stratton.

Allen, C., & Rupp, R. R. (1975, November). *Comparative evaluation of a self-assessment hearing handicap scale given to elderly women from low and high socioeconomic groups.* Paper presented at the Convention of the American Speech-Language-Hearing Association, Washington, DC.

Berkowitz, A., & Hochberg, I. (1971). Self-assessment of hearing handicap in the aged. *Archives of Otolaryngology, 93,* 25–28.

Carhart, R. (1946). Selection of hearing aids. *Archives of Otolaryngology, 44,* 1–18.

Carhart, R. (1950). Hearing aid selection by university clinics. *Journal of Speech and Hearing Disorders, 15,* 106–113.

Demorest, M. E., & Erdman, S. A. (1987). Development of the Profile for the Hearing Impaired. *Journal of Speech and Hearing Disorders, 52,* 129–143.

Gaitz, C., & Warshaw, M. S. (1964). Obstacles encountered in correcting hearing loss in the elderly. *Geriatrics, 19,* 83–86.

Grossman, B. (1955). Hard of hearing persons in a home for the elderly. *Hearing News, 23,* 11–12, 17–18, 20.

Hayes, D., & Jerger, J. (1978). A new method of hearing aid evaluation. *Journal of the Academy of Rehabilitative Audiology, 11,* 57–65.

High, W. S., Fairbanks, G., & Glorig, A. (1964). Scale for self-assessment of hearing handicap. *Journal of Speech and Hearing Disorders, 29,* 215–230.

Hull, R. H. (1982). *Rehabilitation audiology.* New York: Grune & Stratton.

Jeffers, J. (1960). Quality judgment in hearing aid selection. *Journal of Speech and Hearing Disorders, 25,* 259–266.

McConnell, F., Silber, E. F., & McDonald, D. (1960). Test-retest consistency of clinical hearing aid tests. *Journal of Speech and Hearing Disorders, 25,* 273–280.

Noble, W., & Atherly, G. (1970). The hearing measure scale: A questionnaire for the assessment of auditory disability. *Journal of Auditory Research, 10,* 229–250.

Reddell, R. C. (1966). Selecting a hearing aid by interpreting audiological data. *Journal of Auditory Research, 6,* 445–452.

Rupp, R. R., Higgins, J., & Maurer, J. F. (1977). A Feasibility Scale for Predicting Hearing Aid Use (FSPHAU) with older individuals. *Journal of the Academy of Rehabilitative Audiology, 10,* 81–104.

Shotola, R., & Maurer, I. (1974). *The development and use of a short screening form for detection of hearing loss in older adults.* Paper presented before the annual meeting of the Western Gerontological Society, Tucson, AZ.

Ventry, I. M., & Weinstein, B. E. (1983). The Hearing Inventory for the Elderly: A new tool. *Ear and Hearing, 3,* 128.

CHAPTER 22

Techniques of Aural Rehabilitation Treatment For Older Adults

■ RAYMOND H. HULL, Ph.D. ■

The process of aural rehabilitation for older adult clients is exciting, to say the least. To be involved in the recovery of communication skills that previously have caused the older adult to withdraw from a communicating world is indeed rewarding. Both the client and the audiologist can rejoice in the recovery of those skills. Some elderly clients recover skills that allow them to participate on a social basis again, at least, with a greater degree of efficiency. Others simply may regain the ability to communicate with their families with greater ease. In light of those gains and, perhaps, a step toward a reinstatement of communicative independence, the client and his or her audiologist have reason to rejoice.

This chapter presents the components and process of aural rehabilitation services for the older adult client. Theory is deemphasized here, because process is of primary importance.

In some ways, the two most difficult clients the audiologist faces are the young child and the elderly person. Because the majority of older clients who are hearing impaired have experienced normal to near-normal auditory function during their younger years, and because they are generally fully aware of the communicative difficulties they face, it is important that clinicians provide the client the opportunity to make them aware of his or her communicative needs.

Because it is being confirmed that the auditory disorder found in older adults is not only peripheral in nature, but also involves the central auditory system (Bergman, 1980; Hull, 1988; Kasten, 1981; McKroskey and Kasten, 1981; Welsh, Welsh, & Healy, 1985), approaches to aural rehabilitation must accommodate the communication difficulties experienced as a result of those compounding problems (see Chapter 17). The audiologist is, indeed, working with complex people who possess a complex auditory disorder.

COMPONENTS OF AURAL REHABILITATION TREATMENT FOR ELDERLY CLIENTS

Following are the important components of an aural rehabilitation service program for older adult clients that are applicable for either the well older adult in the community or those who are confined to a health care facility.

1. Counseling
2. Hearing aid orientation
3. Adjusting/manipulating the listening environment
4. Development of positive assertiveness
5. Developing compensatory skills through the use of residual hearing and supplemental visual cues
6. Involvement of family and other significant others

COUNSELING

As this author talks with his students about aural rehabilitation services for older adult clients, it is emphasized that counseling is one of the most important aspects, and is intertwined throughout the process of aural rehabilitation. Counseling is not something that occurs alone and out of context, but is an integral part of everything the audiologist does when working with his or her clients. It is called *talking*. It is called *instilling* confidence in a client who becomes discouraged when he or she does not do as well as expected on a given communicative task. It is called *listening* to the innermost feelings a client reveals about him- or herself and that person's relationship with an intolerant family or roommate. And it is called *trust* that must develop between audiologist and client. Counseling is the discussion that develops when the client desires to talk about an incident in which he or she had particular difficulty understanding what another person was saying, and it also includes *problem solving* to unravel the reasons for the difficulty.

When an audiologist comes face to face with an elderly client who is hearing impaired who says, "I do not desire to be helped. I am old and I do not know how much longer I will live," the attitude of that elderly person certainly will impact on how much potential progress that person will make. This is particularly true if that person has isolated him- or herself from the outside world as a result of that attitude and is resigned to not seek help because of advanced age.

The Audiologist as Counselor

If there are no other significant contraindicating factors which would hinder responsiveness to aural rehabilitation services, the audiologist is in a position to intervene in a counseling role. It is possible that this person has said what was said because he or she has been told by others that, "You are too old." Or, a child may have said unthinkingly, "Mom, you know you can't care for yourself as well as you used to, so we should start thinking about moving you to a nursing home," not realizing that the older adult is convinced that placement in a nursing home will be terminal. Such statements, perhaps said in a well-meaning way, are understandably defeating to the elderly adult. They may cause the person to develop doubts regarding his or her survival. One of my clients, a female of 89 years, told me that when her 50-year-old daughter told her that they should sell her house and she should move into an efficiency apartment, she was so hurt and angry that she could not think of anything to say. She felt convinced that if her mature daughter felt that she could not care for her house, then she must be doing a worse job than she thought. I asked her what she would have said if her daughter had suggested that to her when she was 45 years old and her daughter was 15. She said she would have asked her why she would say such a thing, but, she said, when you are 89 years old, perhaps it is not worth it to argue.

If the medical records of an individual indicate satisfactory health, and there appears to be nothing that would contraindicate the provision of aural rehabilitative services, then the self-defeating attitude of the potential client may be the only thing that stands between the provision of services and reasonable progress in aural rehabilitation. Although an older person's realistic view of becoming older may be a healthy one, long-term mourning because of age and the possibility of death is not. The audiologist can be a positive catalyst in helping people adjust to aging, particularly for those who are barred from social interaction as a result of their auditory deficit.

Feelings to Which the Audiologist Must Respond

The audiologist must not be afraid to work with these clients in a close but professional manner. He or she must not be hesitant to intervene in a counseling role, but must be cognizant of those instances when a client's emotional state and personal problems are beyond the scope of the audiologist's knowledge. For those persons, it is the responsibility of the audiologist to refer the individual to other appropriate professionals. Above all, the elderly client must be confident in the audiologist who is providing the aural rehabilitation service. The client must realize that the audiologist understands the communicative impact of presbycusis through his or her experience in working with other elderly clients. The elderly client must know that the audiologist feels that he or she can, indeed, be helped to communicate more efficiently through aural rehabilitative services, and that that feeling has justification on the basis of *evaluation*, not sympathy. A feeling of *justified trust* is the true key to motivational counseling.

Listen — talk — empathize — listen — encourage where appropriate — remember the status and age of the client — provide support — counsel — listen — ask questions — expect answers — listen — provide guidance. Add an appropriate amount of inspiration and we may have the key to successful motivational counseling.

HEARING AID ORIENTATION

Information in Chapter 22 deals with considerations on hearing aids for older adults. As stated in that chapter, the process of adjust-

ment to the use of a hearing aid can be facilitated with greater ease for some elderly clients than others; this adjustment depends on prior exposure to and knowledge of the use of hearing aids and factors of memory, manual dexterity, and such. The process of adjustment to a hearing aid and orientation to its use logically can be carried over into daily or weekly aural rehabilitation treatment sessions, as can the trial use of various assistive listening devices.

Through carryover of orientation to hearing aid usage into the aural rehabilitation treatment program, slight adjustments to the hearing aid can be made pursuant to communicative problems encountered during its use, and discussions regarding certain difficult listening environments can be entertained that may not only benefit that individual client, but also others in a group session. More experienced hearing aid users can be an important catalyst in the new user's successful adjustment to amplification. Further, experimental adjustments in hearing aid gain and frequency response can be made in accordance with the activities in various treatment sessions.

Carryover of the hearing aid orientation process into aural rehabilitation treatment sessions can be as important as the orientation process itself, and is a logical extension of it. The consistency of client contact itself is a valuable asset in facilitating adjustment to amplification. In group treatment sessions, the catharsis and camaraderie that arise as various clients describe their own difficulties experienced during the initial adjustment period provide a healthy environment for efficient adjustment to hearing aid use. Procedures for hearing aid orientation that are applicable for the older adult are well outlined by Downs (1970), and modified by Traynor and Peterson (1972). Hearing aid orientation for the confined elderly has been prepared by Smith and Fay (1977).

ADJUSTING AND MANIPULATING THE LISTENING ENVIRONMENT

As will be observed in "The Process" section of this chapter, elderly clients are initially asked to set priorities in favor of communication situations in which they desire to function more efficiently. After this is completed, they are asked to choose one or two in which they most desire to learn to function more efficiently. They are, of course, requested to be reasonable in their selections. In this way, the aural rehabilitation treatment program can be designed to meet their specific communication needs. When a client's auditory difficulties are so severe that group sessions are not practical or cannot be tolerated by the client, individual treatment is scheduled. The goal, if at all possible, is to eventually integrate that client into a group situation. Another situation in which it is desirable that individual treatment be instituted is in the case of a client whose priority communication environment is so unique that it warrants individual work.

A situation in point is a client who was provided services individually by this author. His most difficult communication environment, as a semiretired physician from a small town, was his examination room. His treatment sessions, therefore, centered around physical and environmental adjustments in that specific room. His priority communication environment did not warrant exposure in group sessions. He, further, did not desire that his difficulty be exposed to the group at that time. He had little difficulty in other more social environments.

Group Sessions

Group sessions center around discussions of the clients' chosen and priority communication environments. Priority environments most frequently center around church (understanding the minister or Sunday school teacher, or at church committee meetings), other social environments in which groups of people meet, understanding what women or children are saying, and understanding what people are saying in other environmentally distracting environments, such as on the street corner, in a restaurant, or at the theater. The inevitable commonality of their choices allows for group sessions that are beneficial for everyone, since the majority of clients can enter into each discussion as it relates to their individual experiences.

Creating Positive Assertiveness

Whether an elderly person is residing in a health care facility or in the community, it regrettably becomes more usual for dramatic and sometimes unpleasant things to occur in that person's life as aging progresses. In light of the unexpected occurrences that are prompted by people doing things to elderly persons rather than for them, it becomes easier to remain passive and wait rather than to become assertive and say "no," which may result in the use of force to make you do it anyway. "Dad is getting stubborn in his old age" may be the label placed on that elderly person. Many elderly persons feel powerless because of a lack of independence. It is difficult to respond to a rapidly changing world when one does not possess the finances, transportation, physical mobility, quickness of analytical thought, or strength to manipulate one's environment.

Examples of Passive Behavior

An example that illustrates the feelings of many elderly persons who are hearing impaired is one that involved a 72-year-old woman client of this author who had just returned from a lecture on Southeast Asia, which she had been looking forward to attending for some time. She explained that the lecturer, a woman who had a rather soft voice, began talking and then walked away from the public address system microphone and sat down in front of the podium with the statement, "I'm sure that you all can hear me without the microphone."

The client said that she hardly understood a word that the speaker said throughout the next hour, but she was too embarrassed to leave the auditorium. When I asked her why she did not say, "Please use the microphone," when the speaker moved away from it, her reply was that she just could not bring herself to do it. She wanted to, but was too embarrassed. "Besides," she said, "maybe I was the only person who couldn't hear her." When I asked her whether she was important enough to warrant that speaker's consideration, this client's response was simply, "I hope so." I said, "Don't you think that the microphone was there for a purpose? A public address system generally helps everyone to hear more comfortably. If you would have said something, I am sure that others in the audience would have been pleased that she had returned to the podium and used the microphone." Her reply was that she had not thought of that. "But still," she said, "I didn't want to make a nuisance of myself. I'm just an old woman who can't hear very well."

That attitude among many older clients is one that must be combatted, or at least altered, if these persons are to learn to cope and function more efficiently in the world outside, and in their homes. In light of the fact that apparently some people are not willing to accommodate elderly persons who are hearing impaired, or perhaps are not aware of what accommodations can be made to facilitate communication, elderly persons themselves must be taught ways to become assertive enough to manipulate their communication environments and those with whom they desire to communicate.

INVOLVEMENT OF FAMILY AND OTHERS

The client's family and significant others in the client's life are critical elements for a successful aural rehabilitation treatment program. This is particularly true if, for example, the client's spouse is willing to become involved in the aural rehabilitation process. This includes attending the individual or group treatment sessions and participating in follow-up assignments.

A significant other's involvement in aural rehabilitation treatment sessions provides that person with a better understanding of the difficulties and frustrations with which the friend, spouse, or family member undergoing treatment is faced, particularly if they can attend the first sessions when discussions of hearing loss and difficult communication situations are emphasized. It, further, aids the client's significant other to understand the commonality of communication difficulties when other clients discuss similar problems. That involvement prompts a realization that the communication difficulties that

have arisen because of the auditory deficit are not limited only to their spouse, family member, or friend, but are found in others as well. That enhanced understanding may be passed on to others who are close to that client.

A case in point is that of a 70-year-old man who had been a widower for four years. On the first day of his group aural rehabilitation program he brought with him a woman companion. They both enjoyed attending social gatherings together, but the client was experiencing great difficulty hearing and, in particular, understanding what was being said in such environments. His companion was willing to explain what was being said, but was becoming discouraged at the consistency with which she had to function in the capacity of interpreter. In this instance, she attended all treatment sessions with the client — she was wearing her ear plugs and he his hearing aid. A great deal of warmth and understanding developed between them, and as his ability to function communicatively increased so did her willingness to aid in the treatment process through carryover. The assignments, which included experimentation at social gatherings, were carried out in an excellent manner. Problem situations that were to be addressed during treatment sessions became less, and so did his dependence on his companion for communication support.

The support and carryover by this significant other was instrumental in this client's achievements in learning to use his residual hearing, to use supplemental visual clues, and to manipulate his most difficult listening environments. Without such support and assistance, the audiologist may have great difficulty facilitating such improvements. In the end, he or she may never be able to aid the client in making such significant and positive strides as will the significant other.

THE PROCESS OF AURAL REHABILITATION

The aural rehabilitation program for the older adult client should include:

1. Knowledge of the client's desires and needs for communication through setting priorities;
2. Ongoing motivational counseling as an integral part of the process of aural rehabilitation;
3. Carryover of hearing aid orientation;
4. Learning how to manipulate one's environment to enhance communication;
5. Learning to become positively assertive; and
6. Learning to use one's residual hearing and supplemental visual cues to enhance comprehension of verbal messages.

To put all of these factors together into a meaningful aural rehabilitation treatment program for the older adult can be a positive experience. And, the process becomes quite logical once a number of older clients have critiqued the clinician's approach in relation to its meaningfulness and benefit to them.

Following is an example of an approach to aural rehabilitation treatment for the elderly adult client, utilizing and intermingling the six areas just listed. There are subtleties involved in clinician-client interaction that can make or break an effective treatment program. Those subtleties are difficult to discuss, but the process is presented herewith. This process has been found to be effective with both confined and community-based older adults.

THE ONGOING AURAL REHABILITATION PROGRAM

Some structure in the treatment process is desired by the majority of older clients. However, overly structured sessions can be counterproductive. For example, it is not uncommon for audiologists who use traditional speech-reading (lip-reading) approaches that emphasize a progression from phoneme analysis to syllables, words, phrases, sentences, and stories (which, for example, stress several like-phonemes) to begin to realize in a fairly short period of time that the clients who seemed motivated initially are attending speechreading sessions with less regularity. Excuses generally range from, "My family is coming to visit and I will be spending time with them," to "We have several church suppers coming up and I have to help with them." They may, further, call to tell your secretary that they really do not feel the need to come to "class" anymore, even though the audiologist knows that they have made little or no progress in treatment.

Those clients are telling clinicians something that they *should* hear loudly and clearly. That is, if they felt that aural rehabilitation services were benefiting them they probably would still be attending, because when they began they evidently were motivated. If the aural rehabilitation treatment program was geared to their specific needs, they probably would be taking advantage of the audiologist's services.

Treatment procedures used by speech-language pathologists, occupational therapists, physical therapists, and others are based on a *treatment plan* that is designed around the assessed needs of the client. Why are some audiologists, then, still opening their "lipreading" lesson book at page one to provide services to clients who have varied and individual communication deficits and needs?

INDIVIDUALIZING YOUR APPROACH

How does the audiologist develop a meaningful approach to aural rehabilitation treatment for the elderly client? Hardick (1977) described basic characteristics of a successful aural rehabilitation program for older adults. They are well defined, and provide comprehensive guidance for those who intend to provide services for older clients. Those characteristics are:

1. The program must be client centered.
2. The program must revolve around amplification and/or modifying the client's communication environment.
3. All programs consist of group therapy with some individualized help when necessary.
4. The group must contain normally hearing friends or relatives of the person who is hearing impaired.
5. Aural rehabilitation programs are short-term.
6. The program is consumer oriented. (pp. 60–62)

These characteristics are extremely important for consideration prior to the initiation of aural rehabilitation programs for the older adult. They go far beyond the more traditional "lip-reading" procedures that continue to be utilized by some.

Other more current client-centered approaches to aural rehabilitation are those discussed in Chapter 15 of this text, including procedures by Alpiner (1963), Miller and Ort (1965), Colton and O'Neill (1976), McCarthy and Alpiner (1978), Colton (1977), O'Neill and Oyer (1981), Hull (1982), Sanders (1982), Alpiner and McCarthy (1987), and others. The aspect stressed throughout is that older adult clients possess needs that are specific to them, and each client's aural rehabilitation program must be centered on his or her needs and priorities.

If the ingredients presented on the previous pages are combined properly, a possible sequence of services emerges. An example of such a sequence follows.

An Awareness of Reasons for Auditory Dysfunction

Facilitating an awareness of the reasons for auditory communication difficulties through an understanding of the aging process and its effect on the auditory mechanism is an important part of the aural rehabilitation process. Included is a discussion of the central processing of auditory/linguistic information and the effect of aging on the speed and precision of that important component in communication, particularly in noisy or otherwise distracting environments. The level of terminology is determined by the individual or group in question. The audiologist is cautioned *never* to speak down to clients. It is important to use the correct technical terminology, but immediately explain it at the level of the persons involved. Always remember that you are speaking to adults, no matter what their educational level. They deserve to be treated as such.

Charts, diagrams, slides, and blackboard drawings are used for this discussion, and presentations on the aging ear, hearing aids and their uses, benefits, and limitations, environmental factors that affect communication, poor speakers versus good speakers and their makeup, and a general discussion of the aging process are included.

The premise behind this first session (or sessions) is to provide a base for the remainder of the treatment program, to develop a better understanding among the clients of what has occurred to them, and to assure them that in all probability they can improve, at least to some degree. Most persons come away from such sessions with a better understanding and greater acceptance of what is occurring to them and a desire to participate in the aural rehabilitation treatment program. It cannot be emphasized enough that a significant other in each client's life should attend these sessions. Whether it be a spouse or a family member such as a child, or a friend, he or she will gain much greater insight into the auditory/communication problems with which that person is attempting to cope.

Priority Communicative Needs

The second step in the aural rehabilitation treatment program is to ask each client to list and prioritize the difficulties in communication that affect them most. The UNC Communication Appraisal and Priorities Scale, or another of the available scales, can be used in this process (see Chapter 24). These may include specific communication environments, such as a meeting room, church, certain restaurant, table arrangement at their child's home, and so on. Clients also may list individuals whom they have trouble understanding.

The next step is for clients to set priorities in those situations (or persons), from most important to least important. And, if they had their choice, in which of those would they most like to improve. They are asked, of course, to be realistic in their final choices. For some, the choice is simple. For others, it is more difficult. It is important to note, however, that if gains are made in one category, improvement also may be observed in others.

The clients then are asked to discuss their choices, present a situation in which they have experienced difficulty, and explain what prompted them to make their choices. Particularly in a group situation, it is interesting to note the general consistency of priority areas that emerge. The clients also generally feel a sense of camaraderie develop out of this discussion. For the first time, many of them realize that they are not the only ones who experience difficulty in those environments.

In many instances, clients put part of the blame for their auditory/communicative difficulties on others who possess poor speech habits. That is acknowledged and discussed. The discussion centers around the fact that there are, indeed, many poor speakers in this world, and a demonstration of some of their habits which interfere with efficient communication is appropriate. Immediate identification with those habits generally is evident among the clients. Even though there are many poor speakers, clients must develop ways to cope in those communication environments. The encouraging acknowledgment that they can, in many instances, manipulate those difficult situations in such a way as to at least be able to function more efficiently in them, and that they will be working on avenues for resolving difficult listening situations, ends that discussion on a positive note.

ON BECOMING ASSERTIVE

Clients are given weekly assignments which include noting a communication situation in which they had particular difficulty with communication. They are to write them down and diagram the physical environment, if necessary (or simply be able to recall it as accurately as possible). They bring the specifics of the situation to the next treatment session for presentation and discussion. Each client (or in the case of individual treatment, the client) presents his or her difficult situation, if one has been noted. It is imperative that the client who was involved in the situation be the one who presents it and not the significant other who may have been present with the client.

After a thorough presentation, with diagrams if possible, the situation is discussed by the group (or in the event of individual treatment, by the client, the audiologist, and the significant other who is present, if he or she was involved). Suggestions regarding possible ways the client might have manipulated the communication to his or her best advantage, including the physical environment or the speaker, are made by the group under the guidance of the audiologist, and are accepted as viable or discarded. According to Hull (1980), insights into ways of manipulating the communication environment to their best advantage, along with methods of coping with and adjusting to frustrating situations are, in turn, developed among clients under the guidance of the audiologist. This form of self- and group analysis is an important part of the aural rehabilitation program. Clients, then, are helped to develop their own insights into methods of adjusting to situations where communication is difficult.

Examples of these discussions include one that was initiated by one of this author's clients who was being seen on a group basis. The woman was discussing a situation involving another woman with whom she had morning coffee on almost a daily basis for a number of years. The client's complaint was that her friend was an incessant gum chewer, and her manner of chewing gum almost negated ongoing conversation since chewing continued as she talked, thus, interfering with precise articulation. Her friend interpreted the client's inability to understand what she was saying to be the result of the hearing impairment, not her imprecise manner of speaking, which resulted from her enthusiastic gum chewing, compounded by the client's hearing loss. This apparent interpretation of the situation infuriated my client. But, she continued the morning coffee time because there were few other women her age in her geographic area, and besides, they had been friends since childhood.

This woman's major concern was how to tell her friend that her manner of speaking and gum chewing had, for several years, interfered with her ability to understand what she was saying and, in the end, made what might have been a pleasant conversation, an almost intolerable one. She was particularly afraid to say anything because of the embarrassment her friend might feel since the situation had been going on for so long, and nothing had been said. "Almost like," as the client said, "being associated with a person for a long time and never knowing her name. As the days pass, you become increasingly embarrassed about asking her name, particularly when she knows yours." The suggestions that came from the group varied from an enthusiastic, "Tell her that if she wants to talk to you, to take the gum out of her mouth," to a timid, "If you value your friendship, maybe it is best to say nothing and simply tolerate the situation." The latter suggestion was discarded.

The ultimate conclusion was simply to tell the truth. It was the consensus of the group that they would respect their own friend more if he or she would simply tell her that chewing gum doesn't allow her to utilize the facial cues that are important for speech understanding.

Positive assertiveness are the key words in this instance. For that client, the strategy she and the remainder of the group determined as most effective did prove to be successful. And, she maintained the friendship.

Other Topics

Other topics for discussion and development of strategies may include weekly socials at private homes where the furniture arrangements interfere with efficient communication. Some, as experienced through this author's work with older clients, involved the table arrangement at one client's son's home where they usually had Thanksgiving dinner, the television set at a male client's friend's home, the seating arrangement and acoustics at a church meeting room, and others. Even though the discussions and thought-provoking suggestions generally aid the individual whose situation is being discussed, they also provide insights for the remainder of the group on how they, too, can manipulate their communication environments.

These assertiveness discussions can be extremely stimulating for the clients involved and for their significant others in attendance. Clients have told this author that those sessions are probably the most valuable for them, particularly because we are working and sharing on behalf of *their* problems in communication.

THE USE OF RESIDUAL HEARING WITH SUPPLEMENTAL VISUAL CLUES

Even though the use of visual clues and every possible bit of residual hearing individual clients can muster is discussed and practiced throughout all aspects of the aural rehabilitation program, sessions should emphasize those aspects of communication. Again, it is not suggested that strict approaches to speechreading/ auditory training be stressed. Rather, the fact that the majority of older clients possess normal to near-normal language function should be capitalized on to encourage the use of innovative and useful approaches toward an increased efficiency in the use of a very natural facilitating element in communication — that is, the complement of vision to audition.

These sessions are based on the premise that speech (including the phonemic and linguistic patterns of speech in the English language, the use of gestures, inflectional clues, and the English language itself) is generally quite redundant, even though there are individual differences in speech patterns, use of gestures, words, and such. Another premise is that the average listener has been taking advantage of the redundancies inherent in American English speech and language patterns to aid in verbal comprehension for the majority of his or her life. When hearing declines with age — as does the precision and speed of the processing of phonemic verbal/linguistic elements of speech — it becomes more difficult to understand what others are saying. This is particularly true in environmentally distracting or otherwise difficult listening situations.

The purpose of these sessions, therefore, is to remind clients of what they have been doing for years at an almost subliminal level, that is, using important parts of auditory/verbal messages, when heard, and supplementing what was not heard with visual clues. A further purpose of these sessions is to discuss the redundancies of the phonemic and linguistic aspects of spoken American English, and to encourage clients to take advantage of them when they are communicating with others. This aspect of the aural rehabilitation treatment program is called "A Linguistic Approach to the Teaching of Speechreading," and has been described by this author elsewhere (Hull, 1976).

Linguistic Closure

As the reader will observe in this section, clients are asked to determine the correct information within sentences from the least number of words provided. The clients are asked to imagine that the word, or words, given on the blackboard are those that were heard. The blanks provided between words are imagined as those not heard or not heard well. Clients, first of all, are asked to tell the audiologist what the sentence is about (out of context), when perhaps only one word is provided out of a total of seven, with six blanks indicating that those words were not heard. Clients are encouraged to venture guesses as to what the sentence might be. Let us say, for example, that the word presented is "street" located as the last word of the sentence. The clients are asked to let their minds wander. "Take a guess." As clients accept that encouragement and begin to guess, the fear of being wrong appears to decrease. Many genuinely are surprised, in fact, to find that their "educated" guesses are often extremely close, if not correct. Guesses in this instance, for example, may range from "the man was walking down the street," to "a giraffe was seen running up the street." They are, however, encouraged to be rational in their decisions, and to think more realistically about the possibilities. The word "street" as the last word in a sentence tells you what? It tells you, generally, that *something* is happening. If the word came as the second word in a sentence, maybe

after the word "the," I may have been describing the street, such as "the street was very bumpy." But, since it is located at the end of the sentence, we know that something is probably happening either on or to the street. Now, let us set the stage. Let us say that your friend's horse, Zorba, has run away. You and other people from around the area are searching for him. Suddenly, someone runs to you and says something about, "_____ _____ _____ _____ _____ _____ street!" You observed that the speaker obviously had been running, and was pointing up the street as he was talking. Now, what do you imagine the speaker was telling you? Since the audiologist has now set the stage for the clients, their guesses will probably be quite close to what he or she had intended.

The audiologist's next step is to say, "Now I am going to allow you to fill in the gaps by observing my face and gestures as I take the place of the excited neighbor who is talking to you." The audiologist then presents the sentence in a slightly audible manner with full visible face and gestures. If clients are not able to "make closure," then another word is added at the blackboard, and the clients are allowed to try again. An example of presentation, if additional words are required, is presented below.

1. _____ _____ _____ _____ _____ _____
   street!
2. _____ _____ is _____ _____ _____
   street!
3. _____ _____ is _____ down _____
   street!
4. _____ _____ is running down _____
   street!
5. _____ _____ is running down the street!
6. A _____ is running down the street!
7. A horse is running down the street!

As clients become aware of what the message is, the audiologist continues by discussing (1) the importance of the position of each word within the sentence that was required before they were able to determine its content; (2)

their linguistic value in terms of the probability of determining the meaning of the sentence; (3) the importance of the environmental clues which were available to them; and (4) the supplemental use of visual clues.

An important element involved in any of these sessions is the audiologist's enthusiasm over the fact that, perhaps, the clients needed only to "hear" one or two words out of a sentence to make closure and grasp the meaning of the sentence. It is encouraging for older clients to be made aware that with their knowledge of the English language and their successful use of visual and auditory clues, they were able to determine what the message was at least at the thought level.

Linguistic, Content, and Environmental Redundancies

LINGUISTIC REDUNDANCY. American English language is redundant in its formal usage of the position of various parts of speech. In other words, the position of principal words such as nouns, pronouns, and direct objects is generally constant, as are function words, descriptors such as adjectives and adverbs, and action words such as verbs. Some dialects within the United States do, however, deviate from those standard rules. During these sessions, although the technical names of the parts of speech are not stressed at all, the importance of those words that fall within various positions in verbal messages are discussed as they relate to deriving the meaning of those messages.

This aspect of treatment capitalizes on the fact that most older clients who are hearing impaired will possess at least near-normal language function. It stresses the fact that as people listen to others, they zero in on words in conversations that permit them to at least derive the thought of what is being said so that the conversation can be followed. In some distracting environments, less of the message may actually be heard, but most persons can still maintain the gist of what is being said. It is normal in those circumstances, if a word was missed, to ask the speaker to repeat it, because

it appeared to be an important one in regard to the content of the statement. The point that is stressed to the clients here is that the reason the listener was able to determine that the word was an important one in permitting him or her to continue to follow the conversation was an almost innate knowledge of the structure of the American English language, which has progressively expanded since childhood.

The treatment sessions that stress this important aspect of efficient listening revolve around bringing that functional language capability to a more conscious level. Occasionally, clients have become so despondent over an inability to communicate with others that such otherwise natural compensatory skills become repressed.

CONTENT AND ENVIRONMENTAL REDUNDANCIES. These discussions stress the fact that, as we observe human behavior, it is discovered that not only do the same people generally say similar things on similar occasions, but they also say them in similar ways. In other words, in a given environment, depending on who the person is with whom one is speaking, what the listener knows about him or her, and if the listener is aware of those influences, the general content of some conversations can be predicted with reasonable accuracy.

Clients are asked to describe the environments they frequent. In all probability they will be those that were set as priorities earlier. They are also asked to describe those persons who are generally there, including their speaking habits, their facial characteristics, and their known interests. During these treatment sessions, clients also are asked to write down the more frequent topics of conversations that are observed among those whom they have described. These not only include frequent topics, but also words and phrases that those people may use habitually. They are asked to keep those lists and add to them as they remember additional items, or as they find out more about the person after speaking with him or her. Clients also are asked to begin new lists as they meet new people. The more one knows and remembers about a person, the more communication is enhanced.

An awareness of the predictability, or redundancy, of people and what they say within known environments is sometimes surprising to older adults who are hearing impaired. If it is surprising, generally it is because they had not really thought about it prior to that time. If nurtured, however, this awareness can facilitate increased efficiency in communication.

REDUCING AUDITORY OR VISUAL CONFUSIONS

Other activities which, by necessity, are important for adults may include information on why certain confusions of words occur in conversations. This particularly concerns older adults because word confusions may be occurring with some frequency. These discussions include not only information on the fact that the nature of the majority of auditory disorders that older adults face enhances the probability of auditory confusions, but also that the nature of certain sound and visual elements in many words enhances the probability of confusions because they may either sound like or look like other words. When words are confused with others, the meaning of a sentence or conversation may appear to be different than what was intended.

The discussions involve on-the-spot decisions required to solve misunderstood messages by determining *why* a sentence in a conversation was visually and/or auditorily confusing, or otherwise did not make sense. The process generally involves:

1. Analyzing the information derived from the previous portions of the conversation.
2. Determining that a confusing word has been received that may change the content of what is being said.
3. Mentally sifting through other words that look and/or sound like the one that would make more sense in light of the previous portions of the conversations.
4. Simultaneously projecting what the word "should have been" from the continuing conversation.

COMMUNICATING UNDER ADVERSE CONDITIONS

One of the frequent communication problems that older adult clients view as their most difficult is communication in noisy environments, for example, social events and meetings. Many clients' primary complaint, after finding themselves in an adverse listening environment, is that the noise and the resulting difficulties they experience in attempting to sort out the primary message from the chatter of other voices makes them tense and nervous. The nervousness, as they describe it, results in a further deterioration of their ability to cope in that environment, and thus their ability to sort the primary message from the noise. For many, the only alternative that appears to be available is to excuse themselves from the situation. By submitting to that less-than-satisfactory option, however, they generally feel some embarrassment. Unless they are quite resilient, many will simply avoid those situations in which they consistently fail. Since those situations include social events, meetings, the theater, church, and other desirable environments, the decision to avoid them can be quite self-defeating. Nervousness in that sense, and as they describe it, may not lessen because they are concerned over their inability to function communicatively in those environments, and they are torn between making another attempt at coping or giving up altogether.

In regard to this communication problem, treatment sessions are not only designed to assist clients in the development of skills for communicating in those distracting environments, but also to develop coping behaviors. The terms "desensitization," "reciprocal inhibition," and others may be appropriate to use here, but "coping behaviors" will stand as the most meaningful for this discussion. Within this framework, clients again choose as priorities those environments in which they have the most difficulty and/or those in which they most desire to function more efficiently. Those situations are recreated in the treatment room as accurately as possible around the individual cli-

TABLE 22-1. RESPONSES STRESSED DURING AUDITORY TREATMENT SESSIONS

Relaxation under stressful conditions.

Confidence that clients can, indeed, piece together the thought of the verbal message, even though not all of it was heard.

Remembering that because of their normal language function and their knowledge of the predictability of American English, they can determine what is being said if supplemental visual cues are used, along with as much auditory information as is possible under the environmental circumstance.

Knowledge that other people in the same environment may also be having difficulty understanding what others are saying, and they also may or may not be coping successfully with the stress.

Freedom to manipulate the communication environment as much as possible by, for example, asking the person with whom they are speaking to move with them to a slightly quieter corner where they can talk with greater ease, move their chair to a more advantageous position so the speaker can be seen and/or heard more clearly, or other positive steps to enhance communication.

Remembering that if difficulty in that communication environment seems to be increasing and feelings of concern or nervousness begin to become evident, they should feel free to interrupt the conversation and talk about the noise or the activity around them that seems to be causing the difficulties in understanding what the person with whom they are speaking is saying. The other person will probably agree with that observation, and in talking about it, feelings of stress may be reduced and communication enhanced.

Remembering that the amount of noise used in treatment sessions was probably greater than will be experienced in most other environments. If success was noted in their treatment sessions, then similar success may be carried over into other stressful environments.

ent's description of his or her chosen difficult environments. It is stressed that in the treatment environment no one can fail, but he or she can feel free to discuss their concerns or frustrations as they arise. Use of the language-based speechreading instruction previously discussed is emphasized during these sessions. Those areas that are stressed in the discussions during these noise exercises, but not in order of importance, are outlined in Table 22-1.

Other components of effective aural rehabilitation sessions, as described by Hull (1976, 1988, 1989) involve:

1. *The Use of Time Compressed Speech.* Because of a slowing of the speed of central nervous system processing of auditory linguistic information that accompanies advancing age (Marshall, 1981; Schmitt & McCroskey, 1981;

Madden, 1985), the use of time compression of speech is a method through which clients can compensate to some degree for that decline and increase their ability to comprehend speech with greater speed and precision than they possessed prior to the training. Clients practice by listening to sentences and paragraphs that are progressively time-compressed, attempting over an 8 to 10 week sequence of sessions to increase their speed and accuracy of comprehension for recorded speech. Clients who increase their accuracy of speech comprehension to 80 to 90% for sentences and paragraphs at time-compression levels of 35% (65% of the message received over-time), for example, have been found to correspondingly increase their accuracy of auditory-alone speech discrimination scores by as much as 24% (Hull, 1988).

This is a very exciting and tangible method for enhancing the speed and accuracy of speech comprehension among individual clients who can tolerate the demands of the process. Usable aided or unaided hearing is a prerequisite, however, because this is an auditory-only task.

2. *Interactive Laser-Video Training in Speed and Accuracy of Visual Synthesis and Closure.* New interactive laser video technology recently has evolved for use in training olympic athletes, air force fighter pilots, and radar observers to increase their speed and accuracy in visual closure, tracking, and synthesis. This technology also has been found to possibly be an effective and motivating way of training adults who are hearing impaired to increase their visual compensatory skills, particularly as it relates to speed, accuracy, and visual vigilance (Hull, 1989).

3. *Environmental Design.* Hull (1989) describes avenues for the training of older clients who are hearing impaired in techniques and strategies of environmental design. These involve training in the acoustical/environmental design of their homes, offices, and other communicative environments to their listening/communicative advantage. Training also involves how to make modifications in other situations in which they find themselves, including social environments, meetings and business environments that otherwise may have placed them at a communicative disadvantage. These can be very powerful aural rehabilitation sessions that provide clients with tangible methods for modifying their most difficult communication situations.

These methods are bringing the aural rehabilitation process into the era of modern technology. They not only are being found to be effective, but they are tangible and motivating forms of training for clients who can perform these tasks. Except for the client who is severely hearing impaired, who may find time-compressed speech tasks too difficult, because it involves listening-only tasks, this author has not found older clients who cannot benefit from these techniques, at least to some degree.

CONCLUSION

It is important for older clients to be given the opportunity to make decisions regarding areas of communication in which they desire to improve. Even though many may feel discouraged because of the embarrassing difficulties they experience in their attempts at understanding what others are saying, and because of the whole process of aging that they are experiencing, they generally are totally aware of the specific communication situations that cause them the most difficulty.

As adults who probably possessed normal hearing and were once vital social beings (whose case histories may reveal nothing except the fact that they have become older), these clients deserve to participate in the decisions regarding their treatment program. These persons, above all, are adults, and deserve to be treated as such. Prescription of certain aspects of treatment by individual clients must be permitted simply because they feel they are important for enhancement of their ability to function in their own communicating world. However, guidance in the decision-making process must be provided by the audiologist.

REFERENCES

Alpiner, J. G. (1963). Audiological problems of the aged. *Geriatrics, 18,* 19–26.

Alpiner, J., & McCarthy, P. (Eds.). (1987). *Rehabilitative audiology: Children and adults* (Vol. 3). Baltimore, MD: Williams & Wilkins.

Bergman, M. (1980). *Aging and the perception of speech.* Baltimore, MD: University Park Press.

Colton, J. (1977). Student participation in aural rehabilitation programs. *Journal of the Academy of Rehabilitative Audiology, 10,* 31–35.

Colton, J., & O'Neill, J. (1976). A cooperative outreach program for the elderly. *Journal of the Academy of Rehabilitative Audiology, 9,* 38–41.

Downs, M. (1970). *You and your hearing aid.* Unpublished manual, University of Colorado Medical Center, Department of Otolaryngology, Division of Audiology, Denver.

Hardick, E. J. (1977). Aural rehabilitation programs

for the aged can be successful. *Journal of the Academy of Rehabilitative Audiology, 10,* 51–66.

Hull, R. H. (1976). A linguistic approach to the teaching of speechreading: Theoretical and practical concepts. *Journal of the Academy of Rehabilitative Audiology, 9,* 14–19.

Hull, R. H. (1980). Aural rehabilitation for the elderly. In R. L. Schow & M. A. Nerbonne (Eds.), *Introduction to aural rehabilitation* (pp. 311–348). Baltimore, MD: University Park Press.

Hull, R. H. (1982). *Rehabilitative audiology.* New York: Grune & Stratton.

Hull, R. H. (1988, December). Presentation before the National Invitational Conference on Geriatric Rehabilitation, Department of Health and Human Services, Public Health Service, Washington, DC.

Hull, R. E. (1989, November). *The use of interactive laser/video technology for training in visual synthesis and closure with hearing impaired elderly clients.* Presentation before the convention of the American Speech-Language-Hearing Association, St. Louis, MO.

Kasten, R. N. (1981). The impact of aging on auditory perception. In R. H. Hull (Ed.), *The communicatively disordered elderly* (pp. 205–212). New York: Thieme-Stratton.

Madden, D. (1985). Age-related slowing in the retrieval of information from long-term memory. *Journal of Gerontology, 40,* 208–210.

Marshall, L. (1981). Auditory processing in aging listeners. *Journal of Speech and Hearing Disorders, 46,* 226–240.

McCarthy, P. A., & Alpiner, J. G. (1978). The remediation process. In J. G. Alpiner (Ed.), *Handbook of adult rehabilitative audiology* (pp. 88–111). Baltimore, MD: Williams & Wilkins.

McCroskey, R. L., & Kasten, R. N. (1981). Assessment of central auditory processing. In R. Rupp & K. Stockdell (Eds.), *Speech protocols in audiology* (pp. 126–142). New York: Grune & Stratton.

Miller, M., & Ort, R. (1965). Hearing problems in a home for the aged. *Acta Oto-Laryngologica, 59,* 33–44.

O'Neill, J. J., & Oyer, H. J. (1981). *Visual communication for the hard of hearing.* Englewood Cliffs, NJ: Prentice-Hall.

Sanders, D. A. (1982). *Aural rehabilitation.* Englewood Cliffs, NJ: Prentice-Hall.

Schmitt, J. F., & McCroskey, R. L. (1981). Sentence comprehension in elderly listeners: The factor rate. *Journal of Gerontology, 36,* 441–445.

Smith, C. R., & Fay, T. H. (1977). A program of auditory rehabilitation for aged persons in a chronic disease hospital. *Journal of the American Speech and Hearing Association, 19,* 417–420.

Traynor, R., & Peterson, K. (1972). *Adjusting to your new hearing aid.* Unpublished manual.

Welsh, J., Welsh, L., & Healy, M. (1985). Central presbycusis. *Laryngoscope, 95,* 128–136.

CHAPTER 23

Visual and Multiple Impairments in Older Adults

■ JANE E. MYERS, Ph.D. ■

Most older persons are affected to some extent by visual impairments, with significant impairment affecting one in four persons over age 65 (Heinemann, Colorez, Frank, & Taylor, 1988). These impairments can create a variety of adjustment problems and activity limitations. When coupled with other physiological losses normally associated with the aging process (e.g., hearing impairment), multiple and compounding complications occur. In fact, older persons who are visually impaired are more likely to experience multiple handicapping impairments (Kirchner, 1985).

In this chapter, the visual decrements experienced by older persons are explored and the effects of visual losses are discussed. The causes and effects of visual changes are viewed in terms of the behavioral limitations they impose on older individuals. Visual impairments in combination with hearing impairment or other handicapping conditions are considered, along with strategies for helping persons cope with the multiple handicapping conditions often present in later life.

DEFINITIONS AND DEMOGRAPHY

Visual acuity, or sharpness of vision, rates along a continuum from very good (20/20) through various levels of defect to legally blind. Kohn (1980) defined blindness as "central visual acuity of 20/200 or less in the better eye after correction, or visual acuity of more than 20/200 if there is a field defect in which the widest diameter in the visual field subtends an angle distance of no greater than 20 degrees" (p. 230). Defective vision is defined as less than 20/40 without correction.

Two-thirds of the 14 million persons in the United States who have significant visual impairment (e.g., unable to read newspaper print with conventional correction) are over age 65 (Belsky, 1984). More than half of the 500,000 legally blind persons are in this age group (Kohn, 1980). Older persons who are severely visually impaired comprise 4% of the noninstitutionalized older population and at least 3% of nursing home residents. Another 26% of nursing home residents experience partial visual impairment, resulting in an estimated 8.4 million older people with significant visual impairments.

Defective vision represents a major area of loss for older persons, with 85% of those 75 to 79 having visual acuity of less than 20/40 (Hess & Markson, 1980). A 50-year-old person needs twice as much light to see as well as a youth of 20, and an 80-year-old person needs three times as much light (Manney, 1975). Defective vision among persons 12 to 17 years of age is found in only 22% of the population. This proportion actually decreases until age 40, at which point the proportion of persons who have defective vision again increases (Saxton & Etten, 1987). Although defective vision is the norm in old age, serious visual defects are less common. Overall, almost 95% of older people wear corrective lenses (Ferrini & Ferrini, 1986), yet only about 7% of those 65 to 74 and 16% of those 75 years of age and older experience serious defects. The incidence of blindness and other serious visual difficulties increases with age, with the incidence of blindness being twice as high among nonwhites as whites. The rate of "absolute" blindness (no light or dark perception) is three times as high among nonwhites (Hess & Markson, 1980).

VISUAL CHANGES IN OLD AGE

A variety of visual changes are associated with aging — making fear of visual loss one of the most common fears of older persons. Visual losses are due to changes in the lens, pupil, composition of the vitreous humor, and ability to shift from near to far vision. The aging eye needs more light to adequately stimulate visual receptors. Age-related visual decrements result in decreased sharpness of visual images.

Among the normal visual changes associated with advancing age is decreased lens transparency. Yellowing of the lens results in decreased ability to discriminate all colors in the spectrum, and particularly shades of blue, green, or purple. Red and yellow discrimination remains much better, while pastels of all shades are less readily discriminated (Saxon & Etten, 1987).

The lens also loses elasticity and becomes rigid, contributing to improved accommodation to distant objects, decreased near vision accommodation, and reduced speed of adaptation from near to far and far to near vision. In addition, reduced adaptation to light or dark is common, causing a gap of up to several minutes to adapt to changes resulting from walking into bright sunlight or dark rooms.

Also common are decreased flicker adaptation, decreased peripheral vision, decreased pupillary response (smaller pupil), and decreased intraocular fluid reabsorption (making glaucoma more likely). Additionally, less tearing is present in the eyes of older persons. The combined effect of these changes is an 80% loss of visual acuity by age 85 compared to age 40.

EYE DISEASES
IN OLDER PERSONS

Several visual disorders are more common among older persons, primarily cataracts, glaucoma, macular degeneration, and diabetic retinopathy. Each of these conditions is discussed briefly in this section. When combined with normal changes in vision, these conditions contribute to reduced mobility and an increase in the probability of an accident or injury (Malasanos, Barbanskas, Moss, & Stoltenberg-Allen, 1981). Disabilities frequently associated with these conditions include reduced ability to read, to recognize faces or facial expressions, and to recognize important features of the environment (National Advisory Eye Council, 1983).

Cataracts are the most common visual disorder affecting older persons, with three-fourths of persons over age 60 having some degree of cataract formation (Ferrini & Ferrini, 1986). However, less than 1 in 10 are legally blind as a result of cataracts, 15% experience significant vision loss, and only 5% need surgery (National Society to Prevent Blindness, 1980). This condition, the yellowing and ultimate opacity of the lens, is common to some degree in most persons who live to extreme age. It is correctable through surgical removal of the affected lens and prescription of contact lenses or glasses (Villaverde & MacMillan, 1980).

Glaucoma is the second leading cause of blindness in older persons. It can develop slowly and without symptoms, and can cause blindness if not detected and treated early. It is recommended that all persons over 30 years of age should have periodic glaucoma screening (Saxon & Etten, 1987). The increased production of ocular fluid and inability of the fluid to drain leads to the increased interocular pressure present in glaucoma. Irreparable damage to the optic nerve can result, causing early loss of peripheral vision. Treatment includes surgical intervention and/or drug therapy to reduce interocular pressure by diminishing and/or withdrawing the aqueous humor (fluid) production within the eye.

Senile macular degeneration is caused by decreased blood supply to the macula. It results in damage to the receptors and loss of central vision. Peripheral vision may be unaffected. Early signs of macular degeneration usually appear in persons in their fifties and include inability to discriminate fine print, blurring or cloudiness of vision, and/or loss of central vision.

Reduced and fluctuating visual acuity is a common complication of diabetes. Uncontrolled or poorly regulated diabetes creates the greatest fluctuations. *Diabetic retinopathy*, a disease affecting vision which is caused by a diabetic condition, is sometimes accompanied by retinal detachment and loss of central vision. Continuous medical control is essential if irreversible vision loss is to be prevented (DiStefano & Aston, 1986).

VISUAL AND MULTIPLE IMPAIRMENTS IN OLDER PERSONS

Loss of vision can impair or severely restrict an older person's ability to function within their environment. Not surprisingly, the visual losses experienced by older persons affect their mobility and performance of even the most routine activities of daily living. Examples are difficulty reading dials on stoves, faces of clocks, medication instructions, or the print in telephone books. Safety both in and outside the home may be endangered.

Equally important is the fact that decreased ability to function independently can have serious social and psychological consequences, with a resultant negative impact on physical health. Ainlay (1988) studied the disruptions of time and space that occur for older persons who experience vision loss. These disruptions cause older persons who are visually impaired to question their ability to manipulate and control their environment as well as their ability to engage in social relationships. "Consequently, these perceptual disruptions make them vulnerable to both self-imposed tentativeness and externally generated labeling processes that identify them as incompetent" (Ainlay, 1988, p. 79).

An example of the interactive nature of health or disability and emotional functioning is apparent when an older person's declining visual acuity creates an inability to read road signs, leading to difficulty in driving. Combined with reductions in reaction time, such older persons can become unsafe drivers or even find themselves involved in accidents. Loss of a driving license can lead to increased dependence on others and a reduced sense of personal efficacy or capability. Another example is the isolation experienced by some 10 to 15% of older persons who find themselves largely homebound as a result of various physical and emotional disabilities. Social isolation contributes to decreased self-esteem, which further erodes both physical and emotional capacities.

These are just two of the many examples that could be provided of the cyclical, interactive nature of physical change and aging. Older persons experience declines in all body systems (Saxon & Etten, 1987), and multiple chronic, degenerative diseases (Williams, 1986). Older persons also experience numerous other losses, both psychological (e.g., status, self-esteem) and social (e.g., friends, spouse). When visual decrements are combined with these other conditions and losses, a complex of symptoms and problems can and often does result. Rehabilitative efforts are difficult, at best, and professionals working with older persons increasingly find themselves challenged to keep trying in the face of seemingly insurmountable odds. Some case examples may serve to clarify the points made here.

CASE STUDIES

To consider more accurately the feelings, thoughts, frustrations, and plight of older persons who are multihandicapped, three case studies are presented (Murphey, 1980). In each case, the impact of the visual difficulty is exacerbated when coupled with hearing loss, economic loss, mobility loss, inability to communicate effectively, and other limitations. Not surprisingly, reactions to multiple impairments in old age include a range of emotions from frustration, anxiety, and hostility, through depression and despair. The isolation many older persons experience may be exacerbated by multiple handicaps. On the other hand, the examples that follow show that the goals of improved quality of life and increased feelings of self-worth among older persons who are multihandicapped can be achieved in spite of extensive physical losses.

CASE 1

The first case is that of a 92-year-old, widowed housewife, who at the time of contact was living alone in rural central Mississippi. Her two primary handicaps included gradual onset, non-specific macular degeneration resulting in light perception only, and presbycusis with resulting near total deafness. Her initial limitations were loss of driver's license and substantial oral communication difficulty. Later, she was unable to crochet or play her organ (two favorite activities), and she could not correspond with her friends due to her loss of ability to read and write legibly. Since her mid-eighties, she had not been able to attend church, cook, wash clothes, or accomplish her basic personal hygiene needs. She continually expressed frustration, saying, "What can I do? What can be done for me? I feel worthless and I am ready to die."

Her almost total blindness and deafness left her experiencing only fragments of what was occurring in her environment, and she often expressed the desire to become totally blind and deaf so she would not be aware of any of the occurrences around her. The effect of the cumulative losses was that she was unable to cope with the fragments of perception that she experienced. She stated, "Life as I experience it is stifling." A housekeeper was employed for her during the evenings to clean the house, cook, and serve as a companion. As she continued to live in the home she occupied when she was sighted, she was able to maintain a relatively high degree of mobility. Illumination was increased throughout the home; contrasting colors in red, yellow, and orange were used to color code certain areas (doors, medication containers, steps, telephone) so that she could distinguish them more easily. All persons with whom she came in contact were advised to speak slowly, to repeat if necessary, to speak in a lower pitch, to give basic information first, and to touch while speaking.

These efforts enabled her to function in her home, but did not address her isolation, deprivation, anxiety, and feelings of worthlessness. She experienced the disinterest of her physician and often had hypochondriacal reactions, which further reduced the physician's patience with her. She accelerated her attempts to converse with the family and friends, resulting in heightened anxiety among all who came in contact with her.

The first and only non-drug-related therapy that partially improved her feelings of self-worth and resulted in mood elevation was her introduction to swimming at the age of 91. She found that exercise in the buoyant medium of water gave her an uplift in both physical feeling and mental outlook. She enjoyed the exercise, kept count of her lap progress, and seemed to feel better. She left the house for her daily swim, enjoyed "getting out" without endangering herself, falling, or other possible negative outcomes. Further, she did not require communication for success in this activity. Visual acuity was not a requirement, and a full-time support person to pursue her new, healthful activity was not necessary. At age 93, she continued to swim and had a reasonably positive outlook for the future. Family members were supportive and provided transportation for her daily swim, as the benefits of her mood elevation were apparent to all concerned.

CASE 2

Another case of interest concerns an 81-year-old male with no relatives, who at the time of initial contact was living in a long-term care facility in Florida. He was a diabetic amputee, had tunnel vision secondary to glaucoma, and had severe bilateral hearing impairment. He had little interest in activity of any kind. He could not read, was immobile, and was considered "senile" by institutional staff. He was docile and appeared confused by his environment and the daily routine of the facility. He received meals regularly, was fed by an aide, was escorted to the bathroom on a regular basis, and received occasional visitors. However, he did not respond to any of these activities in a positive or interested manner. He said he "worried about others because he couldn't see or hear them" and, therefore, "did not know who they were."

Intervention for him came when a graduate student in gerontology counseling began visiting him as part of a supervising practicum and attempted to relieve the anxiety and confusion he was experiencing. This occurred at the same time that a unique elementary school program called "Adopted Grandparents" began to have children visit the facility twice each week, resulting in his "adoption" by a child (Whitley, 1976). The student/counselor and the "adopted grandchild," over an extended period of time, were able to isolate certain vocal levels and words that the older man could hear and understand. Further, since the client would talk and was lucid mentally, it was discovered that he felt "trapped inside his physical prison." As he began talking about himself, his life, and the limitations his physical decrements imposed on him, he became more alert, talkative, and responsive. He responded to the touch and affection of the child and looked forward to her visits each week. His mood improved, he began feeding himself, and he was less passive. Communication between the student/counselor, the child, and himself, had been virtually one-way, but through talking with these concerned and interested others, he had become better able to function within his institutional life setting. At the time of case closure, he was still a resident of the same institution and did not have any reasonable prospect of living in a noninstitutional setting. He was no longer acting confused and anxious, and he maintained a positive attitude concerning his life and its meaning. He often talked of the feelings of being needed as the adopted grandparent of the child and how much that meant to him.

CASE 3

The third case study involved a 76-year-old woman living in the home of a daughter. At 61, she began to experience mild confusion, and following the death of her husband, she became increasingly unable to accomplish personal care tasks in her own home. When she developed cataracts, her daughter became distressed and invited her to move to Florida from her home in Michigan. Following surgery for the cataracts at age 66, it was discovered that she was unable to hear female voices. She was examined and found to possess hearing impairment bilaterally, which was not amenable to medical treatment. Her confusion continued to exacerbate, and when she was 70 she was diagnosed as having irreversible chronic brain syndrome. She was often very loud, physically active, and had a tendency to wander if not attended constantly. She did not have control of bowel or bladder function, and as a result became an embarrassment to the family.

Ultimately, when she was age 74, her daughter's marriage ended in divorce. Reluctant to place her in a nursing home, the daughter relocated with her to a small trailer, leaving her husband and children in the home.

The resolution of this case is the least satisfactory of the three cases presented. At 76 years of age, she was living with her daughter, in poor health, and continued to be loud, very active, and have no control of body functions. The daughter spent virtually all of her time caring for her mother, with both subsisting on the mother's Social Security income and a small alimony from the daughter's former husband.

COMMENT ON CASE STUDIES: IMPACT OF MULTIPLE IMPAIRMENT

The three case studies described are illustrative of typical situations involving multiple handicaps including vision, hearing, physical disabilities, and organic brain impairments in older persons. The outcomes in each case depended to a considerable extent on the availability of special services or on the presence of interested persons with commitment or family ties. The outcomes were more or less satisfactory, in terms of improved quality of life for the older persons, depending on the severity, number, and type of disabilities that were experienced.

Heinemann et al. (1988) noted that visual impairments comprise one of the most prevalent health conditions affecting social participation in later life. Vision loss is accompanied by "a host of physiological, psychological and sociological changes" (Ainlay, 1988). This is true even when vision loss is the only physical impairment experienced. Clearly, older persons with multiple handicapping conditions face significant changes in themselves and their relationship to other persons and their environment. Personal doubts, fears of dependency, low self-esteem, and reduced feelings of self-efficacy are common responses, all of which may be accompanied by frustration, depression, or even despair. Social isolation, bewilderment, and general pessimism about the world may result.

Feelings of vulnerability may contribute to a view of oneself as incompetent, leading to a negative spiral of social and personal breakdown. Left untreated, this process eventually leads to severe disability and death (Kuypers & Bengston, 1973).

REHABILITATION OF OLDER PERSONS WHO ARE MULTIHANDICAPPED

It is possible to slow, stop, or even reverse the social breakdown process, for an indefinite period of time. The needs of older persons who are multiply handicapped are multifaceted, thus comprehensive approaches to treatment are required. DiStefano and Aston (1986) refer to such approaches as "total rehabilitation." Medical treatment combined with team interventions that employ the skills of counselors, social workers, physical therapists, occupational therapists, speech-language pathologists, audiologists, family members, and other care providers are necessary. Residential, inpatient treatment in a rehabilitation facility may be required to teach older persons daily living skills that will enable them to continue living independently in the community. These skills may include training in the use of optical aids to maximize residual vision, mobility training for severe visual impairments, vocational training or retraining, housekeeping and personal care management skills, or personal adjustment counseling, to name a few.

When interdisciplinary approaches are implemented, cooperation and mutual respect among the various professionals involved are essential. A "team leader" or case manager must be specified to coordinate all aspects of care and assure continuity for the older person and his or her family. Dealing with one familiar, friendly, supportive individual while negotiating a maze of agencies and services is not merely important, it is an essential resource for frail older individuals. Where possible, services can and should be provided in community rather than institutional settings.

The Older Americans Act, originally authorized in 1965, provides funds for senior centers and nutrition programs throughout the country. The overall goal of these programs is to maintain older persons in community settings as long as possible. Among the services provided through such programs are congregate and home-delivered meals, transportation, shopping assistance, health screening, chore service, escort service, home repairs, and legal aid. A network of more than 600 Area Agencies on Aging administers funds for Older Americans Act services nationwide. One of the most significant mandates of this Act is the requirement for information and referral services. Thus, most communities in the United States offer telephone counseling, referral, and follow-up for older persons needing a variety of care and social services.

BARRIERS TO TREATMENT

A number of difficulties exist in treating older persons with visual and multiple impairments. Among the most pervasive is the lack of knowledge among older persons of the diseases that occur most frequently in old age. Additionally, there are many misconceptions among older persons regarding prognosis, treatment, and limitations imposed by such conditions. Thus, many older people fail to seek treatment in the early stages of their diseases — when treatment would be most effective.

Lack of training of physicians in dealing with older patients is another serious barrier to effective treatment. Among the major issues of concern for medical practitioners are:

1. Lack of knowledge among the general public concerning visual and other handicapping conditions in old age.
2. Fear and anxiety of older persons regarding eye diseases.
3. Lack of knowledge of the probability of occurrence and/or prognosis for various eye diseases.
4. Concern over how to most appropriately inform an older patient of the presence of eye disease in order to reduce anxiety, fear, stress, and other psychological trauma due to the diagnosis.
5. Lack of information predictive of level of impairment in older persons who are multiply handicapped.
6. Need for counselors to assist when dealing with older persons who are severely visually and/or multiply impaired.
7. Desire for information on how best to work with family members of the older person who is severely multiply impaired.
8. Interest in developing positive approaches to working with older patients who are visually impaired and institutionalized, with a goal of improving the quality of life for those persons.
9. Willingness to accept maintenance rather than cure as the goal of treatment with older patients.

The cumulative effect of these barriers to treatment and information deficits results in the need for physicians to spend greater amounts of time with older persons and their families than with younger patients. Communication may be difficult due to the time constraints faced by busy physicians and the anxieties experienced by older patients, which lead them to question or even distrust their physicians' recommendations. As one 86-year-old woman remarked, "He (the first doctor) just ruined my eyes! All of my life I went to him, got a new prescription, and I was fine. That time he put those drops in my eyes, then he said there is nothing more he can do. I could see if not for him!" Unfortunately, attempts to explain the nature of her senile macular degeneration only resulted in tears and denial.

These issues are areas in which further research is indicated so that the physician-patient link may become a more positive experience for both. Certainly, the presence and use of support staff trained in counseling can be important adjuncts for physicians in treating older patients. The result of improvements in medical and supportive care could enhance the ability of older persons to deal effectively with multihandicapping conditions.

PRESENT AND FUTURE NEEDS

The last three decades have seen a rapid expansion of programs and services for older persons. At the same time, the paucity of trained persons available to work with older persons and develop and implement new and innovative programming for them has become evident. Further, coordination of services for older persons who are multiply handicapped has emerged as an important need nationally. To address this need, the Administration on Aging, the Rehabilitation Services Administration, and the National Institute of Mental Health have begun to work together. Notable developments have included the funding of two Rehabilitation Research and Training Centers focused on the needs of older persons and two national conferences on aging and rehabilitation (see Brody & Ruff, 1986).

Among possible new approaches to assisting older persons who are multihandicapped are the establishment of regional and local comprehensive geriatric ophthalmology/audiology/internal medicine centers. Such centers could be jointly funded by the Administration on Aging, the Rehabilitation Services Administration, and other sources, and could include staff with training and experience in gerontology and rehabilitation. A comprehensive, holistic health care model could be implemented in these centers which would not consider "time left to live" as a constraint to avoid providing positive services to older persons who are

severely handicapped. Multidisciplinary research, treatment, and therapy could be conducted at these centers to expand the knowledge base of effective strategies for working with this special and growing population.

Sheltered workshops have been successfully developed for persons with retardation, delinquent youth, individuals who are severely physically handicapped, and persons with mental illness. A few workshops have been implemented to meet the needs of older persons who are multihandicapped. These include adult day care centers as well as more traditional sheltered employment settings. Such programs are almost nonexistent in the private sector, and in one of the more logical settings: long-term care facilities. With special funding, selected long-term care facilities could implement programs that included counseling, recreational programs, physical therapy, and sheltered work opportunities.

To realize fully the benefits of new and innovative programs for older persons, new and expanded facilities staffed by trained personnel are needed. Clearly, such programs cannot be developed in the absence of funding. Both private and public sector funds are needed, backed by national policies which result in legislative and funding priorities designed to enhance the quality of later life.

CONCLUSION

Social psychologist Anselm Strauss stated that "the chief business of a chronically ill person is not to stay alive or to keep his symptoms under control, but to live as normally as possible despite his symptoms and his disease" (Manney, 1975, p. 10). Many older people fail at the task of living as normally as possible. Many succumb to the limitations of multiple handicapping conditions because they lack the knowledge or assistance required to enable them to continue living independently. The challenge we face, individually, as service providers, and as a society, is to provide a continuum of care that will enable all persons to live to the fullest extent of their potential regardless of disability, age, or life circumstances. In effect, we need to consider that growing old is really not so bad when you consider the alternative.

If we live, we grow old, so we may as well do it as gracefully as possible. But we have to work at it. When the print gets smaller, the steps get higher, and the sounds get softer, we have to make adjustments that may not come easily. If we learn to cooperate with the inevitable, life can be a joy to the very end. (Nemeth, in Saxon & Etten, 1987, p. 177)

REFERENCES

Ainlay, S. C. (1988). Aging and new vision loss: Disruptions of the here and now. *Journal of Social Issues, 44*(1), 79–94.

Belsky, J. K. (1984). *The psychology of aging.* Pacific Grove, CA: Brooks/Cole.

Brody, S. J., & Ruff, G. E. (Eds.). (1986). *Aging and rehabilitation: Advances in the state of the art.* New York: Springer.

DiStefano, A. F., & Aston, S. J. (1986). Rehabilitation for the blind and visually impaired elderly. In S. J. Brody & G. E. Ruff (Eds.), *Aging and rehabilitation: Advances in the state of the art* (pp. 203–217). New York: Springer.

Ferrini, A. F., & Ferrini, R. L. (1986). *Health in the later years.* Dubuque, IA: William C. Brown.

Hess, B. B., & Markson, E. W. (1980). *Aging and old age.* New York: Macmillan.

Heinemann, A. W., Colorez, A., Frank, S., & Taylor, D. (1988). Leisure activity participation of elderly individuals with low vision. *The Gerontologist, 28*(2), 181–184.

Kirchner, C. (1985). *Data on blindness and visual impairment in the U.S.: A resource manual on characteristics, education, employment, and services delivery.* New York: American Foundation for the Blind.

Kohn, J. (1980). A new look at the aging blind. In C. W. Hoehne (Ed.), *Opthalmological considerations in the rehabilitation of the blind.* Springfield, IL: Charles C. Thomas.

Kuypers, J. A., & Bengtson, Y. Competence and social breakdown: A social-psychological view of aging. *Human Development, 16,* 181–201.

Malasanos, L., Barbanskas, V., Moss, M., & Stoltenberg-Allen, K. (1981). *Health assessment.* St. Louis, MO: C. V. Mosby.

Manney, J. D. (1975). *Aging in American society: An examination of concepts and issues.* Ann Arbor: University of Michigan Press.

Murphey, M. (1980). *Case study of the multi-handicapped elderly.* Unpublished manuscript, University of Northern Colorado, Greeley.

National Advisory Eye Council. (1983). *Vision research: A national plan.* Washington, DC: Department of Health and Human Services.

National Society to Prevent Blindness. (1980). *Vision problems in the United States: A statistical analysis.* New York: Author.

Saxon, S. V., & Etten, M. J. (1987). *Physical change and aging: A guide for the helping professions.* New York: Tiresias Press.

Villaverde, M. M., & MacMillan, D. W. (1980). *Ailments of aging: From symptom to treatment.* New York: Van Nostrand Reinhold.

Whitley, E. (1976). *From time to time; A record of young children's relationships with the aged* (College of Education Research Monograph No. 17). Gainesville: University of Florida.

Williams, T. F. (1986). The aging process: Biological and psychological considerations. In S. J. Brody & G. E. Ruff (Eds.), *Aging and rehabilitation: Advances in the state of the art* (pp. 13–19). New York: Springer.

■ PART III ■

Evaluation in the Aural Rehabilitation Process

CHAPTER 24

Evaluation of Communicative Function and Successes in Aural Rehabilitation

■ RAYMOND H. HULL, Ph.D. ■

One of the many historically challenging aspects of aural rehabilitation services on behalf of adult and elderly clients has been the attempts at assessing the impact of those services on their communicative behaviors. Perhaps the most discouraging have been those instances in which persons from audiology or other professions have asked to be shown *how much* improvement a given client has made, when in fact the instruments to measure those gains were not available. It is simpler to note the speech and language progress of a child who is congenitally hearing impaired, or to plot the increase in speech reception thresholds after a hearing aid fitting, than to pinpoint the social gains of an adult who is adventitiously hearing impaired that result from aural rehabilitation services. It is equally challenging to assess the psychosocial and personal handicap of hearing loss on an otherwise active adult client, when

the assessment tools available to us may not be sensitive to the elements of life and communication faced daily by that person.

IMPORTANT ASSESSMENT FACTORS

There are several factors that must be considered when assessing communication skills, or the impact of hearing loss on adult clients. Those include:

1. *The person's emotional response* to his or her auditorily based communication difficulties. Occasionally positive change in a client's emotional response to his or her auditory difficulties will reflect itself in enhanced communication abilities.

2. *The client's most frequented communication environments.* Audiologists must realize that not all persons require an active social life, but rather they may be content to remain at home with family or a friend. Their requirements regarding aural rehabilitation services are, thus, based upon such environments, and the tool for assessing communication abilities and subsequent determination of improvements or lack of them resulting from aural rehabilitation services must be capable of reflecting such differences among adult clients.

3. *The communication priorities of the client.* Linked to the previous factor, but important to discuss further, is the establishment of priorities by the client relative to his or her communication needs. In Chapters 15 and 22, this author discussed prioritization as an important part of the provision of aural rehabilitation services for adult and elderly clients. If the priority communication needs of each client are the basis on which treatment services are developed and provided, then any evaluation of progress also must be based on them. Only then can progress, or lack of it, be determined.

4. *Determining realistic goals for the client.* Besides establishing client needs or desires for communication as a basis for services and subsequent evaluation, the *importance of determining those that are realistic for individual clients is critical.* If, for example, a client who is profoundly hearing impaired has established as a priority the ability to communicate with absolute precision at social gatherings, that goal may not be realistic for that person. If the goal is held at that level, treatment may be doomed to failure, and the evaluation would reflect little or no improvement. However, a realistic goal of increased skill in social communication within optimal environments may be reached, and pre- and postevaluation may reveal those gains. This is not to say, however, that goals should be set so low that improvement in communication skills is inevitable.

The point stressed here is that goals for individual clients should not be set so high that failure is probable. The perceptive audiologist will be aware of communicative heights to be at-

tempted. The most important criteria for goals, however, are the communication needs of individual clients. Usually, most adults are realistic in their expectations and are aware of their limitations. It is tragic to observe audiologists who have established the same aural rehabilitation goals for all clients or, perhaps, had established no real individual goals at all at the time that aural rehabilitation services for a group of adult clients were begun.

ATTEMPTS AT ASSESSMENT

ELEMENTS TO BE ASSESSED

Research designed to investigate factors that influence the ability of persons who are hearing impaired to communicate historically has included such factors as the ability to identify the phonemes of speech, intelligence as a factor in lipreading ability, synthetic abilities among good and poor lipreaders, and others. Those and other studies have led to the conclusion that the person's language level is one of the most important factors that influence compensation for a hearing loss (Lowell, 1969). This language level not only includes vocabulary level, but also the client's ability to efficiently use the language that he or she possesses. This usage involves the rules of language and the ability to make closure when not all of the linguistic information is available in a given moment of communication. This also inevitably involves factors in processing linguistic information from moment to moment.

The mental gymnastics that are involved when a person who is hearing impaired is required to take the threads of phonemic and linguistic information obtained through an impaired receptive auditory system and combine them with what is received visually (if the speaker is visible), and derive information from what is being said is mind boggling, to say the least. To measure that ability appears to be equally difficult, especially when audiologists are dealing with complex adult or elderly clients who differ greatly in relation to:

1. Their response to their hearing impairment;
2. Their communication environments;
3. Their response to noise and other distractions;
4. Those with whom they communicate; and
5. The multiple interrelational parameters of peripheral and central auditory function.

Most of these important aspects are, in one way or another, addressed in the scales of communicative function that are available to clinicians. The scales that are available today have proved most useful in terms of evaluating social/behavioral/personal communication behaviors.

In view of the complex nature of the requirements for efficient communication that may be compounded by a hearing impairment and/or advanced age, the remainder of this chapter will concentrate on sorting through the factors involved in assessment of progress in or handicap of communicative function. Even though there is evident diversity among philosophies relative to assessment of speechreading, general communication abilities, and other factors involved in communication by the hearing impaired, common denominators appear to be emerging. These will be presented during the remainder of this chapter, particularly procedures that appear to have promise in noting progress in communicative function among clients who are hearing impaired.

A HISTORICAL PERSPECTIVE

FILMED TESTS

Studies of filmed tests of lipreading ability generally have demonstrated that persons who are hearing impaired perform at least similarly to persons who have normal hearing. Further, they generally have shown that adult clients perform as well or as poorly on them after completion of a speechreading treatment program as when they began. Most importantly, it has been demonstrated that it is difficult to separate the quality or efficiency of the aural rehabilitation treatment procedures from persons' performances on these tests.

Morkovin Life Situation Films

Filmed tests were introduced in the 1940s as an attempt to both evaluate and teach lipreading. Mason (1943) developed a series of 30 silent films for lipreading instruction. Morkovin (1948) introduced the Morkovin Life Situations films. These films depicted various "real-life" situations for lipreading therapy that advocated a theme approach. They also were utilized as an approach to assessing lipreading skills. The films were made with sound and, for example, depicted a girl and her mother buying shoes at the shoe store, youngsters receiving dancing lessons, and Monty Montana (the roping and cowboy movie star) demonstrating rope tricks for children. The films generally were interesting, but difficult to use either for instruction or for assessment. They, further, became quickly dated due to the actors' clothing and mannerisms. In the majority of instances, they were certainly not suitable for work with adults.

Utley Test

The first actual filmed test of lipreading was developed by Utley (1946). It also has received the majority of attention by researchers. This silent film was developed from the most frequently used words in Thorndike's *First Word Dictionary*. It is not known whether the use of those words hindered the validity of her test or not, since those words contained in that dictionary are the words most frequently written, not the most frequently spoken.

The test contained three parts. Part 1 utilized words, and Part 2 contained sentences. Both Parts 1 and 2 were filmed in black and white. Part 3 was a five-part story test filmed in color. Utley investigated the reliability of the forms of the tests and found that in Parts 1 and 2, the internal reliability of each portion was high enough to be significant. Those parts were presented to 761 subjects who were deaf or hard-of-hearing for purposes of standardization.

The validity of the Utley test has been investigated on numerous occasions. DiCarlo and Kataja (1951), for example, found that the test was probably, although not necessarily, reliable. Even though they found a 0.77 correlation level between the Utley test and the Morkovin "Family Dinner" film, they questioned the validity of the test. They felt, due to the method of filming and its length and speed of presentation, that the test primarily assessed persistence and the frustration tolerance of the viewers.

O'Neill and Stephens (1959) studied the Mason, the Utley, and the Morkovin films. They did not find a significant correlation between the responses of viewers of the Utley and Morkovin films, but did find a correlation between the Mason films and Parts 1 and 2 of the Utley film test and the Morkovin films. They concluded that the lack of correlation between the Utley tests and the Morkovin films probably was because the Morkovin films were originally constructed as a series of lessons and not as an assessment tool.

Simmons (1959) concluded that the Utley and Mason films seem to measure something related to lipreading ability. But the "something" was thought to be only a part of the general ability of persons who were hearing impaired to communicate in face-to-face situations.

Pestone (1962) determined that no filmed tests met all the criteria that are needed in a test. She felt that a filmed test should utilize presentation of material by two speakers — a man and a woman. Further, she advocated that the films should be in color to make them more realistic, two equivalent forms should be developed to facilitate measurements, and the test should have a wide range of difficulty and be easy to score. Pestone used this philosophy to develop a filmed test that utilized sentences evenly divided between statements and questions. She found the test to be reliable, but it has not been heard of again to any extent.

John Tracy Test of Lipreading

Donnelly and Marshall (1967) developed a filmed multiple-choice test of lipreading using the John Tracy Clinic Test of Lipreading (Taaffe

& Wong, 1957). The test was filmed in color and with sound. College-age students who were hearing impaired were used as subjects in a study to assess its reliability. The subjects individually controlled the intensity of the sound. Multiple-choice answers were based on (1) the correct answer, (2) the most frequent incorrect response of persons tested previously, and (3) the second most frequently missed. Donnelly and Marshall found the test to be reliable.

Summary

Even though filmed tests of lipreading consistently have shown at least some level of reliability on test-retest and between tests, their validity continually has been questioned. Perhaps Lashley (1961) stated it best by saying, "It is possible that validity of lipreading tests will not be established until an understanding of what factors involved in lipreading are agreed upon" (p. 182). Alpiner (1978b) has, further, listed criticisms of filmed or videotaped tests (see Table 24–1).

EARLIER ATTEMPTS AT ASSESSMENT

Other attempts at measuring speechreading or lipreading abilities included interview procedures to determine the communicative function of a person who is hearing impaired. These

TABLE 24–1. CRITICISMS OF FILMED OR VIDEOTAPED TESTS OF LIPREADING

The distractions caused by the tester on the film holding up a card with the number of the test item.

The stolid appearance of the presenter.

The usual presentation mode of showing the speaker from the shoulders upward.

The erratic rate of presentation of stimulus materials.

The dated clothing and hair styles, which may prove distracting to the client.

Source: Reprinted with permission from Alpiner, J. G. (1978b). *Handbook of adult rehabilitative audiology* (p. 36). Baltimore, MD: Williams & Wilkins.

attempts have included clients' lipreading ability and attempts to note progress or lack of it. The basis on which Simmons (1959) attempted the use of judges rather than previous standard tests of lipreading was the lack of quantitative measures of lipreading ability. She felt that this was the major problem in attempting to establish a relationship between lipreading ability and other physical or psychological factors.

Interview Methods

Simmons (1959) used five judges who were qualified therapists of adults who were hard-of-hearing to attempt to determine the reliability of an interview method for assessing lipreading abilities. Subjects included 12 men and 12 women. All were hard of hearing, with a mean pure-tone average of 33.8 dB and mean speech discrimination scores of 58.7%. The rating scale devised was based on three simple categories of "good, average, and poor" lipreading abilities. Each classification had its own set of criteria for determining the level of skill. The judges engaged in "everyday" conversation with the subjects, keeping their voices at an intensity level that was below the speech reception threshold of each subject. Comparison of the judges' decision as to lipreading ability of individual clients yielded a relationship of 0.92, indicating a high positive correlation.

If such correlations can be maintained, perhaps such interview techniques could be used successfully. Close monitoring of the intensity level of the judge's voice below, at, or above clients' thresholds could yield important pre- and posttreatment information about their ability to utilize visual and supplemental auditory clues in everyday speech. The most difficult aspect when dealing with such methods, however, is the scoring procedure. It is suggested that further investigation of such approaches be made relative to their possible routine use with older adults.

Multiple-Choice Tests

Other procedures, such as that developed by Hutton (1959), included the use of multiple-choice tests. Hutton's procedure utilized two simultaneous word presentations in visual-only, auditory-only, and auditory-visual modes. The subjects were asked to choose the correct word from a multiple-choice answer sheet of eight words.

Further, Black, O'Reilly, and Peck (1963) developed a self-administered multiple-choice procedure that was presented on silent film. The filmed stimulus items were used for training in lipreading. The projector speed could be slowed or speeded. Subjects first were tested using the normal speed of projection. The film was then slowed to 15%, and subjects were tested again. The subjects, after reviewing their scores, were permitted to adjust the speed of the projector until they could achieve a score of 100%. Results revealed that even with that brief period of practice, subjects improved in their ability to lipread even when viewing a different speaker. Although this procedure was basically self-administered training in lipreading, the assessment aspect was unique.

ASSESSMENT THROUGH BISENSORY MODALITIES

The current consensus of opinion is that assessment of the ability of persons who are hearing impaired to understand speech should involve the combined use of vision and audition. Innumerable studies confirm the reciprocal complement of vision and audition (Binnie, 1973; Binnie, Montgomery, & Jackson, 1974; Duffy, 1967; Erber, 1971; Erber, 1972a, 1972b; Erber, 1975; Ewersten, B. Nielsen, & S. Nielsen, 1970; Hutton, Curry, & Armstrong, 1959; Miller & Nicely, 1955; Neely, 1956; O'Neill, 1954; Prall, 1957; Sumby & Pollack, 1954; and Van Uden, 1960). Their results, and the results of numerous other studies, continually confirm the benefits of bisensory modalities for speech reception.

No matter how restricted the auditory component, the complement continues to exist. If an individual client's ability to recognize the visimes of speech or to discriminate auditorily is to be assessed, then those sensory modalities must be isolated. If assessment of the ability to *communicate* is held as a priority, however, then both vision and audition should be combined.

USE OF LIVE-VOICE TESTS

The criticisms of filmed or videotaped tests of lipreading cited earlier by Alpiner (1978b) are valid ones. Further, people do not communicate with others via film or videotape in the course of everyday conversations. Therefore, the use of live voice for the presentation of assessment materials to determine skill in the reception of speech by clients who are hearing impaired often is preferred.

For live-voice testing, the use of sentences is preferred over single words. Sentences as stimulus items most closely approximate the types of stimuli found in the conversations experienced by clients who are hearing impaired. Sentences also lend themselves to greater ease of scoring. Even though paragraphs most closely resemble the conversations that people listen to in the everyday world, they are more difficult to score, and other compounding factors such as auditory and visual memory have an impact on the results. For a more accurate determination of skill in auditory-visual reception of speech, sentences continue to be beneficial.

Sentence materials that lend themselves well to assessment of speechreading skills include the Central Institute for the Deaf (CID) Everyday Speech Sentences (Davis & Silverman, 1970), the Denver Scale Quick Test (Alpiner, 1978b), and the University of Northern Colorado (UNC) Sentence Test of Speechreading Ability (Hull, 1982).

The CID Everyday Speech Sentences include 10 lists of 10 sentences each. The sentences vary in length and are common to most adults. (See Appendix A of this text for the CID lists of sentences, Lists A through J.)

The Denver Scale Quick Test is made up of 20 simple sentences, 8 questions, and 12 declarative statements. Although no information is available regarding consistency of sentence ease or difficulty or consistency of phonemic visibility, the list lends itself well to assessing client abilities in the identification of sentence material. It is suggested by Alpiner (1978b) that the test be administered under the visual-only condition, although it can be used with an auditory-visual mode. Each stimulus item has a value of 5%, and scoring is based only on identifying the thought of the sentence rather than on verbatim repetition. (See the Denver Scale Quick Test in Appendix B.)

The UNC Sentence Test of Speechreading is based on a study by Hull and Alpiner (1976), in which they investigated linguistic factors in speechreading. Three lists of 36 sentences each were developed based on a sentence length of eight words, which was found by Taaffee and Wong (1957) to be as visually intelligible as shorter sentences. Since shorter sentences are limited in content and complexity, it was felt that longer sentences would provide a greater opportunity for comparisons between conditions and allow for greater experimental manipulation. Further, the sentences were developed according to specific requirements as presented in Table 24–2.

Scoring is based on the thought or idea of the sentence. Each sentence is valued at 2.80 points, and it is suggested that the lists be presented by live voice at a just-audible level for the client. (See Appendix C for the UNC Sentences.) If a verbatim scoring is desired, then each word of each sentence is valued at 1 point each.

PRESENTATION OF SENTENCE MATERIAL

The presentation of the assessment materials can be made in the same room as the client, at a distance of approximately 5 to 6 feet, with the voice of the tester just audible to the client. The determination of audibility can be made by asking the client to close his or her eyes and with the tester reading words or sentences, judge when the tester's voice is audible, but the stimulus items are just not understood. Any level of desired voice presentation can be determined in that fashion, although it is difficult to control across speakers.

Another method of live-voice presentation that has been found to be useful is through the

TABLE 24–2. GUIDELINES FOR DEVELOPMENT OF SENTENCES FOR UNC SENTENCE TEST

An equal number of interrogative and declarative sentences (45 each).

All sentences contained an equal number of words (8).

All words within each sentence were taken from the Jones and Wepman (1966) list of 1,000 most commonly spoken words.

Parts of speech in each sentence were varied as much as possible in terms of position, so that identifying cues could not be obtained from word position.

Percentage of words among parts of speech was based on norms established by Templin (1957) regarding the structure of the English language.

No common phrases such as "good morning," "in the U.S.," or "how are you" were used in the sentences developed.

No contractions that might be confusing in terms of completing written answers were included.

No bisyllabic proper nouns that might be confusing were included.

No highly visible words that could influence the visual intelligibility of sentences were included (Fisher, 1968).

use of a sound-treated audiometric suite, where a window separates the tester from the client. If lighting can be adjusted so that the face and shoulders of the tester are easily observable, the free-field speech system of the audiometer can be used for presentation of the auditory portion. Further, the just-audible level, or other intensity levels of voice presentation can be more easily established, and the intensity levels varied. The most difficult aspect of the use of an audiometric sound-treated suite is the visibility of the tester, particularly through the two to four panels of glass between prefabricated enclosures.

SCALES OF COMMUNICATIVE FUNCTION

A viable approach to assessing the handicap of hearing loss on adult and elderly clients, as well as changes that occur as the result of aural rehabilitation treatment, are rating scales of communicative function. Selected scales that have been tested and published over the past 30 years are as follows:

Hearing Handicap Scale

One forerunner of the current scales is the Hearing Handicap Scale (HHS) developed by High, Fairbanks, and Glorig (1964). Both forms of this scale are presented in Appendix D. The scale concentrates on questions related to communication per se, that is, the impact of hearing impairment on communication in various environments. It does not delve into other aspects related to hearing, such as the social or psychological impact of hearing impairment, which appears to be one of its weaknesses (Giolas, 1970; Sanders, 1975). Responses for this scale include the options of (1) almost always, (2) usually, (3) sometimes, (4) rarely, and (5) almost never.

Even though this scale is somewhat limited by only probing into various communication settings (including the impact of distance on communication), the questions are useful for interviews with adult clients who are hearing impaired. Clients' subjective judgements relative to their ability to function communicatively in typical environments provide important pretreatment data. Since there are two forms for the scale, which are similar in terms of the areas of communication queried, the scale can be used on a pre- and postassessment basis to determine if clients' opinions of their ability to communicate in various similar environments have changed to the positive or the negative. Further, the pretreatment administration can, as with other scales, be used to guide the emphasis of treatment, and procedures.

The Denver Scale of Communication Function

The Denver Scale of Communication Function (Alpiner, Chevrette, Glascoe, Metz, & Olsen, 1978) is an attitude scale which provides adults who are hearing impaired the opportunity to make subjective judgments relative to the impact of their hearing impairment on relationships with family, their ability to communicate with others, image of self, and the impact of the hearing impairment on the social and/or vocational aspects of life and other areas. (This scale is presented in Appendix E of this text.)

It is suggested by Alpiner (1978b) that the scale be administered prior to initiating aural rehabilitation treatment so that the client's responses will not be influenced by discussions that take place there. Clients respond to 25 statements on a seven-level semantic differential continuum, from 1 (agree) to 7 (disagree). The scale contains four categories: family, self, social-vocational, and general communication experience. Alpiner (1978b) recommends a time limit of 15 minutes for administration of the scale.

Client responses are recorded on the Denver Scale Profile form (Alpiner et al., 1978). The abscissa numbers represent the statements on the scale, and the ordinate points represent the clients' responses to each statement, ranging from agree to disagree. The responses are plotted along the abscissa, and lines are drawn from response to response. The profile is studied by the client and audiologist in relation to the communication problems which need attention. That information is then used to design individual clients' aural rehabilitation treatment programs.

One aspect of the scale has been confusing to some clients, and their ratings are probably affected. That is the fact that the middle point on the semantic differential, which is exactly between 1 (agree) and 7 (disagree), is meant to be marked if the statement on the scale is, to an individual client, "irrelevant or unassociated" with his or her communication situation. Some clients, perhaps not understanding the instructions, have placed marks in that position believing that their response would then mean that it is somewhere between agree and disagree, perhaps as a "maybe." Alpiner (1978b) has stated that that aspect will be altered on future revisions of the scale.

Even though this scale is not designed specifically with the older adult in mind, it is applicable and useful for pinpointing areas of communication that concern individual clients. These are important in planning the treatment program. The majority of the Denver scale is applicable for the well noninstitutionalized older adult. Zarnoch and Alpiner (1977) have developed a modified version of the Denver scale which is designed for the older adult who is confined to a health-care facility (nursing home). This scale will be presented later in this discussion.

Test of Actual Performance

A brief scale to assess the communication habits of persons who are hearing impaired has been developed by Koniditsiotis (1971). (The test is shown in Appendix F.) The purpose of the test was to study the extent of relationship between the amount of hearing loss as determined by pure-tone and speech audiometry and the actual disability experienced by the person who possessed the hearing loss. The test contains seven items that are scored 1 (poor), 2 (adequate), 3 (good), or 4 (excellent). Little correlation between the test judgments and actual hearing impairment has been found. The least correlation was found when comparing the test judgment and client scores for speech discrimination.

The strongest limitation to the test is the fact that the test judgments are made by the clinicians who work with the clients and not by the clients themselves.

The Hearing Measurement Scale

Noble and Atherley (1970) devised the Hearing Measurement Scale (HMS), which was designed to probe the handicap of hearing impairment. Even though the purpose of their scale is to assess handicap of hearing loss acquired as the result of industrial noise, all of the questions lend themselves well for use with other persons, including the elderly. (This scale is shown in Appendix G.)

The scale is divided into seven sections:

Section 1: Speech Hearing
Section 2: Acuity for Nonspeech Sound

Section 3: Localization
Section 4: Reaction to Handicap
Section 5: Speech Distortion
Section 6: Tinnitus
Section 7: Personal Opinion of Hearing Loss

The HMS contains a valuable assortment of questions that not only aid in the determination of the client's opinions of the extent of his or her hearing impairment, but also those aspects which interfere most, and their reactions to the handicap. A set of instructions accompanies the assessment forms. Nobel and Atherley (1970) stress that the scale cannot be administered without reading the instruction manual.

Profile Questionnaire for
Rating Communicative Performance

A Profile Questionnaire for Communicative Performance was developed by Sanders (1975). Two aspects of the profile — Communicative Performance in a Home Environment and Communicative Performance in a Social Environment — are applicable for older adults. A third profile is the questionnaire entitled "Performance in an Occupational Environment." For older adult clients in a health-care facility environment, responses to the profile relating to the home environment would need to be interpreted as being their typical environment. (The profiles on social and home environments are presented in Appendix H of this text.)

The Sanders (1975) profiles and the Hearing Handicap Scale (High, Fairbanks, & Glorig, 1964) discussed earlier, differ from the Denver scale since they probe into specific communication environments, rather than clients' attitudes regarding their ability to communicate. All, however, also provide valuable pre- and posttreatment information for assessment of progress or lack of it.

The scales, or profiles, discussed by High, Fairbanks, and Glorig (1964); Alpiner and associates (1978); Noble and Atherley (1970); and Sanders (1975) can be used appropriately with noninstitutionalized adult clients. In some instances they can be used with older clients who are confined at home or in a health-care facility,

but in those instances the questions must be interpreted in relation to their environment(s).

ASSESSMENT BASED ON COMMUNICATIVE PRIORITIES

This procedure, developed by Hull (1982), can be used with both community-based adults and elderly clients and confined older adults. Its premise is that the client's highest priority communication environments should be stressed in planning aural rehabilitation treatment for adults, assessment of successes, or lack of them, also should be based on those environments.

Prior to initiation of treatment, clients are asked to rank the difficulty they experience in a variety of communication environments on a form that can be seen in Appendix J of this text (UNC Communication Appraisal and Priorities, 1982). The ratings of difficulty range from 1 (No Problem), through 2 (Only in Specific Instances), to 3 (Definite Problem). A section for "Other" is included on the form in anticipation that an environment which was not included in the list may be felt to be important to an individual client. After they have rated the 13 communication environments, clients are asked to choose those that are most important to them. When that task is completed, clients are requested to rank the environments in terms of their priority, from highest to lowest. These priorities, if realistic for individual clients, then are used as the basis for the design of clients' treatment programs and to evaluate the program's successes or lack of them.

At the conclusion of a specified number of treatment sessions, clients again are asked to rank the communication environments in terms of the difficulty that they experience in them. The client and the audiologist then review both the pre- and posttest ratings, particularly noting those communication environments considered high priorities by the client. Success, or lack of it, is based only on changes in client attitudes relative to the priority environments. It is interesting to note, however, that on occasion, if positive progress is noted on one priority item, there appears to be a progression of attitude change regarding other "near" environments as they are ranked according to their difficulty. For example, if participation in church group meetings was rated as the highest priority communication environment by an individual client, but other "near" environments such as other formal meetings, at the dinner table, and at parties, were also ranked as being a definite problem, but not as high of a priority, the client's ratings in those other environments also may begin to change toward positive.

In any event, evaluation of progress or lack of it based on clients' priority communication environments appears to have merit. Further, clients feel a sense of confidence in audiologists who hold their priorities as pre-eminent in aural rehabilitation treatment.

Hearing Performance Inventory

This comprehensive assessment tool has been developed by Giolas, Owens, Lamb, and Schubert (1979). It probes six areas that can either impact on communication or involve communication. Those areas are:

1. Understanding the speech of various talkers;
2. Intensity, or the person's awareness of social and nonsocial sounds in his or her environment;
3. Response to auditory failure;
4. Social, or the person's ability to converse in groups of two or more persons in social environments;
5. Personal, or the person's feelings about his or her hearing impairment in relation to its personal impact; and
6. Occupational.

This inventory can be used effectively with adults of all ages. Due to its length, selected categories may be used to establish priorities for aural rehabilitation treatment and for assessment.

The Communication Profile for the Hearing Impaired

The Communication Profile for the Hearing Impaired (CPHI) (Demorest & Erdman, 1987)

was designed to provide systematic and comprehensive assessment of a broad range of communication problems. It was developed at Walter Reed Army Medical Center for use with patients in the Aural Rehabilitation Program. The profile was developed for use with adults of all ages who are hearing impaired. Although it was developed for use with a military population, the authors chose not to use materials specific to military life.

The final version of the CPHI contains 145 items and 24 scores. The scales of the profile are organized into four areas: (1) Communication Performance, (2) Communication Environment, (3) Communication Strategies, and (4) Personal Adjustment. The direction of the scoring for the scales was chosen so that low scores would always indicate potential problem areas, regardless of the name of the scale, and would identify areas in need of rehabilitative intervention. When the scores are plotted graphically, it permits a rapid visual scan of the profile. Thus, according to Demorest and Erdman (1987), a low score on Self-Acceptance, for example, indicates a low level of self-acceptance, but a low score on Communication Need indicates a high level of need for communication. (The Communication Profile for the Hearing Impaired is presented in Appendix L of this text.)

SCALES FOR THE HEARING IMPAIRED ELDERLY

It is evident that all of the scales discussed in this chapter can be used in assessing or discussing the impact of hearing loss on various aspects of older adults' lives. Other than the sections that are specific to one's occupational life, most others are applicable. And, in the long run, because the majority of adults audiologists serve are beyond age 60, all of the adult scales necessarily must be designed to serve them to some degree.

Two scales have been designed with the confined elderly client in mind. One is the Denver Scale of Communication Function for Senior Citizens Living in Retirement Centers (Zarnoch & Alpiner, 1977), and the other is the

Hearing Handicap Inventory for the Elderly (HHIE) (Ventry & Weinstein, 1982).

The Denver Scale of Communication Function for Senior Citizens

The Denver Scale of Communication Function for Senior Citizens Living in Retirement Centers is the result of a modification of the Denver Scale of Communication Function developed by Zarnoch and Alpiner (1977). (This scale can be seen in Appendix I.)

The content of the questions has been designed to be suitable for confined elderly clients. Further, rather than the scale being self-administered as in the original Denver scale (Alpiner, 1978b; Alpiner et al., 1978), the questions are presented to the clients, who then respond verbally. This provides control for variables such as a client's inability to respond to written tests, or fatigue. The Scale for Senior Citizens is based on seven major questions regarding their feelings about themselves and their communication abilities. Each question is followed by Probe Effect questions, which delve more extensively into the principal question. Probe Effect questions range in number from two to five depending on the principal question. To determine the relevance of the Principal Questions and the Probe Effect questions, Exploration Effect questions are also asked.

Each of the seven major questions, including the Probe Effect and Exploration Effect questions, are categorized according to family, emotional, other persons, general communication, self-concept, group situations, or rehabilitation theme. Responses are based on yes or no answers, and scores are indicated by a plus or a minus. Scoring for the Principal Questions, the Probe Effect questions and the Exploration Effect questions is identical.

As stated earlier, the Denver Scale for Senior Citizens appears very useful for interviewing the confined elderly person on a pre- and posttreatment basis. The only drawback observed by this author is the scoring procedure. A semantic differential format, which allows for degrees of yes-to-no responses, generally is more desirable for clients of any age. Otherwise, the scale provides valuable information for the development of aural rehabilitation treatment programs and evaluation of progress based on the attitudes of the client about him- or herself.

The Hearing Handicap Inventory for the Elderly (HHIE)

The HHIE (Ventry & Weinstein, 1982) represents a handicap assessment technique designed to quantify the emotional and social/situational effects of hearing impairment on noninstitutionalized elderly persons. The authors state that this inventory differs from other instruments in that its focus is on the psychosocial effects of hearing impairment specific to the elderly. The inventory consists of 25 questions that address the client's social and personal life, identified as S (social) and E (emotional) on the questionnaire.

The HHIE was studied by comparing self-assessed hearing handicap utilizing that inventory with pure-tone sensitivity and word recognition utility among 100 elderly individuals (Weinstein & Ventry, 1983). The authors found a high correlation between the HHIE responses and subjects' pure-tone sensitivity loss, but found significantly less correlation between the HHIE and word recognition scores. (The HHIE is found in Appendix K in this text.)

SUMMARY OF ATTEMPTS AT EVALUATING COMMUNICATIVE FUNCTION

Whatever method is used to determine whether a person who is hearing impaired can perceive speech, or the symbols of speech, communicative function is being evaluated to some degree. Those methods may include determining if he or she can visually recognize phonemes, words, or sentences, use his or her residual hearing to recognize units of speech, utilize both vision and hearing to recognize units of speech, or use various factors of language to determine the meaning of statements. What matters is the emphasis that is placed on the interpretation of the results of the evaluation.

PHONEME IDENTIFICATION

If lipreading ability for phonemes per se is the object of measurement, then a visible mouth, mandible, and neck may be all that is necessary to determine whether the person who is hearing impaired can identify the various vowels, consonants, and diphthongs as they are viewed on film, on slides, or in ink-drawn pictures. If the person's score is interpreted *only* as that person's score for the recognition of phonemes of American English in isolation, then it would be accurately described. If the score was described as a measure of communicative ability, however, it would be misrepresented, as would that client's probable ability to communicate. The emphasis would have been inappropriately placed, although a high score may indicate that the person has less difficulty recognizing phonemes of speech, which is, indeed, a part of communication. The score does not, however, tell audiologists how well that person may be able to recognize those same phonemes in continuous discourse.

WORD IDENTIFICATION

Tests of lipreading ability that include filmed, videotaped, or live visual-only presentations of single words out of context as test items do not provide information on the ability of a person who is hearing impaired to recognize words in continuous discourse, nor on his or her ability to communicate in various social, business, or personal environments. However, the scores are still used by some audiologists to predict abilities in social communication, even though this type of test provides information only on the person's visual recognition of words. This type of test can, however, provide important bits of diagnostic information regarding auditory and visual speech discrimination. If the mode of presentation includes both the auditory and visual portions of the stimulus items, then information would be obtained regarding that person's ability to utilize the additive complement of visual clues on audition, and vice versa.

Although the components discussed can provide important information regarding the ability of an individual who is hearing impaired to utilize audition and vision in the recognition of phoneme and word elements, they do not provide information as to that person's ability to communicate in his or her most frequented environments.

SENTENCES AND PARAGRAPHS

The use of sentences and paragraphs as stimulus items for assessment of a person's ability to communicate in spite of hearing impairment has been recommended (Hirsch, 1952). However, the use of sentences still leaves the audiologist without important information regarding the client's ability to function communicatively in his or her communication environments. Assessment of a person's ability to receive and interpret at least the thought of sentences does, however, provide audiologists with information on that person's ability to receive and synthesize content while using the visual and auditory modalities. The use of paragraphs in analyzing a person's ability to use visual and auditory clues generally is compounded by such factors as memory and attentiveness, although those are also important in most communication environments.

Difficulties in administration of such test batteries, standardization of the tests, and client variables such as the person's emotional response to his or her hearing impairment and the testing environment, compounded by problems in scoring, result in problems in the use of paragraphs as measures for determination of improvement in communicative ability, particularly among older clients.

VISION VERSUS AUDITION

The visual-only mode of presentation of test batteries generally is not satisfactory. There are very few adults who are hearing impaired who do not possess at least some usable hearing no matter how severe their discrimination problem. Any formal assessment and treatment procedure should include the use of both audition and vision. Since clients also will seldom find themselves in situations where they will not be using both hearing and vision, any assessment of their ability to receive and interpret verbal information should emphasize the advantage of the bisensory mode of presentation. Among elderly persons who possess severe visual disorders, assessment and treatment obviously will involve the use of residual hearing as the primary sensory modality.

COMMUNICATION SCALES AND PROFILES

Scales of communicative function, including those that stress attitudes of people who are hearing impaired and those that concentrate on situations or communication environments, seem to be taking audiologists in the right direction. This is particularly true when attempting to assess the communicative behaviors and needs of the elderly client. The majority of the scales and profiles appear to be based on the important fact that the audiologist is dealing with adult clients, who have communication needs and priorities that are unique to them. Even though many persons may benefit from enhanced visual and/or auditory skills and awareness, they also desire that the efforts involved have meaning for them, and that the treatment have relevance to their specific communication needs.

Assessment and treatment based on the feelings, attitudes, and priority communication environments of adult clients will surely enhance the individual effectiveness of aural rehabilitative services provided by audiologists. These procedures have brought audiologists a long way from the days of the filmed tests of lipreading.

VALIDITY

Scales of communication function face similar questions in regard to validity as have tests of lipreading and other procedures. Test-retest reliability among the various scales and profiles

generally has been found to be acceptable. A major question that inevitably is asked, however, is do we know whether clients are answering the questions or responding to the statements honestly? In that regard, the reliability of the client is in question. Hopefully, a wise audiologist will be able, in the majority of cases, to "see through" the client who appears to be attempting to fool the audiologist or, perhaps more regrettably, fool him- or herself. Occasionally, a client provides answers that he or she feels the provider of services *wants* to hear. Clients do not like to see audiologists fail either. It is up to the audiologist to assure clients that their answers or responses are to be honest ones. How else can real progress, or lack of it, be noted? And, how can adjustments in the treatment program be made, if they are needed?

The question of validity is indeed, for lack of a better phrase, a valid one. However, Alpiner (1978b) responded to that question well when he stated that, "Their (the scales or profiles) successful use depends on the audiologists' judgment, not on tests of validity" (p. 32).

SUMMARY

To recommend an approach for assessment of not only the handicap that adult clients are experiencing as a result of an auditory disorder, but also the gains or lack of them as a result of aural rehabilitation treatment is difficult. The audiologist, however, must be responsible for determining which aspects of communicative function are assessed, treated, and again assessed as to the value of the treatment procedures used.

A comprehensive approach to assessment is recommended. This includes:

1. Observing the results of the case history relative to the possible causes of the auditory deficit, its duration, and the current social and environmental status of the elderly client.
2. Utilizing the audiometric results, particularly the type, degree, and configuration of the hearing loss, and importantly the results of speech discrimination assessment.

3. The results of a hearing aid evaluation and the possible benefits of amplification.

4. Assessment of the client's ability to utilize visual clues with minimal auditory clues. This assessment may include (1) monosyllabic words, (2) sentences, and (3) everyday conversation. Sentence lists recommended are the Denver Quick Test of Lipreading, the CID Everyday Sentences, or the UNC Sentence Test of Speechreading.

5. Assessment of the impact of the hearing impairment by the use of one of the scales of communication function. Those recommended are (1) the Denver Scale of Communication Function, (2) the Denver Scale of Communication Function for Senior Citizens, (3) the Profile Questionnaires (Home and Social), or (4) the UNC Communication Appraisal and Priorities.

6. Plans for aural rehabilitation treatment and posttreatment assessment should be based only on the clients' communicative needs and priorities. Only then will the audiologist be adding validity to his or her treatment goals. "Cookbook" approaches usually do nothing more than consume valuable time.

REFERENCES

Alpiner, J. G. (1978a). *Handbook of adult rehabilitative audiology* (p. 36). Baltimore, MD: Williams & Wilkins.

Alpiner, J. G. (1978b). Evaluation of communication function. In J. G. Alpiner (Ed.), *Handbook of adult rehabilitative audiology* (pp. 236–252). Baltimore, MD: Williams & Wilkins.

Alpiner, J. G., Chevrette, W., Glascoe, G., Metz, M., & Olsen, B. (1978). The Denver Scale of Communication Function. In J. G. Alpiner (Ed.), *Adult rehabilitative audiology* (pp. 36, 53–56). Baltimore, MD: Williams & Wilkins.

Binnie, C. A. (1973). Bi-sensory articulation functions for normal hearing and sensorineural hearing loss patients. *Journal of the Academy of Rehabilitative Audiology, 6,* 43–53.

Binnie, C. A., Montgomery, A. A., & Jackson, P. L. (1974). Auditory and visual contributions to the perception of selected English consonants. *Journal of Speech and Hearing Research, 17,* 619–630.

Black, J. W., O'Reilly, P. P., & Peck, L. (1963). Self-administered training in lipreading. *Journal of Speech and Hearing Disorders, 28,* 183–186.

Davis, H., & Silverman, S. R. (1970). *Hearing and deafness.* New York: Holt, Rinehart and Winston.

Demorest, M. E., & Erdman, S. A. (1987). Development of the profile for the hearing impaired. *Journal of Speech and Hearing Disorders, 52,* 129–143.

DiCarlo, L. M., & Kataja, R. (1951). An analysis of the Utley lipreading test. *Journal of Speech and Hearing Disorders, 16,* 226–240.

Donnelly, K. G., & Marshall, W. J. (1967). Development of a multiple-choice test of lipreading. *Journal of Speech and Hearing Research, 10,* 565–569.

Duffy, J. K. (1967). Audio-visual speech audiometry and a new audio and audio-visual speech perception index. *Maico Audiological Series, 5,* 9.

Erber, N. P. (1971). Auditory and audiovisual reception of words in low-frequency noise by children with normal hearing and by children with impaired hearing. *Journal of Speech and Hearing Research, 14,* 496–512.

Erber, N. P. (1972a). Speech-envelope cues as an acoustic aid to lipreading for profoundly deaf children. *Journal of the Acoustical Society of America, 51,* 1224–1227.

Erber, N. P. (1972b). Auditory, visual, and auditory-visual recognition of consonants by children with normal and impaired hearing. *Journal of Speech and Hearing Research, 15,* 413–422.

Erber, N. P. (1975). Auditory-visual perception of speech. *Journal of Speech and Hearing Disorders, 40,* 481–492.

Ewertsen, H. W., Nielsen, B. H., & Nielsen, S. S. (1970). Audiovisual speech perception. *Acta Otolaryngologica* (Suppl.), *26,* 229–230.

Fisher, C. (1968). Confusions among visually perceived consonants. *Journal of Speech and Hearing Research, 11,* 796–804.

Giolas, T. G., Owens, E., Lamb, S. H., & Schubert, E. E. (1979). Hearing performance inventory. *Journal of Speech and Hearing Disorders, 44,* 169–195.

High, W. S., Fairbanks, G., & Glorig, A. (1964). Scale for self-assessment of hearing handicap. *Journal of Speech and Hearing Disorders, 29,* 215–230.

Hirsh, I. J. (1952). *The measurement of hearing.* New York: McGraw-Hill.

Hull, R. H., & Alpiner, J. G. (1976). The effect of syntactic word variations on the predictability of sentence content in speechreading. *Journal of the Academy of Rehabilitative Audiology, 9,* 42–56.

Hull, R. H. (1982). *Rehabilitative audiology.* New York: Grune & Stratton.

Hutton, C. (1959). Combining auditory and visual stimuli in aural rehabilitation. *Volta Review, 6,* 316–319.

Hutton, C., Curry, E. T., & Armstrong, M. B. (1959). Semidiagnostic test materials for aural rehabilitation. *Journal of Speech and Hearing Disorders, 24,* 318–329.

Jones, L. V., & Wepman, J. M. (1966). *A spoken word count.* Chicago: Language Research Associates.

Koniditsiotis, C. Y. (1971). The use of hearing tests to provide information about the extent to which an individual's hearing loss handicaps him. *Maico Audiological Series, 9,* 10.

Lashley, K. S. (1961). The problem of serial order in behavior. In S. Saporta (Ed.), *Psycholinguistics* (pp. 180–198). New York: Holt, Rinehart and Winston.

Lowell, E. L. (1969). Rehabilitation of auditory disorders. *Human communication and its disorders — An overview* (Monograph No. 10). Bethesda, MD: National Advisory Neurological Diseases and Stroke Council, National Institutes of Health.

Mason, M. K. (1943). A cinematic technique for testing visual speech comprehension. *Journal of Speech Disorders, 8,* 271–278.

Miller, G. A., & Nicely, P. E. (1955). An analysis of perceptual confusions among some English consonants. *Journal of Acoustical Society of America, 27,* 338–352.

Morkovin, B. S. (1948). *Life-situation speechreading through the cooperation of senses (movie).* Los Angeles: University of Southern California.

Neely, K. K. (1956). Effect of visual factors on the intelligibility of speech. *Journal of the Acoustical Society of America, 28,* 1275–1277.

Noble, W. G. (1978). *Assessment of impaired hearing: A critique and a new method.* New York: Academic Press.

Noble, W. G., & Atherley, G. R. C. (1970). The hearing measure scale: A questionnaire for the assessment of auditory disability. *Journal of Audiology Research, 10,* 229–250. [Manual and scale available from Dr. W. Noble, Department of Psychology, University of New England, Anmidale, N.S.W., 2351, Australia.]

O'Neill, J. J. (1954). Contributions of the visual components of oral symbols to speech communication. *Journal of Speech and Hearing Disorders, 19,* 429–439.

O'Neill, J. J., & Stephens, M. C. (1959). Relationships among three filmed lipreading tests. *Journal of Speech and Hearing Research, 2,* 61–65.

Pestone, M. J. (1962). Selection of items for a speech-reading test by means of scalogram analysis. *Journal of Speech and Hearing Disorders, 27,* 71–75.

Prall, J. (1957). Lipreading and hearing aids combine for better comprehension. *Volta Review, 59,* 64–65.

Sanders, D. (1975). Hearing aid orientation and counseling. In M. C. Pollack (Ed.), *Amplification for the hearing impaired* (pp. 327–352). New York: Grune & Stratton.

Simmons, A. A. (1959). Factors related to lipreading. *Journal of Speech and Hearing Research, 2,* 340–352.

Sumby, W. H. & Pollack, I. (1954). Visual contributions to speech intelligibility in noise. *Journal of Acoustical Society of America, 26,* 212–215.

Taaffee, G., & Wong, W. (1957). Study of variables in lipreading stimulus material. *John Tracy Clinic Research Papers III.* Los Angeles: The John Tracy Clinic.

Templin, M. C. (1957). *Certain language skills in children.* Minneapolis: University of Minnesota Press.

Utley, J. (1946). Factors involved in the teaching and testing of lipreading ability through the use of motion pictures. *Volta Review, 38,* 657–659.

Van Uden, A. A. (1960). A sound-perceptive method. In A. W. G. Ewing (Ed.), *The modern educational treatment of deafness* (pp. 3–19). Washington, DC: Volta-Bureau.

Ventry, I. M., & Weinstein, B. E. (1982). The hearing inventory for the elderly: A new tool. *Ear and Hearing, 3,* 128.

Weinstein, B. E., & Ventry, I. M. (1983). Audiometric correlates of the hearing handicap inventory for the elderly. *Journal of Speech and Hearing Disorders, 48,* 379–384.

Zarnoch, J. M., & Alpiner, J. G. (1977). *The Denver scale of communication function for senior citizens living in retirement centers.* Unpublished study, University of Denver, Denver, CO.

■ APPENDIXES ■

Materials and Scales for Assessment of Communicative Abilities

The following appendixes present an array of assessment tools and scales of handicap that are appropriate for use with adults and elderly clients who are hearing impaired. All are designed for use with either adult or elderly clients, except for "The Communication Scale" by Kaplan, Bally, and Brandt (1990), which is designed also for younger adults, including high school and college-age students. However, it is also designed to be utilized with adults beyond college age.

The tools and scales in the appendixes include the following:

A. CID Everyday Sentences;
B. The Denver Scale Quick Test (Alpiner, 1978);
C. The UNC Sentence Test of Speechreading Ability (Hull, 1976);
D. Hearing-Handicap Scale (High, Fairbanks, & Glorig, 1964);
E. The Denver Scale of Communication Function (Alpiner, Glascoe, Metz, & Olsen, 1971);
F. Test of Actual Performance (Konditsiotis, 1971);
G. The Hearing Measurement Scale (Noble & Atherley, 1970);
H. Profile Questionnaire for Rating Communicative Performance in a Home and Social Environment (Sanders, 1975);
I. The Denver Scale of Communication Function for Senior Citizens Living in Retirement Centers (Zarnoch & Alpiner, 1978);
J. University of Northern Colorado Communication Appraisal and Priorities (Hull, 1975);
K. The Hearing Handicap Inventory for the Elderly (Ventry & Weinstein, 1982);
L. The Communication Profile for the Hearing Impaired (Demorest & Erdman, 1987); and
M. Communication Skill Scale (Kaplan, Bally, & Brandt, 1990).

APPENDIX A

CID Everyday Sentences

LIST A

1. Walking's my favorite exercise.
2. Here's a nice quiet place to rest.
3. Our janitor sweeps the floors every night.
4. It would be much easier if everyone would help.
5. Good morning.
6. Open your window before you go to bed!
7. Do you think that she should stay out so late?
8. How do you feel about changing the time when we begin work?
9. Here we go.
10. Move out of the way!

LIST B

1. The water's too cold for swimming.
2. Why sould I get up so early in the morning?
3. Here are your shoes.
4. It's raining.
5. Where are you going?
6. Come here when I call you!
7. Don't try to get out of it this time!
8. Should we let little children go to the movies by themselves?
9. There isn't enough paint to finish the room.
10. Do you want an egg for breakfast?

LIST C

1. Everybody should brush his teeth after meals.
2. Everything's all right.
3. Don't use up all the paper when you write your letter.
4. That's right.
5. People ought to see a doctor once a year.
6. Those windows are so dirty I can't see anything outside.
7. Pass the bread and butter please.
8. Don't forget to pay your bill before the first of the month.
9. Don't let the dog out of the house.
10. There's a good ball game this afternoon.

Reproduced with permission by CHABA (National Research Council Committee on Hearing and Bio-Acoustics). (1951). CHABA No. 5. The testing of hearing in the Armed Services. *Technical Report to the Office of Naval Research*, Bethesda, MD, from the Central Institute for the Deaf under contract No. 1151 (10) NR 140-069.

LIST D

1. It's time to go.
2. If you don't want these old magazines, throw them out.
3. Do you want to wash up?
4. It's a real dark night so watch your driving.
5. I'll carry the package for you.
6. Did you forget to shut off the water?
7. Fishing in a mountain stream is my idea of a good time.
8. Fathers spend more time with their children than they used to.
9. Be careful not to break your glasses.
10. I'm sorry.

LIST E

1. You can catch the bus across the street.
2. Call her on the phone and tell her the news.
3. I'll catch up with you later.
4. I'll think it over.
5. I don't want to go to the movies tonight.
6. If your tooth hurts that much you ought to see a dentist.
7. Put the cookie back in the box!
8. Stop fooling around!
9. Time's up.
10. How do you spell your name?

LIST F

1. Music always cheers me up.
2. My brother's in town for a short while on business.
3. We live a few miles from the main road.
4. This suit needs to go to the cleaners.
5. They ate enough green apples to make them sick for a week.
6. Where have you been all this time?
7. Have you been working hard lately?
8. There's not enough room in the kitchen for a new table.
9. Where is he?
10. Look out!

LIST G

1. I'll see you right after lunch.
2. See you later.
3. White shoes are awful to keep clean.
4. Stand there and don't move until I tell you.
5. There's a big piece of cake left over from dinner.
6. Wait for me at the corner in front of the drugstore.
7. It's no trouble at all.
8. Hurry up!
9. The morning paper didn't say anything about rain this afternoon or tonight.
10. The phone call's for you.

LIST H

1. Believe me!
2. Let's get a cup of coffee.
3. Let's get out of here before it's too late.
4. I hate driving at night.
5. There was water in the cellar after that heavy rain yesterday.
6. She'll only be a few minutes.
7. How do you know?
8. Children like candy.
9. If we don't get rain soon, we'll have no grass.
10. They're not listed in the new phone book.

LIST I

1. Where can I find a place to work?
2. I like those big red apples we always get in the fall.
3. You'll get fat eating candy.
4. The show's over.
5. Why don't they paint their walls some other color?
6. What's new?
7. What are you hiding under your coat?
8. How come I should always be the one to go first?
9. I'll take sugar and cream in my coffee.
10. Wait just a minute!

LIST J

1. Breakfast is ready.
2. I don't know what's wrong with the car, but it won't start.
3. It sure takes a sharp knife to cut this meat.
4. I haven't read a newspaper since we bought a television set.
5. Weeds are spoiling the yard.
6. Call me a little later!
7. Do you have change for a $5 bill?
8. How are you?
9. I'd like some ice cream with my pie.
10. I don't think I'll have any dessert.

APPENDIX B

The Denver Scale Quick Test

REHABILITATIVE AUDIOLOGY (ADULTS)

1. Good morning.
2. How old are you?
3. I live in (state of residence).
4. I only have one dollar.
5. There is somebody at the door.
6. It that all?
7. Where are you going?
8. Let's have a coffee break.
9. Park your car in the lot.
10. What is your address?
11. May I help you?
12. I feel fine.
13. It is time for dinner.
14. Turn right at the corner.
15. Are you ready to order?
16. Is this charge or cash?
17. What time is it?
18. I have a headache.
19. How about going out tonight?
20. Please lend me 50 cents.

Reproduced with permission by Alpiner, J. G. Evaluation of communication function. In J. G. Alpiner (Ed.), *Handbook of adult rehabilitative audiology*. Baltimore, MD: Williams and Wilkins, 1978, p. 36.

■ APPENDIX C ■

The UNC Sentence Test of Speechreading Ability

LIST 1

1. It was such a great day for hiking.
2. Have you read the sports page this morning?
3. The cost of living will make you poor.
4. He serves excellent food in all his restaurants.
5. What kind of a car do you drive?
6. The weather for the game was almost perfect.
7. Why was the picnic called off this time?
8. I like white houses with large covered porches.
9. Did the white-and-black cat have kittens?
10. Slow music always makes me feel like sleeping.
11. Why did you go there for your vacation?
12. How much snow did we have last night?

LIST 2

1. Will you come with me to see him?
2. Snow always looks pretty on the mountain side.
3. Is your whole family getting together for Thanksgiving?
4. Do you have an umbrella with you today?
5. Fathers should spend more time with their children.
6. Are you going grocery shopping while in town?
7. The wind is blowing from the northeast again.
8. It is time to go back home now.
9. Did you forget to shut off the water?
10. (Name) has been considered this state's favorite sport.
11. Where do you usually work during the winter?
12. It is a good day for playing golf.

Hull, R. H. Unpublished materials. University of Northern Colorado, 1976.

LIST 3

1. What time was it when you arrived?
2. Have you any brothers or sisters at home?
3. It has rained for the past 3 days.
4. Do you have a dog or a cat?
5. What does the judge say about him now?
6. A soft rain makes grass grow in spring.
7. Did you buy a new car this year?
8. You should brush your teeth three times daily.
9. Children go to school at around age 6.
10. He let the dog out of the house.
11. Hockey is often a rough and tumble sport.
12. Would you like to go to the show?

■ APPENDIX D ■

Hearing-Handicap Scale

FORM A

1. If you are 6 to 12 feet from the loudspeaker of a radio do you understand speech well?
2. Can you carry on a telephone conversation without difficulty?
3. If you are 6 to 12 feet from a television set, do you understand most of what is said?
4. Can you carry on a conversation with one other person when you are on a noisy street corner?
5. Do you hear all right when you are in a street car, airplane, bus, or train?
6. If there are noises from other voices, typewriters, traffic, music, etc., can you understand when someone speaks to you?
7. Can you understand a person when you are seated beside him and cannot see his face?
8. Can you understand if someone speaks to you while you are chewing crisp foods, such as potato chips or celery?
9. Can you carry on a conversation with one other person when you are in a noisy place, such as a restaurant or at a party?
10. Can you understand if someone speaks to you in a whisper and you can't see his or her face?
11. When you talk with a bus driver, waiter, ticket salesman, etc., can you understand all right?
12. Can you carry on a conversation if you are seated across the room from someone who speaks in a normal tone of voice?
13. Can you understand women when they talk?
14. Can you carry on a conversation with one other person when you are out of doors and it is reasonably quiet?
15. When you are in a meeting or at a large dinner table, would you know the speaker was talking if you could not see his lips moving?
16. Can you follow the conversation when you are at a large dinner table or in a meeting with a small group?
17. If you are seated under the balcony of a theater or auditorium, can you hear well enough to follow what is going on?
18. When you are in a large formal gathering (a church, lodge, lecture hall, etc.) can you hear what is said when the speaker *does not* use a microphone?
19. Can you hear the telephone ring when you are in the room where it is located?
20. Can you hear warning signals, such as automobile horns, railway crossing bells, or emergency vehicle sirens?

Reproduced with permission from High, E. S., Fairbanks, G., & Glorig, A. (1964). Scale for Self-Assessment of Hearing Handicap. *Journal of Speech and Hearing Disorders, 29,* 215–230.

FORM B

1. When you are listening to the radio or watching television, can you hear adequately when the volume is comfortable for most other people?
2. Can you carry on a conversation with one other person when you are riding in an automobile with the windows *closed*?
3. Can you carry on a conversation with one other person when you are riding in an automobile with the window *open*?
4. Can you carry on a conversation with one other person if there is a radio or television in the same room playing at normal loudness?
5. Can you hear when someone calls to you from another room?
6. Can you understand when someone speaks to you from another room?
7. When you buy something in a store, do you easily understand the clerk?
8. Can you carry on a conversation with someone who does not speak as loudly as most people?
9. Can you tell if a person is talking when you are seated beside him and cannot see his face?
10. When you ask someone for directions, do you understand what he or she says?
11. If you are within 3 or 4 feet of a person who speaks in a normal tone of voice (assume you are facing one another), can you hear everything he or she says?
12. Do you recognize the voices of speakers when you don't see them?
13. When you are introduced to someone, can you understand the name the first time it is spoken?
14. Can you hear adequately when you are conversing with more than one person?
15. If you are in an audience, such as in a church or theater and you are seated near the *front*, can you understand most of what is said?
16. Can you carry on everyday conversations with members of your family without difficulty?
17. If you are in an audience, such as in a church or theater and you are seated near the *rear*, can you understand most of what is said?
18. When you are in a large formal gathering (a church, lodge, lecture hall, etc.) can you hear what is said when the speaker *does* use a microphone?
19. Can you hear the telephone ring when you are in the next room?
20. Can you hear night sounds, such as distant trains, bells, dogs barking, trucks passing, and so forth?

■ APPENDIX E ■

The Denver Scale of Communication Function

Preservice _____   Postservice _____

Date _____   Case No. _____

Name _____   Age _____   Sex _____

Address _____

| (City) | (State) | (Zip) |

Lives Alone _____   In Apartment _____   Retired _____
(if no, specify)

Occupation _____

Audiogram (Examination Date _____   Agency _____)

Pure Tone:

	250	500	1000	2000	4000	8000	Hz
RE	___	___	___	___	___	___	
LE	___	___	___	___	___	___	dB (re:ANSI)

Speech:

SRT   *Discrimination Score (%)*
                             Quiet   Noise (S/N = _____)

RE _____ dB   RE _____

LE _____ dB   LE _____

Hearing Aid Information:

Aided _____   For How Long _____   Aid Type _____

Satisfaction _____

                                        EXAMINER _____

Reproduced with permission by Alpiner, J. G., Chevrette, W., Glascoe, G., Metz, M., & Olsen, B. Unpublished materials. University of Denver, 1971.

The following questionnaire was designed to evaluate your communication ability as you view it. You are asked to judge or scale each statement in the following manner.

If you judge the statement to be *very closely related* to either extreme, please place your check mark as follows:

Agree __X__ _____ _____ _____ _____ _____ _____ Disagree

or

Agree _____ _____ _____ _____ _____ _____ __X__ Disagree

If you judge the statement to be *closely related* to either end of the scale, please mark as follows:

Agree _____ __X__ _____ _____ _____ _____ _____ Disagree

or

Agree _____ _____ _____ _____ _____ __X__ _____ Disagree

If you judge the statement to be only slightly related to either end of the scale, please mark as follows:

Agree _____ _____ __X__ _____ _____ _____ _____ Disagree

or

Agree _____ _____ _____ _____ __X__ _____ _____ Disagree

If you consider the statement to be irrelevant or unassociated to your communication situation, please mark as follows:

Agree _____ _____ _____ __X__ _____ _____ _____ Disagree

PLEASE NOTE: Check a scale for every statement.
Put only one checkmark on each scale.
Make a separate judgment for each statement.
ALSO: You may comment on each statement in the space provided.

1. The members of my family are annoyed with my loss of hearing.

    Agree _____ _____ _____ _____ _____ _____ _____ Disagree
    Comments: _____

2. The members of my family sometimes leave me out of conversations or discussions.

    Agree _____ _____ _____ _____ _____ _____ _____ Disagree
    Comments: _____

3. Sometimes my family makes decisions for me because I have a hard time following discussions.

    Agree _____ _____ _____ _____ _____ _____ _____ Disagree
    Comments: _____

4. My family becomes annoyed when I ask them to repeat what was said because I did not hear them.

    Agree _____ _____ _____ _____ _____ _____ _____ Disagree
    Comments: _____

? what's "ongoing" =? outgoing

5. I am not an "ongoing" person because I have a hearing loss.

Agree _____ _____ _____ _____ _____ _____ _____ Disagree

Comments: _____

6. I now take less of an interest in many things as compared to when I did not have a hearing problem.

Agree _____ _____ _____ _____ _____ _____ _____ Disagree

Comments: _____

7. Other people do not realize how frustrated I get when I cannot hear or understand.

Agree _____ _____ _____ _____ _____ _____ _____ Disagree

Comments: _____

8. People sometimes avoid me because of my hearing loss.

Agree _____ _____ _____ _____ _____ _____ _____ Disagree

Comments: _____

9. I am not a calm person because of my hearing loss.

Agree _____ _____ _____ _____ _____ _____ _____ Disagree

Comments: _____

10. I tend to be negative about life in general because of my hearing loss.

Agree _____ _____ _____ _____ _____ _____ _____ Disagree

Comments: _____

11. I do not socialize as much as I did before I began to lose my hearing.

Agree _____ _____ _____ _____ _____ _____ _____ Disagree

Comments: _____

12. Since I have trouble hearing, I do not like to go places with friends.

Agree _____ _____ _____ _____ _____ _____ _____ Disagree

Comments: _____

13. Since I have trouble hearing, I hesitate to meet new people.

Agree _____ _____ _____ _____ _____ _____ _____ Disagree

Comments: _____

14. I do not enjoy my job as much as I did before I began to lose my hearing.

Agree _____ _____ _____ _____ _____ _____ _____ Disagree

Comments: _____

15. Other people do not understand what it is like to have a hearing loss.

Agree _____ _____ _____ _____ _____ _____ _____ Disagree

Comments: _____

16. Because I have difficulty understanding what is said to me, I sometimes answer questions wrong.

Agree _____ _____ _____ _____ _____ _____ _____ Disagree

Comments: _____

17. I do not feel relaxed in a communicative situation.

Agree _____ _____ _____ _____ _____ _____ _____ Disagree

Comments: _____

18. I do not feel comfortable in most communication situations.

Agree _____ _____ _____ _____ _____ _____ _____ Disagree

Comments: _____

19. Conversations in a noisy room prevent me from attempting to communicate with others.

Agree _____ _____ _____ _____ _____ _____ _____ Disagree

Comments: _____

20. I am not comfortable having to speak in a group situation.

Agree _____ _____ _____ _____ _____ _____ _____ Disagree

Comments: _____

21. In general, I do not find listening relaxing.

Agree _____ _____ _____ _____ _____ _____ _____ Disagree

Comments: _____

22. I feel threatened by many communication situations due to difficulty hearing.

Agree _____ _____ _____ _____ _____ _____ _____ Disagree

Comments: _____

23. I seldom watch other people's facial expressions when talking to them.

Agree _____ _____ _____ _____ _____ _____ _____ Disagree

Comments: _____

24. I hesitate to ask people to repeat if I do not understand them the first time they speak.

Agree _____ _____ _____ _____ _____ _____ _____ Disagree

Comments: _____

25. Because I have difficulty understanding what is said to me, I sometimes make comments that do not fit into the conversation.

Agree _____ _____ _____ _____ _____ _____ _____ Disagree

Comments: _____

Test of Actual Performance

How well does he or she:

	Poor	Adequate	Good	Excellent
1. Pay attention in the group? (daydreams, restlessness, changes the subject)	_____	_____	_____	_____
2. Communicate ideas verbally?	_____	_____	_____	_____
3. Use speech intelligibly?	_____	_____	_____	_____
4. Respond to others? (shares similar experiences, agrees, disagrees)	_____	_____	_____	_____
5. Hear speech when noise was going on around him/her? (like at parties)	_____	_____	_____	_____
6. Understand speech when not able to see the speaker?	_____	_____	_____	_____
7. Monitor the loudness of his or her own speech?	_____	_____	_____	_____

Reproduced with permission by Konditsiotis, C. Y. The use of hearing test to provide information about the extent to which an individual's hearing loss handicaps him. *Maico Audiological Library Series,* 1971, 9, 10.

The Hearing Measurement Scale

SECTION 1

SPEECH HEARING

1. Do you ever have difficulty hearing in the conversation when you're with one other person at home?
2. Do you ever have difficulty hearing in the conversation when you're with one other person outside?
3. Do you ever have difficulty in group conversation at home?
4. Do you ever have difficulty in group conversation outside?
5. Do you ever have difficulty hearing conversation at work?
5a. Is this due to your hearing, due to the noise, or a bit of both?
6. Do you ever have difficulty hearing the speaker at a public gathering?
7. Can you always hear what's being said in a TV program?
8. Can you always hear what's being said in TV news?
9. Can you always hear what's being said in a radio program?
10. Can you always hear what's being said in radio news?
11. Do you ever have difficulty hearing what's said in a film at the cinema?

Revised with permission. Noble, W. G., & Atherley, G. R. C. The hearing measurement scale: A questionnaire for assessment of auditory disability. *Journal of Audiological Research*, 1970, *10*, 229–250.

SECTION 2

ACUITY FOR NONSPEECH SOUND

1. Do you have any pets at home? (Type _____) Can you hear it when it barks, mews, etc.?
2. Can you hear it when someone rings the doorbell or knocks on the door?
3. Can you hear a motor horn in the street when you're outside?
4. Can you hear the sound of footsteps outside when you're inside?
5. Can you hear the sound of the door opening when you're inside that room?
6. Can you hear the clock ticking in the room?
7. Can you hear the tap running when you turn it on?
8. Can you hear water boiling in a pan when you're in the kitchen?

SECTION 3

LOCALIZATION

1. When you hear the sound of people talking and they're in another room would you be able to tell from where this sound was coming?
2. If you're with a group of people and someone you can't see starts to speak would you be able to tell where that person was sitting?
3. If you hear a motor horn or a bell can you always tell in which direction it's sounding?
4. Do you ever turn your head the wrong way when someone calls to you?
5. Can you usually tell, from the sound, how far away a person is when he calls to you?
6. Have you ever noticed outside that a car you thought, by its sound, was far away turned out to be much closer in fact?
7. Outside, do you always move out of the way of something coming up from behind, for instance a car, a trolley, or someone walking faster?

SECTION 4

REACTION TO HANDICAP

1. Do you think that you are more irritable than other people or less so?
2. Do you ever give the wrong answer to someone because you've misheard them?
3. When you do this, do you treat it lightly or do you get upset?
4. How does the other person react? Does he get irritated or make little of it?
5. Do you think people are tolerant in this way or do they make fun of you?
6. Do you ever get bothered or upset if you are unable to follow a conversation?
7. Do you ever get the feeling of being cut off from things because of difficulty in hearing?
7a. Does this feeling upset you at all?

SECTION 5

SPEECH DISTORTION

1. Do you find that people fail to speak clearly?
2. What about speakers on TV or radio? Do they fail to speak clearly?
3. Do you ever have difficulty, in everyday conversation, understanding what someone is saying even though you can hear what's being said?

SECTION 6

TINNITUS

1. Do you ever get a noise in your ears or in your head?
2a. to 2e. A series of items on the nature and incidence of tinnitus.
3. Does it ever stop you from sleeping?
4. Does it upset you?

SECTION 7

PERSONAL OPINION OF HEARING LOSS

1. Do you think your hearing is normal?
2. Do you think any difficulty with your hearing is particularly serious?
3. Does any difficulty with your hearing restrict your social or personal life?
4a. to 4f. A series of items on Temporary Threshold Shift, specifically for those with chronic acoustic trauma, on the relative importance of eyesight over hearing and on other difficult hearing situations not mentioned in the interview.

Profile Questionnaire for Rating Communicative Performance in a Home and Social Environment

HOME ENVIRONMENT

1. (a) In my living room, when I can see the speaker's face, I have

+2	+1	−1	−2
little or no difficulty in understanding.	some difficulty (but not a lot in understanding.	a fair amount of difficulty (quite a lot) in understanding.	great difficulty in understanding.

   (b) This happens

1	2	3
seldom.	often.	very often.

Reproduced with permission by Sanders, D. A. Hearing aid orientation and counseling, in M. C. Pollack (Ed.), *Amplification for the hearing impaired.* New York: Grune and Stratton, 1975, pp. 363–372.

2. (a) If I am talking with a person in my living room or family room while the television, radio, or record player is on, I have

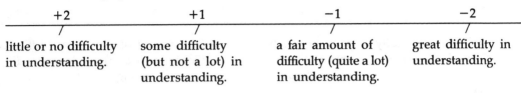

+2	+1	−1	−2
little or no difficulty in understanding.	some difficulty (but not a lot) in understanding.	a fair amount of difficulty (quite a lot) in understanding.	great difficulty in understanding.

(b) This happens

1	2	3
seldom.	often.	very often.

3. (a) In a quiet room in my house, if I cannot see the speaker's face I have

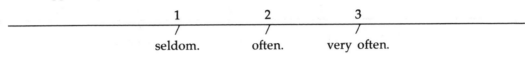

+2	+1	−1	−2
little or no difficulty in understanding.	some difficulty (but not a lot) in understanding.	a fair amount of difficulty (quite a lot) in understanding.	great difficulty in understanding.

(b) This happens

1	2	3
seldom.	often.	very often.

4. (a) If someone in my home speaks to me from another room on the same floor, I experience

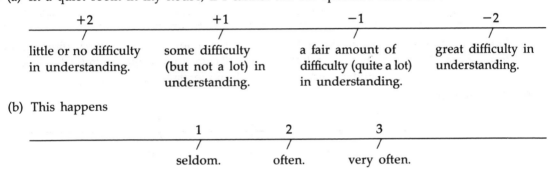

+2	+1	−1	−2
little or no difficulty in understanding.	some difficulty (but not a lot) in understanding.	a fair amount of difficulty (quite a lot) in understanding.	great difficulty in understanding.

(b) This happens

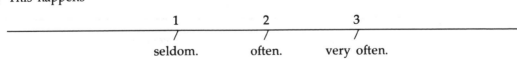

1	2	3
seldom.	often.	very often.

5. (a) If someone calls me from upstairs when I am downstairs, or from the window when I am in the garden, I will experience

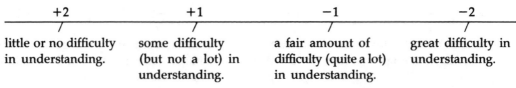

+2	+1	−1	−2
little or no difficulty in understanding.	some difficulty (but not a lot) in understanding.	a fair amount of difficulty (quite a lot) in understanding.	great difficulty in understanding.

(b) This happens

1	2	3
seldom.	often.	very often.

6. (a) Understanding people at the dinner table gives me

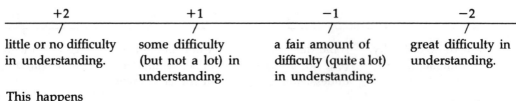

+2	+1	−1	−2
little or no difficulty in understanding.	some difficulty (but not a lot) in understanding.	a fair amount of difficulty (quite a lot) in understanding.	great difficulty in understanding.

(b) This happens

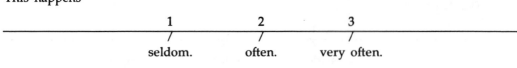

1	2	3
seldom.	often.	very often.

7. (a) When I sit talking with friends in a quiet room I have

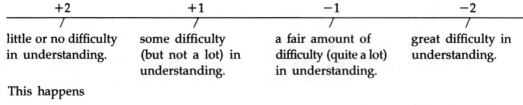

+2	+1	−1	−2
little or no difficulty in understanding.	some difficulty (but not a lot) in understanding.	a fair amount of difficulty (quite a lot) in understanding.	great difficulty in understanding.

(b) This happens

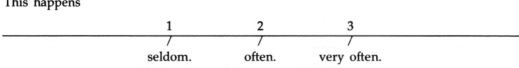

1	2	3
seldom.	often.	very often.

8. (a) Listening to the radio, record player, or watching TV gives me

+2	+1	−1	−2
little or no difficulty in understanding.	some difficulty (but not a lot) in understanding.	a fair amount of difficulty (quite a lot) in understanding.	great difficulty in understanding.

(b) This happens

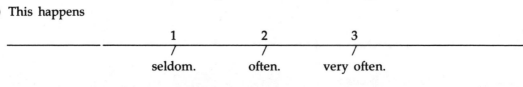

1	2	3
seldom.	often.	very often.

9. (a) When I use the phone at home, I have

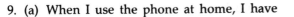

+2	+1	−1	−2
little or no difficulty in understanding.	some difficulty (but not a lot) in understanding.	a fair amount of difficulty (quite a lot) in understanding.	great difficulty in understanding.

(b) This happens

1	2	3
seldom.	often.	very often.

SOCIAL ENVIRONMENT

1. (a) If we are entertaining a group of friends, understanding someone against the background of other talking gives me

+2	+1	−1	−2
little or no difficulty.	some difficulty (but not a lot).	a fair amount of difficulty (quite a lot).	great difficulty.

(b) This happens

1	2	3
seldom.	often.	very often.

2. (a) If we are playing cards, understanding my partner gives me

+2	+1	−1	−2
little or no difficulty.	some difficulty (but not a lot).	a fair amount of difficulty (quite a lot).	great difficulty.

(b) This happens

1	2	3
seldom.	often.	very often.

3. (a) When I am at the theater or the movies, I have

+2	+1	−1	−2
little or no difficulty in understanding.	some difficulty (but not a lot) in understanding.	a fair amount of difficulty (quite a lot) in understanding.	great difficulty in understanding.

(b) This happens

1	2	3
seldom.	often.	very often.

4. (a) In church, when the minister gives the sermon, I have

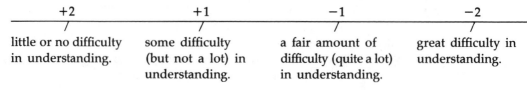

+2	+1	−1	−2
little or no difficulty in understanding.	some difficulty (but not a lot) in understanding.	a fair amount of difficulty (quite a lot) in understanding.	great difficulty in understanding.

(b) This happens

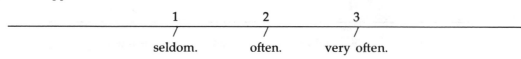

1	2	3
seldom.	often.	very often.

5. (a) When you eat out, following the conversation I have

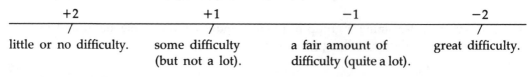

+2	+1	−1	−2
little or no difficulty.	some difficulty (but not a lot).	a fair amount of difficulty (quite a lot).	great difficulty.

(b) This happens

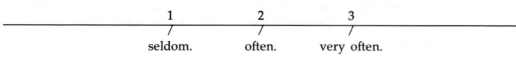

1	2	3
seldom.	often.	very often.

6. (a) In the car, I find that understanding what people are saying gives me

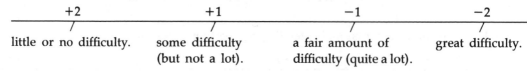

+2	+1	−1	−2
little or no difficulty.	some difficulty (but not a lot).	a fair amount of difficulty (quite a lot).	great difficulty.

(b) This happens

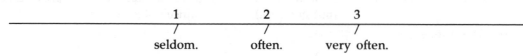

1	2	3
seldom.	often.	very often.

7. (a) When I am outside talking with someone I have

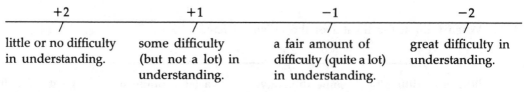

+2	+1	−1	−2
little or no difficulty in understanding.	some difficulty (but not a lot) in understanding.	a fair amount of difficulty (quite a lot) in understanding.	great difficulty in understanding.

(b) This happens

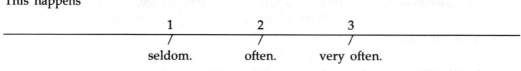

1	2	3
seldom.	often.	very often.

■ APPENDIX I ■

The Denver Scale of Communication Function for Senior Citizens Living in Retirement Centers

Name _____   Date of Pretest _____

Address _____   Date of Post-test _____

Age _____   Examiner _____

Sex _____

1. Do you have trouble communicating with your family because of your hearing problem?

   Yes _____ No _____

   Probe Effect I

   a. Does your family make decisions for you because of your hearing problem?
      Yes _____ No _____
   b. Does your family leave you out of discussions because of your hearing problem?
      Yes _____ No _____
   c. Does your family get angry or annoyed with you because of your hearing problem?
      Yes _____ No _____

Reproduced with permission by Zarnoch, J. M., & Alpiner, J. G. The Denver scale of communication function for senior citizens living in retirement centers, in J. G. Alpiner (Ed.), *Handbook of adult rehabilitative audiology.* Baltimore: Williams and Wilkins, 1978, pp. 166–168.

Exploration Effect

a. Do you have a family?   Yes _____   No _____
b. How often does your family visit you? _____
c. How far away does your family live? _____   In a city _____   Other _____
d. How often do you visit your family? _____

2. Do you get upset when you cannot hear or understand what is being said?
   Yes _____   No _____

Probe Effect I (to be used only if person responds yes)

a. Do your friends know you get upset?   Yes _____   No _____
b. Does your family know you get upset?   Yes _____   No _____
c. Does the staff know you get upset?   Yes _____   No _____

Probe Effect II (to be used only if person responds no)

a. Do your friends realize you are not upset?   Yes _____   No _____
b. Does your family realize you are not upset?   Yes _____   No _____
c. Does the staff realize you are not upset?   Yes _____   No _____

Exploration Effect (to be used only if person responds yes)

a. How does your behavior change when you become upset? _____

3. Do you think your family, your friends, and the staff understand what it is like to
   have a hearing problem?   Yes _____   No _____

Probe Effect

a. Do they avoid you because of your hearing problem?   Yes _____   No _____
b. Do they leave you out of discussions?   Yes _____   No _____
c. Do they hesitate to ask you to socialize with them?   Yes _____   No _____

Exploration Effect

a. Family   Yes _____   No _____
b. Friends   Yes _____   No _____
c. Staff   Yes _____   No _____

4. Do you avoid communicating with other people because of your hearing problem?
   Yes _____   No _____

Probe Effect

a. Do you communicate with people during meal times?   Yes _____   No _____
b. Do you communicate with your roommate(s)?   Yes _____   No _____
c. Do you communicate during the social activities in the home?   Yes _____   No _____

d. Do you communicate with visiting family or friends?   Yes _____   No _____

e. Do you communicate with the staff?   Yes _____   No _____

Exploration Effect

a. Is your roommate capable of communication?   Yes _____   No _____

b. What are the social activities of the home? _____

c. Which ones do you attend? _____

5. Do you feel that you are a relaxed person?   Yes _____   No _____

Probe Effect

a. Do you think you are an irritable person because of your hearing problem?
   Yes _____   No _____

b. Do you think you are an irritable person because of your age?
   Yes _____   No _____

c. Do you think you are an irritable person because you live in this home?
   Yes _____   No _____

Exploration Effect

a. Do you have to live in this home?   Yes _____   No _____

6. Do you feel relaxed in group communication situations?   Yes _____   No _____

Probe Effect

a. Do you get nervous when you have to ask people to repeat what they have said if you
   have not understood them?   Yes _____   No _____

b. Do you feel nervous if you have to tell a person that you have a hearing problem?
   Yes _____   No _____

Exploration Effect

a. Do you watch facial expressions?   Yes _____   No _____

b. Do you watch gestures?   Yes _____   No _____

c. Do you think you are a good listener?   Yes _____   No _____

d. Do you have a hearing aid?   Yes _____   No _____

e. Do you wear your aid?   Yes _____   No _____

7. Do you think you need help in overcoming your hearing problem? Yes _____   No _____

Probe Effect

a. If lipreading training was available, would you attend?   Yes _____   No _____

b. Do you think this home provides adequate activities to make you want to communicate?
   Yes _____   No _____

Exploration Effect I

a. Can a person improve communication ability by using lipreading (or speechreading), which means watching the speaker's lips, facial expressions, and gestures when

 he or she is speaking?   Yes _____   No _____

b. Do you agree with the above as a definition of lipreading?   Yes _____   No _____

Exploration Effect II

a. Is your vision adequate?   Yes _____   No _____

b. Are you able to get around unassisted?   Yes _____   No _____

University of Northern Colorado Communication Appraisal and Priorities

Date _____

Name _____ Age _____ Sex _____

Address _____ Phone _____

Please indicate below those situations in which you are able to communicate best, those that are difficult for you in some instances, and those that are a definite problem. Under "explain," please tell us more if you desire, such as certain instances when you experience more difficulty than others, certain types of speakers, certain places, and so on.

	No problems	Only in specific instances	Definite problem	Priority
1. At parties or other social events	_____	_____	_____	_____
Explain _____
	_____
2. At the dinner table	_____	_____	_____	_____
Explain _____
	_____

Hull, R. H. Unpublished scale. Greeley: University of Northern Colorado, 1982.

	No problems	Only in specific instances	Definite problem	Priority
3. On the telephone	_____	_____	_____	_____
Explain _____				
_____				
4. At home	_____	_____	_____	_____
Explain _____				
_____				
5. With males	_____	_____	_____	_____
Explain _____				
_____				
6. With females	_____	_____	_____	_____
Explain _____				
_____				
7. With children	_____	_____	_____	_____
Explain _____				
_____				
8. In groups	_____	_____	_____	_____
Explain _____				
_____				
9. With certain important individuals	_____	_____	_____	_____
Explain _____				
_____				
10. At church	_____	_____	_____	_____
Explain _____				
_____				

	No problems	Only in specific instances	Definite problem	Priority
11. At meetings	_____	_____	_____	_____

Explain _____

_____

12. Watching TV	_____	_____	_____	_____

Explain _____

_____

13. At the theater	_____	_____	_____	_____

Explain _____

_____

14. At work	_____	_____	_____	_____

Explain _____

_____

15. Other (please specify)	_____	_____	_____	_____

Explain _____

_____

Do you have specific preferences in regard to things you would like to improve as they relate to your ability to communicate with others? _____

_____

■ APPENDIX K ■

The Hearing Handicap Inventory for the Elderly

The purpose of this scale is to identify the problems your hearing loss may be causing. Answer YES, SOMETIMES, or NO for each question. Do not skip a question if you avoid a situation because of your hearing problem. If you use a hearing aid, please answer the way you hear without the aid.

		YES (4)	SOMETIMES (2)	NO (0)
S–1.	Does a hearing problem cause you to use the phone less often than you would like?			
E–2.	Does a hearing problem cause you to feel embarrassed when meeting new people?			
S–3.	Does a hearing problem cause you to avoid groups of people?			
E–4.	Does a hearing problem make you irritable?			
E–5.	Does a hearing problem cause you to feel frustrated when talking to members of your family?			
S–6.	Does a hearing problem cause you difficulty when attending a party?			
E–7.	Does a hearing problem cause you to feel "stupid" or "dumb?"			

Reproduced with permission by Ventry, I. J., and Weinstein, B. (1982). The hearing handicap inventory for the elderly: A new tool. *Ear and Hearing, 3,* 128–134.

		YES (4)	SOMETIMES (2)	NO (0)
S–8.	Do you have difficulty hearing when someone speaks in a whisper?			
E–9.	Do you feel handicapped by a hearing problem?			
S–10.	Does a hearing problem cause you difficulty when visiting friends, relatives, or neighbors?			
S–11.	Does a hearing problem cause you to attend religious services less often than you would like?			
E–12.	Does a hearing problem cause you to be nervous?			
S–13.	Does a hearing problem cause you to visit friends, relatives, or neighbors less often than you would like?			
E–14.	Does a hearing problem cause you to have arguments with your family members?			
S–15.	Does a hearing problem cause you difficulty when listening to TV or radio?			
S–16.	Does a hearing problem cause you to go shopping less often than you would like?			
S–17.	Does any problem or difficulty with your hearing upset you at all?			
S–18.	Does a hearing problem cause you to want to be by yourself?			
S–19.	Does a hearing problem cause you to talk to family members less often than you would like?			
E–20.	Do you feel that any difficulty with your hearing limits or hampers your personal or social life?			
S–21.	Does a hearing problem cause you difficulty when in a restaurant with relatives or friends?			

	YES (4)	SOMETIMES (2)	NO (0)
S–22. Does a hearing problem cause you to feel depressed?	_____	_____	_____
S–23. Does a hearing problem cause you to listen to TV or radio less often than you would like?	_____	_____	_____
E–24. Does a hearing problem cause you to feel uncomfortable when talking to friends?	_____	_____	_____
E–25. Does a hearing problem cause you to feel left out when you are with a group of people?	_____	_____	_____

FOR CLINICIANS USE ONLY: Total Score: _____

Subtotal E: _____

Subtotal S: _____

■ APPENDIX L ■

The Communication Profile for the Hearing Impaired

The purpose of this questionnaire is to find out how your hearing loss affects your daily life and what problems, if any, you may be having as a result. Most of the items deal in some way with communication and your interactions with other people, but there are also items that describe your feelings and your reactions in a variety of situations.

PART I

This section of the questionnaire asks you to describe how often you feel you are able to communicate effectively with others. Mark "1" if you *Rarely* or *Almost Never* communicate effectively in that situation. Use "2" for *Occasionally* or *Sometimes;* use "3" for *About Half the Time;* use "4" for *Frequently* or *Often;* and use "5" if you *Usually* or *Almost Always* communicate effectively.

We would also like to know how important these situations are to you. That is, we would like to know which types of situations really matter to you and which ones don't. If a particular situation occurs quite often, or if it's essential for you to communicate effectively in that situation, indicate this by marking "5" for *Essential* on the response sheet. On the other hand, if the situation occurs rarely, or if it does not really matter if you communicate in that situation, then mark "1" for *Not Important* on the response sheet. Use "2" for *Somewhat Important,* use "3" for *Important;* and use "4" for *Very Important.*

Reproduced with permission by Demerest, M. E., and Erdman, S. A. (1987). Development of the communication profile for the hearing impaired. *Journal of Speech and Hearing Disorders, 52,* 129–143.

_____ 1. Someone in your family is talking to you while you're driving or riding in a car.

_____ 2. You're at a social gathering with music or other noise in the background.

_____ 3. You're at the dinner table with your family.

_____ 4. You're at work and someone is talking to you from another room.

_____ 5. You're at a restaurant ordering food or drink.

_____ 6. You're talking on the telephone when you're at work.

_____ 7. You're at an outdoor picnic.

_____ 8. Someone's talking to you while you're watching TV or listening to the stereo.

_____ 9. You're listening for information at a lecture, briefing, or class.

_____ 10. You're talking with someone in an office.

_____ 11. You're at home talking on the telephone.

_____ 12. You're at a dinner party with several other people.

_____ 13. You're listening to someone speak at religious services.

_____ 14. You're at a meeting with several other people.

_____ 15. You're at home and someone is talking to you from another room.

_____ 16. You're having a conversation at a social gathering while others are talking nearby.

_____ 17. You're talking with a friend or family member in a quiet room.

_____ 18. You're giving or following work instructions outdoors.

PART II

In this section of the questionnaire you're asked to describe the kinds of experiences you have when you're communicating with others. What kinds of things happen when you're trying to carry on a conversation? What do you do when you have trouble understanding what someone has said? What kinds of things do other people do that make it harder or easier for you to communicate with them?

Mark "1" if the item describes something that _Rarely_ happens or that is _Almost Never_ true for you. Mark "2" for _Occasionally_ or _Sometimes_; mark "3" for _About Half the Time_; mark "4" for _Frequently_ or _Often;_ and mark "5" for _Almost Always._

_____ 19. One way I get people to repeat what they said is by ignoring them.

_____ 20. If someone repeats what they've said and I still don't understand, I ask them to repeat again.

_____ 21. I have to talk with others when there's a lot of background noise.

_____ 22. If I hear part of what someone has said, I only ask them to repeat what I didn't hear.

_____ 23. My family gets annoyed when I don't hear things.

_____ 24. I try to give the impression of normal hearing.

_____   25. Others think I'm ignoring them if I don't answer when they speak to me.

_____   26. In difficult listening situations, I try to position myself so that I can hear as well as possible.

_____   27. I have conversations with others when I'm home.

_____   28. People think I'm not paying attention if I don't answer them when they speak to me.

_____   29. I have to communicate with others in a group situation.

_____   30. I interrupt others when listening to them is difficult.

_____   31. I've asked my family to get my attention before speaking to me.

_____   32. I tend to dominate conversations so I don't have to listen to others.

_____   33. Members of my family speak to me when they're not facing me.

_____   34. When I don't understand what someone has said, I ask them to repeat it.

_____   35. People who know I have a hearing loss accuse me of hearing only what I want to hear.

_____   36. When I have trouble understanding someone, I pay close attention to his or her face.

_____   37. If someone seems irritated at having to repeat, I stop asking them to do so and pretend to understand.

_____   38. I tend to avoid situations where I think I'll have problems hearing.

_____   39. I get bothered or upset when I'm unable to follow a conversation.

_____   40. I have to talk to others in noisy areas.

_____   41. I avoid conversing with others because of my hearing loss.

_____   42. If I'm sitting where I can't hear, I'll move to another seat.

_____   43. My job required me to use the telephone.

_____   44. When I don't understand what someone has said, I pretend that I understood it.

_____   45. At parties or other social gatherings I try to stay in a well-lighted area so I can see the speaker's face.

_____   46. People treat me as if I'm stupid because I can't understand what they say.

_____   47. When I'm having trouble understanding friends or family members, I remind them that I have a hearing problem.

_____   48. I avoid talking to strangers because of my hearing loss.

_____   49. People get annoyed when I ask them to repeat what they've said.

_____   50. During the day I have to communicate with others.

_____   51. My job involves talking to people who speak quietly.

_____   52. Members of my family leave me out of conversations or discussions.

_____   53. When I must listen in a group, I try to sit where I'll be able to hear better.

_____   54. Others become impatient because I don't always understand.

_____   55. Members of my family refuse to repeat what they've said more than once or twice.

_____   56. Members of my family talk to me from another room.

_____ 57. I feel stupid when I have to ask someone to repeat what they've said.

_____ 58. When I don't understand what someone has said, I ignore them.

_____ 59. People act frustrated when I don't understand what they say.

_____ 60. People who know I have a hearing loss don't speak clearly enough when they're speaking to me.

_____ 61. People don't remember to get my attention before speaking.

_____ 62. My job involves communicating with others.

_____ 63. I try to hide my hearing problem.

_____ 64. When there's background noise I position myself so that it's less distracting.

_____ 65. I've asked friends and people I work with to get my attention before speaking to me.

_____ 66. People who know I have a hearing loss don't speak up when they're talking to me.

_____ 67. When I don't understand what someone has said, I explain that I have a hearing loss.

_____ 68. People say, "Never mind" or "Forget it" if I ask them to repeat more than once.

_____ 69. When I'm having trouble following a conversation, I listen carefully and try to catch the main points.

_____ 70. I feel foolish when I misunderstand what someone has said.

_____ 71. When I think a person is speaking too softly, I ask them to speak up.

_____ 72. If possible, I try to watch a person's face when he or she is speaking.

_____ 73. People mumble when they're talking to me.

_____ 74. I get mad at myself when I can't understand what people are saying.

_____ 75. Others think I'm not interested in what they're saying.

_____ 76. I feel embarrassed when I have to ask someone to repeat what they've said.

PART III

The items in this section describe a variety of feelings, attitudes, and beliefs about hearing loss and communication. If the statement accurately describes your beliefs, feelings, attitudes, or experiences, mark "4" on the response sheet for _Agree_ or "5" for _Strongly Agree_. If the statement doesn't accurately describe your feelings or reactions, mark "2" for _Disagree_ or "1" for _Strongly Disagree_. Mark "3" if you're _Uncertain_ or if you partly agree and partly disagree.

_____ 77. Sometimes I have trouble understanding what's being said when someone speaks to me from another room.

_____ 78. I feel threatened by many communication situations due to difficulty hearing.

_____ 79. My hearing loss is my problem and I hate to bother others with it.

_____	80. I feel left out of conversations because I have trouble understanding.
_____	81. People should be more patient when they're talking to me.
_____	82. My hearing loss makes me mad.
_____	83. Sometimes I'm ashamed of my hearing problems.
_____	84. I withdraw from social talk because of my hearing loss.
_____	85. I'm not very relaxed when conversing with others.
_____	86. Others feel I use my hearing loss as an excuse for not paying attention.
_____	87. Communicating with others is an important part of my daily activity.
_____	88. I sometimes have trouble understanding others when there's background noise.
_____	89. I feel guilty about asking people to repeat for me.
_____	90. Sometimes I feel left out when I can't follow the conversation of those I'm with.
_____	91. I sometimes get annoyed when I have trouble hearing.
_____	92. I hate to ask others for special consideration just because I have a hearing problem.
_____	93. There's a lot of background noise where I work.
_____	94. When I have trouble hearing, I feel frustrated.
_____	95. Because of my hearing loss, I sometimes have trouble communicating with others.
_____	96. I'm not very comfortable in most communication situations.
_____	97. Sometimes it's hard for me to understand what's being said in meetings, conferences, or other large groups.
_____	98. At social gatherings I sometimes find it hard to follow conversations.
_____	99. At times my hearing loss makes me feel incompetent.
_____	100. It's frustrating when people refuse to repeat what they've said.
_____	101. I get very tense because of my hearing loss.
_____	102. Sometimes when I misunderstand what someone has said I feel foolish.
_____	103. I get aggravated when others don't speak up.
_____	104. Because of my hearing loss I keep to myself.
_____	105. I'm sensitive about my hearing loss.
_____	106. When I have trouble hearing, I become nervous.
_____	107. I feel depressed as a result of my hearing loss.
_____	108. I find it difficult to admit to others that I have a hearing problem.
_____	109. Since I have trouble hearing, I don't enjoy going places with friends as much.
_____	110. If people speak where I can't see them, they shouldn't expect me to answer them.
_____	111. My family doesn't understand the strain and stress I feel from trying to understand what they say.
_____	112. I get discouraged because of my hearing loss.

_____ 113. I worry about looking stupid when I can't understand what someone has said.

_____ 114. Straining to hear upsets me.

_____ 115. Communicating with others is an important part of my job.

_____ 116. I feel bad about the inconvenience I cause others because of my hearing loss.

_____ 117. I get impatient with people who aren't willing to repeat for me.

_____ 118. Because of my hearing loss I have feelings of inadequacy.

_____ 119. Questions about my hearing loss really irritate me.

_____ 120. It bothers me to admit that I have a hearing loss.

_____ 121. The problems I have communicating with others really get me down.

_____ 122. I sometimes get angry with myself when I can't hear what people are saying.

_____ 123. When I can't understand people, sometimes I just don't care anymore.

_____ 124. Sometimes it's difficult for me to follow a conversation when others are talking nearby.

_____ 125. I can't talk to people about my hearing loss.

_____ 126. If people want me to understand them, it's up to them to speak more clearly.

_____ 127. Sometimes I feel tense when I can't understand what someone is saying.

_____ 128. If someone talks to me while I'm watching TV, I sometimes have trouble understanding them.

_____ 129. Others should be more understanding about my hearing problems.

_____ 130. I sometimes feel embarrassed when I misunderstand what someone has said.

_____ 131. Sometimes I miss so much of what's being said that I feel left out.

_____ 132. I let my hearing problems get me down.

_____ 133. I have a hard time accepting the fact that I have a hearing loss.

_____ 134. I really get annoyed when people shout at me as if I'm deaf.

_____ 135. I try not to bother anyone else when I'm having trouble hearing.

_____ 136. I feel self-conscious because of my hearing loss.

_____ 137. When people mumble, they shouldn't expect me to understand them.

_____ 138. Feeling isolated is part of having a hearing impairment.

_____ 139. When I can't understand what's being said, I feel tense and anxious.

_____ 140. I'd rather miss part of a conversation than admit that I have a hearing loss.

_____ 141. I sometimes have trouble understanding what's being said when I can't see the speaker's face.

_____ 142. Not being able to understand is very discouraging.

_____ 143. I get angry when I can't understand what someone is saying.

_____ 144. I don't like to ask other people to help me with my hearing problems.

_____ 145. The difficulties I have with my hearing restrict my social and personal life.

Communication Skill Scale

IDENTIFYING INFORMATION

Name _____
     Last   First   Middle Initial

Social Security # _____
                (Gallaudet Student use ID Number)

Age _____   Sex   ( ) Male   ( ) Female

When did you become deaf:

      ( )   1)   Birth   –   2 years of age
      ( )   2)   Age 3   –   6 years of age
      ( )   3)   Age 6   –   12 years of age
      ( )   4)   Age 12   –   18 years of age
      ( )   5)   After age 18

Education:

      ( )   1)   Less than High School
      ( )   2)   High School Graduate
      ( )   3)   Some College
      ( )   4)   College Undergraduate Degree
      ( )   5)   Postgraduate
      ( )   6)   Ph.D.

The CSS is not reproduced here in its entirety, but rather as an example of the scale.

The Scale, Scoring Form, and Norms can be obtained from Dr. Harriet Kaplan, Department of Audiology, Gallaudet University, Washington, DC. 20002.

How long did you attend each of the following:
(Enter 0 if you did not attend and .5 if you attended less than a full year.)

Residential School for the Deaf	_____ year(s)	_____ months
Private School for the Deaf	_____ year(s)	_____ months
Public School — Mainstreamed	_____ year(s)	_____ months
Public School — Special Class	_____ year(s)	_____ months
Private School — Mainstreamed	_____ year(s)	_____ months
Private School — Special Class	_____ year(s)	_____ months

How long did you attend each of the following:
(Enter 0 if you did not attend and .5 if you attended less than a full year.)

Gallaudet University	_____ year(s)	_____ months
National Technical Institute for the Deaf	_____ year(s)	_____ months
Other program for hearing impaired	_____ year(s)	_____ months
Hearing Jr. College, College or University	_____ year(s)	_____ months
Program not specifically for hearing impaired	_____ year(s)	_____ months

How do you communicate most of the time:

At Home	:	( ) ASL	( ) PSE	( ) Speech
At School	:	( ) ASL	( ) PSE	( ) Speech
At Work	:	( ) ASL	( ) PSE	( ) Speech
In the Community	:	( ) ASL	( ) PSE	( ) Speech

How often do you use a hearing aid now:

( )   1) – Do Not Own a Hearing Aid
( )   2) – Not At All
( )   3) – Occasionally
( )   4) – All the Time

Do you wear an aid in:

( )   One ear
( )   Both ears

Type of aid currently in use:

( )   1) – Behind-the-ear aid
( )   2) – In-the-ear aid
( )   3) – Body-worn or eyeglass aid
( )   4) – Vibrotactile aid
( )   5) – Cochlear Implant

Indicate the degree of your hearing loss:

( )   1)   –   Mild
( )   2)   –   Moderate
( )   3)   –   Severe
( )   4)   –   Profound

INSTRUCTIONS

We want to find out how your hearing loss affects your daily life. The following questions are about different communication situations, ways of managing situations, and attitudes about different situations. If you have never experienced the situation do not answer the question. Go on to the next question.

Some of the items ask you whether you understand conversation. The word "understand" means knowing enough of what is said or signed to be able to answer appropriately.

Always assume you are interested in what is being said.

We know that some people are easier to understand than others. Please answer the questions according to the way most people talk to you or understand you. We know that sounds and speakers vary. Please answer the questions as best you can.

If you wear a hearing aid, answer the questions as though you were wearing your aid.

SECTION I

DIFFICULT COMMUNICATION SITUATIONS

Please read each situation. Decide if the situation is true:

1. Almost always,
2. Sometimes, or
3. Almost never.

If you have not experienced this situation **DO NOT** answer the question. Go on to the next question.

Then indicate if the situation is:

1. Very important to you,
2. Important to you,
3. Not important to you.

Question #1.
 You are in class. The teacher is easy to lipread but is not signing. You understand _____ (frequency)   _____ (importance)

Question #2.
 You meet a stranger on the street and ask for directions. He does not sign. You understand him _____ (frequency)   _____ (importance)

Question #3.
 You are at work. It is quiet. Your supervisor gives you an order. She is not signing but her face is clearly visible. You understand her _____ (frequency)   _____ (importance)

Question #4.
You are at work. It is noisy. A hearing co-worker asks you to eat lunch with her. She does not sign but you can see her face. You understand her _____ (frequency)   _____ (importance)

Question #5.
You are visiting a friend. His hard-of-hearing child speaks to you about his school. The child does not sign. You understand _____ (frequency)   _____ (importance)

Question #6.
You are at a meeting. A hearing person speaks but does not sign. You know the subject. You understand _____ (frequency)   _____ (importance)

Question #7.
You are in class. A hearing person speaks but does not sign. You know the subject. You understand _____ (frequency)   _____ (importance)

Question #8.
You are at the dinner table at home. All your relatives are hearing. Your grandmother is talking. She does not sign. You do not know the topic. You understand her
_____ (frequency)   _____ (importance)

Question #9.
You are introduced to a hearing person. You sign and speak at the same time. He understands you _____ (frequency)   _____ (importance)

Question #10.
You are at a meeting with five hearing people. No one signs but everyone's face can be seen. One person talks at a time. You understand the conversation
_____ (frequency)   _____ (importance)

Question #11.
You are watching a movie on television. There is no captioning. It is quiet in the room. You understand _____ (frequency)   _____ (importance)

Question #12.
You are talking to the doctor. It is quiet. She does not sign. You can see her face clearly. You understand her _____ (frequency)   _____ (importance)

Question #13.
You are ordering lunch at McDonald's. You speak to the person behind the counter. She understands you _____ (frequency)   _____ (importance)

Question #14.
You are talking to one person at a noisy party. The person does not sign. You understand _____ (frequency)   _____ (importance)

Question #15.
You are talking to a family member on the telephone. It is quiet in the room. You understand _____ (frequency)   _____ (importance)

Question #16.
You are reading in a quiet room. Someone calls you from the next room. You hear the person's voice _____ (frequency)   _____ (importance)

Question #17.
You are sitting in a car next to the driver. The driver is talking. He is not signing. You understand him _____ (frequency)   _____ (importance)

Question #18.

You must give directions to hearing people at work. They understand your speech

_____ (frequency)   _____ (importance)

Question #19.

I have trouble hearing fire alarms in buildings when other people can hear them.

_____ (frequency)   _____ (importance)

Question #20.

I have trouble hearing fire engines and ambulances when other people can hear them.

_____ (frequency)   _____ (importance)

Question #21.

I have trouble hearing cars or buses when other people can hear them.

_____ (frequency)   _____ (importance)

Question #22.

I have trouble hearing the telephone when I am in the same room.

_____ (frequency)   _____ (importance)

Question #23.

I have trouble hearing the telephone when I am in the next room.

_____ (frequency)   _____ (importance)

Question #24.

I have trouble hearing the doorbell when other people can hear it.

_____ (frequency)   _____ (importance)

Question #25.

I have trouble hearing a knock on the door when other people can hear it.

_____ (frequency)   _____ (importance)

Question #26.

I have trouble hearing music when it is loud enough for other people.

_____ (frequency)   _____ (importance)

Question #27.

I have trouble hearing a person's voice when he is talking in the same room.

_____ (frequency)   _____ (importance)

SECTION II

COMMUNICATION STRATEGIES

Please read each situation. Decide if the situation is true:

1. Almost always,
2. Sometimes, or
3. Almost never.

If you have not experienced this situation **DO NOT** answer the question. Go on to the next question.

Question #28.

You are talking with someone you do not know well. You do not understand. You ask her to repeat. _____ (frequency)

Question #29.
You are talking with two people. You are not understanding. You change the topic so that you can control the conversation. _____ (frequency)

Question #30.
You ask a stranger for directions. You understand part of what he says. You tell him the part you understand and ask him to repeat the rest. _____ (frequency)

Question #31.
You answer a question but the other person doesn't understand. You repeat the answer. _____ (frequency)

Question #32.
You are at work. Your boss gives you instructions. You do not understand. You ask him to say the instructions in a different way. _____ (frequency)

Question #33.
A friend introduces you to a new person. You do not understand the person's name. You ask the person to spell her name. _____ (frequency)

Question #34.
A person asks you for your name. He does not understand your speech. You spell your name. _____ (frequency)

Question #35.
A stranger spells his name for you. You miss the first two letters. You ask him to say each letter and a word starting with each letter (A as in Apple, B as in Boy). _____ (frequency)

Question #36.
A person tells you his address. You do not understand. You ask him to repeat the street number, one number at a time. _____ (frequency)

Question #37.
You are talking with one person but are not understanding. You interrupt the person before he finishes to say what you think. _____ (frequency)

Question #38.
Your friend asks you to buy seven hamburgers. You do not understand how may he wants. You ask him to start counting from zero and stop at the correct number. _____ (frequency)

Question #39.
You are in a restaurant. The waitress does not understand what you want. You point to the item on the menu. _____ (frequency)

Question #40.
You are in class. The teacher says something you do not understand. You pretend to understand and hope to get the information from the book later. _____ (frequency)

Question #41.
You are at the dinner table with your family. Someone does not understand you. You say the same thing a different way. _____ (frequency)

Question #42.
Someone who does not sign asks you for your phone number. You say each number and show the correct number of fingers as you speak. _____ (frequency)

Question #43.
Two people are talking. You do not understand the conversation. You ask them to tell you the topic. _____ (frequency)

Question #44.
   You are talking with one person in a restaurant. His face is in the shadows. You know you could understand better if you changed seats with him. You ask to change seats. _____ (frequency)

Question #45.
   You are at the airport. You want to buy a ticket for a flight home. The clerk does not understand you. You write the information. _____ (frequency)

Question #46.
   You are visiting the doctor. He tells you what to do for your sickness. You do not understand his speech. You ask him to write. _____ (frequency)

Question #47.
   You are at a meeting. The speaker does not look at you when he talks. You feel angry but do nothing about it. _____ (frequency)

Question #48.
   You meet a deaf friend who is with another person. The other person talks to you but does not sign. You ask her to sign. _____ (frequency)

Question #49.
   You are at a meeting. You realize you are too far from the speaker to understand. There are empty seats in the front of the room. You change your seat. _____ (frequency)

Question #50.
   You are at a meeting at work. You are the only deaf person. You are afraid that you will not understand but you do not ask for help. You do the best you can. _____ (frequency)

Question #51.
   You are talking to the dentist. He speaks very fast. You cannot lipread him. You ask him to slow down. _____ (frequency)

Question #52.
   You are in class. The teacher talks while she writes on the board. You talk to her after class. You explain that you need to see her face in order to speechread. _____ (frequency)

Question #53.
   Your teacher likes to move around the room while she teaches. You have problems reading her signs. You ask her after class to lecture from one place so you can understand her signing. _____ (frequency)

Question #54.
   You are going to a series of meetings or lectures. The speaker does not sign. You ask the speaker to use the slides, pictures or the overhead projector whenever possible. _____ (frequency)

Question #55.
   You are going to a series of meetings or lectures. The speaker does not sign. You ask him to find a person to take notes for you. _____ (frequency)

Question #56.
   You are going to a series of meetings or lectures. The speaker does not sign. You ask for an interpreter. _____ (frequency)

Question #57.
   You are going to a series of meetings or lectures. The speaker does not sign. You ask for an outline or a reading list. _____ (frequency)

Question #58.
You are going to a play. It will not be signed. You read the play or reviews of the play before you see it. _____ (frequency)

Question #59.
You are going to a job interview. You act out the situation in advance with a friend to prepare yourself for the experience. _____ (frequency)

Question #60.
You are talking with a clerk at the bank. A fire truck goes by. You ask him to stop talking until the noise stops. _____ (frequency)

Question #61.
You ask a person to repeat because you don't understand. He seems annoyed. You stop asking and pretend to understand. _____ (frequency)

Question #62.
You ask a stranger for directions to a place. You really want to understand his speech. You ask very specific questions like: "Is this place north or south of here?" "Do I turn left or right at the corner?" _____ (frequency)

Question #63.
You need to ask directions. You avoid asking a stranger because you think you will have trouble understanding him. _____ (frequency)

Question #64.
You must make a phone call to a hearing person. The person does not have a TDD. You ask a hearing friend to make the call and interpret for you. _____ (frequency)

Question #65.
You are at a store. You have trouble hearing the clerk because his voice is soft. You explain you are hearing impaired and ask him to talk louder. _____ (frequency)

Question #66.
You are at home. You ask your family to get your attention before they speak to you. _____ (frequency)

Question #67.
You are with five or six friends. No one is signing. You miss something important. You ask the person next to you what was said. _____ (frequency)

Question #68.
You have trouble understanding a man who is chewing gum. You explain that you need to speechread. You politely ask him to remove the gum when he talks. _____ (frequency)

Question #69.
You try to avoid people when you know you will have trouble hearing them. _____ (frequency)

Question #70.
You hate to bother other people with your hearing problem. So, you pretend to understand. _____ (frequency)

Question #71.
I avoid wearing my hearing aid because it makes me feel different. _____ (frequency)

SECTION III

ATTITUDES

Please read each situation. Decide if the situation is true:

1. Almost always,
2. Sometimes, or
3. Almost never.

If you have not experienced this situation **DO NOT** answer the question. Go on to the next question.

Question #72.
   I feel embarrassed when I don't understand someone. _____ (frequency)

Question #73.
   I get upset when I can't follow a conversation. _____ (frequency)

Question #74.
   I become angry when people do not speak clearly enough for me to understand. _____ (frequency)

Question #75.
   I feel stupid when I misunderstand what a person is saying. _____ (frequency)

Question #76.
   It's hard for me to ask someone to repeat things. I feel embarrassed. _____ (frequency)

Question #77.
   Most people think I could understand better if I paid more attention. _____ (frequency)

Question #78.
   I get angry when people speak too softly or too fast. _____ (frequency)

Question #79.
   Sometimes I can't follow conversations at home. I still feel a part of family life. _____ (frequency)

Question #80.
   I feel frustrated when I try to communicate with hearing people. _____ (frequency)

Question #81.
   Most hearing people do not understand what it is like to be deaf. This makes me angry. _____ (frequency)

Question #82.
   I am ashamed of being hearing impaired. _____ (frequency)

Question #83.
   I get angry when someone speaks with his mouth covered or with his back to me. _____ (frequency)

Question #84.
   I prefer to be alone most of the time. _____ (frequency)

Question #85.
   I am uncomfortable with people who communicate differently than I do. _____ (frequency)

Question #86.
   My hearing loss makes me nervous. _____ (frequency)

Question #87.

My hearing loss makes me feel depressed. _____ (frequency)

Question #88.

My family understands my hearing loss. _____ (frequency)

Question #89.

I get annoyed when people shout at me because I have a hearing loss. _____ (frequency)

Question #90.

People treat me like a stupid person when I don't understand their speech. _____ (frequency)

Question #91.

People treat me like a stupid person when they don't understand me. _____ (frequency)

Question #92.

Members of my family don't get annoyed when I have trouble understanding them. _____ (frequency)

Question #93.

People who know I have a hearing loss think I can hear when I want to. _____ (frequency)

Question #94.

Members of my family don't leave me out of conversations. _____ (frequency)

Question #95.

Hearing aids don't always help people understand speech, but they can help in other ways. _____ (frequency)

Question #96.

I feel speechreading (lipreading) is helpful to me. _____ (frequency)

Question #97.

I feel the only useful communication system for a deaf person is sign language. _____ (frequency)

Question #98.

Even though people know I have a hearing loss, they don't help me by speaking clearly or repeating. _____ (frequency)

Question #99.

My family is willing to make telephone calls for me. _____ (frequency)

Question #100.

My family is willing to repeat as often as necessary when I don't understand them. _____ (frequency)

Question #101.

Hearing people get frustrated when I don't understand what they say. _____ (frequency)

Question #102.

Hearing people get embarrassed when they don't understand my speech. _____ (frequency)

Question #103.

Hearing people pretend to understand me when they really don't. _____ (frequency)

Question #104.

I feel the only useful communications system for a deaf person is speech and lipreading. _____ (frequency)

Question #105.

I feel embarrassed when hearing people don't understand my speech. _____ (frequency)

Question #106.
I do not mind repeating when people have trouble understanding my speech. _____ (frequency)

Question #107.
I prefer to write when I communicate with hearing people because I am ashamed of my speech. _____ (frequency)

Question #108.
I feel that most hearing people try to understand my speech. _____ (frequency)

Question #109.
I feel that my family tries to understand my speech. _____ (frequency)

Question #110.
I feel that strangers try to understand my speech.
_____ (frequency)

■ INDEX ■